NOTES

ON NEW TESTAMENT CRITICISM

NOTES

ON NEW TESTAMENT CRITICISM

BY

EDWIN A. ABBOTT

"Fili mi, monitus esto ut facias libros sapientiae plurimos, adeo ut non sit finis."
   Eccles. xii. 12 (according to the Targum).

WIPF & STOCK · Eugene, Oregon

Wipf and Stock Publishers
199 W 8th Ave, Suite 3
Eugene, OR 97401

Notes on New Testament Criticism
By Abbott, Edwin A.
ISBN 13: 978-1-4982-3204-3
Publication date 6/10/2015
Previously published by Adam and Charles Black, 1907

TO

THE TARGUMISTS

MUCH NEGLECTED BY MOST STUDENTS OF THE SCRIPTURES

YET FOR THOSE WHO DESIRE TO TRACE THE GROWTH OF TRADITION

AND TO DISTINGUISH FACT FROM NON-FACT

UNIQUELY VALUABLE

PREFACE

IN submitting to the public the Seventh Part of *Diatessarica* the author cannot but feel that he may be supposed to be rejecting the warning attributed to Solomon, " And furthermore, my son, be admonished: *of making many books there is no end*: and much study is a weariness to the flesh."

But there are at least two other versions of this saying under either of which I could find shelter; and they appear morally though perhaps not critically sound. One of these warns the son to *beware of those who say* " Of making books there is no end." Another, the Targum, punctuates and expands so as to give the following rendering: "And furthermore, my son, *be admonished to make very many books of wisdom*, so that there may be no end, and to study the words of the Law, and to attain understanding in weariness of the flesh[1]."

---

[1] On the Targums, see Schürer I. i. 154—60. He says (1) that they "belong to the Rabbinical Literature, inasmuch as expression is given in them likewise to the traditional understanding of the Scripture text." But he adds (2) "We mention here only the Targums on the Pentateuch and on the Prophets, for the Targums on the Sacred Writings or Kethubim can scarcely come under consideration by us owing to their late origin." After mentioning the two Targums attributed severally to Onkelos (on the Pentateuch) and to Jonathan ben Uzziel (on the Prophets)—"placed by some about the middle of the first century"—he says (3) "Even if the two Targums were first issued during the third and fourth centuries, it cannot be doubted that they are based upon earlier works, and only form the conclusion of a process that had been going on for several centuries."

The reader will perceive from the second of these extracts that the

PREFACE

Not that I would claim for all the preceding parts of this series that they are "books of wisdom." But I do venture to claim that they are "books of fact." They sometimes add suggested explanations; but seldom, if ever, without alleging facts. It is as a store-house of facts—facts carefully ascertained, fully and impartially stated, and so arranged and indexed as to be readily accessible—that *Diatessarica* appeals to students of the New Testament.

In order to make these facts accessible to students who may wish to refer to the series in some library but may not be able to purchase it owing to its cost, I have decided to publish the Indices to this and the preceding Parts (I—VII) in a separate volume shortly after, if not simultaneously with, the present publication. My hope is that, long after *Silanus the Christian* is forgotten, these Notes—originally entitled *Notes to Silanus* but now *Notes on New Testament Criticism*[1]— together with the *Indices to Diatessarica*, may remain in use for New Testament research.

If some of the Notes appear too full of detail and digression, I must ask my readers to remember that they are (most of them) not intended so much for perusal as for reference. The Note on "The Son of Man," for example, has been

---

quotation from the Targum on the title-page of the present work must not be taken as a specimen of Targums in general.

Schürer arranges the principal Targums thus:

1. ONKELOS ON THE PENTATEUCH.
2. JONATHAN ON THE PROPHETS (this includes "the historical books," outside the Pentateuch, as well as "the prophets properly so called").
3. PSEUDO-JONATHAN AND JERUSALMI ON THE PENTATEUCH. These "are only two different recensions of one and the same Targum," and "both are quoted by older authorities (*Aruch* and *Elia*) under the name 'Targum Jerusalmi.'" Hence "Pseudo-Jonathan" is often referred to as "Jer. I," and Jerusalmi as "Jer. II." But there are reasons for thinking "Jerusalmi," of which only fragments are extant, to be earlier than "Pseudo-Jonathan." Some call "Jerusalmi" the "Palestinian" Targum.

For abbreviated references to the Targums, see below, pp. xxviii—ix.

[1] See *Apologia* pp. vii—viii.

lengthened into a treatise (pp. 140—252) by the necessity (as it appeared to me) of tracing the difference of contextual thought amid which the phrase is used by Balaam, the Psalmists, Ezekiel, Daniel, and the author of the Similitudes of Enoch —with a view to studying the gospel uses of it hereafter.

Again, the Book of Revelation, in special passages, has been minutely commented on (**2942*** (i)—(xxiv), **2998** (xxvi) —(xxxiii)). The question of its date is of great importance for New Testament criticism generally. But it also appeared important to shew that some of the most characteristic thoughts of the Seer of Revelation are reproduced, though in very different language, by his disciple, the Evangelist of the Fourth Gospel.

I do not think some students of the Gospels realise how much, how very much, remains to be done in the way of collecting and classifying facts. Only the facts must be of the right kind, and classified in the right way. And here a caution may perhaps be useful as to that particular class of facts called "authorities," whether ancient or modern.

That Chrysostom thought this or that, is a fact. That Origen thought this or that, is a very much more important fact—because he is a scholar, fearless, frank, thorough, acquainted with Hebrew as well as with Greek, and because he goes fully into contexts and parallels, and seldom or never gives you his opinion without also giving you the historical or documentary facts on which it is founded. Sometimes it is founded on fancy as well as fact. Even when that is the case, Origen never deceives his reader. You can reject his fancies while gratefully accepting his facts and giving them your own interpretation.

The facts, then, must be facts of a solid sort. It is not worth while to record error without a reasonable hope that the error may point to some truth hidden behind it.

After collecting comes the need of classifying. Care having been taken to select, for first research, only such sub-

PREFACE

jects as present most available facts—*e.g.* the subject-matter common to the three Synoptists, in preference to the subject-matter found in the Fourth Gospel alone—we must then tabulate results in such a way as to get a bird's-eye view of parallelisms and divergences, likenesses and differences. If we are to reach the truth we shall reach it not by talking a great deal about matters on which we have little or no evidence, but by toiling[1] a great deal about matters where the evidence is abundant.

For example, Mr Rushbrooke's *Synopticon*, placing the three Synoptic Gospels in parallel columns, prints in red the matter common to Mark, Matthew, and Luke. It also prints in special types the *additional contextual matter in which Matthew agrees with Luke*.

When the eye glances down the columns, the reader is

---

[1] It appears to me a significant fact that a reader of these pages, not unacquainted with the usual methods of N.T. criticism, queried "*toiling*" and suggested "*talking*."

This would make a neat antithesis, "not by *talking a great deal*" about the unknown but "by *talking a great deal*" about the comparatively well-known. But it was not what I meant. Let me explain in detail. I meant that we might take two or three copies of Mr Rushbrooke's indispensable *Synopticon* and utilise the blank pages as follows. First, insert quotations of the text by the Fathers from Resch's valuable *Parallel-texte*, and add others. Then add variations of the great Greek and Latin Codices (sometimes with their contexts) and those of Prof. Burkitt's *Evangelion da-Mepharreshe*. The translation of the Arabic *Diatessaron* should also be written out in full, with quotations from Ephrem Syrus. Illustrations from the LXX, from Aquila, Theodotion, and the rest, may be brought to bear upon the parallelisms of Mark, Matthew, and Luke. Conflations (*Clue* 20 foll.) from O.T. and the Targums should be adduced to throw light on the conflations in Mark.

"Why all this labour?" Because there is evidence to shew that our present gospels are developments; and, if they are, all the phases of their development must be studied by those who hope to discover the original by scientific method. A "scientist" has been defined—not amiss though by a child—as "a man who finds out things." But "things" cannot be found out except from "things." This involves "toiling." One may "toil all the night and take nothing." Still it is the only way to take anything. So I adhere to "*toiling*."

struck by the extreme paucity, and often complete absence, of any such additional matter. Yet the types shew abundance of additional matter in which Matthew agrees with Mark, and also abundance of other additional matter in which Luke agrees with Mark.

Reading on, he is led to the conclusion that, in these portions of their narrative, Matthew and Luke *hardly ever agree except, so to speak, through the intervention of Mark*, and that *they copied, independently, from an edition of the latter*. For the full details, see *Corrections of Mark* **318—30**.

To see this was very difficult until Mr Rushbrooke's laborious classification had been accomplished. Afterwards, even to the merest beginner in Greek, with a few pages of the *Synopticon* before him, the conclusion was patent.

It is not often that an important group of literary phenomena can be traced so simply and surely to a single cause. Least of all can this be expected about phenomena in theological literature where a multitude of causes is mostly at work, causes moral as well as intellectual and literary, national or ecclesiastical as well as individual. In previous parts of this series it has been contended that many divergences in the Gospels may be explained by Semitic obscurity in the earliest traditions. But the author has never intended to deny that other influences were at work, and that research in the Gospels, as in most other provinces of study, requires a student to keep constantly before him the rule, BEWARE OF SINGLE CAUSES.

One reason why Gospel criticism has made no progress proportionate to the vast labour expended on it, is, that we have no *Handbook of Traditional Evolutions* to teach us how traditions have been evolved out of records, or poems, or religious rites, or other sources. One section of such a work should deal with documentary as distinct from oral evolution, although recognising that oral and documentary developments often go together.

Such a Handbook would classify documentary developments under various headings, whether relating to the source or to the source-use and transmission. Under "*Source*" would come (1) original obscurity, (2) original indefiniteness, (3) original austerity, non-edification, or offensiveness.

Under "*Source-use*" or "*Transmission*" would come not only the general desire to be clear, definite, and attractive (covered by (1) (2) (3)) but also special tendencies. One writer, for example, might arrange a biography according to chronology; another according to subject-matter of conversations, letters, or books; another would prefer a series of graphic scenes mingling word and deed together. Less pardonably, a special tendency might exist in a writer to favour a particular nation, *e.g.* Jews or Greeks against the world; or a class against the whole nation, *e.g.* priests against people, or the people against their rulers, and so on. There would also have to be considered the special circumstances that might cause some writers to abridge, although the general tendency has been to amplify.

Such a Handbook, besides containing general rules applicable to all literature, would, of course, keep in view the special rules applicable to transmissions of literature, *e.g.* translation; to special kinds of literature, *e.g.* prophecy; and to special national traditions about literature, *e.g.* those of the Hebrews and the Jews, and then those of the Jewish Christians handed on to the Christian Church at large.

Let us briefly consider a single instance in the Synoptic Gospels where such a work might be useful:

Mk xiii. 14	Mt. xxiv. 15	Lk. xxi. 20
"But when ye see *the abomination* (neut.) *of desolation* [one] standing (masc.) where it is not fit—"	"When therefore ye see *the abomination of desolation* spoken of (neut.) by Daniel the prophet standing (neut.) in a [or, the] holy place—"	"But when ye see *Jerusalem surrounded by camps* (or, *armies*), then know that her desolation is nigh—"

In each column the text continues identically, in order as well as in word, "Then let them that are in Judæa flee unto the mountains."

Three obvious ways (besides others not obvious though possible) present themselves for dealing with the italicised words. One is, to assert that Christ uttered Luke's words as well as the others, and that for some inscrutable reason the definite prophecy about Jerusalem was omitted by Mark and Matthew though they knew it and though it was acted on by the Christians before 70 A.D. Another is, to say that Christ made no mention of Jerusalem, but that Luke, writing after the destruction of the City by the Romans, substituted "surrounded by armies" for "abomination of desolation"; either dishonestly, because the substitution magnified Christ; or honestly, because he thought that Christ meant this.

These two ways have the merit of being short.

The third way is much longer. It has, so to speak, several stations at which we must halt. First, remembering what Papias said about a Hebrew Gospel that was variously interpreted—*i.e.* targumised, for "targum" means "interpretation" —we must consider whether in this case there may have been such a Hebrew original. If so, and if our Greek gospels are, in parts, interpretations of that Hebrew, it follows that, relatively to that Hebrew, they are of the nature of Targums. This is our first station—a hypothesis that the gospels are interpretations or Targums.

From this we go on further to consider the relation between existing Targums and their existing original, *i.e.* the Hebrew Bible. Under this head we must include the Greek Targums of the LXX, Aquila, Theodotion and Symmachus, as well as the Aramaic Targums of Onkelos and of later Targumists. These Targums are scattered over centuries, whereas our hypothetical evangelistic Targums called gospels could be divided only by intervals of mere decads. But a decad in the seething-pot of the first century might well

PREFACE

produce as many developments as ten decades at any other period. And in any case the Targums of the Hebrew sacred books cannot fail to throw some light on the way in which the sacred books of the Jewish Christians in the first century would be interpreted into Greek, or into other languages or dialects. Clearly, therefore, we have to make parallel columns of these ancient Targums, as we made above of our Synoptic gospels, and to ask whether in the divergences of the former we can find any rules that may help us to explain the divergences of the latter.

A preface does not afford room to explain by instances how much these ancient Targums have to teach us about literary developments in general and about our gospels in particular. The reader will find a few facts bearing on the subject in the Note on *The influence of mistranslation illustrated from Shakespeare* (**2830**—7)[1]. Here I can do no more than indicate how our *Handbook* might help us to explain Luke's "Jerusalem surrounded by armies" as something better than a "prophecy after the event," and something far better than an arbitrary alteration of Mark's "standing where it is not fit," or Matthew's "standing in a (or, the) holy place."

First, then, the *Handbook* will teach us that where Old Testament Targumists diverge in prophecies, one fundamental cause of the divergence is, very often, the honest belief of the Targumist that the prophet *meant*, in plain prose, something verbally different from what he *said*, in poetic metaphor.

---

[1] If the Note seems out of place, my apology must be that many think everything relating to Shakespeare interesting, everything relating to grammar uninteresting, and everything relating to Targums supremely dull. So I blended the Shakespearian matter with the Targumistic that the latter might have a better chance of being read. But I would ask the reader to note (**2834**) "Brutus answered him, *being yet but a young man*, 'I...'" instead of "Brutus answered him, '*Being yet but a young man*, I....'" Does not this appear to illustrate Mt. xix. 20 "*The young man* said" parall. to Mk x. 20, Lk. xviii. 21 "He said, '*From my youth*'"?

This leads us to what may be called "The Law of Prosaic Substitution."

Secondly, the *Handbook* will teach us that when a prophecy centres round some obscure word capable of two or even more interpretations, there will often flow from it divergent streams, sometimes running separately, sometimes combining in various ways—the result being two or more versions of the whole context as well as of the central word. This leads us to a second Law. It may be called "The Law of Divergence from Obscurity[1]."

---

[1] See **2837** (i)—(iii) where instances are given of both these Laws, shewing how, for example, such a phrase as Gen. xlix. 22 "branches (lit. daughters) run over the wall," has given rise to a number of different interpretations in which the "daughters" are supposed to be (1) the tribes of Manasseh and Ephraim, or (2) the daughters of Egypt. These, when combined with one another and inserted in the context, have resulted in long expansions that may be almost called separate legends.

See also **2949** foll. quoting Gen. xv. 7 (Heb.) "from *Ur* of the Chaldees,' where Jer. Targ. (because "*Ur*" may mean "*fire*") has "from *the fiery furnace*, from *Ur* of the Chasdai." Hence Gen. xi. 28 (Heb.) "Haran died…in Ur of the Chaldees" becomes, in the Targum, "Haran died…*in the furnace of fire which the Chasdai had made for Abraham.*" The result is a long legend about the deliverance of Abraham from a fiery furnace into which he is cast by Nimrod. See *Beresh. R.* (on Gen. xi. 28).

There are scores of instances of this kind in the Targums alone, not to speak of instances in the Talmuds and other Jewish literature. In the face of these facts, it is futile to assert that, because Greek and Latin mythology is not based—so often as was once supposed—on such verbal divergences, therefore the New Testament is not in any way affected by them.

For an instance in early Christian literature take the astonishing legend gravely recorded by Hegesippus in the second century that James the Just "alone was allowed to enter into the holy place (ἅγια); for he wore no wool but only fine linen, and he would enter into the sanctuary (ναόν) alone…." Some may say that this was simply mendacious exaggeration. Lightfoot (*Gal.* pp. 362—6) suggests misunderstood metaphor as the explanation of what he declares to be "plainly false." But see **2999** (xvii) *c* foll., where an attempt is made to shew that "alone" has been transposed in the tradition "He used to go into the temple wearing *linen alone.*" The meaning has been taken to be "*going alone.*" This implies (Lightf.) "assigning to him a privilege which was confined to the high-priest alone," and is "plainly false."

PREFACE

Let us apply these two Laws to Mark (xiii. 14). Mark does not, it is true, mention any prophet by name (as Matthew does) but he clearly alludes to the prophet Daniel, mentioned by Matthew, and to an expression contained in Dan. ix. 27 "abomination of desolation."

According to our first Law, "the Law of Substitution," we may take, as a point of starting, the hypothesis that Luke honestly thought this "abomination of desolation" to *mean* "the Roman armies closing round Jerusalem," and that he substituted the literal prose for the poetic metaphor.

But further, keeping in view the second Law, that of "Divergence from Obscurity," we must refer to Daniel in order to ascertain whether Daniel's context contains any obscure word that may explain the Synoptic divergences. Indeed Mark himself almost seems to say, "Read Daniel and think of its meaning," when he gives us the warning, "*He that readeth let him understand.*" See p. xviii, n. 1 (*b*).

The detailed results of such a reference to Daniel will be found in **2837** (i) foll. In outline, the facts are these. Daniel

---

From Josephus an interesting instance may be taken in his account of the sweetening of the waters of Marah by Moses (Exod. xv. 25 "And the Lord shewed him a tree and he cast it into the waters, and the waters were made sweet"). Philo (i. 255—6) says, "God cast 'the sweetening tree' into the soul, creating *love of toil* (φιλοπονίαν) in place of *hate of toil*....This is the food of the soul that practises virtue—the belief that *toil* is very sweet instead of bitter." R. Levi (Wünsche on Exod. xxxvii. 1) said that the bitterness was in Israel's mouth: "The generation was 'bitter' in its conduct." Others (*ib.*) illustrated the miracle from 2 K. ii. 22 "The waters were *healed*," and Jerem. xxx. 17 "*From* (ἀπὸ) *thy plagues* (LXX πληγῆς) I will heal thee." Josephus literalises (1) Philo's tradition about πονέω, (2) the tradition about πληγαί. Moses, he says (*Ant.* iii. 1. 2), split the tree so as to use it as a channel for drawing off the water. Then he persuaded the most vigorous of the men to "*toil* (πονεῖν)" to such good purpose that the water was purified *from* (ὑπὸ *i.e.* as the result of) the continuous "*strokes* (πληγαί)." He also says that the fragment of the tree was "cast at the feet" of Moses. For an explanation of this, and of the "splitting," see The Introduction to *Indices to Diatessarica*.

(ix. 27 "*on the wing* [of] abomination[s] one that maketh desolate") has just such an obscure "central word" as will explain all the divergences. Daniel's Hebrew for "wing" may mean (1) tip, or extremity, of anything; (2) "wing" of an invading and desolating army; (2) "pinnacle" (from "pinna," feather, or wing), and hence, more particularly, "*pinnacle* (πτερυγίον) of the Temple" (comp. Mt. iv. 5, Lk. iv. 9). The following table of divergences, taken from Field's *Hexapla*, traces as it were their descent from the parental obscurity:

Daniel ix. 27 (Hebrew)
"ON THE WING"

LXX and Theod.	Aq. and Sym.	"Another (Ἄλλος)"
"*on the temple* (ἐπὶ τὸ ἱερὸν) an abomination of desolations."	"*on the beginning* (ἐπὶ τῆς ἀρχῆς) of the abominations it shall be desolated."	"as far as the *pinnacle* (ἕως πτερυγίου) from destruction."

There is no Targum. But the Syr. has "*super extremitates* (or, *alas*) abominationis." If "the abomination" meant an invading army, this would mean "the wings of the invading army," which the Syriac means in 1 Macc. ix. 12 "the right *wing*."

In the absence of a Targum paraphrasing "wing" in Daniel[1],

---

[1] (*a*) I have found only one reference to Dan. ix. 27 in the Talmud, *Taanith* 28 *b*—29 *a* on which see **2837** (iii) *d*. Dr A. Büchler tells me that, as far as he knows, there is no other in Talmud or Midrash, and Bacher's Index to his "Agada" mentions no other. The tradition (4th cent.) takes "wing" as "hand" (for which meaning of *chânâph* in Talmud see Levy ii. 357) and proceeds to develop a legend about two idols with something written on the *hand* of one of them (rather like the story of Dagon in 1 S. v. 4).

Jerome's commentary says "What the Hebrews think about this passage I will briefly outline (brevi sermone perstringam)." Having unfortunately omitted it below, I will give here his "outline" of the Jewish paraphrase of Dan. ix. 22—7: "(22—3) O Daniel, scito quod a die hac, qua tibi nunc loquor: erat autem annus primus Darii, qui occidit Balthasar, et regnum Chaldaeorum in Persas Medosque transtulit, (24) usque ad septuagesimam annorum hebdomadam, hoc est, annos

PREFACE

the reader will find an equivalent (and an instance of the Law of Prosaic Substitution) in the following parallels:

quadringentos nonaginta, haec populo tuo per partes accident. Primum propitiabitur tibi Deus, quae nunc magnopere deprecaris, et delebitur tibi peccatum, et finem accipiet praevaricatio. Nunc enim urbe deserta et templo usque ad fundamenta destructo, in luctu est populus constitutus, sed non post grande tempus instaurabitur: Et non solum hoc fiet in his septuaginta hebdomadibus, ut aedificetur civitas, et templum instauretur, sed nascetur Christus, *i.e.* justitia sempiterna. Et signabitur visio et Propheta, ut nequaquam Propheta inveniatur in Israel, et ungatur Sanctus sanctorum. De quo in Psalterio legimus: Propterea unxit te Deus, Deus tuus, oleo laetitiae prae consortibus tuis. Qui et in alio loco dicit de se: Sancti estote, quia et ego sanctus sum. (25) Scito igitur, quoniam a die, qua tibi nunc loquor et Dei sermone promitto, quod revertatur populus et Hierusalem instauretur, usque ad Christum ducem et perpetuam desolationem templi, hebdomadae numerentur sexaginta duae, nec non et aliae septem hebdomadae, in quibus juxta ordinem suum duae res fient, de quibus et ante jam dixit, quod revertatur populus et aedificetur platea a Nehemia et Esdra. In fine ergo hebdomadarum complebitur Dei sententia in angustia temporum, quando rursum destruetur templum et capietur civitas. (26) Nam post sexaginta duas hebdomadas occidetur Christus, et non erit ejus populus, qui eum negaturus est, sive ut illi dicunt, non erit illius imperium quod putabat se redempturum. Et quid dico de Christo occidendo et populo penitus deserendo auxilio Dei, cum civitatem et Sanctuarium dissipaturus sit populus Romanus cum Duce venturo Vespasiano? (27) Quo mortuo transactis septem hebdomadis, id est annis quadraginta novem, Ælius Hadrianus, a quo postea de ruinis Hierusalem urbs Ælia condita est, rebellantes Judaeos, Timo Ruffo magistro exercitus pugnante, superavit. Et tunc deficiet hostia et Sacrificium et usque ad consummationem mundi et finem perseverabit desolatio."

Jerome adds, as regards "una hebdomada de qua scriptum est Confirmabit pactum multis hebdomada una," that by some Jews the week (?) is divided for Vespasian and in the case of Hadrian, "dividatur Vespasiano et in Hadriano," because, "juxta historiam Josephi, Vespasianus et Titus tribus annis et sex mensibus pacem cum Judaeis fecerint. Tres autem anni et sex menses sub Hadriano supputantur, quando Hierusalem omnino subversa est et Judaeorum gens catervatim caesa, ita ut Judaeae quoque finibus pellerentur."

(*b*) Mk xiii. 14 "*He that readeth*" assumes that the reader is to read Daniel. Mt. xxiv. 15 expressly mentions "Daniel" for clearness. "Readeth" could not mean "reads to the congregation" except in suitable context, *e.g.* Rev. i. 3 "Blessed is *he that readeth and they that hear*."

PREFACE

Hebrew poetry	Jerem. xlviii. 40 Targum prose
"As it were an eagle shall fly and *extend its wings*."	"Like a flying eagle so shall a king go up *with his army and encamp* on Moab."

Returning to the Christian documents we find that Mark, using the masculine ("the abomination (*neut.*)...[one] standing (*masc.*)") appears to contemplate the Abomination as a Man of Sin (comp. 2 Thess. ii. 3—4) standing erect and obtrusive. Where? The various versions of Daniel suggest some "holy place" or "pinnacle." An evangelist not able to decide between these two places might well paraphrase by "*where it is not fit [for him] to stand.*" Matthew explains "on the wing" in general terms as "*in a holy place.*" Luke, like the Targumist on Jeremiah, takes the "wing" as that of an army, and paraphrases with "*camp*," or "*army.*"

What, then, did our Lord actually say? Or, if we cannot yet venture to answer that question, which of the three Synoptists has been most faithful to His words? That is a question to be discussed in *The Fourfold Gospel*[1] rather than in the present volume. But the evidence points to the conclusion that the earliest tradition made no mention of Daniel by name, and certainly made no mention of "armies" or "camps," but that it did make mention of Daniel's phrase about the "wing"—perhaps meaning "pinnacle" of the Temple.

On this same "pinnacle" Jesus—according to Matthew and Luke—had been placed by Satan when He was tempted to tempt God. On this same "pinnacle," perhaps, the Thes-

---

[1] Some may ask, "Why *fourfold*? Ought not this to be discussed in a treatise on the *threefold* Gospel? For the fourth gospel says nothing about it."

True, but it is contended that, in passages of this kind, *if Luke omits or alters anything in Mark, John intervenes as a rule to give the substance of Mark* (**2965**, and *Paradosis* p. ix). Consequently the passage has to be discussed in *The Fourfold Gospel*; for, if John does not intervene, the rule is here broken.

salonian Epistle describes the Man of Sin as "exalting himself" against God "in the temple." Origen, at all events, quotes Paul and Daniel as saying the same thing[1].

If Origen is right, the Synoptic words about the Abomination of Desolation would need to be studied in the light of the Johannine tradition (Jn xiv. 30) "The prince of the world cometh and hath nothing in me." It would be in accordance with Christ's general doctrine to suppose that He predicted some outburst of spiritual revolt against God, not a merely material or national war. Many considerations combine to make it certain that He did not speak of "Jerusalem surrounded by armies, or camps."

This is a specimen, in outline, of the way in which many Synoptic divergences—so far as documentary causes are concerned—might be studied where they come in the midst of parallel or identical traditions. If only we had such a *Handbook* as has been suggested above, the method would be both briefer and safer. As things are, the way is long, circuitous, and laborious, and sometimes leads the traveller to no conclusion. But negative knowledge is not always to be despised,—as, for example, when a kind ransacker of Concordances and Indices tells his reader that, so far as these helps may be relied on, this or that word is non-existent in these or those authors or papyri. Moreover, even if he finds himself brought to a standstill, the diligent seeker may map out the country as far as he has gone, and thus leave behind him positive knowledge useful for future explorers.

In exploration of this kind it is not lawful for the traveller to feel hopes or fears in such a form as to entice him into reporting non-fact as fact. But it is lawful to feel hope about the untraversed based on knowledge of the traversed region,

---

[1] Orig. *Cels.* vi. 46, after quoting 2 Thess. ii. 4, says, "Now this has been said also in Daniel as follows, '*And on the temple an abomination of desolations.*'"

PREFACE

if he can reasonably believe that he has gained some insight into "the lie of the land."

Hence I venture to express my conviction that the minutiæ of scientific literary criticism are destined to play more than a minute part in the attainment of truths beyond those of grammar and literature. Grammar is not theology, nor is it the handmaid of theology. But it is the handmaid of truth, and truth includes theology. Honest criticism, grammatical as well as historical, will ultimately (so I believe) play a constructive as well as a destructive part for Christian faith, opening our minds to discern more clearly the real meaning of worship and the real meaning of redemption, and gradually preparing us for a purer, firmer, more spontaneous, and more fruitful worship of our Redeemer.

In addition to friends mentioned in the Preface to *Apologia* (Mr H. Candler and the Rev. J. Hunter Smith) I desire to record my thanks to Mr W. S. Aldis and Professor W. H. Bennett, for valuable suggestions. In several passages I have expressed indebtedness to Professor A. Büchler, of Jews' College, London, for special extracts from Rabbinical works, but I have pleasure in here adding that I am under a wider obligation to him for criticisms of a more general character.

EDWIN A. ABBOTT

Wellside, Hampstead,
7 *Aug.* 1907.

CONTENTS

	PAGE
REFERENCES AND ABBREVIATIONS	xxvii

PART I

NOTES[1] TO SILANUS THE CHRISTIAN 1

SUMMARY OF PRINCIPAL NOTES

[2805]	On "orphans" in Jn xiv. 18 and Epictetus . .	5
[2806]	„ Johannine and Epictetian descriptions of the Son of God	6
[2808—9]	„ the divergent accounts of the sayings of Socrates	7
[2813]	„ the "Galilæans"	9
[2824*—(i)]	„ "spiritual body"	15
[2830—7]	„ the influence of mistranslation illustrated from Shakespeare	21
[2837 (i)—(iii)]	„ Targumistic Translations	24
[2839 a—d]	„ the continuity between Mark and Isaiah . .	33
[2840* a—g]	„ "favour," "kindness" etc. in R.V. . . .	36
[2842—9]	„ the "yoke" and the "cross"	37
[2851—6]	„ "faith as a grain of mustard-seed" . . .	40

[1] The Notes, being intended to include references, explanations, and justifications, bearing on *Silanus the Christian*, contain, in each case, a reference to that work. Thus "[2807] Page 34, 'Carriest about God,' Epict. ii. 8. 12, ii. 16. 33" merely gives references to the passages quoted on page 34 of *Silanus*.

But "[2824*] Page 135, 'To describe a *real person*'" introduces a note of considerable length under a separate heading "Spiritual Body"; and "[2942*] Page 304 'The Apocalypse'" introduces a very much longer note (pp. 75—114) about the date of that work.

For the convenience of the reader a Summary of Principal Notes is given here, but his principal help will be the Indices.

CONTENTS

		PAGE
[2860—71]	On "the lost sheep"	42
[2874—8]	„ "the barren fig-tree".	46
[2880—2]	„ the birth of Christ	49
[2885—6]	„ "receiving as a little child"	51
[2892—907]	„ the events between Christ's Resurrection and Ascension	54
[2892 a—c]	„ the interval between the Resurrection and the Ascension	54
[2892—5]	„ Acts i. 4 (R.V. txt) "being assembled together"	55
[2896—907]	„ the traditions concerning Christ's eating after the Resurrection	56
[2910]	„ an alleged eclipse at the Crucifixion.	60
[2917—23]	„ Luke's omission of "Why hast thou forsaken me?"	62
[2924]	„ the end of Mark's gospel	66
[2926—34]	„ the prediction of Peter's crucifixion	67
[2935—41]	„ the modern hypothesis of the early death of John the son of Zebedee	70
[2942* (i)—(xxiv)]	THE DATE OF THE WRITING OF "THE REVELATION OF JOHN"	75
[2942*]	The hypothesis of incorporated documents.	75
(i)	The argument (as to the date) from numbers	77
(i) g—k.	The principle of antithesis	79
(i) l—q.	The Number of the Beast	81
(ii)	Parallelism between John and Ezekiel	83
(ii) a—d.	"The Great City"	84
(iii)	The Seven Churches	86
(iv)	The Measuring for the Temple	87
(v)—(vi)	Other arguments for A.D. 96	88
(vii)—(x)	John's view of the Fall of Jerusalem	90
(viii) a—i.	Does ὀνόματα ever mean "persons"?	91
(xi)—(xv)	The Birth of the "Man-child"	96
(xv) b—f.	The meaning of "virgins" in Rev. xiv. 4	103
(xvi)—(xxiv)	Inferences	105
[2942—7]	On Patmos	114
[2948—51]	„ legends of martyrdom by fire	116
[2952]	„ Jerome's story about John the son of Zebedee	117
[2954—5]	„ "Elder," as a title of teachers	117
[2958]	„ the vagueness of Irenæus's references	118
[2959—61 (i)]	„ the pool of (R.V.) "Bethesda"	119
[2962]	„ Jn ii. 20 "forty-six years"	122

CONTENTS

		PAGE
[2963—5]	On the Washing of Feet, as regarded by Philo and Origen	123
[2966]	„ the "thirsting" of Christ as explained by Catherine of Siena	124
[2969—77]	„ the name "Boanerges"	125
[2978]	„ the use and meaning of τεκνία	127
[2980—4]	„ the preface to Luke's gospel	128
[2986]	„ the metaphor "sweat and watching"	132
[2989—90]	„ Jn viii. 57, "Thou art not yet fifty years old"	133
[2995]	„ Mt. x. 8 "Raise the dead"	134

PART II

LONGER NOTES

NOTE I

"THE SON OF MAN" [2998 (i)—(lvi)]

(i)	§ 1.	Importance of the Title	140
(ii)	§ 2.	Deficiency in Aramaic.	141
(iii)—(iv)	§ 3.	"Son of Man" in the Law	142
(v)—(viii)	§ 4.	"Son of Man" in the Prophets	145
(ix)—(x)	§ 5.	"Son of Man" in the Psalms and Job	149
(xi)—(xix)	§ 6.	Jewish Comments	151
(xx)	§ 7.	Ambiguity of the Title	163
(xxi)	§ 8.	The Fourth Gospel prepares us for misinterpretation	165
(xxii)—(xxiii)	§ 9.	Pauline equivalents	166
(xxiv)—(xxv)	§ 10.	The Epistle to the Hebrews and the Acts	171
(xxvi)—(xxxiii)	§ 11.	The Revelation of John	175
(xxvi)	c—g.	Who is "his angel"?	176
„	h—k.	"Witness" and "martyr"	178
„	l—m.	"The IS" and "the seven spirits"	179
„	n—q.	"The faithful Witness"	180
(xxvii)	a—e.	"The Alpha and the Omega"	182
„	f—m.	"Almighty"	184
„	n—q.	"Angels" not to be worshipped	187
„	r—v.	Did Essenes "offer worship" to the sun?	188
„	w.	The "washing" of the Essenes	192
(xxviii)	b—e.	"The seven golden candlesticks"	193
„	f—k.	"Walking in the midst"	196

CONTENTS

		PAGE
(xxviii) *l—r.*	" One like a son of man "	199
„ *s—x.*	The " stars " and the " sword "	202
(xxx) *b*—(xxxi) *c.*	" Clouds " and " cloud "	207
(xxxii) *b—d.*	The difference between ἀρνίον and ἀμνός	210
(xxxiv)—(xxxvi) § 12.	The Gnostics, Ignatius, and Barnabas	214
(xxxvii)—(xli) § 13.	Justin, Irenæus, and Tertullian	217
(xlii)—(xlv) § 14.	Clement of Alexandria and Origen	224
(xlvi)—(l) § 15.	Conclusion	230
(li)—(lvi) § 16.	Addition on the "*Similitudes of Enoch*"	235
(liv) *e—j.*	" The righteous one "	241
(lv) *d—m.*	The doctrine of " hiding "	246
(lvi) *a—d.*	The resurrection	251

NOTE II

THE SELF-MANIFESTATIONS OF CHRIST [2999 (i)—(xvii)]

(i)—(ii) § 1.	" Touching " and " drawing near "	253
(iii) § 2.	God " meeting " man	255
(iv)—(v) § 3.	" Going to meet," " going before," and " drawing near "	259
(vi) § 4.	Different words employed by the Evangelists	261
(vii)—(viii) § 5.	Matthew's unique use of " anticipate "	263
(ix)—(x) § 6.	Matthew's account of Peter's " fishing " illustrated from John	268
(xi) § 7.	Different symbolisms of " fish "	270
(xii)—(xvii) § 8.	The original meaning of the story of " the stater "	272
(xvii) *a—o.*	The reclothing of Peter	279

INDICES

I.	NEW TESTAMENT PASSAGES	291
II.	ENGLISH	298
III.	GREEK	309

REFERENCES AND ABBREVIATIONS

REFERENCES

(i) *Black Arabic numbers* refer to paragraphs in the several volumes of Diatessarica :—

    1— 272 = *Clue*.
    273— 552 = *Corrections*.
    553—1149 = *From Letter to Spirit*.
    1150—1435 = *Paradosis*.
    1436—1885 = *Johannine Vocabulary*.
    1886—2799 = *Johannine Grammar*.
    2800—2999 = *Notes on New Testament Criticism*.

(ii) The Books of Scripture are referred to by the ordinary abbreviations, except where specified below. But when it is said that Samuel, Isaiah, Matthew, or any other writer, wrote this or that, it is to be understood as meaning *the writer, whoever he may be, of the words in question*, and not as meaning that the actual writer was Samuel, Isaiah, or Matthew.

(iii) The principal Greek MSS. are denoted by ℵ, A, B, etc.; the Latin versions by *a*, *b*, etc., as usual. The Syriac version discovered by Mrs Lewis on Mount Sinai is referred to as SS, *i.e.* "Sinaitic Syrian." It is always quoted from Prof. Burkitt's translation. I regret that in the first three vols. of Diatessarica Mrs Lewis's name was omitted in connexion with this version.

(iv) The text of the Greek Old Testament adopted is that of B, edited by Prof. Swete; of the New, that of Westcott and Hort.

(v) Modern works are referred to by the name of the work, or author, vol., and page, *e.g.* Levy iii. 343 *a*, *i.e.* vol. iii. p. 343, col. 1.

ABBREVIATIONS

Apol. = Justin Martyr's First Apology.
Aq. = Aquila's version of O.T.
Blass = Second English Edition of Prof. Blass's Grammar of New Testament Greek, Macmillan and Co., 1905.
Buhl = Buhl's edition of Gesenius, Leipzig, 1899.
Burk. = Prof. F. C. Burkitt's *Evangelion Da-mepharreshe*, Cambridge University Press, 1904.
C. before numbers = circa, "about" (*e.g.* c. 10).
Canon. LXX = *the canonical books* of LXX.

REFERENCES AND ABBREVIATIONS

Chr. = *Chronicles.*
Chri. = *the words of Christ*, as distinct from narrative, see **1672***.
Clem. Alex. 42 = Clement of Alexandria in Potter's page 42.
Dalman, *Words = Words of Jesus*, Eng. Transl. 1902; *Aram. G.* = *Grammatik Aramäisch*, 1894.
Demosth. 433 = Teubner's marginal page 433 of Demosthenes; but Demosth. (Preuss) xxvii. 3 = p. 3 of Orat. xxvii. in Teubner, as in Preuss's Concordance.
Diatess. = the Arabic Diatessaron, sometimes called Tatian's, translated by Rev. H. W. Hogg, B.D., in the Ante-Nicene Christian Library.
Ency. = *Encyclopaedia Biblica.*
Ephrem = Ephraemus Syrus, ed. Moesinger.
Etheridge = Etheridge's translations of the Targums on the Pentateuch.
Euseb. = the Ecclesiastical History of Eusebius.
Field = Origenis Hexaplorum quae supersunt, Oxford, 1875, also Otium Norvicense, 1881.
Gesen. = the Oxford edition of Gesenius.
Heb. LXX = that part of LXX of which the Hebrew is extant.
Hor. Heb. = *Horae Hebraicae*, by John Lightfoot, 1658—74, ed. Gandell, Oxf. 1859.
Iren. = the treatise of Irenæus against Heresies.
Jer. Targ. (or Targ. Jer.) = the fragments of the Jerusalem Targum on the Pentateuch, sometimes referred to as Jer. II (see Preface, p. viii).
Jon. Targ. (or Targ. Jon.) = the Targum of Pseudo-Jonathan ben Uzziel *on the Pentateuch*, sometimes referred to as Jer. I. The Targum of Jonathan *on the Prophets* is referred to as simply "Targ." (see Preface, pp. vii—viii).
K. = *Kings.*
Levy = Levy's *Neuhebräisches und Chaldäisches Wörterbuch*, 4 vols., Leipzig, 1889; Levy Ch. = *Chaldäisches Wörterbuch*, 2 vols., 1881.
L.S. = Liddell and Scott's Greek Lexicon.
Narr. = *in narrative*, as distinct from (*a*) speech of Christ, (*b*) speech generally (**1672***).
Onk. = the Targum of Onkelos (see Preface, pp. vii—viii).
Origen, Huet, or Lomm., ii. 340 = vol. ii. p. 340 of Huet or Lommatzsch severally. The reader is also sometimes guided by reference to the text, *e.g.* Numb. xiv. 23 in O.'s commentary on Numbers.
Oxf. Conc. = *The Oxford Concordance to the Septuagint.*
Papyri are indicated by *Pap.* [from the] *Berlin* [Museum]; and *Pap.* [of the] *Egypt* [Exploration Society], vols. i—vi, viz. *Oxy*[rynchus] i—iv, *Fayûm* v, *Tebt*[unis] vi.
Pec., affixed to Mt., Lk., etc., means peculiar to Matthew, Luke, etc.
Philo is referred to by Mangey's volume and page, *e.g.* Philo ii. 234, or, as to the Latin treatises, by Aucher's pages (P. A.) (see **1608**).

REFERENCES AND ABBREVIATIONS

Resch = Resch's *Paralleltexte* (4 vols.).
S. = *Samuel*; s. = " see."
Schöttg. = Schöttgen's *Horae Hebraicae*, Dresden and Leipzig, 1733.
Sir. = the work of Ben Sira, *i.e.* the son of Sira. It is commonly called Ecclesiasticus (see **20***a*). The original Hebrew has been edited, in part, by Cowley and Neubauer, Oxf. 1897; in part, by Schechter and Taylor, Camb. 1899.
SS, see (iii) above.
Steph. or Steph. Thes. = Stephani Thesaurus (Didot).
Sym. = Symmachus's version of O.T.
Targ. (by itself) is used where only one Targum is extant on the passage quoted (see Preface, pp. vii—viii).
Targ. Jer., and Targ. Jon., see Jer. Targ. and Jon. Targ. above.
Theod. = Theodotion's version of O.T.
Tromm. = Trommius' *Concordance to the Septuagint.*
Tryph. = the Dialogue between Justin Martyr and Trypho the Jew.
Wetst. = Wetstein's *Comm. on the New Testament*, Amsterdam, 1751.
W.H. = Westcott and Hort's New Testament.
Wünsche = Wünsche's translation of *Rabboth* etc. Leipzig, 1880—5.

(*a*) A bracketed Arabic number, following Mk, Mt., etc., indicates the number of instances in which a word occurs in Mark, Matthew, etc., *e.g.* ἀγάπη Mk (0), Mt. (1), Lk. (1), Jn (7).

(*b*) Where verses in Hebrew, Greek, and Revised Version, are numbered differently, the number of R.V. is given alone.

PART I

NOTES TO SILANUS THE CHRISTIAN

NOTES TO SILANUS THE CHRISTIAN

NOTE TO PREFACE

[**2800**] Page 9 (of *Silanus*) "Detailed proofs." For these the reader will sometimes be referred by black numerals to paragraphs of the various parts of *Diatessarica* as given on p. xxvii of the present volume.

Occasional reference will also be made to a work (mentioned in *Johannine Vocabulary*, Pref. p. ix) to be entitled *The Fourfold Gospel*, which I hope to publish before long[1].

For general remarks as to quotations, and as to the sayings attributed to Epictetus, Arrian, Irenæus, Justin Martyr, and others, the reader's attention is directed to the note on p. 12 of *Silanus*[2].

---

[1] [**2800 a**] Thus, with reference to the argument—which seems to me very slight—for the early date of the fourth gospel, based on Jn v. 2 "Now there is... a pool," the reader will find very little in the text of *Silanus*, and not much in the Notes. But he will be referred for further information to *Fourfold G.* "pool," i.e. *The Fourfold Gospel*, English Index, "pool."

[2] [**2800 b**] Obligations to modern sources will be acknowledged where they occur. But I should like to mention one instance where obligation might be supposed to occur but does not. On p. 188, Scaurus raises the objection that a message to "repent" cannot be regarded as "good news." Wellhausen's *Das Evangelium Marci* p. 8 raises the same objection in very similar words, "Aber wie kann die Busspredigt als frohe Botschaft bezeichnet werden?" This is a case of coincidence. I did not see Wellhausen's work till the notes were written; and the objection raised by him (and by Scaurus) is answered—or an answer is attempted—by Silanus.

[**2800 c**] Concerning "repentance," Luther writing to Staupitz in 1518 A.D. (Martin Luther's Briefe, ed. de Wette, Berlin, 1825, p. 116) says that Staupitz first taught him its true meaning—"quod poenitentia vera non est nisi quae ab amore justitiae et Dei incipit : et hoc esse potius principium poenitentiae quod illis finis et consummatio videtur." By "illis" Luther means the previously mentioned "murderers (carnifices)," who, by their precepts, alike innumerable and insupportable (importabilibus), "teach what they call the method of confession (modum docent, ut vocant, confitendi)." When the true meaning was grasped, and

NOTES TO CHAPTER I

[2801] Page 15, "I forbid...," Epict. i. 2. 19 foll.; p. 15, "Helvidius Priscus," put to death by Vespasian. See Mayor on Juvenal v. 36.

P. 16, "Not from Arrian." Celsus tells this story, and Origen (*Cels.* vii. 54) assumes it to be true; but Arrian makes no mention of it, and it is very doubtful; see Epict. i. 12. 24 (which suggests natural lameness) and Schweig. Epict. vol. iii. p. 126—7; p. 17, "Described," Epict. i. 2. 29; p. 17, "So you philosophers," Epict. i. 29. 9 foll.; p. 17, "Went on to say"; from this point to the end of the chapter, the imaginary lecture consists of quotations—sometimes combined, paraphrased, and transposed—from Epict. i. 9. 15, i. 30. 6—7, ii. 13. 21—7, i. 29. 50 foll., ii. 13. 14, iii. 24. 48, i. 19. 8—9, iii. 22. 30 foll., ii. 9. 1 foll., iv. 5. 16, ii. 9. 3, iii. 22. 72 (quoting *Iliad* ii. 25), iii. 22. 45 foll., iv. 10. 14 foll.

P. 23, "Plato," *Symp.* xxxii (215 E).

NOTES TO CHAPTER II

[2802] Page 25, "It was therefore right...," Epict. i. 1. 7; p. 25, "But what says Zeus?" Epict. i. 1. 10, comp. Epict. iv. 6. 5 "that which Zeus was not able to do."

P. 26, "The difficult words," Epict. i. 2. 12, see Schweig. *ad loc.* The text of Schweighäuser and Schenkl reads ἐδώκαμεν as ἔδωκα μέν, but μέν presents difficulties greater than those involved in the change of number.

P. 26, "Wretched creature!" Epict. i. 12. 24. "The Fates

Scripture was studied in this new light, the consequence, he says, was a delightful transformation: "Ecce jucundissimum ludum! Verba undique mihi colludebant, planeque huic sententiae arridebant et assultabant, ita ut, cum prius non fuerit ferme in Scriptura tota amarius mihi verbum quam poenitentia—licet sedulo etiam coram Deo simularem, et fictum coactumque amorem exprimere conarer—nunc *nihil gratius aut dulcius mihi sonat quam poenitentia.*"

[2800 *d*] While complaining that these spiritual "murderers" have "attached so much importance to works of repentance (poenitentiae) that they have left us scarcely a remnant of repentance [itself]," Luther charitably adds that they have been led astray by the Latin word, "Latino scilicet vocabulo abducti, quod 'poenitentiam agere' actionem magis sonet quam mutationem affectus, et Graeco illi μετανοεῖν nullo modo satisficit (*sic*)."

present at your birth" suggests that the lameness implied in the context was not caused by cruelty (see **2801**); p. 27, "The philosophers say," Epict. ii. 14. 11 foll.

[**2803**] Page 27, "Whom I must needs please," Epict. iv. 12. 11. The context illustrates Gal. i. 10—ii. 6 "Do I seek to *please men?*... From *those who seemed to be something*...*Those who seemed [to be something]* imparted nothing to me." Comp. Epict. iv. 12. 10 "But my friends tell me I have not *pleased* Mr so-and-so. Is Mr so-and-so my life-work? 'No, but he (lit.) *seems* to be someone.' That concerns him and those to whom he *seems* to be someone, not me." In both writers, there is the same disgust at attempting to conciliate a person that "seems to be someone."

P. 27, "Thine...all," see *Silanus* p. 22, quoting Epict. iv. 10. 16. Comp. Jn xvii. 7 "All things whatsoever thou hast given me are from thee." But the Cynic is thinking of himself and his own faculties; Christ is thinking of His body, the Church.

[**2804**] Page 28, "To each...," Epict. i. 14. 12; p. 28, "Cattle...," Epict. ii. 8. 10 foll.; p. 29, "Virtue and vice," Epict. i. 12. 16; p. 30, "Thou art the sun...," Epict. iii. 22. 5—8. Curiously enough, Epictetus mentions Thersites in the context, but without the least recognition of the difficulty mentioned in the text; p. 30, "How grand," Epict. iii. 24. 111—15; p. 31, "In very truth," Epict. iii. 24. 19.

[**2805**] Page 31, "Orphans," see Epict. iii. 24. 14—20. "Not as though he were leaving them *orphans*," resembles Jn xiv. 18 "I will not leave you *orphans*." Comp. Ps. lxviii. 5 "a father of the *orphans*...is God in his holy habitation," and xxvii. 10 "When my father and my mother forsake me the Lord will take me up." The difference between Jn and Epict. is that whereas the latter exhibits Hercules as leaving his children without a regret, and without any suggestion of a future return, Jn exhibits Christ as sympathizing with those whom He is leaving, and as consoling them with the thought that He will come to them, "I will not leave you orphans, I will come unto you[1]."

---

[1] [**2805***a*] Jn xiv. 18 R.V. txt "desolate" does not appear to be justified by Greek usage, which (according to Stephen's *Thesaurus*) always uses ὀρφανός to mean "orphan" except when it is defined by a genitive ("bereaved" of children, of country etc.). The LXX, too, uses it abundantly to mean "orphan" but never to mean "desolate." Origen (*Hom. Ezek.* iv. 5) quotes Jn xiii. 33 "dear children (τεκνία)" along with Gal. iv. 19 "filioli mei quos iterum parturio." He

[2806] The context shews four other Epictetian features in the Son of God that should be compared with corresponding Johannine features.

(1) Epict. "He (Hercules) thought God to be his Father and *fixing his eyes on Him did everything that He did*," Jn v. 19 "The Son can do nothing of himself but *what he seeth the Father doing*." Comp. *Joh. Voc.* 1607 "Philo also uses βλέπω of the Eldest Son in heaven *looking at the acts of the Father as patterns for His own action.*"

(2) Epict. (lit.) "That which is blessed (τὸ γὰρ εὐδαιμονοῦν) ought to be [already] in full possession of (ἀπέχειν) the things that it *wills* (θέλει); it ought to be like something that has been filled, or fulfilled (πεπληρωμένῳ τινὶ ἐοικέναι)." Contrast Jn xv. 11 "that your joy may be filled, or fulfilled (πληρωθῇ)," xvi. 24 "that your joy may be completely filled, or fulfilled (πεπληρωμένη)," xvii. 13 "that they may have the joy that is mine, completely filled, or fulfilled, in themselves." These passages imply a *future* "filling" or "fulfilling." And xvii. 24 "I *will* (θέλω) that, where I am, there they also may be with me" implies that the will of the Son (which is also the will of the Father) is not yet "fulfilled." The only character in the fourth gospel that describes his joy as "fulfilled" is John the Baptist, Jn iii. 29 αὕτη οὖν ἡ χαρὰ ἡ ἐμὴ πεπλήρωται. That implies the finite character of his mission.

(3) Epict. "*Thirst* ought not to attach itself to it (*i.e.* to the blessedness of the Son of God)," Jn xix. 28 "Jesus...in order that the scripture might be perfectly fulfilled, saith, *I thirst*."

(4) Epict. "Ulysses, if indeed he *wept* (ἔκλαιε) and lamented, was not a good man," Jn xi. 35 "Jesus *wept* (ἐδάκρυσεν)."

In (1), Jn agrees with Epict.; in (2), (3), and (4), he disagrees.

P. 31, "Banqueting," Epict. *Ench.* xv.

---

also (on Jn xiii. 33) contrasts the appellation "dear children" with the term (Jn xx. 17) "my brethren" as though the former implied "my" in "dear children," being a term of endearment (ὑποκοριστικοῦ) that also suggested a "littleness" in the souls of the apostles. It must be understood however that the Son will deliver the disciples from orphanhood, not by presenting Himself to them as their Father, but by revealing the Father, or (so to speak) bringing the Father, with the Holy Spirit, into their hearts.

[2805 b] Compare also the Jewish use of "orphan" mentioned by Levy *Ch.* I. 348 b. "Thou orphan!" is addressed metaphorically to anyone regarded as grossly ignorant, "orphaned of his teacher (vom Lehrer verwaister)."

NOTES TO CHAPTER III

[2807] Page 34, "Carriest about God," Epict. ii. 8. 12, ii. 16. 33; p. 34, "Fever and Cholera," Epict. i. 19. 6; p. 34, "Demeter, or the Koré," Epict. ii. 20. 32; p. 34, "Never...Poseidon, Ares, or Aphrodite." They are not in Schenkl's Index; p. 35, "Even Athene...," Epict. ii. 8. 18—20, ii. 19. 26, iii. 13. 4; p. 35, "An oath," Epict. i. 14. 15—17; p. 36, "Profit," Epict. i. 19. 12—15, i. 22. 1, ii. 22. 15, comp. iii. 3. 6.

P. 36, "New work...Tacitus," *Annals* xv. 44 "quos per flagitia invisos vulgus Christianos appellabat," "exitiabilis superstitio," "haud perinde in crimine incendii quam odio humani generis convicti sunt," "sontes et novissima exempla meritos"; p. 37, "His letter to the Emperor," Pliny *Epist. ad Trajan.* 96; p. 38, "Pointed to these words," Plato *Apol.* xix. (31 D); p. 38, "The very words," Xen. *Apol.* xii. 1.

[2808] Page 39, "Entirely different saying," Xen. *Apol.* xxix—xxx. Socrates predicts that the son of Anytus will come to a bad end, because Anytus rejected the advice of Socrates about the boy's training. "Anytus," says Socrates, "exults in having destroyed me,... but how wretched is this man! He does not know that whosoever of us two has achieved for all time the fairer and more profitable results—he is the real victor!"; p. 39, "Condensed version," Epict. i. 29. 18, ii. 2. 15, iii. 23. 21, *Ench.* liii. 4; p. 39, "Much longer," Plato *Apol.* xviii. (30 C—D) "Me Anytus will not harm—nor Meletus either. For he would not have the power. For I do not think that it is God's will that a better man should be harmed by a worse. Kill me he might perhaps, or banish me, or degrade me...."

P. 39, "Very variously reported." See the various readings of the *Manual* in Schenkl's edition as compared with those of the *Lectures*; p. 39, "Sacrifice to Æsculapius," Plato *Phæd.* lxvi. (118 A).

NOTES TO CHAPTER IV

[2809] Page 41, "Quick etc." Comp. Epicharmus quoted by Polyb. xviii. 23, "Be sober and remember to disbelieve."

P. 43, "The same things." See Xen. *Mem.* iv. 4. 6, where Hippias accuses Socrates of always saying the same things, and Socrates replies, "Not only the same things but also about the same subjects," and Plato *Gorg.* xlv. (490—1) where Callicles says, "How you do always say the same things, Socrates!" To which the reply is, "Not only so, Callicles, but also about the same subjects[1]."

[2810] Page 45, "Musonius Rufus," comp. Plin. *Epist.* iii. 11. 5 "C. Musonium...quantum licitum est per aetatem cum admiratione dilexi," and Epict. i. 9. 29 "Thus also Rufus, testing me, used to say, 'This or that will befall you at the hands of your master'." But the context describes Epictetus as replying, "Such things men must put up with," on which Musonius exclaims, in admiration, that the youth, thus armed, is in no need of the philosopher's intercession. Perhaps we should read περὶ σοῦ παρὰ σοῦ...δυναμένου. The context requires the meaning to be "since you are able to draw help from yourself."

[2811] Page 47, "Made money," comp. a treatise printed in the works of Lucian describing a sham philosopher, a Christian (*De Morte Peregrin.* 18) who gained great repute by abusing the Emperor. When the Prefect of the City banished him, the punishment "made him a rival of Musonius, Dion, and Epictetus"; p. 47, "The condition," Epict. iii. 22. 69; p. 48, "Undistractedly[2]... entangled," 1 Cor. vii. 35, 2 Tim. ii. 4; p. 48, "Daniel," see Dan. vii. 1—14; p. 49, "Cudgelled," Epict. iii. 22. 54; p. 49, "I think that God," 1 Cor. iv. 9—13; p. 49, "Never needlessly offending," 2 Cor. vi. 3 foll.; p. 50, "He could give points to Epictetus[3]"; p. 51, "How then dost thou...," Epict. i. 29. 46;

---

[1] [2809 a] The author desires to call attention to the promise of Scaurus (*Sil.* p. 43) and to say that he will be happy to give the same sum (say £5) to the first person that may send him twenty consecutive identical words of Socrates from Plato and Xenophon. Address, Rev. Dr Abbott, Wellside, Well Walk, London N.W.

[2] [2811 a] The word "undistracted," by itself, would prove little. For it is frequent in Polybius and Plutarch, and (which is still more indicative of frequency) had found its way into regular legal forms as early as 13 B.C. See *Berl. Pap.* 1057 (22) (B.C. 13) παρέξεσθαι τὸν Ἡ. ἀπερίσπαστο(ν) καὶ ἀπαρενόχλη(τον), and comp. *Ox. Pap.* 286 (17) (A.D. 82), where the same three words occur, "that they may secure us (παρέχωνται) against any liability or trouble (ἀπερισπάστους κ. ἀπαρενοχλήτους)."

[3] [2811 b] Silanus might have replied to this by quoting Epict. ii. 19. 23—4 "Who then exists, a [genuine] Stoic?...Shew me a man diseased—*and happy* (νοσοῦντα καὶ εὐτυχοῦντα); in peril—*and happy*; dying—*and happy*; exiled—*and happy*; dishonoured—*and happy.*" But I think Scaurus would have retorted that Epictetus was assuredly borrowing here from Paul, and trying to outdo the latter in brevity and epigrammatic point, because he was hopelessly behind the apostle in

p. 51, "Pauline," 2 Thess. i. 11, Eph. iv. 1; p. 51, "Defile the image," Epict. ii. 8. 12 foll.; p. 51, "In this way," Epict. iii. 13. 23; p. 51, "God's temple," 1 Cor. iii. 16—17; p. 51, "The temple of the Holy Spirit," 1 Cor. vi. 19; p. 51, "Cause shame," 1 Cor. xi. 22; p. 51, "Whether therefore," 1 Cor. x. 31; p. 52, "So wrote Pliny," Plin. *Epist.* iii. 11.

NOTES TO CHAPTER V

[2812] Page 56, "Steadfastness," Epict. i. 29. 1 foll.; p. 57, "You are an apparition," Epict. *Ench.* i. 5; p. 57, "Agamemnon," Epict. iii. 22. 30 foll.; p. 59, "Neither good nor evil," Epict. ii. 16. 1; p. 59, "Catechism," Epict. i. 30. 1 foll.; p. 60, "Jew," Epict. ii. 9. 19 foll.; p. 61, "Surgery," Epict. iii. 23. 30; p. 62, "Dipping," see L. S. and Stephen's *Thesaurus*; Schürer (II. ii. 323) thinks Jewish proselytes are denoted. See *Fourfold Gospel* ("baptism").

NOTES TO CHAPTER VI

[2813] Page 65, "The Galilæans," Epict. iv. 7. 6. Some might urge that Epictetus is referring to the followers of Judas of Galilee described by Josephus as "the fourth sect of the philosophies" of the Jews. It is not probable, however, that Epictetus would talk to his class about "the Galilæans," if the class knew them only through book-knowledge, that is to say, through the works of Josephus. Even if Epictetus were referring to those Galilæans, there is nothing in Josephus that suggests "custom," but much that suggests passion, *Ant.* xviii. 1. 6 "unconquerable love (ἔρως) of freedom," "the unchangeableness of their confidence (ὑποστάσεως)," "contempt for pain," "madness (ἀνοίᾳ)." Arrian, however, has "custom"; and he is not responsible for the criticisms fictitiously attributed to him in this and the preceding chapter.

Comp. *M. Ant.* xi. 3 "But this readiness [to meet death]—let it always spring from a man's own deliberate judgment, *not by way of mere obstinate opposition, as the Christians [are ready]*, but

---

force and fervour and fulness of hope. The Stoic could not say "as dying and behold we live," nor "as having nothing yet having all things for ever"; so he repeats "and happy." It is epigrammatic and very fine; but the apostle's language is more than "fine."

[2813] NOTES TO CHAPTER VI

with reasonable conviction (μὴ κατὰ ψιλὴν παράταξιν ὡς οἱ Χριστιανοί, ἀλλὰ λελογισμένως)." Perhaps Epict. iv. 7. 6 ὑπὸ μανίας μὲν... (καὶ ὑπὸ ἔθους οἱ Γαλιλαῖοι)...ὑπὸ λόγου δὲ...οὐδείς may mean "by [the mere force of] habit," because they accustom themselves to think and speak about death in such a spirit (without any reasonable basis for their thoughts and words) that they are able, when the moment comes, actually to die in the same spirit. Bacon's Essay on "Custom" maintains that habits of speech and thought cannot be trusted to produce consistent action. But Epictetus may have thought otherwise. Comp. i. 27. 4—6 where, after deprecating the bad habit of saying, "The poor fellow is dead!" he says, "Against that habit set the opposite habit" (and sim. iii. 12. 6, iii. 16. 13). If so, the clause about the Galilæans in iv. 7. 6 is parenthetical. In iii. 25. 5 ὑπὸ ἔθους is used in a bad sense.

[2814] Page 67, "Who shall separate...," Rom. viii. 35; p. 68, "Never," ἀγάπη does not occur in Schenkl's Index; p. 70, "Ruin and help," Epict. iv. 9. 16, comp. i. 4. 11, i. 9. 30—2; p. 70, "Not only so," Rom. viii. 23.

P. 70, "Foolish...prayers." But it should be added that Epictetus (ii. 7. 10—12) recognises "coming to" God as our guide (though he expressly forbids us (*ib.*) to tell God what we want, which is, he says, as unreasonable as it would be to ask our own eyes to see what we want). Moreover he definitely sanctions "calling on" God in time of moral trial (ii. 18. 29) as mariners in a storm call on the Dioscuri. Comp. iii. 21. 11—12, where he says that the aspirant to teach must have God for his "leader," and must not approach the task "without God" (and sim. iii. 22. 56). The statement, therefore, in the text, *though verbally true about "prayer," is not really true.* It ought to have been said that Epictetus allows us to pray for our own spiritual peace and guidance, but not for anything else, *and for nothing that concerns others.*

P. 70, "Searcheth," 1 Cor. ii. 10; p. 71, "Diogenes," Epict. iii. 24. 64 foll., where he is called "mild and philanthropic"; p. 71, "Such sentences as these," Phil. iv. 13, Col. i. 11, Eph. vi. 10; p. 72, "Power," 1 Cor. ii. 4, Rom. xv. 13; p. 72, "The love of Christ," 2 Cor. v. 14; p. 72, "Adam," Rom. v. 14; p. 73, "Phædo," Plato *Phæd.* lxiv. (115 D); p. 74, "Christ sent me not...," 1 Cor. i. 17 foll.

NOTES TO CHAPTER VII

[2815] Page 77, "Pity me," Ps. li. The translation follows the Septuagint; p. 78, "Country girl," Hor. *Odes* iii. 23; p. 79, "Our own hearts," Epict. i. 29. 4 "Receive from thyself"; p. 80, "A passage," Rom. vii. 18.

P. 80, "Repentant sorrow." It may be urged that Epictetus, though he does not insist on "repentance," makes frequent mention of "turning (ἐπιστρέφω)"—using that very word which, when employed by the LXX to express "turning to God," signifies "repentance." But it will be found that Epictetus' "turning" is, for the most part, to *oneself* (*Ench.* 10 ἐπιστρέφων ἐπὶ σεαυτόν, iv. 4. 7 ἐπ' ἐμαυτὸν ἐπιστρέφω etc.). The meaning appears to be, "fix one's thoughts on one's own nature," and in any case is far removed from the Hebraic "turning to God." The passive, in ii. 20. 22 ἵν' οἱ πολῖται ἐπιστραφέντες τιμῶσι τὸ θεῖον, is put into the mouth of a rhetorician ready to prove anything.

P. 81, "Strangers," Exod. xxii. 21, xxiii. 9, Lev. xix. 10, 33, Deut. x. 19; p. 81, "Vile," Deut. xxv. 3; p. 82, "Base thought," Deut. xv. 9; p. 82, "Covet," Rom. vii. 7, xiii. 9, quoting Exod. xx. 17, Deut. v. 21; p. 82, "Two fundamental precepts," Deut. vi. 5 etc., Lev. xix. 18; p. 83, "Proverbs," Prov. xx. 27 "soul" (R.V. and LXX lit. "belly"); p. 83, "Imputed," by Aulus Gellius, see Epict. ed. Schweig. vol. iii. p. 121.

NOTES TO CHAPTER VIII

[2816] Page 85, "Profit," Epict. ii. 22. 15. Comp. Epict. i. 19. 11 "Even the sun does everything *for its own sake*; and, for the matter of that, so does *Zeus Himself.* Nay, when He wishes to be called Raingiver and Fruitgiver and Father of men and Gods, you see that He cannot attain these actions and these appellations without conferring advantages on the world at large."

In O.T., God is not said to do anything "*for His own sake*," but sometimes "*for His name's sake*," e.g. 1 S. xii. 22, and comp. Is. xlviii. 9 "*For my name's sake* will I defer mine anger," Ezek. xx. 9, 14 etc. "I wrought *for my name's sake* that it should not be profaned," where the meaning seems to be, lest God's "name" and the worship of the true God should be blasphemed among the Gentiles. "Name" is nearly equivalent to "nature as far as it can be revealed in words."

In Mt. v. 44—5 "*Love your enemies...that ye may become sons of your Father in heaven*, for he causeth his sun to rise on evil and good and sendeth rain on just and unjust,"—where the precept is not "*Do good to* your enemies," but "*Love* them"—it is implied that God loves even the "evil" and the "unjust," and does good to them *for their own sake*.

There is no incompatibility between "for His name's sake" and "for Israel's sake." God rewards and punishes Israel, because He loves them. But "God loves Israel" is almost equivalent to "God desires to make Israel righteous," or "to make Israel one with Himself," or "to put His name upon them." Thus, what God does for Israel, He may be said to do *for the sake of Righteousness*, which—Epictetus might say—means "*for the sake of Himself*," and—as the Bible says—means "*for the sake of His name*."

[2817] Page 85, "Given it back," Epict. *Ench.* xi., comp. Epict. iv. 1. 103 and Job i. 21; p. 86, "What does it matter?" Epict. *Ench.* xi.; p. 86, "No philosopher...an enemy," Epict. *Ench.* i. 3; p. 86, "Desire," Epict. *Ench.* viii.; p. 86, "Uneducated," Epict. *Ench.* v.; p. 86, "Take it from yourself," Epict. i. 29. 3—4; p. 86, "Another mention," Epict. ii. 16. 27 foll.; p. 87, "David," Ps. cxix. 97, comp. *ib.* cxix. 131; p. 88, "What he wills...," Epict. ii. 26. 1 foll.; p. 88, "Manliness," Epict. iv. 9. 6 foll.; p. 89, "Abusing," Epict. iv. 9. 12 *i.e.* misusing; p. 89, "Nothing more pliable," Epict. iv. 9. 16.

NOTES TO CHAPTER IX

[2818] Page 92, "Make personal appeals," λέγειν πρός τινα, Epict. iii. 1. 36; p. 92, "Intent on not sinning," Epict. iv. 12. 19; p. 93, "Immortal," see Epict. i. 2. 21, ii. 6. 27, ii. 8. 28, ii. 17. 38, iii. 24. 8, iv. 10. 31, iv. 5. 28. These are all Schenkl's instances from the Dissertations; p. 93, "The death of the whole," Epict. iii. 22. 21.

NOTES TO CHAPTER X

[2819] Page 97, "Desolation," Epict. iii. 13. 1 foll.; p. 98, "Henceforth no evil," Epict. iii. 13. 13; p. 98, "But if at any moment," Epict. iii. 13. 14; p. 98, "Such part as was fire," Epict. iii. 13. 15—if the reading is correct—may indicate a shade of difference between the "fire" and the other element. But Schweig. and Schenkl follow a MS. that reads "*of fire*" parall. to "*of earth*," "*of air*" etc.; p. 99, "The soul," Epict. ii. 12. 20—1, iii. 7. 4, comp. iii. 3. 2—4; p. 100, "Mind, knowledge, right logos," Epict. ii. 8. 2.

P. 100, "Fire." The soul was declared to be of the nature of fire by the Stoics (Cicero *Tusc.* I. xviii—xix) consisting of "inflammata anima," and soaring upwards after death till it found rest in "naturam sui similem." The Stoics (Steph. *Thes.* s.v. τεχνικόν) defined Nature as πῦρ τεχνικὸν ὁδῷ βαδίζον ἐπὶ γενέσει.

P. 100, "Be not afraid," Mt. x. 28, Lk. xii. 4.

NOTES TO CHAPTER XI

[2820] Page 102, "Though the number," Rom. ix. 27—9; p. 102, "Isaiah is very bold," Rom. x. 20; p. 102, "Isaiah says," Rom. xv. 12; p. 102, "To whom are entrusted," Epict. iii. 22. 72 (quoting *Iliad* ii. 25); p. 103, "Children," Is. i. 2. The following quotations or descriptions follow Isaiah's order up to Is. xi. 10 "the root of Jesse." R.V. has been generally followed; p. 104, "The Prayers of David," Ps. lxxii. 20 *ad fin.*

P. 104, "Sophocles," *Ant.* 600. Comp. Herod. viii. 55 describing how the sacred olive-tree in the Acropolis, two days after it had been burned down by the Persians, sent up a shoot, a cubit long, from the stock; p. 105, "Come ye," Is. ii. 3; p. 106, "The dead shall arise," Is. xxvi. 19 (LXX); p. 107, "Hezekiah," see Is. xxxix. 10—20; p. 107, "One passage," Is. liii. 1—12, translated from the LXX, which differs greatly from the Hebrew; p. 107, "Romans," Rom. iv. 24—5; pp. 107—8, "Swallowed up," Is. xxv. 8, quoted in 1 Cor. xv. 54; p. 108, "Other passages," Is. xxxvii. 35, xli. 8, xliii. 10; p. 108, "Abraham my friend," Is. xli. 8.

NOTES TO CHAPTER XII

[2821] Page 111, "The government," Is. ix. 6.

P. 112, "Thee have I chosen," Is. xli. 8, 9, xliii. 10, xliv. 1—2, comp. Amos iii. 2 " *You only have I known* of all the families of the earth," followed by " *Therefore I will visit upon you all your iniquities.*"

P. 113, "In the furnace of affliction," Is. xlviii. 10; p. 113, "The Lord was wroth with me," Deut. iii. 26, comp. Numb. xx. 12; p. 114, "Divide the spoils," Is. liii. 12 (LXX); p. 115, "David," Ps. viii. 1—9; p. 116, "Behold, the Lord," Is. xl. 10—13.

NOTES TO CHAPTER XIII

[2822] Page 117, "Be not surprised," Epict. i. 16. 1 foll.; p. 119, "Articulates," Epict. i. 17. 1—4; p. 119, "In the act of blaming," Epict. iii. 17. 1 foll.; p. 120, "Thou seest," Epict. i. 12. 3 quoting *Iliad* x. 279; p. 120, "Why cannot God?" Epict. i. 14. 7—10; p. 121, "Galba," Epict. iii. 15. 14; p. 123, "Look up," Gen. xv. 5 (LXX); p. 123, "Lift up your eyes," Is. xl. 26 foll., from the LXX. The punctuation is doubtful; p. 123, "But sorrow," Is. xl. 29, Heb. has "To him that hath no might he increaseth strength." In the LXX, "them that have no grief" seems to mean "have no experience of chastisement," so that they are unfeeling.

NOTES TO CHAPTER XIV

[2823] Page 125, "Paul, a slave," Rom. i. 1; p. 126, "Cynic," Epict. i. 24. 6, iii. 22. 23 and *passim*; p. 126, "As a shepherd," Is. xl. 11 (LXX); p. 128, "Ye have heard," Gal. i. 13—14; p. 128, "A Hebrew," Phil. iii. 5—6; p. 128, "The chief of sinners," 1 Tim. i. 15; p. 128, "Accursed from Christ," Rom. ix. 3; p. 129, "On the third day," 1 Cor. xv. 4.

P. 129, "Reveal his Son *in me*," Gal. i. 16. Both Jerome (in the earlier and fuller of his two interpretations) and Chrysostom take "in me" as meaning "within me," and not "by me." Jerome perhaps (as he very frequently does) has followed Origen's interpretation.

NOTES TO CHAPTER XIV [2824*]

P. 131, "But whatever things," Phil. iii. 7 foll.; p. 131, "Drama," Shakespeare, *Richard II*, v. 1. 28; p. 132, "If any man be in Christ," 2 Cor. v. 17; p. 132, "Emasculate," Gal. v. 12 (lit.); p. 132, "Add affliction," Phil. i. 17; p. 133, "Ten thousand tutors," 1 Cor. iv. 15.

[2824] Page 133, "Villains!" Epict. iii. 22. 58. Schweig. *ad loc.* quotes Jerome, who says that Diogenes, under a tree, said, "'Haec me nox aut victorem probabit aut victum. Si febrim vicero, ad Agonem (*i.e.* the Olympic games) veniam. Si me vicerit, ad inferna descendam.' Ibique, per noctem, eliso gutture, non tam mori se ait quam febrim morte excludere." According to Jerome, Diogenes appears to have hanged himself in order to stop the fever. Epictetus takes interrogatively ("*Are you going* to Olympia?") what Jerome seems to take imperatively ("*Abite* quaeso et spectatum pergite!"). Silanus is supposed to have heard (though not from Epictetus) that the story ended in the death of Diogenes.

P. 133—4, "Weakness," Gal. iv. 13, 1 Cor. ii. 3, 2 Cor. xii. 5. In 2 Cor. xii. 9 ἡ δύναμις, "the power"—like (*Corrections* 272) "the name [of God]"—prob. means "the power of God," "divine power." As "the power" is hardly intelligible to English readers, "the" has been dropped, and the noun has been printed with a capital letter.

P. 134, "Satan hindered," 1 Thess. ii. 18; p. 134, "Fever is worshipped," Epict. i. 19. 6; p. 134, "Have the fever rightly," Epict. iii. 10. 13; p. 135, "Who is made to stumble?" 2 Cor. xi. 29. The following reff. are to 2 Cor. xi. 28, 2 Tim. iv. 7, Rom. xv. 19, 2 Cor. xii. 10.

"Spiritual Body"

[2824*] Page 135, "To describe a 'real person.'" The "spiritual body" is not to be regarded as the "real person." It is rather conceived to be a spiritual shape expressive of a spiritual being. An angel might be said to have a spiritual body: and this, when made visible to men, would be seen as the body of a man. 2 Cor. v. 1—2 calls the spiritual body provided for men "a house...eternal in the heavens," and teaches us to think of ourselves as "putting on the clothing [of this house] over" our former earthly being, so that we are encompassed with an atmosphere of incorruptibility, not "unclothed," but "clothed upon." But 1 Cor. xv. 35—45 describes the spiritual body as bearing the same relation to the earthly body that

the flower bears to the seed. Probably the Apostle did not intend us to infer that the spiritual body was as different in shape from the earthly body as the flower is from the seed, and that the spiritual body resembled the earthly body in being tangible. He seems to have used these metaphors to express his conviction that the human being is raised up in Christ *whole*—that is, preserving a continuity of spiritual identity—and *real*, and *incorruptible*.

[2824* (i)] The difficulty attending the use of "*body*," in connexion with resurrection, may be illustrated by the ambiguity of the word "*bodiless*." "*Bodiless*" may be used to signify (1) "immaterial" in a good sense, or philosophic sense; (2) "unreal," "unsubstantial," "weak," in a popular sense—especially when applied to the dead, or in a bad sense applied to *bodiless* evil spirits, which (according to Jewish belief), having no bodies of their own, tried to find homes in human bodies[1]. Luke repeats a tradition that Jesus after the Resurrection said to the disciples (R.V. txt), "See my hands and feet that it is I myself: handle me and see; for *a spirit* hath not flesh and bones, as ye behold me having." R.V. txt proceeds, "And when he had said this he shewed them his hands and his feet." But W.H. doubly bracket this sentence, and there are many variations in the context[2]. Moreover Ignatius has the following, "For I know and believe that also after the resurrection He was in the flesh: and when He came to Peter and his friends He said to them, Take, handle me, and see that I am not a *bodiless* demon," as to which Jerome

---

[1] [2824* (i) a] For Origen's remarks on this difficulty, see below, 2824* (i) e. Ἀσώματος is not used in LXX or N.T. Steph. gives "Carphyl. Anth. Pal. 9, 52, 3 οἰκτείρας δὲ νέκυν τὸν ἀσώματον," implying "helpless," like Virgil, *Æn.* vi. 292 "tenues *sine corpore* vitas...volitare cava sub imagine formae," but on the other hand Plato *Phil.* p. 64 B κόσμος τις ἀσώματος and *Phæd.* p. 85 E ὡς ἡ ἁρμονία ἀόρατόν κ. ἀσώματον κ. πάγκαλόν τι ἐστίν. Lewis and Short quote Aul. Gel. v. 15. 1 "Corpusne sit vox an incorporeum: hoc enim vocabulum quidam finxerunt proinde quod Graece dicitur ἀσώματον."

[2] [2824* (i) b] Lk. xxiv. 39—40. SS omits "And when...feet." Epiphanius *Adv. Hær.* I. iii. 78 (p. 349 C)—perh. quoting Marcion, for elsewhere he quotes differently—has ἴδετε τὰς χεῖράς μου καὶ τοὺς πόδας μου· ὅτι πνεῦμα ὀστᾶ οὐκ ἔχει, καθὼς ἐμὲ θεωρεῖτε ἔχοντα. In Lk. xxiv. 37 "they thought they saw a spirit (πνεῦμα)," D has φάντασμα, and in xxiv. 39 it has τὸ πνεῦμα (? meaning "the Holy Spirit," as in 2 Cor. iii. 17 "the Lord is the Spirit," on which Origen says (*Hom. Exod.* xii. 4) "Verbum Dei...nunc via, nunc veritas, nunc vita...: *nunc vero spiritus dicitur*"). Φάντασμα occurs elsewhere in N.T. only in Mk vi. 49, Mt. xiv. 26, where SS has "devil." Thus φάντασμα in Lk. xxiv. 37 (D) shews how πνεῦμα in that passage might be interchanged with δαιμόνιον "devil."

makes the "repeated and explicit[1]" statement that this is from the Gospel according to the Hebrews which he had himself translated. Origen quotes it, with condemnation, as from the *Teaching of Peter*. But the important point to note is that as early as the beginning of the first century, if not before, difficulties appear to have arisen as to Christ's post-resurrectional "body." Some seem to have argued thus: "Christ could not have said, *I am not a spirit*, for (2 Cor. iii. 17) *The Lord is the Spirit*. He must have meant, I am not *a bodiless demon*. Even if He did not use these words, they express His meaning." Others, Marcion for example, may have turned Luke's tradition round—unless indeed Luke turned the original round and Marcion kept closer to it—so as to mean, in effect, "[I am a spirit. And] a spirit has not bones as also ye see me [not] having [them][2]." Curiously enough, Origen appears to say that the tradition about the "bodiless demon" was similarly used in two senses. His remarks on the passage deserve careful study[3]. They

---

[1] [2824* (i) *c*] See Lightf. on Ign. *Smyrn.* 3 shewing that Jerome renders οἶδα by "vidi" ("in carne eum vidi") and "evidently supposes that Ignatius had seen our Lord in the flesh."

[2] [2824* (i) *d*] Tertull. *Marc.* iv. 43 *ad fin*. "Quum haesitantibus eis ne phantasma esset, immo phantasma credentibus, Quid turbati estis, inquit, et quid cogitationes subeunt in corda vestra? Videte manus meas et pedes, quia ego ipse sum; quoniam spiritus ossa non habet, sicut me habentem videtis. Et Marcion quaedam contraria sibi, illa credo industria eradere de Evangelio suo noluit, ut ex his quae eradere potuit, nec erasit, illa quae erasit, aut negetur erasisse, aut merito erasisse dicatur. Nec parcit nisi eis quae non aliter interpretando quam delendo subvertit. Vult itaque sic dictum, quasi, Spiritus ossa non habet, sicut me videtis habentem, ad spiritum referatur, sicut me videtis habentem; id est, non habentem ossa sicut et spiritus. Et quae ratio tortuositatis istius? quum simpliciter pronuntiare potuisset, Quia spiritus ossa non habet, sicut me videtis *non* habentem." Here it may be noted that Tertullian apparently admits that Marcion *quoted* correctly and fully, though he *explained* perversely. If so, Tertullian read "phantasm" as D does ("phantasma credentibus"). It is not quite so clear that he omitted "flesh." As regards "bone," it may be noted that the context mentions "I *myself*," and that in N. Heb. (Levy iii. 679) עֶצֶם, "bone," may mean "self" with persons as well as things (in Bibl. Heb., only with things, Gesen. 783 *a*). The punctuation in Tertullian is doubtful, and perhaps "spiritus" should be printed "Spiritus" (comp. D τὸ πνεῦμα) throughout.

[3] [2824* (i) *e*] See Orig. *De Princip. Praef.* 8 "Appellatio autem ἀσωμάτου, id est, incorporei, non solum apud multos alios, verum etiam apud nostras scripturas est inusitata et incognita. *Si vero quis velit nobis proferre* ex illo libello, qui Petri Doctrina appellatur, ubi Salvator videtur ad discipulos dicere: 'Non sum daemonium incorporeum': primo respondendum est ei, quoniam ille liber inter libros ecclesiasticos non habetur; et ostendendum quia neque Petri est ipsa

shew that the word "bodiless," if applied to Christ's manifestations after death, would have been misleading and essentially false, and they help us to appreciate St Paul's motives in using the expression, "spiritual body."

NOTES TO CHAPTER XV

[2825] Page 136, "The lecture," Epict. i. 24. 1 foll. and i. 25. 1 foll.; p. 138, "I am not ashamed," Rom. i. 16; p. 139, "Shall judge," Rom. ii. 16; p. 139, "Abraham had faith," Rom. iv. 3, 9 etc., Gal. iii. 6; p. 140, "Shall not the judge," Gen. xviii. 25.

scriptura, neque alterius cujusquam, qui spiritu Dei fuerit inspiratus. Quod etiamsi ipsum concederetur, non idem sensus ibi ex isto sermone ἀσωμάτου indicatur, qui a graecis et gentilibus auctoribus ostenditur, quum de incorporea natura a philosophis disputatur. *In hoc enim libello* incorporeum daemonium dixit pro eo, quod ipse ille, quicunque est, habitus vel circumscriptio daemonici corporis, non est similis huic nostro crassiori et visibili corpori: sed *secundum sensum ejus, qui composuit illam scripturam*, intelligendum est quod dixit; id est, non se tale corpus, quale habent daemones, quod est naturaliter subtile, et velut aura tenue, et propter hoc vel putatur a multis vel dicitur incorporeum, sed habere se corpus solidum et palpabile. In consuetudine vero hominum omne quod tale non fuerit, incorporeum simplicioribus vel imperitioribus nominatur: velut si quis aërem istum, quo fruimur, incorporeum dicat, quandoquidem non est tale corpus, ut comprehendi ac teneri possit, urgentique resistere.

"Quaeremus tamen si vel alio nomine res ipsa, quam graeci philosophi ἀσώματον, id est incorpoream, dicunt, in Scripturis sanctis invenitur. Deus quoque ipse quomodo intelligi debeat, inquirendum est, corporeus, et secundum aliquem habitum deformatus, an alterius naturae, quam corpora sunt: quod utique in praedicatione nostra manifeste non designatur. Eadem quoque etiam de Christo et de Spiritu sancto requirenda sunt: sed et de omni anima, atque omni rationabili natura nihilominus requirendum est."

[2824* (i) *f*] It is not clear whether Origen distinguishes an unnamed controversialist or an allusion to such a one ("si vero quis velit nobis proferre") who *quotes* the *Doctrina Petri*, from the actual composer of the *Doctrina* ("qui composuit illam scripturam"). There appears also an antithesis between the meaning of this "composer" and the meaning intended in the treatise previously mentioned ("in hoc enim libello"). But in any case the passage clearly indicates Origen's difficulty, and the popular difficulty, in connexion with the use of "body" applied to spiritual beings.

[2824* (i) *g*] Compare the following passage from Clem. Alex. 970—1 in which, starting from Mt. xviii. 10 "the face of the Father," he asks, "How can there be a face of Him that is not fashioned (πρόσωπον δὲ τοῦ ἀσχηματίστου πῶς ἂν εἴη;)?" He apparently maintains that the "bodies" of angels, archangels, and the Son, differ in respect of "bodilessness and invisibility," "definite measurement and perceptibility," as compared with the Father (ὡς πρὸς τὴν σύγκρισιν τῶν τῇδε σωμάτων, οἷον ἄστρων, ἀσώματα καὶ ἀνείδεα, ὡς πρὸς τὴν σύγκρισιν τοῦ υἱοῦ, σώματα μεμετρημένα καὶ αἰσθητά, οὕτως καὶ ὁ υἱὸς πρὸς τὸν πατέρα παραβαλλόμενος).

NOTES TO CHAPTERS XV—XVII [2827]

P. 141, "Shew us," Epict. iii. 7. 33—4. The text has "the quasi-ruler," which is rather flat. Perhaps ὅτως (*i.e.* ὄντως) has been corrupted to ὁ ὥς (a somewhat unusual combination).

P. 141, "If I knew," Epict. ii. 6. 10—13; p. 142, "Wisdom of word," 1 Cor. i. 17.

NOTES TO CHAPTER XVI

[2826] Page 144, "What Epictetus had said," see *Sil.* p. 98; p. 144, "the enigma" of the "mirror," 1 Cor. xiii. 12. I had at first adopted R.V. txt "darkly," but a friend justly objected, as follows: "'Darkly' is a poor rendering of ἐν αἰνίγματι. I suppose two men to be standing before a mirror, and the mirror to be a very bad one, as the *common* mirrors of that time must have been. One of the two sees the image of the other *through* the mirror, a dimmed and distorted image which *puzzles* him; turning round, he sees his companion 'face to face.' So there is an immediate contrast between a puzzling (say, confusing) image and the reality"; p. 144, "Work together," Rom. viii. 28; p. 145, "Elijah," Rom. xi. 2, and comp. 1 K. xix. 10 foll.; p. 145, "Cry aloud," Is. xlii. 2; p. 146, "Be with Christ," Phil. i. 23; p. 146, "I have fought," 2 Tim. iv. 7 (Silanus is represented, perhaps wrongly, as having the Pastoral Epistles in his Pauline volume); p. 146, "Fallen asleep," 1 Thess. iv. 15; p. 148, "To the Galatians," the reff. are Gal. i. 11—12, i. 16—17, iv. 25, i. 18—19, ii. 1; p. 149, "Spiritually prepared," comp. Acts xxvi. 16[1].

NOTES TO CHAPTER XVII

[2827] Page 151, "The Lord Jesus said," 1 Cor. xi. 23—4; p. 154, "A divine Artist," Epict. ii. 8. 21 foll.; p. 154, "Inveighed," see Epict. iv. 13. 4—19, ii. 23. 13, and comp. ii. 20. 7; p. 155, "Medea," Epict. ii. 17. 19 foll., iv. 13, 14; p. 155, "If you pity," Epict. ii. 17. 26; p. 155, "Observe and test," Epict. ii. 19. 20 foll.; p. 157, "Is not this matter," Epict. ii. 19. 32—4.

---

[1] [2826 a] This version of Christ's words, uttered to Paul at the moment of his conversion, indicates that the substance of the apostle's testimony was to be based on the *future* "appearing" of Jesus as well as on the things that he saw at the moment, "For to this end appeared I (ὤφθην) unto thee to appoint thee a minister and witness both of the things wherein thou sawest me (ὧν τε εἶδές με) and of the things wherein I will appear unto thee (ὧν τε ὀφθήσομαί σοι)."

NOTES TO CHAPTER XVIII

[2828] Page 160, "Thyestean meal," comp. Euseb. v. 1. 14, Iren. fragm. ed. Grabe p. 469, Origen *Cels.* vi. 27.

P. 161, "'Giving' or 'delivering over.'" More literally, this would be (1) "Giving or giving over," or else (2) "Delivering or delivering over." But it is impossible to reproduce in English ἔδωκε and παρέδωκε in either of these ways when St Paul uses the two Greek words in the same context to describe the Father as "delivering over" the Son for the redemption of mankind.

P. 161, "Homer," *Iliad* ii. 702 foll.; p. 162, "New covenant," "old covenant," 2 Cor. iii. 6, 14, Gal. iv. 24, Exod. xxiv. 8; p. 162, "Create in me," Ps. li. 10; p. 164, "When Socrates is dead," Epict. iv. 1. 169; p. 164, "Playing at ball," Epict. ii. 5. 15 foll.; p. 164, "Transferred his habitation," Plato, *Phæd.* 117 C, *Apol.* 40 C; p. 165, "Thy image," Virgil *Æn.* vi. 695—6; p. 165, "Scaurus's saying," see *Sil.* p. 43; p. 166, "A living sacrifice," Rom. xii. 1; p. 167, "Si nunc," Virgil *Æn.* vi. 187; p. 168, "The reign of Domitian," on the date of the Apocalypse, see **2942***; p. 169, "The three gospels," Mk xiv. 22—4, Mt. xxvi. 26—8, Lk. xxii. 17—20; p. 169, "No mention." This is not quite accurate, see *Sil.* p. 172.

P. 170, "Sophocles," *Ant.* 1195. But it is a messenger that says "Truth is always right"; and the message causes the wife of Creon to commit suicide. It is to be feared that it is an instance of "Sophoclean irony." The messenger may be intended to speak as a fool.

NOTES TO CHAPTER XIX

[2829] Page 172, "Benefactors," Lk. xxii. 25. Comp. *Joh. Voc.* **1571** "Luke appears to be alluding to the name *Euergetes*, or Benefactor, assumed by several Eastern Kings, one of whom, it is said, was called by the Alexandrians *Kakergetes*, or Malefactor."

P. 173, "A ransom for many," Mk x. 45, Mt. xx. 28; and see Lk. xxii. 27 "he that serveth."

P. 174, "And they drank," see *Clue* **141—2, 240—3**, quoting similar instances, *e.g.* Josh. xxii. 8 "Return ye," LXX "and they departed."

P. 174, "To you" and "for you," see *Paradosis* **1321—4** p. 175, "I am become...Jews," 1 Cor. ix. 22 and 20.

NOTES TO CHAPTER XIX   [2832]

The influence of mistranslation illustrated
from Shakespeare

[2830] Page 178, "'Ilices' or 'silices,'" see *Clue*, 1—2. Procopius (I think) has made a mistake of this kind, but I cannot give the reference. The best instance known to me is one in which Shakespeare might be said by some to have been led into a complete misrepresentation of the words of Marcus Brutus, before the battle of Philippi, as to the lawfulness of suicide. I think it can be shewn that, in the context, where he was not "misled," he used North's text as potter's clay for his dramatic images. Still, in one point, he has certainly been misled by North, who has mistranslated Amyot's French translation of the passage. Amyot wrote "fis," "*made.*" North (ed. 1657, p. 831) took it as "fie," "*trust*[1]."

[2831] In answer to the question of Cassius as to what Brutus would do in case of defeat, Plutarch represents Brutus as replying, "When I was a young man, Cassius, and without experience of practical life, *I uttered* (or, *published*)—*I know not how or why* (2833)—*a grandiloquent discourse in philosophy*. I blamed Cato for making away with himself, as though it were an unholy and cowardly action to give way before the face of one's fate, and to run away, instead of fearlessly awaiting that which is to befall. But now, in the events that have chanced, I find myself becoming changed. And in the event of Providence not awarding the present contest favourably, I have no desire again to put to the test other hopes and enterprises, but I shall pass away [from life], acquiescing[2]."

[2832] Amyot renders this as follows: "Estant encore ieune & non assez experimenté és affaires de ce monde, *ie fis*, ne scay

---

[1] The Clarendon Press edition of *Julius Cæsar*, p. xxxvii, quotes Amyot as "ie feis," and says "North translated *feis* (=*fis*) as if it were from *fier*." My edition of Amyot (1571) has (p. 592 F) *fis*. The C. P. ed. also says in the notes that "I trust," "although evidently a past tense (Old English *truste*) must have been read by Shakespeare as the present." I cannot accept "evidently." It would seem to me probable that North used "trust" as the present tense, unless it could be shewn that he elsewhere uses it as a past. See **2834**.

[2] [2831 a] Plut. *Vit. Brut.* 40 Νέος ὢν ἐγώ, Κάσσιε, καὶ πραγμάτων ἄπειρος οὐκ οἶδ' ὅπως ἐν φιλοσοφίᾳ λόγον ἀφῆκα μέγαν. Ἠτιασάμην Κάτωνα διαχρησάμενον ἑαυτόν, ὡς οὐχ ὅσιον οὐδ' ἀνδρὸς ἔργον ὑποχωρεῖν τῷ δαίμονι καὶ μὴ δέχεσθαι τὸ συμπῖπτον ἀδεῶς, ἀλλ' ἀποδιδράσκειν. Νυνὶ δ' ἀλλοῖος ἐν ταῖς τύχαις γίνομαι· καὶ θεοῦ καλῶς τὰ παρόντα μὴ βραβεύσαντος, οὐ δέομαι πάλιν ἄλλας ἐλπίδας ἐξελέγχειν καὶ παρασκευάς, ἀλλ' ἀπαλλάξομαι τὴν τύχην ἐπαινῶν.

[2832] NOTES TO CHAPTER XIX

comment, vn discours de Philosophie, par lequel ie reprenoye & blasmoye fort Caton de s'estre desfait soy-mesme, cõme n'estant point acte licite ny religieux, quãt aux dieux, ny quant aux hommes vertueux, de ne point ceder à l'ordonnance diuine, & ne prendre pas cõstamment en gré tout ce qui luy plaist nous enuoyer, ains faire le restif & s'en retirer: mais maintenant me trouuant au milieu du peril, ie suis de toute autre resolution : tellement que s'il ne plaist à dieu que l'issuë de ceste bataille soit heureuse pour nous, ie ne veux plus tẽter d'autre esperãce, ny tascher à remettre sus derechef autre equipage de guerre, ains me deliureray des miseres de ce monde, me contentãt de la fortune." I give the spelling exactly (*e.g.* "quãt" and "quant").

[2833] Amyot has perhaps read μεγᾶ, *i.e.* μέγαν, as μέγα, "greatly," *fort*, and connected it with ἠτιασάμην ("blasmoye *fort*"). Also—taking ὑποχωρεῖν δαίμονι in a good sense, "submit (céder) to fate," whereas it appears to be in a bad sense "give way before fate"—he has inserted a negative ("de ne *point* ceder") which is not in the Greek. The apologetic phrase οὐκ οἶδ' ὅπως may refer to the *manner*, or to the *motive*, of the "discourse." In the former case, it might imply haste; in the latter, self-conceit and ostentation. It is certainly apologetic, but it is difficult. Amyot has rendered it literally, leaving it ambiguous.

[2834] North (ed. 1657) commits two errors at the very outset. First, he takes the words "being a young man" as being *uttered by Plutarch about Brutus, not by Brutus about himself—a specimen of a very frequent source of ambiguity in the fourth gospel*. "Brutus answered him, being yet but a young man, and not over greatly experienced in the world." This leads him and his readers all wrong. Brutus really says, in effect, "Many years ago, when I was a foolish young man, I did so-and-so." North makes Plutarch say that Brutus, at the time of the battle of Philippi, was a foolish young man[1].

In the next place, North takes "fis," "*made*," as "fie," "*trust*." To make the sense agree with this error, he renders λόγον ("discourse") by "rule" (following Amyot as to "greatly") thus : "*I trust* (*I know not how*)[2] *a certain rule* of Philosophy, by the which I did *greatly*

---

[1] [2834 a] Comp. Mt. xix. 20, Mk x. 20, Lk. xviii. 21 (Pref. p. xiv).

[2] Perhaps North took the meaning to be "I entertain a lingering illogical trust" in this "rule," but in practice "I am of a contrary mind." He has translated the passage very carelessly. It seems more probable that "trust" is a careless use of the present than an antiquated use of the past ("trust" for "trusted").

blame and reprove Cato for killing himselfe, as being no lawfull nor godly act, touching the gods; nor, concerning men, valiant; not to give place and yeeld to divine Providence, and not constantly and patiently to take whatsoever it pleaseth him to send us, but to draw back and flie: but being now in the midst of the danger I am of a contrary minde. For if it be not the will of God that this Battell fall out fortunate for us, I will look no more for hope, neither seek to make any new supply for War againe, but will rid me of this miserable world, and content me with my fortune."

[2835] Shakespeare, then, found Brutus (in North) saying two inconsistent things (1) "I trust (I know not how) a certain rule of Philosophy," (2) "Now...I am of a contrary mind." How does he deal with the difficulty?

He omits this change of mind in Brutus, or perhaps *transfers it to Cassius*, whom he represents as saying (*Julius Cæsar* v. 1. 77—8) "You know that I held Epicurus strong And his opinion: *now I change my mind.*" Thus he exhibits Brutus as still consistently retaining his old condemnation of suicide—for "even by the rule" implies "consistently adhering to the rule that I approved when I blamed Cato." I give the text, with its strange punctuation, as in Booth's (1864) representation of the folio of 1623:

> "Euen by the rule of that Philosophy,
> By which I did blame Cato, for the death
> Which he did giue himselfe, I know not how;
> But I do finde it Cowardly, and vile,
> For feare of what might fall, so to preuent
> The time of life, arming myselfe with patience,
> To stay the prouidence of some high Powers,
> That gouerne vs below."
>
> *Julius Cæsar* v. 1. 101 foll.

[2836] Yet it was necessary for Shakespeare to express in *some* way the fact that Brutus does not intend to survive defeat. This the dramatist does by inserting a question from Cassius, not in Plutarch. Will Brutus be content to be "led in triumph"? To this Brutus replies with an indignant "No, Cassius, no," and a protest not in Plutarch. Brutus adds that this same day "must end that work the ides of March begun." Of these words there is a vestige in Plutarch's text (possibly corrupt) "having given my life to my country on the ides of March." By thus breaking Brutus's speech in two, and by

[2836]   NOTES TO CHAPTER XIX

interpolating as above, Shakespeare prepares the way for Brutus's change of mind in practice, while avoiding any avowal of Brutus's change of mind in theory. On the other hand, Cassius does distinctly change his mind in theory as well as in practice—according to Shakespeare. Plutarch, on the contrary, represents Cassius as retaining his Epicurean beliefs till the last and as applying them to (North) "comfort and quiet Brutus" in his misgivings about the vision of an "evil spirit" seen by the latter. All this, of course, Shakespeare leaves out.

Targumistic Translations

[2837] A promise was made in the Preface that some illustrations should be given from the Targums of two tendencies, or what might be called laws, of translation or paraphrase :—(i) The Law of Prosaic Substitution, (ii) The Law of Divergence from Obscurity. Others might easily be enumerated (*e.g.* the Law of Definiteness[1]), but space will confine illustration almost entirely to these two.

[2837 (i)] The Law of Prosaic Substitution may be illustrated from the following description, in Isaiah, of an impending invasion. The passage has a special bearing on Lk. xxi. 20 "Jerusalem surrounded by camps (or armies)," because (as has been shewn in the Preface to this work) the parallels of Mark and Matthew to

---

[1] [2837 *a*] "Definiteness." Comp. Gen. i. 2 "without form and void," where Targ. Jon. and Jer. add "solitary *of the sons of men* and void *of every animal*," and they define "Spirit of the Lord" as "the Spirit *of mercies* from before the Lord" (where Onk. has simply "Spirit from before the Lord," Etheridge "Wind from before the Lord"). So in Job i. 6 "There was a day when the Sons of God came to present themselves before the Lord," the Targum has "And it came to pass *on the day of judgment* at *the beginning of the year* that the hosts of angels came...."

[2837 *b*] In Gen. xxii. 1 "After these *things* (lit. *words*) the Lord tempted Abraham," a tradition (*Sanhedr.* 89 *b*) taking the Heb. as "words," says, "What *words*?" and gives a dialogue between God and Satan, like that in Job i. 8 foll. Targ. Jon. and Jer., making the "*words*" consist of a contention between Ishmael and Isaac, supply a suitable dialogue. No doubt, the Targumists often borrowed from pre-existing traditions of the Agadists; but that does not affect the argument in this section.

[2837 *c*] In Job iii. 17 "*the wicked* cease from troubling," the Targum has "the wicked *who have repented* cease from the trouble *of Gehenna*." Comp. Mk ii. 17, Mt. ix. 13, Lk. v. 32 "I came not to call the righteous but *sinners*," where Lk. alone adds "*to repentance*."

24

Lk. xxi 20 allude to a prophecy of Daniel obscurely mentioning *"wing"* (כָּנָף); and, somewhat similarly, the Hebrew of Isaiah mentions a *"wing"* while the Targum of Isaiah mentions an *"army."*

Isaiah viii. 8

Hebrew	Targum
"And he [*i.e.* the king of Assyria] shall sweep onward into Judah; he shall overflow and pass through; he shall reach *even to the neck*; and *the stretching out of his wings* shall fill the breadth of thy land, O Immanuel." See **2837** (iii) *d*.	"And he shall pass through the land of the House of Judah as an inundating torrent; *even to Jerusalem* shall they attain; and *the people of his army* shall fill the fulness of thy land, O Immanuel." [Comp. also אֲגַף, "wing (of an army).")]

Another instance occurs where we can compare the earlier Targum (Onkelos) with two later Targums, one called by the name of Jonathan ben Uzziel, or Jerusalem I, another called Palestinian or Jerusalem II. I give them from Etheridge's translation, unaltered. They all expand into detailed simile the metaphor contained in:—

Gen. xlix. 16—18 (Heb.)

"Dan shall judge his people, as one of the tribes of Israel. Dan shall be a serpent in the way, an adder in the path, that biteth the horse's heels, so that his rider falleth backward. I have waited for thy salvation, O Lord."

Onkelos	Jonathan	Jer. II
"From the house of Dan will be chosen and will arise a man in whose days his people shall be delivered, and in whose years the tribes of Israel have rest together. A chosen man will arise from the house of Dan, the terror of whom shall fall upon the peoples; (a man) who will smite the Philistines with strength, as the serpent, the deadly serpent, lurking by the way, he will slay the mighty of the Philistines' host, the	"From the house of Dan there is to arise a man who will judge his people with the judgment of truth. All the tribes of Israel will hearken to him together. A chosen man shall arise from the house of Dan, like the basilisk which lieth at the dividing of the way, and the serpent's head which lurketh by the way, that biteth the horse in his heel, and the master from his terror is thrown backward. Even thus	"He will be the deliverer who is to arise, strong will he be and elevated above all kingdoms. And he will be like the serpent that lieth in the way, and the basilisk which lurketh at the dividing of the road, which striketh the horse in his heel, and thinketh by the terror of him to throw his rider backward. He is Shimshon bar Manovach, who will be a terror upon his adversaries, and a fear upon them that hate

[2837] NOTES TO CHAPTER XIX

Onkelos	Jonathan	Jer. II
horsemen with the foot; he will weaken (loosen) the horses and chariots, and throw their riders backward. For thy salvation have I waited, O Lord!"	will Shimshon bar Manovach slay all the heroes of Philistia, the horsemen and the foot; he will hamstring their horses and hurl their riders backwards. When Jakob saw Gideon bar Joash and Shimshon bar Manovach, who were established to be deliverers, he said, I expect not the salvation of Gideon, nor look I for the salvation of Shimshon; for their salvation will be the salvation of an hour; but for thy salvation have I waited, and will look for (*sic*), O Lord; for thy salvation is the salvation of eternity."	him, and who will slay kings with princes. Our father Jakob said, My soul hath not waited for the redemption of Gideon bar Joash which is for an hour, nor for the redemption of Shimshon which is a creature redemption, but for the redemption which thou hast said in thy Word shall come for thy people the sons of Israel, for this thy redemption my soul hath waited."

It will be observed that Onkelos, who is generally very faithful to the Hebrew, and not given to expansions, here expands freely, so as to explain the historical fulfilment of the prophecy in Samson's destruction of the Philistines whom he mentions twice. The two later Targums expand still more, but they dwell less on the historical fulfilment. Jer. II does not mention the Philistines by name. They enlarge on the contrast between "salvation" past and future.

[2837 (ii)] The Law of Divergence from Obscurity may be illustrated from obscure passages of two kinds, (1) obscurities of reading, *e.g.* where one has to choose between ר and ד (*Clue*, 5—7); (2) obscurities arising from a rare and difficult word.

The first class has been illustrated in several volumes of *Diatessarica*, and especially in **1069** (i) *Addendum on Jewish Legend*, where various traditions are given about the ram substituted for Isaac. They appear to have arisen in the later Targums from the various meanings of אחר and אחד meaning "after," "behind," "one," "hold fast." This class is largely increased by the Jewish habit of saying (Levy iv. 367) "Read, not this, but that," sometimes seriously where the reading is in doubt, but sometimes with a playful intention of giving a new moral meaning to a scriptural passage where the reading is not in doubt.

Instances of the second class are comparatively rare in narrative. But the strange use of "bareness" to signify "a bare hill top" has caused the following variations in:—

Numb. xxiii. 3 (Heb.) " He [Balaam] went [to] *a bare height.*"

Onkelos	Jonathan	Jer. II
"And he went *solitary.*"	" He went *bending as a serpent.*"	" He went *with a humbled heart.*"

Here the LXX conflates two renderings "(1) He went *to ask God* and (2) he went *straight*" (but "Ἄλλος" has συρόμενος "trailed," or "trailing"). Any one of the three Jewish renderings might obviously have given rise to an explanatory and picturesque amplification of Balaam's action.

And in the next instance we find such an amplification. It occurs in Jacob's prophecy about the future of Judah:—

Gen. xlix. 9 (Heb.) "Judah is a lion's whelp. From the *prey* (טרף lit. *rending,* or *tearing*), my son, thou art gone up (עלית)."

Onkelos	Jonathan
"The dominion shall be [thine] in the beginning, and in the end the kingdom shall be increased from the house of Jehuda, because *from the judgment of death, my son, hast thou withdrawn* (marg. *gone up*)."	" I will liken thee, my son Jehuda, to a whelp, the young of a lion; for *from the killing of Joseph, my son, thou didst uplift thy soul, and from the judgment of Tamar thou wast free.*" (Jer. II is similar.)

The LXX has "Whelp of a lion, Judah, from *a sucker* (βλαστοῦ, טרף), my son, *didst thou mount up,*" taking טרף as in Gen. viii. 11 "freshly plucked [twig]" Ezek. xvii. 9 "leaf."

The clue to these divergences lies in the double meanings of טרף and עלה. The former may mean "torn prey" or "leaf"; the latter may mean "go up," or "shoot up" like a tree. "Went up from [tearing] the prey" is taken by Onkelos as meaning "withdrew from shedding blood," and he applies this to Judah's reversal of the judgment on Tamar (Gen. xxxviii. 26). Perhaps he also included the meaning "shot up from a leaf" in the word "increased"; which however may be a mere expression of the metaphor of the "whelp" becoming a lion. Jonathan, besides definitely mentioning Tamar, adds a reference to (Gen. xxxvii. 26—7) Judah's preventing the shedding of Joseph's blood. Comp. Gen. xxxvii. 33, xliv. 28, טרף טרף, twice connected with Joseph.

NOTES TO CHAPTER XIX

The next and last instance that will be given is of interest partly because it shews how one or two metaphorical or allusive phrases, variously translated and combined, may absolutely transmute one passage into two widely divergent traditions, and partly because it illustrates Josephus (*Ant.* ii. 8. 1) "He also enlarged upon the praises of Joseph," on which Whiston has this note, "As to this encomium upon Joseph, as preparatory to Jacob's adopting Ephraim and Manasses into his own family, and to be admitted for two tribes, which Josephus here mentions, all our copies of Genesis omit it (ch. xlviii); nor do we know whence he took it, or whether it be not his own embellishment only." It will be seen that Onkelos and Jer. Targ. assign to Jacob an express prediction of this kind concerning the "*two tribes.*"

After Jacob has compared Joseph to a fruitful bough by a fountain, the literal Hebrew proceeds as follows:—

Gen. xlix. 22—4 "His *daughters* [*i.e.* the small branches of "the bough"] run over the wall...There shot at him *the lords of arrows.* But there abode in strength his *bow* and the arms of his hands *were made supple* by the hands of the Mighty One of Jacob."

The main causes of obscurity here are four: (1) "daughters," (2) "lords of arrows," (3) "bow," (4) "were made supple."

(1) "Daughters" of a parent city means (*Clue*, **40**) surrounding towns or villages, and the metaphor may represent the superabundant and overflowing towns of the descendants of Joseph, denoted by the small branches of the "bough." Others might take it literally of "daughters" looking at Joseph "over a wall." The LXX renders it "son."

(2) "Lords of arrows," if taken of the "arrows" of the tongue, may refer to Joseph's brothers, who quarrelled with him; or to some in Egypt, who slandered him. So LXX ἐλοιδόρουν.

(3) "Bow" might be interpreted as "steadfastness" since the same Aramaic word represents both (Levy *Ch.* ii. 393). Comp. Ps. lx. 4 (R.V.) "*the truth*," marg. "anc. auth. *the bow*," LXX τόξον.

(4) "Made supple" is an extremely rare word, identical with a word meaning "refine [gold]" (Gesen. 808 *a*) whence comes a common word for "refined gold." The Scripture, in Gen. xli. 42, speaks of a "signet ring" and a "gold chain" placed on Joseph by Pharaoh. Onkelos says vaguely here that "gold was laid upon his [Joseph's] arm." The later Targums say that the daughters of Egypt cast their bracelets or ornaments of gold before Joseph.

TARGUMISTIC TRANSLATIONS [2837]

These explanations will suffice to explain the following divergent accounts:—

Onkelos
"...as a vine planted by a fountain of waters. Two tribes will come forth from his sons, and they shall receive a portion and inheritance. The mighty men, the men of division, were bitter against him; they afflicted him and sorely grieved him; and his prophecy shall be fulfilled in them, because he was faithful to the law in secret, and set his confidence firmly. Therefore was gold laid upon his arm, and the kingdom was strengthened and confirmed. This was to him from the mighty God of Jacob,..."

LXX
υἱὸς ηὐξημένος μου ζηλωτός· υἱός μου νεώτατος· πρὸς μὲ ἀνάστρεψον. εἰς ὃν διαβουλευόμενοι ἐλοιδόρουν, καὶ ἐνεῖχον αὐτῷ κύριοι τοξευμάτων· καὶ συνετρίβη μετὰ κράτους τὰ τόξα αὐτῶν, καὶ ἐξελύθη τὰ νεῦρα βραχιόνων χειρὸς αὐτῶν διὰ χεῖρα δυνάστου Ἰακώβ....

Jonathan
"...to a vine planted by fountains of water, which sendeth forth her roots, and overrunneth the ridges of stone, and covereth by her branches all unfruitful trees; even so didst thou, my son Joseph, subject by thy wisdom and thy good works all the magicians of Mizraim; and when, celebrating thy praises, the daughters of princes walking on the high places cast before thee bracelets and chains of gold, that thou shouldst lift up thine eyes upon them, thine eyes thou wouldst not lift up on one of them, to become guilty in the great day of judgment. And all the magicians of Mizraim were bitter and angry against him, and brought accusations against him before Pharoh, expecting to bring him down from his honour. They spake against him with the slanderous (marg. triple) tongue which is severe as arrows. But he returned to abide in his early strength, and would not yield himself unto sin, and subdued his inclinations by the strong discipline he had received from Jakob,..."

Jer. II
"...to a vine planted by fountains of water, which sendeth her roots into the depth, and striketh the ridges of the rocks, uplifting herself on high and surmounting all the trees. So hast thou, O Joseph my son, risen by thy wisdom above all the magicians of Mizraim, and all the wise men who were there, what time thou didst ride in the second chariot of Pharoh, and they proclaimed before thee and said, This is the father of the king, Long live the father of the king, Great in wisdom, though few in years. And the daughters of kings and of princes danced before thee at the windows, and beheld thee from the balconies, and scattered before thee bracelets, rings, collars, necklaces, and all ornaments of gold, in hope thou wouldst uplift thine eyes and regard one of them. But thou, my son Joseph, wast far from lifting thine eyes on any one of them, though the daughters of kings and of princes spake one to another, This is the holy man Joseph, who walks not after the sight of his eyes nor after the imagination of his heart; because the sight of the eyes and the imagination of his heart

[2837] NOTES TO CHAPTER XIX

Onkelos	Jonathan	Jer. II
		make the son of woman to perish from the world. Therefore will arise from thee the two tribes Menasheh and Ephraim, who shall receive portion and inheritance with their brethren in the dividing of the land. The magicians of Mizraim and all the wise men spake against him, but could not prevail over him; they spake evil of him before his lord, they accused him before Pharoh king of Mizraim, to bring him down from his dignity; they spake against him in the palace of Pharoh with a slanderous tongue severe as arrows. But the strength of his confidence (or, fidelity) remained in both his hands and his arms, and he sought mercy from the strength of his father Jakob,..."

[2837 (iii)] This note on Targumistic translations was written to illustrate the divergences arising (Preface, p. xvi foll.) from the obscure word "*wing*" in Dan. ix. 27 in connexion with "abomination of desolations," and it was contended in the Preface that Christ actually used the word "*wing*," perhaps in the sense of "pinnacle ($\pi\tau\epsilon\rho\acute{\upsilon}\gamma\iota\text{o}\nu$)" and that it was variously interpreted by Christians—Luke, for example, taking the word to mean "a surrounding army." A confirmation of this conclusion, namely, that our Lord did not mention "army" and did mention "wing," is afforded by the following facts. According to Josephus (*Ant.* xx. 9. 1) James the Just was unjustly condemned to death and stoned. Origen (*Cels.* i. 47) is supported by Eusebius (ii. 23. 20) in quoting Josephus as saying that retribution befell the Jews for this crime. No such statement is in our text of Josephus. But Eusebius quotes (ii. 1. 5) Clement of Alexandria as declaring that there were two Apostles named James, "One, the Just, he that was cast down from the *pinnacle* (πτερυγίον) and clubbed to death by a fuller." Eusebius afterwards (ii. 23. 4 foll.) quotes Hegesippus' largely fabulous account (Lightf. *Epist. Galat.* p. 330) of James's death in which the Pharisees place him "on the *pinnacle* of the temple" and afterwards throw him down. Then they "stone" him (see Josephus above). Then a fuller clubs him to death. The narrative concludes with the words "And straightway Vespasian besieges them." The inference suggested by this abrupt conclusion is that Hegesippus considered this cruel and sacrilegious murder on "*the wing*," or "pinnacle," of the temple, as being an "abomination" that might well be regarded as fulfilling Christ's prediction about "*the abomination of desolation.*" If so, it would seem probable that Hegesippus' account was based on an earlier narrative by someone who reasoned thus: "The death of James the Righteous one was 'the abomination of desolation.' But the Lord said it was to be '*on the wing,*' that is, *on the pinnacle of the temple.* Therefore the Righteous one must have been placed on that 'pinnacle' and thrown down[1]."

---

[1] [2837(iii)*a*] It is antecedently natural that, before the siege of Jerusalem, many questionings and traditions would be current among Christians in the city about the meaning of the Lord's warning words, "the abomination of desolation." This is confirmed by Eusebius' mention (iii. 5. 3) of "a certain oracle (τινὰ χρησμόν)," given to "those of approved reputation there (τοῖς αὐτόθι δοκίμοις)," in accordance with which the Christians "were commanded to remove from the city and dwell in a certain city of Peræa, [people] call it Pella." If the Christians had had Luke's clear words before them, "When ye see Jerusalem encircled by armies," they would hardly have needed an "oracle." As it was, they seem to have needed one. When it was announced, it might be expressed in Greek thus: "What the Lord *meant* was (ἔλεγεν δὲ ὁ Κύριος ὅτι) that, when ye see Jerusalem etc." This, in Greek (and in Semitic too) would be indistinguishable (**1300, 2467—70**) from "Now the Lord *said*, When ye see...."

[2837(iii)*b*] Before this "oracle" had become current, and long before it was adopted in Luke's gospel, amid the horrors that preceded the siege, the Christians within the walls might naturally say, "Surely this or that is the Abomination of Desolation"; and no event that we know would take precedence of the Martyrdom of James the Just in its claim to be so called. We might naturally expect that the Martyrdom would be recorded in various traditions, and that the central word "*pinnacle*" would reappear in some other shape.

[2837(iii)*c*] Accordingly, in *Recognitions of Clement* (transl. Clark, bk i, ch. 55), the apostles "*go up to the temple,*" and stand "*on the steps*" and repeat this action (ch. 66) on the following day. Then, Peter is introduced as saying (ch. 70) "One of our enemies," namely Saul, "seized a strong brand from the altar," and,

[2838] Page 178, "Flavius Clemens," Suet. 15 "contemptissimae inertiae," see Lightfoot *Philipp.* p. 22; p. 179, "Mark in the middle," see *Corr. of Mk* 322; p. 180, "Old Hermas," an imaginary character, not the author of the *Pastor*; p. 181, "Bond and free," comp. Lucian *Hermotim.* 24 (i. 763) as to the city in which "the words '*inferior*' and '*superior*,' '*noble*' and '*lowborn*,' '*bond*' and '*free*,' have absolutely no existence."

---

attacking the Christians with his followers, threw James headlong down "from the top of the steps, and, supposing him to be dead, he cared not to inflict further violence upon him." In this narrative, the "pinnacle" becomes "the top of the steps." "The fuller"—a term applied in the Talmud to a Rabbi (**522** n.)—becomes "the enemy," Saul, as is indicated by the next chapter which describes him as "going to Damascus with letters" from the high priest. That the "fuller's club" should become "a strong brand" would be intelligible if Saul were regarded as (Zech. iii. 2) "a brand plucked from the fire" of an ordinary hearth, and if the writer meant to describe him as ultimately converted. But "brand *from the altar*" suggests sacrilege, and the writer is bitterly hostile to Paul.

The passage is quoted to shew the early currency of traditions about the martyrdom of James the Just in connexion with some obscure mention of a "pinnacle" or "high place."

[**2837** (iii) *d*] It should be added that Gesen. 1055 *a* suggests as prob. the sing. "abomination" in Dan. ix. 27 and also כנו "its place" instead of כנף "wing" (comp. Gesen. 489 *b*). *Taanith* 28 *b*—29 *a* after quoting Dan. xii. 11, *where the sing. is used*, "the *abomination* that maketh desolate," says, "Was there then only one?" and asks how this can be *reconciled with the plural* in Dan. ix. 27 "Und auf dem Flügel werden die entsetzliehen (?-ichen) Scheusale stehen. Raba erwiderte: Es waren zwei Götzen, da fiel einer auf den anderen und brach ihm eine Hand ab; auf dieser fand man folgende Aufschrift: Du wolltest den Tempel zerstören, deine Hand ist ihm aber übergeben worden." This suggests that כנף was taken as "hand" (for which meaning, see Levy ii. 357 *a*, Levy *Ch.* i. 371 *b*). Compare the story of the fall of the truncated Dagon (1 S. v. 4) of whom it is said that "the *palms* (כפות) *of his hands*" were broken off and lay on "the threshold." Having regard to the extant divergences in rendering "*wing*," it is perhaps worth adding that the Heb. for "*threshold*," in the Dagon story מפתן, is usually rendered by LXX αἴθριον (Lat. atrium) and also once βαθμός, "step" (comp. the use of "steps" above in the martyrdom of James the Just), also πρόθυρον etc. But Aquila and Symmachus twice render it οὐδός. Hesychius has οὐδός, βαθμός....

Οὔδει (Steph. *Thes.*) is a freq. dat. of οὖδος or οὖδας, "ground," "pavement," meaning "on the ground," whereas ἐπ' οὐδῷ means "on the threshold," sometimes metaph. The facts suggest that על כנף may have been rendered επογΛω, επογΛει, and that the latter may have produced Mk xiii. 14 οποιογΛει. But paraphrase seems a more probable explanation.

32

NOTES TO CHAPTER XX

[2839] Page 184, "The time is fulfilled," Mk i. 15; p. 184, "Comfort ye," Is. xl. 1 (LXX). Aquila, like R.V. marg., has "time of service[1]." The LXX has prob. confused the Hebrew letters;

THE CONTINUITY BETWEEN MARK AND ISAIAH

[1] [2839 a] The continuity between Mark and Isaiah may be illustrated (2839 b) by their use of the word "preach." This, in Hebrew, is קרא, which means "call," "cry aloud"—sometimes "call [to a place]" or "call [by name]," καλέω: sometimes "cry as a public crier," βοάω: sometimes "proclaim as a herald," κηρύσσω. In later Hebrew this "crying" or "proclaiming" came to be applied technically to the "crying aloud," or public reading, of the scriptures. The written scriptures had no vowel points. But the scriptures read aloud were necessarily pronounced with definite vowels; and the oral text, thus defined, was called (from the Hebrew verb) *Kri* (which by accident agrees somewhat in sound with the French "cri" and our "cry").

This Hebrew verb (from which *Kri* is derived) is used both in the Scripture and in Targums in two passages (Lev. xxv. 10, Is. lxi. 1) relating to the "*crying*" (as though by God's "public crier") of "the year of remission." One of these passages is said by Luke (iv. 18) to have been read by our Lord at His first appearance in public life, "He hath anointed me...to *cry* remission to the captives...to *cry* the acceptable year of the Lord." Here the LXX uses 1st, κηρύξαι, "preach" (or "proclaim"), 2nd, καλέσαι, "call." But Luke uses κηρύσσω twice. Κηρύσσω, too, is the word used regularly in the Pauline epistles to denote Christian "preaching" *i.e.* "announcing the gospel." The Targum of Onkelos on Leviticus (xxv. 10) uses the old Hebrew word, the root of "Kri," to denote this "announcement" of remission. It may be taken as certain that Christ used it, too, if He read Isaiah to His countrymen. It is true that the Targum of the Prophets (as also Targ. Jon. in Lev. xxv. 10) often renders the Hebrew "cry" by *câraz*, a Hebraized form of κηρύσσω "proclaim as a herald": but this does not hold in the passage of Isaiah in question, in which the Targum uses the old Hebrew word "cry." The Syriac also uses the root of Kri, "cry," in Lev. xxv. 10 and Is. lxi. 1, 2.

[2839 b] Now let us pass to the opening words of Mark quoting Is. xl. 3 "the voice of one *crying*." LXX has βοῶντος. But Aquila has καλοῦντος "calling," and we have seen above that, in Is. lxi. 1, the LXX renders the word first by "proclaim" and then by "call," while Luke renders it twice by "proclaim." The latter, κηρύσσω, might well seem to some a more dignified word than βοάω which often means "shout." Hence we cannot be surprised that Mark, after quoting the prophecy with the LXX word, βοάω, describes the fulfilment in his own word, κηρύσσω. But the result is, that English readers may fail to realise that Mark means, in effect, "Isaiah predicted 'the voice of one *crying*,' and accordingly John the Baptist came '*crying.*'" This "crying," LXX παρακαλέω and βοάω, recurs in Isaiah's context, Is. xl. 1 foll. "*Cry* unto her (παρακαλέσατε αὐτήν)... (3) The voice of one that *crieth* (βοῶντος)...(6) The voice of one saying, *Cry*

[2839] NOTES TO CHAPTER XX

p. 185, "Having authority," Mk i. 22; p. 185, "Flavius Josephus," *Ant.* viii. 2. 5; p. 185, "Would not allow," Mk i. 34, Lk. iv. 41; p. 186, "Authority on earth," Mk ii. 10; p. 186, "In the habit of quoting," 1 Cor. xv. 27—8, Eph. i. 22, Heb. ii. 8 quoting Ps. viii. 6 (comp. Phil. iii. 21). Silanus is allowed to quote the Epistle to the Hebrews as Pauline. Origen quotes it thus. But perhaps the allowance is a fault. Almost all deny its Pauline authorship.

The doctrine of the exaltation of the Son by the Father may be illustrated by Jewish tradition likening God to the father of a

---

(βόησον), and I said, What shall I *cry* (βοήσω)?" Then Isaiah gives the message that is to be "*cried*," namely, "All flesh is grass...but the word of our God abideth for ever." Mark and Isaiah alone might suffice to shew the connexion between the Hebrew "*crying*," or *Kri*, and the Christian "*preaching*" or "*gospel*." But we have, besides, the confirmation of 1 Pet. i. 24—5 quoting the words of the "*cry*" ("All flesh...but the word of God abideth for ever") and adding, "*Now this is the 'word' that was preached as gospel to you.*" Both Isaiah and Peter take the "gospel" to be the abiding fulfilment of "the word of God," as Ibn Ezra says (on Is. xl. 6) "This verse explains 'the glory of the Lord' to consist in the fact that His word alone is fulfilled, not so the word of man." Ibn Ezra also explains Is. xl. 3 "the voice of him that *crieth*," as "the voice of him that *brings the good tidings*," thus connecting "*crying*" with "*good tidings*" or "*gospel*." The Syriac uses the root of "Kri" in Is. xl. 2, 3, 6. Another meaning of the root of "Kri," "call," is expressed in Christ's saying that He "came to *call* sinners," and in many parts of N.T. that speak of the "*calling*" of Christians and describe them as "*called*."

[2839 *c*] All these Hebrew, Jewish, and Greek traditions may help to explain the first mention of κηρύσσω in Christ's words, as given by Mark (i. 38) "Let us go hence...that there also I may *proclaim*"—*i.e.* carry on and fulfil the "*crying aloud*," the "*proclaiming*" of the true "year of remission" in the highest sense, the "*calling*" of men to accept the "remission" of sins. By itself, "that I may *proclaim*" must have been unintelligible to Greek readers of Mark. But it pointed back to Mk i. 14 "Jesus came...*proclaiming* (κηρύσσων) the gospel of God," and that, again, to Mk i. 7 "John *proclaimed*, saying, There cometh he that is stronger than I," and to Mk i. 4 "John...*proclaiming* the baptism of repentance for remission of sins." Finally, Mk i. 4 "*proclaiming*" pointed back (though not clearly for a Greek reader) to Mk i. 3 "the voice of one *crying aloud*," *i.e.* "proclaiming"; and this led the reader back to the "good tidings," or "gospel" "cried aloud," or "proclaimed," in Isaiah.

[2839 *d*] Mark is open to the objection that readers of Christ's words, "that I may proclaim," may well ask, in perplexity, "proclaim what?" Luke meets this objection in Christ's first public discourse:—"*proclaim* remission to prisoners... *proclaim* the acceptable year of the Lord (*i.e.* the year of remission)." John perhaps considered that κηρύσσω, meaning "proclaim, as a herald proclaims the advent of a king," was entirely inappropriate to the Son declaring the will of the Father. At all events John never uses κηρύσσω either in Christ's words or in his own narrative, though it is frequent in all the Synoptists.

NOTES TO CHAPTER XX [2840]

household, and Israel, or Abraham, to the son. Thus Exod. rab. (on Exod. xii. 2, Wünsche pp. 108—9) says, "Even as a King that had a Son, whom he loved above all things. The Son said to the Father, 'If thou givest me not thy throne, how shall all know that thou lovest me?'…Even so God gave to Abraham the world (Gen. xviii. 17 foll.). When He had given him all, Abraham said, 'If thou givest me not the Temple, which is 500 ells long and as many broad, thou hast given me nothing.'" The Temple is apparently regarded as the "throne." Comp. Rom. iv. 13 "heir of the world," applied to Abraham.

[2840] Page 186, "Socrates had the power," see Epict. iii. 7. 34, which adds, "Make us enamoured (lit. *zealots*) of you, as Socrates made people enamoured of himself." Comp. *ib.* i. 19. 6 "Who becomes enamoured of you [lit. thy *zealot*] as of Socrates?" ii. 6. 26 "We shall be *zealots* of Socrates, in the moment (and not till the moment) when we can write paeans in prison," where "zealot" implies imitation.

P. 186, "In Matthew," Mt. xxi. 16.

P. 187, "Wild beasts." The word transl. "field" (שָׂדַי) in Ps. viii. 7 (R.V.) "the beasts of the *field*," means (Gesen. 961 a) "home of wild beasts" there and in Joel ii. 22, Is. lvi. 9 etc. The word שָׂדֶה means (Gesen. *ib.*) "specif. home of beasts…of beasts in gen. and of wild beasts." For "beasts in gen." Gesen. quotes 2 S. xvii. 8 "as a bear robbed of her whelps in the *field*," which indicates a "wild beast" of the carnivora; and Jer. xiv. 5 "the hind also in the *field* calveth," which indicates a "wild beast," but not carnivorous. Gesen. gives no instance where "field" is used as the home of "cattle" in the English sense[1].

P. 188, "He goes about," Epict. iii. 22. 73; p. 188, "Reconnoitrer," Epict. i. 24. 6; p. 188, "I came not," Mk ii. 17, Mt. ix. 13, Lk. v. 32; p. 189, "Healthy," Epict. iii. 22. 72; p. 189, "Bear ye," Gal. vi. 2; p. 189, "meekness," Gal. vi. 1; p. 190, "Pronouncing righteous," see Gesen. Oxf. 842—3; p. 191, "That men should repent," Mk vi. 12; p. 191, "The sabbath…for man," Mk ii. 27;

---

[1] [2840 a] In Ps. viii. 7, LXX renders "*beasts of the field*" by "*cattle of the plain*," τὰ κτήνη τοῦ πεδίου, perhaps misled by the word "field." But comp. 1 S. xvii. 44 "I will give thy flesh to…the *beasts of the field*," LXX "*cattle of the earth*," where A corrects κτήνεσιν to θηρίοις. Here LXX does not retain "field," and yet mistranslates "beasts." Probably the Psalmist included in one brief phrase the subjection of "beasts of prey," and "beasts of the chase," to man.

[2840]

p. 191, "I desire kindness," Mt. xii. 7 quoting Hos. vi. 6; p. 191, "If ye have any charge," Mk xi. 25.

[2840*] Page 192, "The favourite of a bad God." In O.T. (R.V.) the notions of "favour," "grace," "kindness," and "compassion" so run into one another that it may be well to state a few leading facts about the terms here, for future reference. The Heb. *noun*, "favour," חֵן, is rendered by LXX χάρις about 60 times; but the *verb*, "favour," is never rendered by LXX χαριτόω etc., but (besides other renderings) ἐλεέω 45 times, οἰκτείρω 10; and (in hithp.) δέομαι about 17 times. Aquila renders the verb by δωρέομαι, "make a free gift," "give freely," thus suggesting the notion of "grace" or "favour." R.V. varies remarkably[1].

"Favour," "kindness," etc. in R.V.

[1] [2840* *a*] In Ps. vi. 2, ix. 13, xxx. 10 etc., LXX has ἐλεέω, Aq. δωρέομαι (Targ. חוס, in O.T. = (22 times) φείδομαι, "spare"). In Ps. cxix. 29, both A.V. and R.V. have "grant graciously." In Ps. xxxvii. 21 where A.V. has "sheweth mercy," R.V. has "dealeth graciously." In Ps. iv. 1, lxxxvi. 16, R.V. has txt "have mercy," marg. "be gracious." In Ps. vi. 2, ix. 13, xxv. 16, xxvii. 7, xxx. 10, xxxi. 9, cxxiii. 2, 3, R.V. has "have mercy," without marg. note. In all these cases the Heb. is a form of חנן. In Gen. xxxiii. 5 (R.V.) "The children which God hath graciously given," Onk. follows Heb. חנן, but LXX and Jon. Targ. have ἐλεεῖν and a form of חוס; so, too, in Exod. xxxiii. 19 "I will be gracious to whom I will be gracious."

[2840* *b*] As regards חסד, *chesed*, "kindness," Aq. freq. renders it by ἔλεος, *e.g.* Ps. xliv. 26 "for the sake of thy kindness," LXX "for the sake of thy name," Aq. Sym. διὰ τὸ ἔλεός σου: also li. 2 LXX κατὰ τὸ μέγα ἐλεός σου, Aq. κατὰ ἔλεόν σου, Sym. κατὰ τὸ ἔλεός σου. Oxf. Conc. gives Aq. as using ἔλεος in Ps. xxxi. 7, 16, 21, xxxii. 10, and xxxiii. 18, 22 etc. Symmachus renders *chesed* by χάρις in Ps. xxxi. 7, 16, xxxiii. 18 etc., and it is similarly rendered in Sir. vii. 33 (txt χάρις, א χάρισμα).

[2840* *c*] The Vulg. mostly uses some form of "miser" (such as "misereri," "misericordia" etc.), where "mercy" occurs in our A.V., *e.g.* Gen. xix. 19, xxiv. 27, xxxix. 21, Exod. xv. 13, xx. 6, xxxiv. 7, Numb. xiv. 18, 19. All these passages have *chesed*.

[2840* *d*] "Lovingkindness" (sing. or pl.) occurs in A.V. 30 times, and always as the representative of *chesed*, 23 times in the Psalms, 7 in the Prophets. In Ps. lxxxix. 33 "But my lovingkindness will I not utterly take from him," and Jer. xxxii. 18 "shewest lovingkindness unto thousands," R.V. substitutes "mercy"; and in Ps. cvii. 43 "They shall understand the lovingkindness of the Lord," R.V. has "the mercies of the Lord."

[2840* *e*] On the other hand, R.V. freq. introduces "lovingkindness" where A.V. has "mercy," *e.g.* 2 S. xxii. 51 "sheweth lovingkindness unto his anointed," and so too in Ps. v. 7, xviii. 50, xxi. 7, xxv. 7, 10, xxxvi. 5, lxi. 7, cxliii. 12.

[2840* *f*] The American Revisers (Strong's *Comparat. Conc.* p. 123 *b—c*) have

NOTES TO CHAPTER XXI

[2841] Page 193, "Outside the man," Mk vii. 15, Mt. xv. 11; p. 193, "A vision," Acts xi. 5—10, x. 9—16; p. 194, "Confuse." Instances could be quoted from letters written by intelligent and well-read students of Scripture, published in English journals of the highest class, where such confusion has occurred in recent times; p. 195, "Leaven," "loaves," "crumbs," see "loaves" in Index of *The Fourfold Gospel*; p. 195, "Take up his cross," Mk viii. 34, Mt. xvi. 24, Lk. ix. 23; p. 195, "Paul's epistles," 2 Cor. v. 15, Gal. ii. 20, Rom. vi. 6, Gal. vi. 14; p. 196, "Reproached," Mt. xi. 3, Lk. vii. 19, "Art thou he that should come, or must we look for another?"

The Yoke and the Cross

[2842] Page 197, "Yoke-bearer," see *From Letter* **928** (i) foll. on "furca," the yoke of punishment, and on "furcifer"; p. 197, "Take my yoke," Mt. xi. 29; p. 197, "Babes," Mt. xi. 25, comp. Is. xxviii. 7—13.

P. 198, "Akiba," see *From Letter* **928** (v) *a* Jerem. *Lam.* iii. 27 "It is good for a man that he bear the yoke in his youth....Let him give his cheek to him that smiteth him; let him be filled full with reproach" is paraphrased in the Targum "si docuerit animam suam ut portet jugum præceptorum in adolescentia sua" and "sustinebit castigationes quæ eveniunt, *propter unitatem nominis Dei.*" The final words are illustrated by the tradition that the spirit

---

gone still further in altering "mercy"—for example, where Abraham's servant, on meeting with Rebekah, blesses God because (Gen. xxiv. 27) (R.V.) "he hath not forsaken his *mercy* and his truth toward my master." They adopt the same course in Gen. xix. 19, Exod. xv. 13, xx. 6 and very many other passages, besides more than sixty instances in the Psalms.

[2840* *g*] Luke and John, alone of the evangelists, use the word χάρις. But they apply it to Christ very differently. Lk. ii. 40 uses it of the "grace" of God that was on Jesus as a child when He was "becoming full of wisdom"; ii. 52 says that Jesus "advanced in wisdom and age and grace (or, favour) with God and man"; iv. 22 says that people "wondered at the words of grace which proceeded out of his mouth," immediately before they exclaimed, "Is not this Joseph's son?" and not long before they attempted to stone Him. In Jn i. 14—17, the phrases "grace and truth," and "grace in the place of grace," help to describe not only the "glory of the Only begotten," but also the gifts that came to men from Him, from whose "fulness," says the writer, "we all received" (**1775** *c*, **2285**, **2743** *a*).

of Akiba passed away while he was uttering the word ONE in proclaiming the unity of God, see Taylor's *Aboth* p. 54.

[2843] Page 198, "Yoke," Gal. v. 1, Acts xv. 10, Barnabas ii. 6.

P. 198, "Matthew's tradition." The Greek word for "yoke" may mean (1) "balance," (2) the crosspiece of a sail, *i.e.* "yard," (3) the crosspiece of a cross, (4) the yoke of oxen. The *Acts of Thomas* § 3 connects "*yokes* and *balances* and *ships*," and says, later on, § 28 "receive the *yoke* of meekness and the light burden...come unto Him that is truly good that ye may receive His *grace*; and His *sign* [*i.e.* the *cross* in baptism] shall ye place in your souls." In Plato *Timæus* 26 (63 B) the phrase αἴρειν ζυγόν refers to a "*balance*." Clem. Alex. 663, after quoting a maxim of Pythagoras, "not to overpass the *balance*," adds "For this cause the Lord says, Take my *yoke*," apparently playing on the word. Elsewhere he uses the word "take" to mean "take away," thus (440) "*Take* from yourselves, says he, the heavy yoke, and receive the meek" [? meek yoke or ? Meek One (comp. Mt. xi. 29)], "the Scripture says," ἄρατε ἀφ' ὑμῶν, φησὶν, τὸν βαρὺν ζυγὸν καὶ λάβετε τὸν πρᾶον, ἡ γραφή φησι.

[2844] A treatise attributed to Cyprian says, *Adv. Jud.* 7 "He broke His old Covenant and wrote a new one....We Gentiles carry on our shoulders the *cross, which the Lord of Israel confessed* (? *confessed to Israel*, quam confessus est Israel Dominus) who gently (placide) addressed them [*i.e.* the Jews] in these words (Mt. xi. 28—30) 'Come unto me all that toil under burdens and I will refresh you. *For my yoke is gentle* (placidum) and [my] burden very light.'" The writer appears to regard "*my yoke*" as the Cross, rejected by the Jews but accepted by the Gentiles. In *Testim.* i. 13 (and iii. 119) Cypr. quotes the whole of Mt. xi. 28—30 (as in R.V.) in order to shew that the old yoke is made of no effect and a new one substituted.

[2845] Origen frequently quotes the context, but seldom or never the words "*Take my yoke*." In *Cels.* ii. 7 Origen quotes "Learn from me..." to defend Christ from the charge of "*pompous arrogance* (ἀλαζονείας)." Clem. Rom. xvi. says "the Lord Jesus Christ came not in the boasting of *pompous arrogance* (ἀλαζονείας)" but does not quote "Learn from me." He concludes however with the words, "If the Lord was thus humble minded, what ought to be done by us who, through Him, have come under the *yoke of grace*?"

[2846] Justin Martyr, alluding to the ass and the colt mentioned in the Entry into Jerusalem, says (*Tryph.* 53) that the Gentiles were "like a *colt not having a yoke* on its neck" until they "bore the yoke *of His word*," and that the "*saddled ass*" was a symbol of the Jews. "*Saddled ass*" alludes to Mt. xxi. 5, which describes the colt as (literally) "the offspring of *one under the yoke*." In this might be seen an implied contrast between the Jews, *i.e.* the ass, which had been under the yoke, and the Gentiles, *i.e.* the colt, which had not.

[2847] Clem. Alex. 106 makes no such contrast between the "ass" and the "colt," apparently regarding the two as one, and saying that, although the animal is called "ass" in the Scripture, it is also "colt" and "young" (*i.e.* "new," with allusion to the "new man" in Christ). The context in Clem. regards "yoke" as evil, speaking of the Gentiles as "colts unyoked to vice."

[2848] Origen (on Jn *lib.* x. 18, Lomm. i. 330) says that the "ass" is a beast of burden, and of heavy burdens, but "the colt is not a beast of burden in the same way as the ass is." Then he mentions the view that the colt means the Gentiles, who, "before they receive *the word of Jesus*, are free from control." Here, if the precedent of Clem. Rom. and Justin had been followed, we should have had "before they receive *the yoke of Jesus*," or "*the yoke of grace*."

On Mt. xxi. 1 foll., Origen says (Lomm. iv. 47) that perhaps the ass and the colt are the symbols of the Jews and Gentiles, both having been "bound" by sins, and both being loosed by the Saviour. He adds that Jesus "sat on the ass *that He might give rest*, rather than *find rest*." This evidently refers to Mt. xi. 29 "and *ye shall find rest* for your souls," where the "rest" is associated with "my yoke."

[2849] Chrysostom (on Mt. xi. 28—30) in a very long commentary on the "yoke," although he nowhere identifies it with the Cross, frequently declares that it may imply persecution, insult, and a violent death.

The impression given by the early quotations (and by the non-quotations) of Mt. xi. 28—30 is that Christian writers avoided connecting the name of Christ with "yoke" except in passages where the new yoke was contrasted with the old one.

NOTES TO CHAPTER XXII

[2850] Page 201, "Shall be ashamed," Mk viii. 38; p. 201, "Of the present day." This is doubtful. Such traditions are recorded in the Talmud about Hillel and about much earlier personages (including Biblical characters): but the date of these traditions cannot be determined. See the remarks on *Bath Kol* in *From Letter* 725—85; p. 201, "Thou art my beloved Son," Mk i. 11; p. 201, "Above," see *Sil.* p. 184 foll.; p. 202, "Repeated," Mk ix. 7 "This is my beloved Son"; p. 203, "David and Daniel," see *Sil.* pp. 48 and 186; p. 203, "Matthew," Mt. xvi. 27 instead of "shall be ashamed," has "shall render to each according to his doing"; p. 203, "A very instructive parable," Mt. xxv. 31—46.

P. 204, "Who is this Son of man?" Jn xii. 34. For the early Christian explanations of "Son of Man," and for its Aramaic equivalents, see **2998** (i) foll.

"Faith as a grain of mustard-seed"

[2851] Page 204, "Fast," Mk ix. 29 (see R.V. marg.). Mk ix. 29 (R.V. txt) has "This kind can come out by nothing save by prayer." The parall. Mt. xvii. 20 has "Because of your little faith. For verily I say unto you, *if ye have faith as a grain of mustard-seed*, ye shall say unto this mountain...." Again, where Mk xi. 22—3 has "Have faith *in* (lit. *of*) *God*....Whosoever shall say to this mountain...," the parall. Mt. xxi. 21 has "If ye have faith *and be not divided* [in mind]...even if ye say to this mountain...," but Lk. xvii. 6 has "If ye have faith *as a grain of mustard-seed*, ye would say to this sycamine-tree, Be uprooted...."

[2852] Hippolytus (Dunck. p. 168, v. 9, and p. 244, vi. 14) says that certain very early heretics—whom he calls Phrygians—and also Simon Magus (in his *Announcement*) spoke of *growing, or being generated*, "*from the indivisible point*." This the Phrygians illustrated by "the grain of mustard" (in Mt. xiii. 31), saying, "This is the kingdom of the heavens, the grain of mustard, which is the indivisible point existing in the body." Simon Magus applies this to the generation of man both in Paradise and in the womb.

[2853] Origen (on Mt. xvii. 20, Lomm. iii. 219) explains "faith as a grain of mustard-seed" as signifying its *small repute in the eyes of men.* Both here and later on (Lomm. iii. 223) he identifies it with Paul's "*all faith*," and likens it to the faith of Abraham.

[2854] On the other hand, Clem. Alex. *Theodot. Excerpt.* 993 says, "The Saviour shewed his faithful apostles that *prayer was stronger than faith*...saying 'Such [evils] as these are set right by prayer.'" This indicates a different view from Origen's. Origen takes the meaning to be, not that prayer is stronger than faith, but that "all faith," or "faith in its entirety," was needed, and not possessed, by the apostles.

[2855] These facts shew (what is *a priori* probable) that the expression "*faith as a grain of mustard-seed*" caused difficulty in very early times. It would naturally be taken to mean "*a very little faith.*" But Origen's conclusion seems right—though his arguments are not convincing—that it means "*a living faith.*" It seems to have been paraphrased by Mark, both in ix. 29, and in xi. 22—3, as "faithful and fervent prayer." In Mk ix. 29, "fasting" may have been added by many authorities in order to express that the prayer was of a special nature.

[2856] The speculations of Simon Magus and others shew that the doctrine about the "mustard-seed" was liable to corruption through undue emphasis laid on the "littleness" of the "grain." Paul, in arguing about the resurrection, mentions "grain" of any kind. The fourth gospel (xii. 23—4) mentions "a grain of wheat" in connexion with "the Son of man," implying that as the "grain" must "die" to "bear fruit," so "the Son of man" must be "glorified" through death. In expression, this somewhat resembles the Egyptian doctrine about Osiris. But the thought is implied in the Synoptic gospels, which teach that "whosoever will lose his life (or soul, $\psi\upsilon\chi\acute{\eta}$) shall find it," if it is "lost" for "the Son of man." See **2998** (lv) *m.*

[2857] Page 204, "Of men," Mk ix. 31. Origen, on the parall. Mt. xvii. 22, calls attention (*Paradosis* 1221—2) to this difficult phrase. It is probably based (**1223**) upon Isaiah liii. 12. Origen is referred to, in an anachronism, as "one of the brethren," later on.

P. 204, "Above," see *Sil.* pp. 107 foll. and 160 foll.; p. 205, "Desires to be first," Mk ix. 35; p. 205, "As a little child," Mk x. 15; p. 205, "First sentence," Mk i. 15; p. 206, "One thing is lacking," Mk x. 21; p. 207, "Loved (or embraced)," Mk x. 21, see *Joh. Voc.* **1744** (iii); p. 207, "The Son of man came," Mk x. 45; p. 207, "All things that ye pray," Mk xi. 24; p. 207, "In the moment when ye stand praying," Mk xi. 25; p. 207, "Have salt in yourselves," Mk ix. 50; p. 208, "The commandments of men," Mk vii. 7; p. 208, "What Plutarch says," see his Introduction to the Life of Alexander.

[**2858**] Page 209, "Salted with fire," Mk ix. 49; p. 209, "All things are possible," Mk ix. 23, x. 27, xiv. 36, Mt. xix. 26; p. 209, "Be at peace with one another," Mk ix. 50. Concerning "salting with fire," see *Fourfold G.* "fire," "salt." Since "salt" represents the Holy Spirit, the precept "*Have salt in yourselves*" implies, in effect, "Have in yourselves the fellowship of the Holy Spirit," which includes, "Have peace with one another." In Jn xiii. 34, xv. 12, "love one another" is a wider expression of the same precept.

P. 209, "Unbelievers." Cramer, on Mk x. 24 foll., prints this cavil, "Can it be then that this includes evil things?"; p. 209, "Fashion anew," Phil. iii. 21; p. 209, "Nowhere uses it," see *Joh. Voc.* **1686** "mighty (possible, able)"; p. 209, "Is able to do," see *Joh. Gram.* **2605** quoting Jn v. 19, 30, and **2516**. Comp. *Joh. Voc.* **1607**; p. 210, "Prefers 'authority,'" see *Joh. Voc.* **1576—94**.

NOTES TO CHAPTER XXIII

[**2859**] Page 211, "It is not fit," Mk vii. 27.

P. 212, "The disciples tried." If so, the circumstances would resemble those in Mk v. 35, x. 13—14, where the disciples of Jesus try to prevent people from coming to Him. "They said" and "he said" might be confused in Greek through the interchange of two similar letters (*Joh. Gram.* **2650—2**), and then the narrative would be modified to suit the error.

"THE LOST SHEEP"

[**2860**] Page 212, "As in Matthew," Mt. xv. 24 "I was not sent save to the lost sheep of the house of Israel." In the gospels, the phrase "house of Israel" is found only in Mt., and only in connexion with "lost sheep." The emphasis may have originally been not on "Israel," as distinct from "Gentiles," but on "lost."

P. 212, "By extraction," Acts iv. 36; p. 212, "Dogs," Phil. iii. 2 comp. Rev. xxii. 15.

NOTES TO CHAPTER XXIII [2865]

[2861] Page 213, "The lost sheep." All the Synoptists have traditions about a man's "losing" or "saving" *his own* "*soul*" (or "*life*"). But, apart from these, the word "lost" occurs freq. in Lk. to represent the "lost sheep," and in parables (peculiar to him) about "saving the lost." Lk. also describes the shepherd as (Lk. xv. 4) "having lost one" of his sheep. But "save the lost" does not occur in the other gospels (Mt. xviii. 11 being an interpolation).

[2862] Matthew has "lost" in this sense only twice, and that in the phrase Mt. x. 6, xv. 24 "lost sheep of the house of Israel." In the parall. to Mt. x. 6, Mk and Lk. omit the phrase—and also omit the context, which forbids the disciples to go to Gentiles or Samaritans. In the parall. to Mt. xv. 24—the story of the Syrophœnician woman, which is wholly omitted by Lk.—Mk omits the phrase and its context.

[2863] "Lost" may be ambiguous in Hebrew and in Greek (as to some extent in English) since it may mean (1) "*destroyed*," (2) "*strayed*." SS renders Mt. x. 6, xv. 24 "the flock that hath *strayed* from the house of Israel" and Palest. Lect. has "from," but with a different word meaning "lost" or "destroyed" (comp. Levy i. 6 *a*, where "lost from the world" means "vanish (or, be destroyed) out of the world").

[2864] Hence some evangelists might avoid, as being paradoxical, the expression "save that which is lost." They might prefer (1) "*find* that which is *lost*," or (2) "*save* that which is *on the point of being lost*." Compare:—

Mt. xviii. 12.	Lk. xv. 4.
"What think you? If a man have a hundred sheep and one of them have *strayed* (πλανηθῇ)…he seeketh *that which is straying*…."	"What man of you having a hundred sheep and *having lost* (ἀπολέσας) one of them…he goeth after that which is *lost*…."

[2865] Here SS has in Lk. xv. 4 "and one of them be lost." This avoids the inference that the shepherd has by carelessness "lost" the sheep. Luke however does not consider this an objection, as is clearly seen in his parable of the drachma "lost" by the woman, which is peculiar to him. Lk. xix. 10 "hath come to seek and *save* that which is lost" is quoted by Clem. Alex. 579 "having come to-day hath *found* that which was lost," and Epiphanius *Haer*. xlvi. 4 quotes Mt. xv. 24 "I have not come except to the strayed sheep (sing.) of the house of Israel."

43

NOTES TO CHAPTER XXIII

[2866] Mark nowhere speaks of "lost sheep," or "strayed sheep," or "saving the lost"; but he describes the Saviour as having compassion on the multitude because they were (Mk vi. 34) "as *sheep that have no shepherd.*" W. H. print this as alluding to Numb. xxvii. 17 "that the congregation of the Lord *be not as sheep that have no shepherd*"—which is just before the appointment of "Jesus," or Joshua, to be the "shepherd." The Jon. Targum paraphrases the italicised words thus, "*may not be without the wise, nor go astray among the nations, as sheep who go astray, having no shepherd.*" This shews how words of our Lord might be variously expressed.

[2867] Are we to suppose that Matthew's expression, "*the lost sheep of the house of Israel*," was really uttered by Christ and dropped by Mark in the story of the Syrophœnician woman, or that it was erroneously inserted by Matthew? The former supposition is more probable, especially in view of the great difficulty found by Origen (*Cels.* iv. 3, 17, *De Princip.* iv. 1, and Lomm. i. 367, ii. 206, iv. 51) in explaining the phrase. He refuses to take it literally "as the Ebionites do."

[2868] But it is quite possible that Christ's precept to His missionaries did not originally mention "Gentiles" or "Samaritans." The emphasis may have been on "lost," thus, "Go to the *lost sheep* of the house of Israel, that is, to the outcasts and sinners, *not to the 'just persons.'*" The former were to be dealt with first. A subsequent interpretation, not recognising this antithesis, may have supposed that a different antithesis was intended, "of the house of Israel, *not of Samaritans or Gentiles.*" Then the italicised words may have been inserted in the text. If the tradition was thus variously interpreted at a very early date, we can understand why Mark and Luke may have honestly omitted all reference to "the lost sheep of the house of Israel" as being of doubtful meaning.

[2869] What then were the facts that confronted the author of the fourth gospel? (1) He found Luke continually mentioning "*the lost*" as the objects of salvation, but not "those who were on the point of being lost." (2) Luke frequently *implies* a "shepherd" but *never mentions the word.* When Luke speaks of a "man" owning sheep, he once describes him as "*losing*" one of his sheep. (3) Mark (followed by Matthew) twice mentions "shepherd" (Mk vi. 34, xiv. 27). In the first of these passages he (followed by Matthew, though not in the same context) uses the old phrase of the Law "*sheep that had no shepherd*" to describe the condition of Israel at the coming of Jesus. (4) Matthew alone twice uses "the lost sheep of the house of Israel" in a manner that suggests national exclusiveness. How does John deal with these facts?

[2870] As regards "losing," John emphasizes the doctrine that Christ came (iii. 16) "that every one that believeth in him *might not be lost*" (comp. the mystical (vi. 12) "*that nothing may be lost*"), (vi. 39) "*that I may not lose* aught of that which thou hast given me." It is only the thief that comes to the sheepfold (x. 10) "that he may steal...and (lit.) *lose*, i.e. *destroy*." The sheep that hear the shepherd's voice (x. 28) "shall *never* be *lost*, or *destroyed*," (xvii. 12) "*not* one of them *was lost*," (xviii. 9) "I have *not lost* one of them."

[2871] As regards the "shepherd," John (x. 1—18) describes Him as not only caring for the sheep outside the fold, but also coming to the sheep in the fold and taking them in and out of it. He also explains how the shepherd may "save" the sheep (not merely "find" them) by "laying down his life" for them. Lastly, "other sheep" are mentioned, not of the same fold as the first, which are to be united with the first. There is nothing in all this that is contrary to the spirit of Christ's teaching, and there is much that is in obvious conformity with it. It seems exactly adapted to remove misunderstandings likely to have been current at the end of the first century.

[2872] Page 213, "Bury," Mt. viii. 21, Lk. ix. 59; p. 213, "Esau," Gen. xxvii. 41; p. 213, "In Latin," Hor. *Sat.* i. 9. 28 "omnes composui"; p. 213, "My rabbi," see *Sanhedr.* 52 a "We shall see who will bury whom," *i.e.* who will survive. This conjecture has been made, or mentioned, in some recent review, which I cannot recall.

[2873] Page 214, "Tacitus's story," *Hist.* iv. 81.

P. 215, "Ass's Jawbone," Strabo (p. 363) "Onou Gnathos (Ὄνου γνάθος) (*i.e.* ass's jawbone) a lowlying peninsula."

P. 215, "Believe that ye have received," Mk xi. 24; p. 216, "To this sycamine-tree," Lk. xvii. 6; p. 216, "Uprooter of mountains," see *From Letter* 764, which also quotes an instance of a Rabbi "uprooting a tree"; p. 216, "The deed of the fig-tree," Mt. xxi. 21: see Mk xi. 12—14, Mt. xxi. 18—19.

"The barren fig-tree"

[2874] Page 216, "Barren." The LXX (Trommius) translates the same Hebrew root, עָקַר, 12 times "barren" and 3 times "root out" or "pluck out." Levy *Ch.* ii. 238 gives this word as meaning "cut down," "exterminate," "uproot," "barren"—all very frequent. For the "parable," see Lk. xiii. 6—9. But see also Mk xiii. 28 (Mt. xxiv. 32) "But from the fig-tree learn its (τὴν) *parable*," where Lk. xxi. 29 has "And he spake a parable to them, See the fig-tree *and all the trees*"—apparently missing the point of difference between the fig-tree and "all the trees," namely, that the fig-tree puts forth *fruitbuds before leafbuds and fruit before leaves*. Lk. xxi. 30 προβάλωσιν is the word used by Aquila in Cant. ii. 13 describing the (lit.) "spicing (חנטה)" or "fragrant budding" of the green figs which took place (Levy ii. 81 *a*) *a hundred days before the* "*plucking*," so that R.V. "*ripeneth* her green figs" seems an error. In *The Fourfold Gospel* (Index "End") it will be shewn that there is a very close connexion between (1) "the [Messianic] end," (2) "summer," (3) "ripe-fig-time[1]." The last two may be identical in Hebrew,

---

[1] [2874 *a*] "Ripe-fig-time," comp. Amos viii. 1—2 "The Lord God shewed me ...a basket of *ripe figs* (קיץ) (see Levy iv. 300 "bes. Feige ")...Then said the Lord unto me, *Ripeness* (קץ) is come upon my people Israel." Here R.V. has "*the end* is come," but I adopt Ewald's "*ripeness*" to keep the play on the words. The LXX completely misses the meaning. The Syr., for "basket of *ripe figs*," has "the goal of the *end* (קצא)." Mk xi. 13 "season of figs" might be expressed by קיץ alone. For the thought of the Messiah seeking early figs comp. Hos. ix. 10 "I saw your fathers as the first ripe in the fig-tree at her first season." And for the Messiah's disappointment comp. *ib.* "but they came to Baal Peor and consecrated themselves unto the shameful thing."

[2874 *b*] In Jer. viii. 20 "Harvest is passed, *ripe-fig-time* (קיץ) is finished, and we are not saved," the Targum renders or paraphrases קיץ by קצא "the end," reducing the metaphor to literal expression.

[2874 *c*] On Cant. ii. 13 "The fig hath *put forth with fragrance* her green figs," the Targum is, "The assembly of Israel, which is likened in a parable to the early ripe figs of the fig-tree, opened its mouth and sang a song on the shore of the Red Sea, and even boys and infants praised the Lord of the World with their tongues" —which resembles the tradition peculiar to Matthew (xxi. 15) about the "children" crying Hosanna to Christ in the Temple.

[2874 *d*] In *The Fourfold Gospel* it will be maintained that Origen, although partially misled by Luke's interpolation of "all the trees," has correctly explained "the parable of the fig-tree" as enjoining fruitfulness and ripeness; and that originally much that Luke supposed to apply to the siege of Jerusalem really applied to the development of the human soul through pain and trouble, and

NOTES TO CHAPTER XXIII [2874]

through what is called by Mark and Matthew "pangs of child-birth," illustrated by John's tradition about "a woman when she is in travail" (Mk xiii. 8, Mt. xxiv. 8, Jn xvi. 21—2).

[2874 e] Contrast the following predictions:

Mk xiii. 14	Mt. xxiv. 15—16	Lk. xxi. 20—21 a
"But when ye see the abomination of desolation standing where he ought not (let him that readeth understand), then let them that are in Judæa flee unto the mountains."	"When therefore ye see the abomination of desolation, which was spoken of by Daniel the prophet, standing in the holy place (let him that readeth understand), then let them that are in Judæa flee unto the mountains."	"But when ye see Jerusalem compassed with armies, then know that her desolation is at hand. Then let them that are in Judæa flee unto the mountains."

Then add Origen's comment (*Cels.* ii. 13) ὁ δὲ ἀπιστῶν παρὰ τῷ Κέλσῳ Ἰουδαῖος περὶ τοῦ Ἰησοῦ, ὅτι πάντα τὰ συμβάντα αὐτῷ προῄδει, κατανοησάτω τίνα τρόπον, ἔτι συνεστώσης τῆς Ἰερουσαλήμ, καὶ πάσης τῆς Ἰουδαϊκῆς λατρείας γινομένης ἐν αὐτῇ, προεῖπεν Ἰησοῦς τὰ συμβησόμενα αὐτῇ ὑπὸ Ῥωμαίων. Οὐ γὰρ δὴ τοὺς αὐτοῦ Ἰησοῦ γνωρίμους καὶ ἀκροατὰς φήσουσι χωρὶς γραφῆς τὴν τῶν εὐαγγελίων παραδεδωκέναι διδασκαλίαν, καὶ καταλιπεῖν τοὺς μαθητὰς χωρὶς τῶν περὶ Ἰησοῦ ἐν γράμμασιν ὑπομνημάτων. Γέγραπται δὴ ἐν αὐτοῖς τό "ὅταν δὲ ἴδητε κυκλουμένην ὑπὸ στρατοπέδων τὴν Ἰερουσαλήμ, τότε γνῶτε ὅτι ἤγγισεν ἡ ἐρήμωσις αὐτῆς."

[2874 f] Here Origen, with an inaccuracy or unfairness quite unusual in his writings, describes the definite prophecy about the "surrounding of Jerusalem" as being *in the gospels* (ἐν αὐτοῖς), whereas it is only in Lk. It seems obvious that Luke means (1) the "surrounding of Jerusalem" to be the equivalent of (2) "the abomination of desolation." Both are the objects of "when ye see." But the former would be intelligible to Greek readers, the latter would not be. Perhaps Luke found the "surrounding" mentioned in some oral or written tradition of Christ's words as being what Christ really "*meant* (ἔλεγε)," and took it as representing what He "*said*" (2469). In the Targums such substitutions are very frequent. It is incredible that Christ should have uttered these words about the surrounding of Jerusalem and that only Luke, the third of the evangelists, should have been aware of them, or else that only Luke should have thought them worth recording. Origen is perfectly alive to the advantage given him over his Jewish adversaries by Luke's version of Christ's words, and we may be sure that Mark, Matthew, and John would have been equally alive to it—if they had recognised such words as authentic. Origen quotes Lk. xxi. 20 again in his *Comm. Gen.* tom. iii. 4 (Lomm. viii. 17) as a specimen of prophecy, and incidentally in *Comm. Matth.* tom. xvi. 2 (Lomm. iv. 5). In neither passage does he quote it as the utterance of only one evangelist, but at all events he does not assign it to the gospels in the plural ("it is written in *them*").

[2874 g] The passage in Lk. affords an instructive warning that even a diligent evangelist with a historical turn of mind could not be trusted always to refrain from—if one may use the word—"Targumizing" even the words of the Lord, where clearness as well as edification seemed to recommend it. No doubt, the Jewish habit of using Targums in the synagogues would contribute generally to a Christian habit of Targumizing the earliest traditions of the gospels; and here, there were special reasons (2837 (i)) for the rendering "armies."

as well as in Greek; and it will be maintained that θέρος in Mk xiii. 28, Mt. xxiv. 32, Lk. xxi. 30 (which occurs nowhere else in N.T.) meant "fruit-time," rather than "summer," and that it was intended to impress on the disciples that the time was at hand for judging men by their "fruits." If so, the underlying thought is that which is expressed by Edgar in *King Lear* v. 2. 11, "*Ripeness is all.*"

[2875] Page 217, "Remembering it," Mk xi. 21; p. 217, "Marvelled," Mt. xxi. 20; p. 217, "Ezekiel's saying," Ezek. xvii. 24; p. 217, "The green tree," Lk. xxiii. 31.

P. 218, "Qui cum eo erant," see *Corr. of Mk* 370 and *Joh. Voc.* 1802 *a*. Add *Pap. Fayûm* 34 (11) (A.D. 161) where "Panesneus and Maron," partners, are afterwards described as "you that are around (περὶ) Panesneus," *i.e.* P. and Co., comp. Dan. iii. 23, 49 (LXX). The only passage in which Lk. uses "Those around him" (xxii. 49) prepares the way for a story about "one of them," whom Jn xviii. 11 defines as "Peter." See **2999** (xvii) *f* foll.

P. 218, "An error," *e.g.* comp. Numb. xvi. 5 "*in the morning,*" LXX "*visited*"; 2 K. xvi. 15 "*inquire by*," LXX "*in the morning.*"

P. 218, "The disciples...remembering," Jn ii. 22, xii. 16; p. 218, "Dark sayings," Jn xvi. 25; p. 218, "Call them back to their minds," Jn xiv. 26.

[2876] Page 219, "By no means improbable." Comp. Epict. iv. 8. 36—43 which combines two thoughts, 1st, the necessity of gradual growth (εἶτα...εἶτα...εἶτα, comp. Mk iv. 28 εἶτεν...εἶτεν), 2nd, the danger of premature bloom, which exposes the tree to "frost-burn" (ἀποκαύσει σε ὁ χειμών), "cutting off by frost even to the root" (ἀποπαγήσῃ, μᾶλλον δ᾽ ἀποπέπηγας ἤδη ἐν τῇ ῥίζῃ κάτω), "withering away" (τί οὖν με πρὸ ὥρας ἀποξηρᾶναι θέλεις ὡς αὐτὸς ἐξηράνθης;). But this illustration of human precocity is so frequent that the borrowing cannot be proved.

[2877] In John, the words "wither" and "burn" are applied, not to a tree but to the boughs of a tree. Concerning the bough that bears no fruit (presumably having leaves alone) it is said (xv. 6) ἐξηράνθη...καὶ καίεται. But the agency that produces the "*drying up* (or, *withering*)" and the "*burning*" is not frost, as in Epictetus; nor is it a miracle, as in Mark. It is the Powers of divine Retribution. "THEY cast them into fire" (*Joh. Gram.* **2426**).

[2878] Origen attempts to explain Mk xi. 13 "for it was not the season of figs," at great length, in his commentary on the parall. Mt., but not satisfactorily. Nor are the comments published by

Cramer on Mk xi. 13 satisfactory. The thought appears to be this, "He came from afar off to look, on the chance of (εἰ ἄρα) finding... and he found nothing but leaves. [*I say, 'on the chance,' because a fig-tree having leaves would usually have fruit as well, since its fruit precedes its leaves; but it was hardly to be expected*] *for the season of figs had not arrived.*" But the notion of Christ's doing anything "on the chance," and also the suggestion that He could not see "from afar off" whether there were figs or not, might be a stumbling-block to some. This difficulty would make it all the more desirable that John should intervene to shew how God prepares man to bear "fruit," and (so to speak) expects it from him.

P. 219, "For they were afraid," see Mk xvi. 8—9 with note in R.V., and Westcott and Hort's note on the spurious Appendix; and see below, **2924**.

NOTES TO CHAPTER XXIV

[**2879**] Page 221, "Everyone agrees." Papias says so (Euseb. iii. 39. 16) and this was the general belief among the early Fathers.

P. 221, "Ignorant of letters," Acts iv. 13, *i.e.* (*Corr. of Mk* **317** *a*) "unlettered and ignorant men," as in Epict. ii. 14. 15, comp. Epict. ii. 2. 22. In both passages it means "not knowing how to write the letters of the alphabet correctly." Comp. Berlin *Pap*. 664 (1st cent.) ἔγραψα ὑ[πὲρ αὐτ]ων ἀγραμμάτου (*sic*) and Papyri *passim*.

P. 221, "Physician," Col. iv. 14; p. 221, "Is not this the carpenter?" Mk vi. 3, comp. Mt. xiii. 55 and Lk. iv. 22.

THE BIRTH OF CHRIST

*[**2880**] Page 222, "Born of a woman," Job xiv. 1, xv. 14, xxv. 4. In Gal. iv. 4, γενόμενον ἐκ γυναικός, R.V. has "born of a woman" (A.V. "made of a woman"). Γίνομαι = Heb. יִלֵּד " to be born," freq. in LXX, espec. (Tromm.) Genesis (iv. 25, xxi. 3, 5 etc.); comp. Ezr. x. 3 τὰς γυναῖκας κ. τὰ γενόμενα (הַנּוֹלָד) ἐξ αὐτῶν (al. exempl. γενηθέντα) parall. to 1 Esdr. viii. 90 τὰς γυναῖκας ἡμῶν...σὺν τοῖς τέκνοις αὐτῶν. Lightf. on Gal. iv. 4 says "Comp. Job xiv. 1, Matth. xi. 11. These passages show that the expression must not be taken as referring to the miraculous incarnation."

P. 222, "Philo." The quotations are from Philo i. 130—1,

[2880] NOTES TO CHAPTER XXIV

147—8. Comp. Philo i. 273, 598—9 where similar language is used about Samuel the son of Hannah, Isaac the son of Sarah, and the sons of Leah and Tamar[1].

P. 223, "Narratives," Mt. i. 18—25, Lk. i. 26—35; p. 223, "Isaiah," Is. vii. 14, where the LXX has "virgin," but Aquila "young woman," as stated later on; p. 224, "Out of the school of Diodorus." This is an imaginary incident, but the charge erroneously brought by Justin against the Jews is not imaginary, see *Tryph.* 71—3.

[2881] Page 225, "Marginal notes," see Prof. Burkitt's translation of the Syriac Gospels, and his commentary in vol. ii. p. 261 foll.

(i) In Mt. i. 24—5 "he took his wife (Burk. txt "Mary") and knew her not (Burk. txt "purely was dwelling with her") until she bare a son," the Syro-Sinaitic version omits "knew her not until."

(ii) In Mt. i. 21, the Syro-Sinaitic version makes the Angel say of Mary to Joseph, "She will bear *thee* a son[2] and *thou shalt* call."

---

[1] [2880 a] Justin justifies his belief in the miraculous birth of Christ by saying to the Gentiles (1 *Apol.* 21 foll.) "We do not go beyond the sons assigned to Zeus among you, alleging something new (οὐ παρὰ τοὺς παρ' ὑμῖν λεγομένους υἱοὺς τῷ Διῒ καινόν τι φέρομεν)." Then he mentions Mercury, Æsculapius, Bacchus, Hercules, the Dioscuri, and Perseus. Then he takes three hypotheses. First, even if Jesus were born after the common fashion (κοινῶς), He would be worthy to be called God's Son "on account of wisdom," for Zeus is called "Father of Gods and men." Secondly, if He were "born in a peculiar way beyond common generation (ἰδίως παρὰ τὴν κοινὴν γένεσιν γεγενῆσθαι)" from God as God's Word, this would be analogous to the birth of Hermes. Thirdly, "if we allege that He has been actually begotten through a virgin (εἰ δὲ καὶ διὰ παρθένου γεγεννῆσθαι φέρομεν) this, too, may be accepted as analogous to the birth of Perseus (κοινὸν καὶ τοῦτο πρὸς τὸν Περσέα ἔστω ὑμῖν)"—who was begotten from Danae by Zeus descending in a shower of gold. Otto *ad loc.* compares *Tryph.* 66 ἐκ παρθένου γεννητὸς κ. διὰ παρθένου γεννηθῆναι, and *ib.* ἀπὸ παρθένου.

[2] [2881 a] Comp. Gen. xvii. 19 "And God said, Nay, but Sarah thy wife shall bear *thee* a son and thou shalt call his name Isaac." Philo i. 617 omits "*thee*" in quoting the text, but subsequently (*ib.*) inserts it in paraphrase, "Learn therefore, O soul, that also Sarah, [that is] virtue, shall bear *thee* a son"; and again (i. 618) "Virtue therefore shall bear *thee* a son...and thou shalt call the name of the son according to the feeling that thou shalt feel about him, and thou shalt verily feel *joy* (χαράν)." Comp. Lk. i. 13—14 "Thou shalt call his name John; and thou shalt have *joy* and gladness"—where it seems probable that Luke connected the name "John" etymologically with "*joy*." Philo, in "*joy*," is referring to the etymology of "Isaac," i.e. "*laughter*." Comp. Origen *Hom. Genes.* viii. 10 (Lomm. viii. 205) "generas *gaudium*" (i.e. Isaac) after which he quotes Jn xvi. 17, 22 concerning the "*joy*" that "no man shall take away"—where Jn's context (xvi. 21) speaks of "the woman in travail."

(iii) Syriac versions differ between "*she called*" and "*he called*" (in Mt. i. 25 "*she called* his name Jesus").

(iv) In Mt. i. 16, the Syro-Sinaitic version has "Jacob begat Joseph; *Joseph*, to whom was betrothed Mary the Virgin, *begat Jesus* called the Messiah." There are many other variations.

[2882] Page 226, "Three consecutive kings," see Alford on Mt. i. 8; p. 226, "Write ye," Jer. xxii. 30; p. 227, "Irenæus," quoted from iii. 21. 9.

P. 227, "That of Mary." Some differ from Scaurus. See Alford's note on Lk. iii. 23. Justin says (commenting on Ps. xxii. 4 "*our fathers* hoped in thee," which he regards as uttered by Christ) *Tryph.* 101 "The words are significant of the fact that He also owns as His '*fathers*' those that '*hoped in God*' and were saved by Him, who also were '*fathers*' *of the Virgin through whom He came into being, coming into being as man.*" This suggests that Justin, who favours Luke's gospel, imagined that Lk. iii. 23 could mean "being the son, as was supposed, of Joseph, [*but in fact*], descendant of Heli, descendant of Matthat...," and that "Heli" was the father of Mary. On "son of Joseph" in Lk. and Jn, see *Joh. Voc.* 1776—8.

[2883] Page 228, "Dreams," comp. 1 K. iii. 5, 15 with 2 Chr. i. 7; p. 229, "Thy father and I," Lk. ii. 48; p. 229, "He is beside himself," Mk iii. 21. This, being omitted by Mt. and Lk., might naturally be referred to by Jn. On this, see *Fourfold G.* "Brethren (of the Lord)"; p. 230, "Out of Egypt," Mt. ii. 15 quoting Hos. xi. 1; p. 230, "Rachel weeping," Mt. ii. 18 quoting Jer. xxxi. 15; p. 232, "In earthen vessels," 2 Cor. iv. 7; p. 232, "The foolishness of God," 1 Cor. i. 25.

NOTES TO CHAPTER XXV

[2884] Page 234, "Must love," Epict. iii. 22. 54; p. 236, "King and master," Epict. iii. 22. 49; p. 237, "Jesus is represented," see *Joh. Voc.* 1685 *a*; p. 237, "Phalanx," Col. ii. 5, where see Lightfoot's note.

"Receiving as a Little Child"

[2885] Page 238, "Ambiguously...earlier," see Mk x. 15, ix. 36 (comp. Lk. xviii. 17, ix. 47). Origen (Matth. tom. xiii. 18, Lomm. iii. 243) suggests that the little child placed by Jesus in the midst of the disciples is the Holy Spirit, which they are to receive so as to become little children. Thus, "receiving the child" and "becoming as children" would be two aspects of one thing. Later on (Lomm. iii. 247) Origen says that "receiving as a little child" is "ambiguous." Mt. xviii. 3–4 "turn and become as little children....humble himself as this little child," which is peculiar to Matthew, describes a third aspect of Christ's doctrine (*Joh. Voc.* 1865 *a*), using language not found in Mark and John. It implies regeneration.

[2886] Cramer (on Mk x. 13 foll.) prints a striking comment, "It is well said that He blessed them *taking them in His arms.* For once again as it were into the arms of the Creator the creation is [by this act of Jesus] brought back." Origen would probably connect the "child" taken into "Christ's arms" and the "disciple" that "lay in Christ's bosom," and would say that by receiving these we receive Christ.

Matthew alone (x. 41) has preserved a doctrine about "receiving" the "reward" of a "prophet" etc. by receiving a "prophet." This implies that by receiving *any character* we to some extent approximate to, or appropriate, *that character*. Receiving "a little child," and receiving "the Son of man," imply receiving the innocent spirit of the former, and the human and humane spirit of the latter. See *Joh. Voc.* 1689, 1721, and 1826—30, and *The Fourfold Gospel* ("Receiving").

[2887] Page 238, "Diffinget," Hor. *Odes* iii. 29. 47—8; p. 238, "Babes in respect of malice," 1 Cor. xiv. 20; p. 238, "Born from above," see *Joh. Gram.* 1903—8, 2573; p. 239, "Mountain," Mt. v. 1; p. 239, "Plain," Lk. vi. 17; p. 239, "Would sooner give it up," Epict. iv. 1. 153[1]; p. 239, "Binding and loosing," Mt. xvi. 19, xviii. 18. On the Jewish use of the term, see *Hor. Heb.* on Mt. xvi. 19; p. 240, "Arise, kill and eat," Acts x. 13, xi. 7; p. 240, "In the fourth gospel," Jn xx. 23, see *Joh. Gram.* 2517—20; p. 240, "But if he refuse," Mt. xviii. 17; p. 240, "I am there in the midst of them," Mt. xviii. 20; p. 240, "I am with you always," Mt. xxviii.

---

[1] [2887 *a*] Elsewhere, however, Epictetus agrees with Matthew in recommending non-resistance under "pressing" (Mt. v. 41 ἀγγαρεύσει, Epict. iv. i. 79 ἀγγαρεία). But Epict. merely says, "Do not resist, do not even murmur." He does not say, "Go two miles where only one is required."

20; p. 240, "When ye are gathered together," 1 Cor. v. 4; p. 241, "Eat those things that are served up to you," Lk. x. 8, comp. 1 Cor. x. 27.

[2888] Page 241, "Lord, appoint," Acts i. 24 "appoint [him] whom thou hast chosen," where R.V. has "shew," although the verb is the same as in Lk. x. 1 R.V. "appointed."

P. 242, "A tradition of Matthew's," Mt. xix. 10—12; p. 242, "Paul's advice," 1 Cor. vii. 1—40; p. 243, "Blessed are the poor," Lk. vi. 20, comp. Mt. v. 3; p. 243, "Hungering after righteousness," Mt. v. 6, comp. Lk. vi. 21; p. 243, "A staff only," Mk vi. 8, comp. Mt. x. 10, Lk. ix. 3; p. 243, "My staff," Gen. xxxii. 10, comp. Philo i. 83. This seems to me to complete and strengthen the explanation offered in *Clue* 264—7; p. 243, "Thy rod," Ps. xxiii. 4; p. 243, The "rabbi" is represented by Rashi on Gen. xxxii. 10; p. 244, "Sandals," see *Corr. of Mk* 390 (ii) (ε) *a*; p. 246, "John sent," Mt. xi. 2—3, Lk. vii. 19; p. 246, "Timæus," Plato *Tim.* § 3, 22 B "O Solon, Solon, you Greeks are always boys."

NOTES TO CHAPTER XXVI

[2889] Page 248, "Come and let us return," Hosea vi. 1—2.

P. 248—9, On "deliver over," "betray," and "Galilee," see the Indices to the author's *Paradosis* and *From Letter to Spirit*, where the matters here touched on are fully discussed.

P. 249, "Took hold of his feet," Mt. xxviii. 9; p. 250, "As I have explained above," see *Silanus* p. 134—5.

P. 250, "Would have," *i.e.* ἄν, is dropped by the LXX, or by MSS, in 1 S. xiii. 13, Ps. lv. 7, lvi. 2, lxxxi. 14, 16, Jer. li. 9. But a much more potent cause of confusion exists in ambiguities of Hebrew or Aramaic words. On these, and on other points of verbal criticism bearing on the self-manifestations of Christ, see below, **2999** (i) foll.

[2890] Page 251, "Walking," Gesen. 236 *b* quoting Deut. xxiii. 14 etc. Barnabas i. 4 says "The Lord *journeyed with* (συνώδευσεν) *me*" (where the word is the same as in Acts ix. 7 "the men that *journeyed with* him)." In Barnabas, the meaning is made clear by the following words, "in the way of righteousness."

P. 252, "Their Jewish enemies," comp. Orig. *Cels.* ii. 70; p. 252, "Delusion," Lk. xxiv. 11; p. 252, "Josephus," see *Ant.* iv. 8. 15.

[2891] Page 253, "They touched him," Ign. *Smyrn.* 3.

P. 253, "They fed on one another," Diod. Sic. i. 84. For the saying of Pythagoras, see Steph. *Thes.*

P. 253, "'Take' as in Mark and Matthew," Mk xiv. 22, Mt. xxvi. 26. The active verb naturally means, not "take hold of" (which would almost require the middle) but "take" in the sense of "receive."

P. 253, FISH, see *Joh. Gram.* 2703.

P. 254, "Instances," *e.g.* Ps. xii. 2 "*They* speak," LXX "*he* spake"; Ps. xxxiii. 9 "*it* was done," LXX "*they* were created" etc.

The Events between Christ's Resurrection and Ascension

[2892] It will be convenient to place here, for future reference, some facts bearing on the interval between the Resurrection and the Ascension[1], and on the traditions concerning Christ's eating after the Resurrection.

---

[1] [2892 a] The following remarks bear on—

The Interval between the Resurrection and the Ascension.

The only basis for statements as to the duration of the period after the Resurrection during which our Lord remained with the disciples is Acts i. 3 "appearing unto them (R.V.) *by the space of forty days.*" It has been shewn however (*Joh. Gram.* 2331 c) that there is no authority for this rendering. To the proofs there given add the following from Origen *Cels.* ii. 63 "For in truth to us also it is manifest (according to the Gospel) that He did not appear in the same way after the resurrection as He was wont to manifest Himself before in public and to all ('Ἀληθῶς γὰρ κ. ἡμῖν φαίνεται...οὐχ οὕτω...ὀφθεὶς ὡς τὸ πρότερον... ἐφαίνετο). But in the first place (μέν) in the Acts it is written '*after an interval of forty days*' appearing (δι' ἡμερῶν τεσσαράκοντα ὀπτανόμενος) to the disciples He was announcing (κατήγγελλεν) 'the things concerning the kingdom of God'; and on the other hand (δέ) in the Gospels [it is] not [written] that He was always in company with them, but on some occasions (ἀλλ' ὅπου μέν) *after an interval of eight days* He appeared (δι' ἡμερῶν ὀκτώ) the doors being shut, in the midst of them; but on other occasions in some such similar ways (ὅπου δὲ κατά τινας τοιούτους τρόπους)."

[2892 b] The words "*after an interval of eight days*" refer to Jn xx. 26 μεθ' ἡμέρας ὀκτώ. Origen quotes this with διά and the genitive, as in the previous quotation from the Acts: and he alleges both passages in such a way as to shew that the "forty" and the "eight" *do not indicate days of duration but days of interval.* He also proceeds to quote 1 Cor. xv. 3—8 "after that,...after that,... last of all," to shew that Christ did "not appear to the people at large (μὴ δημωδῶς αὐτοῦ ὀφθέντος)": but incidentally these phrases also indicate that an "interval" elapsed between them.

§ 1. *Acts* i. 4 (*R.V. txt*) "*Being assembled together*"

P. 254, "Being incorporated." This is suggested as a literal approximation to the meaning of Acts i. 4 συναλιζόμενος, A.V. and R.V. txt "being assembled together with them." Shakespeare never speaks of one person as "being assembled" with a number of companions. It sounds like scholastic English of 1611 attempting to give an exact rendering of a difficult word. "Assembled with" is hardly strong enough: "assimilated with" would perhaps be too strong.

[2893] The rendering, "feeding with"—which is not (I believe) supported by any contemporary authority—would assume a derivation from σύναλος, "partner of salt," which however is not recognised in Steph. *Thes.* as used except in glosses. Ἀλίζομαι, when derived from ἅλας, "salt," means "I am salted."

[2894] In Ignat. *Magn.* 10 ἁλίσθητε, meaning "be salted," is corrupted (Lightf.) by A to "conjungamini" (taking the word in the sense "incorporated") and by g to αὐλίσθητε. In *Clement. Hom.* xiii. 4, although (Thayer) Dressel, with Cod. Ottob., reads συναλιζόμεθα, the sense demands (as Schwegler) συναλιζόμεθα and the meaning is "eat with."

[2895] This suggests that, at a very early period, the "*incorporation*" implied in the Christian Eucharist had conveyed to the word that strictly meant "*be incorporated with*," the new and Christian meaning "*eat with*." Steph. *Thes.* quotes Manetho v. 339 πῆμα λυγρῷ γαμέτῃ συναλιζόμενον κακόηθες: but this does not appear to necessitate any other meaning than "closely united with." On Ps. cxli. 4 "let me not *eat of* their dainties," Field gives LXX συνδοιάσω μετά, Sym. συμφάγοιμι, "Ἄλλος" συναλισθῶ ἐν, and adds "In editis Chrys. hodie legitur μὴ συναυλισθῶ."

P. 254, "One loaf," comp. 1 Cor. x. 17; p. 254, "Gathered

[2892 c] Origen, who enters fully into the nature of the appearances of Christ after death, *nowhere implies that they were compressed into a period of forty days.* He says that they were given (*Cels.* ii. 66) "with a certain discrimination (κρίσεως) measuring to each what was due (τὰ δέοντα)." He adds "As it is written, 'God appeared (ὤφθη) to Abraham (Gen. xii. 7)' or to one of the saints, and this 'appearing' (τὸ ὤφθη τοῦτο) was not always going on (οὐκ ἀεὶ ἐγίνετο) but *at intervals* (ἐκ διαλειμάτων) and was not manifested (ἐφαίνετο) to all, so I would have you understand (νόει μοι) that the Son of God also has appeared (ὤφθαι) with the same sort of discrimination (τῇ παραπλησίᾳ...κρίσει)...." The text is perhaps slightly corrupt in detail. But the general meaning is clear.

[2895] into one," comp. *Didach.* ix. 4; p. 254, "Mixed," Ign. *Smyrn.* 3 κραθέντες τῇ σαρκὶ αὐτοῦ, where Lightf. gives below, "*convicti* (κρατηθέντες?) L; *quum prehendissent eum* C; al. g. A has *crediderunt qui eucharistiæ-participes-fuerunt* (lit. *communicaverunt*) *et cænaverunt antea corpus et sanguinem ejus*. The first clause is evidently a gloss (prob. later and certainly erroneous) of the second; and the rendering generally points to κραθέντες. The rendering of C may represent κρατήσαντες, but prob. is a loose paraphrase of κραθέντες." He adds " The same confusion of κραθῆναι, κρατηθῆναι, appears three times in Iren. i. 6. 4."

P. 255, "Testifying," Acts x. 41; p. 256, "In the fourth gospel," Jn xxi. 13.

§ 2. *The traditions concerning Christ's Eating after the Resurrection*

[2896] Page 256, "Punctuated...differently." See Origen *Cels.* ii. 20 which quotes from a Jewish opponent this ironical attack on Christ's prediction concerning Judas Iscariot: "God, then, it seems, brought round His own disciples and prophets, *with whom He was in the habit of dining and drinking*, to a state of impiety and iniquity"; and comp. *ib.* ii. 9, and ii. 70 "*his fellow-revellers.*" These phrases refer to the period before the Resurrection. It should be stated that the Jew says "*was in the habit of drinking*" (imperf.) whereas Peter says "*drank*" (aor.). W. H., to judge from their punctuation, apparently take Acts x. 41 as Scaurus does. But the aorist and the imperfect might easily be interchanged (especially in rendering from Semitic tradition where distinctions of tense are comparatively few).

[2897] Page 256, "In other ways." As to "convivo" and "convivor" see Lewis and Short. In Syriac the same verb that means "abide with," "put up for the night," lit. "loose," means also, in its reflexive form, "take breakfast," "feast" etc., Thes. Syr. 4312. The following passage deserves particular attention because it combines two acts of Jesus, one of which, "*hymning,*" is placed by Mark and Matthew (not by Luke) at the Eucharist; while the other, "*standing in the midst,*" is placed by Luke (not by Mark or Matthew) at a meal after Christ's resurrection.

[2898] It occurs in Justin Martyr, who combines these two acts with a mention of Jesus as "*living,*" or "*passing the time,*" with the disciples, *Tryph.* 106 "And that He *stood in the midst* (comp. Lk. xxiv. 36) of His *brethren* the apostles...and, *living* with them, He *hymned* God (as also in the memoirs of the apostles is shewn to have taken place) was indicated by the rest of the psalm." Justin is referring to Ps. xxii. 22 "I will declare thy name unto my *brethren*; *in the midst of* the congregation will I *hymn* thee," which is applied to Christ in Heb. ii. 12. "*To hymn*" occurs nowhere else in N.T. except Mk xiv. 26, Mt. xxvi. 30, Acts xvi. 25, see below.

[2899] "*Stood in the midst*" is applied to Christ in Luke's and John's accounts of His manifestation to the disciples (*Joh. Gram.* 2307). But how are we to explain Justin's phrase "*living* (διάγων) *with them*"? He perhaps means, "continuing," "abiding"—to distinguish the manifestation from a mere fitful transient apparition. Comp. Jn xiv. 23 "My Father will love him and we will come unto him *and make our abode with him*," Rev. iii. 20 "If any man hear my voice and open the door, *I will come in to him and sup with him and he with me.*" This last sentence shews that, *if* διάγω *could in any way be connected with "eating,*" it might naturally be so rendered in a tradition like that of Justin's "*living* with them."

[2900] Stephen's *Thesaurus* ii. 1132 shews that διάγειν is sometimes thus used to mean "entertain," "feed," mostly active (and with a dative of the food), but once middle: "To nourish and *entertain* with (ἐν) many good things," "To *supply* the barbarians with (ἐν) abundance of water" (like our phrase "We will keep you, or find you, *in* tobacco"), "He *fed* (διήγετο) on honey-cakes and loaves," "He *fed* the army with wild herbs," "They *entertained* the populace with spectacles...and feasts."

[2901] Steph. *Thes.* has the following comment on ξενίζων τε αὐτὸν πολὺν χρόνον διῆγε, "Haud accuratissime versum est, 'Multo autem tempore ejus hospitio usus est.' Verbum διῆγε est activae sign. et notat Oblectare, Tempus alicui gratum reddere, sive bene nutriendo, s. diebus festivis ipsi institutis." This indicates another source of confusion as to traditions about Christ's "*living* with the disciples," some of which might, or might not, mean "*eating* with them."

[2902] The only passage in the gospels where "hymning" is mentioned is Mk xiv. 26, Mt. xxvi. 30. This takes place at the conclusion of the Lord's Supper. Luke omits the word "hymning." It is used in the plural so that it would include the disciples as well as Christ. The *Acts of John* § 11 represents Christ on the night before the Passion as "gathering" or "entertaining" (συναγαγών) all the disciples, and as saying "Let us *hymn* the Father." Then He placed Himself "*in the midst* of" them, and "began to hymn a hymn," which is given in full.

[2903] The verb "hymn" is so rare in N.T., and the prophecy about "hymning" was applied to Christ at such an early date, that Mark and Matthew may well be supposed to have had it in view though they do not quote it. They may have thought it was fulfilled *before* the Resurrection. John assigns to Jesus before the Resurrection a long utterance of prayer and praise that might well be called a "hymn." Luke may have thought (like Justin) that it was fulfilled *after* the Resurrection. Luke does not mention a "hymning," any more than John does; but Lk. xxiv. 44—9 implies a long discourse shewing the fulfilment of "the Law, the Prophets, and the Psalms" in the Gospel.

[2904] Returning to *Tryph.* 106 καὶ μετ' αὐτῶν διάγων ὕμνησε τὸν θεόν, we see that the aorist "*He hymned* [*on that occasion*]" prevents us from taking διάγων as referring to "forty days"—the period of "abiding" (2892 *a*) erroneously deduced in Acts i. 3 (*Joh. Gram.* 2331 *c*)—but it may mean, "Instead of vanishing away as at Emmaus, as soon as the meal began, He, *remaining*...." If that was the sense, with punctuation before and after διάγων, "and with them— [*not vanishing away but*] *abiding*—He hymned God," most students will recognise that the meaning was very obscurely conveyed and liable to misunderstanding.

[2905] Among misunderstandings, one might be the rendering "with them—*entertaining* [*them at a meal*]—He hymned God." The word διαγωγή "spending the time," *ought not* to be confused with διατροφή or δίαιτα; but that it *was* in danger of being thus confused appears from a warning of Thom. M. Δίαιτα· οὐ διαγωγὴ οὐδὲ διατροφή, Steph. *Thes.* ii. 1133 where see Steph.'s note.

[2906] Justin quotes the "*standing in the midst*," and the "*hymning*," as two of the Messianic fulfilments of Ps. xxii. 22, "*In the midst* of the congregation will I *hymn* thee." "The whole Psalm" (*Tryph.* 99) appears to Justin to be fulfilled in Christ. Consequently, although he passes rapidly over the last part (*Tryph.* 106) as "the remainder," it is probable that he found a fulfilment (in Luke's post-resurrectional meal) of Ps. xxii. 26 "*the meek shall eat and shall be satisfied.*" Those who took the same view would be prepared to believe that Christ gave food to the disciples after the Resurrection, and perhaps to render διάγων, "entertaining [them]."

[2907] T. & T. Clark's translation of *Tryph.* 106 (1) does not print, or annotate, "stood in the midst" as an allusion to Lk. xxiv. 36; (2) brackets, as part of a parenthesis, the part of the sentence containing the words "after He rose from the dead" so as to give the connexion thus: "The remainder of the Psalm makes it manifest that...and that He stood in the midst of His brethren the apostles... *and when living with them* sang praises to God." The translator apparently takes the words that I have italicised, as meaning, "and *while still living with them before the crucifixion.*" This seems improbable, in view of (2307) "stood in the midst." But it is possible. And the possibility illustrates the great uncertainty attending every attempt to elicit the exact truth amid conflicting traditions of alleged fact largely based on poems and prophecies.

As a whole, however, the facts indicate that Luke's tradition about Christ's eating has sprung from expressions that have been misunderstood; that Matthew was justified in not inserting any such tradition; and that John was justified in declining to reproduce the tradition of Luke, except in a form where the disciples eat and Christ gives them to eat.

NOTES TO CHAPTER XXVII

[2908] Page 257, "The Jews," see *Beresh. Rabb.* on Gen. xxix. 2—3. Philo i. 596 (on Exod. ii. 16) describes Moses as "nourishing the Father's flock with draughts of the word."

P. 257, "A veil," 2 Cor. iii. 14; p. 258, "Veiled from them," Lk. ix. 45; p. 258, "Opening the scriptures," Lk. xxiv. 32; p. 258, "Isaiah," Is. viii. 14 (quoted in Rom. ix. 33), xxviii. 16, comp. 1 Pet. ii. 4—6; p. 259, "Someone," Mk xvi. 3 SS "Now who hath rolled...?"; p. 259, "The Psalmist," Ps. xciv. 16—17, cviii. 10—11. Comp. Deut. xxx. 12 quoted in Rom. x. 6; p. 259, "Traditions," an anachronism. See *Evang. Pet.* § 8 and Lk. xxiii. 53 (Codex D).

[2909] Page 260, "I think it means 'saw in a vision'." For ἀναβλέπω, meaning "I see angels, a vision etc.," comp. Gen. xxxii. 1 (ins. LXX) ἀναβλέψας...ἴδεν παρεμβολὴν θεοῦ, Dan. viii. 3 "I lifted up mine eyes...a ram...," LXX ἀναβλέψας εἶδον, Theod. ἦρα τοὺς ὀφθ. μου κ. ἴδον, Mart. Polyc. § 2 τοῖς τῆς καρδίας ὀφθαλμοῖς ἀνέβλεπον. In N.T. it mostly means "recover sight." In Gen. xxii. 13 "lifted up his eyes.,.a ram," no vision is intended as in Daniel, but the word probably implies divine intervention. Onk. has "lifted up his eyes *after these words*" (*i.e.* the words just spoken by the angel of the Lord), Targ. Jon. (Etheridge) "lifted up his eyes and saw...a certain ram which had been created between the evenings of the foundation of the world."

P. 260, "Right up to heaven." Origen (on Jn xi. 39) contrasts Gen. xxix. 2—10 "rolled away" with "lifted up" (or "taken right away") the word used in Jn, saying that the latter implies that "the stone is altogether taken away and is not to be rolled back again." Schöttg. ii. 88 gives a tradition from Sohar of the ascent of "the stone" in a different sense; the "corner stone" of the temple (which the builders rejected) is carried up to heaven.

P. 260, "Ascension of angels," see codex k, which (in Mk xvi. 3) describes angels as "descending" and "rising" and ascending with Him; or possibly it may mean that those saints who rose with Christ ascended with Him, see Mt. xxvii. 53.

P. 260, "An angel," Mt. xxviii. 2, 5; p. 261, "Bless them," Rom. xii. 14 foll.; p. 263, "One like unto a son of man," Dan. vii. 13 (see **2998** (xxvi)—(xxxi)); p. 263—4, "Deuteronomy," Deut. xxx. 12 foll., quoted in Rom. x. 6 foll.

NOTES TO CHAPTER XXVIII

[2910] Page 267, "Last utterance," Mk xv. 34, Mt. xxvii. 46 (?) parall. to Lk. xxiii. 45; comp. Mk xv. 37, Mt. xxvii. 50, parall. to Lk. xxiii. 46.

P. 268, "An eclipse." Origen (on Mt. xxvii. 45, Lomm. v. 54) suggests that either (1) someone has ignorantly altered "the sun was darkened" into "eclipsed" (as being the ordinary explanation of such darkening), or that (2) "the crafty enemies of the Church of Christ (insidiatores ecclesiae Christi)" have done this, in order to accuse the evangelist of falsehood. He reads "the sun was darkened." But the best Greek MSS. have "eclipsed," and W. H. adopt this, without alternative[1].

---

[1] [2910 *a*] Thucydides makes it clear that a solar eclipse was generally recognised at a very early date to be impossible except at new moon, ii. 28 νουμηνίᾳ κατὰ σελήνην, ὥσπερ καὶ μόνον δοκεῖ εἶναι γίγνεσθαι δυνατόν, ὁ ἥλιος ἐξέλιπε. In *Acta Pilati* 11 (A and B) the Jews tell Pilate that there has been merely "an eclipse of the sun in the usual way." In *Acta P.* (A), one MS. makes Pilate reply, "*I know that that never happens but at new moon.*"

NOTES TO CHAPTERS XXVIII, XXIX [2915]

P. 268, "Of the sun" or "Of Elias," see *From Letter* 1057—60.
P. 268, "Why hast thou forsaken?" Ps. xxii. 1.

[2911] Page 269, "We let him kill it." Tertull. *Ad Nat.* 15 says that the laws against infanticide are deliberately evaded, and that the evasion is deliberately permitted, comp. Tertull. *Apolog.* 9. It would seem that an infant might be killed with impunity if the parents avoided steel and left the business to "drowning, cold, hunger, or dogs."

[2912] Page 269, "Got a nurse," so Mrs Carter, *Introd.* p. xxix. But the words (Schweig. iii. p. 134, quoting Simplic. § 46 p. 272) may mean that he, "after remaining alone the greater part of his life, quite late in life *took to himself a wife*, to nurse a child (ὀψέ ποτε γυναῖκα προσελάβετο, παιδίου τροφόν) that he had taken and reared, belonging to a friend, who was purposing to expose it because of his poverty." See Steph. *Thes.* vi. 1958—9.

[2913] Page 271, "His own son," Epict. iv. 5. 3; p. 271, "Apollo," Epict. iii. 1. 16; p. 271, "one in a thousand," Epict. iii. 1. 19; p. 271, "Hear ye indeed," Is. vi. 9 foll., comp. Mk iv. 12, Mt. xiii. 13 foll., Lk. viii. 10, Rom. xi. 8; p. 272, "The universe," Epict. iii. 24. 19; p. 272, "Ulysses," Epict. iii. 24. 18; p. 272, "How long," Mk ix. 19, Mt. xvii. 17, Lk. ix. 41; p. 273, "As Diogenes did," Epict. iii. 24. 64—8; p. 273, "Not from within," Epict. *Ench.* xvi, comp. i. 18. 19; p. 273, "The subject of 'distress'," Epict. ii. 2. 1 foll., comp. ii. 13. 10; p. 274, "Played at ball," Epict. ii. 5. 15—20; p. 274, "These portents," Epict. *Ench.* xviii; p. 274, "Nothing to do with my father," Epict. iii. 3. 5; p. 274, "Am I to neglect," Epict. iii. 3. 7; p. 275, "A contrast," Epict. i. 4. 24—7; p. 276, "It is among the rich," Epict. i. 24. 15 foll.

NOTES TO CHAPTER XXIX

[2914] Page 288, "Not on the same level as scripture." Barnabas iv. 14 "Let us give heed lest, *as it is written*, we be found many called but few chosen," is sometimes alleged as proof that the writer quoted Mt. xxii. 14 with the formula "as it is written," *i.e.* as "scripture." But Barnabas also twice quotes Enoch either as (xvi. 5) "scripture" or (iv. 3) with the form "it is written." See *Enc. Bibl.* (col. 1828) "Gospels" § 89.

[2915] Page 288, "Mark committed no error." The "elder"

here mentioned is quoted by Papias; who, in turn, is quoted by Eusebius thus, iii. 39. 15 "And this too *the Elder* used to say, Mark in the first place becoming Peter's interpreter...so that *Mark committed no error* (οὐδὲν ἥμαρτε)...." In the preceding sentence, Eusebius says that Papias hands down diegetic works of Aristion and traditions of "the Elder, John." And Eusebius previously quotes Papias as mentioning together (iii. 39. 4) "Aristion and *the Elder, John.*" It appears therefore that "the Elder" described as here defending Mark was called "John." See *Silanus* p. 306 foll.

[2916] Page 289, "Wrote in Hebrew," see p. 221; p. 289, "Never did quote it." For proof of this, see *Enc. Bibl.* (col. 1832—7) "Gospels" § 101—4; p. 290, "Irenæus" iii. 11. 8 foll. "It is not possible that there should be more gospels than there are, nor again fewer. For since there are four zones...and four principal winds...."

NOTES TO CHAPTER XXX

On Luke's omission of "Why hast thou forsaken me?"

[2917] Page 293, "Luke...something about the sun." The following remarks bear on the possibility of explaining Luke's omission in a manner consistent with an honest though unsuccessful attempt to elicit the facts. It will be shewn that other early authorities, besides Luke, had traditions about the "sun" and "light" at this point of the gospel narrative.

P. 293, "Some of our brethren." Justin says (*Tryph.* 98) "And further I will if you please quote *the whole psalm* (xxii.), that you may hear His piety to the Father, and how He [*i.e.* the Son] *refers all things to Him.*" He proceeds to quote the entire psalm. Chrysostom, though he does not say that "the whole of the psalm" was in Christ's mind, implies it thus: "He says, Eli, Eli...that men may see that up to the last breath He honours the Father and does not oppose Himself to God." Cramer prints similar comments on Mt. xxvii. 46 and on the parall. Mk xv. 34. The Valentinians said that when Jesus said these words He indicated (Iren. i. 8. 2) that Sophia (by which they meant the lower Wisdom) was forsaken by light.

[2918] An extract preserved by Clem. Alex. (1003, *Theodot. Excerpt.*) mentions Christ's "Heli" in connexion with "Helios," the sun (comp. *Silanus* p. 267—8) quoting Ps. xix. 4 "In them hath he set a tabernacle for the sun," as in LXX, "In the sun he placed his tabernacle" (**2920**). Tertullian says (*Adv. Prax.* 30) that the Father "forsook" the Son inasmuch as (Rom. viii. 32) He "did not spare" the Son, and "delivered Him up (Is. liii. 5—6, 12) for our transgressions." Comp. Cypr. Spur. (*De Mont. Sina et Sion* 10) "Caro ligno confixa emisit verbum dominicum dicens: *Heli, heli*: et adimpletum est propheticum spiritale ante dictum: 'De Sion exiet lex et verbum domini ab Hierusalem.'" Does "dicens" agree with "caro" or with "verbum"? Does "caro" mean "the flesh forsaken by the spirit"?

[**2919**] Page 294, "One of the brethren" is to some extent represented by Origen. Origen (on Mt. xxvii. 46—7, Lomm. v. 58 foll.), after quoting the text as in Mt., says, "It is not lawful to believe that He lied, when saying, *Why hast thou forsaken me?* Now some under cover of reverence for Jesus (colore religionis pro Jesu), and because they cannot explain the meaning of Christ's being forsaken by God, think [thus] and say [thus] 'It is true that it was so said, (or, What was said is true) but it was said in humility (per humilitatem).'" Brushing aside this evasion, Origen seriously asks what the words mean, and his conclusion apparently is that the Son is questioning the Father as to the future results of His being "forsaken," so that "why?" means "What is thy desire or object?"

[**2920**] Origen, although (**2921**) he resembles the author quoted above (**2918**) by Clement of Alexandria in connecting the cry to God with a mention of the "sun," differs from him in spirit and in detail. For the older writer, presumably a Valentinian, says, "Can it be that the words (Ps. xix. 4) 'In the sun he placed his tabernacle' are to be understood thus:—'*placed in the sun*,' that is, '*in God*'...?" The following words are obscure, ἐν τῷ θεῷ τῷ πλησίον θεός, ὡς ἐν τῷ εὐαγγελίῳ ἠλὶ ἠλί, ἀντὶ τοῦ θεέ μου, θεέ μου. But they seem to express the Valentinian belief that Jesus, ascending, laid aside His body in the sun because it was not possible that it should ascend to the highest height. So Hermogenes (180 A.D. or earlier) declares that (Hippol. *Haer.* viii. 10) Christ, as He went up to heaven, left His body in the sun, but Himself proceeded to the Father. Irenæus himself (iv. 33. 13) quotes Ps. xix. 6 "His going forth is from the height of heaven and his returning even to the highest heaven" as referring to the Incarnation and the Ascension, although the Psalmist is referring to the sun. Origen (on Ps. xix. 4) says, "the sun of righteousness is our Lord, and in Him the Father tabernacles." Elsewhere he condemns the Valentinian view ("quidam quidem dicebant") and defines his own more fully (Lomm. *ib.* xii. 73 "in sole justitiae ecclesiam suam collocavit").

[2921] But in quoting Ps. lxxxix. 36—8 "his throne as the sun before me...but thou hast cast off and rejected," Origen (Lomm. v. 60—5) paraphrases the words as follows: "As long as the sun's light lasted, enduring His great sufferings, He did not say, Why hast thou forsaken me? But when He saw darkness spread over all the land of Judæa until the ninth hour, He said with His loud voice, *Why hast thou forsaken me?* desiring by these words to indicate that, namely (illud...quoniam), 'Deliberately (volens) hast thou forsaken me, Father...that the people [of the Jews]...may be in darkness....But thou hast also forsaken me for the salvation of the Gentiles....'" And then Origen adds further questions supposed to be addressed by the Son to the Father.

[2922] Elsewhere Origen says (*Cels.* iii. 32) "Since He had 'authority to lay down His life,' He laid it down when He said, '*Father*, why hast thou forsaken me?' And, having cried with a loud voice, He dismissed His Spirit, anticipating the executioners that were to deal with those crucified." It will be observed that Origen here uses "Father" in quotation. Above (Lomm. v. 58—65) he used "My God" in quotation, but "Father" in paraphrase.

[2923] Page 294, "I am not alone," Jn xvi. 32.

P. 295, "A complete answer." Origen (Lomm. v. 65—6) suggests that the last words and acts of Christ, as described in the four gospels, constitute a *"cause"* of the resurrection, "*Propter hoc* enim non dereliquit animam ejus in inferno nec dedit eum videre corruptionem." He has just said, "Quod si vis audire *quid profuit Christo* magnam vocem clamasse, et sic emisisse spiritum, id est, in manus Domini commendasse spiritum, et sic emisisse, aut inclinasse caput super gremium Patris, et tradidisse spiritum, audi quod dicit Propheta: *Propter hoc* enim...." The original is Ps. xvi. 9—10 "*For this cause* my heart is glad...*because* thou wilt not forsake my soul in Sheol." No version has "*for this cause* thou wilt not forsake." Possibly the Latin transl. of Origen is inaccurate. But his language as a whole indicates that he regarded Christ's utterance as revealing *an act that causatively prepared the way for the resurrection*[1].

---

[1] [2923 *a*] The Valentinians (Iren. i. 8. 2) regarded the words of the Saviour

on the cross as shewing that Sophia ("a kind of abortion" outside the Pleroma) was deserted by "the light," which "had *forsaken* her." So previously (i. 4. 1) "she strained herself to discover *that light which had forsaken her,*" impelled by the passion of "desiring to return to Him who gave her life." These last words suggest the earnest desire for God's presence, expressed in the Johannine words "I thirst": the former accord with the connexion seen by Origen between the "light" (or its absence) and the "forsaking."

[2923 b] Philo i. 412 quoting Jer. xv. 10 "Mother, what manner of man hast thou borne me, a man of strife!" says that the Mother is Wisdom. Origen (Lomm. xv. 261 foll.), agreeing with Philo, adds that Christ uttered this, "not as God but as man," like many other passages in the Psalms and prophecies, and that Jer. xv. 10 (LXX, Heb. diff.) "My strength hath failed (ἡ ἰσχύς μου ἐξέλιπεν)" was fulfilled when Christ "emptied himself" (Phil. ii. 7), that is, in the Incarnation. It will be remembered that *Evang. Pet.* gives Christ's words as "My Power (ἡ δύναμίς μου)! Thou hast abandoned me."

[2923 c] The facts indicate that every word of this Aramaic utterance was much scrutinized, explained, and sometimes explained away. D, in Mk xv. 34 σαβαχθανεί, has ζαφθανεί (sim. in Mt. xxvii. 46, where, however, the photograph seems to shew ζ corrected into σ). This is D's attempt to transliterate עזבתני, *azabthani*, dropping *a*, and changing *b* to *p* (perhaps for euphony). But why does D, while rendering ζαφθανεί in Mt. ἐγκατέλιπες, render it in Mk ὠνίδισας (sic), "didst reproach," thus making the moral difficulty perhaps greater than before?

Dalm. *Words*, p. 54, suggests that D's ζαφθανεί has been "transformed" back into a form of זעף. But זעף means in Heb. (Gesen.) "be out of humour, vexed; be enraged," and in Aram. (Levy) "toben, stürmen." It is not quoted by either authority as a transitive verb; nor is it ever rendered ὀνειδίζω by LXX, or others. Ὀνειδίζω may come from an Aram. gloss, "*My strength hath failed*." "Strength" is called by Eusebius (*Dem. Evang.* p. 494, Field on Ps. xxii. 1) the correct rendering. "*Fail,*" ἐκλείπω—which occurs in parall. Lk. xxiii. 45 ἡλίου ἐκλείποντος—is expressible in Heb., Syr. (*e.g.* Lk. xxii. 32) and Aram., by חסר. This is confused with חסד, "*reproach,*" in Sir. xiv. 2 "*reproached*" (Heb. "*failed,*" but edd. "וחסרת, read חסדתו"), *ib.* xli. 6 ["*want*"] Syr. חסר, but LXX ὄνειδος, Prov. xiv. 34 "*reproach* (חסד)," LXX ἐλασσονοῦσι *i.e.* חסר. In Mk xv. 34, a, b, etc. are wanting, k has "dereliquisti" ("*a m.* 3") over erasure. Swete does not mention ὠνείδισας, and gives B ζαβαχθανει, but the photograph clearly has ζαβαφθανει.

[2923 d] With reference to the last utterance of the Saviour on the cross as recorded by Jn (xix. 30), it should be noted that τετέλεσται mid. is the regular official word in a custom-house receipt to signify that the carrier of goods "*has paid duty*" in passing "*through a gate.*" It is regularly defined by (Fayûm Pap. p. 195) "διὰ πύλης followed by a village name." The editors of the Fayûm P. (p. 200) say that "the receipts range in date from the reign of Titus to the third century," and Berlin Urk. 766 gives such a receipt beginning with τετέ[λεσ]ται of A.D. 91, besides many of later date. These facts go far to prove that, when the fourth gospel was written, the word τετέλεσται would suggest, even to the poorest classes of Greeks, the meaning "*duty paid,*" and a thought of "*passing through a gate.*" This would lend itself to a mystical suggestion—that Jesus, at the moment of this utterance, passed "through the grave and gate of death," taking mankind with Him, and paying the tax with His blood. Such mysticism is almost incredible to modern readers, but it is hardly more difficult than other instances in Jn (see *e.g.* "lifted up," *Joh. Gram.* **2211** *b, c,* **2642** *b*).

A.

[2924] Page 296, "Forsaken yet not forsaken." Comp. Is. liv. 6 "The Lord hath called thee as a wife *forsaken*," *ib.* lxii. 12 "a city not *forsaken*," and Hos. i. 6—11; p. 297, "Him that knew not sin," 2 Cor. v. 21; p. 298, "I taught Ephraim," Hos. xi. 3—4; p. 298, "Mark never mentions 'love,'" see *Joh. Voc.* 1716; p. 299, "A new commandment," Jn xiii. 34; p. 300, "The Lord's Prayer," see *From Letter* 967—71.

THE END OF MARK'S GOSPEL

P. 300, "I am disposed to think." Great difficulties attend the two suppositions (1) that Mark deliberately stopped short in his narrative so as not to record any manifestations of the risen Saviour, (2) that Mark described such manifestations in the last part of his gospel but that the last part is lost. As to (1), the objections hardly need to be stated: and the ill-omened end, "for they were afraid," adds to their weight. As to (2), it requires us to believe that in every one of the copies of Mark's gospel made at the time of its being first circulated, that part which would be of most interest to Christians was destroyed, without being transcribed. The least difficult supposition is (3) that Mark's work was cut short by his death, or by some other preventive cause. That would account for the general roughness of the gospel and for the errors in various parts of it.

The following passage from Tertullian about a work of his own may illustrate the view that Mark may have been "opusculum properatum," and also "nondum exemplariis suffectum." It also suggests an explanation of some of the additions in Luke. (*Against Marcion* i. 1) "My original tract, as being a hasty composition (primum opusculum quasi properatum) I had subsequently superseded by a fuller treatise. This, too, I lost, *before it had been adequately copied* (nondum exemplariis suffectam). A brother, who afterwards turned apostate, stole it. He happened to have transcribed portions of it, in a transcript full of faults, and this he published (exhibuit frequentiae). It became necessary to correct [this] (emendationis necessitas facta est). The opportunity afforded by this new edition (Innovationis ejus occasio) induced me to make some additions. So my pen—which I now take up for the third time in place of the second, but must ask my readers to regard henceforth as first in place of the third—necessarily prefixes this explanation of the issue of its work, for fear anyone should be perplexed by the various versions that might be found in scattered forms (ita stilus iste nunc de secundo tertius, et de tertio jam hinc primus, hunc opusculi sui exitum necessario praefatur, ne quem varietas ejus in disperso reperta confundat)."

P. 301, "Bear ye," Gal. vi. 2; p. 301, "Love one another," Jn xiii. 34.

NOTES TO CHAPTER XXXI

[2925] Page 303, "The texts vary," Jn xxi. 24, see *Joh. Gram.* 2166. On the whole passage, see 2386, 2427—35; p. 303, "The disciple whom Jesus loved," Jn xxi. 20; p. 303, "Hath borne witness," Jn xix. 35; p. 303, "Sons of Zebedee," Jn xxi. 2.

THE PREDICTION OF PETER'S CRUCIFIXION

[2926] Page 303, "Crucified." Westcott, on Jn xxi. 19 "what manner of death" and the context, says, "Though the language of the Lord has very commonly been adapted to the details of crucifixion, it does not appear that it points directly to anything more than martyrdom, when 'another girded him' and he was taken 'whither he would not.' The 'stretching forth the hands' can hardly be referred primarily to the position on the cross, since this detail is placed first."

But, as regards the last objection, "*the stretching out of the hands* [on the cross]" mentioned (see *Joh. Gram.* 2797) may mean the "stretching out of the hands" on the σανίς, or "crosspiece of the cross" (*From Letter* 928 (vii) *c* foll., 928 (x) *a*) which was often *preliminary* to the "girding" (with a rope) and to the "lifting up" of the condemned, on the upright part of the cross. So Theodorus (Cramer *ad loc.*) "The stretching out (ἔκτασις) of the hands and the bond of the girdle (ὁ δεσμὸς τῆς ζώνης) signified nothing else but the manner of death by crucifixion (τὸ σχῆμα τοῦ σταυροῦ)." In Rome it sometimes preceded (928 (vi)) the going to the cross.

[2927] Westcott himself does not deny (though he does not explain) that xii. 33 "what manner of death," and its contextual "lifted up," refer to crucifixion. Also on xviii. 32 "what manner of death," he says, "Crucifixion was not a Jewish punishment," apparently admitting that, there, "what manner of" implies something "more than martyrdom," namely, a *particular kind of martyrdom*, crucifixion. The words would not apply to beheading or stoning.

[2928] Westcott says "*Stretch forth thy hands*, as helpless and seeking help." But Steph. *Thes.* (ἐκτείνω col. 581, ὕπτιος col. 493, where add Aristoph. *Eccles.* 782) indicates that ἐκτείνω χεῖρας pl. (when χεῖρας is not qualified by ὕπτιος or some special context) does not mostly imply "seeking help," but may imply *giving* help, or self-confident action as in Polyb. i. 3 ἐθάρσησαν ἐπὶ τὰ λοιπὰ τὰς χεῖρας ἐκτείνειν. In LXX, "*stretch out the hands*"—though much rarer than "*stretch out the hand*"—occurs in Exod. ix. 33, B "*and he stretched out his hands*," Heb., A, and Aquila "*and he spread abroad his hands*," that is, in prayer; 1 Esdr. viii. 73 "*stretched out my hands*," where the parall. Ezr. ix. 5 has, correctly, "*spread out*"; Is. i. 15 LXX "when ye *stretch out your hands*," without v.r., though Heb. has "*spread out.*"

[2929] It appears therefore that there is enough of LXX usage to make intelligible a play on the double meaning (1) "*stretch out the hands*" in prayer to God, (2) "*stretch out the hands*," literally, at the bidding of the executioner. The latter was probably familiar in vernacular Greek and connected with crucifixion. Artemidorus (*Joh. Gram.* 2211 c) like Theodorus above, mentions "*the stretching out of the hands*" as a sign of crucifixion. Epictetus iii. 26. 22 ἐκτείνας σαυτὸν ὡς οἱ ἐσταυρωμένοι, may imply that the condemned had to obey the order of the executioner "Stretch yourself out," *i.e.* stretch out your arms, in order that they may be bound to the σανίς or crosspiece of the cross. Thus, when Prometheus is to be nailed to the rock "with his two hands spread out," Hermes says to him, "Go up," "Make yourself ready to be fastened to the mountain," and then, "*Stretch out your right hand*," "*Stretch out the left*." But there (Lucian i. 185—7, *Prom.* 1—2) no "crosspiece" was needed, no "girding," and no "uplifting," as Prometheus himself could "go up" to the place of crucifixion, which was on a steep cliff.

[2930] As to the words, Jn xxi. 18 "shall *carry thee* (οἴσει) whither thou wouldest not," the same word "*carry*" occurs in Mk xv. 22 (R.V.) "bring (φέρουσιν)" in connexion with crucifixion (*Corrections*, 449). Possibly in Mk it means "*bring*," but in Jn "*carry*." It was suggested (*Joh. Gram.* 2797) that there was a double meaning in Jn's words, one meaning being "*Another* [i.e. *the Lord*] shall gird thee [for thy martyrdom] and shall carry thee [to the cross, obedient now to His will]."

[2931] In connexion with this "carrying," see Artemidorus ii. 57 "On carrying and being carried," where he says that "carrying" is sometimes a bad sign, meaning "crucifixion," but that "being carried" is worse because, as a rule, it indicates helplessness. But it is a good sign when "*the servant*" is "*carried by the Master.*" Artemidorus uses βαστάζω, not φέρω, but his words rather favour the view that in Jn the "carrying" was contemplated mainly as the act of "*the Master.*" One executioner (*Joh. Gram.* **2796**) could hardly "carry" the condemned.

[2932] "*Stretch out the hands*" must be distinguished from "*stretch out the hand.*" The latter implies action, and often violence. The first instance of the latter is in Gen. iii. 22 "Behold, the man is become as one of us...and now, lest he *stretch out his hand*, and take also of the tree of life."

[2933] Alluding to this, and to "the tree" as also meaning the "wood" of the cross, Ephrem says (p. 261) "No one so exalted himself as man, who *stretched out his hands* (sic) (extendit *manus*) to the tree, and would fain have made himself equal to his Creator; and no one so humiliated himself as God, who *stretched out His hands* on the wood (super lignum) and blotted out those transgressions which, by *stretching out of the hand* (extensione manus), had entered for the first time [into the world] (primae intraverant). The Lord *stretched out His hands* on the wood of the cross (in ligno crucis) that He might slay death which had come into being through the wood of the tree [of knowledge] (mortem quae per lignum erat)."

[2934] Ephrem confuses two phrases quite distinct in meaning though very similar in word. Nevertheless his words may possibly illustrate the meaning of Jn xxi. 18, which clearly means, "When you were young, you acted in your own strength, and went your own way." An instance of Peter's "acting in his own strength" is given in Mt. xxvi. 51 "*Having stretched out his hand*...smote the servant of the high priest." "*Stretch out the hand*" is nowhere else applied in the gospels to any disciple: Jn may be alluding to this. Also the impulsiveness of Peter is indicated by Jn in xxi. 7 "girt on his garment...and threw himself in the sea" (whereas the other disciples came in the boat). The whole passage (Jn xxi. 2—23) is so full of allusion that it is not fanciful to suppose a contrast between Peter's being "*girt*" by "*himself*" recently, and by "*Another*" henceforth (**2796-7**).

The Modern Hypothesis of the Early Death of John the Son of Zebedee

[2935] Page 303, "Survived his martyrdom." The prediction of Christ that James and John would (Mk x. 39) drink of His cup and be baptized with His baptism would lead some Christian writers to infer that John was actually put to death. But a "martyr" or "witness" to Christ might be tortured, maimed, imprisoned, condemned to the mines for life, and yet not actually die under his sufferings (2939–40). The parallel in Matthew (xx. 23) omits "baptized." Perhaps Matthew confined himself to that part of the tradition which was accepted by all as applying to both James and John, namely, that they testified and "suffered" for their testimony. This "suffering" Matthew may express by "cup" (as distinct from "dying," which he might take to be expressed by "baptism").

[2936] Luke has no parallel to Mk x. 39. John steps in to explain that there are more ways of "following" Christ to the cross than one. Peter "followed" to the literal cross (Jn xxi. 18—19). John also is described as (xxi. 20) "following[1]," yet he lived to a great

---

[1] [2936a] In the context of Jn xxi. 20 ἐπιστραφεὶς ὁ Πέτρος βλέπει τὸν μαθητὴν... ἀκολουθοῦντα, there is no mention of Christ's rising from the meal (as in Jn xiii. 4) and going away from the disciples, or beckoning Peter to "follow" Him. Chrysostom, Theodorus, and Anastasius (Cramer) imply that "Follow me" is metaphorical. But they throw no light on the words "seeth the disciple...following." Westc. says, "The command of the Lord appears to have been accompanied by some symbolic action. As St Peter literally obeyed the call thus expressed under a figure, and moved away from the group of the apostles, something attracted his attention, and he 'turned about' to the direction indicated (ἐπιστραφείς, Mark v. 30). The whole picture is full of life." But if a "picture" in words is "full of life," ought we not to see the living figures doing, not "*some* action," but a *definite* action? And are not the words "*appears*" and "*some* symbolic action" equivalent to a confession that it is difficult to realise the picture of our Lord literally walking away, and bidding Peter alone to "follow" Him in a literal sense?

But if the narrative refers to a vision, to be taken separately from what precedes, then "following" may denote literal symbolic "following," seen by Peter in that vision. After hearing and beginning to obey the call " Follow me [to the cross]!" Peter "turns round," in his vision, and sees the beloved disciple also "following"— as indeed he did, according to tradition, to the very brink of death by martyrdom. Then he asks for a revelation of the future in store for his brother-apostle.

Compare, however, Lk. xxii. 32. There, ἐπιστρέψας (preceding στήρισον τοὺς ἀδελφούς σου), applied to Peter, might indeed possibly be taken, as in Lk. i. 16, transitively; but it is much more probably intransitive, "having turned again," and it suggests that there may have been various versions of an ambiguous tradition about Peter's "turning again" after Christ's resurrection.

age after his "martyrdom" in Patmos. This is one of the cases where John seems to have intervened to explain something difficult in Mark and omitted by Luke.

[2937] In modern times a hypothesis that John died early as a martyr like his brother James (Acts xii. 2) has been supported from two writers quoting Papias (see *Enc. Bibl.* col. 2509). Their lateness weakens their evidence[1]. But besides, they may easily have

---

[1] [2937 a] The earlier of the two is (*Enc.* ib.) Philip of Sidè (c. 430 A.D.). But the extant evidence is only "from an epitome," dating from the 7th or 8th cent. and "probably based" on his writing. Moreover (*Dict. Christ. Biogr.* iv. 356) "the chronological order of events" is said to be "constantly disregarded" by Philip, and "his details" are pronounced by Neander (*ib.*) "unworthy of confidence." The epitome says, Παπίας ἐν τῷ δευτέρῳ λόγῳ λέγει, ὅτι Ἰωάννης ὁ θεολόγος κ. Ἰάκωβος ὁ ἀδελφὸς αὐτοῦ ὑπὸ Ἰουδαίων ἀνῃρέθησαν. This is more fully expressed (Burkitt, *The Gospel History* etc. p. 252) "in the oldest MS. of the Chronicle of George the Monk, a writer of the 9th century." George, after understanding Origen, wrongly, as asserting that John was a martyr to the death, proceeds (*Enc.* ib.) Παπίας γὰρ ὁ Ἱεραπόλεως ἐπίσκοπος αὐτόπτης τούτου γενόμενος ἐν τῷ δευτέρῳ λόγῳ τῶν κυριακῶν λογίων φάσκει ὅτι ὑπὸ Ἰουδαίων ἀνῃρέθη, πληρώσας δηλαδὴ μετὰ τοῦ ἀδελφοῦ τὴν τοῦ Χριστοῦ περὶ αὐτῶν πρόρρησιν καὶ τὴν ἑαυτῶν ὁμολογίαν περὶ τούτου καὶ συγκατάθεσιν.

[2937 b] Note here that both writers use ἀναιρεῖν, to mean "kill." This is a rare word in N.T. (exc. in Acts). It is also non-existent in the Indices of Eusebius. Yet Eusebius uses it in describing the death of James the brother of John, thus, iii. 5. 2 Ἰουδαίων...κατὰ τῶν ἀποστόλων...πλείστας ὅσας ἐπιβουλὰς μεμηχανημένων, πρῶτον τοῦ Στεφάνου λίθοις ὑπ' αὐτῶν ἀνῃρημένου, εἶτα δὲ μετ' αὐτὸν Ἰακώβου, ὃς ἦν Ζεβεδαίου μὲν παῖς, ἀδελφὸς δὲ Ἰωάννου, τὴν κεφαλὴν ἀποτμηθέντος, ἐπὶ πᾶσί τε Ἰακώβου...τὸν προδηλωθέντα τρόπον μεταλλάξαντος. Now ἀναιρεῖν is the word used in the Acts to describe the death of James the brother of John, thus, Acts xii. 1—2 Ἡρῴδης ὁ βασιλεὺς...ἀνεῖλεν...Ἰάκωβον τὸν ἀδελφὸν Ἰωάνου μαχαίρῃ.

[2937 c] Origen (Lomm. iv. 18, *Comm. Matth.* tom. xvi. 6), also referring to Acts xii. 1—2, says, Ἡρώδης μὲν ἀπέκτεινεν Ἰάκωβον τὸν Ἰωάννου μαχαίρᾳ, omitting ἀδελφόν. This would naturally mean "James the son of John," an absurdity, but it points to a possibility that the tradition of Acts xii. 1—2 may have existed in a form where ἀδελφός was not mentioned, and where Ἰωάνης *meant, as it usually does,* "*John the Baptist*" (see 2937 e). Moreover it has been acutely observed (*Oxford Magazine*, 1907, p. 175) that Eusebius' own words might be carelessly translated, "Stephen having been first slain by them [*i.e.* the Jews] with stones, and then, after him, James, who was *on the one hand the son of Zebedee and on the other hand the brother of that John who was beheaded* (ὃς ἦν Ζεβεδαίου μὲν παῖς, ἀδελφὸς δὲ Ἰωάνου τὴν κεφαλὴν ἀποτμηθέντος)."

[2937 d] Early writers lay great stress on the variety of the deaths suffered by God's "martyrs" or "witnesses," *e.g.* Heb. xi. 37 "sawn asunder etc.," Tertull. *Scorp.* 15 "This I perceive...running through the Acts (Acta decurrens)...(1) prisons, bonds, scourges, stones (saxa), swords, onsets of Jews and gatherings of Gentiles.... That (2) Peter is scourged (caeditur), Stephen crushed [with stones] (opprimitur), James [the son of Zebedee] immolated (immolatur), Paul torn in pieces (distra-

[2937] NOTES TO CHAPTER XXXI

mistaken some such expression as "*James was perfected with the death of John.*" (This actually occurs in Tertullian *De Praescr. Haer.* 36 "Paulus *Johannis exitu* coronatur.*") This might be taken to mean, "James the son of Zebedee died as a martyr like his brother John the son of Zebedee[1]." But it means, "*James was put to death, not on the cross but with the sword, with the death of John the Baptist.*"

[2938] A more plausible argument for John's execution is, that Heracleon, as quoted by Clement of Alexandria (p. 595), does not mention John as dying a natural death along with "Matthew, Philip, Thomas, Levi, and many others." Of these he says, "They did not confess the confession of voice [before a magistrate] and go forth [in death] (ὡμολόγησαν τὴν διὰ τῆς φωνῆς ὁμολογίαν καὶ ἐξῆλθον)."

[2939] Probably "*go forth*" means "depart," "die," as in the Letter of the Church of Lyons (A.D. 177)[2] and Epictetus ii. 15. 6.

---

hitur)...." The writer closely follows the order of the Acts, in his lists of (1) persecutions, (2) names:—iv. 3, v. 18, 23, 40 Peter's "imprisonments" and "scourging"; vii. 58 Stephen's "stoning"; xii. 2 the "immolation" of James with the "sword," perhaps with some allusion to the severing of the throat as connected with "immolation"; xiv. 5 "an onset of Gentiles and Jews" on Paul and his companions; xxiii. 10 Paul's rescue from being "pulled in pieces (Vulg. discerperetur)." From missing the force of Tertullian's "distrahitur," some have translated it "beheaded"! Others have taken "James" to mean James the Just, who (**2837** (iii)) was *not* slain with the "sword."

[**2937** *e*] Having regard to the general carelessness of Philip and to the ease with which "John" the Baptist might be confused, in his days, with "John" the son of Zebedee, it is a reasonable and charitable supposition that Philip has not invented, but misunderstood a saying of Papias, to the effect that "*James—as also John—was put to death by the Jews with the sword.*"

[1] [**2937** *f*] Such a mistake is very natural. Comp. Clem. Alex. 145, as transl. by T. & T. Clark p. 167, "And *in the Gospel by John* He says, 'Serpents, brood of vipers,'" with the footnote, "Nothing similar to this is found in the fourth Gospel; the reference may be to the words of the Baptist, Matth. iii. 7, Luke iii. 7." But the Gk is, Κἀν τῷ εὐαγγελίῳ, διὰ Ἰωάννου, '"Ὄφεις," φησί, i.e. "And *in the Gospel, through John [the Baptist]*, He says, 'Serpents, generation of vipers....'" The previous sentence describes the Instructor as "*speaking through Isaiah*"; this describes Him as "*speaking through*" *John the Baptist*, whom the translator appears to have mistaken for *John the son of Zebedee*.

[2] [**2939** *a*] Euseb. v. 2. 3. Such "confessors" as did not actually "depart (ἐξέρχομαι)" modestly disclaimed the title of "martyr." But it is clear that people were disposed to give it to them, ἡδέως γὰρ παρεχώρουν τὴν τῆς μαρτυρίας προσηγορίαν τῷ Χριστῷ, τῷ πιστῷ καὶ ἀληθινῷ μάρτυρι καὶ πρωτοτόκῳ τῶν νεκρῶν καὶ ἀρχηγῷ τῆς ζωῆς τοῦ θεοῦ, καὶ ἐπεμιμνήσκοντο τῶν ἐξεληλυθότων ἤδη μαρτύρων, καὶ ἔλεγον· ἐκεῖνοι ἤδη μάρτυρες, οὓς ἐν τῇ ὁμολογίᾳ Χριστὸς ἠξίωσεν ἀναληφθῆναι, ἐπισφραγισάμενος αὐτῶν διὰ τῆς ἐξόδου τὴν μαρτυρίαν, ἡμεῖς δὲ ὁμόλογοι μέτριοι καὶ ταπεινοί. Note the belief that the "departed" witnesses, or martyrs, had been "*taken up* (ἀναληφθῆναι)," and comp. Tertull. *Scorp.* 15 "Then is Peter 'girt by

John was in a peculiar position. He *did*, according to tradition, "confess" before a magistrate; he *did*, according to some traditions, "*go forth*" *to die*; but he *did not actually* "*go forth*," i.e. *depart this life*, under the punishment to which he was subjected. It is highly improbable that Heracleon would venture to reckon John along with Matthew and the rest, who neither "confessed [before a magistrate]" nor "went forth." For John, according to Tertullian, had not only been condemned to the mines at Patmos, but had also been cast into burning oil, and had survived, *De Praescr. Haer.* 36 "in oleum igneum demersus...relegatur."

[2940] Tertullian, speaking about announcements referring to martyrdom, says (*Scorp.* 12) "Cui potius figuram vocis suae declarasset quam cui effigiem gloriae suae revelavit, *Petro, Jacobo, Joanni, et postea Paulo*, quem paradisi quoque compotem fecit ante martyrium?" The context implies that Tertullian regarded John as no less a "martyr" than Peter, James, and Paul, although he asserts that John had survived martyrdom (**2939**). Hegesippus, quoted by Eusebius, says that the grandsons of Jude, *after having been let go by Domitian*, "became leaders of the Churches, *as being at once martyrs* (μάρτυρες) *and relatives of the Lord*," and that they "lived on till the reign of Trajan[1]."

[2941] Origen (Lomm. iv. 18 on Mk x. 38) though the text ("it seemed to some") may be corrupt, clearly shews that there was a difference of opinion as to the fulfilment of the prediction about the sons of Zebedee. And he inclines to think that the "relegatio" constituted martyrdom.

Summing up the evidence for and against the hypothesis of John's

---

another' (Jn xxi. 18) when he is made fast to the cross. Then is Paul (Acts xxii. 28) 'born free' of Rome indeed, when, in Rome, he *springs to life again* ennobled by martyrdom "—a passage that would suggest to Roman Christians—familiar with the story of the martyrdom of the two apostles on one and the same day—another instance of God's "two witnesses," martyred and "taken up" to heaven: comp. also **2942*** (xix) foll.

[1] [**2940** *a*] Euseb. iii. 20. 6 (rep. iii. 32. 6). Lightf. on Clem. Cor. 5 refers also to Apollonius (Euseb. v. 18. 5—7) as using μάρτυς thus "several times." Apollonius is *condemning* people who did this or that, posing as "martyrs," although they had procured immunity from punishment, or were unworthy of the name (*e.g.* ὡς μάρτυς καυχώμενος ἐτόλμησε...). Still, the passage shews that μάρτυς was freely used for confessors who had suffered, but not died, for Christ. Eusebius also quotes a letter alleged by Serapion, beginning (v. 19. 3) "I, Aurelius Cyrenius, *martyr*, greet you ('Α. Κ., μάρτυς, ἐρρῶσθαι ὑμᾶς εὔχομαι)."

early death by martyrdom, we find, in favour of it, (1) a non-mention by Heracleon of John, among the list of apostles that did not "confess and depart," *i.e.* die as martyrs; (2) two very late and unauthoritative documents loosely quoting a saying of Papias—not quoted by the more early, and accurate, and diligent Eusebius—to the effect that John "was killed (ἀναιρέω) by Jews."

Against it we find that (1) in the first century and for some time afterwards the name of "martyr" was freely given to *those that "confessed" and suffered for Christ, even though not actually killed*, so that Heracleon would not mention John along with Matthew; (2) the two late writers above-mentioned have probably confused some statement of Papias mentioning the death of James and the *death of John* [*the Baptist*] *together*, or else the death of James and the *name of John* [*the Apostle*] *together*, from which they inferred that James and his brother John had been simultaneously killed.

Against it are also (3) Luke's non-mention of any martyrdom of John in the Acts; (4) the silence of Eusebius about any such account of martyrdom (in Hegesippus, Papias, or other writers); (5) the mention by Paul of John as still living and as one of the three "pillars" (Gal. ii. 9) "James, Cephas, and John," where James is (*ib.* i. 19) "the Lord's brother"; (6) the evidence of the fourth gospel as to the belief that (Jn xxi. 23) "the disciple was not to die" (**2998** (xxv) *b*); and (7) the consensus of testimony recorded by Eusebius. These facts, taken all together, constitute overwhelming proof that John the son of Zebedee lived to a great age. Traditions that he died as a martyr would spring up so naturally from Christ's prediction to the sons of Zebedee, that we may well be surprised that only one such tradition exists, and that one so poorly supported.

P. 304, "We know," Jn xxi. 24; p. 304, "Revealed to Andrew," see *Enc. Bibl.* "Gospels" § 78.

The Date of the Writing of "the Revelation of John"

§ 1. *The Hypothesis of incorporated Documents*

[2942*] Page 304, "The Apocalypse." The question of the date of the Apocalypse *as a whole* is not affected by the possibility that it may combine documents of different dates. *The date of the work as a whole must be later than the latest events described or alluded to;* and these descriptions or allusions confirm the statement of Irenæus (v. 30. 3) "It" [not "he" (2997 a)] "was not seen long ago but nearly in our generation at the close of the reign of Domitian." Justin Martyr describes the author (*Tryph.* 81) as "John,...one of the Apostles of Christ"; and that Justin's words are genuine is shewn by two facts. (1) They present great difficulty to those who believe that the Apostle John wrote the Fourth Gospel, so that there would be no temptation to interpolate them; (2) Eusebius says (iv. 18. 8) "He [*i.e.* Justin] makes mention also of John's Apocalypse saying unmistakeably that it is the work of the Apostle."

The following discussion deals not only with the date of the work as a whole, but also with its unity of authorship, and with the character and purpose of the author so far as they can be inferred from his work. As to the date, reasons will be given for thinking that chronological inferences cannot be safely drawn from the numbers mentioned in the book, but that the evidence points to A.D. 96, or thereabouts (the date asserted by Irenæus). As to its unity, an attempt will be made to shew that it is of the nature of an epic poem describing what a Christian Homer might describe as "the Good News of the accomplishment of the righteousness and the wrath of God."

Homer begins by saying that by the anger of Achilles "the purpose of Zeus was being fulfilled." The Epistle to the Romans says (i. 16—18) "I am not ashamed of the gospel: for it is *the power of God unto salvation*....For therein is revealed *a righteousness of God*....For *the wrath of God is revealed from heaven against all ungodliness and unrighteousness of men.*" So, in Ezekiel, the slaughter of the sinful by the six Destroying Angels follows hard on the marking of the redeemed by the Recording Angel in their midst (**2998** (xxviii) *n*); and both acts precede the measuring for the New Temple. The author of Revelation, though frequently using the language of Daniel, is permeated through and through with the thought of Ezekiel. He constantly realises, through various emblems, the domination exercised over the inanimate, irrational, and bestial forces of the Universe by One whom Origen calls "the Charioteer" of the Four Living Creatures. His poem, for it is one poem, though also a succession of poems—in spite of episodes and inconsistencies of imagery and expression indicating perhaps a combination of the visions of many years by a Seer, now in extreme old age, who will not alter what God has at any time uttered or revealed to him—appears to be a series of poetic visions of "the power of God" typified from the outset by the Figure with the "two-edged sword." The sword, as Philo says, separates Light from Darkness. It is characteristic of our author that he delights in differences expressive of unity. Nothing can be more different from a sword than a lamb. Yet the Lamb—who is also the Lion of the tribe of Judah—accomplishes the work of the two-edged sword. A closely following vision reveals the Lamb, in heaven, opening the seven seals of doom and preparing the way for "salvation" by "revealing God's wrath against all ungodliness and unrighteousness." This is the tenor of all the visions even to the end.

There is no attempt to keep chronological order. But the spiritual significance of the visions sometimes perhaps gains from the non-attempt. There is, as in a drama, a sense of the retarded but inevitable accomplishment, perhaps all the more vivid because the reader is taken at times back from the present to the past and then hurried into the future; or suddenly lifted up to the spectacle of God's purpose in heaven, and then brought down again to behold the vain and furious raging of the heathen upon earth—all things alike, evil as well as good, being ultimately subjected to one divine will. The literary form is rough-hewn. But it may be roughly said to describe a Purpose, a growth of Good, a growth of Evil, a Conflict, and a Victory. Those who deny that the work could have been written by a personal disciple of Christ should reflect that the book may be almost said to begin and end with the name of Jesus. Behind all the angelic visions there is unity in the thought that Jesus sends them. Moreover the book has poetic refrains, mystical repetitions of words and phrases, mystical uses of number. These and many other considerations strengthen the feeling that as a whole the prophecy proceeds not only from one mind but also—with the exception of a few passages—from one hand, though probably the hand of one recording, late in life, the most prominent and most vividly remembered of many visions and many revelations.

If Revelation was written by John the son of Zebedee, and if the same John supplied to a disciple traditions that form the basis of the Fourth Gospel, then some of the characteristics of Revelation may be expected to reappear in the Gospel, though tinged by a different personality and expressed in entirely different language. It is for this reason that Revelation is so fully discussed here, as to its date and unity, and later on (2998 (xxvi)—(xxxiii)) as to some of its visions, and as to the influence exerted on the Seer by Ezekiel and by Daniel.

§ 2. *The Argument (as to the date) from numbers*

[2942* (i)] Bishop Lightfoot maintained that the Apocalypse was written before the fall of Jerusalem. And it has been argued with much apparent cogency that the language used about the heads and horns of the Beast points to that conclusion. But the number of the heads can be made to vary (1) by including or excluding the great Dictator Julius—as in the two widely differing alternative lists of Roman Emperors given by Clement of Alexandria (405—6) —and the three short-lived rivals for Nero's throne (Galba, Otho, and Vitellius), (2) by reckoning the three emperors of the Flavian House as "under one [head] (ὑφ' ἕν)" as in Barnabas and the Sibylline Oracles, (3) by playing on the popular saying that Domitian was, as Juvenal says, "a bald Nero," or (as Tertullian) "a Sub-Nero"—and this at a time when it was believed by many that Nero would really return to take vengeance on Rome[1]. It can

---

[1] [2942* (i) a] See *Orac. Sib.* v. 222 :
Πρῶτα μὲν ἐκ τρισσῶν κεφαλῶν σὺν πληγάδι ῥίζης
Στησάμενος μεγάλως, ἑτέροις δώσειε σπάσασθαι,
Ὥστε φαγεῖν σάρκας γονέων βασιλῆος ἀνάγνου.

The previous lines shew the meaning. The returning Nero is to destroy the "three heads" of the Flavian dynasty. Barnabas says (iv. 4—5) λέγει δὲ οὕτως καὶ ὁ προφήτης· (Dan. vii. 24) Βασιλεῖαι δέκα ἐπὶ τῆς γῆς βασιλεύσουσιν, καὶ ἐξαναστήσεται ὄπισθεν αὐτῶν μικρὸς βασιλεύς, ὃς ταπεινώσει τρεῖς ὑφ' ἓν τῶν βασιλέων. ὁμοίως περὶ τοῦ αὐτοῦ λέγει Δανιήλ (Dan. vii. 7 foll.) καὶ εἶδον τὸ τέταρτον θηρίον πονηρὸν καὶ ἰσχυρὸν καὶ χαλεπώτερον παρὰ πάντα τὰ θηρία τῆς γῆς, καὶ ὡς ἐξ αὐτοῦ ἀνέτειλεν δέκα κέρατα καὶ ἐξ αὐτῶν μικρὸν κέρας παραφυάδιον, καὶ ὡς ἐταπείνωσεν ὑφ' ἓν τρία τῶν μεγάλων κεράτων. He changes Daniel's order and might give a reader the impression that "the prophet" is distinct from the subsequently mentioned "Daniel." Also where Daniel says (vii. 24) "ten *kings*," he says "ten *kingdoms*"

also be shewn that the numbers in the Apocalypse are in very many cases obviously mere symbols, as when the Seer speaks of "seven churches," and "one hundred and forty-four thousand" of the "sealed," and that (as Origen suggests) he has almost always in view spiritual Powers of evil rather than (like Daniel) earthly kings or emperors. More particularly, his interest in numbers is of an antithetical nature. He shews the "seven" churches, and the "seven" spirits, and the "seven" angels, of God, conquering the Dragon as the Beast with the "seven" heads, and the Harlot that sits on "seven" hills[1].

(comp. Dan. vii. 17 "four *kings*," LXX and Theod. "*kingdoms*"). He twice inserts ὑφ' ἕν, which is not in either passage of Daniel. Similarly 2 Esdr. xii. 23 explains the three heads as "three *kingdoms*," but goes on to say, as though they were "*kings*" (*ib.* 26) "unus ex eis [Vespasian] super lectum suum morietur et tamen cum tormentis," and, of the two next (*ib.* 28) "unius [Domitian] enim gladius comedet [eum, *i.e.* Titus] qui cum eo, sed tamen et hic [Domitian] gladio in novissimis cadet." The legend that Domitian killed Titus may reflect a current tradition that the former not only (Suet. *Titus* 9) "plotted" his brother's death, but also effected it.

[2942* (i) *b*] On Domitian, regarded as a second Nero, comp. Juvenal (iv. 38) who describes how "the last Flavian lacerated the almost lifeless world, and Rome served *bald Nero*"—for which utterance, the Scholiast says, he was banished. Mayor *ad loc.* quotes also Pliny *Pan.* 53, and Auson. *Monost. de ord. xii imper.* 11—12, who speaks of Titus as followed by "Frater quem *calvum* dixit sua Roma *Neronem.*" Tertull. calls Domitian (*Apol.* 5) "Portio *Neronis* de crudelitate," and (*De Pall.* 4) "*Subnero.*" Comp. Euseb. iii. 17 τῆς Νέρωνος θεοεχθρίας διάδοχος.

[1] [2942* (i) *c*] Origen has left no commentary on the Apocalypse. But in *Comm. Johann.* tom. i. 1—2 he questions the literal accuracy of the numbering in Rev. vii. 2—8, and implies that the passage has a mystical meaning. In his *Comm. Ps.* lxviii. 21 he suggests that "the heads of his enemies" may mean τὰ πρώτως ἐκ τῶν δαιμόνων ἐπισυμβαίνοντα νοήματα τῇ ψυχῇ, and this indicates that he would have at all events included a spiritual meaning in interpreting the "heads" of the Dragon and of the Beast in Rev. xii. 3 &c. if he had written his intended commentary, referred to at the end of this paragraph. He speaks of churches as being (*Comm. Numb.* iii. 3, Lomm. x. 28) "non solum in terris sed et in *coelis* ecclesias ex quibus et septem quasdam Joannes enumerat." Concerning Rev. xi. 8 "the great City, which is called spiritually Sodom and Egypt, where their Lord was crucified," he raises the question (*Comm. Matth.* Lomm. iv. 314) whether "the whole world" or "Judæa" is signified. On Rev. xii. 3 "seven heads and ten horns," he says (Lomm. iv. 307) "Omnia haec exponere singillatim de capitibus septem draconis, quae forsitan possunt referri ad aliquos principes rerum nequitiae, sive ad tanta ducentium ad mortem peccata, non est temporis hujus; exponentur autem tempore suo in revelatione Joannis. Sed et decem cornua dicere, quoniam sunt regna serpentinae malitiae, et habentis serpentis naturam...."

[2942* (i) *d*] The only striking exception to this rule—of the spiritual, not literal, significance, of numbers—is the mention of (Rev. xvii. 9—11) the "seven

THE DATE OF THE APOCALYPSE [2942*]

hills" of Rome, followed by a mention of "seven kings," of whom " five have fallen, the one is, the other hath not yet come, and when he shall have come he must remain a little and the beast that was and is not" [the punctuation is here doubtful] " even he [or, and he] is eighth and from the seven and goeth into destruction (καὶ ὅταν ἔλθῃ ὀλίγον αὐτὸν δεῖ μεῖναι καὶ τὸ θηρίον ὃ ἦν καὶ οὐκ ἔστιν καὶ αὐτὸς ὄγδοός ἐστιν καὶ ἐκ τῶν ἑπτά ἐστιν καὶ εἰς ἀπώλειαν ὑπάγει)."

Comp. *Enoch* 18 "*seven mountains*," of which the middle one "reached to heaven like the throne of God," contrasted with "*seven stars, like great burning mountains*," and like spirits"—afterwards (*En.* 21) described as "bound together" in chaos, "*like great mountains*, and flaming as with fire." The seven stars, or mountains, have (*ib.*) transgressed the commandment of God, and are bound in "the prison of the angels."

[2942* (i) *e*] Here, doubtless, the Seer has been influenced by Daniel's description of Antiochus Epiphanes, as a Portent of Evil, who is to be (Dan. vii. 8) "*among* (Theod. ἐν μέσῳ, LXX ἀνὰ μέσον)," and yet (Dan. vii. 24) "*after*," the previously mentioned ten "horns." Applying this to the popular belief in a returning Nero—identified with Domitian, who is said by Pliny to have "avenged" the former—he is struck, as a poet might be, by the similarity between the Beast (who is to be "*from the seven*" and yet "*the eighth*") and Daniel's horn (which is to be "*among*," and yet "*after*," the other horns). Perhaps, in the quarries of Patmos, he may have heard from fellow-toilers, fresh from the streets of Rome, something about the "seven" ancient kings of Rome repeated in the "seven" imperial kings from Augustus to Titus, to whom there is now added the returning Nero, in his imitator and avenger, Domitian.

[2942* (i) *f*] This mysterious (Rev. xvii. 9—11) "king"—whether he is regarded as the Beast, or as one of the heads of the Beast, or as both, is uncertain, but in any case the masc. αὐτός denotes a "king"—is called "*eighth*." The only other instance of "*eighth*" in N.T., applied to persons, is 2 Pet. ii. 5 "Noah the *eighth* person," meaning "with seven others." At first sight there would appear to be no possible connexion between a number applied to Noah, and also applied to the Beast or the Beast's representative. But a brief consideration will shew that the numbers in this book (as well as occasional expressions) are influenced by what may be called the writer's recognition of:—

THE PRINCIPLE OF ANTITHESIS

[2942* (i) *g*] This is expressed by Sir. xxxiii. (xxxvi.) 14—15 "Good is set over against (ἀπέναντι) evil, and life over against death. So is a sinner over against a saint (εὐσεβοῦς); and thus discern thou (ἔμβλεψον εἰς) all the works of the Most High *two* [*and*] *two, one right against the one* (ἓν κατέναντι τοῦ ἑνός)."

[2942* (i) *h*] The unity of the Roman Empire has been typified by Virgil in the line

"*Septem*que *una* sibi muro circumdedit arces."

This material unity has been taken by the Seer of the Apocalypse as a symbol of spiritual unity of a bad kind, a unity of consistent policy, dominating and (as Juvenal says) "lacerating" the nations of the earth, and compelling them to receive its "brand (χάραγμα)" (xiii. 16, 17 etc., 7 times mentioned) which is opposed to the (vii. 2) "seal (σφραγῖδα) of the living God" with which believers are "sealed," and perhaps also opposed to the (v. 1) "seven seals" of the Book of Redemption.

[2942* (i) *i*] This contrast is especially manifest in the use of "seven," which is applied to a very great number of the manifestations of God, or to their adjuncts, *e.g.* "spirits," "candlesticks," "stars," "angels," "torches," "seals," the "horns" of the Lamb, the "eyes" of the Lamb, "trumpets" and "thunders." Antithetically, "seven" is applied to the (xii. 3) "heads" and "diadems" of the "dragon" and (xvii. 3, 7) to the "heads" of the "scarlet beast," and it is said that (xvii. 9—11) the "seven heads" are "seven hills" (*i.e.* the seven hills of Rome) and that they are also "seven kings," and that the "eighth" is one of "the seven." This (with the exc. of xxi. 9) is the last mention of "seven," and it shews the spirit in which the writer uses "seven" throughout the book, as indicating spiritual antithesis, "good over against evil, life over against death."

[2942* (i) *j*] Note also the following antitheses relating severally to God or the Lamb on one side, and to the Beast on the other, or to the two causes for which they contend:—

Lamb	Beast
v. 6 "A Lamb standing *as though* (ὡς) *slain* (ἐσφαγμένον)."	xiii. 3 "One of his [*i.e.* the Beast's] heads *as though* (ὡς) *slain* (ἐσφαγμένην) unto death."
v. 11—13 "Myriads of myriads" acclaim "the slaughtered Lamb," and "all creation" gives glory to Him that sitteth on the throne and to the Lamb.	xiii. 3—4 The deadly wound is healed and "all the earth" worships the Dragon and the Beast.
iv. 8 "The WAS and the IS and the COMING."	xvii. 11 *a* "The Beast, which *was* and *is not*."
	xvii. 11 *b* "And he is eighth, and is from the seven, and goeth into destruction."

In xvii. 11, taken with iv. 8, there appears to be a bitter antithesis, contrasting the past present and future, as applied to God, with the past present and future, as applied to the Power of Evil—the only abiding positive statement about the latter being that it "*was*."

[2942* (i) *k*] Returning to Rev. xvii. 11 in the light of these illustrations of numerical antithesis, we may reasonably suppose that antithetical allusion exists in "the *eighth* [king]," as contrasted with 2 Pet. ii. 5 Noah "the *eighth* [person]." Also the Valentinians early in the second century (Iren. ii. 24. 1, comp. i. 14. 4 Clark's note, and i. 15. 2) recognised 888 as a number symbolic of the Saviour. "Eighth" is connected with circumcision in the familiar phrase "circumcised the *eighth* day," and with baptism, the ark, and Noah, in 1 Pet. iii. 20, 21 "in the days of *Noah*...few, that is, *eight* souls, were saved through water... even *baptism*." That being so, the "eighth [king]," who is to precede the fiery destruction of the world, may be called "eighth" in antithesis to Noah. Elsewhere the writer thinks it well to tell us that the "number" of the Beast, instead of being 888, is (Rev. xiii. 18) 666. Philo (*P. A.* 101) deals with the latter indirectly in connexion with Noah. He speaks of 6, 60, and 600, and says that God would never have destroyed mankind "sub forma sexti" except for their excessive wickedness. Elsewhere he adds (*P. A.* 124) "in sexti numeri ratione corruptio." Apparently he would have thought that 666 represented the essence of diabolical power as the Valentinians found the essence of its opposite in 888.

What precise name, or word, the Seer may have had in view, we do not know. But we may feel sure that he laid stress upon it, not solely because it represented any of the conjectured historical names, but also (if not entirely) because it represented spiritual evil.

THE DATE OF THE APOCALYPSE [2942*]

The Number of the Beast

[2942* (i) *l*] In connexion with Rev. xvii. 11, must be considered Rev. xiii. 18 "Here is wisdom. He that hath understanding *let him count the number of the beast, for it is the number of a man, and his number is 666.*" Compare an obscure passage in Clem. Alex. 812 about Christ going up to the Mount of Transfiguration "*fourth*," *i.e.* with three others. Then He "becomes *Sixth*," *i.e.* because Moses and Elijah join Him. Then He is "proclaimed Son of God, *through the Voice as Seventh* (δι' ἑβδόμης ἀνακηρυσσόμενος τῆς φωνῆς υἱὸς εἶναι θεοῦ)." Clement proceeds, ἵνα δὴ οἱ μὲν...ὁ δὲ διὰ γενέσεως (ἣν ἐδήλωσεν ἡ ἑξάς) ἐπίσημος, ὀγδοὰς ὑπάρχων, φανῇ θεός...ἀριθμούμενος μὲν ὡς ἄνθρωπος, κρυπτόμενος δὲ ὃς ἦν, τῇ μὲν γὰρ τάξει τῶν ἀριθμῶν συγκαταλέγεται καὶ ὁ ἕξ, ἡ δὲ τῶν στοιχείων ἀκολουθία ἐπίσημον γνωρίζει τὸ μὴ γραφόμενον. Apparently he is referring to the ancient *sixth* letter of the alphabet (the digamma *F*) which had dropped out of the alphabet, and only remained as an arithmetical symbol (ϛ). Comp. Gow's *History of Greek Mathematics* p. 45 "The tickets of the ten panels of Athenian jurymen were marked with the letters of the alphabet from α to κ, ϛ being omitted. So also the books of Homer as divided by Zenodotus (flor. c. B.C. 280) were numbered by the 24 letters of the ordinary Ionic alphabet, ϛ and ϙ being omitted: and the works of Aristotle were also at some ancient time divided into books numbered on the same principle."

Irenæus quotes from the Valentinians an apparently similar use of ἐπίσημος (i. 14. 4) 'Ιησοῦς μὲν γάρ ἐστιν ἐπίσημον ὄνομα (Lat. insigne nomen) ἐξ ὧν γράμματα. Here Grabe says, "'Επίσημον hic non *insigne* vel *celebre nomen* denotare puto, sed *sex constans literis*, ut mox additur. Cum enim ἐπίσημον βαῦ sextum in Alphabeto locum teneret, indeque numeri 6 nota esset, tam hic ipse numerus, quam quae illum haberent, ἐπίσημα dici sueverunt." Comp. i. 14. 6—7 and ii. 24. 1 "Jesus enim nomen...aliquando quidem *episemon* esse dicunt *sex habens literas*, aliquando autem plenitudinem Ogdoadum, 888 numerum habens." Hesych. and Steph. *Thes.* do not recognise any technical use of ἐπίσημος. It means "sign-bearing," "stamped," "conspicuous [for good or ill]." There may be different views as to the ways in which the word might be played on and applied to Christ; but it was certainly used by the Valentinians (*e.g.* Iren. i. 15. 2) to denote the incarnate Jesus, the *Hexad*, as distinct from the celestial Christ, the *Ogdoad*; and it bears on Rev. xiii. 18 because it shews that there were early heretical disquisitions on the number six.

[2942* (i) *m*] The extract given above from Clem. Alex. may have some bearing on the possibility of early glosses and corruptions in Rev. xiii. 18, where 666 has been most variously transliterated. *A priori* the conjecture entitled to most consideration would be the very early one favoured by Irenæus (v. 30. 3) TEITAN. This, in itself, would be suitable as denoting a Monster of earth rising up against the Powers of heaven. The word occurs in 2 S. v. 18, 22 to represent "Rephaim," "giants," and in Judith xvi. 6 (8). An objection against it is, that it is not (Rev. xiii. 18) "*the number of a man*" in the sense of representing a man's name. But, even if that phrase ("the number of a man") is regarded as above suspicion of being a gloss, it may be replied that (1) every one of the three Flavian emperors was called TITUS, (2) the name TITUS was used as early as the middle of the first century in Rome in bitter satire on vicious and degenerate Roman nobles—

> "Hic neque more probo videas neque voce serena
> Ingentes trepidare TITOS cum carmina lumbum
> Intrant" Persius i. 19—21

[2942*] THE DATE OF THE APOCALYPSE

(3) Hesychius has Τιτάν παιδεραστής (as well as καὶ τὸ τοῦ 'Αντιχρίστου ὄνομα), (4) the name Titus occurs in the Talmud in connexion with profanity, cruelty, and licentiousness, *e.g. Beresh. Rab.* (on Gen. ii. 1, Wünsche p. 42), R. Nathan on *Aboth* i. 1, (5) the hatred felt by the Jews for the second of the " Titi " (Titus) would be transferred by the Christians to the third (Domitian), (6) a vernacular use of the word, as applied to the Flavian dynasty in the streets of Rome during the later years of the unpopularity of Domitian, might easily reach John, working as a convict in Patmos; and (7) its Greek and Roman associations with rebellion against heaven, penetrating far below literary circles, would appeal even to a Jew attempting to represent that outburst of evil against good which (he felt) must precede the final triumph of the latter. It is true that the *i* in "Titus" is short. But the Jews transliterated it as "Teitous," see **2942*** (i) *q*.

It has been shewn above (**2942*** (i) *b*) that Domitian was called "a second Nero." Pliny *Pan.* 53 ("*vindicatus* Nero...qui mortem *ulcisceretur*") seems to speak of the former as "avenging" the latter. "Vengeance" is also associated with "Titan" by Irenæus (v. 30. 3 "ut etiam *sol* Titan vocetur ab his qui nunc tenent [?"who now hold fast [to belief in the sun]," comp. Tertull. *Prax.* 3 "monarchiam *tenemus*"]: et ostentationem quandam continet *ultionis et vindictam inferentis, quod ille simulat se male tractatos vindicare*") arguing, no doubt, from τίομαι, "I exact vengeance," but agreeing with what might be popular talk about Domitian. Nor should Irenæus's mention of the "sun" be forgotten, in view of the fact that the colossal statue of Nero (the one that gave name to the Coliseum) was remade by Vespasian and dedicated to the Sun (Pliny *N. Hist.* xxxiv. 7. 18 (45), Suet. *Vesp.* 18). When Domitian claimed to be worshipped as Lord God, the Christians in Rome might well say that the old Nero had been "new made as Domitian, the Sun-God, the Titan." That the Jews would associate such worship with a special "abomination" is indicated by Ezek. viii. 16—18, where the worship of the sun at the door of the temple comes as the climax of "abominations" and prepares the way for the slaughter of Israel by the six destroyers.

[**2942*** (i) *n*] These facts may have a two-fold importance. In the first place, if the author supplied material for the Fourth Gospel, they prepare us for symbolical uses of numbers in that work (not indeed for symbolism of the same openly poetic character, but still for numerical symbolism). In the second place, they shew the insecurity of arguments as to chronology based on the numbers in this book. Suppose a tradition about " three heads " (borrowed from Daniel's tradition about Antiochus Epiphanes) to have referred originally not to the Flavian family but to the three short-lived successors of Nero—namely, Galba, Otho and Vitellius—during a time when the Empire was supposed to have received a deadly wound. As time went on, it might be adapted to the Flavian family, with a suggestion of the returning Nero.

[**2942*** (i) *o*] We may illustrate the state of things by the old prophecy (Bacon's *Essays*, 35) "When HEMPE is spun, England's done." At first, " Hempe " might be spelt with a final P, and the meaning would be that England would be ruined when Mary and Philip reigned: then, the E being added, it might suit those who (before the Armada) regarded England as destined to be destroyed under Elizabeth. The last interpretation would be that, after Elizabeth's reign was over, " England " was merged in " Great Britain."

Comp. Jerome's account of the Jewish interpretation of the end of Dan. ix, where a period of "three and a half years" is mentioned as occurring (1) under Vespasian, (2) under Hadrian, so as to make up a divided "week" (of years).

THE DATE OF THE APOCALYPSE [2942*]

§ 3. *Parallelism between John and Ezekiel*

[2942* (ii)] The determination of the date of the Apocalypse might not be affected, but our estimate of the writer or of the writing would be affected, by the proof of a hypothesis that he or his editor had incorporated, in his accounts of things that he *had* seen, whole documents—and, amongst them, pre-Christian documents—about things that he *had not* seen. Such a hypothesis does not seem to me proved or probable. The undoubted differences of view taken in different parts of the book are easily explicable if the author had been, from his youth, one of the "Boanerges" in the sense given by Origen (2969—77), a receiver of "thunders," or voices, from heaven, accompanied by visions, a genuine Seer. Even those who dispute his claims to be a Seer must admit that he is a poet—imbued indeed

---

Irenæus, when giving his conjectures as to the Number of the Beast, says that there is (v. 30. 3) "no want of names possessing this number." This remark, and the early variation of 666 and 616, imply that, from the first, the Number was obscure and probably based on some local and transient vernacular talk.

[2942* (i) *p*] Not that the author of this book would be himself likely to manipulate prophecies in this fashion. But he might accept them as manipulated by others, and as reported to him in the quarries of Patmos by Roman fellow-Christians. And these predictions, in various shapes, blending with his dreams and visions, might be moulded by him into harmony with his own broad and general conception of the pending and imminent conflict between the WAS and the IS and the COMING on the one side, and, on the other, the *was*, and the *is not*, and the *going into destruction*.

[2942* (i) *q*] For "Titus" transliterated as "Teitous" in the Talmud, see Levy ii. 154 *a*. "Teit" (*ib.* 153 *b*) means "mire," "slime," and a demon is addressed as "Son of *mire*, son of *the unclean* (טמא), son of *clay* (טינא)!" According to Kohut, the last two should be read as names of spirits of darkness, "*Temo, Tena.*" Compare the variations of the name of *Tineius* Rufus A.D. 132 governor of Judæa (Schürer Div. i. Vol. 2, p. 263). In his Chron. Jerome calls him "*Tinnius* Rufus," but on Dan. ix 25 foll., *quoting from Jews*, he calls him "*Timus* Ru(f)fus," and on Zech. viii. 16, again quoting from Jews, he has (abl.) *T. Annio* Rufo. This has been corrected conjecturally into *Turannio*. But it is perhaps Jerome's attempt to give a Jewish nickname. The name *Tineius* lent itself to Jewish jests (somewhat like "Boney" in English for "Buonaparte"). TANNIUS may represent a form of the Jewish "Tena," "*clay*," and TIMUS may represent "Temo," "*the unclean.*" Another name for this Rufus in the Talmud is "Turnus," *i.e.* "*Tyrant.*" Schürer (Div. i. Vol. 2, pp. 304—5)—who also gives, as a frequent form, "מונוסטרופוס" (sic) Tunustrufus" (like "Istrahel")—says that this is "only a corruption" of Tineius. I should prefer to call it possibly a nickname, or play upon "Tineius," a *wilful* "corruption." Playing upon names is a characteristic of Hebrew literature from the earliest times.

with the prophetic poetry of Israel, as the *Pilgrim's Progress* is imbued with Scripture, but no more a copyist than Bunyan—and must recognise that poets cannot be expected to have, or to aim at, the exactness of historians.

John's treatment of history may be illustrated from Ezekiel, who, more than any other writer, has contributed to shape and inspire the Apocalypse—in its outline, its imagery, its expressions, and its profound sense of the correspondence between the visible and the invisible and of the domination of the latter. Now Ezekiel, whose prophetic work (Hastings' *Dict.* "Ezek." p. 814) "extended over a period of not less than 22 years," instead of cancelling an unfulfilled prophecy, is said to have written (*ib.* 818) "a supplementary oracle," many years afterwards, "to counteract the impression produced by the non-fulfilment of the original prediction"; he also (*ib.* 816) "calls up from the past the vanished cities of Samaria and Sodom, and treats them as if they had a present and real existence and a real interest in the unfolding of the divine purpose"; and again (*ib.* 817) "in the signs of chap. iv the prophet appears to represent simultaneously two facts—the siege of Jerusalem and the captivity of the two branches of the Hebrew nation."

Yet almost all commentators agree that the book of Ezekiel is written (subject to a little revision) by one hand. The same inference appears to me true about the Apocalypse, in spite of one or two difficult passages—in particular, the Measuring for the Temple, and the Birth of the Messiah. As to the latter, see **2942*** (xi) foll. As to the former, see **2942*** (ii) *a—c* and (iv) *a—c*. The reader should note that both in Ezekiel and in Zechariah the Measuring for the Temple takes place *after* the old Temple has fallen. The fall is the *raison d'être* of the "measuring." As to all the visions, it may be usefully borne in mind that the visions of John, the son of thunder, say in A.D. 40 in Jerusalem, might be very different from those that he had in A.D. 96 in the quarries of Patmos[1].

"THE GREAT CITY"

[1] [**2942*** (ii) *a*] No doubt, the Measuring for the Temple (Rev. xi. 1—13) presents the appearance of (*Enc. Bibl.* col. 209) "a fragment interpolated." Hastings' *Dict.* Vol. iv. p. 252 *a* asserts that "its Jewish origin is unmistakable," and that "its evident date (before 70)" is "much earlier than the book as a whole." But the description of the two Witnesses (Rev. xi. 8, "And their *carcase* (sic) [is] on the street of the Great City, which is called spiritually Sodom and Egypt, where also their Lord was crucified") would be admitted by all not to proceed, in its entirety, from a

THE DATE OF THE APOCALYPSE [2942*]

"Jewish origin," not, at least, in the sense of "non-Christian." On this, see **2942*** (xix) foll.

[**2942*** (ii) *b*] "Great city" occurs elsewhere in the Bible, but always applied to foreign cities as also in this book (Gen. x. 12; Josh. x. 2; Jonah i. 2 etc. (Nineveh); Rev. xvi. 19, xvii. 18, xviii. 10, 16, 18, 19, 21 (Babylon)). Jer. xxii. 8 "Why hath the Lord done thus unto this *great city*?" can hardly be called an exception, as it is not uttered by the prophet but is put into the mouth of foreigners. In Rev. xxi. 10 (A.V.) "that *great city*, the holy Jerusalem" is a corruption; and R.V. omits "great" without even mentioning it in the margin. Prof. Swete says, "The epithet ἡ μεγάλη is one which a Jew might not unnaturally give to the capital of his native land (cf. *Orac. Sibyll.* v. 154, 226, 413)...." Instead of "not unnaturally," I should prefer to say "as a rule, only where the Jew regards the capital of his native land as estranged from Jehovah." But I must admit that the use in *Orac. Sibyll.* breaks the rule because v. 154 (rep. 226) μεγάλην τε πόλιν λαόν τε δίκαιον couples "great city" with "righteous people." This suggests a Jewish hand, and *Orac. Sibyll.* v is generally attributed to an Alexandrian Jew. But comp. *ib.* 422—3 ἅγιόν τε νεὼν ἐποίησεν Ἔνσαρκον, and 256—7 ἀπ' αἰθέρος ἔξοχος ἀνήρ, Οὗ παλάμας ἥπλωσεν ἐπὶ ξύλον πολύκαρπον, Ἑβραίων ὁ ἄριστος ὃς ἠέλιόν ποτε στήσεν. These references to "the *Temple in the flesh*," and the return of Jesus the Son of Nun in Jesus of Nazareth who "*stretched out His hands on the fruitful Tree* [*of the Cross*]," indicate a Christian. The book, then, may be from a Jew but from a Christian Jew, or it may contain Christian interpolations. In either case μεγάλη πόλις may be borrowed from Rev. xi. 8.

[**2942*** (ii) *c*] If the writer of the Apocalypse called Jerusalem "the great city," he probably meant that it had become foreign to Jehovah, like Nineveh or Babylon—"great" instead of "holy." Otherwise the passage (xi. 8) might refer to Rome, the New Babylon, which is elsewhere always, in this book, "the Great City." The "two witnesses" cast out unburied in the Great City—two being the number prescribed by the Law ("in the mouth of two witnesses")—might represent the Christian martyrs destroyed by Babylon the Great. To be left "unburied" was the fate of many Christian martyrs, who "fed the crows" on the cross. Origen (on Mt. xxiv. 30, Lomm. iv. 314) says, with reference to Rev. xi. 8, "sive totus mundus, sive Judæa."

[**2942*** (ii) *d*] It should, however, be added that the description of these two Witnesses may have been suggested by the fate of Ananus the High Priest and his kinsman Jesus, who were killed by the Idumæans (A.D. 67) and cast out unburied. Josephus—although in his *Antiquities* xx. 9. 1 (if his text has not been Christianized) he takes a somewhat unfavourable view of Ananus as causing the death of James the Just—declares in his *Wars of the Jews* that this brutality (which was quite abhorrent to Jewish feeling) indicated that Jerusalem was a "polluted" city. "God," he says (*Bell.* iv. 5. 2) "cut off its best friends because He had sentenced it to destruction, and because He willed that the Holy Places should be thoroughly purged with fire." And he describes the horror with which the citizens saw "those who had but lately worn the sacred vestments" now slain and "cast out naked to be the food of dogs and wild beasts." Some Jewish tradition of this outrage may have been blended with a Christian vision in which it was predicted that a doom would fall on the Great City of Rome or Jerusalem, when the two Martyrs, or Witnesses, of the Christians, rose up from the dead, to bring down vengeance on the persecutors of the Church. But see **2942*** (xix) foll.

§ 4. *The Seven Churches*

[2942* (iii)] The later date of the Apocalypse is favoured by the authoritative tone of the Apostle in addressing the Seven Churches; by his intimate knowledge of their characteristics and circumstances; and by the long standing of heresies and of persecutions[1].

---

[1] [2942* (iii) *a*] The language of the author to the Seven Churches indicates that he had already lived a long time among or near them, and that he held a position of recognised authority among them. Now it is generally supposed that John the Apostle remained in Jerusalem till a short time before the siege, say A.D. 66 or 65: and, up—or nearly up—to that time, St Paul, and not St John, would be the prominent Apostle among the Seven Churches (and especially at Ephesus where he had spent (Acts xix. 10) two years). Suppose John to have left Jerusalem A.D. 65. He comes to Asia, remains at Ephesus for, say, a couple of years till A.D. 67; is then (according to the Neronian theory) arrested, tried, sentenced, banished to Patmos, sees the Apocalypse, writes the Apocalypse—and all this in the short space of one or two years: is it likely that he should write to the Seven Churches as he does, not only in a tone of high authority, but with so detailed a knowledge of their circumstances and antecedents?

[2942* (iii) *b*] The descriptions of the Seven Churches (Rev. ii, iii) point rather to A.D. 96 than to A.D. 68. The mention of the first Christian "sect" by a sectarian name ("Nicolaitans," Rev. ii. 6, not "the followers of Nicolaos") suggests a date much later than any of the Epistles of St Paul. To the same conclusion, though less directly, tends the use of such terms and names as "the deep things of Satan" (ii. 24), "the teaching of Balaam" (ii. 14) and the allusion to "Jezebel" (ii. 20). "The deep things of Satan" appears to be an ironical parody of the Gnostic phrase "the deep things of Gnosis, or Knowledge"; and the names "Balaam" and "Jezebel" presuppose in the Asian Churches a familiarity of considerable standing with the allusions to certain heretics and heretical habits. The use of "their Lord" (for Christ) in the nom. (xi. 8) and of "Lord's day" (i. 10) for the Sunday, are also indications of a late date.

Also it is hard to suppose that in A.D. 68 the Church of Sardis had lived long enough to shew such signs of advanced corruption as appear in iii. 1: "Thou hast a name that thou livest and thou art dead": even the Church of Ephesus has so far lost its first love that its "candlestick" will be moved out of its place unless it repents. There is nothing in St Paul's Epistles nor in the Acts of the Apostles (even in the way of predictions such as are found in the Pastoral Epistles, written, says Lightfoot, probably as late as A.D. 66 or A.D. 67) which would prepare us for such a state of things in A.D. 68—9.

[2942* (iii) *c*] Note in particular the allusions to martyrs, who had been slain for the name of Christ some time before. The phrase "in the days of" (ii. 13) ("*in the days of* Antipas, my martyr, my faithful one, who was slain among you where Satan dwelleth") suggests that Antipas lived several years before the date of writing; and, if that date were A.D. 68—9, an early and exceptional martyrdom occurring, say, A.D. 48 or 58, would probably have found mention, if not in the New Testament, at least in ecclesiastical writers. But if the author wrote about A.D. 96, he might naturally allude thus to a martyrdom that took place about

§ 5. *The Measuring for the Temple*

[2942* (iv)] The measuring for the Temple, which is sometimes taken as an indication that the building was regarded by the author of the Apocalypse as still standing, is, on the contrary—when taken in conjunction with the precedents of "measuring" in Ezekiel and Zechariah—an indication that the Temple *had been* destroyed[1].

A.D. 76 or 86 (one of the sporadic persecutions that followed the persecution of Nero in A.D. 64).

To the same effect is vi. 10, 11 "How long, O Master, the holy and true, dost thou not judge and avenge our blood on them that dwell on the earth?" This is the utterance that accompanies the opening of "the fifth seal," and it comes from "the souls of them that had been slain for the word of God"—intelligible enough in A.D. 96 when the souls of those who had suffered in the terrible Neronian persecution (A.D. 64—5) had waited unavenged for more than thirty years, but less intelligible in A.D. 68—9 when they had only waited for four or five years.

[2942* (iii) *d*] Moreover, it is implied, 1st, that in the persecution contemplated by the author, the Christians are to be condemned not for secret or open crimes but as part of a systematic war of the Beast against the Church, in which the test applied to the martyr is, "Wilt thou worship the Beast?"; 2nd, that the whole world is divided into those who will and those who will not thus worship, and that the latter alone are to be saved (xiii. 8): "And all that dwell on the earth shall worship him, everyone whose name hath not been written in the book of life of the Lamb...."

This does not apply so well to the persecution under Nero as to that under Domitian. The latter, claiming systematically to be called "dominus deusque," prepared the way for the anticipations of the Apocalypse.

[1] [2942* (iv) *a*] John borrows (2998 (xxvi) foll.) from Ezekiel (Ezek. i. 5—28) the four "living creatures," the "throne," the "appearance of a man," the "rainbow," (*ib*. ix. 2) the man with the ink-horn who sets a mark on the foreheads of those who are to be saved, (*ib*. iii. 3) the roll or book of prophecy which is to be sweet first and afterwards bitter, and (above all) the New Jerusalem (beside the river of life (*ib*. xlvii. 9) with trees that are to bring forth new fruit each month and leaves that are to be for healing (*ib*. 12)) whose gates are named after the twelve tribes (*ib*. xlviii. 31) and whose name shall be (*ib*. 35) "the Lord is there." When, therefore, John borrows from the same prophet the "measuring for the temple," we should be prepared to find that he uses this last imagery in the spirit, and with something of the purpose, of his predecessor. Now Ezekiel tells us that his "measurement" occurred (xl. 1) "*in the fourteenth year after that the city was smitten*": and the object of the vision is clearly to encourage his deserted countrymen with the thought that *their Temple will be restored hereafter.*

By "borrowing" it is not meant that John plagiarizes or copies. For example, his "four living creatures" are in many respects different from those of Ezekiel. But he gives us the impression of having meditated long on Ezekiel's prophecies and on the events that caused them, and of writing like a prophet who had lived through similar events and had received similar revelations and visions—similar, yet not the same, because of the Voice that said, "Behold I make all things new."

THE DATE OF THE APOCALYPSE

§ 6. *Other arguments for* A.D. 96

[**2942*** (v)] The later date is also favoured by apparent allusions to special events in the reign of Domitian, such as the coincidence of corn-famine and vine-plenty, and the wealth and pride of Laodicea,

[**2942*** (iv) *b*] Again, John borrows from Zechariah (Zech. i. 8, comp. vi. 2, 3) the "four horses," (*ib*. iv. 2) "the candlestick with the seven lamps," (*ib*. iv. 2, 3, 14) the "two olive-trees on the right and left of the candlestick" (which represent, for Zechariah, "the two anointed ones that stand by the Lord of the whole earth," and for John (Rev. xi. 3, 4) the "two witnesses," whose emblems also "stand before the Lord of the earth"). Also, the Woman whose name is Wickedness (Zech. v. 7, 8), who is carried into the land of Shinar or Babylon, is the prototype of the Woman (Rev. xvii. 3, 5) who is Babylon the Great, the Mother of the harlots and abominations of the earth. Now by Zechariah, as by Ezekiel, the "measurement" for the Temple is introduced as a consolation to those who are mourning for its destruction (Zech. i. 16): "Therefore thus saith the Lord, I am returned to Jerusalem with mercies; my house shall be built in it, saith the Lord of hosts"; and then, after a vision of the "four horns" that scattered Israel, and the four friendly "smiths" who are to cast down the "horns," the prophet sees "*a man with a measuring line*" who is to *measure Jerusalem with the view of rebuilding it*. All this occurs (Zech. i. 12) "three score and ten years" after the desolation of Jerusalem. Thus the argument of the last paragraph applies here again. Borrowing so much from Zechariah's imagery, John seems likely to have borrowed it with something of his predecessor's spirit and meaning. And the argument is all the stronger because the precedent is twofold. *When two great prophets had thus stamped the "measuring" of the Temple with a definite apocalyptic meaning, it is not likely that John would have departed from it.*

[**2942*** (iv) *c*] Not, of course, that John hoped (as Ezekiel and Zechariah hoped) that the *material* Temple would be rebuilt. His revelation taught him that this was not to be. Even in the beginning of his vision of the measurement he diverges significantly from Ezekiel. The measurement of Ezekiel had begun from the outer courts and worked inwards; John (Rev. xi. 2) is warned to "reject and measure not the court that is without the Temple, for it hath been given unto the nations." He therefore measures only the "sanctuary of God and the altar and them that worship therein." And he gives us none of Ezekiel's "cubits." He has already given us the mystical numbers of those who are saved, twelve times twelve thousand (vii. 4). And in the end, when New Jerusalem at last appears, he sees "no temple therein; for the Lord God Almighty and the Lamb are the temple thereof." For him, therefore, the New Temple was the Church, the Body of Christ, the Congregation of the Saints.

All this confirms—and indeed almost suffices by itself to prove—a date some time after the fall of Jerusalem. John's attitude is (except in respect of good taste and beauty of expression) like that of the Pseudo-Barnabas who wished to persuade "the unhappy Jews" (xvi. 1) that their cravings for the rebuilding of the Temple were useless. Barnabas urges that the Temple is to be (xvi. 10) "a spiritual temple built unto the Lord." Both apparently assume that the material Temple has fallen long ago; both agree that it is vain to expect that the structure will be otherwise than spiritually rebuilt.

after that luxurious city had repaired its ruin (caused by a well-known disastrous earthquake) without having recourse to aid from the imperial treasury[1].

[2942* (vi)] The Apocalypse, for the most part, uses numbers mystically, not historically; and the author seems to deal with historical facts in the same way, believing that what has been in the past will be repeated in the future. This applies, perhaps, not only to events predicted by Ezekiel and Zechariah, but also to traditions about the past horrors of the siege of Jerusalem. His imagery was derived from what he had heard, as well as from what he had read. And what he had heard about the woes of Jerusalem

---

[1] [2942* (v) *a*] Rev. vi. 6 "a measure of wheat for a denarius......and the oil and the wine hurt thou not," *i.e.* a day's bread alone would cost a whole day's wage. This would mean famine for the poor, and the continuance of luxury for the rich. The *Chronicon* of Eusebius states that Domitian, apparently towards the close of his reign, prohibited the planting of vines "in the cities." Suetonius (*Domitian* ch. vii) gives us the reason. Wine was extremely abundant, and corn scarce. Domitian issued an edict that no one was to plant new vineyards in Italy and that at least half of the vines in the provinces should be cut down. A coincidence of cheap wine and dear corn might have happened before; but it needed an imperial edict to stamp the event with the importance attached to it in the Apocalypse. Not that the author intended to gain credit by a "prophecy after the event." Such prophecies, common in the Sibylline Poems, are not to be found in the Apocalypse. But he has in mind future scourges, in which, as in the past, misery will cause moral evil. In describing these anticipations, he borrows from recent historical fact.

[2942* (v) *b*] Rev. iii. 17 represents Laodicea as saying "I am rich and have gotten riches and have need of nothing." Now although this city was indeed famous for its wealth, it was not wealthy at the alleged paullo-post-Neronian date of the Apocalypse (A.D. 68—9). At that time such language would have been peculiarly inappropriate. For it was then still suffering from the effects of an earthquake which had utterly prostrated it (Tacit. *Ann.* xiv. 27, Euseb. *Chronicon* ii. p. 154). Eusebius places the earthquake A.D. 64, and Lightfoot gives good reasons (*Coloss.* p. 39) for preferring his date to that given by Tacitus (A.D. 60). But in any case we know from inscriptions (Boeckh 3935 and 3936) that the amphitheatre was not rebuilt till A.D. 79 and its race-course a little later.

In A.D. 80, the year after the amphitheatre was rebuilt, the author of the Fourth Sibylline Poem (l. 107) after mentioning the terrible earthquake that had cast down "hapless" Laodicea, might naturally congratulate it on "again standing erect," and in A.D. 96 the only result of the calamity might be the proud consciousness of the citizens that (Tacit. *Ann.* xiv. 27) they had remedied it without imperial aid. But in A.D. 68—9 how could a Greek city that had neither amphitheatre nor stadium—and no prospect of either for some ten years—be represented as saying "I am in need of nothing"?

in the past might naturally suggest forms and combinations in his visions of woes to come[1].

§ 7. *John's view of the Fall of Jerusalem*

[2942* (vii)] It has been thought by some that the author must necessarily have written before the siege of Jerusalem, because he feels a hope that, even if God should inflict punishment on Jerusalem, only a part of the city and its inhabitants will perish; that such as remain will amend, and the city, together with the temple, will be preserved until the appearing of the Lord.

Presumably, this inference is drawn from the following passages:

(*a*) (xi. 2) "The court which is without the temple leave without and measure not; for it hath been given unto the nations: and the holy city shall they tread under foot forty and two months." This is, seemingly, supposed by some to mean that the temple itself will *not* be "given to the nations."

(*b*) (xi. 13) "And in that hour there was a great earthquake, and the tenth part of the city fell; and there were killed in the earthquake

---

[1] [2942* (vi) *a*] In the First Woe a description is given of (ix. 3—11) locusts with scorpions' stings, like horses prepared for war, taken from Joel's (i. 4—ii. 9) well-known description of the locust-plague. These, however, are not to destroy herbage but to "*torture* (βασανισθήσονται)" men for "five months"; they are to have the teeth of lions but "*the hair of women*."

It is not at all likely that the "five months" refer to the actual duration of the investment of the city, from April to September. Such literal arithmetical allusions to the past (or perhaps they might be called collusions with the past) are not in the manner of the Apocalypse. "Five," as often throughout the Old Testament, means "a few." "The hair of women" is doubtless intended to indicate a kind of monstrosity of cruelty. It is to be unexpectedly revolting, combining feminine aspect with masculine ferocity. Now Josephus, describing the "tortures," or "torments," perpetrated on the citizens by some of the Idumæans or Galilæans, declares that they *assumed the garb of women*. He says of their victims (*Bell*. iv. 6. 3) "Those who so survived congratulated those who had died before them, as being at rest already. So did those *under torture* (αἰκιζόμενοι) in the prisons declare that even the unburied corpses were by comparison happier": and (v. 1. 5) "*they were tormented* (ἐβασανίζοντο) without even daring to open their lips in groaning." Of some of these murderers (iv. 9. 10) he says that in the midst of plundering, outrage, and murder, they dressed, walked, painted and "*dressed their hair* (κόμας συνθετιζόμενοι) *like women*," and again, "*While wearing the appearance of women* they slew with their right hands." It is probable that some account of these *torturing women-fiends*, brought to John in Asia, suggested this particular feature in his account of the locust-torturers of the Second Woe.

names of men seven thousand; and the rest were affrighted and gave glory to God." This is, seemingly, supposed by some to mean that "only a part"—and a very small part—only "seven thousand" of the citizens of Jerusalem, will perish. Now that anticipation is glaringly contradicted by the history of the siege. Hence (it has been inferred) the prediction must have been before the siege.

[2942* (viii)] Against this view it may be repeated that John's general tendency is to use numbers mystically; that the forty and two months, that is, three and a half years, may represent the period described as (Dan. vii. 25, xii. 7) "a time, times, and half a time." This is a prophetic phrase that might be variously applied. For example, it was interpreted by the Jews themselves (according to Jerome (2942* (i) *o*)) as referring both to the war against Vespasian and to the war against Hadrian. Similarly, before the First Woe (ix. 12 "one woe is past") "a third part" of "trees," "rivers" etc. is destroyed; and, before the Second Woe (xi. 14 "the second woe is past") mention is made of the destruction of the (ix. 15—18) "third part" of men. But the number would seem not intended to be taken literally. There is only one passage in O.T. where "a third part" is connected with destruction, and that is in Ezekiel's (v. 2—12) prediction of the destruction of Jerusalem. There the context is different. But still it seems probable that it was from Ezekiel that John derived the phrase though he modified its application.

As regards the difficult expression (following "the tenth part of the city") (xi. 13) "there were killed...(lit.) *names of men*[1] *seven thousands*"—which has not as yet been satisfactorily explained from merely Greek usage—it seems probable that it may contain some

---

Does ὀνόματα ever mean "persons"?

[1] [2942* (viii) *a*] On Rev. xi. 13 "there were killed in the earthquake names of men seven thousands," Prof. Swete says "i.e. ἄνθρωποι, 'persons': cf. iii. 4, note; to the examples of this use of ὄνομα given by Deissmann, *Bible Studies* p. 196 f., may now be added those published by Grenfell and Hunt in the Index to the *Tebtunis Papyri*."

This use of ὄνομα appears to me not proved. It appears to be occasionally used in such a way that we might *substitute for it "person" without injury to the sense*. But even this is in contexts that imply writing, or accounts; and even there the word is not identical with "person." As John's use of the term here may illustrate his style, I give, below, some facts bearing on the subject.

[2942* (viii) *b*] *Tebt. Pap.* 24 (64—5) speaks of dishonest officials who "have transferred their duties to their sons (εἰς τοὺς υἱούς) who are quite young men (edd.) *and sometimes to other persons altogether* (ὅτε δὲ καὶ τύχοι καὶ εἰς ἄλλον (i.e. ἄλλων)

[2942*] THE DATE OF THE APOCALYPSE

ὀνόμ[α]τα)." The writer might have said "*to others*," εἰς ἄλλους, parall. to εἰς τοὺς υἱούς. But he means "to *names* of other people." The editors take this, apparently, as "not even [like their sons] of the same name as themselves." I should prefer "to [mere] names of others," *i.e.* "to people nominally so-and-so, but really themselves in disguise, their tools." The foll., xxviii. (Introd.) ὀνόματος παστοφόρου, xxxii. 22 τοῦ υἱοῦ τὸ ὄνομα, xxxviii. 13 οὗ τὸ(ν) [ὄνο]μα ἀγνοῶι, xxxix. 28 ὧν τὰ ὀνόματα ἀγνοῶι—are not instances of ὄνομα = person. These are all the instances of ὄνομα in *Tebt.* Index. I have found no instance of the above use of ὄνομα in the Indices of *Oxyr. Pap.* vols. iii and iv.

[2942* (viii) *c*] Deissmann's *Bible Studies* pp. 196—7 quotes B. U. 113 (11) (143 A.D.) ἑκάστῳ ὀνόματι παρα(γενομένῳ). This is possibly more correct than the B.U. text, which gives παραγ(ενομένῳ). It should be compared with B.U. 265 (18) (148 A.D.) [ἑκάστῳ ὀνόμ]ατι παράκ[ει]ται. Both of these are "claims (δικαιώματα)" from "veterans" (see *Egypt Expl. Pap. Fayûm* 319 ἀντίγρ(αφον) [δ]ικαιωμάτων ἐπικρ[ίσεως]) for ἐπίκρισις. Comp. B.U. 780 (154—6 A.D.) where it is stated that the "veterans" παρεγένον[το πρὸς ἐπίκρισιν...] and then that "*the claims they presented are attached to each name*," ἃ δὲ παρέ[θεντο δικαιώματα ἑκάστῳ ὀνό]ματι παράκιται.

From these facts I should infer that ὄνομα means "*name*" in all these formularies, and that, in the first of them, παρα (not παραγ) should be read as a short form of παράκειται. In all of them, "the claim is attached to each *name*." For παρακεῖσθαι thus used, comp. *Tebt. Pap.* No. 27 (8—9) πέμψαθ' ἡμῖν τὰς κατ' ἄνδρα γραφάς, παρακειμένων οὗ ἕκαστος ἔχει κλήρου, "You will send us the lists of individuals, *with a statement, attached to each,* of their several holdings."

[2942* (viii) *d*] Deissmann also alleges B.U. 531, ii. 9 τὰ περιγεινόμενα ἐνοίκια πρὸς ἕκαστον ὄνομα τῶν τρυγώντων γραφήτωι. But this seems simply a request that the amount should be written "against the *name* of each of the vintagers."

Somewhat more to the point is B.U. 388 i. 16 ταβέλλαι δύ[ο] ἐλευθερώσεων τοῦ αὐτοῦ ὀνόματος διαφόροις χρόνοις (cf. ii. 35 πῶς [ο]ὖν τοῦ Εὐκαίρου δύ[ο] ταβέλλαι ἐλευθερίας εὑ[ρί]σ[κον]ται;). But the context explains this. Two deeds of emancipation had been found, *made out for the same name* (Eukairos) *but at different dates.* It was suspected that one was a forgery. A barrister, suspecting this, would not be safe in assuming that the two deeds referred to the same person, but he was safe in stating that they *belonged to the same name*: "There have been brought into court two deeds of emancipations *belonging to the same name* (τοῦ αὐτοῦ ὀνόματος) of different dates, and I doubt whether the writing was that of the deceased. For how can he have emancipated *the same man* (τὸν αὐτόν) twice?" Here it would hardly have been possible to use "name" with the *verb* ("emancipate a name"); but, in the special circumstances, the use of "name" with the *noun* ("emancipations of the same name," meaning "deeds of emancipation connected with, or referring to, the same name") is intelligible for brevity.

[2942* (viii) *e*] The frequent use of "nomen" in Latin lists and accounts suggests that ὄνομα may have a Latin derived meaning in B.U. 390 (A.D. 200) where ἀπορικὰ ὀνόματα καὶ ἄλλα τετελευτηκότα seems to mean "names," in the sense of "securities," like the Latin " bonum nomen ": "*names*, some little better than those of paupers, others deceased." 'Απορικά perhaps means "not quite ἄποροι but nearly." It is not in Steph. *Thes.*

[2942* (viii) *f*] But all this is quite different from Rev. xi. 13 "there were killed in the earthquake *names of men* seven thousands." And that it needs explanation is indicated by a commentary printed by Cramer on Rev. xi. 13, "ἰδικώτερον, for

THE DATE OF THE APOCALYPSE [2942*]

allusion to numbers mentioned in ancient Hebrew history as well as to the notion of "names" written in the book of life. "Seven thousand," in the days of Elijah, represented the faithful remnant, and the Epistle to the Romans had reminded Christians of this, long before the destruction of Jerusalem. "Seven thousand," also, conquering Ben-hadad, are described as (1 K. xx. 15) "all the people

---

the 'names' were not [literally] 'killed'." Perhaps the commentator takes the meaning to be that the "names," or "memorials," perished metaphorically, as well as the bodies literally (comp. Ps. ix. 6 "their very *memorial* is perished"), and regards the former, the metaphorical meaning, as predominant. There may be an allusion to "the book of life," or "the book of the living."

[2942* (viii) *g*] "The book of life" or "the book of the living" (see Lightf. and Wetstein on Phil. iv. 3 and Charles on *Enoch* 47) means "the register of the covenant people" (Lightf.) "perhaps confined originally to temporal blessings," but "in itself a witness to higher hopes." In N.T. it is very rare, not occurring apart from Rev. (iii. 5, xiii. 8, xvii. 8, xx. 12, 15, xxi. 27) except in Phil. iv. 3. But Lk. x. 20, Heb. xii. 23 have the phrase "written in heaven." With the "*names*" on such a "*register*" the notion of "numbering" was naturally connected as in the numbering of Israel (Numb. i. 2) "according *to the number of the names*." So a parenthesis in the Acts tells us that, when the Church met for their first public act, the election of a twelfth Apostle, (Acts i. 15) "there was a multitude of *names* [gathered] together about a hundred and twenty." The next mention of a number in connexion with the Church is (Acts ii. 41) "there were added in that day about three thousand *souls*." As "souls" suggests salvation, so "names" suggests the first "numbering" of Israel after the spirit, and an enrolling in the Book of Life.

[2942* (viii) *h*] The "blotting out" of a name from the Book of Life meant originally a disfranchisement of a citizen of Israel, but conveyed a notion of perishing in the sight of God, that is, of real perishing. Ezekiel says concerning the false prophets, who (xiii. 16) prophesied "peace" for Jerusalem when there was "no peace," (*ib*. 9) "they shall not be in the council of my people, *neither shall they be written in the writing* (marg. *register*) *of the house of Israel*." Origen interprets this (Lomm. xiv. 213) "They shall *be blotted out from the book of the living*." Some meaning of this kind appears to be indicated by Rev. xi. 13.

[2942* (viii) *i*] Wetstein, on Rev. xi. 13, says, "*Nomina virorum* sunt viri nobiles et principes," and refers to 2 K. xxiv. 16 "all the men of might, even seven thousand" (on which *Sanhedr*. 38 *a* interprets the context about "smiths" metaphorically, as meaning "teachers," but says nothing about "the men of might"). Did Wetst. regard "names of men" as identical with the Hebrew "men of name(s)" which occurs in Gen. vi. 4, Numb. xvi. 2, 1 Chr. v. 24, xii. 30? "Men of name(s)" may mean "notorious" as well as "glorious" (see *Beresh. R.* on Gen. vi. 4). The thought of "a name" among men, simultaneous with a "death" in the sight of God, may be illustrated by Rev. iii. 1 "Thou hast a *name* that thou livest, but thou art *dead*." But "*men of name(s)*," in any sense, is quite distinct from "*names of men*." The latter implies names on a list. In Rev. iii. 4, the "names" are regarded as still on the list; but in Rev. xi. 13, as "names of men once inscribed on the register of the Kingdom of God and now struck off as dead."

of Israel"! But again, in the days of Jeremiah—in a context difficult to reconcile with itself and with Jeremiah lii. 28—the position is reversed (2 K. xxiv. 16) "and all the men of might, even seven thousand...the king of Babylon brought captive to Babylon," and (*ib*. 15) "none remained save the poorest sort of the people of the land." Christian Jews at the end of the first century might say that history had repeated itself—only spiritually. The "men of might" had perished from the Kingdom of God; the citizenship of the New Jerusalem had been given to "the poorest sort." And this feeling may be latent here in the Seer's description of the fall of Jerusalem as he looks back to it through the interval of a quarter of a century, rejoicing in the growth of Israel after the Spirit: "The 'court without the temple' was given unto the nations, but the 'temple,' the body of Christ, remained. The whole City of God was shaken by His judgment, but mercy prevailed. In Elijah's time, the 'remnant' was but 'seven thousand' and the rest were to perish. But in this last judgment, the numbers were as in the days of Jeremiah. Only seven thousand names were written down for death, 'The rest were affrighted and gave glory to the God of heaven.' This is the Second Woe. It is past. But there is a heavier Woe to come, the third Woe, which is to fall on Babylon! Behold, the third Woe cometh quickly." See **2942*** (xiii)*f*.

[**2942*** (ix)] Some may feel it difficult to believe that a Jew could take such a view of the destruction of Jerusalem, even when softened by the lapse of twenty-five years. Yet Paul wrote, " All Israel shall be saved," when half a generation of Israel had passed away, from the Christian point of view, unsaved. We can hardly make sufficient allowance, in our days, for the Christ-absorption of those early Jewish Christians who found the true Israel and the true Temple nowhere but in Christ.

In any case there is much more difficulty in the hypothesis of a literal meaning and a Neronian date. If we take the writer's words literally and not mystically, he anticipates that only 7000 of the citizens of Jerusalem will perish! But already, before March A.D. 68, there were (Joseph. *Bell*. iv. 5. 1) 8500 corpses lying in the outer court of the temple! The city, too, was divided into three factions warring against each other (*ib*. v. 1. 3) and causing constant slaughter. Josephus (*ib*. vi. 9. 3) makes the numbers of those who perished in the city during the whole of the war, 1,100,000, besides those who were slain in Palestine and the surrounding districts. Grant that Josephus exaggerates, yet would not contemporary rumour also exaggerate? And would not John, if he had dealt in literal numbers, have been compelled to rely on contemporary rumour? Is it possible then that, in the midst of such literal reports of the deaths of thousands of his countrymen, John, about A.D. 69, should predict in a literal sense that the number of those who would fall would be 7000? A quarter of a century afterwards, when this mass of horrors was ancient history, he might represent it under symbolical numbers as a contrast to the far more terrible retribution that he saw impending on Rome; but about A.D. 69, when the tales of daily slaughter and the numbers of those who were slain, were continually reaching his ears, was it possible for a Jew to indulge, even symbolically, in an understatement so cold if regarded as a symbol, and so false if regarded as a fact?

[2942* (x)] If the fall of Jerusalem, and the destruction of the Temple for ever, were accepted by John not only as matters of ancient history, but also as parts of the revealed will of God, then we can understand how it is that a few lines suffice to describe them, while whole chapters are reserved for the doom impending on Rome.

On the supposition that the writer, or inserter, of Rev. xi. 1—13 was a Christian, we may also allege, in favour of A.D. 96, the Synoptic predictions (probably based on actual predictions of Jesus) that the Temple, in a literal sense, would be utterly cast down and that the city would suffer terrible and unprecedented tribulation. If these Synoptic predictions have any substantial likeness to what Jesus said, how could any Christian writer, and especially an Apostle, at a time when the Roman armies were closing round Jerusalem, anticipate—as some maintain that he did—that "the City, together with the Temple," in a literal sense, would be "preserved until the appearing of the Lord"?

Some may reply, "This favours our view that the writer of this separate passage was not a Christian." But these have to explain how the Christian writer or editor of the whole book came to insert a non-Christian vision that, literally speaking, was completely falsified by results.

The safest conclusion is, that the vision was seen by John long after (or, less probably, long before) the Fall of Jerusalem; and that, in either case, the numbers of persons, days, months etc. have no historical significance.

§ 8. *The Birth of the "Man-child"*

[**2942*** (xi)] It has been contended that a non-Christian origin must be assigned to the Birth of the Messiah in xii. 1—5 foll. "And a great sign was seen in heaven; a woman arrayed with the sun, and the moon under her feet, and upon her head a crown of twelve stars; and she was with child...and behold a great red dragon...stood before the woman...that...he might devour her child...and she bare a son, a man [child] who is to shepherd all the nations with a rod of iron; and her child was caught up unto God and unto his throne."

But, far from this being the case, is it not, at bottom, the conception of a personal disciple of Christ, imbued with His doctrine about the exaltation of the "babes and sucklings" who are the signs of God's glory "above" the heavens? The Seer is so rapt with this thought of the domination of the mere "child ($τέκνον$)" that he describes Him as simply born and then "snatched up" at once to heaven away from the "dragon," who represents the prince of this world. It is very doubtful whether any Jew uninfluenced by Christ's doctrine would have ventured to describe a "child" as snatched up to the "throne of God." A somewhat similar tradition in the Jerusalem Talmud, perhaps shewing traces of Christian influence, makes no mention of God's throne[1].

It would be more reasonable to contend that Pagan combined with Christian thought to shape this story. Looking due West from his convict island, John would see Delos daily, a few leagues off. He might naturally hear from his fellow-convicts the story of its preparation for becoming the birth-place of the God of the Sun (**2942*** (xiii) *b*). This might blend with his thoughts of the preparation for the birth of the Sun of Righteousness.

John's vision of the Mother giving birth is (doubtless) influenced by Isaiah; but his vision of the Mother in heaven is not like anything in any prophet. It is, however, like what a Christian Jew might dream, or see, working in chains among convicts from Rome, when

---

[1] [**2942*** (xi) *a*] Jer. *Berach.* ii. The mother, when questioned as to what has become of her child, says (Schwab i. 42) "Storms have carried him away." Comp. *Echa Rabb.* (on Lament. i. 16, Wünsche p. 88) where the story is similarly told. In both, it is said that the birth of the babe will bring the destruction of the Temple, and also its rebuilding. But neither describes the babe as carried up "to the throne of God."

he had learned to understand the Roman reverence for the imperial Mother who (Virg. *Æn.* vi. 782—8) would "raise her spirit to the height of Olympus...like the Berecynthian Mother, rejoicing in her offspring of Gods, all dwellers in heaven, all throned on the heights above." The Vision is the answer, coming from a Christian Jew: "We, too, have our Mother in heaven, ordained from the beginning."

[2942* (xii)] The writer is saturated, no doubt, with Jewish as well as Hebrew tradition, but this saturation, and the application of Jewish symbolism to Christian illustration, are characteristics of the whole book, and not merely of parts capable of being detached from the rest. The description of the birth of the Child, not from a Virgin but from a Woman—Woman in the Greek sense of Wife, the Bride of Jehovah—is what we might have expected from a personal disciple of Christ to whom Christ's personality was everything, and by whom He was regarded as summing up all the revelation of God from the beginning, so that He seemed not the Son of Mary of Nazareth, but the Son of the crowned Mother in Heaven, the celestial Sion, the Bride of Jehovah. Nor is there anything inconsistent in the mention of the "travail" of the Mother. On the contrary we may discern in it the hand of the disciple who heard Jesus Himself say "These things are the beginning of travails," and who gave to the author of the Fourth Gospel the grounds for our Lord's Discourse containing the words, "The woman when she is in travail hath sorrow," as an illustration of the necessary trials through which the Church must pass. The non-mention of the Virgin does not prove that the writer was a non-Christian. It tends to prove that he was a Jewish disciple recognised by the Asiatic Churches as having the highest authority and the fullest knowledge of facts. From any other, towards the end of the first century, some of the Churches of Asia would have expected some mention of the Virgin, and would hardly have accepted the picture of the "Woman...being in travail[1]."

---

[1] [2942* (xii) *a*] The description of the birth is preceded by Rev. xi. 19 "And there was opened the *sanctuary* (ναός) of God that is in heaven, and there appeared the ark of his covenant...." Victorinus says "The *sanctuary* of God is the Son" and quotes Jn ii. 19—21 "the *sanctuary* (ναός) of his body."

Iren. iv. 18. 6 connects a reference to this opening of the "sanctuary" with a reference to the divine "tabernacling" (which in Jn i. 14 denotes the Incarnation) thus, "Est ergo altare in coelis (illuc enim preces nostrae et oblationes nostrae diriguntur) et templum—quemadmodum Joannes in Apocalypsi ait (xi. 19) Et *apertum est templum Dei*—et tabernaculum: *Ecce* enim, inquit (xxi. 3), *tabernaculum Dei in quo habitabit cum hominibus* (ἰδοὺ ἡ σκηνὴ τοῦ θεοῦ

[2942*] THE DATE OF THE APOCALYPSE

[2942* (xiii)] This passage (Rev. xii. 1—17), in many details, bears the impress of the mind of the author of the whole book. In particular it shews his habit of regarding history as repeating itself, so that the story of Israel in the desert of Sinai becomes the story of Christ's Church in "the wilderness of this world." The LXX's first use of the phrase "she brought forth a male child" is connected with Moses. The thought of Providence watching over the birth of the Deliverer of Israel from Egypt, might well suggest the thought of the still greater Deliverer of mankind from sin. Moses at birth (through Pharaoh) and Moses after birth (through the monsters of the Nile) is in danger of being "swallowed up" by a "dragon[1]." But

---

μετὰ τῶν ἀνθρώπων καὶ σκηνώσει μετ' αὐτῶν)." As to later commentators, Prof. Swete *ad loc.* says that "the majority take the birth-pangs to symbolize the spiritual travail of the Church," *e.g.* Hippol. *Christ. et Antichr.* 61 οὐ παύσεται ἡ ἐκκλησία γεννῶσα ἐκ καρδίας τὸν Λόγον τὸν ἐν κόσμῳ ὑπὸ ἀπίστων διωκόμενον. Comp. Jn xvi. 21 ἡ γυνὴ ὅταν τίκτῃ.

[2942* (xii) *b*] Origen's commentary on Jn xvi is lost. But in commenting on Gen. xxii. 13—14 he says, "*You, too, will generate a son, Isaac*, in the spirit, when you begin to have the fruit of the spirit—*joy* (gaudium) [and] peace." So Philo i. 618 says—alluding to (Gen. xvii. 19) the birth of Isaac, "laughter," or "joy"— "Virtue will bring forth to you a *son, noble, male* (υἱὸν γενναῖον ἄρρενα)...and thou shalt call his name...*joy* (χαράν)." Comp. the curious phrase in Rev. xii. 5 υἱόν, ἄρσεν. Buhl (218 *a*) gives only Lev. iv. 23, Jer. xx. 15 as instances of a superfluous "male," ἄρρην, applied to a masc. noun. In Lev. iv. 23 the sacrifice of a "he-kid, a male" is distinguished from the inferior sacrifice of a she-kid in iv. 28. Jer. xx. 15 "a son, [yes,] a man-child" (LXX ἄρσεν, v.r. ἄρσην, Aq. Sym. Theod. add υἱός) is parall. to the congratulatory language in Job iii. 3 "a [great] man (גֶבֶר) is born." This perhaps illustrates Jn xvi. 21, "she remembereth no more the anguish for joy that a *man* (not "a son") is born into the world." Although Jn has ἄνθρωπος, not ἀνήρ, it is not prob. that he means "human being." At all events Origen quotes Jn xvi. 17, 22 in connexion with his comment on the sacrifice of Isaac: "Generas autem *gaudium*, si (Jas. i. 2) 'omne gaudium existimaveris cum in tentationes varias incideris,' et istud *gaudium* offeras in sacrificium Deo. Cum enim laetus accesseris ad Deum, iterum tibi reddit, quod obtuleris, et dicit tibi, quia 'Iterum videbitis me, et gaudebit cor vestrum, et *gaudium* vestrum nemo auferet a vobis.'" Hippolytus (*Christ. et Antichr.* 61) quoted by Swete, τὸν ἄρρενα κ. τέλειον Χριστόν, perh. means "full-grown" (as in Heb. v. 14).

[2942* (xii) *c*] Concerning the Dragon, Origen says (iv. 307) "Omnia haec exponere singillatim de capitibus septem draconis, quae forsitan possunt referri ad aliquos principes rerum nequitiae, sive ad tanta ducentium ad mortem peccata, non est temporis hujus; exponentur autem tempore suo in revelatione Joannis. Sed et decem cornua dicere, quoniam sunt regna serpentinae malitiae, et habentis serpentis naturam..."

[1] [2942* (xiii) *a*] Comp. Ezek. xxix. 3 "I am against thee, Pharaoh king of Egypt, the great dragon...." Ibn Ezra, on Is. li. 9—10 "Art thou not it...that pierced the dragon? Art thou not it which dried up the sea?" says, "Pharaoh

is meant," and he compares Ezek. xxix. 3, and says that Isaiah "refers to the division of the Red Sea." So in Ps. lxxiv. 13 "thou brakest the heads of the dragons in the waters," the Targum explains this and the parall. "leviathan" by reference to "Egypt" and "Pharaoh." In Job vii. 12 "sea...sea-monster," Targ. gives two versions, (1) "Egyptians...Pharaoh," (2) "sea...leviathan." Levy (iv. 656 b and *Ch.* ii. 547 a) explains the word as "great sea-fish, crocodile, dragon." Hence it might be applied to any Enemy of Israel, *e.g.* Pompey, the desecrator of the Temple, murdered on the sandy beach of Egypt, *Ps. Sol.* ii. 28—31 (ed. James) "'Delay not, O God, to recompense it upon their heads, to turn the *pride of the Dragon* to dishonour.' And I delayed not until God shewed to me that insolent one (τὴν ὕβριν αὐτοῦ)? His *Dishonourer*) lying pierced upon the high places (ὀρέων, v.r. ὁρίων borders) of Egypt...even his dead body lying corrupted upon the waves in great contempt" [ὕβρει ? *dishonour*, so as to retain the play on the words indicating that the "Dishonourer" is in "dishonour"] "and there was none to bury him." This is probably one of many similar Jewish traditions which, if extant, would explain many things in John. The Dragon has a natural connexion with the "sea," or "abyss." The dragon, Pompey, after dishonouring God, comes from the sea to Egypt and is cast back "on the waves," dishonoured. In Rev., the Dragon (or the Beast) comes from the sea, or from the abyss, and is cast into the abyss. Comp. *Clem. Hom.* viii. 15 δρακοντόποδες sc. Τιτᾶνες (**2942*** (i) *m*).

[**2942*** (xiii) *b*] Rev. xii. 9 "The great dragon, the ancient serpent, he that is called Devil and Satan, he that leadeth astray the whole of the earth," accumulates *many* phrases to shew that they all mean *one* Evil. The mention of "the ancient serpent (ὄφις)" does not oblige us to suppose that the Seer saw the dragon in the actual form of a serpent when he (xii. 4) "*stands* (ἕστηκεν) before the Woman," waiting for the birth of the Child. Swete says, "The δράκων is a glorified ὄφις, which, as Pliny (*H.N.* viii. 21. 33 (78)) says, 'nec flexu multiplici ut reliquae'" [Teubn. -qua, ?-qui] "'corpus impellit sed celsus et erectus in medio incedens.'" Against this is the fact that Pliny describes the creature as (*ib.*) "not more than twelve inches in size," so that its posture would hardly seem applicable to that of a dragon large enough to devour a child. See, however, **2942*** (xiii) *g* on "scorpion." The mention of "dragon" by Artemidorus (ii. 13) mostly as presaging good— whereas "serpent (ὄφις)" (*ib.*) presages evil—and the associations of the Hebrew word with the waters of Egypt rather favour the conclusion that the shape is that of a crocodile, not of a python. On the other hand it is the Python—not "a dragon"—that hunts Latona from land to land so that she finds no refuge wherein to give birth to Apollo till the wandering Delos is made to stand still for her. This story John, in the quarries of Patmos, was sure to hear; and his vision may have blended it with the story in Exodus.

Wetstein says, "In *numis* Imp. Veri Hydra ἐπτακέφαλος" and quotes *Kidduschin* f. 29 *b* "R. Acha pernoctavit in ἀκροατηρίῳ. Mox visus ei est daemon forma draconis septem habentis capita...." In *Test. Abr.* (A) § 17 Death exhibits κεφαλὰς δρακόντων πυρίνους ἑπτά, and says (§ 19) τοὺς ἑπτὰ αἰῶνας ἐγὼ λυμαίνω τὸν κόσμον. Δράκων is Hebraized in New Heb. (though not in Aramaic) and *Baba Bathra* 16 *b* (on Job xxxix. 1) represents God as appointing a "dragon" to bite the "hind" in order that it may bring forth its offspring safely!

[**2942*** (xiii) *c*] For illustrations of the conception of the overflowing Nile going forth in pursuit of its prey comp. Jer. xlvi. 7—8 "Who is this that *riseth up like the Nile*...Egypt *riseth up like the Nile*...and he saith, I will *rise up*, I will *cover the earth*; I will *destroy the city and the inhabitants thereof*," *ib.* xlvii. 1 foll. "The

[2942*] THE DATE OF THE APOCALYPSE

the two thoughts—the picture of the two Sons of the enthroned Mother—mingle in the Seer's vision. He thinks, first, of the greater Deliverer, Christ, as at once ascending—just shewn to mankind ("ostendent terris hunc tantum fata") and then withdrawn—snatched up to heaven and to the throne of God. Then his mind turns to the work of the inferior Deliverer, Moses, triumphantly leading Israel forth into the wilderness. But again this Deliverer, Moses, is merged in the Mother, whom he delivers, Israel led forth from Egypt. The "Dragon" casts forth a "river" to pursue the Mother—the army of Egypt with its horses and chariots and a rushing as of many waters (Is. xvii. 12—13). But the Mother flees, upborne by the two "wings" of the great Eagle[1], "into the wilderness, where she hath a place prepared by God[2]," and the "river" is "swallowed up" by the earth.

---

word of the Lord that came to Jeremiah the prophet...before that Pharaoh smote Gaza...*waters rise up...and shall overflow the land...at the rushing of his chariots*...." It may be called by some "a bold use of metaphor" to describe the swallowing up of Pharaoh's army in the sea as a swallowing up of "waters" in the "earth." But John is not a composer of metaphors but a seer of visions. He describes what he sees. And the language of the prophets made him see things as Jeremiah and Isaiah pictured them.

[1] [2942* (xiii) d] Rev. xii. 14 "the two wings of the great eagle," as the context seems to refer to the deliverance from Egypt, probably alludes to Exod. xix. 4, "Ye have seen what I did unto the Egyptians, and how I *bare you on eagles' wings* and brought you unto myself." But the article ("*the* great eagle") is obscure. Does it refer, literally, to the largest kind of eagle known to the writer, or to some symbolic "great eagle"? If the latter, does it refer to Rev. iv. 7 "the fourth creature like a flying eagle"? Hippol. (*Christ. et Antichr.* 61) illustrates by (1) the outspreading of Christ's hands on the cross, (2) Mal. iv. 2 "the sun of righteousness...with healing in his wings." Origen often quotes Mal. iv. 2 for "sun of righteousness," but only once for the "wings," where he says (*Comm. Ps.* xix. 4 (LXX) (Lomm. xii. 73) "In the sun he placed his tabernacle") that some "used to say (dicebant)" that the Saviour, ascending to heaven, laid aside His body (*i.e.* "tabernacle") in the sun, because the body could not ascend higher. Origen maintains that the "tabernacle" is the Church, and God has placed it "in the sun"—not in the physical sun, but in the sun of righteousness.

[2] [2942* (xiii) e] As to Rev. xii. 6 (comp. xii. 14) "place prepared by God," see *Parad.* **1240—3**, on "place," and **1232—9, 1244**b, **1434—5**, on "prepare a place." It may refer to the Providence of God in the first instance preparing for Israel a "tent of meeting" or "tabernacle" in the Wilderness, whereby God, through Moses, says to Israel (as above quoted) Exod. xix. 4 "*I brought you to myself.*" Comp. 1 Chr. xv. 1 κ. ἡτοίμασε τὸν τόπον and Jn xiv. 2 "I go to prepare a place for you." The allusions may include one to the migration of the Christian Church, before the siege, from Jerusalem to Pella, Euseb. iii. 5. 3 τοῦ λαοῦ...κατά τινα χρησμὸν τοῖς αὐτόθι δοκίμοις δι' ἀποκαλύψεως δοθέντα...καί τινα τῆς Περαίας πόλιν οἰκεῖν κεκελευσμένου, where Eusebius seems to indicate that the warning

The "place" probably alludes to the tabernacle. Other allusions are not wanting to the whole history of Israel. The "dragon," as in the days of Antiochus Epiphanes, casts down "stars"—perhaps from the Woman's coronet. So Daniel (viii. 10) had said. John says a "third part" of the stars—introducing a number, perhaps, symbolical of trial, and, in any case, repeatedly used throughout this book in that symbolism[1].

[2942*(xiv)] Before the birth of the "man-child," and before the "travail," the Seer beholds the opening of the temple of God that is in heaven (Rev. xi. 19) "and there was seen in his temple the ark of his covenant, and there followed lightnings and *voices*...." Compare Isaiah's prediction (lxv. 18—lxvi. 7) "I create Jerusalem a rejoicing...the heaven is my throne...what manner of house will ye build unto me?...To this man will I look, even to him that is poor and of a contrite spirit...*a voice from the temple, a voice of the Lord that rendereth recompense to his enemies. Before she travailed she brought forth; before her pain came she was delivered of a man-child.*" Here the LXX has "*Before she that was in travail brought forth, before the pain of her travail came, she fled away and was delivered of a man-child.*" Perhaps the writer had this passage of the LXX in view, treating it freely after his custom, when he wrote that the Woman "*fled*" into the wilderness after bearing the "man-child." In any case, in his context (Rev. xii. 5) "who shall surely shepherd

---

(Mk xiii. 14, Mt. xxiv. 16, Lk. xxi. 21) "Let those in Judæa flee unto the mountains" was defined more clearly in a revelation to disciples "of repute."

[1] [2942* (xiii) *f*] "Third part" is used in Zech. xiii. 8—9, apparently to describe the remnant that is saved. Reversely, Rev. uses it repeatedly (viii. 7, 8 &c., ix. 15, xii. 4) to describe that which is destroyed. So 1 K. xix. 18 applies "seven thousand" to the remnant saved, but Rev. xi. 13 to the number killed (**2942*** (viii)). (Comp. *Test. Abr.* (A) § 17 ἐτελεύτησαν...ὡσεὶ χιλιάδες ἑπτά). "Third part" in Zech. is variously interpreted in *Rosh-hashanah* 17 a, *Sanh.* 111 a. Jerome makes it refer to Christians as distinct from Jews and unbelieving Gentiles.

[2942* (xiii) *g*] As regards the dragon drawing down the stars with its tail, my friend Mr W. S. Aldis informs me that the splendid constellation of the Scorpion, for an observer in the Isle of Patmos soon after dark in the summer, would be entirely above the horizon, speedily plunging into the sea from which it rose, and that, when he was residing in New Zealand, it often reminded him of the Great Red Dragon. Virgil implies that the Scorpion encroaches on two neighbouring constellations but gives place to Augustus (*Georg.* i. 33—5, where "panditur" expresses the protrusive form of the constellation). Comp. Ovid *Metam.* ii. 195—6 "geminos ubi brachia concavat arcus Scorpios, et *cauda* flexisque utrinque lacertis, Porrigit in spatium signorum membra duorum," and *Fast.* iv. 163—4

"Dum loquor, elatae metuendus acumine *caudae*
Scorpios in virides praecipitatur aquas."

(μέλλει ποιμαίνειν) all the nations with an iron rod," he quotes an erroneous LXX rendering of Ps. ii. 9, where the "shepherding" should be "breaking." The erroneous "shepherding" is also quoted in Rev. ii. 27, xix. 15. This use of LXX appears inconsistent with the hypothesis of a Jewish non-Christian authorship for the narrative of the birth of the Child, but consistent with the view that all the three passages where the error occurs proceed from the same writer, and that writer, a Christian.

[2942*(xv)] The last quoted passage of Isaiah, "to him will I look that is *poor*...," should be studied in conjunction with such doctrines of Christ as "blessed are *the poor*" (meaning "blessed are *the poor in spirit*"), "blessed are *the little ones*," "blessed are *the babes and sucklings*." Then we should perceive that Isaiah also, in effect, declares that no house of stone can be a "throne" or even a "footstool" for the Highest. His "throne" is to be the heart of man—man "poor," *i.e.* "hungering and thirsting" after God. It is a kindred metaphor to describe His "temple," or His "throne," as the "child." Thus regarded, the birth of the Child is, in the mind of the Seer, identified with the revelation, not only of the Temple, but also of the Ark. The material Ark had been destroyed with the Temple of Solomon, nor had a substitute been provided in the Temple of Ezra. But the Seer goes back, like the author of the Epistle to the Hebrews, to "the pattern in the heavens"—probably, like that writer, seeing in the Ark not only the Tables of the Covenant, but also the hidden "manna" of which the Epistle speaks, and which John mentions to the Church of Pergamum[1]. But the main meaning in John's vision of the Ark appears to have been this, that the Old Covenant of the Law was on the point of being fulfilled and superseded by the New Covenant embodied in the Child, the Poor, the Little One, the Lamb (ἀρνίον). If so, the twofold mention of a (xii. 1, 3) "sign in heaven" in this passage is intended to prepare us for a passage in which the phrase occurs for the third and last time, introducing the final stage of the fiery purification of the saints ("a glassy sea mingled with fire"). Here Moses, instead of being merely suggested as a type of the "man-child," is actually mentioned. It is

---

[1] [2942* (xv) *a*] Rev. ii. 17 "I will give to him of the hidden manna." See Wetstein's note, which shews a widely diffused Jewish belief that the pot of manna was "hidden," along with the ark. Rev. ii. 17 is generally accepted as coming from a Christian source.

the only mention of his name in the book; and it is most instructive, as a proof of the writer's reverence for the great Lawgiver, and of his belief that the Lawgiver testified, as a subordinate, to the Redeemer (xv. 1—3): "And I saw another sign in heaven...seven plagues...for in them is finished the wrath of God. And I saw as it were a glassy sea mingled with fire, and them that come victorious from the beast... having harps of God. And they sing *the song of Moses the servant of God, and the song of the Lamb*[1]."

THE MEANING OF "VIRGINS" IN REV. xiv. 4.

[1] [2942* (xv) *b*] On Rev. xiv. 4 "These are they that were not defiled with women; for they are virgins," Wetstein says simply "Οὐκ ἐμολύνθησαν, *non polluti* idololatria." But in modern times "ascetic celibacy" has been confidently asserted to be John's meaning. Which is right? On the one hand, Wetstein does not, and presumably could not, allege any instance where μολύνεσθαι μετὰ γυναικῶν (including γυναικῶν) is metaphorically used. Moreover Epictetus, and passages in the Pauline Epistles, recommend celibacy as best for a missionary; and this view may have prevailed in some Christian Churches at an early date, especially under Essene influences. On the other hand, Revelation magnifies "apostles," of whom one (Peter) was married, and includes them in the "twenty-four elders." [Any allusion in "twenty-four" to (Diod. Sic. ii. 31) a double zodiac, if existent, is subordinate to the thought of the twelve tribes, the Old Church, and the twelve apostles, the New Church, combined together (Rev. xxi. 12—14).] Would the writer exclude Peter from those that "have not defiled themselves with women"? This would be in express contradiction to Heb. xiii. 4 "marriage honourable and the bed undefiled." The passage therefore requires discussion.

[2942* (xv) *c*] The first question is, "When and where in *pre-Christian* Greek or Hebrew literature is 'virgin' applied to man?" The answer is (so far as O.T., Steph. and Levy indicate) "Nowhere." The next question is, "Is 'virgin' used in any pre-Christian writing likely to be known to the Seer and of such a character that he might have it in his mind during his visions of the 144,000 who (Rev. xiv. 3—4) sing 'a new song' that 'no man could learn' except themselves, and who 'follow the Lamb whithersoever he goeth'?" The only mention of "virgins" (pl.) in the gospels is connected with (Mt. xxv. 1—11) "going to meet" a "bridegroom"—presumably (see Wetstein, on the Arabian custom not rightly represented by Alford) as the Bride's escort. Now in Revelation the Lamb is a Bridegroom— the Bridegroom of the New Jerusalem. And the wedding of the Lamb with the "bride adorned for her husband" forms the climax of this book (xxi. 1 foll.). This suggests that the "virgins" in Revelation are regarded as following the Lamb on the way to the Bride or returning in a procession with the Bride, and leads us to ask, 1st, whether O.T. contains any description of a wedding that might be regarded as Messianic, 2nd, whether such description, if it exists, makes any mention of "virgins" such as the Seer might apply to Christian visions of the wedding of the Lamb of God.

[2942* (xv) *d*] The forty-fifth Psalm appears to be just such a writing as we are in search of. Iren., Clem. Alex., Tertull., and Origen, all regard it as applying to Christ. Its marginal reff. (at verses 3, 4 [for Rev. xvi. 2 rd vi. 2], 16) contain several minor parallelisms to Revelation about the Messiah as a warrior riding to victory &c. But it is preeminently a Wedding Psalm. In correspondence with Rev. xxi. 2 the "bride adorned," the clothing of the Bride is described in detail (*ib.* 13 "her clothing is inwrought with gold..."). Afterwards, when she is led to the royal Bridegroom, mention is made of (*ib.* 14) "*the virgins her companions that follow her*": Origen's comment is, "The undefiled, and pure, and consequently (διὰ τοῦτο) '*virgin*' *souls, having departed* [*this life*] *will be brought to Christ.*" Clement of Alexandria (874—5) speaks of the married man as having "the Apostles as his patterns," and says that the man "who restrains his passion, like the widow, *becomes a virgin again.*" See Lightfoot's note on Ign. *Smyrn.* 13 "I salute the *virgins*—the so-called widows," *i.e.* "I salute those women who though called widows *are really virgins because of the purity of their devotion to God.*"

[**2942*** (xv) *e*] John's mention of "defilement" and "virgins" must not be considered by itself but as issuing from a consistent reversal of prophetic metaphor. Both John and the prophets agree that the *true* Bridegroom of the Church is One, namely, God, or, in John, God represented by the Lamb of God; but they differ as to the *false* gods, the seducers. The Old Testament regards them always as male; Revelation, often, as female. Space does not admit of discussing the reason—more probably reasons—for this reversal. But it is at all events a fact. In Ezekiel, the gods of Assyria are described repeatedly (xxiii. 6, 12, 23) as "desirable young men." Samaria and Jerusalem are described as "playing the harlot," going after their Assyrian or Babylonian lovers and being (*ib.* 17) "polluted with them;" (*ib.* 37 foll.) "with their idols they have committed adultery...ye have sent for men...for whom thou didst wash thyself...and satest upon a stately bed...." Isaiah, it is true, (xxiii. 15—18) briefly mentions Tyre's "merchandise" with the nations as a "harlot," but he nowhere suggests that she seduces Israel: Ibn Ezra says "In reality, he does not speak of a harlot at all." Again, Babylon is described by Jeremiah (li. 7) as "a golden cup in the Lord's hand that made all the earth drunken," but nowhere as a wanton leading Israel astray.

[**2942*** (xv) *f*] Our author, on the other hand (Rev. xiv. 8, xvii. 1—2, 4, xviii. 5—9), though reproducing old prophetic phrases about Tyre and Babylon, is really seeing an entirely new vision of the supreme Polluter—"Babylon the Great, the Mother of the Harlots," who rides, supreme for a time, upon the Beast, and with whom the kings of the earth committed fornication, until (xvii. 16) they turn to hate and destroy her. This feeling induces him elsewhere (as it seems) to apply Jehu's brief reference to (2 K. ix. 22) the "fornication" of Jezebel, and to use the name (Rev. ii. 20) in connexion with "committing fornication and eating things sacrificed to idols," very much as Ezekiel invents the names Oholah and Oholibah to describe the idolatry of Samaria and Jerusalem. No doubt, the writer also has in view the "strange women" that led Solomon (1 K. xi. 1—8) into idolatry, and the daughters of Moab who (Numb. xxv. 1—2) "called the people unto the sacrifices of their gods." The main truth for us to keep in view is that the Seer sees, so to speak, more visions than one, and yet tries to express them in one. He sees the Virgin daughter of Sion, the Church, the Bride, faithful to her one Lord (comp. 2 Cor. xi. 2 "I espoused you to one husband...a pure virgin to Christ"); but he also sees the members of the Virgin Church triumphing over the temptations of "strange women" such as Jezebel and the daughters of Moab, and over the temptations of the idol-worship to which they led, and over all the temptations of the Harlot's "golden cup." He sees a procession, so to speak, of the members

THE DATE OF THE APOCALYPSE [2942*]

§ 9. *Inferences*

[**2942*** (xvi)] Attention has been called above to the fact that the same prophecy (about "shepherding the nations with a rod and beating them to pieces") is quoted in three passages of Revelation—passages ascribed by some to different authors. This is but one of many quotations, phrases, or images (pointed out in the course of this discussion) recurring again and again in this book—somewhat like the recurrences in the Fourth Gospel—and implying unity of authorship. There are also traces of a natural, though not chronological, arrangement. Like Ezekiel, the Seer is first sent to testify to his own immediate circle, the "seven churches." These are God's Temple on earth, with the "candlestick" of the Jewish Temple, multiplied according to the promise of Isaiah concerning the sun (Is. xxx. 26) "sevenfold." Thence he is led to the vision of the heavenly causes that led to this new temple on earth, and then to the remeasuring for the new temple, which suggests a mention of the destruction of the old one. This introduces the causes of the destruction of the temple on earth, namely, Evil, in various shapes, the Evil that caused the sin of Adam and the many lapses and captivities of Israel; and hence come visions of future outbreaks of sin and God's future judgments. Amidst all these conflicts between good and evil are seen glimpses of the divine purpose, which finally drives the Seer forward to the vision of a consummation where he beholds the descent of the New Jerusalem coming down as a Bride from heaven.

[**2942*** (xvii)] For modern readers, a more serious doubt than any that concerns the mere date or literary character of the Apocalypse may present itself in its moral character. The Seer appears sometimes vindictive. He seems to exult in fire and sword and to need the repetition of Christ's words (Lk. ix. 55, R.V. marg.) "Ye know not of what spirit ye are." This objection is difficult to meet because of his constant use of language undoubtedly intended by Psalmists and Prophets to mean literal slaughter and vengeance, *e.g.* the passage in the Psalm above-quoted, as to the "breaking" of the "nations." Origen's assertion (on Ps. ii. 9) that it is good for us

---

of the Virgin Church faithful to the Lamb, on the one side, and a procession of the kings of the earth, the slaves of Circe, on the other side. The latter have succumbed to the Harlot and to her daughter harlots. They have "defiled themselves with women." The former have not. They are "virgins."

[2942*] THE DATE OF THE APOCALYPSE

to be thus "broken," and even to be "killed," seems to modern readers the height of absurdity. Yet even modern readers admit that Christ's "two-edged sword" is spiritual, and that He not only forbade Peter to use the earthly sword but also pronounced, in effect, the verdict, "Thou shalt perish" on any of His disciples that should resort to it. He also said that He had come to send a "sword" and "fire" upon earth. Surely, in the face of these facts, we ought not to find it hard to infer—however strange the inference may appear at first—that the words (Rev. ii. 26—7) "I will give to him [*i.e.* to the faithful conqueror] authority over the nations, and he shall shepherd them with an iron staff *even as the vessels of the potter are broken in pieces*," did not mean that the Thyatirans to whom this promise was made might look forward to revenging themselves on Roman oppressors with clubs or maces.

[2942* (xviii)] The reply, then, to this objection is, 1st, that, if it were valid, it would affect the *whole* of the book, including those parts that are recognised by all as coming from a Christian source, 2nd, that it is not valid, since the language of "blood and iron" must not be taken literally[1], 3rd, that modern readers will do well to recognise the extreme difficulty of putting themselves in the place of

---

[1] [2942* (xviii) *a*] "Must not be taken literally." It may be asked, "Did not John, then, really believe that there would be literal famines, literal earthquakes, literal pestilences, before the Coming of the Saviour and the Last Judgment?" Probably he did. But he looked on these visible movements mainly as the external signs of invisible movements intended to rescue men at all costs from the greatest evil of all—servitude to the Beast. 2 Thess. i. 8 "the Lord Jesus...in flaming fire *rendering vengeance* (διδόντος ἐκδίκησιν)," is rendered by Lightfoot "*awarding retribution*," and Lightfoot says that a "double aspect" of the words "will hold equally whether the 'fire' be taken in a literal or a figurative sense: for the revelation of Christ will in itself inflict the severest punishment on the wicked, by opening their eyes to what they have lost." "*Avenger*," at all events, is not the right word, as used in modern English, to apply to a magistrate called by Greeks (Rom. xiii. 4) ἔκδικος, *i.e. exactor of justice*. There is a feeling in John as in Paul that ἐκδίκησις is connected with δίκαιος, *just*, or *righteous*, and that the *justice* of the Father—who sent His Son into the world as the Sacrifice or Lamb of Redemption—cannot be other than δικαιοσύνη, *righteousness*.

The cry in Rev. vi. 10 "How long dost thou not judge and *exact justice* (ἐκδικεῖς) for our blood?" means, in effect, "How long dost thou delay to *right the oppressed? How long dost thou delay to open the eyes of the sinful to their sins? How long dost thou suffer a Nero, or a Domitian, to exult as Lord over the world? How long dost thou delay to lift up the Man who is now prostrate under the claws of the Beast?*" Into the exact nature of the ultimate destruction of Evil and evil beings the Seer gives us no clear vision. But he himself seems clearly to see that they will be destroyed—and this, by the agency of "the Lamb."

such an original Seer as John, and of realising the influence exerted on him by Jewish associations and by his Master's abundant use of metaphor. It may be added that what has been preserved from Origen, bearing on the Apocalypse, is always worthy of consideration; and he seems, as a rule, to have regarded the book as dealing with spiritual forces. Probably he is right. Daniel deals with political Powers, but Ezekiel—much more, though by no means wholly—with spiritual and natural Powers. John follows both, but mainly Ezekiel. Or rather, he follows neither, but he assimilates both, and has assimilated in the main the thoughts of the earlier prophet.

Perhaps, instead of calling the writer "cruel," some may be disposed to call him an inconsistent optimist: "He calls God 'Almighty,' 'the First and the Last,' 'the Beginning and the End'; yet what is the 'end' of God's drama? Is it the New Jerusalem? No, that is only half the end. The other half is what is outside the City: (Rev. xxii. 15) 'Without are the dogs, and the sorcerers...and everyone that maketh a lie.' Who is responsible for this if not the 'Almighty' and 'the Beginning'? And is not such an 'end' a failure?"

A charge of this kind—though it might be slightly extenuated by metaphysical arguments about "Almighty" (**2998** (xxvii) *f—m*)—cannot be denied. The fault (if it is a fault) arises from the Seer's feeling that he can realise what we cannot at present logically realise—a future when God's "Kingdom" will have "come" in such a manner that the saints, looking back on (Rev. xx. 14) "Death and Hades...cast into the lake of fire," may be able to see that God after all was "Almighty"—though the word is one that Jesus Himself never applied to God. Perhaps all men ought to be, in some sense, guilty of "inconsistent optimism."

At all events, this feeling is compatible with compassion for the sinful in themselves, along with a horror of them in so far as they identify themselves with the Beast that preys on the Man, dragging their fellow-creatures under the Beast's feet. The Epistle to the Romans says (xi. 32—3) "God hath shut up all unto disobedience," and yet "O the depth of the riches both of the wisdom and the knowledge of God!" Elsewhere, it says (ix. 3) "I could wish that I myself were anathema from Christ for my brethren's sake," and yet (xi. 26) "All Israel shall be saved." Paul, though he had never seen Christ in the flesh, was forced to utter these "inconsistent optimisms" by the conviction that, in Christ, death was swallowed up by victory. Might not the same conviction explain even greater inconsistencies in the beloved disciple? The gulf between Jews and Christians was wider in John's time than in Paul's. John, we may think, had not so much right as Paul to be sanguine. But on the other hand, if John had "lain in Christ's bosom," might he not be unable to keep down a predominant exultation—predominant over individual and national sympathies and sorrows—in the thought of the Lamb of God, wielding the judgments of heaven, and controlling the forces of the universe for the salvation of mankind?

[2942* (xix)] There are undoubtedly instances of Jewish works appropriated by Christians, and either revised, or interpolated and amplified, for Christian purposes. But in such cases any predictions that are retained or added are generally found to be in fair accordance with subsequent facts, since one of the reviser's objects is to claim credit for the prophetic truth of the work as a whole. The *Book of Enoch*, for example, is manifestly a compilation; it has been certainly revised; possibly also it has been here and there touched by a Christian hand; and it is full of differences of style and inconsistencies of detail. But it does not, so far as I know, insert prophecies that have been manifestly falsified by subsequent facts. If there are any, they are few.

The Revelation of John, as compared with *Enoch*, may be pronounced quite homogeneous in style and thought. If the book proceeded from an interpolator or compiler, the ban (Rev. xxii. 18—19) on anyone adding to or taking from it would bespeak an extraordinary audacity of self-confidence in the compiler[1].

---

[1] [2942* (xix) *a*] Rev. xxii. 18 ἐάν τις ἐπιθῇ...καὶ ἐάν τις ἀφέλῃ, comp. Deut. iv. 2 (rep. xii. 32) οὐ προσθήσεσθε...κ. οὐκ ἀφελεῖτε, and Prov. xxx. 6 μὴ προσθῇς τοῖς λόγοις αὐτοῦ. Prof. Swete *ad loc.* says, "It was not uncommon for writers to protect their works by adding a solemn adjuration to the scribes to correct the copies carefully, and in no case to mutilate or interpolate the original; cf. *e.g.* Irenæus ap. Eus. *H. E.* v. 20...." But does this prove that such adjurations were "not uncommon" at the end of the first century? If no such adjuration can be found at the end of books of, or before, that date, does not its existence here indicate an "uncommon" attitude in the writer? The Seer seems to apply the warning of Moses about "adding to" or "taking from" the Words of the Law to "the words of the prophecy" of this book (with a play on words, as Prof. Swete justly notes, gained by altering Deut. προστίθημι to ἐπιτίθημι, so as to introduce Rev. xxii. 18 ἐπιθήσει πληγάς, "lay on lashes"). This seems a vast assumption of authority. Perhaps the Seer was moved by his Master's warnings against "false prophets," and by his own knowledge of their forgeries. But in any case, until this adjuration can be shewn to have been "not uncommon" in the first century, it goes some way to prove that the writer occupied an eminent position in the Christian Church.

It also differs from *Enoch* in containing at least one prophecy that appears not only to have been not fulfilled but also to call attention to a different fulfilment from that contemplated by the Seer. And it utters this prophecy in curiously condensed and definite language as though the writer had long had it in his mind. It is the story of the Two Witnesses (Rev. xi. 1—13): "These are the two olive-trees and the two candlesticks, that [are] before the Lord of the earth, standing." They are to prophesy 1260 days. They can consume their adversaries with fire, shut up the rain in heaven, turn waters to blood, and smite the earth with plagues. When their witness is accomplished, "*the beast*"—yet no "beast ($\theta\eta\rho\iota\text{ον}$)" has been mentioned—"that comes up from the abyss shall kill them," and their carcase (*sic*) shall lie unburied in the street of the Great City. The nations gaze on "their carcase" three and a half days and do not suffer "their carcases" (**2942*** (xxii) *b*) to be entombed. The dwellers on earth rejoice to be freed from their torturers. But a spirit of life makes the dead Witnesses stand up. A Voice from heaven says, "Come up here," and they "went up to heaven in *the cloud*"—no cloud has been mentioned—"and their enemies beheld them."

[**2942*** (xx)] Suppose this not to have proceeded from John. Then it must have been inserted among his genuine visions either by John himself or by some editor of his work. In either case, we have to face the question, "Why?" No one can say that it is a prophecy after the event, or that it has ever been literally fulfilled. No one can deny that it perplexes us with its assumptions about things defined in the Seer's mind but not in that of his reader—"*the* two candlesticks," "*the* beast," "*the* cloud"—to which we might add "*the* Great City" if it were not defined by a suspicious addition, "which is called spiritually Sodom and Egypt, where also their Lord was crucified[1]." It is very difficult to answer the question *Cui bono*—"Whose interest was it to make this incoherent insertion?"

---

[1] [**2942*** (xx) *a*] Comp. Rev. xvi. 13 "Out of the mouth of the dragon, and out of the mouth of the Beast, and out of the mouth of *the false prophet* three unclean spirits, as frogs"—where no false prophet has been previously mentioned. He is probably (Swete *ad loc.*) to be identified with the second Beast in xiii. 11. The Seer assumes that there is a threefold evil, the Dragon, the first Beast (i.e. *the* Beast) and the Word of the Beast, *i.e.* "the false prophet." He is mentioned thrice altogether, namely, here and xix. 20, xx. 10. The "three" unclean spirits are perhaps (antithetical to the Pauline triad) faithlessness, hopelessness, and hate. There seems an implied antithesis to a divine triad never mentioned in this book but implied in (**2998** (xxvi) *l*, (xxvii) *e—f*) IS, WAS,

[2942*] THE DATE OF THE APOCALYPSE

[2942* (xxi)] But on the other hand let us suppose it to have proceeded from John the son of Zebedee. According to the Fourth Gospel this John was a disciple of the Baptist, and the Baptist came to "bear witness" to Christ. According to Revelation, Christ Himself was "the faithful and true Witness." Here, then, were "*two witnesses.*" The Fourth Gospel (like the Law) lays stress on the necessity of "*two witnesses.*" These "*two witnesses,*" the Baptist and the Christ, were closely associated together in all the gospels. Nay, the Synoptists agree in asserting—an assertion scarcely credible but for their combined testimony—that some people in Galilee declared *Christ to be the Baptist raised from the dead*! These facts point to the conclusion that the Seer may have had in his mind Jesus of Nazareth and John the Baptist (as well as Moses and Aaron, and Elijah and Elisha) as the culminating pair in a series of Witnesses, sent "two and two" into the world by God to testify against men's sin and for God's righteousness, and to prepare them for God's righteous judgments—bringing purification to the penitent, destruction to the persisters in sin.

[2942* (xxii)] We cannot indeed assert that the vision is historically true. It is not a photograph of a single definite past. More truly might we say that it is of the nature of a superimposed photograph shewing traces of many pasts. If the Baptist and the Christ are among the "two witnesses," then it is not true that they died at the same time; or that they both died in Jerusalem; or that they were left unburied; or that they destroyed their enemies with fire; or that both visibly ascended to heaven. No historian could assert these things. But it does not follow that a Poet and Seer—"jumping o'er times" and giving body and place to spiritual imaginings—might not assert them. He might behold the two witnesses in a series of pictures, thus. First, they would be "standing" before the Lord like Zechariah's two bright "sons of oil[1]" before the altar. Then, in

---

COMING. All this gives the impression of having been thought out by the writer so long ago and meditated on so constantly that images are defined in his mind as "the," where the reader would expect "a." As to "the cloud" see **2998** (xxx) *b*—(xxxi) *c*.

[1] [2942* (xxii) *a*]. Zech. iv. 2—14 "I have seen...two olive-trees by it [*i.e.* by the candlestick]...what are these two olive-branches which are beside the two golden spouts that empty the gold [*i.e.* the golden oil] out of themselves?...These are the two *sons of oil* that stand by the Lord of the whole earth." Aq. has "sons of *brightness* (στιλπνότητος)," Theod. λαμπρότητος. John, who before (i. 12 foll.) mentioned "seven candlesticks" as representing the seven Christian Churches,

THE DATE OF THE APOCALYPSE [2942*]

accordance with the Baptist's and Christ's utterances about "fire" (and about the "axe," and about "bringing a sword, or fire, into the world") they would be seen dividing, as with a two-edged sword, the false from the true in Israel, terrifying the rulers of the land, and destroying evil, as with flame from their mouth. Then he would see them meeting death together—for what difference would a few months make in a vision that concerned all time and destiny?—killed and cast out from the vineyard by the rebellious vine-dressers of Israel, who exulted in being rid of their persecutors. No doubt the Baptist died in Machærus; and (according to Mark) his "corpse" was allowed by Herod Antipas to be buried by his disciples. Christ's "corpse," too, was allowed by Pilate to be buried by Joseph of Arimathæa[1]. But, in the eyes of the Seer, Jerusalem was the real scene of both murders. It was not Antipas, or Pilate, but the Jewish rulers who were responsible[2]. Christ's own word held good,

---

later on (xi. 4) describes God's "two witnesses" as being "the two olive-trees and the two candlesticks, standing before the Lord of the earth," whereas Zechariah speaks of "one candlestick" and "two olive-trees" (or "olive-branches") interpreted as "sons of oil." The Targ. has "sons of rulers." John, as before, deals freely with the ancient symbol. He seems to regard the "sons of brightness" as lights. We might be prepared for this from him but hardly from a non-Christian Jew.

[1] [2942* (xxii) b] Mk vi. 29, Mt. xiv. 12 πτῶμα, of John the Baptist, Mk xv. 45 πτῶμα, of Jesus. In Mk xv. 43, πτῶμα is the reading of D, and SS, but is not adopted by W.H. In Mt. xxiv. 28, πτώματα (pl.) means "carcases." In LXX πτῶμα sometimes means "carcase" or the body of one slain (but more often "downfall" or "fall"). In Rev. xi. 8—9, R.V. has, twice, txt "dead bodies," marg. Gr. "carcase" concerning the sing. πτῶμα, but "dead bodies," without marg. "carcases," for πτώματα.

[2] [2942* (xxii) c] Comp. Origen iii. 206 (on Mt. xvii. 10) where he says that Christ implied that the scribes were "jointly guilty (συναίτιοι)" of the imprisonment and execution of John the Baptist by Herod Antipas. He is also actually driven to suppose (Lomm. i. 252, *Comm. Joann.* tom. vi. 30 foll.) that Christ was confused with the Baptist διὰ τὸ κοινὸν τῆς μορφῆς. The Cod. Bodl. has sought refuge from this hypothesis by changing μορφῆς to γραφῆς. Eusebius iii. 5. 2 says Στεφάνου...ὑπ᾽ αὐτῶν ἀνῃρημένου...εἶτα δὲ...'Ιακώβου .. ἀποτμηθέντος, which would lead the reader to infer that "the Jews" were as much responsible for the death of James as for that of Stephen. But he has some justification in Acts xii. 3 "when he saw it pleased the Jews."

[2942* (xxii) d] That the office and the personality of John the Baptist were regarded by the earliest Christians in aspects differing from one another and differing from modern aspects, appears from several facts. Acts xviii. 25—xix. 3 describes Apollos as "teaching accurately the things concerning Jesus," but "knowing only the baptism of John," and certain disciples as ignorant of any other baptism. Josephus says that (*Ant.* xviii. 5. 2) some of the Jews thought

"It is not possible that a prophet can perish outside Jerusalem." The "two Witnesses," then, were virtually killed by the rulers of the corrupt City—once called Jerusalem but now Sodom and Egypt—killed, and cast out, and (so far as the rulers were concerned) left unburied. Then was fulfilled the saying of the Lord about the blood of all the prophets "from Abel to Zechariah" falling on the people. As Abel's blood went up to the Lord to call down vengeance on Cain, and as Elijah went up to heaven leaving a curse of the sword on idolatrous Israel, so the two Witnesses went up to heaven in the cloud in the sight of their enemies, some of whom repented while others were destroyed.

[2942* (xxiii)] Such a hypothesis—briefly described above as a hypothesis of photographic superimposition—may seem beneath the level of a historian's consideration. But not if the historian has to deal with the history of Seers and visions; not if the particular Seer in question has passed through fifty or sixty years of history and experience. And such history, and such experience! Including discipleship under John the Baptist, discipleship under Christ, the death and resurrection of the Saviour, the rise of the Christian Churches, the apparently imminent death of the Roman empire—wounded and restored to life—the actual and absolute destruction of the Temple in Jerusalem! Then, the variations of place and circumstance! Fisherman in Galilee, apostle in Jerusalem, bishop and chief of bishops in the region round Ephesus, convict among

---

that the destruction of Herod's army came from God as a punishment for his killing John. Christian Jews, and especially those who had been disciples of John as well as Jesus, might attribute to God's wrath for both John and Jesus the calamities that fell on their country during the first century. Origen (*Comm. Johann.* ii. 25, Lomm. i. 146 foll.) asks whether John was an "angel" before he became a man. Hippolytus (*Christ and Antichrist* 45) says that John the Baptist "preached to those in Hades" before Christ. Justin Martyr (*Tryph.* 87, comp. 51) says that the Spirit "ceased" in John when it "rested" on Jesus, and perhaps implies that which Tertullian (*Marc.* iv. 18, comp. *Adv. Jud.* 8) actually ventures to say, that the Spirit went back from John into Jesus. Perhaps the Synoptic tradition about Christ's being "John the Baptist raised from the dead" simply meant what we should express by saying that any departed Master "lives again in his pupil." But Galilæan poetry might very well expand this thought into a conception of the Two Witnesses (1) prophesying together, in one and the same spirit, before the Lord; and then (2) both of them, after their ministration was accomplished, slain and raised up together. For the "taking up [to heaven, or Paradise]" of martyrs, comp. the Letter of the Churches of Lyons (Euseb. v. 2. 3) ἐκεῖνοι ἤδη μάρτυρες οὓς ἐν τῇ ὁμολογίᾳ Χριστὸς ἠξίωσεν ἀναληφθῆναι (comp. v. 1. 10 ἀνελήφθη κ. αὐτὸς εἰς τὸν κλῆρον τῶν μαρτύρων).

convicts in the quarries of Patmos! These antecedents are not unworthy of the consideration of a historian endeavouring to assign date and authorship to "the Revelation of John."

Nor must the historian despise grammar. And from a grammatical point of view the hypothesis of the compilation of documents is most unlikely. Differences of style undoubtedly exist, in different portions of Revelation, but not a tenth part of such differences as separate *The Tempest* from *Richard II*. In contrast with all the other books of N.T., the Apocalypse of John is written in a language of its own, a blend of Hebraic Greek and vernacular Greek, defiant of grammar. Its peculiarities stamp the whole work—barring a few brief phrases—as not only conceived by one mind but also written by one hand.

[2942* (xxiv)] As regards the exact dates of the several visions, and the exact amount of influence on the Seer exerted by oral and written traditions—some of them still extant in apocryphal books connected with the names of Enoch, Esdras, and others—a critic must be very self-confident if he ventures to utter detailed decisions[1]. But the case is different in deciding that particular allusions necessi-

---

[1] [2942* (xxiv) *a*] In studying Revelation, some notice ought perhaps to be taken of the influence likely to be exerted on men's minds by the approaching centenary (according to ordinary computation) of Christ's birth 101 A.D., the third year of Trajan. The Book of Elchasai (Hippol. ix. 13) connects "a new remission of sins" with "*the third year of Trajan*." Comp. *ib.* 16 "When the time comes again for the fulfilment of *three years of the Emperor Trajan from the time when he subjected the Parthians* to his authority [when three years have been fulfilled] war is to rage (ἀγριζεται) between the angels of wickedness of the north." This repetition of a date that has no recognised historical importance (whatever may be the explanation of the modification in the second passage) suggests an early date for the Book of Elchasai and also reminds us that Christians, a century after Christ's birth, would begin to ask with special emphasis, "Will not the Lord Jesus come now?" The second passage also illustrates the note on the Parthians in **2998** (li) *a* foll.

[**2942*** (xxiv) *b*] Lightf. *Coloss.* p. 375 renders the precept of Elchasai in Epiphan. xix. 3 p. 42 "men ought to pray there at Jerusalem (λέγει ἐκεῖ δεῖν εὔχεσθαι εἰς 'Ι.)." But that εὔχεσθαι εἰς 'Ι. means "pray *towards* Jerusalem" is indicated by what precedes (*ib.*) "he forbids them *to pray towards* (εἰς) *the East* (εἰς ἀνατολὰς εὔξασθαι), saying that they must not pray thus, but *must have their face towards* (ἐπὶ) *Jerusalem*, from all parts." So 1 K. viii. 29—30, 2 Chr. vi. 20—1 προσεύχεσθαι εἰς τόπον 4 times. Comp. Ps. xxviii. 2, cxxxviii. 2 and Tobit iii. 11 (where ℵ adds "*spreading out her hands*"). For ἐκεῖ meaning "thither," comp. Mt. ii. 22, xvii. 20, etc. This does not wholly destroy Lightfoot's argument (*Coloss.* 87—8) that sun-worship was practised by the Essenes; but it indicates possibilities of misunderstanding "*towards* the sun" as meaning "*to* the sun," which must be taken into account. See **2998** (xxvii) *r*—*v*.

tate particular pre-existent historical facts. It is these allusions that (in my opinion) almost necessitate the conclusion that large portions of the Apocalypse were written—as Irenæus says—at the close of the reign of Domitian. Having regard to the general unity of thought and style, I should be disposed to go further, and to say that practically the whole of the book was written or revised at that date. It would follow, as an inevitable conclusion, for those who compare the style of the Apocalypse with that of the Fourth Gospel, that the author of the former could not have written the latter till late in the reign of Trajan, so as to allow time for a complete transformation of language and idiom. Even with this allowance, the hypothesis that the author of the Apocalypse was also the author of the Gospel, would involve something approaching to "a miracle." See **2967** *a*.

PATMOS

[**2942**] Page 304, "To the mines in Patmos." So Victorinus of Pettau (Migne v. 333) on Rev. x. 11 "Hoc dicit propterea quod quando haec Joannes vidit erat in insula Pathmos in metallo damnatus a Domitiano Caesare. Ibi ergo vidit Apocalypsin. Et cum jam senior putaret se per passionem accepturum receptionem, interfecto Domitiano omnia judicia ejus soluta sunt. Et Joannes de metallo dimissus sic postea tradidit hanc eamdem quam acceperat a Deo Apocalypsin." But see *Dict. Christ. Biogr.* iv. 1128—9 on the doubtfulness of the works assigned to this writer.

[**2943**] Guérin (*Descr. de l'île de Patmos* 1856, p. 2) quotes Meletius (*Geogr.* p. 488, ed. 1728) describing the island as μεταλλοφόρος. "Metallum" may mean "mine" or "quarry." Sir W. M. Ramsay (*Letters to the Seven Churches*, p. 85) says, "There were no mines in Patmos. Whether any quarries were worked there might be determined by careful exploration of the islet." I presume that Sir W. M. Ramsay, who quotes no authorities, has convinced himself that there never were any mines—by a personal inspection that has not sufficed to settle the rather more difficult question whether there were ever any quarries.

On this point I am permitted to quote a letter from the Rev. Prof. Alexander Nairne, describing his inferences from a visit to Patmos in March and April 1887: "I do not remember any mines or quarries. I am almost certain none were being worked while we were there, and I don't think we saw any disused ones."

[2944] Mayor's exhaustive note on "relegatio" (Juvenal i. 73) mentions a great number of islands, described by various historians as selected for this purpose, and, among these, Patmos, but adds no authority except Rev. i. 9. Several other islands, however, are mentioned by him in connexion with only one instance. Pliny iv. 69 gives the circuit as 30 miles; Meletius says "40 or, according to others, 50." The discrepancy might be explained if Pliny took a walker's estimate and Meletius a sailor's. And the indentations of the island might make even a walker's estimate vary very much. Pliny iv. 69—74 contains the names of more than sixty islands. About many he gives no particulars. About many he merely gives their distance from other points. But he specifies the circuit in six cases. Of these six, one is Patmos. Another is Gyaros—the well-known place of exile. Pliny may have ascertained the circuit of Gyaros from his friend Musonius Rufus, who was sent there by Nero.

[2945] In Rev. xiii. 1, A.V. has "And I stood upon the sand of the sea and I saw," but R.V. "And he [*i.e.* the beast] stood upon the sand...." The MSS. favour R.V., but on this point (*Joh. Gram.* 2687 *d*) good MSS. might go wrong. The precedents of Ezek. i. 1 foll., Dan. viii. 2, x. 4 "by the river," and Gen. xli. 17 "upon the brink of the river," suggest that standing by the side of water would be a feature in dreams and visions. But had the rocky island of Patmos any "sand" on which the Seer could "stand" whether in fact or in vision? Prof. Nairne writes, "There were bits of sandy beach here and there along the coast"; and I gather that there is a beach in the principal bay looking eastward on which the Seer might stand, or imagine himself standing, beholding the rising sun and "the Beast coming up from the sea."

[2946] In describing the group of islands to which Patmos belongs, Pliny says, iv. 70 "When Thera first emerged it was called Calliste, Therasia was afterwards torn off from it, and between the two there soon sprang up Automate (also called Hiera), and in our times Thia, which sprang up next to the above-mentioned islands." These words, and the frequent references to earthquakes in the Sibylline books, and our knowledge of multitudes of earthquakes about the Ægean sea from 100 A.D. onward, must be taken into account in estimating the value of negative evidence, even when coming from most careful and trustworthy eye-witnesses, as to the non-existence of mines and quarries in Patmos in the reign of Domitian. Comp. *Orac. Sibyll.* iii. 363 "Samos shall be sand (*ammos*); Delos shall be no Delos (*adēlos*)," and many other passages.

[2947] Since writing the above, I have received from the Rev. T. C. Fitzpatrick, President of Queens' College, Cambridge (through the kindness of Prof. Swete), an article in *Christ's College Magazine*, Easter Term, 1887, describing a fortnight spent in Patmos in the spring of 1887. It says (p. 19) "Down the middle of the island run a succession of hills; in one of them, in the northern half of the island, *there are quarries.*" [I italicize.] "This perhaps is the explanation of the statement that St John was 'damnatus in metallum,' as there do not appear to have been any mines properly so called."

In a letter to Prof. Swete dated 30 April 1906, Mr Fitzpatrick says, "There are quite a number of little bays with sandy shore."

Legends of Martyrdom by Fire

[2948] Page 304, "The fiery trial." Comp. 1 Pet. iv. 12 "the fiery trial among you," lit. "the *burning* (πυρώσει) among you." Πύρωσις occurs elsewhere in N.T. only twice, Rev. xviii. 9, 18 "smoke of her *burning.*" In Prov. xxvii. 21, πύρωσις corresponds to Hebrew "*smelting pot,*" or "furnace," which Heb. is rendered by the LXX "furnace" in Is. xlviii. 10, Deut. iv. 20. Πύρωσις, in the LXX of Amos iv. 9, means "blight," which is substituted by the other translators. Stephen's *Thesaurus* indicates that πύρωσις is very frequent as literal "burning," but gives no instance of "trial," "probation," except from Hesychius. These facts shew that "*saved from burning,*" in an old tradition about John, might be taken literally by error (as Tertullian, "fiery oil") although it really meant "*saved from a fiery trial of suffering in prison, mines, torture etc.*"

[2949] Compare Gen. xi. 28 "And Haran died in the presence of his father Terah, in the land of his nativity, in *Ur* of the Chaldees," and xv. 7 "I am the Lord that brought thee out of *Ur* of the Chaldees." The word "*Ur*" means "*flame.*" The Jerusalem Targum in the latter passage has, "I am the Lord who brought thee out of *the fiery furnace, from Ur of the Chasdai,*" thus combining "*furnace*" and "*Ur.*" (Targ. Jon. omits "from Ur.")

[2950] So far, a reader might suppose that Ur, being given up to idolatry, was regarded as being a place of trial for Abraham and called metaphorically a "furnace," as Egypt is in Deut. iv. 20, "from the *iron furnace, even out of Egypt.*" But in Gen. xi. 28 the metaphor has been developed into a literal fact by Targ. Jon., "And Haran died in the presence of his father Terah, where *he was burned* in the land of his nativity, *in the furnace of fire which the Chasdai had made for Abraham*," and sim. Targ. Jer. On the phrase "*in the presence of*," i.e. "*in the life-time of*," see Gesen. 818 *b*.

[2951] In this form, Gen. xi. 28 is made the basis of a long legend in which Abraham is brought by God out of the furnace that the Chaldees had made for him; but Haran, his brother, being faithless, is consumed in the furnace, before the eyes of Terah. The legend of the furnace in Daniel may have had a similar origin, in the metaphor of a "furnace," though without the special mention of "Ur."

[2952] Page 304, "I have heard it said." Jerome (on Gal. vi. 10) relates, without question, that John, "tarrying (moraretur) at Ephesus up to the last limits of old age (ad ultimam senectutem), being with difficulty carried down into the congregation in the hands of the disciples, and being unable to frame voice for more words (nec posset in plura vocem verba contexere [? many words, or more words than the following]) was wont to utter at each assembly nothing more than this: '*Dear sons (filioli), love one another.*' At last the disciples and brethren present, tired of always hearing the same thing, said, 'Master, why do you always say this?' His reply was worthy of John, 'Because it is the Lord's command; and this by itself, if done, is enough.'" It should be noted that Jerome does not say that this comes "from tradition," or that "some report this." He relates it as a fact.

[2953] Page 305, "Mix vision with fact," comp. 2 Cor. xii. 2—3 "Whether in the body or out of the body I know not." See also, as an extreme instance, *Sons of Francis* (by Anne Macdonell) on "Giles the Ecstatic," p. 72 "Soon he lost control over his comings and goings between the world of sense and vision."

[2954] Page 305, "Something of the kind," Epict. i. 9. 10—12, where see Schweig.'s note. He refers to Diog. Laert. vii. 182 where Hübner (Leipzig 1828) reads (as given me by a friend) πρεσβύτερον,

"'Cease,' said he, 'distracting *the Elder* [*i.e.* the teacher] from more serious occupations: propound these things to us, the young [*i.e.* the pupils].'" Comp. 1 Pet. v. 1 "The elders I exhort, who am a fellow-elder." In Diog. Laert., Cobet's text varies greatly from Hübner's and reads πρεσβύτην for πρεσβύτερον.

[2955] On Philem. 9 (R.V.) "such a one as Paul the aged (marg. an ambassador) (πρεσβύτης)" Lightfoot quotes Theophylact ("to be respected both because of his claim as a *teacher* and because of *age* (lit. time)") who apparently finds a play on the double meaning of the word, (1) "advanced in authority as an Elder or Teacher," (2) "advanced in years." Theophylact does not recognise "*ambassador*" as one of the meanings here. To the passages in Lightf.'s note add that (Steph. *Thes.* vi. 1589) πρεσβύτης is freq. "vitiose scriptum pro πρεσβύτερος," and that some (*ib.*) make πρεσβύτης older than γέρων, others younger. The latter view is more probable, and, if adopted, will remove the difficulty (discussed by Lightf.) as to Paul's calling himself "an old man." Πρεσβύτης probably means, not "old," but "advanced in years."

[2956] Page 306, "The Wisdom of Solomon." See the Muratorian Fragment (Westcott's *Canon of N.T.* p. 530). The text is corrupt, but fairly clear as to a connexion between the composition of the Wisdom of Solomon and that of the Johannine letters: "Epistula sane Iudae et superscriptio Ioannis duas in Catholica habentur; et Sapientia ab amicis Salomonis in honorem ipsius scripta," where the second "et" is corrected by some to "ut," but it may represent καὶ...δέ.

[2957] Page 306, "In the same sentence," Eus. iii. 39. 4. Eusebius calls attention to the distinction, as shewing the truth of the account of those who assert that there were two Johns and two tombs of John in Ephesus, comp. Eus. vii. 25. 16; p. 306, "Above," see *Silanus* p. 288.

[2958] Page 307, "He that is greater than we are" etc., see Iren. *Pref.*, and i. 13. 3, i. 15. 6, iii. 17. 4. Of these, i. 15. 6 is printed in Greek iambic verse, and *Pref.* and iii. 17. 4 shew signs of a similar origin. Comp. the saying of Polycrates in Eus. v. 24. 7, "For *they that are greater than I* have said, 'We must obey God rather than man,'" referring to Peter and John in Acts v. 29; p. 308, "Hard to say," see *Joh. Gram.* Pref. pp. vii—viii.

THE POOL OF (R.V.) "BETHESDA"

[2959] Page 310, "There *is* in Jerusalem a pool," Jn v. 2, see *Fourfold G.*, "pool." The text abounds in variations and is probably corrupt. Perhaps therefore not much stress can be laid on the fact that SS and Nonnus have "*was* in Jerusalem." Apart from the reason suggested by Clemens for the present, "is" might naturally be used here in accordance with the regular habit of geographers to use "is" in mentioning such remarkable phenomena as intermittent springs. Having used "*is*," the writer does not break off into the past to say that in old times it had five porches, but uses the participle "having," which may, or may not, represent the indicative imperfect ("which used to have"). Perhaps he thought the porches were not destroyed. Perhaps he did not know whether they were destroyed or not.

[2960] The following facts—which will be more fully given, with authorities, in *The Fourfold Gospel*—make it probable that the pool mentioned by John was not "intermittent" in the ordinary sense of the term, nor medicinal. Some of them point to the conclusion that the pool was used for purification, and especially before the beginning of the New Year. Such a pool, regarded as regularly and perhaps as annually intermittent, just before the Day of Atonement, might be contrasted by John with the "fountain for sin and uncleanness" opened in Jerusalem by the Messiah, not intermittent but always at hand for the sinful.

The Talmud, and other Jewish literature (so far as alleged), and Josephus, while mentioning remarkable springs in various parts of Palestine or Syria, are silent about this one. So is Pliny, though he is diffuse on medicinal and intermittent springs, and though he mentions one (*N. H.* xxxi. 18) "in Judæa," that ceased on Sabbaths. Tertullian (*Adv. Jud.* 13) implies that after Christ's resurrection and the institution of baptism the spring lost its curative power. Eusebius and Jerome use the *past* to declare that the bathing-place "formerly *had* five porches"; they use the *present* about two "pools (λίμναι, lacus)." The water of one of these, they say, is remarkably "red" (Jerome says "as it were bloody")—but not a word about their being intermittent or curative. "Each (ἑκατέρα)" says Eusebius ("one (unus)," says Jerome) is filled "from the *yearly* rains (ἐκ τῶν κατ' ἔτος ὑετῶν, Jerome *hibernis* pluviis)."

[2961] The Jewish Prayer-Book says (p. 254) "On the First

[2961] NOTES TO CHAPTER XXXI

Day of New Year, or, when New Year falls on Sabbath, on the Second Day, after the Afternoon Service, it is customary to go to the banks of a river or any other piece of water." A prayer is subjoined containing the words "thou wilt cast all their [*i.e.* Israel's] sins into the depths of the sea." SS describes the pool mentioned by John as "*a certain place of baptism.*" *Hor. Heb.* (on Jn v. 2) quotes a Targum about a man going "down to Siloam," in consequence of uncleanness, and washing himself "on the shortest day in winter," on which it may be remarked that the Talmudic tract entitled *Rosh-Hashanah*, "Beginning of the Year," recognises four beginnings of the year, of which the winter solstice would be one. We cannot indeed assert that Jn v. 1, "a feast of the Jews," meant New Moon of the beginning of the Year; but at all events Origen appears to have dissented from Irenæus' confident assertion that it was the Passover[1]. Wetstein quotes from the Talmud a tradition about a rivulet flowing from the Holy of Holies, at first as thin as the horns of a grasshopper, and then growing to a river capable of purifying the unclean[2]. But he omits, at the end of his extract, the words "*For it is said,* (Zech. xiii. 1) *In that day there shall be a fountain opened...*" These would have shewn that the tradition was based upon prophecy and apparently intended to be of a spiritual or mystical character.

[2961 (i)] If (Jn v. 1) "feast" was connected with *Rosh-hashanah*,

---

[1] [**2961 a**] Iren. ii. 22. 3. Origen's comm. on Jn v. 1 foll. is lost, but on Jn iv. 35 he says (Lomm. ii. 75) ἐὰν δὲ αὐτὴ ἡ ἑορτὴ τοῦ Πάσχα ἦν, οὐ πρόσκειται τὸ ὄνομα αὐτῆς. στενοχωρεῖ τε τὸ ἀκόλουθον τῆς ἱστορίας, καὶ μάλιστα ἐπεὶ μετ' ὀλίγα ἐπιφέρεται ὅτι "ἦν ἐγγὺς ἡ ἑορτὴ τῶν Ἰουδαίων ἡ σκηνοπηγία." Westcott (on Jn v. 1, Add. Note) does not quote this, but seems to me right in suggesting that the "feast" is the September New Moon, unless indeed it is the Day of Atonement. As regards the latter, Westcott says, "It is scarcely likely that the *Day of Atonement* would be called simply 'a festival,' though Philo (*de Septen.* § 23) speaks of it as 'a festival of a fast' (νηστείας ἑορτή)." But Philo (ii. 296) adds ἦν ἑορτὴν (Mang. -τή by error) τὴν μεγίστην Μωυσῆς ἀνεῖπεν...σάββατον σαββάτων ὀνομάσας. (Comp. Lev. xvi. 31, xxiii. 32 σάββατα σαββάτων.) And אC read ἡ ἑορτή. It is therefore possible, though strange to us, that Jn meant the Day of Atonement.

[2] [**2961 b**] *Joma* 77 b " Dixit R. Pinehas nomine Hunae Zipporensis: Rivulus, qui emanavit e sancto sanctorum, principio tenuissimus erat, ut cornua cicadarum; attingendo ostium porticus referebat filum staminis; cum pervenisset ad ostium templi referebat filum subtegminis; denique circa portam atrii excreverat in oris urceoli magnitudinem; deinceps valde augebatur et invalescebat, ad portam usque arcis Davidicae; atque porro fluminis instar exundabat, inque eo qui passi fuerant gonorrhoeam, menstruatae ac puerperae lavabantur."

NOTES TO CHAPTER XXXI   [2961]

special interest would attach to a remark at the beginning of that tract as to the method of dating (Schwab vi. 53) "*since the going forth from Egypt.*" The sick man is said to have been sick (Jn v. 5) "thirty-eight" years. He is generally regarded (see the comments in Cramer) as a type of Israel after the flesh. The only other Biblical use of "thirty-eight" is in Deut. ii. 13—14 where it is applied to Israel crossing the brook Zered, on the point of deliverance, after "thirty-eight years" of wandering in the wilderness, *dating from "the going forth from Egypt.*"

The number of porches may have been specified in order to suggest the influence of "the flesh," like the (Jn iv. 18, s. Origen *ad loc.*) "five husbands" of the woman of Samaria. On the whole, several details point to the conclusion that there was actually some place of purification of the kind described by John; that Christ actually performed an act of healing there; and that the circumstances lent themselves so easily to allegory that John took this one act of healing as typical of the whole class of similar acts mentioned by the Synoptists. It is easy to see how the "year by year[1]" filling of the pool mentioned by Eusebius—as the result of "rains"—might give rise to the notion of an annual and miraculous agency adopted by Tertullian. A 6th or 7th century inscription given below[2], late

---

[1] [**2961** (i) *a*] See **2960**. Κατ' ἔτος occurs in N.T. only in Lk. ii. 41, of going up to the feast of the Passover, and κατ' ἐνιαυτόν only in Heb. ix. 25, x. 1, 3 of the Highpriest making atonement. For ἔτος interchanged with ἐνιαυτός, s. 1 K. xiv. 21 parall. 2 Chr. xii. 13, Ezr. vii. 8 parall. 1 Esdr. viii. 6. According to Jerome, one pool was of the colour of "blood," the other (presumably) of the ordinary colour of water. Eusebius and Jerome agree in connecting the blood-red colour with sacrifices, Ἴχνος, ὥς φασι,...τῶν πάλαι καθαιρομένων ἐν αὐτῇ ἱερείων, "quasi cruentis aquis antiqui operis in se signa testatur. Nam hostias in eo lauari a sacerdotibus solitas ferunt." We may accept the Bordeaux Pilgrim's "piscinae gemellares" (Geyer p. 21) (A.D. 333) as being those described by John, while regarding his "porticos" as doubtful. Comp. *ib.* "crepta (*sic*) ubi Salomon dæmones torquebat" &c.

[2] [**2961** (i) *b*] Boeckh *Inscr.* 9060.

Ἐν τῷ Σωλοάμ, προβατικῇ κολυμβήθρ[ᾳ]
([ὄ]νομα αὐτοῖς ἑβραεστὶν Βηδσαιδά), εὗρηθε ὁ κ[ύριο]ς, ἐν τῇ στοουᾷ τὸ Σολομῶντος εὗρηθε ὁ τησπότης τὸν ἄνθρ(ωπον) καταγείμενος ἀργόν· ἠθεράπευσεν καὶ τὸν δυψλὸν ἀνέβληψεν. ὅθεν καὶ ὑμεῖς ματὰ τὸν ἀρχανγγέλον τὸν ἀζωμάτων ἀναβῶντα καὶ γεγρακόντα καὶ λέγοντες· ἅγιος ὁ θεός, ὃ ἀνυμνῖ τὰ χερουβὶν καὶ προσκυνοῦσ-[ιν οἱ...]οι· ἅγιος ἰσχυρ[ός], ὃ ἐνδοξάσσοι ὁ χορὸς τῶν ἀζωμάτων ἀγγέλο[ν].
[ἅγιος, ἀθάν]ατος, ὁ [ἐ]ν φωνῇ τὸν ἀλόγον γνορισθείς· ἠλέησον ὑμᾶς.

though it is, shews how these picturesque surroundings of this particular act of Christ might be blended with other acts. And it is not impossible that Luke's account of a dropsical man healed on the Sabbath may have some connexion with John's story of the man lying sick and helpless by the water[1].

JN ii. 20 "FORTY-SIX YEARS"

[2962] According to some commentators, another indication of date—not indeed of the date of the writing of the gospel but of an event in the gospel—occurs in ii. 20 "forty-six years was this temple in building." But it can be shewn that this is simply an erroneous statement made by the Jews about the Temple of Ezra. It may have been current even before the first century (*Joh. Gram.* 2021—4). Many Jews may have refused to regard the Idumæan Herod as building the Temple; in their eyes, he merely "repaired" it[2].

The Editor says, "Aetatem tituli certo definiri non posse fatendum est. Mihi si credis, ad secula referas post Chr. septimum vel octavum."

[1] **[2961** (i) *c*] "Dropsical" occurs in N.T. only in Lk. xiv. 2, of a man healed on the sabbath. There is no single word of native Heb. or Aramaic to express "dropsical." SS transliterates ὑδρωπικός, but Syr-Pesh. gives "who had *gathered* waters," and *Thes. Syr.* (1774) quotes a saying that Hadrian died "in (ב) a *gathering* of waters." But in Gen. i. 10 "the gathering together of the waters," rendered by Vulg. "*congregationes* aquarum," is, in Onk. and Jon., "*house of gathering* of the waters." And this phrase "*house of gathering together* (or, *of congregation*)" is regularly used for "*synagogue*."

[2961 (i) *d*] Again, *Thes. Syr.* 1549 shews that עַל יַד in Syriac, as well as in Hebrew (Buhl 306 *b*), means "by the side of," so that a man "lying sick by the side of the water," might be described as κατακείμενος νοσῶν ἐπὶ χεῖρα ὑδάτων. But to a Greek this might convey the notion of some *disease of the hand*. Hence it is not to be passed over that Luke's account of the cure of the *dropsical* man in a private house (xiv. 1—2) on the sabbath is in many respects parall. to his account (vi. 6) of a man with a withered *hand* cured in a *synagogue* (parall. to Mk iii. 1, Mt. xii. 10). The word "*waters*," whether inserted or omitted, is not so easy to explain. It may however be noted that in vi. 6, Lk. alone says it was the "*right* hand," יְמִין, and this is confusable with מַיִם "waters." Details must remain uncertain, but there is evidence enough to shew that many of the divergences in the accounts of sabbath healing may be explained by divergent interpretations of one and the same obscure Semitic original.

[2] **[2962** *a*] Some, who favour an early date for the fourth gospel, allege, in favour of it, an expression in the first epistle, 1 Jn ii. 18 "*It is the last hour*," as being language likely to have preceded the fall of Jerusalem, to which fall, as an accomplished fact, they find no allusion in the gospel. But Jn xi. 48—52 appears to be just such a prophecy as the author might repeat, a generation after its accomplishment, "The Romans will come and *take away both our place and*

[2963] Page 310, "Connected with sacrifice." Lev. i. 6—9 refers to the washing of the "feet" and the "inward parts" of sacrificial victims. Origen *ad loc.* (Lomm. ix. 181) says, "Pedes abluit qui consummationem suscipit sacramenti, et scit quia qui mundus est non indiget nisi ut pedes lavet." In his comment on Jn xiii. 5 Origen, after contrasting Christ with Abraham (Gen. xviii. 4) and Joseph (Gen. xliii. 23—4) who did not themselves wash the feet of their guests, says "But He who said (Lk. xxii. 27), 'I came (*sic*) not as the guest but as the attendant,' and who with justice says (Mt. xi. 29), 'Learn from me, for I am meek and lowly in heart'— He Himself puts water in the basin."

[2964] Origen's "I came" is a reminiscence of the parallel to Lk. xxii. 27 in Mk x. 45, Mt. xx. 28, "the son of man *came* not to be ministered unto but to minister and *to give his life a ransom for many*." This is a slight indication of Origen's recognition of the notion of "expiation," "ransom," or "sacrifice," as underlying "the washing of feet." He adds that Christ "wiped off" the uncleanness from the feet of the disciples with the towel with which He girt Himself (Lomm. ii. 401) "perhaps to make their feet cleaner, but perhaps to take into His own body the filth on the feet of the disciples...for (Is. liii. 4, comp. Mt. viii. 17) '*He bears our infirmities.*'"

[2965] Philo, i. 115 and ii. 242, comments on Lev. i. 9, ix. 14, and in both passages explains the washing of the "feet," and the washing of the "inward parts," with reference to spiritual purification.

P. 310, "John intervenes," see *Joh. Gram.* Index, "John, intervention of." Comp. Dom J. Chapman (*Journal of Theological Studies*, April 1906, p. 426), "In the *Revue Bénédictine* (July 1905) I have expressed my full agreement with Dr E. A. Abbott's re-

---

our nation." And surely a Christian teacher in the days of Domitian might well think, and say, "It is the last hour"! Even after that date, the thought would still be natural. Who would argue that Ignatius wrote before the fall of Jerusalem because he says to the Ephesians § 11 "*The last times [are at hand]*," ἔσχατοι καιροί?

[2962 *b*] In Jn xxi. 18—23, there is nothing to shew that the death of Peter had recently occurred. What is shewn, or at least made probable, is that an old tradition had contrasted Peter's comparatively early death with the unusually protracted life of the "disciple whom Jesus loved," leading some disciples to a conclusion that the latter might possibly not die till the coming of the Saviour. This conclusion appears to have been contradicted by the death of the disciple at a very advanced age. The contrast suggests that Peter had died long ago.

markable discovery that the fourth Gospel takes up, with explanation, the points in Mk which Lk. omits (*Encycl. Bibl.*, art. 'Gospels'), and I have shewn that the account of St Mark given by the Presbyter of Papias affords a very clear confirmation of this theory. Now in our present subject," the Brethren of the Lord, "we shall find Lk. carefully omitting certain things which he found in his authority Mk, and we shall find John explaining the apparent difficulty."

[2966] Page 311, "O God, my God," Ps. lxiii. 1 (LXX) ὁ θεὸς ὁ θεός μου, (Aq.) θεὲ ἰσχυρέ μου; p. 311, "My soul thirsteth," Ps. xlii. 2. In Hebrew, "my soul" is often used where Greek or English would use "I" or "myself" (*Paradosis* 1326).

The thirst for God's presence may also be a thirst to consummate God's will, which is the redemption of mankind. Compare *Saint Catherine of Siena, As seen in her Letters* (transl. by V. D. Scudder, Dent & Co., 1905) p. 120 "Do we wish to have that glorious hunger which these holy and true shepherds of the past have felt, and to quench in ourselves that fire of self-love? Let us do as they, who with fire quenched fire; for so great was the fire of inestimable and ardent charity that burned in their hearts and souls, that they were an-hungered and famished for the savour of souls....Should one ask me how men attained that sweet fire and hunger—inasmuch as we are surely in ourselves unfruitful trees—I say that those men grafted themselves into the fruitful tree of the most holy and sweet Cross, where they found the Lamb, slain with such fire of love for our salvation as seems insatiable. Still He cries that He is athirst, as if saying: 'I have greater ardour and desire and thirst for your salvation than I shew you with my finished Passion.'"

[2967] Page 311, "Rested his head," Jn xix. 30, see *Joh. Gram.* 2644 (i) quoting Origen, who interprets the words thus, and who is referred to here in *Silanus* as "one of the ablest Greek scholars among the brethren."

P. 311, "In Aramaic," see *Corr. of Mk* 510—14.

[2967 a] ADDENDUM ON 2942* (xxiv). See *Journal of Theol. Stud.*, Apr. 1907, pp. 436—44, indicating that Hegesippus testified to the exile of John under Domitian. The argument would be still stronger if the two names alleged by an unknown writer from Hegesippus (*ib.* p. 437) ὁ μὲν ἐκαλεῖτο Ζωκήρ, ὁ δὲ Ἰάκωβος, could be shewn to be a corruption of the term quoted correctly in Euseb. iii. 20. 1 .Ἰουόκατος (*i.e.* "evocatus," "veteran") v.r. Ἡκόβατος, Πριβοκάτος &c., Ruf. "revocatus"—conflated as (1) καλούμενος, (2) a pair of proper names.

NOTES TO CHAPTER XXXII

[2968] Page 312, "He meant," see *Joh. Gram.* 2467 foll.; p. 313, "Give me to drink," Jn iv. 7; p. 313, "If anyone be athirst," Jn vii. 37; p. 313, "Thirsting to free them from thirst," see the words of St Catherine of Siena quoted in 2966.

THE NAME "BOANERGES"

[2969] Page 314, "Translated the term correctly." See *Hor. Heb.* on Mk iii. 17, shewing that the *o* in "Boanerges" may have been the result of Jewish pronunciation in Galilee, so that it may represent "sons of," and quoting a passage where the Hebrew *rgs* (represented by *-erges* in "Boanerges") means the "rushing sound" of the divine glory, or Shechinah: Megill. 29 *b* "The father of Samuel sat in the synagogue...the Shechinah came. He heard the voice of the *rigsha* [*i.e.* the rushing sound of the Spirit] and went not out: the angels came and he was affrighted."

[2970] Comp. the account of the descent of the Holy Spirit in Acts ii. 2 "*the sound as of a mighty rushing wind.*" It happens that the same word means "perception," "understanding," so that there might be a double meaning in the title, (1) "sons of *perception*," (2) "sons of *divine revelation*." Levy i. 239 *b* quotes "sons of the *rigsha*" as meaning "Spürende, die Empfindung haben"; but the context of Levy's extract indicates that the meaning there is physical and special[1], and it would be inappropriate here.

[2971] Josephus, describing the Shechinah as abandoning the temple to the Romans, mentions (*Bell.* vi. 5. 3) "a moving, and a beating [of the air] and afterwards a voice as of a great multitude [saying], 'Let us depart hence.'" Comp. Ezek. iii. 12—13 "Then the spirit lifted me up and I heard behind me the voice of a great rushing....And I heard the noise of the wings of the living creatures... and the noise of the wheels...even the noise of a great rushing." The Syriac Thesaurus 3815—6 gives the word in its masc. and fem.

---

[1] [2970 *a*] Levy *Ch.* ii. 407—8 gives רגש as "rauschen," and (Af.) "merken, nachspüren," also רגש as "das Rauschen," not Nachspürung, but (*ib.* 408) רגישתא as "das Empfinden" in Job xx. 2, where LXX and Targ. ("*sensus* meus in me est") differ from Heb.

NOTES TO CHAPTER XXXII

forms as meaning (1) "uproar," "tumult," "sound of a multitude," "rushing," (2) "sense," "perception."

[2972] It may be regarded as almost certain that the title "Boanerges" was meant by Mark in a good sense, like "Peter." This Origen assumes. In modern times, it has been suggested that it may record a name of rebuke incidentally used by Jesus (just as He is said to have incidentally called Peter "Satan" and "stumbling-block"). But is it credible that Mark could place such a dishonourable title here in his account of the appointment of the Twelve, in contrast with the honourable title given to Peter?

[2973] A difficulty, felt by some, has been that in Hebrew, men would not be said to thunder (as Aristophanes says of Pericles that he lightened and thundered) except in a *bad* sense, meaning "murmur," "rebel" etc. But the explanation suggested above (2970) excludes the notion—which is the popular one about a modern "Boanerges"—that *the man "thunders." It is from God* that there comes the *"rushing mighty sound,"* which Mark has, not very correctly, translated *"thunder."*

[2974] Origen has no comment on Mark; but he may perhaps refer to the correct interpretation *i.e.* "sons, and receivers, of the voices of divine revelation," when he speaks of the "thunder" (Lomm. iv. 14) as "the true mother" of the sons of Zebedee, who "*have taken in* (χωρήσαντας) her mighty sound." "Take in," χωρέω, may imply spiritual "perception" (comp. Mt. xix. 11—12). To the same effect is Orig. *Cels.* vi. 77 "And those who have obtained as their lot birth from words of loud utterance (ἐκ λόγων τὴν γένεσιν λαχόντες μεγαλοφώνων), who in no respect fall short of being sons of thunder." This follows a comment on Peter as "having taken in (χωρήσας) the building of the Church in himself from the word." Both "Peter" and "Boanerges" are regarded as honourable titles.

[2975] Elsewhere Origen (Lomm. i. 165) refers to John thus, "What as to him that lay on the breast of Jesus, who has left [only] one gospel, [though] avowing that he was able to compose so many that the world would not hold them? But he also wrote the Apocalypse, having been commanded to be silent (Rev. x. 4) and *not to write the voices of the seven thunders.*" This implies, *not that John himself "thundered," but that he received "thunders" of God*, that is, voices of God (the Hebrew word "voice" is repeatedly used for "thunder"). Compare *Enoch* 59, where the Patriarch says, "I saw the secrets of the thunder...how it ministers unto well-being and blessing, or serves for a curse before the Lord of Spirits."

[2976] It would naturally be displeasing to judicious friends of John the son of Zebedee to find that the name "sons of thunder," as given by Mark, was interpreted in the west as meaning merely loud-tongued or sonorous—preachers of the gospel with a voice of thunder. Since Luke omits the name (as also does Matthew) the fourth gospel (according to its custom) might be expected to intervene.

[2977] There is no trace of direct intervention; but indirectly it represents John (1) as anything but "thunderous," and (2) as being peculiarly "a son of perception." (1) Although he and Andrew are the first to join Jesus, John's name is not mentioned. Nor does John receive a new name (as Simon does in the context, "thou shalt be called Cephas"). (2) John and Andrew simply receive a promise of revelation (Jn i. 39 "Come and ye shall see"). This perhaps prepares the way for constituting him a Boanerges in the sense "son of vision" or "son of perception." He is certainly a disciple of "perception" later on, for he is the first to "catch a glimpse of, and note" (παρακύψας (*Joh. Voc.* 1798—1804) βλέπει) the bands of the grave discarded by Christ. He is also the first disciple mentioned as "believing" (Jn xx. 8) after the Resurrection. Moreover, on the sea of Gennesaret, when the disciples have failed to recognise Jesus, it is the "son of perception" who first recognises Him (Jn xxi. 7) "That disciple whom Jesus loved saith to Peter 'It is the Lord.'"

[2978] Page 315, "Simon son of John," Jn xxi. 15—17; p. 315, "sons of Zebedee," Jn xxi. 2; p. 316, "Be not little children," 1 Cor. xiv. 20. Here, and in all that follows, "little children" represents παιδία (not τεκνία); p. 316, "Calls to them and says 'Little children,'" Jn xxi. 5. See *Joh. Voc.*, **1676** *b*, *Joh. Gram.*, **2235** *c*; p. 316, "Born from above," Jn iii. 3, on which see *Joh. Gram.* **1903—8**.

P. 316, "Mother's word," Jn xiii. 33 τεκνία. The nearest equiv. is perhaps "darlings." It does not occur in LXX, and Steph. gives no instances of it in prose writers before N.T. But it occurs in Epict. iii. 22. 78, Anton. ix. 40, x. 34 etc., always with some notion of contempt. In N.T. it occurs only in Gal. iv. 19 (v. r. τέκνα) τεκνία

[2978] NOTES TO CHAPTERS XXXII, XXXIII

μου οὖς πάλιν ὠδίνω, and 1 Jn ii. 1, 12 etc. Origen (on Jn xiii. 33) says that it indicates fondness (ὑποκοριστικοῦ) on the part of Christ and also spiritual childishness (βραχύτητα...ψυχῆς) in the apostles.

P. 316, "Orphans," Jn xiv. 18. See **2805** *a*; p. 316, "In Himself," Jn xv. 4, 5, 6 etc.; p. 316, "Paul never mentions it." It occurs, however, in Heb. ii. 13, 14, xi. 23; p. 316, "I have written unto you, little children," 1 Jn ii. 14; p. 317, "The Son of God chose," *Catherine of Siena* p. 46.

[2979] Page 318, "The son of Joseph," "from Nazareth." This is implied for all the disciples mentioned in Jn i. 37—46, except that Nathanael at first raises an objection to "Nazareth," an objection almost immediately dropped. In the case of Philip, it is not only implied but expressed, i. 45 "We have found Jesus son of Joseph, Jesus of Nazareth."

P. 319, "Taking hold of Christ's feet," Mt. xxviii. 9, comp. Jn xx. 17, and s. **2999** (i) foll.; p. 320, "Agreed with Scaurus," see *Silanus* p. 252 foll.; p. 320, "Before the Resurrection," Mt. xviii. 18, xiv. 29—30.

NOTES TO CHAPTER XXXIII

[2980] Page 322, "What did (Jn i. 1—2) '*with*' mean?" See *Joh. Gram.* 2363—6.

THE PREFACE TO LUKE'S GOSPEL

P. 323, "The *facts*," Lk. i. 1 περὶ τῶν πεπληροφορημένων ἐν ἡμῖν πραγμάτων. For the very emphatic position of πραγμάτων, comp. Heb. xi. 1 as punctuated by Field in his edition of Chrys., and as interpreted by Chrys., ἔστι δὲ πίστις, ἐλπιζομένων ὑπόστασις πραγμάτων, ἔλεγχος οὐ βλεπομένων: so punctuated by W. H. marg., but without comma after πίστις. It has the same meaning ("*facts*, not fancies") in Heb. x. 1, and is also best taken thus in Heb. vi. 18. Lommatzsch v. 85—6 prints a Gk fragm. of Origen (not in the Latin transl.) on Lk. i. 1 "He used the word πραγμάτων to destroy the heresy of those who assert (λεγομένων ? λεγόντων) that the acts of the Saviour *occurred only in phantasms* during His incarnation (τὴν αἵρεσιν τῶν κατὰ φαντασίαν λεγομένων τὰ διὰ τοῦ Σωτῆρος γεγενῆσθαι κατὰ τὴν σάρκωσιν αὐτοῦ)."

[2981] Page 323, "Consummated," πεπληροφορημένων, "solidly

NOTES TO CHAPTER XXXIII [2984]

fulfilled." Heb. x. 1 speaks of three degrees of reality: (1) "shadows," (2) "likenesses," (3) "facts." Comp. Herm. *Sim*. ii. 9, where the prayers of the poor are said to "*give fulness to*" the wealth of the rich, and the alms of the rich "*give fulness to*" the souls of the poor —in both cases using πληροφορεῖν, and playing on the double meaning of the word. Applied to *things*, it means "give full realisation to an act"; applied to *persons*, it means "satisfy."

[2982] In *Pap. Ox.* vol. iii. 509 (10) it means "*I have been fully paid* my debt," and so perhaps in Berlin Urk. (1st cent.) 665 II. 2; in *ib*. 747 I. 22 the context leaves the meaning uncertain. By saying "solidly fulfilled among us," *i.e.* among us Christians, Luke probably intends to convey more than would have been conveyed by πεπληρωμένων. Lightfoot (on Col. iv. 12) is right in saying "there is no justification for translating it 'most surely believed' in Lk. i. 1": but some *notion of the writer's strong conviction of reality is suggested*. This is confirmed by the fragm. of Origen, above quoted, Περὶ δὲ τῶν πεπληροφορημένων εἰπὼν, τὴν διάθεσιν αὐτοῦ ἐμφαίνει, and he continues "for *he had been fully satisfied* (πεπληφόρητο sic) and was in no doubt whether things were so or not." Similarly a schol. in Cramer on Lk. i. 1.

[2983] Page 323, "Eyewitnesses...accessories." "Eyewitness" does not occur in N.T. except in Lk. i. 2. Ὑπηρέται—too loosely paraphrased in *Silanus* as "accessories," in order to distinguish it from διάκονοι, the ordinary word for "ministers"—in N.T. almost always means the "officers," or "attendants," of the chief priests. But it is used in connexion with the gospel in Acts xiii. 5 "they had John as *attendant*" (called previously *ib*. xii. 25 "John surnamed Mark"), xxvi. 16 "to appoint thee" [*i.e.* Saul] "a *minister* (ὑπηρέτην) and a witness both of the things wherein thou hast seen me, and of the things wherein I will appear unto thee," 1 Cor. iv. 1 "Let a man thus reckon of us as *ministers* of Christ."

[2984] Although Luke in the Acts applies the word ὑπηρέτης to Mark, and although he borrows largely from Mark, it is not probable that in the words οἱ ἀπ' ἀρχῆς αὐτόπται κ. ὑπηρέται γενόμενοι τοῦ λόγου he intends to draw a distinction between two kinds of witnesses and to include Mark in the latter. It is true that Papias says about Mark (Euseb. iii. 39. 15) "He was neither a hearer of the Lord nor a follower of Him, but, later on, as I said, [a follower] of Peter." But, if Luke had intended such a distinction, would he not have omitted γενόμενοι and repeated the article (οἱ...

[2984] NOTES TO CHAPTER XXXIII

αὐτόπται καὶ οἱ ὑπηρέται)? He appears to mean (as Origen implies) "those who consistently became [in the first place] eyewitnesses from the very beginning and [in the next place] servants of the Word." Probably Luke would have placed Paul also in this class. Chronologically and literally, Paul could not be thus classed. But spiritually, the words of Christ (Acts xxvi. 16 "thou hast seen... I will appear") covering both past and future, when combined with mentions of "visions" and "revelations" in the Epistles and Acts, might seem to Luke to justify the classification[1].

---

[1] [2984 a] Iren. iii. 14. 2 quotes Paul's farewell to the Ephesians, including Acts xx. 27 "I have not shunned to declare unto you the whole counsel of God." Then he says, "Thus did the Apostles......deliver to all what they had themselves learned from the Lord. Thus also does Luke...deliver to us what he had learned from them, as he has himself testified, saying (Lk. i. 2) '*Even as...from the beginning eyewitnesses and ministers of the Word.*'" Here, and in iv. pref. 3, he implies that Luke means "the apostles," including Paul. But he does not explain how "from the beginning" and "eyewitnesses" could apply to Paul.

[2984 b] Origen suggests various explanations of "eyewitnesses" (Lomm. vol. xx. Proleg. x. foll.) (1) those that saw Christ in the flesh (comp. Jn i. 14); (2) ἢ τοῦτό φησιν· ὑπηρέται τοῦ λόγου γεγόνασιν οἱ ἀπόστολοι, ὡς τὸν λόγον τῆς ἀληθείας παραδιδόντι τῷ Ἰησοῦ, meaning (?) "Or else he says this, 'The apostles are said to have become servants of the Word, as [being servants] to Jesus, who delivers the Word of Truth'"; (3) then follows, "But another says, 'If to have seen the Lord in the body had been to become an eyewitness of Him (τούτου) then Pilate would have been an eyewitness of the Word....Knowing the Word therefore (τὸ οὖν εἰδέναι τὸν λόγον) must be understood as the Saviour says (Jn xiv. 9) *He that hath seen me hath seen the Father.*'" Comp. a Latin version of this in Orig. *Lk. Hom.* 1, Lomm. v. 88—9, and a fragment in Lomm. v. 237 πραγμάτων δὲ εἶπεν ἐπεὶ οὐ κατὰ φαντασίαν, κατὰ τοὺς τῶν αἱρετικῶν παῖδας ἐδραματούργει ὁ Ἰησοῦς....

[2984 c] Neither the Latin nor the Greek version of Origen's comment explains what meaning he attaches to "from the beginning (ἀπ' ἀρχῆς)" and whether it would apply to Paul. But, as he spiritualises the context, he probably gives to this phrase also something more than a chronological meaning. Ἀπ' ἀρχῆς, in N.T., means "consistently, from the first"—for good in Jn xv. 27 "ye have been (ἐστέ) with me *from the beginning* (ἀπ' ἀρχῆς)," 1 Jn ii. 7 "the old commandment, which ye had *from the beginning*," implying a spontaneous reception and retention of the good. On the other hand it is applied to evil in Jn viii. 44 "he was a murderer *from the beginning.*" In Mk x. 6, Mt. xix. 4, 2 Pet. iii. 4, ἀπ' ἀρχῆς refers to God's arrangement; and the negation of ἀπ' ἀρχῆς in Mt. xix. 8, Mk xiii. 19, Mt. xxiv. 21 refers to man's disarrangement or to exceptional miseries caused by man's sin. This differs from the chronological meaning of ἐξ ἀρχῆς in Jn vi. 64, xvi. 4. In 1 Jn, ἀπ' ἀρχῆς is very freq. to denote the eternal and continuous Word, or Command, and the spontaneousness and continuity of the Christian reception of it.

NOTES TO CHAPTER XXXIII [2985]

[2985] Page 324, "John...Epictetus." A very interesting coincidence appears on the surface in Jn x. 1 "He that entereth not *through the door* (διὰ τῆς θύρας)...is a thief and a robber," and Epict. ii. 11. 1 on the right initiation into "philosophy," at least "for those that attach themselves to it fitly and *by the door* (ὡς δεῖ καὶ κατὰ θύραν)." But comp. Plutarch *Mor.* ii. p. 617 A–B "Lest we should seem, while excluding conceit by *the hall-door, to let her in by the side-door* (τῇ αὐλείῳ...ἀποκλείοντες εἰσάγειν τῇ παραθύρῳ)," and Clem. Alex. 897 "not throwing open the hall-door...but *cutting open* (ἀνατεμόντες) *a side-door*," with which comp. Lucan *Phars.* ii. 443 "Non tam portas intrare patentes quam *fregisse juvat.*" Lucian (*Nigrin.* 31, i. p. 73) seems to assume that the phrase is familiar (τὸ λεγόμενον) to theatre-goers when he says that the seekers after unseasonable and unnatural pleasure are guilty of the fault of which "mention is made both in tragedies and comedies," forcing their way in "*beside the door* (παρὰ θύραν εἰσβιάζεσθαι)." From all this it

---

[2984 *d*] This sense, of spontaneous reception from the first, might be illustrated by Gal. i. 15 "It pleased God, *who set me apart* [*i.e.* for the gospel] *from my mother's womb*," and it is really supported—not contradicted—by Acts xxvi. 14 "It is *hard* for thee to kick against the goads." The Galatian Epistle also represents the Pauline gospel (Gal. ii. 2) as at one with that of the older Apostles; and, as has been said above, "revelation" might be supposed to convey to Paul the gospel as it was "from the beginning."

[2984 *e*] Iren. iii. 14. 1 describes Luke as "inseparable from Paul," and Luke's phrase was probably intended not to distinguish Paul from the "eyewitnesses from the beginning" but to claim for him a place among them. Perhaps Luke had in view Paul's self-description as (1 Cor. iv. 1) "a minister of Christ and steward of the mysteries of God," as distinguished from those who were unfaithful "stewards" and who tampered with the Word. "Ministers of the Word" is perhaps a brief way of suggesting (1) "servants of the incarnate Logos," and (2) "stewards of His logos," in a single phrase. The saying in Plato's *Theætetus* (p. 173), "We...are not ministers (ὑπηρέται) of the *logoi*, but the *logoi* are as it were our own house-slaves (οἰκέται)," might hold good of some *logoi* but did not hold good of the Logos of the Gospel. Some Christians, however, at a very early date—perhaps before Luke wrote his preface—acted as though they were not ὑπηρέται, and as though the Christian history contained, not πεπραγμένα, but (as Origen says) φαντασίαι. In some critical details these heretics may have been right, but in their heresy of a non-human Christ they were fatally wrong. In some sayings, *e.g.* about refusing to "know" Christ "after the flesh," Paul may have seemed to support the heretics against the other Apostles. Against this view Luke contends, saying, in effect, "My story is one of facts, not fancies; and my teachers are those who had personal knowledge, and insight into the meaning of facts, from the beginning; instead of shaping the truth to accord with their imaginations, they devoted themselves to the service of the Word."

would seem that both John and Epictetus inherited the metaphor of "forcing entrance *beside the door.*" But it is not at all improbable that John borrowed the application from Epictetus. It seems to be Greek, not Jewish, in phrase, and perhaps in thought.

P. 324, "When a wolf snatches away," Epict. iii. 22. 35, contrast Jn x. 11—12; p. 325, "Blames Ulysses," Epict. iii. 24. 18—20, contrast Jn xi. 35 ; p. 325, "This is eternal life," Jn xvii. 3, on which see *Joh. Gram.* 1936; p. 325, "Thrice troubled," Jn xi. 33, xii. 27, xiii. 21; p. 326, "Ye are clean," Jn xv. 3; p. 326, "Epictetus...with the Logos," Epict. iv. 11. 4; p. 327, "Look at the passages," Mk xiv. 58, Mt. xxvi. 61, Jn ii. 19—21.

[2986] Page 328, "Watching and sweat." Comp. 2 Macc. ii. 26 "The business was one *of sweat and watching,*" where the Syriac, for "*sweat,*" has (Walton) "sudore et labore lassitudineque." In quoting Lk. xxii. 44, Justin Martyr omits "of blood," *Tryph.* 103 "sweat streamed down like drops," or rather, "like clots." This suggests how the interpolation developed. First it was merely "sweat," used metaphorically, meaning "anxious toil" or "travail." Then it was taken literally. Then, in order to indicate that there was something unusual, and also perhaps in order to explain how it was visible to the disciples at some distance, "like clots" was added. But Wetstein *ad loc.* quotes Galen, "*clot,* for this is the customary Greek word for congelated *blood.*" Hence it would be natural to add "*of blood.*" The Arabic diatessaron has "*as a river of blood.*" The passage is omitted by the best Gk MSS. and by SS, and is placed in double brackets by W. H. But it must have been a very early interpolation, for Irenæus iii. 22. 2 speaks of Christ's "sweating clots of blood." "Clot" is θρόμβος in all these passages.

[2987] Page 328, "He that hath seen...may believe," Jn xix. 35, on which see *Joh. Gram.* textual Index.

P. 328, "He that seeth (ὁρῶν)," comp. 1 Chr. xxi. 9, 2 Chr. ix. 29, xii. 15, also used by Theod. and Sym. in 1 S. ix. 9. The phrase in the present tense, "he that seeth God," is regularly applied to Israel by Philo i. 483, 526, comp. 124, 369 etc. For the sake of distinguishing Christian vision, and to emphasize its permanence, John might prefer to use the perfect of ὁράω. He never uses the present. His non-use of it cannot be explained by contemporary disuse of the present, for it is very freq. indeed in the second century.

P. 329, "Zechariah," Zech. xiii. 1 "In that day there shall be a fountain opened."

P. 329, "A marginal note," Mt. xxvii. 49 enclosed by W. H. in double brackets, see *Joh. Voc.* 1756.

[2988] Page 329, "Acts of John," 12—15 "I therefore, having seen Him, did not even abide at His passion but fled to the Mount of Olives.... And our Lord stood in the midst of the cave...and having said these things He shewed me a cross of light...and the Lord Himself I could see above the cross not having shape but a kind of voice....'Thou hearest that I suffered, yet I did not suffer; [thou hearest] that I did not suffer, yet I did suffer...; thou hearest that blood flowed from me (αἷμα ἐξ ἐμοῦ ῥεύσαντα (*sic*)) and it did not flow.'" But the *Acts of John*, though a very early work, could not have been known to Scaurus in 118 A.D.

P. 329, "Crib," see *Joh. Voc.* 1673, 1736; p. 329—30, "Ambiguities," "Philo," and "lifted up," see *Joh. Gram.* Index.

[2989] Page 330, "Thou art not yet fifty...," Jn viii. 57. On this see *Hor. Heb.* referring to Numb. iv. 3 and iv. 47. But Numb. viii. 25—6 shews that, after the age of fifty, the Levite was not (as *Hor. Heb.* says) "superannuated" but *relieved from laborious service*. Hence Philo says i. 204 "the fiftieth logos is *complete*, or *perfect* (τέλειος)." Origen (on Numb. iv. 3—47, Lomm. x. 35 and x. 41—3) also says "usque ad quinquagesimum annum et fit iste *praecipuus numerus et electus*"; p. 331, "The young Irenæus," ii. 22. 5—6.

[2990] Page 331, "Another of the brethren." This is an anachronism, referring to Chrysostom, who reads "forty" both in his text and in his comment. Cyril says that, though Jesus was only thirty-three, the Jews thought that He was nearly fifty; p. 331, "Twofold and threefold attestation," see *Joh. Gram.* 2587—2623.

NOTES TO CHAPTER XXXIV

[2991] Page 334, "Seven before the resurrection." In *Joh. Gram.* 2624, "John records only seven 'signs,'" the words "*before the resurrection*" were assumed, but should have been added; p. 334, "Fourteen generations," see *Silanus* p. 226.

[2992] Page 334, "Mighty works," see *Joh. Voc.* 1686; p. 334, "The stronger," see *Joh. Gram.* 2799 a; p. 334, "Greatness," see *Joh. Voc.* 1683; p. 334—5, "No mention of repentance," "never uses the noun faith" etc. For these and other points see 1670 and the English alphabetical lists in *Joh. Voc.*; p. 335, "Ceres and

Pluto," Epict. ii. 20. 32 ; p. 335, "On the edge of the sea," see *Joh. Gram.* 2340—6, and *Fourfold G.* "sea."

[2993] Page 335, "A curious book," Fourth (or Second) Book of Esdras, on which see *Enc. Bibl.* col. 1392—3. The vision is described in ix. 38—x. 55.

[2994] Page 336, "David...'a son of thirty years'" is the lit. rendering of 2 S. v. 4, comp. Lk. iii. 23. Epiphanius says (*Adv. Hær.* Lib. ii. tom. ii. 34, p. 652) "We have also found in traditions that Lazarus was thirty years old at the time when he is recorded to have been raised from the dead, and after [the Lord] had raised him up he lived another thirty years"; p. 336, "The raising of Lazarus," see the author's article in *Enc. Bibl.* 2744—51.

P. 337, "Philo sees......Barnabas." Philo i. 481 comments on the two aspects of the name Eliezer, as denoting that man is "dead" without God: "Being interpreted, Eliezer means 'God my help,' since the lump of flesh and blood, which is by itself liable to dissolution and dead, is kept together and enkindled by God's providence." *Beresh. Rabb.* (on Gen. xiv. 14 "three hundred and eighteen") says that the number means "Eliezer," and Barnabas ix. 8 says that the number means "Jesus and the cross"; p. 337, "Christians," Justin Martyr *Tryph.* 134, Iren. iv. 21. 3.

[2995] Page 338, "Some leave it out," that is, Mt. x. 8 "raise the dead." Chrysostom and Jerome leave it out, as also do some good MSS. The Scholia published by Cramer say nothing about it. Nor does Alford. But it must be remembered that Origen also (once) omits "*the dead are raised*" in Mt. xi. 5, where the words, if taken literally, create great difficulty—because the Baptist's disciples are supposed *to see this and the other mighty works* ("Go, tell John the things that ye *hear* and *see*"). Luke meets the difficulty by (1) changing the present into past tenses (Lk. vii. 22 "the things that ye *saw* and *heard*"), and (2) introducing a raising of the dead just before the arrival of the Baptist's messengers, so that Christ is able to say with literal truth, "*the dead* (pl.) are raised," which Matthew (having mentioned no revivification except that of Jairus' daughter) could not consistently say except in a spiritual sense. A kindred difficulty occurs in Matthew's combination of a precept about "lepers" (Mt. x. 8), "*raise the dead, cleanse the lepers.*" This is mentioned by no other evangelist and (so far as we know) fulfilled by no Apostle. It will be maintained in a future treatise that Matthew has preserved a spiritual tradition of great value (which perhaps Luke may have taken literally and consequently omitted as erroneous). The Babylonian Talmud mentions a tradition that the Messiah would be a "leper." Of far greater importance is the fact that in Isaiah's account of the Suffering Servant as "*stricken*, smitten of God, and afflicted," Aquila and Symmachus render "*stricken*" by "*leprous*." According to Matthew, the first act of the Saviour, after descending from the mountain where He had promulgated the New Law, was to break the letter of the Old Law (while fulfilling its spirit) by touching a leper—thereby symbolizing His mission to "bear the infirmities and carry the pains" of sinful mankind. See *Fourfold Gospel* (Index, " Healing ").

P. 340, "Isaiah and Horace in one," Is. x. 33, Hor. iv. 4. 57; p. 341, "Arms of war," Cicero, *De Offic.* i. 22. 77; p. 341, "Laws are silent," *ib. Pro Mil.* 4; p. 342, "Frustra," Virgil, *Æneid* vi. 294.

NOTES TO CHAPTERS XXXV AND XXXVI

[2996] Page 351, "The kingdom of God," Lk. xvii. 21; p. 352, "So Paul," Acts xvii. 23 foll.; p. 353, "One year," see Irenæus (ii. 22. 1—5) who vehemently attacks heretics for holding this view, which however (see Grabe's note, p. 156) seems to have been held by Tertullian, Lactantius, Julius Africanus, and Clemens Alexandrinus; p. 353, "The acceptable year," Is. lxi. 2; p. 354, "Aio te, Æacida," see Shakespeare, *2 Hen. VI.* i. 4. 65; p. 357, "A woman," see "Letters of Saint Catherine of Siena," *passim*; p. 357, "one of our poets," Cowper; p. 358, "The Son of man," Mk x. 45, Mt. xx. 28, parall. to Lk. xxii. 27; p. 358, "Philo," see Philo i. 187—8 and *Paradosis*, 1285; p. 358, "Dry bones," Ezek. xxxvii. 1—14.

[2997] Page 364, "The Promise of the Man," Epict. ii. 9. 3. The word "promise," or "profession," ἐπαγγελία, occurs about 15 times in Epictetus and about as many times in the epistle to the Hebrews. It is also freq. in the Acts and the Pauline epistles. Bonitz gives it as only occurring once in Aristotle (and there in a bad sense), and Mitchell does not give it as occurring in Plato. It is also rare in Plutarch. It does not occur at present (1906) in the indices of the *Berl. Urkund.* and the *Egypt Expl. Pap.* Marc. Ant. does not use it. In canon. LXX, it occurs only thrice. It may be taken as characteristic of a few writers in N.T. and Epictetus. But Epictetus speaks of "the promise of the Man," "the promise of

Virtue," "the promise of the philosopher," whereas the N.T. writers mostly regard it as "the promise of God."

P. 364, "All...in subjection," Epict. ii. 10. 1; p. 364, "Thou hast put," Ps. viii. 6; p. 364, "Man...in honour," Ps. xlix. 12 (LXX).

ADDENDUM ON **2942***

[**2997** a] Page 75 above, "*It*, not *he*." See an able paper (*Journ. of Theol. Stud.*, Apr. 1907, pp. 431—5) on Iren. v. 30. 3 εἰ γὰρ ἔδει ἀναφανδὸν τῷ νῦν καιρῷ κηρύττεσθαι τοὔνομα αὐτοῦ [sc. τοῦ 'Αντιχρίστου] δι' ἐκείνου ἂν ἐρρέθη τοῦ καὶ τὴν 'Αποκάλυψιν ἑωρακότος. οὐδὲ γὰρ πρὸ πολλοῦ χρόνου ἑωράθη (*visum est*) ἀλλὰ σχεδὸν ἐπὶ τῆς ἡμετέρας γενεᾶς, πρὸς τῷ τέλει τῆς Δομετιανοῦ ἀρχῆς, urging (1) that the connexion requires "*He* (not *it*) was seen"; (2) that "he" harmonizes with v. 30. 1 μαρτυρούντων τῶν κατ' ὄψιν τὸν Ἰωάννην ἑωρακότων, and with similar phrases about "having *seen* apostles, elders &c.," *e.g.* iii. 3. 3 and 4, iv. 27. 1; (3) that "*visum* est" may be a corruption of "*visus* est," for, if the meaning were "*it* was seen," the Latin ought to be "*visa* est [sc. Apocalypsis]."

But (1) the connexion may be explained thus: "If it had been needful that the name should be openly proclaimed for the present season, it would have been mentioned by the same man that has also seen [the vision about the name], for [*the vision*] *was seen*...almost in our own generation [*so that it may almost be said to belong to 'the present season'*]." (2) Against Dr Chase's suggested paraphrase, "For the author was seen on earth, he lived and held converse with his disciples not so very long ago but almost in our own generation," there is the objection that Irenaeus' usual expression for prolonging life is παρέμεινε, *e.g.* ii. 22. 5 "He (John) *remained with* them up to the times of Trajan," iii. 3. 4 (*bis*) about John and Polycarp, iii. 4. 3 about Valentinus. Dr Chase would seemingly distinguish παρέμεινε "remained (alive)" from "was seen," *i.e.* was active. This hardly agrees with the Irenæan and Pauline (Phil. i. 25, Heb. vii. 23) use of παραμένω. Besides, Jerome implies (**2952**) that John "*was seen*" when bedridden. If "*was seen*" meant "*lived and held converse*," we should expect, not the aorist ἑωράθη, but an imperf. (to denote continuance) or some mention of "being heard," as in iv. 27. 1 "seen and heard." (3) "Visum" (neut.) may well refer to ὄνομα, or, κατὰ σύνεσιν, to ἡ 'Αποκάλυψις, *i.e.* τὸ ἀποκεκαλυμμένον ἐν τῇ 'Αποκαλύψει. Against the conjectural "visus," applied to John, there is this objection, that the passive of ὁράω (which is much rarer than the active) when used at all, seems mostly applied by Aq. and Iren. to *divine manifestations*, *e.g.* Aq. in Exod. vi. 3, Numb. xiv. 14, 1 S. iii. 21, Iren. i. 19. 2 ἑωρᾶσθαι "visum (masc.)," iv. 20. 5 "videtur," "visus" (*bis*), "videbitur," ἀόρατος ὀρώμενον (visibilem) ἑαυτὸν παρέσχεν.

Dr Chase—whose paper deserves careful study—endeavours to meet the objections based on the aorist ἑωράθη and on the naturalness of what he admits to be an "obvious" interpretation. But he does not appear to me successful. And compare Eusebius v. 8 ὅπως ὁ Εἰρηναῖος τῶν θείων μνημονεύει γραφῶν, quoting the ἑωράθη-clause with its preceding context. If the clause referred to John, Eusebius might have stopped short without quoting it. But he expressly says, "This is what Irenæus has recorded *about the Apocalypse*" (not, "*about John*").

PART II
LONGER NOTES

CONTENTS OF PART II

NOTE I

"THE SON OF MAN" [2998 (i)—(lvi)]

(i)　§ 1.　Importance of the Title
(ii)　§ 2.　Deficiency in Aramaic
(iii)—(iv)　§ 3.　"Son of Man" in the Law
(v)—(viii)　§ 4.　"Son of Man" in the Prophets
(ix)—(x)　§ 5.　"Son of Man" in the Psalms and Job
(xi)—(xix)　§ 6.　Jewish Comments
(xx)　§ 7.　Ambiguity of the Title
(xxi)　§ 8.　The Fourth Gospel prepares us for misinterpretation
(xxii)—(xxiii)　§ 9.　Pauline equivalents
(xxiv)—(xxv)　§ 10.　The Epistle to the Hebrews and the Acts
(xxvi)—(xxxiii)　§ 11.　The Revelation of John
　　(xxvi) c—g.　Who is "his angel"?
　　　 " h—k.　"Witness" and "martyr"
　　　 " l—m.　"The IS" and "the seven spirits"
　　　 " n—q.　"The faithful Witness"
　　(xxvii) a—e.　"The Alpha and the Omega"
　　　 " f—m.　"Almighty"
　　　 " n—q.　"Angels" not to be worshipped
　　　 " r—v.　Did Essenes "offer worship" to the sun?
　　　 " w.　The "washing" of the Essenes
　　(xxviii) b—e.　"The seven golden candlesticks"
　　　 " f—k.　"Walking in the midst"
　　　 " l—r.　"One like a son of man"
　　　 " s—x.　The "stars" and the "sword"
　　(xxx) b—(xxxi) c.　"Clouds" and "cloud"
　　(xxxii) b—d.　The difference between ἀρνίον and ἀμνός
(xxxiv)—(xxxvi)　§ 12.　The Gnostics, Ignatius, and Barnabas
(xxxvii)—(xli)　§ 13.　Justin, Irenæus, and Tertullian
(xlii)—(xlv)　§ 14.　Clement of Alexandria and Origen
(xlvi)—(l)　§ 15.　Conclusion
(li)—(lvi)　§ 16.　Addition on the "*Similitudes of Enoch*"
　　(liv) e—j.　"The righteous one"
　　(lv) d—m.　The doctrine of "hiding"
　　(lvi) a—d.　The resurrection

NOTE II

THE SELF-MANIFESTATIONS OF CHRIST [2999 (i)—(xvii)]

(i)—(ii) § 1. "Touching" and "drawing near"
(iii) § 2. God "meeting" man
(iv)—(v) § 3. "Going to meet," "going before," and "drawing near"
(vi) § 4. Different words employed by the Evangelists
(vii)—(viii) § 5. Matthew's unique use of "anticipate"
(ix)—(x) § 6. Matthew's account of Peter's "fishing" illustrated from John
(xi) § 7. Different symbolisms of "fish"
(xii)—(xvii) § 8. The original meaning of the story of "the stater"
(xvii) a—o. The "reclothing" of Peter

NOTE I

"THE SON OF MAN"

§ 1. *Importance of the Title*

[2998 (i)] This title is applied by our Lord to Himself in all the gospels. But it has been divergently explained from very early times. The divergence may cause a corresponding divergence in estimates of Christ's doctrine. For example, some have considered that it implied a claim to be the Messiah; others, that it implied an identification of Himself with ordinary mankind; and it has been already indicated (*Apologia* p. 62) that very early patristic interpretation favoured the view that ἄνθρωπος, "man"—which might mean "human being," male or female—meant, in this phrase, *the female parent*, so that "Son of man" meant "Son of the Virgin Mary." The task of throwing light on Christ's meaning by a comparison of evangelistic passages must be deferred to *The Fourfold Gospel* (Index, "Son of Man").

But evidence will be collected here bearing on the use of it in (1) Biblical Hebrew, (2) Jewish and Aramaic, (3) Early Christian writings. (4) An attempt will also be made to deduce from the facts here collected an inference as to the fundamental thought of the Law and the Prophets on which Christ based His adoption of this title.

§ 2. *Deficiency in Aramaic*

[**2998** (ii)] The regular Biblical Hebrew for "*man*" in "son of *man*" is *adam*, regularly rendered ἄνθρωπος, corresponding to *homo*. Hebrew has other words to express "man," *e.g. īsh*, regularly rendered ἀνήρ, corresponding to *vir*. "*Adam*" dropped out of Aramaic except as meaning the patriarch. This placed Aramaic at a disadvantage with Hebrew because the former could not distinguish so well as Hebrew could, between "homo" and "vir," ἄνθρωπος and ἀνήρ (Germ. "Mensch" and "Mann"). In English and French we are under the same disadvantage. The distinction is regularly recognised in the LXX, which (with a few exceptions in Proverbs) may be almost said never to use ἀνήρ to represent *adam*, whereas it uses ἀνήρ to represent *īsh*, the Hebrew "vir," many hundreds of times. This deficiency in Aramaic forces us to rely less on the precise Aramaic words in which Jesus may have called Himself "Son of man," and more on the context and circumstances in which He gave Himself this title. But still more must we rely on the *thought*—as distinct from the words—set forth in the best Biblical writings, and especially those parts of the Law, the Prophets, and the Psalms, from which our Lord quotes. Another reason for laying stress on the thought rather than the words is, that we have very little knowledge of the exact kind of Aramaic used in Galilee in 1—30 A.D. It was probably very different from that of the later Targums composed four or five centuries afterwards.

§ 3. "*Son of Man*" *in the Law*

[**2998** (iii)] For these reasons special attention is due to the only instance of "Son of man" (sing.) in the Pentateuch. It occurs in Balaam's Song and deserves attention from the point of view both of *thought* and of *word*. As to "*thought*," it represents Balaam as saying that God could not "repent" because He was not "Son of man." But God often "repents," in the Old Testament. The Talmudists much discussed this passage[1], naturally. And how could Jesus fail to have it in His mind, whether He accepted it, as from Scripture, or rejected it, as from Balaam? As to "*word*," the passage exhibits, both in Onkelos and in the two other Targums, paraphrases of "son of man" (either as "sons of flesh," or as "sons of men," without using the word *adam*), and all three paraphrases differing.

[**2998** (iv)] The Hebrew is (Numb. xxiii. 19) "God is not a *man* (*īsh*) that he should lie nor *son of* (*ben*) *man* (*adam*) that he should repent." Premising that *ben*, "son of" (Aramaic *bar*) may mean specimen of a class,—*e.g.* "*son of the herd*," (Gesen. 121*b*) "in general, *one of the herd*"—we might imagine a Targumist meditating thus concerning the best method of rendering the ancient Hebrew: "We do not use the singular *īsh* for 'vir,' but we have a plural form of it meaning men in general, 'homines.' Using this, I will paraphrase '*man*' as '*sons of men.*' As to *ben adam*, if I were to call it *bar adam*, it would mean 'son of Adam,' which is not the meaning. *Adam* suggests an earthly source, a corruptible or fleshly nature. I will therefore substitute '*flesh*,' and throw this phrase, too, into the plural, so as to indicate that it means a class. Since the plural, 'sons of,' is the same in Aramaic as in Hebrew, there

---

[1] See Schwab *Jer. Talm.* vol. vi. p. 156, Wünsche *Bemidb. R.* on Numb. xxiii. 19, and below, **2998** (xviii) foll.

will be no need to use *bar*." This is what Onkelos has done, as will be seen in the footnote[1].

A later Targumist might say, " In order to express *īsh*—which does not here mean emphatically 'vir'—I will use the Aramaic *bar nash*, 'son of man,' that is, 'ordinary man,' 'a specimen of humanity.' In order to express *ben adam*, I will follow Onkelos and say 'sons of flesh.'" This is what the Targum of Jonathan has done[1].

Again, a third Targumist has said, in effect, " I shall not try to express the difference between the Hebrew 'man' and 'son of man.' But, to shew that both terms signify a class, I will throw both, as Onkelos does, into the plural, 'sons of men,' and will use that phrase twice—not following him in the use of the term 'flesh[1].'"

The LXX mistranslates the passage. Philo repeatedly quotes it as " God is not *as man* (ὡς ἄνθρωπος)" and there stops short. He twice contrasts Balaam's saying favourably with Deut. i. 31, " The Lord thy God bare thee as a man doth

---

[1] [2998 (iv) *a*] Walton's translations, which are generally fairly accurate, exemplify, in these Targumistic passages, the differences that might be expected in early Christian attempts to render the Aramaic *bar nash*, or similar titles. I therefore give them in full. In Targ. Jon., Walton represents *bar nash* first by "hominum," and then by "homo." In Targ. Jer., he represents one and the same title by (1) "filiorum hominis," (2) "hominum," (3) "homines."

Onk. Non sicut verba filiorum hominum est sermo Dei; filii hominum (Walt. אנש by error, Lagarde אינשא, ed. Wien 1859 אנשא) dicunt et mentiuntur; nec juxta opera filiorum carnis, qui....

Jon. Non sicut verba hominum sermo Dei viventis......at homo dicit et renuit; et etiam non similia sunt opera ejus operibus filiorum carnis, quia....

Jer. Non sicut sermo filiorum hominis fuit sermo Dei viventis, nec secundum opera hominum [sunt] opera Dei. Homines dicunt et non faciunt....

This Pentateuchic use of " Son of man " derives additional importance from the fact that it is alluded to by a Jewish Rabbi at a very early date in a hostile reference to Jesus, in connexion with this title. See below 2998 (xviii).

bear his son," which is also mistranslated—by him in one way and by the LXX in another. "There are two fundamental principles," he says in effect, "One is, *God is not as man.* The other is, that [*He is*] *as man*; the former is confirmed by fundamental truth, the latter is for the sluggish, or for the teaching of the multitude¹."

The gospels indicate that our Lord judged the doctrine of Deuteronomy to be—at all events in His days, and perhaps

---

¹ [2998 (iv) *b*] Numb. xxiii. 19 LXX οὐχ ὡς ἄνθρωπος ὁ θεὸς διαρτηθῆναι (to be put off the scent) οὐδὲ ὡς υἱὸς ἀνθρώπου ἀπειληθῆναι (to be deterred by threats). It would be interesting to know whether Philo, when quoting it above (i. 280) and elsewhere (i. 181, 453, 656) was deterred from quoting more than οὐχ...θεός by an uneasy feeling that the LXX was inaccurate.

[2998 (iv) *c*] Deut. i. 31 "The Lord thy God bare thee as a man doth bear his son." This metaphor is explained by Rashi from the thought of a child attacked by robbers from the front; on which the pillar of cloud goes to the front; then, when he is attacked by wild beasts behind, the pillar of cloud goes behind. But presently he is attacked both behind and before. Then the Father "takes the child into His arms." Comp. Jon. Targ. "And in the desert where thou sawest burning serpents full of deadly venom, the Lord thy God bare thee with the glorious clouds of His Shechinah, as a man carrieth his child" [an exceptional use of "clouds" (2998 (xxx—xxxi)) meaning apparently the pillar of cloud and the pillar of fire].

[2998 (iv) *d*] This beautiful metaphor is spoiled by a mistranslation of "bear" in the LXX, which has "give food to (τροφοφορεῖν)" with v.r. "endure the ways of (τροποφορεῖν)." Philo when quoting it (twice) has παιδεύω, "chasten," i. 656 "And indeed it may be said that there are these two, and only these two, lines of thought in the whole Law (δύο εἰσὶν αὗται αἱ μόναι τῆς νομοθεσίας ἁπάσης ὁδοί), one that inclines to the truth, through which we reach the settled decision (δι' ἧς κατασκευάζεται), *God is not as Man*, but another—the one better fitted for the notions of the more sluggish sort, from which (ἀφ' ὧν) comes the saying (λέγεται) 'The Lord thy God shall chasten thee as if one should chasten—*a* [*mere*] *man* [should chasten] —his son (Παιδεύσει σε κύριος ὁ θεός, ὡς εἴ τις παιδεύσει ἄνθρωπος τὸν υἱὸν αὐτοῦ).'" Simil. i. 280—281 ὡς ἄνθρωπος παιδεῦσαι (sic) τὸν υἱὸν αὐτοῦ is quoted as "brought in [?temporarily, as if on a stage] for the teaching of the multitude (πρὸς τὴν τῶν πολλῶν διδασκαλίαν εἰσάγεται)," whereas Balaam's dictum "is confirmed by fundamental truth (ἀληθείᾳ βεβαιοτάτῃ πεπίστωται)."

for all days—necessary for the enlightenment of all classes as well as for "the multitude."

§ 4. *"Son of Man" in the Prophets*

[**2998** (v)] Isaiah twice uses *ben adam*, "*son of earthy man*," and both times parallel to a preceding *enôsh*. The etymology of the latter is variously given by experts, who define it as originally meaning "frail man" or "social man"; but in Isaiah, *enôsh* clearly means "*frail man*": Is. li. 12 "I, even I, am he that comforteth you. Who art thou that art afraid of *frail man*, who shall die, or the *son of earthy man*, who shall be appointed to be as grass?" In the other passage, there is a climax, or rather a descent, of frailty or transience, Is. lvi. 2—3 "*frail man* (enôsh)...*earthy man* (ben adam)... *stranger* (lit. *son of stranger*)...*eunuch*[1]." All these are comforted with the thought (in effect) that God, though He is in heaven, humbles Himself to behold the things that are on earth and helps the meanest of them. This thought runs through the Old Testament, as well as the New—that the "little one" is "great" in God's eyes, that the "poor" are to be raised up to the seat of judgment or the throne, and that "man" on earth is to be lifted up towards heaven.

Both passages of Isaiah imply a contrast, or relation, between God and *ben adam*. (1) "Man's son" is not to be feared in comparison with God; (2) "Man's son" is to feel comfort in the assurance that he is not forgotten by God.

[**2998** (vi)] *Ben adam* occurs in Jeremiah in a refrain about a desolate land "where no *man* (*ish*) shall abide nor *son of man* (*ben adam*) dwell." The Targum ignores the difference of nouns (having *enâsh* (**2998** (v) *a*) and *bar enâsh*), and there is hardly any distinction of meaning except a suggestion that "nor son of man" means "nor even man of the lowest rank[2]."

---

[1] [**2998** (v) *a*] The Targum does not attempt to preserve Isaiah's distinction. It has *enâsh* (the Aram. form of *enôsh*) followed by *bar* and *enâsh* (genit.), in both passages.

[2] Jer. xlix. 18, 33, l. 40, li. 43.

[**2998** (vii)] *Ben adam* is frequent in Ezekiel. The prophet is addressed for the first time thus, "Son of man," when he is receiving "spirit" for prophecy[1], after falling on his face because of the splendour of a vision in which he has seen (i. 26) "above the appearance of the throne, an appearance like the aspect of *man (adam)*." Then a Voice says to him, "*Son of man (ben adam)*, stand upon thy feet, and I will speak with thee." Then "the spirit entered into" the prophet, and he is commanded, with reiterations of "son of man," to convey God's message to rebellious Israel. Throughout all these reiterations, readers may find a double suggestiveness in *ben adam*. As being "son of earthy man" the prophet falls down and needs lifting up and strengthening; but as being "son of Adam" he is a fit medium for conveying God's message to all the other sons of Adam, including Israel.

Reasoning thus, perhaps, the Targumist does not now, as in Jeremiah, render *adam* by *enâsh*. He treats it as the patriarch's name, and represents the prophet as being called by God "son of Adam[2]."

---

[1] [**2998** (vii) *a*] Ezek. ii. 1, 6, 8 etc. Levy *Ch.* i. 11 *a* has אדם "Mensch und *N. pr.* Adam," but he gives no instance of its Aramaic use as "man," and he renders Ezek. ii. 1, iii. 1, 3 foll., "son of Adam."

[2] [**2998** (vii) *b*] But in Ezek. i. 26 "like the aspect of *man (adam)*" the Targumist renders *adam* by *enâsh*, on which see Levy *Ch.* i. 11 *a*.

[**2998** (vii) *c*] Ezekiel, apparently for the sake of reverence, uses a long periphrasis when he speaks of man, *adam*, in connexion with the enthroned figure that he beholds in a vision: contrast Ezek. i. 5 "there was *the likeness of a man* in (lit. to) them [*i.e.* in the four living creatures]," ὁμοίωμα ἀνθρώπου ἐπ' αὐτοῖς, with *ib.* i. 26 "Upon the likeness of the throne was *a likeness* (דמות) *as the appearance of a man*," ὁμοίωμα ὡς εἶδος ἀνθρώπου. Ezek. viii. 2 repeats the phrase in connexion with fire, thus, "Lo, *a likeness* (דמות) *as the appearance of a fire*," and so Targ.; but LXX has ἰδοὺ ὁμοίωμα ἀνδρός, "similitudo *viri*," reading איש for אש (**434**).

[**2998** (vii) *d*] In Ezek. i. 26—7 "And I saw as the colour of amber, *as the appearance of fire within it round about*, from the appearance of his loins and upwards; and from the appearance of his loins and downwards I saw as it were the appearance of fire," LXX omits the italicised words (inserted by A, Aq. and Theod.). Origen, who also

[**2998** (viii)] As regards *ben adam*, Daniel follows Ezekiel in representing the prophet as affrighted by a vision and falling on his face, after which the Voice says (Dan. viii. 17): "Understand, *son of man* (*ben adam*)"; and then, says the prophet, "he touched me and set me upright."

But the Aramaic portion of Daniel (vii. 13) differs from Ezekiel as to the description of a human form in heaven. It describes "[one] like unto a *Son of man* (*bar enâsh*)" as "coming with the clouds of heaven to the Ancient of days." There is no Targum, but the title is paraphrased by the Syriac translation as "Son of *men*," perhaps meaning "Son of humanity." It seems to denote the human empire of Israel as contrasted with the "beasts" denoting foreign empires. Writing in Aramaic the author could not use *ben adam*. But the meaning seems to be that frail earthy

---

omits them, draws a distinction between "fire above" and "fire below" as follows (Lomm. xiv. 181, on Ezek. i. 26) ὁ ἡνίοχος...οὐχ ὅλος ἦν πῦρ ἀλλ' ἀπὸ ὀσφύος ἐπὶ τὰ κάτω, καὶ ἀπὸ ὀσφύος καὶ ἕως ἄνω ἤλεκτρον...Κολάζει δὲ διὰ τῶν κάτω δυνάμεων. Οὐ γὰρ εἶδε πῦρ περὶ τὴν κεφαλήν, οὐδὲ ἀπὸ τῆς ὀσφύος ἐπὶ τὰ ἄνω ἡνίοχος πῦρ ἦν, ἀλλὰ ἀπὸ τῆς ὀσφύος ἐπὶ τὰ κάτω πῦρ ἦν· ἵνα δηλώσῃ ὅτι οἱ ἐν γεννήσει τυγχάνοντες οὗτοι δέονται πυρός. Jerome inserts the words that Origen omits, yet seems to adopt Origen's view, "Quod electrum et intrinsecus et extrinsecus habebat quasi ignis aspectum. A lumbis vero et deorsum, ignis erat resplendens in circuitu: ut ostenderet ea quae supra lumbos sunt...*non indigere igne nec flammis*.... Ea vero quae a lumbis deorsum—ubi coitus, ubi generatio, ubi incentiva vitiorum—*purgatione indigere* flammarum." The Targum has a long insertion about the glory of the upper parts as being beyond the scope of human vision, but no insertion about the lower parts.

[**2998** (vii)*e*] In Ezek. viii. 2 "from the appearance of his loins and downwards, fire; and from his loins and upwards, as the appearance of brightness, as the colour of amber," fire is seen below the loins; and hence, if Origen's view were correct, the notion of punishment (κολάζει δὲ διὰ τῶν κάτω δυνάμεων) would predominate. In x. 1 there is neither "man" nor "fire," but only "as it were a sapphire stone, as the appearance of the likeness of a throne." The visions of the "fire" in viii. 2, and that of the "sapphire stone," are followed by destruction or denunciation. These variations may have some bearing on the visions of John in Rev. i. 14 &c. See **2998** (xxvii) foll.

humanity, representing oppressed mankind in general but Israel in particular—as contrasted with the beasts that represent foreign empires—is to be exalted to heaven[1].

---

[1] [2998 (viii) a] Daniel (x. 5 foll.) sees a vision of a man, "vir," אִישׁ, described in a context that suggests that the writer has borrowed from Ezekiel viii. 2, adopting (2998 (vii) c) אִישׁ for אֵשׁ. A little afterwards comes x. 16 "and behold as the likeness (כִּדְמוּת) of *the sons of man* (*bne adam*) touched my lips," and x. 18 (lit.) "and he added and there touched me as the appearance of (כְּמַרְאֵה) *man* (*adam*). The LXX has x. 16 ὡς ὁμοίωσις χειρὸς (Theod. υἱοῦ) ἀνθρώπου, x. 18 (LXX and Theod.) ὡς ὅρασις ἀνθρώπου. Neither in these passages, nor anywhere in Daniel, is there any mention of a "man" or "son of man" as "sitting" on a "throne." The only mention of "throne" is in Dan. vii. 9, "Thrones were placed, and one that was ancient of days did sit...his throne was fiery flames...." "Sit" refers to God, not to any "son of man." But the plural "thrones" suggests that, when the "son of man" is "brought" to the "Ancient of days," the redeemed race as a whole will sit on "thrones" judging mankind (comp. Dan. vii. 10 "the judgment was set," *ib.* 22 "judgment was given to the saints of the Most High," Rev. xx. 4 "I saw thrones and [figures] sat on them and judgment was given to them").

[2998 (viii) b] 1 Cor. vi. 2—3 "Know ye not that the saints shall judge the world...that we shall judge angels?" should be compared with Rev. iii. 21 "I will give unto him to sit with me in my throne, as I also...have sat with my Father in his throne," and with Mt. xix. 28 "ye, too, shall sit on twelve thrones" (uttered in reply to Peter), Lk. xxii. 30 "that...ye may sit on thrones," where both add, "judging the twelve tribes of Israel." Taken together, these passages suggest that *our Lord habitually connected the judgment of the world by the Son of man with a notion of collectiveness or assessorship.*

[2998 (viii) c] Comp. *Enoch* 45 (ed. Charles, where see note) "On that day Mine Elect One will sit on the throne of glory," but *ib.* 47 "I saw the Head of Days when He had seated Himself on the throne of His glory, and the books of the living were opened before Him, and His whole host which is in heaven above and around Him stood before Him," *ib.* 51 "And the Elect One will in those days sit on My throne and all the secrets of wisdom will stream forth from the counsels of his mouth; for the Lord of Spirits hath given it to him and hath glorified him," *ib.* 69 "The name of the Son of Man was revealed unto them: and he sat on the throne of his glory, and the sum of judgment was committed unto him, the Son of Man...." All these passages are from the *Similitudes* (on which see 2998 (li) foll.). Another section of *Enoch* (90) says "I saw till

§ 5. *"Son of Man" in the Psalms and Job*

[**2998** (ix)] By far the most important passage bearing on the title is in the Psalms as follows :—Ps. viii. 4 " What is [*frail*] *man* (*enôsh*) that thou art mindful of him, and the *son of* [*earthy*] *man* (*ben adam*) that thou visitest him ? " where the whole context implies 1st, that man, though a " babe and suckling," is created for " strength," so that God, through " the mouth of babes," may " still the enemy and the avenger "; 2nd, that man, though a creature of earthy origin, is to be but " little lower than God," and that, in uplifting man, God will " set his glory above the heavens."

From a different point of view, the Psalmist, thinking of " man " as apart from God, a boaster, hostile to Israel, and destined to perish as a mere thing of earth, says (cxliv. 1—4) " Blessed be the Lord my rock....who subdueth my people under me! Lord, what is [*earthy*] *man* (*adam*) that thou takest knowledge of him, or the son of [*frail*] *man* (*ben enôsh*) that thou makest account of him ? [*Earthy*] *man* (*adam*) is like to vanity[1]." And the meaning is similar— the son of man apart from God—in Ps. cxlvi. 3 " Put not your trust in princes, nor in the *son of man* (*ben adam*) in whom there is no help." In Ps. lxxx. 17 "[Let thy hand] be upon the man (*îsh*) of thy right hand, and upon the *son*

---

a throne was erected in the pleasant land, and the Lord of the sheep sat Himself thereon, and THAT OTHER took the sealed books and opened them before the Lord of the sheep." This has points of resemblance with the Lamb opening the sealed book in Rev. v. 7.

[1] [**2998** (ix) *a*] The difference of order in poetic exclamations like those in Ps. viii. 4, cxliv. 1—4, and the distinctions of words in poetic parallel clauses, may not be susceptible of exact grammatical explanation. Perhaps, in the former, the meaning is "*enôsh*...and [still more] *ben adam*" ; in the latter, "*adam*...and [even] *ben enôsh*." In both, there is a suggestion of weakness ; but the latter may mean that *ben enôsh* is somewhat above the level of *adam*, yet far below the level of a claim to God's consideration.

of man (ben adam) whom thou madest strong for thyself," the Psalmist first prays for the hero and champion of Israel as *īsh* i.e. "vir," and then adds "yea, upon that [*weak*] *son of* [*earthy*] *man* whom thou hast made strong for thy glory." In all these passages, from two opposite points of view, *ben adam* means the same thing; when leaning on God, raised from earth to heaven; when rebelling against God, perishing into his native earth—but always "*son of* [*earthy*] *man*¹."

[**2998** (x)] In Job xxv. 4—6, Bildad says (R.V.) "How then can man be just with God? or how can he be clean that is born of a woman? Behold, even the moon hath no brightness, and the stars are not pure in his sight. How much less *man* (*enôsh*), that is a worm! And *the son of man* (*ben adam*), which is a worm!" This is not the view of the eighth Psalm. There, the heavens are not denied to be glorious, but the "glory" of God, revealed in the son of man, is "set" by God "above" the heavens. According to Bildad, even the stars are not "pure"; *enôsh* is less pure, and *ben adam* most impure of all. This, under the guise of magnifying God, seems unduly to condemn His works—even the stars. But a much lower depth is reached by the cynical Elihu, who implies that man's righteousness or sinfulness does not affect God, but merely weak man, Job xxxv. 8 "Thy wickedness [may hurt] a man (*īsh*) as thou art; and thy righteousness [may profit] a *son of man* (*ben adam*)²."

---

¹ [**2998** (ix) *b*] Targ. has *bar nasha* for Ps. viii. 4 *ben adam*; *bar nash* for Ps. lxxx. 17 *ben adam*, for Ps. cxliv. 3—4 *adam*, and for Ps. cxlvi. 3 *ben adam;* and, in Ps. cxliv. 3, *bne enâsha* "sons of man" for *ben enôsh*.

² [**2998** (x) *a*] The Targ. has "viro impio, qui similis est tui, iniquitas tua est, et filio hominis justo justitia tua." In any case, Elihu is bitterly contemptuous both of Job and of humanity, implying that both are comparatively strong ("vir") for wickedness, and weak ("filius hominis") for righteousness, and that neither their wickedness nor their righteousness is a loss or a profit to God. I think Matthew Arnold, in *Literature and Dogma*, or some other of his works, quotes

But although the thought of these two disputants is different from the thought of the eighth Psalm, the meaning of *ben adam* is the same throughout—"son of earthy man."

§ 6. *Jewish Comments*

[**2998** (xi)] Early Christian literature recognises a kind of paradox in the exaltation of man—a mystery "not revealed" at the beginning, a mystery that "the angels desire to look into." Jewish tradition, of the first two centuries, is very scanty. But it may have been preserved, by oral transmission, in later writings; and these occasionally recognise, in God's dealings with man, not only a paradox, but a paradox that disappoints angels and creates a rivalry between them and the exalted "son of man." In at least two passages of the Talmud this feeling is connected with Ps. viii. 4 "son of man." When Moses went up on high to receive the Law, the angels said to God (*Sabbath* 88 *b*, quoting from 3rd century tradition) "What business hath this [*creature*] *born of a woman* among us? Wilt thou give thy secrets to this *flesh and blood*?" Then the angels quote Ps. viii. 4, "What is *man* that thou art mindful of him, and the *son of man* that thou visitest him?" This indicates, perhaps, a paraphrase of the terms of the Psalmist as "*born of a woman*" and "*flesh and blood*," but at all events an assumption that the Psalm uses the terms to denote the weakness and corruptible nature of man.

[**2998** (xii)] The hostile angels go on to quote Ps. viii. 1—2 "O Lord, our Lord...Set[1] thy glory above the heavens,"

---

one of Elihu's sayings—a saying of this character—with the preface, "The Hebrews said," apparently meaning that it was a customary expression of Hebrew thought. "The Hebrews" would scarcely choose Elihu for their spokesman.

In Job xxv. 6, Targ. has *bar nash* twice (for *enôsh* and *ben adam*); in Job xxxv. 8, Targ. has *bar nash* for *ben adam*.

[1] Ps. viii. 1 אֲשֶׁר תְּנָה הוֹדְךָ, Field "quam gloriam tuam *pone*," Goldschmidt (*Sabb.* 88 *b*) "(welcher) *verleihe* deine Pracht"; הוֹד "splendour," "vigour" (Gesen. 217 *a*), is applied to sound as well as to sight.

apparently meaning that God is not to stoop to "set" His glory below, on the frail "son of man." On this the Holy One bids Moses reply to the angels; but he cannot, for fear of the fire from their mouths: "Then He said, Hold fast to the throne of my majesty and give them their answer; for it is written (Job xxvi. 9) *He closeth in the face of his throne, and spreadeth his cloud upon it.*" The Targum on these last obscure words from Job is, "Who holds the darkness of His throne that the angels may not see Him, who extends it like a veil upon the clouds of His glory"—which illustrates the suggestion of a rivalry between "angels" (who may not see God) and men (to whom, as represented by Moses, God manifests Himself). And fresh light is thrown on it, and perhaps on the phrase "*face of his throne,*" by the Targums on Jacob's Ladder, where some angels, expelled from heaven, go up to those in the high heavens and say, "Come! See Jacob the pious, *whose likeness is inlaid in the throne of glory, and whom you have so greatly desired to behold.*" Then "the rest of the angels of the holy Lord descended to look upon him." Jer. Targ. describes the ascending angels as "those who had accompanied him [*i.e.* Jacob] from the house of his father," but it agrees with the Targum of Jonathan in saying that the "likeness" of Jacob is "in the throne of glory."

In the light of these passages, and of those in Ezekiel and Daniel which describe "as it were the appearance of a man," or a "son of man," either "on a throne," or "coming to the Ancient of days," it would seem that the Rabbi quoting Job above—as though Job supplied the answer to the angels assailing the claims of the "son of man"—meant "he closeth in the face of his throne" to suggest that the "face" of man had a place in or near the very throne of the Supreme, far above the heaven and the heaven of heavens[1]. It is not

---

[1] The passages from the Targums about Jacob are quoted from Etheridge's translations. Another Talmudic passage puts Ps. viii. 4 into the mouths of two classes of angels, who, on two occasions,

contended that the Rabbi was right, but only that he was influenced by some traditional connexion between the "face" of man and the "throne" of God.

[**2998** (xiii)] It is necessary to dwell on this Jewish connexion of "angels" with "son of man," because it may shew the Jewish origin of similar connexions expressed or implied in the gospels. For example, a tradition peculiar to John mentions "angels ascending and descending on the Son of man." Another, peculiar to Matthew—of which Origen recognises the difficulty much more clearly than it is recognised by modern commentators—mentions "angels" of Christ's "little ones," who would naturally be identified with despised humanity, frail "son of man." A tradition peculiar to Luke describes an "angel" standing by shepherds at night, announcing the birth of the Babe to be found lying in a manger in Bethlehem: upon which there comes "a multitude of the heavenly host praising God" in a song that implies that God's "glory in the highest" is connected with man's "peace on earth." When "they go away to heaven," the shepherds find the future Son of man in accordance with their message. The story may freely be described as one that represents, from a Christian point of view, angels from heaven descending to earth and then reascending, after they have caused men to behold the face of the sleeping Son of man, which is "inlaid in the throne of God."

[**2998** (xiv)] *Genesis Rabba* (ed. Wünsche pp. 332—4) contains many Jewish traditions about Jacob's ladder. The first says, The ladder is placed on the earth, that is, (Exod. xx. 24) on the altar. The top of the ladder, reaching up to heaven, signifies the offerings. The angels are the Highpriests. But "according to the Rabbis," the ladder is Sinai, and the angels that go up are Moses and Aaron. God shews

---

deprecate God's purpose of making man. Both classes are destroyed. A third class acquiesces (*Sanh.* 38 *b*).

him [*i.e.* Jacob] His throne, which has "three feet" (Abraham, Isaac and Jacob); and a Rabbi declares that the fathers must be "not less than three." Some, who (differing from the majority) maintain that the angels descend on Jacob, not on the ladder, explain that the angels leap on him for joy because (Is. xlix. 3) they have found the servant in whom God's glory will be fulfilled, and whose image is engraved above. The two classes of angels saw two different things (presumably, according to their natures):—"Those that went up saw his image [on the throne]; those that came down to earth saw him sleeping. [The matter is] like a King sitting on his judgment seat: those who go up into the palace find him as Judge, those who go out into the street find him sleeping."

[**2998** (xv)] Another tradition explained the ascending and descending thus: "In heaven, the angel that defends Israel goes up, and the angel that accuses Israel falls down; on earth, the one defending falls down, and the one accusing goes up[1]." According to another view, the ascending angels

---

[1] [**2998** (xv) *a*] Wünsche p. 333, "Wer für das Volk oben (im Himmel) spricht, dessen Verdienst steigt empor und seine Schuld sinkt herab, wer aber unten (auf der Erde) für das Volk spricht, dessen Verdienst sinkt herab und seine Schuld steigt empor." I give the words in full because they seem to me obscure and capable of more than one meaning. I am indebted to Dr Büchler for the rendering given above.

[**2998** (xv) *b*] Mt. xviii. 10 "*their angels* in heaven do always behold the face of my Father in heaven"—on which Ephrem (Moes. p. 165) says that "their angels" are prayers, "*orationes eorum*"—if the text is correct, might seem to justify a belief in "guardian angels" attached, so to speak, specially to individuals, during their lives. But there is very little basis for supposing that such a belief existed among Jews, except Acts xii. 13—15, concerning which Origen, while in some sense accepting the belief (*ad loc.* Lomm. iii. 262) apparently suggests—in a somewhat obscure passage—that Rhoda's utterance, and the reply made to it, are "not a dogma." The Heb. of Ben Sira shews that "the cry of the poor" is personified in Sir. xxxv. 17 "*it will not remove* till God shall visit," *i.e.* it is a petitioner that goes up to heaven, taking no refusal, like the importunate widow in Luke. The context in Sir. xxxv. 14 mentions "the cry of the widow." This favours Ephrem's view. Comp. Rev. viii. 3—4.

A very slight change would convert Mt. xviii. 10 into "I say unto you that *the angels before the face of my Father do always behold them* (or, *their faces*)," *i.e.* the faces of the little ones. This would resemble *Enoch* civ. 1 "*In heaven the angels are mindful of you for good before the glory of the Great One.* Your names are written before the glory of the Great One." Comp. Lk. x. 20 "your names are written in heaven."

[2998 (xv) *c*] I am indebted to Dr Büchler for quotations from passages (*Tosefta Sabbath* xvii. 2, *Tosefta Aboda Zara* i. 17) indicating that there was a Jewish belief in angelic guardianship of some kind. Levy iii. 121 *b* quotes the former as mentioning "angels of *ministration* (השרת) accompanying the good" (Ps. xci. 11 "He shall give his angels charge over thee") and "angels of *Satan* accompanying the bad" (Ps. cix. 6 "Set thou a wicked man over him and let an adversary stand at his right hand"). Comp. *Sabbath* 119 *b* "R. Jose b. R. Jehuda (A.D. 160—200) says, Two angels (dual) of ministration" [marg. "angels" (pl.)] "accompany the man (לו לאדם) on the eve of the Sabbath from the synagogue to his house." Then, said R. Jose, if preparations for the Sabbath are found duly made, the good angel blesses, and the evil angel unwillingly says, Amen. Else, the evil angel pronounces an evil wish, and the good angel unwillingly says, Amen.

[2998 (xv) *d*] Comp. *Taanith* 11 *a* "Die Rabbanen lehrten: Wenn Jisraél sich in Schmerz befindet, und einer sich ausschliesst, so kommen die zwei Dienstengel, die den Menschen begleiten, legen die Hände auf sein Haupt und sprechen: Dieser da, der sich von der Gemeinde ausgeschlossen hat, soll den Trost der Gemeinde nicht sehen." This represents "the two angels of ministration" as excommunicating the offender by laying their hands on him. "The man," lit. "him, the man," seems to mean "the man, whoever he may be," or "the man in question." But the same "two angels" might conceivably do duty for all mankind.

[2998 (xv) *e*] I am indebted to Dr Büchler for the following extracts. *Tanḥumâ*, ed. Buber, on Genes. xxxii. 3 "This is what Ps. xci. 11 says: 'For he shall give his angels charge over thee to keep thee in all thy ways.' When a man is in Palestine, the angels of Palestine guard him. You see this, in the case of Jacob (in Genes. xxviii. 12) when the angels were leaving who guarded him in Palestine, and who now ascended. Other angels came down from heaven to guard Jacob abroad. When he returned from Padan Aram, the angels who guarded him in Palestine descended again." *Ib.* on Exod. xxiii. 20 § 19 : "'Behold I send an angel before thee.' This is what Ps. xci. 11 says: 'For he shall give his angels charge over thee, to keep thee in all thy ways.' To a man who fulfils one commandment one angel is given; who fulfils two commandments, two angels are given to him. Who fulfils all commandments, many angels are given to him, according to Ps. xci. 11. Who are these angels? Those that guard him from the demons according to Ps. xci. 7."

are those that bring Jacob back to the Holy Land, and the descending ones are those that accompany him into exile. The latter appear to be regarded as "fallen," and thence follow discussions of the reasons for the banishment of the fallen angels, and of the length of its duration. Other traditions pass from Jacob and his ladder (which "reached to heaven") to Nebuchadnezzar and his tree (which "reached to heaven"), apparently contrasting the true empire of God with the false empires of this world.

There is some approach to the Jewish notion of angelic jealousy of man in the recently published *Apostolic Preaching* of Irenæus (ch. 11—16, ed. Harnack, 1907) which confirms the Greek text of Iren. iv. 40. 3 ἄγγελος αὐτοῦ (see *Fourfold Gospel*, "Angels").

[2998 (xv)*f*] The influence of angelology is remarkably illustrated by Origen's theory that John the Baptist may have been an angel incarnate, and by the still earlier *Prayer of Joseph* which he quotes in support of it (*Comm. Johann.* ii. 25) εἰ δέ τις προσίεται καὶ τῶν παρ' Ἑβραίοις φερομένων ἀποκρύφων τὴν ἐπιγραφομένην Ἰωσὴφ προσευχήν, ἄντικρυς τοῦτο τὸ δόγμα καὶ σαφῶς εἰρημένον ἐκεῖθεν λήψεται· ὡς ἄρα οἱ ἀρχῆθεν ἐξαίρετόν τι ἐσχηκότες παρὰ ἀνθρώπους, πολλῷ κρείττους τυγχάνοντες τῶν λοιπῶν ψυχῶν ἀπὸ τοῦ εἶναι ἄγγελοι, ἐπὶ τὴν ἀνθρωπίνην καταβεβήκασι φύσιν. Φησὶ γοῦν ὁ Ἰακώβ· "ὁ γὰρ λαλῶν πρὸς ὑμᾶς, ἐγὼ Ἰακώβ, καὶ Ἰσραήλ, ἄγγελος θεοῦ εἰμι ἐγώ, καὶ πνεῦμα ἀρχικόν, καὶ Ἀβραὰμ καὶ Ἰσαὰκ προεκτίσθησαν πρὸ παντὸς ἔργου· ἐγὼ δὲ Ἰακὼβ ὁ κληθεὶς ὑπὸ ἀνθρώπων Ἰακώβ· τὸ δὲ ὄνομά μου Ἰσραήλ, ὁ κληθεὶς ὑπὸ θεοῦ Ἰσραήλ, ἀνὴρ ὁρῶν θεόν, ὅτι ἐγὼ πρωτόγονος παντὸς ζώου ζωουμένου ὑπὸ θεοῦ."

The evidence of Jewish tradition supports the evidence derived from almost every book of N.T., and also from the earliest heresies, indicating a very general though undefined belief in the widely diffused operations of angels of good and evil, *but not a belief in the existence of a special good angel attached as a guardian to each human being from his entrance into life until his departure from it.* In Tobit iii. 17—v. 4, the angel Raphael is represented as being sent to fulfil the prayers of Tobit and Sara, and he takes the form of a man named (v. 12) Azarias in order to guide Tobit's son, Tobias; but he would not be called a "guardian angel," *in the modern sense of the phrase*, to Tobias or his parents, any more than the angels sent to Gideon, or to Manoah's wife, or to Elijah, would be called, severally, their "guardian angels."

[**2998** (xvi)] This conception of angels from above and from below coming together to behold the sleeping son of man, would naturally be combined by Christians with the words put into the mouth of the Creator in Job xxxviii. 4—7 "Where wast thou when I laid the foundations of the earth ...when the morning stars sang together and all the sons of God shouted for joy?" The LXX, perhaps not understanding how "stars" could "sing," corrupts the Hebrew "sang" into "were created." It also changes "shouted for joy" into "praised me," and substitutes "angels" for "sons of God." The parallelism between "angels" and "stars" may be illustrated by Rev. ix. 1 "I saw *a star* from heaven fallen unto the earth, and the key of the pit was given unto *him*," *i.e.* to the star, regarded as an angel, like "Lucifer" (Is. xiv. 12). "Stars" is also used symbolically of angels in *Enoch* (ch. 86). In Job, by connecting "stars" with a parallel clause about "angels," the LXX prepares the way for Luke's narrative, "There was with the angel *a multitude of the heavenly host* [marg. *of the host of heaven*] praising God[1]." A commentary on Job printed in Origen's works connects the "singing" of the "angels" in Job with the "singing" in Luke[2]. In O.T., "*host of heaven*" almost always means the *stars* in a bad sense, regarded as objects of worship[3].

[**2998** (xvii)] Another source of confusion might arise from Greek traditions about the angels chanting songs over the cradle of Christ. This kind of "chanting over" persons may be expressed by ἐπαείδω, as where the chorus in Euripides appeals to Electra, "Sing a song of victory over

---

[1] Lk. ii. 13. There are many variations in the Latin versions. SS has "There appeared *by him* [*i.e.* by, or near, the first angel] a host and the many angels [of heaven]."

[2] [**2998**(xvi)*a*] *Anon. in Job*, lib. i., Lomm. xvi. 49. Origen also (Lomm. iv. 304—5) interprets Mt. xxiv. 29 "sun," "moon," and "stars," as including "Satan" and powers of evil.

[3] Deut. xvii. 3, 2 K. xvii. 16, xxi. 3, 5 etc.

my chorus[1]." It is applied to the strains of Orpheus[2], and Lucian uses it of the Delphian oracular utterance thus, "I will chant, *Know thyself*, over you[3]." But in the LXX the verb ἐπᾴδειν is always (4 times) used of "charming," and the noun ἐπαοιδός always means "magician," "charmer," "sorcerer," and is frequently parallel to μάγος. This and other points in Luke's narrative, and in quotations of it by early authorities, suggest that Luke's "*singing*" may be connected with Matthew's "Magi[4]," *i.e. magicians*, and with his narrative about the miraculous star. If that were the case, we should have to recognise that the influence of the old Hebrew tradition on Christian literature was still more extended.

---

[1] Eurip. *Electr.* 865 ἀλλ' ἐπάειδε καλλίνικον ᾠδὰν ἐμῷ χορῷ.
[2] Eurip. *Iph. Aul.* 1212 εἰ μὲν τὸν Ὀρφέως εἶχον...λόγον πείθειν ἐπᾴδουσ' ὥσθ' ὁμαρτεῖν μοι πέτρας.
[3] Lucian *Dial. Mort.* ii. 2 ἐγὼ δὲ τὸ Γνῶθι σαυτὸν...ἐπᾴσομαι ὑμῖν.
[4] [2998 (xvii) a] Μάγος is probably "magician" in a bad sense, in conformity with O.T., N.T. (and Greek generally exc. Philo ii. 456) and the express testimony of Origen, who assumes the "magicians" to be converted from their errors. He blames Celsus, who called them "Chaldæans," for not understanding the difference of "profession" between the two: (Orig. *Cels.* i. 58) "The Jew in Celsus' book, instead of the Magi mentioned in the Gospel, says that *Chaldæans* have been asserted by Jesus to have come to worship Him at His birth, while still a babe, as being a God, and to have revealed [the matter] to Herod the *Tetrarch* (sic)." Presumably Origen means that "Chaldæans" were astrologers, and not necessarily "magi," *i.e.* "sorcerers" or "magicians."

[2998 (xvii) b] Beside the possible confusion between "singers" and "magicians" above mentioned, it should be noted that, in Mt. ii. 1, Syr. Palest., and Delitzsch, all have *magushēm* in some form, for "magi." Now this word, though not in Levy *Ch.*, is freq. in New Heb. (Levy iii. 23 a) always in a bad sense. It is easily confused with "*magēshĕm*," which in Mal. i. 7, iii. 3, is used of "bringing" offerings. In Mal. i. 11 the passive describes incense "offered" throughout the world, even "among the Gentiles." 1 K. iv. 21 mentions foreigners "*bringing* (*magēshēm*)" gifts, or tribute, to Solomon. If this word were applied to the angels that "brought" their tribute of praise to the Saviour, it might give rise to, or might confirm, a story about "Magi."

[2998 (xvii) c] The "Magi" are called, from very early times, "kings" (see Tertull. *Adv. Jud.* 9). This might arise in part from Ps. lxxii. 10 "The *kings* of Sheba and Seba shall bring gifts." But the confusion between "king" and "angel" is so frequent (**105** *a*) that the fact favours the hypothesis that the "Magi" are derived from an original "angels."

[**2998** (xvii) *d*] Ignatius *Eph.* 19 says, concerning Matthew's "star," that it "shone above all the stars...and all the rest of the constellations became a *chorus* to the star." Substitute "*angel*" for "*star*," and there is a resemblance between Ignatius and Luke, who says that one angel of great glory shone forth first, bringing the glad tidings, and that then the other angels joined in a chorus, "praising God." As regards one star, preceding the rest in glory, comp. *Paradise Lost*, IV. 605—6 "Hesperus that led The starrie Host, rode brightest."

[**2998** (xvii) *e*] When some of the angels came to be supposed "magi," then Phosphorus (for Phosphor, not Hesper, would be here the leading star or angel) would be said to "lead forward" the "magi" to their destination (instead of "leading the starry host"). Comp. Mt. ii. 9 προῆγεν αὐτούς, a suitable phrase for the "leader" of a "host."

[**2998** (xvii) *f*] Is. xlvii. 13, and the Targum, and LXX, imply that astrologers are "watchers by night," and Lk. ii. 8 mentions "watchers by night." This adds another point of possible similarity between the sources used by Matthew and by Luke.

[**2998** (xvii) *g*] Luke adds "flocks." Now in Judg. v. 16 "flocks (עדרים)" is confused by A with "waking up (ἐξεγειρόντων) (עוררים)," and the text of B gives ἀγγέλων (prob. an error for ἀγελῶν). Levy iii. 285 *a* quotes a saying that "the night-watches in heaven correspond to the night-watches on earth," and it is possible that there may have been some early confusion between (*Arab. Evang. Infant.* 6) "angels...like life-guards standing by a king," and shepherds "guarding" their flocks. Although Greek corruption is probably not a frequent source of error in the gospels, yet in a poetic tradition of this kind, so widely divergent in many versions, the chance of confusion between αγγελων and αγελων is not to be ignored.

[**2998** (xvii) *h*] "Watcher (עיר)" means "angel" in Dan. iv. 13, LXX "*angel*," Theod. "*eir*" (transliterating)—but οἱ λοιποί have "*watcher* (ἐγρήγορος)"—and in Dan. iv. 17, 23. In *Enoch* (ed. Charles, Index) "watchers" means archangels in xx. 1 etc. and "fallen angels" in i. 5 etc. In *Enoch* xv. 2 "watchers of heaven" are fallen angels. In *ib.* lxxxvi. 1, 3 "stars" is used symbolically of "angels" (**2998** (xvi)).

[**2998** (xvii) *i*] It will be shewn (**2999** (v) *a* foll.) that ἐπέστησεν (v.r. ἐστάθη), sometimes with ἐπάνω, is used of sudden angelic apparitions. Hence, a slight additional confirmation of parallelism is afforded by Mt. ii. 9 ἐλθὼν ἐστάθη ἐπάνω οὗ ἦν τὸ παιδίον and Lk. ii. 9 ἄγγελος Κυρίου ἐπέστη αὐτοῖς. Luke adds καὶ δόξα Κυρίου περιέλαμψεν αὐτούς, but D, *b*, and *ff* om. the 2nd κυρίου, *b* having simply "claritas." The paral-

[2998 (xviii)] There are several Jewish comments on Numb. xxiii. 19, "God is not a man that he should lie, nor *son of man* (*ben adam*) that he should repent. Hath he said and shall he not do it? Or hath he spoken and shall he not make it good?" Most of them are unimportant for our purpose as they merely reconcile the passage with others that describe God as repenting. But a saying of Abbahu is important, as it appears to jest against Jesus for calling Himself "son of man": "If a man says to thee, *I am God*, he speaks falsely. [If he says] I [am] *son of man* (*ben adam*) his end is to rue it"—playing on "*son of man* that he should *repent*[1]." Abbahu then takes up Balaam's following words: "*Hath he* [*i.e.* God] *said...and shall he not make it good?*" and applies them to Jesus, reading them non-interrogatively thus: "'*He that hath said* [*so*] *shall not make it good*,'" so as to contrast God's power to "*make good*" what He says with the impotence of the Christian Messiah to do the

---

lelism, the twofold expression in Luke, and the variations, suggest that the original may have simply stated that "the angel, or the star, stood over, or near, the cradle of the sleeping Son of man."

[2998 (xvii) *j*] Comp. *Arab. Evang. Infant.* 7, which does not mention the "star" till the Magi are going home, "And in the same hour there appeared to them an *angel in the form of that star* which had before guided them on their journey." Instead of a "brightness" or "star" appearing to the shepherds, the Arab. gospel says that the shepherds "*lighted a fire*"—another specimen of confusion arising from Semitic sources (617—25). The same gospel says § 6 "Simeon saw Him shining *like a pillar of fire*," and instead of calling the Magi "kings," says that, on their return, "their *kings and chief men* came together to them" questioning them—an apparent duplication of Matthew's statement that *king Herod* questioned the Magi. This gospel carries "conflation" to excess. Comp. Clem. Alex. *Fragm.* 986 ἀνέτειλεν ξένος ἀστὴρ κ. καινός.... αὐτὸς ὁ Κύριος ἀνθρώπων ὁδηγός, ὁ κατελθὼν εἰς γῆν, where "*the Lord*" is the "*strange and new star*" and the "*guide of men.*" By themselves, the first words would mean "*There rose a strange star.*"

[1] [2998 (xviii) *a*] See *j. Taanith* 65 *b* quoted in Dalm. *Words* p. 246. Abbahu lived about 280 A.D. For Heb. "repent (נחם)," Abbahu substitutes תהא as Targ. Jon. does in Exod. xiii. 17 (Levy *Ch.* ii. 530 *a*).

same. The special instance of impotence that he selects is connected with "ascension to heaven." In order to give dramatic vividness to his jest, he represents Christ as boasting, like the king of Babylon in Isaiah (xiv. 13—15), "I will ascend into heaven." Then, by a non-interrogative version, Abbahu twists the sentence round to this:—"[If he, the Christian Messiah, says] '*I will ascend to heaven*'—*he that hath said* [*so*] *shall not make it good*[1]."

[2998 (xix)] This comment is important for two reasons. First, it shews that this early Jewish controversialist assumed— no doubt from his intercourse with Christians—that Jesus habitually *called Himself* "son of man." Abbahu does not say that the friends or followers of Jesus gave Him this title: and indeed, as we have seen and shall see, they did not give

---

[1] [2998 (xviii) *b*] Prof. Dalman, commenting on the interpretation of *j. Taan.* 65 *b*, calls it "a divergence from Dan. vii. 13," and says, "The dictum forms a *crux interpretum* only for those who find the obvious sense disagreeable. It is correctly rendered by *Laible*, Jesus Christ im Talmud (1891), 48, and by *Bacher*, op. cit. 118; incorrectly, by *Levy*, Neuhebr. Wörterbuch under אדם; *Wünsche*, Der jerus. Talmud, 141; *M. Schwab*, Le Talmud de Jérusalem, vi. 156. The explanation of *F. Cohn* given by *Lietzmann*, Der Menschensohn, 50, is quite impracticable."

I am unable to see any "divergence from Dan. vii. 13," if at least deliberate "divergence" is intended. Abbahu appears to me not to be thinking about Dan. vii. 13. He seems intent simply upon making a bitter play upon Numb. xxiii. 19. Levy (i. 29 *a*) translates the latter part of Abbahu's saying thus, "[Wenn er aber sagt:] Ich steige in den Himmel [so ist zu entgegnen:] Wird er [Gott] denn sprechen und es nicht thun? und sagen, aber nicht erfüllen?" That is, he translates Abbahu's quotation "correctly," according to the scriptural meaning, but supplies a wrong context in brackets, and thereby fails to give the jesting and incorrect application intended by Abbahu. Prof. Dalman fails to give—or at least I should not have guessed it from his remarks—the literally "correct" rendering under which Abbahu masks his attack.

Dr Schmidt (*Enc.* 4706) proposes to alter the text of *Taanith*. But, with the explanation suggested by a play upon the words, no alteration appears necessary.

it to Him, speaking in their own persons. The jest would be no jest if the title were not self-given.

In the next place, the jibe is quite consistent with the view that the phrase used by Jesus, whatever it was, meant "ordinary man" with a sense of weakness. Abbahu does not say, "If he calls himself Son of man, he lies," but, in effect, "If he calls himself—to quote Balaam's phrase—*son of man*, he will '*repent*' it—to quote Balaam again—only too keenly, when he finds himself suffering like a *son of man*, and when he finds himself '*repenting*' as *sons of men* do repent."

As regards the other above-mentioned Jewish traditions, many of them (apart from Messianic views about the Son of man on the clouds) shew traces of a belief in the essential unity of human nature with the divine, and of the destined exaltation of *ben adam* to the throne of the Maker.

"Son of man" occurs frequently in the *Similitudes of Enoch*. On this, Westcott (*Gospel of St John*, p. 34) says that, in *Enoch*, "The Messiah is 'a Son of man' and not properly 'the Son of man' (ch. xlvi. 1, 2, 3, 4, xlviii. 2)." Dr Charles (*Enoch* p. 18) says "Dr Westcott asserts that the title in Enoch is 'A Son of Man'; but wrongly; for it is as definitely 'The Son of Man' as the language and sense can make it." The truth, however, is that Enoch *first introduces the term as undefined, then defines it, and always afterwards speaks of it as defined.* Owing to (what appears to me) the uncertain date of the *Similitudes*[1], I had not intended to quote from them: but in view of Westcott's verbal mistake, and a possibility that the mistake may not be so substantially serious as it appears, I have added a section (**2998** (li) foll.) on this subject.

---

[1] [**2998** (xix) *a*] Contrast Dalm. *Words* p. 243, "It cannot be proved that they originate from a pre-Christian period," with Charles *Enoch* p. 108, which states the latest date as 70—64 B.C., but suggests as a reasonable date 94—79 B.C.

§ 7. *Ambiguity of the Title*

[**2998** (xx)] Owing to the defining force of the genitive, it is not always easy to tell, in Greek translations of a Semitic original, whether υἱὸς θεοῦ, "God's son," means "*a* son of God" or "*the* son of God." A somewhat similar ambiguity attends υἱὸς ἀνθρώπου, "a son of a man," or "a son of man, *i.e.* of man typically," or "man's son." In Aramaic, "*bar nāšā*," *i.e.* "man," "the individual of the human species," is distinguished from the indeterminate *bar 'nāš*, "a man." But we are told on high authority that "it is quite possible... that the emphatic ending had already lost its force[1]." The

---

[1] [**2998** (xx) *a*] *Enc. Bibl.* col. 4728, "Son of Man" (Dr Schmidt). As regards the genitive with υἱός, see Jn x. 36 υἱὸς τοῦ θεοῦ εἰμί where W.H. are justified—by the recognised rule of preferring the more difficult text when well supported—in inserting τοῦ, though it is omitted by אD, Chrys., and (Alf.) some minor authorities. Υἱὸς θεοῦ εἰμί, "I am God's son," leaves it an open question whether there are more sons than one; but υἱὸς τοῦ θεοῦ εἰμί, "I am a son of God,"—"God" being defined, and "son" not being defined—suggests "*a* son of God." So Satan contemptuously says to the Saviour (Mt. iv. 3, 6, Lk. iv. 3, 9) εἰ υἱὸς εἶ τοῦ θεοῦ: but Nathanael (Jn i. 49) σὺ εἶ ὁ υἱὸς τοῦ θεοῦ. In Jn, the Saviour does not hesitate to speak of "the Son," in connexion with "the Father," as implying the type of filial dependence and obedience; but when He adds "I am," John (x. 36) does not add "the" (as he does in "I am *the* light of the world"), but prefers, by the words "I am a son of God," to suggest that there are other sons.

[**2998** (xx) *b*] Hence Origen, after enumerating the titles given to Himself by "*the son of God* (ὁ υἱὸς τοῦ θεοῦ)" does not say that Christ *calls Himself* "*the son of God*." He prefers to use the ambiguous phrase "*God's son*," while at the same time quoting Christ's actual words, which suggest as their meaning, "*I am a son of God*": (*Johan. Comm.* tom. i. 23, Lomm. i. 44—5) Ἀλλὰ καὶ υἱὸν εἶναι θεοῦ σαφῶς ἑαυτὸν καταγγέλλει λέγων...ὑμεῖς λέγετε ὅτι βλασφημεῖς ὅτι εἶπον, υἱὸς τοῦ θεοῦ εἰμί. This explains the error of D and Chrys. They have adopted in their text what the more scholarly Origen reserved for a reverential commentary. Nonnus paraphrases Jn x. 36 υἱ. τ. θεοῦ εἰμί simply as θεοῦ ζώοντος ἐγώ παῖς (where ζώοντος may well represent the article, "[the] living God").

attempts of Christian Semitic versions of the gospels give widely divergent results and convey no clue to Christ's original language. Nor must we forget the possibility that a Jewish prophet of the first century might call himself "son of Adam," throwing in his lot with the prophets Ezekiel and Daniel, who prophesied under this ambiguous title to their brethren in captivity. We do not know the precise time when *ben adam* ceased to include, grammatically or verbally, "son of man," and came to mean merely "son of Adam." There are many occasions where "son of Adam" might well be used to mean "son of man." We have seen (**2998** (xviii)) that Abbahu scoffs at Jesus for calling Himself *ben adam*. This is in a Biblical allusion, and of course it does not follow that Abbahu imputed to Jesus the actual words *ben adam*, or *bar adam*. Still, the jest illustrates the possibility that Jesus might describe Himself in the old Biblical term as "son of Adam," that is, "son of man," and that for this reason, among others, Luke might think it well to trace up the Lord's pedigree to "Adam the son of God[1]."

He is much more full and emphatic in paraphrasing Jn i. 50 ὁ υἱ. τ. θ. as σὺ Χριστὸς...υἱὸς ἀειζώοιο θεοῦ λόγος...καί σε θεοῦ ζώοντος ἐτήτυμον υἱόν, besides adding ὑψίθρονε ποιμήν and θεόν.

[1] [**2998** (xx) c] Lk. iii. 36. For variations between A.V. and R.V., and also between txt and marg. of R.V., comp. Gen. ii. 15 A.V. txt "the man," marg. "Adam," ii. 19 (*bis*) A.V. (1) txt "Adam," marg. "the man,"... (2) "Adam," R.V. (*bis*) "the man," ii. 20 A.V. (*bis*) "Adam," R.V. (1) "the man,"...(2) txt "man," marg. "Adam," ii. 21, 23, iii. 8, 9, 20 A.V. "Adam," R.V. "the man"; Deut. xxxii. 8 A.V. "sons of Adam," R.V. "children of men," Aq. "sons of man"; Hos. vi. 7 A.V. txt "like men," marg. "like Adam," R.V. txt "like Adam," marg. "as men."

[**2998** (xx) *d*] That "son of man" in the gospels is incapable of being illustrated by classical Greek metaphors such as "a child of fortune," a true "son of his country," and by uses of "son" as a complimentary title in Greek inscriptions, appears evident from a careful examination of Greek usage. Paton and Hicks give three identical inscriptions (*Inscriptions of Cos*, Nos. 95—97) θεοῖς πατρῴοις ὑπὲρ ὑγείας Μάρκου Αἰλίου Σαβεινιανοῦ υἱοῦ πόλεως καὶ γερουσίας, εὐεργέτα τᾶς πατρίδος. Waddington (*Inscriptions Gr. et Lat.* vol. iii. part ii. p. 26) gives Ἡ

§ 8. *The Fourth Gospel prepares us for misinterpretation*

[2998 (xxi)] In the gospels, "Son of man" is almost exclusively reserved for the utterances of Christ Himself, and the study of these passages must be deferred to *The Fourfold Gospel*. Our business now is not with these, but with the rare instances where it is used about Christ by others, *e.g.* the martyr Stephen, or by the earliest Christian apologists or commentators. One of the most striking is Jn xii. 34: "We have heard from the Law that the Christ abideth for ever, and how sayest thou that the Son of man must be lifted up? Who is this Son of man?" These words exhibit the multitude as, so to speak, recoiling from

---

γερουσία ἐτείμησεν ἐκ τῶν ἰδίων προσόδων Φερ....τὸν υἱὸν τῆς γερουσίας ἀγορανομήσαντα, etc. He says "La qualification de υἱὸς τῆς γερουσίας... est nouvelle. On trouve souvent dans les inscriptions de l'Asie les titres υἱὸς τῆς πόλεως, υἱὸς τοῦ δήμου, et sur les médailles υἱὸς τῆς πόλεως, υἱὸς Ἀφροδισιέων, Κοπαέων etc., mais on ne sait rien de positif sur la nature de ces adoptions. On peut les comparer aux bourses entretenues dans les colléges par nos départements et nos communes...."

[2998 (xx) *e*] Ὁ υἱὸς τοῦ ἀνθρώπου, regarded as a translation from the Aramaic, does not receive much illustration from the LXX, except so far as to shew that Christian translators of the Aramaic phrase would in most cases translate it literally, at least when used by our Lord about Himself, in the singular. When applied to animals, the Hebrew "son of" is sometimes paraphrased by LXX (see Index υἱός), but when applied to persons, it is rendered literally except in a few cases not worth mentioning except as interesting proofs of *exceptional, and, so to speak, "experimental" translation in a few books of the Bible*, notably Genesis. For example, πολίτης in Gen. xxiii. 11 is used to render "son of my people." *But it is never used again as a rendering of this phrase*, although "son of people" (Gesen. 121 *a*) is freq. in Hebrew.

[2998 (xx) *f*] It is indeed possible that, here and there, our Lord's "sons of men" to signify "men," may have been rendered "men" by Greek gospels, partly because "sons of men" and "Son of man," *together*, might cause obscurity and misunderstanding. But the view that any Greek interpreter of Christ's Aramaic would represent Christ as calling Himself "Son of man"—when He did not do so—owing to any influence of Greek thought or language, is extremely improbable.

the phrase "son of man"—which, as used by Jesus, bewildered them owing to their false notions of the vileness of human nature—in order to take refuge in a technical term that they thought they understood, namely, Christ, or Messiah[1]. Perhaps John had in his mind similar misunderstandings among Christians, orthodox as well as heretical, of his own time. At all events, his words should serve to prepare us for them, and these we must now discuss, after mentioning the few very early instances where "son of man" is used in the Epistle to the Hebrews (quoting from the Psalms) in the Acts, and in the history of Hegesippus.

§ 9. *Pauline Equivalents*

[2998 (xxii)] The Pauline Epistles, though not quoting "*son of man*" from the eighth Psalm as referring to Christ, repeatedly quote from this Psalm the closely following phrase about "*subjecting all things*" (Heb. "*put all things under his feet*"), *and always with reference to the expressed or implied*

---

[1] [2998 (xxi) *a*] Comp. Jn i. 41 "We have found the Messiah," iv. 25 "I know that Messiah cometh." These are the only instances of "Messiah" in N.T., and both may be taken as *voces populi*. In Jn xii. 34 the multitude will not attempt to take in the Psalmist's view—set before them by Jesus—of the divinely destined exaltation of "the son of man." They prefer a title (like Messiah) that does not give them the trouble of thinking, because—so they would have said—"Everybody knows what 'Messiah' means."

[2998 (xxi) *b*] We are not to suppose that the multitude took "Son of man" to be another title for "Messiah." There is no evidence to shew that they could have had this notion, and much to shew that they could not have had it. What they said was, in effect, "We do not understand this strange use of the phrase 'Son of man,' which the new Teacher is continually dinning into our ears. Even a prophet was never called 'son of man' except to shew how weak he was. A 'son of man is a poor creature. Does this Jesus mean to call himself 'a poor creature'? What we want is a Messiah—and a Messiah, not to be 'lifted up'—another perplexing phrase of his—but to stay with us on earth, after delivering us from all enemies."

"*subjection*" *of death*[1]. The first epistle to the Corinthians quotes Psalm viii along with Psalm cx ("The Lord said unto my Lord...until I make thine enemies thy footstool") adduced by Jesus against Pharisæan views concerning the Messiah as "*the son of David.*" Any quotation of the latter Psalm, in any Semitic original of the gospels, would probably contain the word "footstool," retained in the LXX thus, "until I *put thine enemies as the footstool of thy feet.*" But in the Apostle's mind the two passages "all things under his feet," and "footstool of thy feet," seem to have referred to the same Person, or at least to the Person and the type of the Person. At all events he has dropped "*the footstool*" so that the two Psalm-quotations are conformed in expression: "For he [*i.e.* Christ] must reign until (Ps. cx. 1) '*he* [i.e. God] *hath put all his* [*i.e.* Christ's] *enemies under his feet.*' The last '*enemy*' to be destroyed is death; [but he, too, must finally be destroyed] for (Ps. viii. 6) *he* [i.e. *God*] *hath subjected all things* [*without exception*] *under his feet* [*i.e.* under the feet of the '*man*' or the '*son of man*'

---

[1] [2998 (xxii) *a*] The allusion is always made without any mention of "Scripture," or "he saith," as though Christians were quite familiar with it:—1 Cor. xv. 27 "The last enemy that is to be destroyed is death, for *He hath subjected all things beneath his feet.*" Here anyone unfamiliar with the Psalm might very naturally suppose that "He" means Death, who had, up to a certain time, "subjected all things" and was now to be himself subjected. But the writer assumes that the Corinthians will recognise his quotation from the Psalm "Thou [*i.e.* God] hast subjected all things under his feet." He proceeds to speak of "*him that subjected,*" and "*the subjecter,*" on the same assumption. Comp. Eph. i. 19—22 "according to the inward working of the might of his strength which he has inwardly worked in Christ, having raised him from the dead and caused him to sit at his right hand...and he '*subjected all things under his feet,*'" Phil. iii. 20—1 "the Lord Jesus Christ, who shall change the fashion of the body of our humiliation so as to share in the form of the body of his glory according to the inward working of his power to *subject all things* to himself." W. and H. do not print this third passage as a quotation. But, though the writer here represents the Son, and not the Father, as the "subjecter," and omits "feet," he appears to me to allude to the Psalmist's phrase.

mentioned by the Psalmist, whom I, Paul, take to be Christ]."
This juxtaposition is of great importance. For it shews that,
although the Apostle does not mention "*man*" or "*son of
man*," he takes them as pointing to Christ. And indeed "*the
Adam*," or "*the first man*," is in his mind all through this
chapter on the resurrection. He regards Christ as being
chronologically the Second Man, or Second Adam—although
spiritually the First Man, because He is the express image of
God in whose image humanity was designed[1].

[2998 (xxiii)] This Pauline combination of the two Psalm-
traditions—the former tradition dealing with "babes and
sucklings" and with the subjection of all things to "the son
of man," and the latter tradition with "sitting at the right
hand" of God till "all enemies" are subdued—takes us back

---

[1] [2998 (xxii) *b*] Perhaps this very early Christian combination of
"subjecting *underneath* (ὑποκάτω) the feet" and "making *the footstool*
(ὑποπόδιον) of the feet" may account for the very great confusion in the
text of the latter as quoted in the Synoptic gospels. W.H. give Mk xii. 36
ὑποκάτω τῶν ποδῶν σου, Mt. xxii. 44 *ib*., but Lk. xx. 43 ὑποπόδιον τῶν
ποδῶν σου. But SS has "underneath" in Mk, Mt., Lk. (prefixing "as
the footstool" in Lk.). The Lat. versions are divided between "sub"
(*d* in Mt. has "suptus") and "scabellum" (Mk xii. 36, in *k*, "suppeda-
neum," D ὑποκάτω, but *d* "scamillum"). In Mk, D has θωσω (with η
above the first ω) and εκχθους, and L has εχρους, and the three versions
have been more than usually "counterchanged," so that it is difficult
to ascertain the right readings.

[2998 (xxii) *c*] St Paul may have felt that "making one's enemies
a *footstool*" had a barbaric sound for Greek ears. At all events he freely
paraphrased ὑποπόδιον as ὑπό. But the Pauline writers of Acts ii. 35,
Heb. i. 13, quote the Psalm and (Heb. x. 13) refer to it in the 3rd pers.
with the correct ὑποπόδιον. Origen, commenting on Mt. xxii. 44, appeals
to the Biblical use of God's "footstool" (as referring to the sanctuary
or ark (Is. lx. 13, lxvi. 1, Lam. ii. 1)) to shew that the "enemies" are
benefited by being made "the footstool." If our Lord interpreted the
words thus and applied them to Himself, it would be in accordance with
His own precepts about the treatment of "enemies." Jerome (on Mt.)
reads "scabellum," but concerns himself with little more than a con-
troversial argument that the words must refer to Christ, and not to
Abraham.

to Christ's fundamental doctrines about "the little ones" who are "great" and to whom "the kingdom of heaven" belongs; and about the bestowal of "authority"—apparently on these same "babes"—to "tread upon serpents and scorpions"; and about God's revealing His truth to none but "babes" and only through "the Son"; and about God's "ordaining praise (Heb. strength) through the mouths of babes and sucklings"; and about "the Son of man" as destined to "sit at the right hand of God[1]." It is the doctrine of Isaiah about the "little child" playing with the "asp" and leading the "lion." Only by "little child" Christ does not mean anything that excludes full-grown wisdom and power; He would say in effect, with His apostle, "in malice be ye babes but in minds full-grown men." Many other passages in the

---

[1] [2998 (xxiii) *a*] "Babes," Mt. xi. 25, Lk. x. 21, followed in Mt.-Lk. by the doctrine that "none knoweth the Father save the Son," and preceded, in Lk., by Lk. x. 19 "I have given you the authority to tread on serpents." The same passage contains a warning as to "subjection." The Seventy are not to rejoice that the evil spirits "are subjected" to them, but that their "names" are "written in heaven." Mt. xxi. 16 quotes Ps. viii. 2 "strength" (and so Targum) as LXX "praise."

[2998 (xxiii) *b*] "The right hand of God" is expressed (or implied) by Christ on only two occasions. (1) In His last utterance to the Pharisees, where they have replied to Him that the Messiah is "the Son of David," He quotes "The Lord said unto my Lord, Sit thou *on my right hand,*" and asks how the Person thus addressed can be both "son" and "lord" to David (Mk xii. 36, Mt. xxii. 44, Lk. xx. 42). (2) He tells the Pharisees that they shall see (Mk xiv. 62, Mt. xxvi. 64, Lk. xxii. 69) "the Son of man seated *at the right hand of the power* (Lk. adds *of God*)." There Mk-Mt. add "and coming with (Mt. 'on') the clouds of heaven." But Lk.'s omission of it almost demonstrates that it was an insertion, intended by the inserter to explain the "son of man" as being the one mentioned by Daniel. When this insertion is omitted, "the son of man" may very well mean the *ben adam* of the eighth Psalm, weak with the weakness of earthly nature now, but destined to be exalted to "the right hand of the *Power*" hereafter. As was said above (2998 (xx)) *bar adam*, though meaning "son of Adam" in Aramaic, might yet convey allusively the meaning that *ben adam* has in Scripture, "son of man."

Pauline epistles suggest that the apostle, though aware that Christ called Himself "son of man," preferred to express the meaning in other ways[1].

---

[1] [2998 (xxiii) *c*] When St Paul speaks of the incarnation of the Son of God as a self-humiliation, with a view to the exaltation of all mankind, in Himself, to the Father, he uses the phrases (Gal. iv. 4) "born of a woman," (Phil. ii. 7) "having taken the likeness of a servant," "having become in the likeness of men (ἀνθρώπων)." Here "*men*"—*i.e.* "man" in the sense of "mankind"—is much more intelligible to Greeks than "*son of man*"—which, as we shall see below, soon caused difficulty to non-Jewish Christians, as they naturally asked, "son of what man?" or "son of what human being?"

[2998 (xxiii) *d*] The Pauline contrasts—between (Phil. ii. 6—9) "humbled himself" and "God highly exalted him," "emptied himself" and "God gave him the name that is above every name," "servant" and "that in the name of Jesus every knee should bow"—may be illustrated by Mt.-Lk.'s tradition about "the Son of man" and "all things" in connexion with "being delivered over." There is an implied assumption of the Law, "To him that giveth shall be given." Because the "Son of man," humiliated, is "delivered over" by the Father to "men"—in the original, perhaps, "to the sons of men," *i.e.* to sinful men—therefore to the "Son of man," glorified, there shall be delivered over all mankind, or "all things." Comp. Lk. ix. 44 (Mt. xvii. 22) "*The Son of man* is destined to be *delivered over* into the hands of men," Lk. x. 22 "all things have been *delivered over* to me by my Father." Luke's order seems preferable—first the prediction "I shall be delivered over (as a ransom)," then the consequence "all things have been delivered over to me."

So, after the Passion, Christ says in Matthew (xxviii. 18) "All authority hath been given to me in heaven and on earth."

[2998 (xxiii) *e*] These gospel traditions about "delivering over," or "giving," are equivalent to saying, "Because the Son of man has subjected Himself to all mankind, 'making Himself their servant through love (Gal. v. 13 διὰ τῆς ἀγάπης δουλεύετε ἀλλήλοις)' therefore God has subjected all mankind to Him." John says the same thing, using δίδωμι instead of παραδίδωμι. Having said (Jn iii. 16) "He [*i.e.* the Father] *gave* the only begotten Son" for the world, he subsequently reiterates the phrase "all that the Father hath *given* unto me"—meaning the world saved by the Son. Here it may be added that Jn never mentions "the right hand of God." Origen's comment on the literalistic interpretation of the phrase (Mt. xxii. 44) may perhaps explain why Jn avoids it. But it is implied in the Johannine "lift up" and "glorify," both of which signify (1) Christ's Passion (2) His Ascension—the two

§ 10. *The Epistle to the Hebrews and the Acts*

[**2998** (xxiv)] The Epistle to the Hebrews takes up and quotes more fully the Pauline combination of the two Psalm-passages above mentioned[1]. This writer, unlike St Paul, inserts "Son of man"[2] in his quotation from the eighth Psalm. But he does not venture to say, "Jesus *was this 'son of man' mentioned by the Psalmist.*" He prefers to quote in full, and then, taking phrase by phrase, to say, "This, and that, were fulfilled, or will be fulfilled, in Jesus." Apparently, he feels that he must meet an objection "How could Christ be called (LXX) *'a little lower than the angels?'"* At great length, he points out that the "Son," mentioned in the Psalms, is superior to the angels, "all" of whom are "ministering

---

being regarded as inseparable parts of one divine foreordained act of Redemption.

[1] [**2998** (xxiv) *a*] One reason for prefixing the quotation about "enemies" from Ps. cx. to the quotation about "subjugating" from Ps. viii., may be that the latter also contains a mention of an "enemy" though somewhat brief and obscure (viii. 2) "because of thine adversaries (LXX enemies, ἐχθρῶν) that thou mightest still the enemy and avenger." For Origen's comment on this see **2998** (xxiv) *e*.

[2] [**2998** (xxiv) *b*] Westcott's note on Heb. ii. 6 "son of man," υἱὸς ἀνθρώπου, "בן־אדם" not ὁ υἱὸς τοῦ ἀνθρώπου (בן־האדם)" might give rise to erroneous inferences—if at least it led the reader to suppose that the Hebrew writer might have written the latter but preferred the former. The pl. *bne ha-adam* sometimes occurs in the Bible, but the sing. *ben ha-adam* nowhere (so far as Mandelkern's Concordance shews). Dr Schmidt says (*Enc. Bib.* 4706) "Christians like Sason...probably translated ὁ υἱὸς τοῦ ἀνθρώπου by *ben hā-ādām*, as, in modern times, Delitzsch." But that fact does not justify us in supposing that a Jew in the first century could have used such a phrase: it merely shews that modern Jews felt the ambiguity caused in ancient Hebrew by the absence of the article. I am informed by Dr Büchler that he has not found *ben ha-adam* in Talmudic literature. My friend Dr W. H. Bennett suggests to me, "Perhaps if it had been possible for a Jew, while Hebrew was a living language, to have had the idea of 'The Son of Man' in our sense, he might have used *ben ha-adam*." Perhaps this was Westcott's meaning. But it seems to me that the words "in our sense" might themselves be interpreted in different senses.

spirits." He also supplies some things that the Corinthian Epistle merely implies—*e.g.* about the "subjection" being universal, and "not yet" completed. He includes in his quotation the words "thou didst crown him with glory and honour." "Crown" has Greek associations with the thought of a victorious conflict for an honourable prize, and Christians had probably long connected the word with the "crown" of martyrdom ("Stephen," or "Crown," being the first martyr). The result is a sort of Targum on the Pauline passage: "But, as it is, we see not yet 'all things subjected' to him. But him who hath been 'made a little lower than the angels' we see—namely Jesus—because of the suffering of death, 'crowned with glory and honour,' in order that, by the grace of God, he might taste of death for all [mankind]¹."

---

¹ [2998 (xxiv) *c*] An instructive contrast is supplied in the different qualifications of "all things have been subjected":—(1) 1 Cor. xv. 27 "But when he says 'all things have been subjected' it is clear that it is with the exception of him [i.e. *God*] who *subjected all things* to him [i.e. *Christ*]," (2) Heb. ii. 8 "For in subjecting [to him, *i.e.* the Son of man] all things that are, he [*i.e.* God] left nothing unsubjected to him. But as it is at present, we see not yet subjected to him all things that are." As regards the "not yet"—implying that some of the fulfilment of the Psalm was future—it may be noted that the Hebrew text of the Psalm quoted leaves loopholes for variations of tense throughout, and that in viii. 6 Aquila had "thou *wilt give* him authority," LXX and R.V. "thou *madest* him to have dominion," Field "dominari *facies* eum."

[2998 (xxiv) *d*] Comp. Ps. viii. 5 "Thou crownest him with *glory and honour*" with Ps. xlix. 12 (R.V. marg.) "Man being in *honour* abideth not, he is like the beasts that perish." The meaning is that there are two sorts of human "glory and honour" (Jn xii. 43), one coming "*from God*," the other "*from men*." The latter, apart from the former, tends to make men (Jn xii. 40) "blind," and (Ps. xlix. 12) "like the beasts that perish."

[2998 (xxiv) *e*] God's "glory"—so far as it comes *from* men—consists (according to Christ's doctrine) in men's sonship towards Himself and brotherhood towards one another. It consists—so far as it is manifested in its coming *to* men—in His righteousness, kindness, and truth. Origen's commentary on the words "Thou that hast set *thy glory* above the heavens" is lost. But we may infer from his comment on Mt. xvi. 27

[2998 (xxv)] Another N.T. mention of "Son of man" "in the glory of his Father," that he considered the real glory of Christ not to be confined to that which is popularly associated with His "second advent," but to consist in "the grace and truth" of (Jn i. 14) "the only begotten." We have his comment on Ps. viii. 2 "Because of thine enemies to still the enemy and avenger." "In the enemy and avenger," says Origen, "understand the true Nebuchadnezzar"—that is, the persecutor, used by God as an instrument for purifying the Three Children, and Job, in the furnace of affliction. "The devil," he continues, "was brought down to nothing (κατέλυσεν) by Christ through fishermen and unlettered folk and 'babes in malice' (1 Cor. xiv. 20)."

[2998 (xxiv) *f*] The words of the Psalm "set thy *glory* (R.V. marg.) *above the heavens*," combined with "*babes and sucklings*," present a parallelism to Luke's version of the song of the disciples on the entry into Jerusalem (xix. 38) "in heaven peace, *glory in the highest*," followed by Matthew's tradition of Christ's words (xxi. 16) "*Out of the mouth of babes and sucklings.*" Origen (on Ps. viii. 2) identifies the (Mt. xxi. 15) "boys (παῖδας)" with the previously mentioned (Mt. xxi. 9) "multitudes (ὄχλους)" and with the Saviour's (Mt. xxi. 16) "babes and sucklings." He also suggests a scribal error in Matthew as to "house of David" and "son of David" (Lomm. xii. 16) ζητήσεις δὲ πότερον ταὐτόν ἐστιν οἶκος Δαυὶδ καὶ υἱὸς Δαυίδ· καὶ εἰ μὴ ταὐτόν ἐστιν, ἡμάρτηται τὸ κατὰ Ματθαῖον γραφικῶς, ὄφειλον ἔχειν ἤτοι δὶς τῷ οἴκῳ Δαυὶδ ἤτοι υἱῷ Δαυίδ. This is somewhat obscure. But it rather confirms a hypothesis suggested by internal evidence, that the Semitic original mentioned "*those who were of his house,*" that is (616 *c*) *Christ's disciples*. This may have been conflated by Mt. as (1) "servants (παῖδας)" (2) "in the House [of God]" *i.e.* ἐν τῷ ἱερῷ.

[2998 (xxiv) *g*] Luke's above-quoted Song of the Disciples (xix. 38) "*In heaven peace,* glory in the highest," and his Song of the angels (ii. 14) "Glory in the highest to God and *on earth peace* among men with whom he is well pleased," taken together, exhibit (as Ephrem p. 27 points out) the "angels" proclaiming "*peace on earth*" and the "babes and sucklings" proclaiming "*peace in heaven.*" The latter is a bold expression, but intelligible as the antithesis of Rev. xii. 7 "There was *war in heaven.*" The suggestion is, that when there is absolute "peace on earth," there can be no sin or evil, and when there is no sin or evil there is nothing against which the powers of heaven need contend. Taken together, Luke's two traditions supply an antidote against the notion that there is any rivalry or jealousy between the angels and man, and suggest that as the songs of angels descend, so the songs of the men with whom God is well pleased ascend, through one and the same Being—the Son of man.

is in Acts vii. 55—6 " And being full of the Holy Spirit he [*i.e.* the protomartyr Stephen] gazed steadfastly on heaven and saw the glory of God and Jesus *standing* on the right hand of God; and he said, ' Lo, I behold the heavens wide opened and the Son of man *standing* on the right hand of God.'" This resembles an extract from Hegesippus, concerning James called the brother of the Lord, who, when questioned about "Jesus the crucified," replied (Euseb. ii. 23. 13) "Why question ye me concerning Jesus *the Son of man*? And He is seated in the heaven on the right hand of the Great Power, and is destined to come upon the clouds of the heaven." The latter utterance may have been shaped by Hegesippus in accordance with some gospel tradition, but the former is clearly independent, since it represents Christ as "standing," not "sitting." The Epistle to the Hebrews (x. 11) describes an ordinary high priest as "*standing*" (**2998** (xxxii) *a*). "*Standing*," used by Stephen—whose death was witnessed by Saul and whose dying words may fairly be supposed to be more exactly reported than the rest of his speech—betokens a very early tradition indeed, which reverence for the martyr retained though it was contrary to customary expression. Thus, in the Acts and Hegesippus we have two traditions, independent of each other—and the former also independent of gospel traditions—shewing that the thought of "*the Son of man at God's right hand*" was connected with the thought of *martyrdom*, or, to use our Lord's word, "*being delivered up*[1]."

---

[1] [**2998** (xxv) *a*] According to these precedents, to "see the Son of man at the right hand of God" would be (or rather, might naturally be) a special vision vouchsafed to a martyr; and this raises an interesting question as to the variations in Christ's prediction before the Transfiguration:

Mk ix. 1	Mt. xvi. 28	Lk. ix. 27
"There are some here of those that stand (*v.r.* "stand	"There are some of those here standing who shall not	"There are some of those here (αὐτοῦ, *v.r.* ὧδε) standing who

§ 11. *The Revelation of John*

[**2998** (xxvi)] The Revelation of John nowhere contains the gospel phrase "*the Son of man.*" But it twice, in prophetic language, describes visions of "*one like a son of man*[1]." The

here," not "some here"; D, a, b etc. add "with me") who shall not taste of death till they see *the kingdom of God having come* (ἐληλυ-θυῖαν) *in power.*"	taste of death till they see *the Son of man coming in his kingdom.*"	shall not taste of death until they see *the kingdom of God* (but D *the Son of man coming in his glory*)."

Immediately after this prediction, Peter, James, and John are taken up to the mountain of Transfiguration where (according to Lk. ix. 30) our Lord holds discourse with Moses and Elias concerning His forthcoming Passion or Martyrdom. Peter and James are recognised by all as "martyrs," and John, though not a martyr so far as actual death was concerned, was generally recognised as a "martyr" (**2935** foll.). The exact words of the prediction are obviously doubtful: but it may not improbably be interpreted as being fulfilled in this special way (besides others) that the three disciples in question enjoyed, before death, the martyr's privilege, the vision of the Son of man in heaven.

[**2998** (xxv) *b*] The variations, leaving it open whether the "kingdom" was to "have come," or the "Son of man" was to be beheld "coming," may be connected with the tradition, about one of the three martyrs, John, that Jesus said, "If I will that he tarry *till I come*, what is that to thee?" On this see **2936** foll.

[1] [**2998** (xxvi) *a*] Rev. i. 13 ὅμοιον υἱὸν (marg. υἱῷ) ἀνθρώπου, and rep. Rev. xiv. 14 (no marg. *v.r.*). Yet in i. 15, ii. 18 and freq. this writer has ὁμ. with the usual dat. It is perh. a "confusion of two constructions" (1) εἶδον ὡς υἱόν, (2) εἶδον ὅμοιον υἱῷ. Comp. Dan. vii. 13 ὡς υἱὸς ἀνθρώπου ἤρχετο or ἐρχόμενος, *i.e.* "there came one like a son of man," equiv. to ὅμοιός τις υἱῷ. In Rev. i. 13 (and in xiv. 14 after parenth.) εἶδον precedes, and might govern υἱόν if ὅμοιον is taken as ὡς. Another explanation might be that ὅμοιον = κατά, "according to," "after the manner of." Comp. Job i. 8, κατ᾽ αὐτόν = Heb. "like him (כמהו)" al. exempl. ὅμοιος αὐτῷ. In either case the originator of the phrase seems to have used ὅμοιος with a deliberate indefiniteness. In the same spirit Ezekiel, after saying (i. 26) "the *likeness* of a throne...the *appearance* of a sapphire stone," duplicates the indefiniteness when he has to describe what is enthroned, "*a likeness as the appearance* of a man."

[2998]

latter may help us to understand the former. Moreover the contexts in Revelation throw light on many questions that will have to be discussed in *The Fourfold Gospel*. Hence they are annotated below at considerable length—rather for reference than for perusal.

Before the first vision comes a preface—largely made up of quotations—to the book as a whole:—(lit.) "The Revelation of Jesus Christ, which God gave him to shew unto his servants—'the things that must needs come to pass' quickly[1]; and he signified them having sent through his angel[2] to his

---

[1] [2998 (xxvi) *b*] Comp. Dan. ii. 28, 29 ἃ δεῖ γενέσθαι and ii. 45 (Theod.) ἃ δεῖ γενέσθαι, also Mk xiii. 7 δεῖ γενέσθαι and comp. Mt. xxiv. 6, xxvi. 54, Lk. xxi. 9, always used of tribulation. It is repeated by "a voice" in Rev. iv. 1 "Come up here, and I will shew thee *the things that must needs come to pass* hereafter," and by (xxi. 9) "one of the seven angels that have the seven bowls" in xxii. 6 "And he said to me, These words are faithful and true, and the Lord, the God of the spirits of the prophets, sent his angel to shew to his servants *the things that must needs come to pass* quickly. And behold, I come quickly."

(xxvi) *c—g* WHO IS "HIS ANGEL"?

[2] [2998 (xxvi) *c*] Rev. i. 1 "Through his angel." Who is "his angel"? Apart from the "angels" of the Seven Churches, "angel," in the sing., does not occur till Rev. v. 2 "I saw a strong angel" and then (vii. 2) "I saw another angel." But this and the following angels do not speak to the Seer till x. 9 ("take it and eat it up"). And no angel is described as "shewing" anything till xvii. 1 ("Come hither, I will shew thee...")— repeated in xxi. 9, and, in both cases, referring to "one of the seven angels that had the seven bowls." It seems therefore that in the earlier part of the book the "angel" is the "*voice* that he (i. 12) turns to see," the same that is called, later on (iv. 1), "the first *voice* that I heard,... namely a [*man*] *saying* (λέγων) 'Come up hither,'" and again (x. 8) "And [behold] the *voice* (καὶ ἡ φωνή) that I heard from heaven—[I heard it] again saying (πάλιν λαλοῦσαν)." The commentary called by the name of Victorinus commenting on iv. 1 says (ed. T. & T. Clark) "That is, the Spirit, whom, a little before, he confesses that he had seen walking as the Son of man in the midst of the golden candlesticks." That is a possible explanation. The Paraclete is said (Jn xv. 26) to be "sent" by the Son to the disciples and might be referred to in Rev. i. 1 "sent." It might be called popularly a "messenger" or "angel" in Rev. i. 1, and

yet a "voice" later on. So in Jn xii. 28 "there came *a voice* from heaven," the "voice" is that of the Spirit, but some of the crowd said it was an "angel." In Rev. xix. 5—9 "And a voice came from the throne, saying, Give ye praise....And *he* (or, it) *saith* (λέγει) unto me, 'Write...,'" there is the same indefiniteness.

[2998 (xxvi) *d*] The Seer's use of "voice" as a spiritual messenger, *i.e.* ἄγγελος or "angel," may be illustrated by Jn iii. 8 "*thou hearest its* [*i.e.* the Spirit's] *voice*, but knowest not whence it cometh nor whither it goeth"—a passage that suggests a "messenger" invisible as the wind. On Rev. i. 12 "I turned to *see the voice*," see 727—8, and comp. Exod. xx. 18 (LXX) "all the people *saw the voice* and the torches and the voice of the trumpet." Philo (728 *b*, 781 *c*—*d*) emphasizes the "seeing" as referring to the eye of the soul.

[2998 (xxvi) *e*] The difficulty of answering the question "Who is 'his angel'?" is increased by the fact that "his" may mean "God's" or Christ's. Compare:—

Rev. i. 1	Rev. xxii. 6—16
"The revelation of Jesus Christ, which God gave him [*i.e.* Christ] to shew to *his* [whose?] servants, namely the things that must come to pass quickly, and (*he*) [who? God or Christ?] signified them having sent through *his* [whose?] angel, to *his* [whose?] servant, John...."	"And he [*i.e.* xxi. 9 "one of the seven angels..."] said to me, '...and the (ὁ) Lord, the God of the spirits of the prophets, sent his angel to shew to *his* servants the things that must come to pass quickly. And behold, I come quickly...'...and he saith unto me, '...Behold I come quickly...I am the Alpha...I Jesus sent my angel to bear witness to you (pl.) these things upon the churches.'"

In the second of these passages (xxii. 6) "the Lord the God" might possibly mean "Christ," regarded (as He is by ancient Fathers) as the Inspirer of the Hebrew prophets and called by the Seer "their God" (comp. xix. 10 "the witness of Jesus is the spirit of prophecy"), although, in any other book but this, it would be far more probable that the title should indicate the Father (Phil. ii. 11 does not say that Jesus Christ is "the Lord the God," but "Lord, to the glory of the Father"). It should also be noted that the "angel" speaks in the person of Christ ("I come quickly") so that the Seer (xxii. 8) falls down to worship the angel, but is prohibited. The writer perhaps means to teach that all the visible figures that bring messages from the Father or the Son, throughout the book, are of the nature of "angels," and not to be "worshipped."

[2998 (xxvi) *f*] Comp. Rev. xxi. 22—3 "And I saw no sanctuary (ναόν) in it [*i.e.* in the city], for the Lord God (ὁ γὰρ Κύριος ὁ θεός) the All-ruler (ὁ παντοκράτωρ) is its sanctuary—and the Lamb....For the glory of God

servant John, who bare witness[1] [of] the word of God and

was its light (ἐφώτισεν αὐτήν) and the Lamb [was] its lamp." Here W.H. print xxi. 22 ὁ γὰρ κύριος as a quotation from Amos iv. 13, but Amos has no article. By inserting the article, did John intend to signify "the Lord Jesus"? In favour of this supposition it may be urged that it is more usual to speak of "Christ" or "the body of Christ," than of "God," as being "the sanctuary." If Christ were meant, there would be (in "All-ruling...Lamb") paradoxical antithesis—a characteristic of this book (compare the paradox in Rev. v. 5—6 "the Lion...a Lamb"). But outside the gospels (**2998** (xxvii) *h*) the distinction between ὁ Κύριος and Κύριος is not regularly observed. On "All-ruler," παντοκράτωρ, see also **2998** (xxvii) *i* foll.

[**2998** (xxvi) *g*] So far, in this conflicting evidence, the definite statement in xxii. 16 "I Jesus sent my angel" turns the balance in favour of supposing that the angel is sent by Jesus, and that it is the Holy Spirit represented by "voices" and "angels." But it also appears that the writer does not make any clear distinction between the Spirit, and Jesus, and the Father. He writes as a Seer, not as a theologian.

(xxvi) *h—k* "Witness" and "Martyr"

[1] [**2998** (xxvi) *h*] i. 2 ὃς ἐμαρτύρησεν, "who bare witness." With the dative, μαρτυρέω would mean "testify to." With the accusative, it means "testify," "state this or that, as evidence." Comp. xxii. 20 ὁ μαρτυρῶν ταῦτα, *i.e.* Jesus, who, throughout this book, through an angel or in His own person, is regarded as "testifying," or "stating in evidence," the will of the Father, which He sees in heaven and which is to be revealed, in act, upon earth.

[**2998** (xxvi) *i*] Μαρτυρία and μάρτυς, in this book, almost always convey the notion of "bearing witness under persecution, or with one's life," comp. μαρτυρία in vi. 9, xi. 7, xii. 11, xx. 4, and μάρτυς in ii. 13, xi. 3, xvii. 6; and this justifies us in supposing that Jesus Himself is called (i. 5) "the faithful *Witness*" and (iii. 14) "the faithful and true *Witness*," with reference to His death, which is regarded as an act of "bearing witness" to the will of the Father. As to xii. 17, xix. 10 (lit.) "those that *keep* (ἐχόντων) the *witness of Jesus*," comp. vi. 9 "slain because of the word of God and because of *the witness* that they *would keep* (εἶχον *i.e.* continued to keep in spite of persecution)." "The witness of Jesus" might mean "the witness borne by Jesus," *i.e.* His martyrdom, or "the witness borne to Jesus," *i.e.* the martyrdom of the saints. The writer perhaps combines the two meanings. The martyrs (2 Cor. iv. 10) "bear about in their bodies" the dying, or martyrdom, of the Lord Jesus, and die in the power of His dying. Thus they make His martyrdom their own.

[**2998** (xxvi) *j*] R.V. has substituted "witness" for A.V. "martyr"

[of] the witness of Jesus Christ...." Then, after a blessing on the observant reader, comes a salutation:—"John to the seven churches that are in Asia, grace to you and peace from the 'IS[1]' and the WAS and the COMING,

---

in Acts xxii. 20, "the blood of thy *martyr* Stephen was shed," Rev. ii. 13 "Antipas was my faithful *martyr*." In Rev. xvii. 6 "the blood of the *martyrs* of Jesus," R.V. retains "martyrs" but places "witnesses" in the margin. Perhaps it would have been better to place "witness" in text, but "martyr" in margin, in all three passages. Comp. Clem. Cor. 5 "Peter, who, on account of unrighteous zeal [*i.e.* persecution], having undergone, not one or two but several (πλείονας) painful burdens (πόνους), *and thus having borne witness*, went to his due place of glory"—a passage that may be compared with 1 Pet. v. 1 where Peter calls himself "*witness* of the sufferings of Christ," perhaps meaning that he had "borne witness" in a practical way, by suffering pain. Clem. Cor. and Rev. were written at a time when μαρτυρία had come to mean "bearing witness *at the risk of death*," but had not yet come to mean necessarily "bearing witness *by actual death*" (see Lightf. on Clem. Cor.)—a distinction not definitely made till the third century. The use of μάρτυς and kindred forms in Rev. shews, 1st, that the writer regarded "the faithful Witness," that is, Christ, as the Martyr for the world, 2nd, that he regarded himself as in some sense a "martyr," "bearing witness" to "the faithful Witness" in the isle of Patmos.

[**2998** (xxvi) *k*] The word μάρτυς is applied to God Himself and to His Servant in Is. xliii. 10 (LXX) (twice quoted thus by Origen, Lomm. i. 153, xx. 282) "Be witnesses to me and I [am] witness, saith the Lord God, and my Servant (where the Targum adds "Messiah") whom I have chosen." Comp. Jn viii. 17, 18 "The witness of two men is true. I am he that beareth witness of myself, and the Father that sent me beareth witness of me." Origen (Lomm. i. 153) calls attention to the narrow sense of μάρτυς prevalent in his time as distinct from that in Acts i. 8.

(xxvi) *l—m* "The IS" and "the seven spirits"

[1] [**2998** (xxvi) *l*] Rev. i. 4 ἀπὸ Ὁ ῶΝ. Comp. Exod. iii. 14 R.V. txt "And God said unto Moses, I AM THAT I AM (marg. I AM, BECAUSE I AM, or, I AM WHO AM, or, I WILL BE THAT I WILL BE)...I AM (marg. I WILL BE, Heb. *Ehyeh*) hath sent me," where Onkelos has (Etheridge) "And the Lord said unto Mosheh, EHEYEH ASHER EHEYEH...EHEYEH hath sent me," LXX ἐγώ εἰμι ὁ ὤν (but Aq. and Theod. ἔσομαι (ὃς) ἔσομαι)...ὁ ὢν ἀπέσταλκέν με, Jon. Targ. "And the Lord said unto Mosheh, *He who spake and the*

and from the seven spirits[1], which [are] before the face of his throne, and from Jesus Christ [He is] 'the faithful witness[2],' 'the first-born of the dead,' and 'the ruler of the

---

world was; who spake and all things were...I am He who is and who will be hath sent me unto you," Jer. Targ. "And the Word of the Lord said unto Mosheh, *He who spake to the world, Be, and it was; and who will speak to it, Be and it will be*...EHEYEH hath sent me." As the two later Targums add the past and the future to the present (imperat. in Jer.), so does John; but, instead of ὁ ἐσόμενος (which would resemble Aq.) he uses ἐρχόμενος in a double sense (1) of "coming" time, (2) of the "coming" Deliverer and Judge.

[1] [2998 (xxvi) *m*] Rev. i. 4 τῶν ἑπτὰ πνευμάτων. Swete compares Targ. Jon. on Gen. xi. 7 "dixit Deus vii angelis...," and Wetst. quotes it thus. But Walton and Etheridge have "*seventy*," and so has the Aramaic, and I have pointed out (see **668** *a* where Rev. i. 4, iii. 1, iv. 5 are discussed) that "*the seventy angels* correspond to the seventy nations of the earth." Possibly (**668** *a*) "the author...derived his 'seven spirits' from meditation on Zech. iv. 2—10 'seven *lamps*...by my *spirit*...these *seven* which are the *eyes* of the Lord,' with an infusion of Eastern tradition about seven angels before the throne." The Targ. on Zech. iv. 10 substitutes for the clause about eyes, "*septem lapidum ordines* quasi hos. Coram Domino revelata sunt opera filiorum hominis in universa terra." The Targumist means by "quasi hos" such stones as that just mentioned, *i.e.* the "plummet," which tests and tries man's works. To the facts in **668** *a* may be added that Origen *Hom.* iii. *Isaiah* (Lomm. xiii. 256) accepts the LXX rendering of Is. xi. 1—3 (as elsewhere) so as to favour the inference that there are seven spirits.

(xxvi) *n—q* "THE FAITHFUL WITNESS"

[2] [2998 (xxvi) *n*] Rev. i. 5 ὁ μάρτυς ὁ πιστός. Comp. Ps. lxxxix. 36—7 "His [David's] throne [shall endure] as the sun before me. It shall be established for ever as the moon, and as *the faithful witness* in the sky," where R.V. gives several various renderings. The Targ. has "like the moon which has been established as a sign for ever and a witness in the sky faithful to the ages," and Gesen. (729 *b*) takes "witness" as referring to the moon, by which the times of the festivals were determined. John perhaps has in view the relation between the moon and the sun as illustrating that between the Son and the Father. The Son receives light from the Father to convey to the dark world, and He makes Himself a "witness," or "martyr," for the Father. Πιστός, in this book, goes with (ii. 10) "unto death," and (ii. 13) "my witness," *i.e.* martyr. Probably "faithful *unto* death" is meant here, and in iii. 14, xix. 11. Perhaps also it is implied as a climax in xvii. 14 "called and chosen and faithful [in spite of persecution or death]."

kings of the earth[1]." Then a doxology is inserted: "To him that loveth us and loosed us from [our] sins in his blood, and made us a kingdom, priests[2] to his God and Father—

---

[1] [2998 (xxvi) *o*] Comp. Ps. lxxxix. 27 (R.V.) "I also will make him [my] firstborn, the highest of the kings of the earth." Perhaps the Psalmist referred to David, the youngest of the sons of Jesse, made "firstborn." The Targum—reducing, as often, poetry to literal prose— has "firstborn of the kings of the house of Judah" (David being, as a fact, the first king of the house of Judah, as well as the chief of all the kings of Judah). John paraphrases it from the Christian point of view, "firstborn of the dead." This may imply (1) "the *first* [*in time*] of the dead to arise," (2) "the *first* [*in precedence and honour*] of the dead," and possibly (3) what is expressed in Rom. i. 3 "of the seed of David after the flesh...*defined as the* [*firstborn*] *Son of God*...from the resurrection of the dead."

[2998 (xxvi) *p*] The Heb. עֶלְיוֹן, "highest" (Ps. *loc. cit.*), is followed by "to," but in Deut. xxvi. 19, xxviii. 1 by "above" ("highest above all the nations of the earth") and Gesen. 751 *a* gives only these three instances of personal application to human beings. When personally applied elsewhere it is a name of God, "Most High," and perh. Aq.'s rendering is best, ὕψιστον τοῖς βασιλεῦσι, "[as] Highest, *i.e.* as God, to the kings of the earth." LXX has ὑψηλὸν παρά "exalted as compared with," Sym. ἀνώτατον τῶν (the least satisfactory of all the renderings). John paraphrases it as ἄρχων, "ruler"—his only use of the word in this book. "Ruler of the kings of the earth"—which differs from (Jn xii. 31, comp. xiv. 30) "the ruler of this world," *i.e.* "the [transient or apparent] ruler of the flesh"—signifies the sole Emperor (αὐτοκράτωρ) who, from behind the veil, controls the kings of the earth, whether with or against their will, subjecting them to the will of the Father, who is called (i. 8) παντοκράτωρ "all-ruler."

[2998 (xxvi) *q*] There is a paradoxical antithesis or climax in the thought. "Witness" and "faithful" mostly imply an attitude of subordination or service; "firstborn" implies birth, growth, and (at all events in the beginning) inferiority to a father. Then "of the dead"— where one might have expected "from the dead"—seems to perplex the reader by suggesting "firstborn of the corpses." And then suddenly comes a note of triumph and exaltation, "the ruler of the kings of the earth."

---

[2] [2998 (xxvi) *r*] Rev. i. 5 λύσαντι ἡμᾶς ἐκ τῶν ἁμαρτιῶν [ἡμῶν] ἐν τῷ αἵματι αὐτοῦ. Swete illustrates this by Is. xl. 2 λέλυται αὐτῆς ἡ ἁμαρτία, and W.H. add Ps. cxxx. 8 λυτρώσεται τὸν Ἰσραὴλ ἐκ πασῶν τῶν

to him [is] the glory and the might for the ages [of ages], Amen." Then come well-known Messianic quotations "Behold, 'he cometh with the clouds,' and every eye shall 'see' him, and whosoever 'pierced' him, and 'there shall mourn over him all the tribes of the earth,' yea, Amen[1]."

[**2998** (xxvii)] Then comes a divine proclamation, "I am the Alpha and the Omega[2], saith the Lord God, the IS and

---

ἀνομῶν αὐτοῦ. But the resemblance is distant. The next words, "a kingdom, priests," perhaps give a clue to what is in the writer's mind, namely, the affectionate address of Jehovah to Israel in Exod. xix. 4—5 as amplified in Targ. Jon. (Etheridge) "I bare you upon the clouds... to solemnize the *Pascha*...you shall be more *beloved* before me than all the peoples on the face of the earth. And before me you shall be crowned *kings*, and sanctified *priests*, and a holy people." Bearing in mind what "the Pascha" would mean to John, we find in his words a striking parallelism to the Jewish tradition :—(1) "loveth" ("beloved"), (2) "a kingdom, priests" ("kings...and...priests"), (3) "loosed us from our sins in His blood" ("the Pascha").

[1] [**2998** (xxvi) *s*] Rev. i. 7. These quotations resemble Dan. vii. 13, Zech. xii. 10 foll., but not as in LXX. Comp. Mt. xxiv. 30, Jn xix. 37 and *Didach*. xvi. 7. All the passages taken together suggest that these passages from Daniel and Zechariah were much quoted by Christians and in a more accurate form than that of Zech. xii. 10 (LXX).

(xxvii) *a—e* "THE ALPHA AND THE OMEGA"

[2] [**2998** (xxvii) *a*] Rev. i. 8 ἐγώ εἰμι τὸ ἄλφα καὶ τὸ ὦ, occurs in this book thrice, but in xxi. 6, xxii. 13, without εἰμι. The context in xxi. 5—6 is "He that sitteth on the throne said (εἶπεν) 'Behold, I make all things new.' And he saith (λέγει) 'Write, because these words are faithful and true.' And he said to me (εἶπέν μοι) 'They are come to pass (γέγοναν). *I [am] the Alpha and the Omega, the beginning and the end*....'" In xxii. 13, after John has fallen to the ground as though to worship "one of the seven angels," the angel says—unless there is some change in the speaker, of which no warning is given—"*I [am] the Alpha and the Omega, the first and the last, the beginning and the end.*" "The first and the last" occurs thrice in this book, i. 17, ii. 8, xxii. 13.

[**2998** (xxvii) *b*] This threefold repetition of "first" and "last," in connexion with God, is also found in Isaiah, from whom John has probably derived it.

(1) Is. xli. 4 (lit.) "I Jehovah first, and with (את) [the] last (pl.) (Field, "et cum posteris"), I he," LXX ἐγὼ θεὸς πρῶτος καὶ εἰς τὰ ἐπερχόμενα ἐγώ εἰμι. Targ. "Ego Dominus creavi seculum a principio,

etiam secula seculorum mea sunt, et absque me non est Deus." Ibn Ezra says "*and with the last*, with the last generations."

(2) Is. xliv. 6 (lit.) "Thus saith Jehovah, the King of Israel, and his Redeemer, Jehovah of hosts, 'I, the first, and I last, and beside me there is no (אין) God'," ἐγὼ πρῶτος καὶ ἐγὼ μετὰ ταῦτα· πλὴν ἐμοῦ οὐκ ἔστιν θεός, Targ. "Ego sum ab initio; etiam secula seculorum mea sunt, et absque me non est Deus." The reader will perceive that, in (1), the Targ. has added the last six words belonging to (2).

Ibn Ezra says, "'*The Lord of Hosts*':—He is always King, and the hosts of heaven testify it. '*I am the first*':—the first king." The LXX here has θεὸς σαβαώθ, transliterating the Heb. *sabaoth*, "hosts." It invariably transliterates *sabaoth* in Isaiah, but almost invariably renders it in other books by παντοκράτωρ, "All-ruler." Παντοκράτωρ is (**2998** xxvii) *i* foll.) remarkably frequent in the Apocalypse, and it is practically certain that to John—who is not in the habit of transliterating—it represents "[Lord] of hosts." Consequently it is almost certain that John would take Is. xliv. 6 as mentioning not only "First and Last" but also "All-ruler," παντοκράτωρ. Hence παντοκράτωρ here (Rev. i. 8) should be regarded as coming not from Amos iv. 13 but from Is. xliv. 6.

(3) Is. xlviii. 12 "I [am] he; I [am] first; yea (אף), I [am] last," ἐγώ εἰμι (Qmg+ἐγώ) πρῶτος καὶ ἐγώ εἰμι εἰς τὸν αἰῶνα, Field, Οἱ λοιποί· ἐγὼ πρῶτος καὶ ἐγὼ ἔσχατος. For "I he," Field says "LXX vacat, ※ Aq. Sym. Theod. ἐγώ εἰμι," Targ. "Ego ipse, ego ipse qui sum ab initio: etiam secula seculorum mea sunt, *et absque me non est Deus*." The Targ. has again—as in (1)—added the last six words, borrowing them from (2).

[**2998** (xxvii) *c*] In (1), (2), (3), both the LXX and the Targum avoid the term "*last*." But in (3) it appears that the other Gk translators retain it. John also uses it thrice, but not here (Rev. i. 8). Why not? Probably because, like the LXX and the Targumist, he felt that "*last*" was liable to be misunderstood until he had prepared the way for it, by shewing that the context implied not only "first *and* last" but "*from* first *to* last," so as to imply totality. Now it happens that the letters meaning "with," את, which in (1) above have caused difficulty to translators (Is. xli. 4)—ignored by Vulg. and Syr., LXX εἰς, R.V. "with," Targ. paraphr.—mean also (Levy i. 183 *b*) *a grouping of the letters of the alphabet on the principle of uniting* "*first and last*," "*first but one and last but one*," &c. "First and last" would be expressed in Hebrew by *a* and *th* making את (*ath*), but in Greek by Alpha and Omega. In Heb. *ath* might mean the sign of the accusative. In Gen. i. 1, 16 etc., where it is thus taken by LXX, Aquila renders it by σύν. John—who closely follows Ezekiel's opening chapters and who describes himself, like Ezekiel, as (Rev. i. 17) falling lifeless at the feet of the Figure that brings him his first vision—must have been familiar with Ezek. i. 28—ii. 2

"THE SON OF MAN"

the WAS and the COMING[1], the ALL-RULER[2]."

"I fell upon my face and I heard [a] voice of one speaking....I heard *the* (את) one speaking unto me"; and Schöttg. i. 1086 quotes Jalkut Rubeni 3 *b*, as asserting that את means the *Shechinah, i.e.* the Divine Glory, and also "*all the letters, the beginning and the end.*" Such a mystical interpretation would be favoured by the fact that the prophet distinguishes between i. 28 "I heard [a] voice of one speaking" and ii. 2 "I heard the (את) one speaking unto me."

[2998 (xxvii) *d*] The Semitic origin of this use of Alpha and Omega is confirmed by the absence of any similar use in Greek or Latin literature (the use of "Alpha" to mean our "AI" being quite different) and also by the early origin of the name (Iren. i. 4. 1) Ἰαώ. It is generally supposed to be an attempt to represent "Jehovah." Perhaps it is more probably Alpha and Omega preceded by the initial Iota which was the first letter of "Jesus," in Hebrew and in Greek.

[2998 (xxvii) *e*] It will be noticed above that, in (3), LXX renders "I he, I first," by "I am first." This arises from the fact that Heb. "*he*" is freq. (2224) equivalent to "*is*" "*am*," etc. in LXX. Ibn Ezra says (on Is. xliii. 10 "I he") "This is the sublimest expression of the unity of God"—the reason being that created beings cannot say "*I am that which I ever was and shall be,*" but God can say this, "*I* [*am*] *he.*" It is improbable (though not impossible) that John meant "I AM HE, the ALPHA and the OMEGA, saith the Lord God, the IS and the WAS and THE COMING." But in any case, the writer probably meant emphasis by inserting εἰμι here alone, compared with xxi. 6, xxii. 13, where its absence is compensated for by additional clauses "first and last," "beginning and end." In the fourth gospel the mystical meaning of ἐγώ εἰμι is well known. In Rev. it occurs thrice at the beginning of a sentence, i. 8 ἐγώ εἰμι τὸ ἄλφα, i. 17 ἐγώ εἰμι ὁ πρῶτος, xxii. 16 ἐγώ εἰμι ἡ ῥίζα (the only other ἐγώ εἰμι being ii. 23 γνώσονται ὅτι ἐγώ εἰμι ὁ ἐραυνῶν, where it is not at the beginning of a sentence).

(xxvii) *f—m* "ALMIGHTY"

[1] [2998 (xxvii) *f*] Rev. i. 8 ἐγώ εἰμι τὸ ἄλφα καὶ τὸ ὦ, λέγει Κύριος ὁ θεὸς ὁ ὢν καὶ ὁ ἦν καὶ ὁ ἐρχόμενος ὁ παντοκράτωρ. On this Prof. Swete remarks "In xxi. 6, xxii. 13, where it [*i.e.* τὸ ἄλφα καὶ τὸ ὦ] occurs again, it is applied to Christ, and this reference is assumed by the ancient interpreters in the present case...but incorrectly, as the next words shew." Of these "ancient interpreters," (1) Hippolytus *adv. Noet.* 6 quotes ὁ ὤν...ὁ θεὸς ὁ παντοκράτωρ and says καλῶς εἶπεν παντοκράτορα Χριστόν, supporting his view from Mt. xi. 27 ; (2) Clem. Alex. 635 merely says διὰ τοῦτο ἄλφα καὶ ὦ ὁ λόγος εἴρηται, which may refer to Rev. xxi. 6, xxii. 13, so that it proves nothing as to i. 8 ; but (3) Origen *de princ.*

i. 2. 10, after quoting Rev. i. 8 with "qui venturus est," says, "'*Qui* enim *venturus est*,' quis est alius nisi Christus?" May not Origen be right?

Origen's argument would apply also to Rev. i. 4 ὁ ἐρχόμενος and would indicate that Origen regarded that verse also as applying to the Son. He supports the epithet "all-ruling" (*de princ.* i. 2. 10, Lomm. xxi. 61) by quoting Jn i. 3 "all things were made through him," adding "per Filium enim omnipotens est Pater." In favour of his view, is the fact that the Fourth Gospel speaks of the Son, or of the Light, as "coming," but seldom or never uses the word concerning the Father (except with the Son (Jn. xiv. 23) "*we* will come").

[2998 (xxvii) *g*] Origen's view seems to agree with that of the Fourth Gospel, and with Heb. i. 3, which describes Christ as "the express image of God's real being, and *bearing* (φέρων) *all things* [to their consummation] *by the word of his power.*" And accordingly Origen elsewhere (*Comm. Rom.* ix. 39, Lomm. vii. 351) introduces Rev. i. 8 by saying that Christ, "ut creator omnium, et potestatem gerens universorum, vi majestatis et necessitate potentiae habet cuncta subjecta... idcirco enim et *omnitenens* vel *omnipotens* dicitur, secundum quod Johannes (Rev. i. 8)...." Origen's "omnitenens vel omnipotens" indicates his feeling that παντοκράτωρ was quite a different word from παντοδύναμος "being able to do all things." Παντοκράτωρ, as he implies in the context, meant holding, swaying, and keeping together, the Universe, by controlling all its forces, evil as well as good, for the ultimate accomplishment of the divine will.

[2998 (xxvii) *h*] This seems a consistent Johannine view. And it seems inconsistent to deny that Rev. could call Christ "All-ruler" in the face of Rev. xvii. 14 "Lord of lords and King of kings"—titles reserved in O.T. for the Supreme God and in 1 Tim. vi. 15 ὁ βασ. τῶν βασιλευόντων, for the Father. Moreover Rev. i. 14 transfers to the Figure that is "like a son of man" the "white hair" that Daniel vii. 9—13 attributes to the Ancient of Days, *i.e.* God, as distinct from the Son of man.

It may be objected, however, that here John could not mean Christ because he has Κύριος, not ὁ Κύριος: and the former, in the gospels, is applied to God, the latter to the Lord Jesus. But the usage varies in LXX, *e.g.* Ezr. iii. 3 ὁλοκαύτωσις τῷ κυρίῳ parall. to 1 Esdr. v. 50 ὁλοκαυτώματα κυρίῳ. And in this very book, Rev. xxi. 22 ὁ γὰρ κύριος ὁ θεὸς ὁ παντοκράτωρ appears to mean God the Father (although closely connected with "the Lamb"). Perhaps, too, we have the article in Rev. xxii. 6 ὁ κύριος (marg. Κύριος) ὁ θεὸς τῶν πνευμάτων...ἀπέστειλεν τὸν ἄγγελον αὐτοῦ, where the meaning may be God, or Christ regarded as God. In Ezra and 1 Esdras, ὁ κύριος freq.=God, *e.g.* Ezr. iii. 10 τοῦ αἰνεῖν τὸν κύριον. See **2998** (xxvi) *f* on Rev. xxi. 22.

² [**2998** (xxvii) *i*] Rev. i. 8 παντοκράτωρ, R.V. "Almighty," raises most important questions. The answer to them will help us to under-

[2998] "THE SON OF MAN"

stand the whole book. Why does the author of Rev. use παντοκράτωρ 9 times, while the rest of N.T. (apart from the quotation in 2 Cor. vi. 18) never uses it? What Hebrew word, or words, does παντοκράτωρ represent in O.T.? Do any writers in O.T. differ in this respect from one another as this author differs from the rest of N.T.?

[**2998** (xxvii) *j*] Παντοκράτωρ in LXX represents two words, 1st, *Shaddai*, 2nd, *Sabaoth*. *Shaddai* occurs, as a title inferior to "Jehovah," in Exod. vi. 3 "I appeared unto Abraham...as God (*El*) *Almighty* (*Shaddai*)." "*Shaddai*" is interpreted by Aq. and the Rabbis, "self-sufficient" (Gesen. 994 *b*). The LXX renders it in various ways, but nowhere as παντοκράτωρ except in Job where it is freq. (15). We may put aside the supposition that John would derive his use of παντοκράτωρ from *Shaddai*—an inferior revelation.

[**2998** (xxvii) *k*] "*Sabaoth*," "hosts" (Hastings' *Dict*. Prof. Driver on "Lord of Hosts") forms part of what "is preeminently the *prophetical* title of God." It is transliterated by LXX as *Sabaoth* (Tromm.) 57 times, of which 52 are (*ib*.) in Isaiah. Much more frequently (*ib*.) it is rendered παντοκράτωρ, but never in Isaiah. John, however, who often deviates from LXX, might naturally use παντοκράτωρ, even when alluding to Isaiah. For it is a term intelligible to Christian Greeks, who would naturally compare it with αὐτοκράτωρ, "emperor." Domitian, who claimed to be "Lord and God," might call himself αὐτοκράτωρ, but Christ was παντοκράτωρ.

[**2998** (xxvii) *l*] Origen (*Comm. Johann*. tom. i. 34 foll., Lomm. i. 67) on the Apocalyptic "First and Last," and Alpha and Omega, says that Christ, as being (Eph. i. 21) "above every name," is above those who are called "Gods," whether good or bad, in Scripture: "One kind of these," he says, "the Hebrew used to call *Sabai*, whence the form *Sabaoth*, their ruler, no other than God (παρὸ ἐσχηματίσθαι τὸν Σαβαώθ, ἄρχοντα ἐκείνων τυγχάνοντα, οὐχ ἕτερον τοῦ θεοῦ)....The Saviour...became a man to men, and an angel to angels...as when the angel of the Lord appeared in a flame of fire...and he said, 'I am the God of Abraham.' And Isaiah (ix. 6) too, says (LXX) 'His name is called angel of great counsel.'" His view is that Christ, being Alpha and Omega, includes the totality of spiritual being, whether divine, angelic, or human; and that He is ruler of the "hosts," whether the "hosts" be good angels or bad.

[**2998** (xxvii) *m*] Ibn Ezra, regarding the "hosts" as good, says (on Is. xliv. 6) "*The Lord of hosts*. He is always king, and 'the hosts of heaven' testify it." But "the hosts of heaven," in O.T., often represents the heavenly bodies as, so to speak, intercepting the worship of men, so that they become "false gods," or "evil angels." It is remarkable that Ezekiel and Daniel, and all but eight of the Psalms (Hastings, *Dict*. iii. 138 *a*) do not use the title "Lord of hosts." In other words, *it is absent from the prophets that speak of "man," or "son of man," on the* *throne or in heaven.* It is also rare, or altogether wanting, in the later chapters of Isaiah, which include the description of the Suffering Servant of God—occurring only once (liv. 5) in the last fifteen chapters, whereas it occurs 21 times in the first fifteen.

(xxvii) *n—q* "ANGELS" NOT TO BE WORSHIPPED

[2998 (xxvii) *n*] John combines the mention of the "Son of man" on the throne, with a very frequent mention of "angels" and with a protest that *they are not to be worshipped.* On three occasions the Seer "falls down" before angelic or other representations of God (i. 17, xix. 10, xxii. 8). On the first, he is touched by the Figure's "right hand," and it is implied that (as in Ezek. ii. 1—2, comp. viii. 1—3, and as in Dan. x. 12, 19) he is either caused to stand, or lifted, and prepared to receive the divine message. Here there is no mention of "worshipping." On the second and third occasions, he "falls down *to worship*" and is expressly forbidden to worship, in identical words, "See [thou do it] not.... Worship God." The imperative, "worship," occurs thrice in this book—the third instance being xiv. 7, "Worship ye him that created the heaven and the earth."

[2998 (xxvii) *o*] The Seer appears to have deprecated all worship of visible symbols. "God" was to be worshipped through them. But they were not to be worshipped, not even He that was "like unto a Son of man," with the "white hair" that was a characteristic of the Ancient of Days. And he so combines appearances of angels with words of Christ that it is sometimes impossible to say whether the angel is not identified with Christ, or at least with a representation of Christ.

[2998 (xxvii) *p*] On the angel Michael, mentioned in Rev. xii. 7, Prof. Charles says (Hastings, *Dict.* iii. 362 *b*) "Here the figure of Michael thrusts aside that of the Messiah." I should prefer to say that the Alpha and the Omega (2998 (xxxiii)), behind the veil, is seen working through "Michael" as through many other agencies, including the numerous "angels" mentioned in this book. Michael is called in Daniel x. 13 "one of the first rulers," (Theod.) "one of the rulers," x. 21 (LXX) "the angel," (Theod.) "your ruler," and may be denoted (Hastings *ib.*) by Dan. viii. 11 ἀρχιστράτηγος, "chief of the host." Prof. Charles compares Enoch Slav. xxii. 6 and xxxiii. 10 where he is called "the chief captain" and "the great captain." Jude 9 attributes to Michael words assigned in the Bible (Zech. iii. 2) to Jehovah. The name "Michael" means (Levy iii. 100 *a*) "*Who is like God?*" implying, "There is none like God," so that it combines a recognition of high angelic powers with a recognition of their inexpressible inferiority to the One God.

[2998 (xxvii) *q*] (1) The general consensus of ancient authorities, and especially Origen, (2) the LXX tradition about the name of the "Child" in Isaiah as being (ix. 6) "Angel of Great Counsel," (3) the evidence from the Pauline Epistles and other sources as to the Jewish belief in angels of good and evil, (4) the mention of a special angel called (Rev. i. 1) "his angel" as the conveyer of the revelation of Jesus Christ, and (5) the tenor of the Apocalypse as a whole (see **2998** (xxvi) *c* and **2998** (xxviii) *m*), make it probable that (as maintained by Primasius on Rev. x. 1, quoted by Swete, who however dissents) *some of the angels, figures, and voices mentioned in this book, represent Christ in various aspects.* It is possible that He may be even represented in one and the same context by (Rev. v. 2 foll.) the "strong angel" who asks the universe "Who is worthy to open the book and to loose the seals thereof?" and the "slain Lamb," who opens the book—just as in Isaiah lix. 16 foll. the Redeemer first "saw that there was no man and wondered that there was no intercessor" and then became the Saviour Himself. But none of these visible angels, individuals of "the host of heaven," is to be worshipped by man, not even the visible Figure "like a son of man." The doctrine is that of the Fourth Gospel (Jn iv. 24), "God is Spirit, and they that worship him must worship in spirit and truth."

(xxvii) *r—v* DID ESSENES "OFFER WORSHIP" TO THE SUN?

[**2998** (xxvii) *r*] In connexion with the worship of angels and of "Titan" (**2942*** (i) *l—m*) must be considered the tendency to sun-worship imputed to the Essenes in Lightfoot's *Colossians* p. 87 alleging passages from Josephus, from the close parallel in Hippolytus, and from Philo.

(1) Lightfoot compares Joseph. *Bell.* ii. 8. 5 πρός γε μὴν τὸ θεῖον ἰδίως εὐσεβεῖς· πρὶν γὰρ ἀνασχεῖν τὸν ἥλιον οὐδὲν φθέγγονται τῶν βεβήλων, πατρίους δέ τινας εἰς αὐτὸν εὐχὰς ὥσπερ ἱκετεύοντες ἀνατεῖλαι with Philo ii. 475 (*Vit. Cont.* § 3) ἡλίου μὲν ἀνίσχοντος εὐημερίαν αἰτούμενοι τὴν ὄντως εὐημερίαν φωτὸς οὐρανίου τὴν διάνοιαν αὐτῶν ἀναπλησθῆναι, and speaks of "this worship which Josephus states to be offered to the sun (εἰς αὐτόν)." Elsewhere Lightfoot repeats about Josephus (*ib.* p. 374) "he says plainly that they addressed prayers to the sun," and he adds, "Similarly Philo relates of the Therapeutes (*Vit. Cont.* 11, ii. p. 485) that 'they stand with their faces and their whole body towards the East'" [ἕω, perh. better rendered "dawn" here] "and when they see that the sun is risen, holding out their hands to heaven they pray for a happy day (εὐημερίαν) and for truth and for keen vision of reason (ὀξυωπίαν λογισμοῦ)."

[**2998** (xxvii) *s*] But in this last passage from Philo the "stretching upward" (ἀνατείναντες) of the hands is not "to the sun," but "to heaven," and εὐημερία seems to mean, as in the preceding quotation from Philo, τὴν ὄντως εὐημερίαν, *i.e.* "Good Day in the truest sense." This he explains as "having their minds filled with the light of heaven," *i.e.* the light given by God. Moreover Philo in the preceding context (ii. 485) says that these Therapeutae sing "hymns made *to God* (πεποιημένους εἰς τὸν θεὸν ὕμνους)" in accordance with the precedent of the choirs of Moses and Miriam, who "sang the songs of thanksgiving *to the God [that was their] Saviour* (τοὺς εὐχαριστηρίους ὕμνους <u>εἰς τὸν σωτῆρα θεὸν</u> ᾖδον)." These facts indicate that the prayer of the Therapeutae was addressed *to God*. They wait, it is true, for the moment of sunrise before uttering their prayer. But the prayer is addressed (in Philo's opinion) to the God of Moses and Miriam, and εἰς τὸν θεόν does not mean "to the God of the Sun."

[2998 (xxvii) *t*] On the custom of orthodox Jews, to wait till sunrise for certain religious utterances, see *Berach*. Mishn. i. 2 (5) "R. Eliezer says, From what time do we recite the *Shema* in the morning? This prayer should be finished until (lit.) the sun shine forth...." R. Joshua adds a licence of extension to the 3rd hour "for such is the custom of kings to rise at the 3rd hour"; but the pious apparently did not avail themselves of this. *Jer. Berach.* comments thus (p. 16 Schwab, Eng. Transl.) "The reading of the morning *Shema* has been prescribed for the hour at which the sun darts its rays, so that the prayer *Amida* may immediately follow the passage relating to the Deliverance and be said by daylight." Both Talmuds quote Ps. lxxii. 5 as meaning "They shall adore thee *at the rising of the sun*" (R.V. "while the sun endureth"). Jer. Talm. adds "Zealous people rose at the first hour and recited the *Shema* and then the other prayers so as to finish at the time that the sun darts its rays." The practice is emphatically recommended by R. Jose (2nd cent.) *Sabb.* 118 *b*, where Ps. lxxii. 5 is again quoted as meaning "at the rising of the sun."

It must not be forgotten that the Heb. verb זרח, "dawn," Gk ἀνατέλλω, *might be applied to God as well as to the sun*, e.g. Is. lx. 2 "Jehovah shall *dawn* (יזרח) on thee," LXX φανήσεται, but Aq. and Sym. ἀνατελεῖ (as also LXX, Aq., Sym., and Theod. in lx. 1, ἀνατέταλκεν). The same Heb. is used of Jehovah in Deut. xxxiii. 2 LXX ἐπέφανεν. Jews therefore might be said by a Jew to "*supplicate God to dawn*," ἱκετεῦσαι τὸν θεὸν ἀνατεῖλαι. This modern classical scholars might take to mean the sun-god. But it would mean Jehovah.

Ps. lxxii. 5 is rendered by LXX συμπαραμενεῖ τῷ ἡλίῳ. Aq. (Field) had σὺν ἡλίῳ, and LXX apparently meant παραμενεῖ σὺν τῷ ἡλίῳ "shall abide *with*, that is, *as long as*, the sun." But παραμένω might be applied to the worshipper of Jehovah—as "fear" is in the correct rendering of the Hebrew ("they shall fear, *i.e.* reverence, thee, with the sun"). In that case παραμένω would mean "I am persistent," or (comp. Rom. xii. 12) "instant in prayer," παραμένω εὐχαῖς, or εὐχόμενος. Then the meaning of the LXX might be taken to be, "He shall abide (παραμενεῖ) praying (εὐχόμενος) *along with the sun*, i.e. *from the dawn onwards* (ἔωθεν)." Now this is just what Hippolytus has, only that he adds "orderly and steadfastly" to "abide," thus (ix. 21) παραμένουσι δὲ εὐτάκτως καὶ ἐπιμόνως εὐχόμενοι ἔωθεν.

We do not know for certain what caused the LXX reading in Ps. lxxii. 5 παραμένω, but it might easily arise from (1) a gloss on "fear," (2) a confusion of the difficult עִם "with"—as follows. "Fear" here means "worship"; "worship" implies "pray"; "pray" (944) is often expressed by "*stand*." Also "*stand*" is confusable (943) with "*with*"; and עמד "*stand*," besides its regular rendering ἵστημι, is, in LXX, παραμένω and διαμένω. Hence we might expect from Ps. lxxii. 5, besides Hippolytus' παραμένουσιν εὐχόμενοι ἔωθεν, some similar phrase with forms of ἵστημι and of ἕως. This we have in Philo quoted above (2998 (xxvii) *r*) τάς τε ὄψεις καὶ ὅλον τὸ σῶμα πρὸς τὴν ἕω στάντες.

Philo's curious expression "*standing with their eyes and their whole body towards*" seems intended to express steadfastness and persistence like ἐπιμόνως in Hippolytus. And a natural inference from the similarities (amid dissimilarities) between Josephus, Philo, Hippolytus, Ps. lxxii. 5 (Heb.) and *ib*. LXX, is, that they are all based on the Heb. of the Psalm and that they all refer to the worship of Jehovah at sunrise, not to any worship of the sun.

[2998 (xxvii) *u*] From these considerations returning to εἰς αὐτόν in Josephus, we have to ask whether it may not mean "*to Him*"—referring to the previous τὸ θεῖον which is a philosophic and cosmopolitan way of saying "God." For τὸ θεῖον followed by the masc. αὐτός, comp. Clem. Alex. 708 (quoting Epicharmus) "Nothing escapes *God* (τὸ θεῖον)...*He* (αὐτὸς) is our Overseer." In that case, we might render *Bell*. ii. 8. 5 "Toward God they shew a peculiar piety; for before the sun is up they will not utter a word about business but only certain prayers made-by-their-fathers (πατρίους) to Him *as though supplicating* [*Him*] *to dawn* [*on them*]." The following passages suggest, though they do not prove, that Josephus might occasionally refer to τὸ θεῖον as αὐτός, *Ant*. xi. 6. 11 (Whiston) "I cannot forbear to admire *God* (τὸ θεῖον) and to learn hence *His* wisdom (τὴν σ. αὐτοῦ) and justice" (where "its wisdom" seems less suitable than "His") and *Ant*. iii. 7. 7 (about the Highpriest's breastplate) (Whiston) "That it was also illustrated with a crown, and that of gold also, is because of that splendour (αὐγήν) with which *God* is pleased (ᾗ μάλιστα χαίρει τὸ θεῖον)" where the personality implied by "pleased" indicates that Josephus might naturally follow the usage of Epicharmus.

[2998 (xxvii) *v*] (2) The second passage quoted from Josephus by Lightfoot (*Coloss*. p. 87) is *Bell*. ii. 8. 9 ὡς μὴ τὰς αὐγὰς ὑβρίζοιεν τοῦ θεοῦ, relating to the carefulness of the Essenes "to conceal and bury all polluting substances so as not 'to insult the rays of the god.'" He adds "There can be no doubt, I think, that by τοῦ θεοῦ is meant the 'sun-god'; comp. Eur. *Heracl*. 749 θεοῦ φαεσίμβροτοι αὐγαί, *Alc*. 722 τὸ φέγγος τοῦτο τοῦ θεοῦ...."

But in *Heracl*. 749 Dindorf and Steph. read φαεσιμβρότου (which is almost demanded by the usage of φ.). With this reading, the text proves nothing as to the absolute use of θεοῦ. In *Alc*. 722 τοῦ θεοῦ may be taken (and, I think, better taken) as referring to "God's" gift of light, comp.

Διὸς φέγγος *Iph. Aul.* 1506. Steph. gives αὐγάς with Zeus twice (from Homer and an epigrammatist) (and once with Helios Hyperion) but not with Phœbus or Apollo. Even if classical tragic Gk regularly used ὁ θεός absol. (without special context) to mean "the sun," a similar use in Josephus would be so antecedently improbable that it would require to be proved by abundant instances taken from Josephus himself. But it does not seem to be proved even about tragic Gk.

Moreover Josephus must be interpreted by reference to the Law of Moses. He is referring to Deut. xxiii. 13—14 "thou shalt cover...*that he* [*i.e.* Jehovah] *see no unclean thing in thee.*" The LXX and the Targums avoid the anthropomorphism ("he see") by a passive rendering "that there be seen." Josephus very skilfully suggests the Hebrew meaning by using αὐγαί, a word capable of two meanings. It may mean, especially in poetic style, (Steph.) "*eyes*" (for the thought, comp. Hab. i. 13 "thou art of purer eyes than to behold evil"). But it may also mean the "rays" of the divine ubiquitous Glory, of which the sun might be taken as the visible type. And there is some evidence, as follows, to indicate that Josephus would use the word in these two ways. Zechariah (iii. 9, iv. 10) speaks of "the eyes of the Lord"—in connexion with the "engraving" of a "stone" "set before" the Highpriest—as "running to and fro through the whole earth"; and Chronicles (2 Chr. xvi. 9) says that "the eyes of the Lord run to and fro" to give victory to a king that trusts Jehovah. Now Josephus (*Ant.* iii. 8. 9) says that the special sign of God's presence at the sacrifices of the Hebrews was an αὐγή that flashed from the precious stone on the right shoulder of the Highpriest, and that by means of the twelve stones on his breast "God foretold victory in battle; for such an αὐγή flashed from them before the army began to march that all the host were aware of God's being present to help them." Elsewhere (*Ant.* iii. 7. 7) he speaks, in the same connexion, of the "αὐγή that is close to (προσοῦσα) all things" and the "αὐγή in which God rejoices (τὸ θεῖον χαίρει)."

Hippolytus (ix. 25), not understanding the force of τοῦ θεοῦ, omits the defining genitive phrase. But it is emphatic: "that they might not outrage the light of *the God* [*of heaven*]." The precept was certainly not limited to times when the sun was shining.

To these facts must be added *a priori* considerations. Would Jews with any pretensions to piety be likely to salute the sun in such a way as to suggest what Job calls (Job xxxi. 28) "an iniquity to be punished by the judges: for I should have lied to God above"? If they did, would Philo and Josephus be likely to praise such worshippers for their special piety? Note also the context in Joseph. *Bell.* ii. 8. 9 μετὰ (1) τὸν θεὸν (Jehovah)...τὰς αὐγὰς (2) τοῦ θεοῦ. Would any Jew be likely to use ὁ θεός in the same context to mean (1) "Jehovah," (2) "sun-god"? Sooner than accept these improbabilities, it would be reasonable to seek some explanation arising from a confusion between "praying *to* (εἰς)," and "praying

[2998 (xxviii)] Now at last the author drops into the first person: "I John, your brother and fellowpartner in the tribulation and kingdom and patience in Jesus, came to be on the island called Patmos because of the word of God and [because of] the witness[1] of Jesus. I came to be in the

---

towards (εἰς)" mentioned above (**2942*** (xxiv) *b*). But the arguments alleged from the use of τὸ θεῖον, ἀνατέλλω, and αὐγή, appear sufficient, without recourse to the ambiguity of εἰς.

(xxvii) *w*   THE "WASHING" OF THE ESSENES

[2998 (xxvii) *w*] In connexion with Lightfoot's discussion of the Essenes, it may be worth remarking that he (*Coloss.* p. 96) also quotes *Orac. Sib.* iv. 160 ἐν ποταμοῖς λούσασθε ὅλον δέμας ἀενάοισι to shew that "with Essenism also it [*i.e.* this Sibylline book] inculcates the duty of frequent washings." But, if that had been the meaning, (1) would not the author probably have written λούεσθε and (2) made some mention of frequency? (3) The epithet ἀέναος is applied in *Clem. Hom.* ix. 19, xi. 35 to water used in Christian baptism, and *Didach.* 7 urges the use of "running (ζῶν)" water, if possible. (4) The phrase "the whole of the body" as distinguished from sprinkling on the head, points to Christian baptism by immersion which is implied by *Didach.* 7 (as desirable where possible), by *Clem. Hom.* (baptism in or near the sea or river) xi. 35—6, xiv. 1, and by *Const. Apost.* iii. 17 κατάδυσις. (5) The context of *Orac. Sib.* iv. 160 begins, "Alas, wretched mortals, lay aside these crimes," and is practically an exhortation like that of Isaiah i. 16 "*Wash you* (λούσασθε)...put away the evil of your doings," being equivalent to, "Repent and *be baptized.*" (6) That the Essenes did not enjoin frequent immersions is indicated by Joseph. *Vit.* 2, which says that Josephus did not resort to a teacher that practised these things until he had made trial of the Essenes, and by other facts for which see *Fourfold Gospel* (Index "Baptism"). For the present it is safe to say that *Orac. Sib.* iv. 160, taken by itself, does not prove that the writer inculcates the duty of frequent washings.

---

[1] **[2998** (xxviii) *a*] Origen (*Comm. Mt.* tom. xvi. 6, Lomm. iv. 18) says, "John informs us about his *bearing witness* (μαρτυρίου, *i.e.* martyrdom) not saying who *condemned* him (Rev. i. 9)...," regarding the passage as confirmatory of the tradition that Domitian "condemned" John, so that John thereby fulfilled Christ's prediction (Mk x. 39) that he should drink His cup and be baptized with His baptism—being a martyr, though not a martyr unto death. The order of the words "tribulation, kingdom, patience," favours the view that the "martyrdom" itself is regarded as

spirit on the Lord's day, and I heard behind me a great voice as of a trumpet, saying, 'That which thou seest write in a book and send to the seven churches....' And I turned to see the voice,...and I saw seven golden candlesticks[1];

---

a kind of "reigning" or "kingdom" (comp. Justin *Tryph.* 73 on "*reigning* from the tree," *i.e.* from the cross), so that John has already partaken in it, but has still to "endure," if he is to attain to the consummated "kingdom." Comp. 1 Pet. v. 1 "Fellow-elder and witness of the sufferings of Christ, who am also a partaker of the glory that shall be revealed," which may refer to Peter's "partaking" in the revelation of the Transfiguration (or of other visions)—as an anticipation of the future "glory." John may include a reference to similar "partaking" in the Kingdom. The suffering, and the visions of the Kingdom, go together. See 2998 (xxv) *a*.

(xxviii) *b—e* "THE SEVEN GOLDEN CANDLESTICKS"

[1] [2998 (xxviii) *b*] Rev. i. 12 ἑπτὰ λυχνίας χρυσᾶς. Comp. Zech. iv. 2 foll. "I have seen, and behold, a candlestick (λυχνία) all of gold, with its bowl (λαμπάδιον) upon it and its seven lamps (καὶ ἑπτὰ λύχνοι) thereon; there are seven pipes to each of the lamps which are upon the top thereof (καὶ ἑπτὰ ἐπαρυστρίδες τοῖς λύχνοις τοῖς ἐπάνω αὐτῆς)....This is the word of the Lord unto Zerubbabel, saying, Not by might, nor by power, but by my Spirit, saith the Lord of hosts....They shall see the plummet in the hand of Zerubbabel, even these seven, [which are] the eyes of the Lord; they run to and fro through the whole earth." How the "eyes" of the Lord are a "plummet"—that is, a measure or test— is seen from Ps. xi. 4 "His eyes behold, his eyelids try, the children of men." It is implied by the prophet that the golden "candlestick" in the Tabernacle is the symbol of the Lord's "Spirit" as against "might and power." It is also the symbol of His judging and testing men, bringing to light their secret sins that they may repent, so that it both illuminates and revivifies. For, as Irenæus says (iv. 20. 7) "the glory of God is a living man (vivens homo) and the life of man consists in beholding God"; and "the Word...reveals God indeed to men, but presents men to God, and preserves at the same time the invisibility of the Father." The "plummet" in Zechariah may be illustrated by the Psalms (xix. 4) where the "*measuring line*" (Aq. κανών) of the heavens is said to have "gone out" to all the nations and tongues of the world, testifying to them about God so that they are (Rom. i. 20) "without excuse." [Ps. xix. 4 (LXX) "their sound," in spite of Gesen. 876 *a*, seems a very natural and commonplace corruption, and Aq.'s authority is strong against it.]

[2998 (xxviii) *c*] Those who believe that John actually saw this vision, and that visions of prophets are shaped by their environments, and that a "candlestick" was the first thing he saw in his long series of visions, must ask what caused him to see it; what associations (over and above those connected with Zechariah) the golden "candlestick" would have for him; and what led him to see the Figure "in the midst of the seven candlesticks," or perhaps as he says later on (ii. 1) "walking in the midst of the seven candlesticks."

[2998 (xxviii) *d*] The following facts may suggest the answer. Philo (i. 520) describes the candlestick as representing "the archetypal pattern of the imitation," or correspondence, in virtue of which the Temple on earth was believed by Jews and Christians alike to have corresponded with a pattern in heaven (see Heb. viii. 4—5, ix. 23—4). Josephus (*Bell.* vii. 5. 5), describing the spoils of Jerusalem exhibited in the Roman triumph, devotes almost all his space to "the golden candlestick," with its "seven lamps," "exhibiting the honour paid to the *hebdomad* among the Jews, *i.e.* to the Jewish idea of the *hebdomad* (τῆς παρὰ τοῖς Ἰουδαίοις ἑβδομάδος τὴν τιμὴν ἐμφανίζοντες)"—where ἑβδομάς seems to mean "number seven," not "week" or "sabbath." He adds that Domitian rode on horseback (not in a chariot like Vespasian and Titus) on a noble horse, which, as Suetonius *Vit. Domitian.* § 2 informs us, was "white."

Here, then, we have the Emperor that sentenced John to the mines, the persecutor of the Churches, the successor on the throne of the Beast, who called himself "Lord God," "riding on a white horse"—with "images of Conquest (Νίκης)" adds Josephus—in triumph over the spoils wrested from Jehovah, foremost among them being the "golden candlestick." Few Jews in the Roman Empire—none, probably, in the Patmos quarries—could fail to know this. Some would hear of it with the reproach addressed to the Psalmist "Where is now thy God?" How natural that John, receiving from the One Allruling God visions in accordance with which the fallen Temple was to be remeasured and rebuilt in spiritual and human form, should see first of all seven golden candlesticks beyond the grasp of any imperial conqueror! We may also note here how Domitian, on the "white horse," with "Niké," would suggest to the Seer the antithesis (Rev. vi. 2) of the crowned Figure, on the "white horse," "going forth conquering and to conquer," and then a second vision (Rev. xix. 11) of the "white horse" with a Figure whose garment is sprinkled with blood, "King of kings and Lord of lords."

[2998 (xxviii) *e*] Zechariah, Philo, and Josephus, speak of the golden "candlestick (λυχνία)," or lampstand, as *one*, with seven "candles (λύχνοι) in it." Why does not John follow them? Apparently he takes advantage of some detailed traditions about the six branching λύχνοι, and the seventh central λύχνος (which Philo ii. 150—1 calls τῆς μέσης λυχνίας, and refers to in the words, ὁ γὰρ ἥλιος, ὥσπερ ἡ λυχνία, μέσος τῶν ἐξ τεταγμένος, comp. Exod. xxv. 33, 35 τοῖς ἐξ καλαμίσκοις τοῖς ἐκπορευομένοις ἐκ τῆς λυχνίας) and about the "seven pipes"—attached to "*each of the lamps*" (Zech. iv. 2) so that each of the seven λύχνοι is, *in some sense, sevenfold*.

Using these, he conveys the impression that (1) there are, in effect, "seven lampstands," (2) they are supplied with light, by the presence of the Figure that "walks about in the midst of them." Zechariah apparently speaks of "the seven lamps" as "*the eyes of the Lord*"— though at the same time referring to the "stone" with (Zech. iii. 9) "*seven eyes.*" John says that the Lamb has (Rev. v. 6) "seven horns and *seven eyes*, which are *the seven spirits of God*," and also that there are (Rev. iv. 5) "*seven torches* (λαμπάδες) *of fire*, burning before the throne, which are *the seven spirits of God*." Previously he has said (Rev. i. 20) "The seven stars are angels of the seven churches, and the seven candlesticks are seven churches." Yet the Figure holds the "seven stars" in His hand. This seems confusing. How can He "hold" the angels of the Churches in His hand and yet "walk about" in the Churches?

It is confusing, if we take the words literally and locally. Taken literally, the number "seven" is also confusing. For who can suppose that in heaven the Seven Churches actually mentioned by John are favoured each by a special candlestick to the exclusion of others, so that, for example, Laodicea is thus honoured while the neighbouring Colossae (Col. iv. 15—16) is not? The Seer was probably influenced by the general belief (Philo ii. 150—1, Joseph. *Ant.* iii. 6. 7, *Bell.* v. 5. 5) that the "seven lamps (λύχνοι)" represented the "planets" (including the sun). The "stars," in Jewish thought, were associated with "angels." The angels that stood in God's immediate presence were generally regarded as "seven." Having special messages for seven of the Asian Churches the Seer regarded them as represented by the seven lampstands, the seven stars, and the seven angels through whom the Figure sent His message. In addressing them, the Lord addressed indirectly all the Churches, for all had similar temptations.

John accumulates images, not for the sake of confusing his reader, but because they crowded in on his mind revealing various aspects of the ubiquitous Presence sent as an angel by Jesus, and he felt that each had its truth, and its consolation for the saints suffering under the temporary triumph of the Beast: "If," he seems to say, "you desire to see 'the sevenfold golden candlestick' you must not seek it in the Temple of Peace (Joseph. *Bell.* vii. 5. 7) where Vespasian has placed it. It is to be found on earth wherever there are 'seven churches' like candlesticks duly receiving (Rev. xxi. 23) the light of the 'candle' of 'the Lamb.' Or again it is to be found in heaven, where 'the seven torches' flame continually before the throne, being 'the seven spirits of God.' Or again it is to be found in 'the seven eyes of the Lamb,' for these also are 'the seven spirits of God' 'walking to and fro' throughout the churches like 'the seven eyes of the Lord,' according to the saying of Zechariah."

(xxviii) *f—k* "WALKING IN THE MIDST"

[2998 (xxviii) *f*) The centre of the "seven golden candlesticks" is a Figure that "*walks to and fro* (περιπατῶν)" in the midst of them. This phrase, though it is not used till later on (Rev. ii. 1), must be discussed here. God is very seldom said to "*walk to and fro*" (הלך hithp., Gesen. 236) in Scripture. Apart from Gen. iii. 8 (comp. Job xxii. 14 διαπορεύεται) "*walking to and fro* in the garden," it is perhaps (Gesen. 236) limited to passages connected with the (Deut. xxiii. 15) "encampment" of Israel, or with the "*tabernacle*," or with "*tabernacling*," e.g. 2 S. vii. 6—7 "I have not dwelt in a house...but have (lit.) *walked to and fro* in a tent and a *tabernacle*. In all places wherein I have *walked to and fro* in (ב) all Israel..." (comp. parall. 1 Chr. xvii. 5—6 "I have been from tent to tent and from one *tabernacle* to another. In all places wherein I have *walked to and fro* in (ב) all Israel..."). We may safely infer that John is alluding to Lev. xxvi. 11—12 "I will set my *tabernacle* among you... and I will *walk to and fro among you* (בתוככם) and will be your God and ye shall be my people," where LXX has ἐνπεριπατήσω ἐν ὑμῖν, but ἐν μέσῳ ὑμῶν would be a more literal rendering. Onkelos reproduces the Heb. "tabernacle" exactly, but, for "I will walk to and fro," has "I will make my Shechinah to dwell" (and sim. Jon. "the glory of my Shechinah"). Comp. Ezek. xxxvii. 26—7 "*I will set my sanctuary in the midst of them* (בתוכם) (LXX θήσω τὰ ἅγιά μου ἐν μέσῳ αὐτῶν, and R.V. "in the midst of them")...my *tabernacle* also shall be (R.V. marg.) *over* (על) them," giving a different order from that of Leviticus, and having "set my sanctuary" instead of "*walk to and fro*." The second Epistle to the Corinthians vi. 16 ἐνοικήσω ἐν αὐτοῖς καὶ ἐνπεριπατήσω combines Lev. and Ezek. and, while paraphrasing the "*tabernacling*" (as ἐνοικήσω), retains "walk to and fro." Jn i. 14 ἐσκήνωσεν ἐν ἡμῖν retains the "*tabernacling*." Rev. xiii. 6, xv. 5, xxi. 3, thrice mentions "*the tabernacle of God* (or, *of God's testimony*)." It predicts twice (vii. 15, xxi. 3) that God "will tabernacle" (Rev. vii. 15) "over (ἐπί)" men (as in Ezek. xxxvii. 26—7, Heb. "over," LXX ἐν) or (xxi. 3) "along with (μετά)" them.

[2998 (xxviii) *g*] W.H. print σκηνόω as allusive in Rev. xxi. 3, but not in vii. 15. But the facts suggest (1) that σκηνόω *should be printed as allusive in both cases*; (2) that the divine "walking to and fro (περιπατέω)," which would be associated in the Jewish mind with God's "tabernacling," should be printed as allusive in Rev. ii. 1. It should be added that Rev. twice (xii. 12, xiii. 6) speaks of "those who tabernacle in the heaven(s)," and once (xiii. 6, "to blaspheme his name and his

and, in the midst[1] of the candlesticks, one like *a son of man*,

tabernacle, [namely] those that tabernacle in the heaven") in such a way as to suggest that the Tabernacle, like the Church or Body of Christ, is composed of spiritual beings.

[2998 (xxviii) *h*] What is the use of prefixing to the sharp rebukes addressed to the Seven Churches the statement that the rebuker "*walks to and fro* in the midst of the seven golden candlesticks"? The answer is given by St Paul, as above quoted—being in effect, "I will walk to and fro among you—*therefore* (διό) come forth out of the captivity of uncleanness (2 Cor. vi. 17, ἐξέλθατε ἐκ μέσου αὐτῶν)." These last words are from Isaiah lii. 11 "Go ye out from them...*be ye clean, ye that bear the vessels of the Lord.*" These again may be illustrated by the only other instance of ἐμπεριπατέω applied to Jehovah (Deut. xxiii. 14—15) "For the Lord thy God walketh to and fro in the midst of thy camp to deliver thee...*therefore* shall thy camp be holy; that he see no *nakedness* of anything in thee and turn away from thee." This the Prophets and Apostles would interpret as referring to spiritual defilement, and probably this was in the mind of John as he wrote down the warning (iii. 17—18) "Thou knowest not that thou art...*blind and naked....*" The Figure that "walks to and fro in the midst of the seven candlesticks" comes to the Church of Laodicea asking whether the Church really has the light or is "blind," whether it is clothed with "white garments" or is "naked." The "walking to and fro" is for the good of the Churches. But it may begin by detecting their faults (Rev. iii. 19) "As many as I love I reprove and chasten." So Adam and Eve heard the Word of the Lord when He "*walked to and fro* in the garden," and they "hid themselves" and Adam said, "I was afraid because I was *naked.*"

[1] [2998 (xxviii) *i*] As regards "*in the midst* (ἐν μέσῳ)," besides i. 13, ii. 1 "*in the midst of* the candlesticks," compare iv. 6 "*in the midst of* the throne, and round about the throne, four living creatures" (comp. Ezek. i. 5 (LXX) "*in the midst* [of the fire] as [it were] the likeness of four living creatures," (Heb.) "*from the midst of it* [*i.e.* of the fire]"); v. 6 "I saw *in the midst of* the throne and [*in the midst*] *of* the four living creatures and *in the midst of* the elders a Lamb standing"; vi. 6 "I heard as [it were] a voice *in the midst of* the four living creatures"; xxii. 2 "A river of the water of life...going forth from the throne of God and the Lamb *in the midst* of the street thereof and (lit.) of the river on this side and on that the tree of life (ἐκ τοῦ θρόνου τοῦ θεοῦ καὶ τοῦ ἀρνίου ἐν μέσῳ τῆς πλατείας αὐτῆς καὶ τοῦ ποταμοῦ ἐντεῦθεν καὶ ἐκεῖθεν ξύλον ζωῆς)" where the meaning would vary with punctuation, but ἐν μέσῳ (as W.H.) prob. alludes to Gen. ii. 9 "the tree of life *in the midst of* the garden." The object of the writer (as in Jn xiv. 20 "Ye in me

and I in you," and xvii. 21 "Thou in me and I in thee" (**1881**—2)) is to delocalise and spiritualise the meaning. For how can the four living creatures be *literally* (iv. 6) "in the midst of the throne" and at the same time "round about the throne"? But they can be in both places at the same time *spiritually*, just as Christ's saints can simultaneously (iii. 21) sit with Him "in" His throne, and yet worship before His throne (according to the more usual picture). So in v. 6, "in the midst of the throne and of the four living creatures, and in the midst of the elders," the meaning is doubtful, because, in Hebraic Greek, "betwixt this and betwixt that" may mean "betwixt this and that." But it is probable that the writer conceives of the Lamb as being, so to speak, the spiritual centre of the "throne," the "creatures," and the "elders" simultaneously (or at least he includes that conception over and above any literal meaning). On the use of the phrase στῆναι εἰς τὸ μέσον, and ἐν τῷ μέσῳ, in connexion with Christ's resurrection, see **1793** foll., **2307, 2710**.

[**2998** (xxviii) *j*] A unique use of another phrase for "in the midst," ἀνὰ μέσον, occurs in Rev. vii. 17 τὸ ἀρνίον τὸ ἀνὰ μέσον τοῦ θρόνου ποιμανεῖ αὐτοὺς καὶ ὁδηγήσει αὐτοὺς ἐπὶ ζωῆς πηγὰς ὑδάτων—a very beautiful and Johannine thought, that "the Lamb," though "in the midst of the throne," can none the less, nay, all the more, act as a shepherd and leader (comp. vii. 15 "He that sitteth on the throne shall tabernacle over them"). But why does the writer here alone use ἀνὰ μέσον—which in O.T. almost always represents בין "between," as to which Gesen. (107) says, "once with a sing. (unusual) Dan. viii. 16 'between the Ulai (אולי),' that is, between its banks"? The context ("I heard a man's voice *between the Ulai* which called and said, 'Gabriel, make this man to understand the vision'") indicates that the author of Rev. would have meditated on this passage of Daniel in connexion with his own visions.

"Ulai" in Dan. viii. 16 is, in Theod., Οὐβάλ. Comp. Dan. viii. 2 "on the *river* (אובל) *Ulai* (אולי)," Theod. "on the Oubal," LXX "at the *gate Ailam*," Aq. "on the *Oubal Oulai*," Sym. "on the *lake* (ἕλους) *Oulai*"—where the LXX "gate Ailam," and viii. 3, 6 "gate" (Heb. "river") indicate that the LXX has transliterated or translated a reading אולם, frequently transliterated elsewhere as αἰλάμ, meaning the "porch" of the temple (also I K. vii. 7, "porch" of the throne in Solomon's palace): comp. Ezek. viii. 16 LXX ἀνὰ μέσον τῶν αἰλάμ, καὶ ἀνὰ μέσον τοῦ θυσιαστηρίου, Sym. μεταξὺ τοῦ προπύλου (or, τοῦ προθύρου, Aq. τῆς προστάδος or τοῦ αἰλάμ, Theod. τοῦ αἰλάμ) κ. τοῦ θ. A connexion between "*porch*" and "*waters*" is recognised by Philo i. 573, on Exod. xv. 27 εἰς Αἰλείμ...δώδεκα πηγαὶ ὑδάτων...Αἰλείμ πυλῶνες ἑρμηνεύονται, and between "*throne*" and "*water*" in Rev. xxii. 1 "*a river of the water of life*...proceeding out of the *throne of God and of the Lamb*," apparently borrowed from Ezek. xlvii. 1 "waters issued out from under *the threshold of the House* [*i.e.* the Temple] eastward." The "threshold of the house" appears to be homonymous with the "porch."

clothed in a garment that reached to the feet, and girt about at the breasts with a golden girdle[1]; and his head

---

[**2998** (xxviii) *k*] Ἀνὰ μέσον generally means "between *two* things." Here it may mean "between [the two sides of] the throne" as in Dan. viii. 16 "between [the two sides of] the river," dimly suggesting the co-assessorship of the Father and the Spirit. Or it may suggest that the Lamb is between "the Throne" and the world, as Mediator, somewhat like 1 Cor. vi. 5 ὃς δυνήσεται διακρῖναι ἀνὰ μέσον τοῦ ἀδελφοῦ αὐτοῦ, "one able to judge between his brother [and the opposing brother]," an abridgment of the Hebrew idiom "between this and between that." Perhaps it suggests both these thoughts. In any case the sevenfold mention of ἐν μέσῳ is probably intentional, and so is this unique mention of ἀνὰ μέσον as compared with the seven uses of ἐν μέσῳ. In the whole of the Bible no book equals this book in the stress it lays on mystical numbers; and on no number does this book lay so much stress as on "seven." See **2998** (xxviii) *d* on τῆς...ἐβδομάδος τὴν τιμήν.

(xxviii) *l—r* "ONE LIKE A SON OF MAN"

[1] [**2998** (xxviii) *l*] Rev. i. 13 ὅμοιον υἱὸν ἀνθρώπου ἐνδεδυμένον ποδήρη, καὶ περιεζωσμένον πρὸς τοῖς μαστοῖς ζώνην χρυσᾶν. On ὅμοιον υἱὸν ἀ. see **2998** (xxvi) *a*. As to the ποδήρης, comp. (1) Ezek. ix. 2—11, where six men come, each with his "instrument of destruction," καὶ εἷς ἀνὴρ ἐν μέσῳ αὐτῶν ἐνδεδυκὼς ποδήρη καὶ ζώνη σαπφείρου ἐπὶ τῆς ὀσφύος αὐτοῦ...ὁ ἐνδεδυκὼς τὸν ποδήρη κ. ἐζωσμένος τῇ ζώνῃ τὴν ὀσφὺν αὐτοῦ: (2) Dan. x. 5 καὶ ἰδοὺ ἄνθρωπος εἷς ἐνδεδυμένος βύσσινα καὶ τὴν ὀσφὺν περιεζωσμένος βυσσίνῳ καὶ ἐκ μέσου αὐτοῦ φῶς, Theod. καὶ ἰδοὺ ἀνὴρ εἷς ἐνδεδυμένος βαδδείν, καὶ ἡ ὀσφὺς αὐτοῦ περιεζωσμένη ἐν χρυσίῳ Ὠφάζ.

The "golden girdle" seems clearly derived from Dan. x. 5 (Theod.) and may typify "judgment according to truth," since "gold" (Theod. "gold of Ophaz") includes the metaphorical meaning of "that which has been refined, or tested, so that it is truly what it professes to be, without alloy." Comp. Eph. vi. 14 "your loins girt about with *truth*," and Rev. xv. 6 ζώνας χρυσᾶς. Now the Hebrew transliterated by Theod. in Dan. x. 5 as βαδδείν, is in Ezek. ix. 2—11 rendered ποδήρης. This, so far, favours the view that John is borrowing from Daniel, only substituting ποδήρης for βαδδείν.

[**2998** (xxviii) *m*] But there are reasons for thinking that Dan. x. 5 may be itself borrowed or corrupted from Ezek. ix. 2—11. For the "man" in Ezek. is really "girded," not with "*sapphire*" but with "a writer's inkhorn (lit.) upon his loins." The author of Daniel—who freely adapts Ezekiel, as for example, when he (x. 6) takes the "beryl" from the "wheels" of Ezekiel i. 16, x. 9 and applies it to the "body" of his Figure—having before him the Hebrew of Ezekiel, namely, "*writer's*

and his hair were white as white wool—as snow[1], and his

---

inkhorn," and the Greek, "*sapphire*," may have chosen "*gold of Uphaz*" as a paraphrastic compromise; expressive of the fact that the Recording Angel was "girt with the pure gold of judgment according to truth." John may have followed Theodotion, against the LXX, taking the metaphor in that sense. Origen (on Ezek. x. 2—8 οὐκ ἀνενδέδυτο ποδήρη ἀλλὰ στολήν) implies that the στολή in Ezek. x. 2 was connected with purification but the ποδήρης in Ezek. ix. 2—11 with destruction. If John has in view Ezekiel's picture of the Man in the midst of the Six Destroyers, this may explain his use of ποδήρης. And it would also illustrate his apparent tendency to identify Christ occasionally with one of the Seven Angels (**2998** (xxviii) *x—y*). Compare Hermas *Sim.* ix. 12 "the glorious Man and the Six glorious Angels on the right hand and on the left."

[**2998** (xxviii) *n*] There is a generally recognised reference to Ezekiel ix. 2—11 in John's account (Rev. vii. 2 foll.) of the "sealing" of the faithful. Now the action of the Recorder in Ezekiel, marking the foreheads of the faithful with a sign, and, by that act, dividing them from the unfaithful, who are slain by the Six—corresponds to the action of the Logos, or Word of God, described by Philo and the Epistle to the Hebrews as a "two-edged sword" or τομεὺς Λόγος (**2998** (xxviii) *t—u*). Verbally, Ezek. ix. 2 "a writer's inkhorn (lit.) upon his loins," is as different as possible from Rev. i. 16 "from his mouth a two-edged sword going forth." But, in fact, is there any real difference between a verdict of "guilty" or "not guilty" written by a Recording Angel "with an inkhorn upon his loins" and the same verdict when uttered by a Proclaiming Angel with what Isaiah (xlix. 2) calls a "mouth like a sharp sword"? The only difference between the cloaked Figure in Ezekiel and the cloaked Figure in Revelation is that the former leaves the guilty to the swords of his six companions, the latter with his own sword deals with good and evil, truth and falsehood, so that his sword is called "two-edged" (**2998** (xxviii) *t—u*). Thus the hypothesis that ποδήρης is borrowed from Ezekiel ix. 2—11 would help us to understand why the writer passed on to speak of the (Rev. i. 16) "two-edged sword," which, though not mentioned by Ezekiel or Daniel in the two passages above quoted, is implied in Ezekiel's context (but not in Daniel's). See **2998** (xxviii) *s—x*.

[1] [**2998** (xxviii) *o*] Rev. i. 14 αἱ τρίχες λευκαὶ ὡς ἔριον λευκόν, ὡς χιών. For this, W.H. refer to nothing but Dan. vii. 9 where the "clothing" is said to be "white as snow," and "the hair of the head" as "pure wool." But in all probability John's expression ("as white wool, as snow") is influenced by Isaiah i. 18 "though your sins be as scarlet they shall be as *white as snow*, though they be red like crimson they shall be *as wool.*" The apparent bathos—which created discussion among the Talmudists (Schwab iv. 122, *Schabb.* ix. 3)—might not be bathos to a Jew alluding to

eyes as a flame of fire[1], and his feet like unto burnished brass[2], as if it had been refined in a furnace; and his voice

---

the tradition that the "*scarlet wool*" (on which see Barnabas vii. 8), used on the occasion of the scapegoat, sometimes became white ("blanchissaient en signe de pardon"). Perhaps Rev. i. 14 should be rendered "as wool [that is] white as snow"—thus alluding to the "whitened wool" referred to in the Talmud. John drops Daniel's mention of "white garments" as being perhaps implied in ποδήρης (*i.e.* βαδδείν, white linen), and he lays stress on the whiteness of the hair because πολιαί, "white hair," is connected with "judgment" as in Sir. xxv. 6 ὡς ὡραῖον πολιαῖς κρίσις, where the Syriac context has Daniel's exact expression, "ancient of days" ("antiquis dierum"). See also Prov. xx. 27—9, where the context implies that "the hoary head" brings with it righteous judgment. Origen (on Numbers, *Hom.* xxvii., Lomm. x. 356) connects the "whiteness" in Isaiah i. 18 with that in Daniel vii. 9. Here, then, John takes from Daniel a characteristic of the prophet's "Ancient of days" to whom the Son of man is "brought," and transfers it to the Son of man Himself, modifying it by an allusion to Isaiah's description of God's purification of sin. Thus he suggests concerning the Son of man (as being the white-haired "ancient of days"), (1) that He is from the beginning, (2) that He judges, (3) that He purifies.

[1] [2998 (xxviii)*p*] Rev. i. 14 καὶ οἱ ὀφθαλμοὶ αὐτοῦ ὡς φλὸξ πυρός... χαλκολιβάνῳ...πεπυρωμένης. "Eyes as a flame of fire" is rep. in ii. 18 and xix. 12. Daniel vii. 9—from which John has borrowed details here—says ὁ θρόνος...φλὸξ πυρός. "Throne" would be inapplicable to this Figure, as it is (Rev. ii. 1) "walking to and fro in the midst of the seven golden candlesticks." John transfers "flame of fire" to the "eyes"—perhaps having in view Zechariah's tradition about the seven candlesticks as being "the eyes of the Lord," and his own tradition about the Lamb as having (Rev. v. 6) "seven eyes," comp. Dan. x. 6, "his eyes as torches of fire (λαμπάδες πυρός)." The sing. concentrates the attention on the one all-seeing and all-testing Judge. He may be also alluding to the first use of a "flame of fire" in the Bible, namely, Exod. iii. 2 the "flame of fire" in which the angel of the Lord appears to Moses, burning but not consuming.

[2] [2998 (xxviii)*q*] Rev. i. 15 οἱ πόδες αὐτοῦ ὅμοιοι χαλκολιβάνῳ is prob. (522 (vi)) a corruption of a paraphrase of Dan. x. 6 (LXX) οἱ πόδες ὡσεὶ χαλκὸς ἐξαστράπτων (Theod. στίλβοντος). John wished to bring out the notion of brass that is being "refined in a furnace" χαλκὸν ἐν κλιβάνῳ: and χαλκοεκλιβανω, or some such phrase, has been corrupted so as to give rise to a compound not occurring elsewhere in Gk (comp. Lev. ii. 4). The phrase ὡς ἐν καμίνῳ πεπυρωμένης is a conflate of this. Both the word

as the voice of many waters[1]; and having in his right hand seven stars; and from his mouth a sword, two-edged, sharp, going forth[2]; and his countenance (or, appearance) was as

---

and the phrase suggest that the Figure will be (Mal. iii. 2) "like a *refiner's fire*."

[1] [2998 (xxviii) *r*] Rev. i. 15 ὡς φωνὴ ὑδάτων πολλῶν is taken from Ezek. i. 24, rep. in xliii. 2 (Heb.), applied first to the "four living creatures" and then to "the glory of the God of Israel." Dan. x. 6 has "the voice of a multitude (המון)," which, though not expressed by the same Hebrew word, also occurs in Ezek. i. 24 "*as the voice of many waters*, as the voice of the Almighty [*i.e.* Shaddai (2998 (xxvii)*j*)] in their going, the voice of *a multitude* (המלה) [Theod. the voice of *the Logos*] as the voice of a camp." Comp. Rev. xiv. 2 "I heard a voice from heaven as the *voice of many waters*...," *i.e.* of the saints singing the New Song, and xix. 6 "I heard as the voice of a great multitude and as *the voice of many waters*," singing Halleluiah. Against this threefold use of "many waters" in a good sense, must be set Rev. xvii 1—15 "the great harlot that sitteth upon *many waters* (comp. Jerem. li. 13)....The waters that thou sawest are peoples and multitudes and nations and tongues," *i.e.* this world, or the flesh—the waters "above the firmament" being contrasted, in the writer's mind, with the waters "below."

(xxviii) *s—x* THE "STARS" AND THE "SWORD"

[2] [2998 (xxviii) *s*] Rev. i. 16 καὶ ἔχων ἐν τῇ δεξιᾷ χειρὶ αὐτοῦ ἀστέρας ἑπτά, καὶ ἐκ τοῦ στόματος αὐτοῦ ῥομφαία δίστομος ὀξεῖα ἐκπορευομένη. Before shewing the connexion between the "seven stars" and the "two-edged sword" it is well to repeat that the Seer, throughout this description, seems to have in view the just Judge, human and therefore able to judge men because He is "like a son of man" (comp. Jn v. 27 "power to execute judgment *because* he is son of man (ὅτι υ. ἀ. ἐστίν)"); but also divine, pure and stainless and wise as the white-haired Ancient of days; girt with the unalloyed "gold" of truth; with eyes that burn as well as see; a form that suggests the fire of the refiner; and a voice that goes forth as that of a sea. All this prepares us for the thought of the Word of God pronouncing sentence and dividing good from evil; and this prepares us for the metaphor of the sword.

[2998 (xxviii) *t*] Heb. iv. 11—12, after warning men against "falling" (like Israel after the flesh), says "For the Logos of God is living and inwardly working (ἐνεργής) and more cutting (τομώτερος) than any *two-edged sword*, and penetrating even to division of soul and spirit, joints and marrow, and a judger (κριτικός) of the thoughts and intents of the heart." Comp. Is. xlix. 2 "He hath made my *mouth as a sharp sword*," and Hos. vi. 5 "I have *hewed them by the prophets*, I have *slain them by the words of my mouth*." This might be interpreted as meaning that the Logos divides truth from falsehood, and "slays" the falsehood in the soul, or else "hews" the soul as long as it retains the falsehood. Comp. Origen—on Ps. cxlix. 6 "two-edged sword"—"The sword is the mind under the influence of Logos (νοῦς λογικός) cutting off the soul from wickedness and ignorance." "The sharp two-edged sword" occurs again (ii. 12) in the beginning of the letter to Pergamum. Afterwards "two-edged" is dropped (ii. 16 "sword of my mouth," xix. 15 "sharp sword," xix. 21 "the sword that goes forth from the mouth of him that sat upon the horse"). In xix. 13—15 it is "the Logos of God" from whose mouth "proceedeth a sharp sword."

[2998 (xxviii) *u*] This last passage is the only one where the Logos of God is described as a personal agent; but all that precedes leads up to it, and so does the mention of the "two-edged sword" here. The Logos is frequently described by Philo as "*cutting*" or "*dividing*," sometimes as a surgeon's knife (i. 212 κακία...λόγῳ τομεῖ τῷ κατ' ἐπιστήμην τέμνεται) but sometimes as the Universal Divider of things really opposite (i. 491 τῷ τομεῖ τῶν συμπάντων αὐτοῦ λόγῳ...οὗτος ὁ τομεύς) "opposing against each other" things that are essentially opposed (*e.g.* ἀληθές and ψεῦδος), and also intervening so as to unite things not opposed; so that the Logos (i. 496) speaks "between the two Cherubim"; and the two Divine Powers, the Giver and the Punisher, are manifested as "coequal (ἰσάζουσιν) using Him as their Divider (αὐτῷ τομεῖ χρώμεναι)." But the "Cherubim" and "the flaming sword" (Gen. iii. 24) are allegorized by Philo (i. 142—3) as referring to "the seven stars (τῶν ἑπτὰ ἀστέρων)," that is, the "planets" (including the sun), and more particularly "the flaming sword is a symbol of the sun (ἡ δὲ φλογίνη ῥομφαία σύμβολον ἡλίου)": "but I once heard," he says, "an even better word [*i.e.* interpretation]" [ἤκουσα δέ ποτε καὶ σπουδαιοτέρου λόγου, perh. a play on λόγος], "and it said to me that, according to the nature of (or, in) the one real God (κατὰ τὸν ἕνα ὄντως ὄντα θεόν), the highest and first Powers are two—Goodness and Authority. He has begotten the All by Goodness; He rules the begotten (τοῦ γεννηθέντος) by Authority. Third is Logos, in the midst, uniting both (τρίτον δὲ συναγωγὸν ἀμφοῖν μέσον εἶναι Λόγον)."

[2998 (xxviii) *v*] The thought of God as "dividing" is brought out by Jer. Targ. (more distinctly than in Targ. Jon.) on Exod. xii. 42 "It is a night to be observed." There are, says the Targum, "four nights written in the memorial." The first was when there was darkness and "the Word of the Lord shone forth and He called it the first night" (comp. Gen. i. 4 "And God *divided* the light from the darkness...and the darkness he called night"). The second night was "when the Word of the Lord was revealed to Abraham between the *divided* parts" (comp. Gen. xv. 10 "*divided* them in the midst," on which see Philo i. 491,

the sun shineth in his strength[1]."

502—6, and *Quæst. Gen.* ad loc.) "and He called it the second night." The third night was "when the Word of the Lord was revealed upon the Egyptians at the" (Etheridge) "dividing of the night" (*i.e.* midnight). "His right hand slew the firstborn of the Egyptians and His right hand spared the firstborn of Israel....And He called it the third night." The fourth night will be "when the end of the age will be accomplished... Moses shall go forth from the midst of the desert and King Messiah from the midst of Rome. The former shall lead (ידבר) on the head of the cloud, and the latter shall lead on the head of the cloud, and the Word of Jehovah shall lead between the two, and they go as one (lit. in one)."

[1] [2998 (xxviii) *w*] Rev. i. 16 καὶ ἡ ὄψις αὐτοῦ ὡς ὁ ἥλιος φαίνει ἐν τῇ δυνάμει αὐτοῦ. Contrast x. 1 τὸ πρόσωπον αὐτοῦ ὡς ἥλιος. Prob. ὄψις here means "appearance" as always in Ezekiel and mostly in LXX. It occurs in Rev. only here, whereas πρόσωπον occurs 10 times (thrice concerning Him that sitteth on "the throne," vi. 16, xx. 11, xxii. 4). In N.T. ὄψις is pec. to Rev. and Jn. Jn never uses πρόσωπον in any sense, but ὄψις twice, Jn vii. 24 "judge not according to *appearance* (ὄψιν)," Jn xi. 44 ἡ ὄψις αὐτοῦ σουδαρίῳ περιεδέδετο, where Origen (*ad loc.* τὴν ὄψιν περιδεδεμένος ἔτι καὶ μήτε βλέπων, and τὴν ὄψιν τῇ ἀγνοίᾳ κεκάλυπται καὶ περιδέδεται) seems to connect ὄψις with "seeing." If ὄψις means "appearance," it sums up the general effect produced by the Figure, "Its appearance [*as a whole*] was as the sun." This is more easy to understand than Mt. xvii. 2 ἔλαμψεν τὸ πρόσωπον αὐτοῦ ὡς ὁ ἥλιος, τὰ δὲ ἱμάτια αὐτοῦ...ὡς τὸ φῶς, for instead of ending with "garments" and "light," the passage in Rev. ends with "sun" as a climax, so dazzling and astounding the beholder that he falls to the ground.

[2998 (xxviii) *x*] Literally, it is inconsistent that the Logos should hold "the seven stars" and yet be as one of them, namely, the "sun." But the same thought pervades the book, that the Logos is sometimes represented by one of the seven angels. For as Philo (i. 632) says, "God is the archetype of light," and as "the sun divides (διακρίνει) the day and the night, so Moses says God walled off (διατειχίσαι) light and darkness (Gen. i. 4)." The vision of the "sun" also prepares the reader for the future, wherein the Logos will be seen both separating light from darkness and good from evil with His sword and also (comp. Origen on Mt. xvii. 2, Lomm. iii. 129) "manifested to the children of light" as (Mal. iv. 2) "the sun of righteousness," and supplying the place of the sun (Rev. xxii. 5) in the New Jerusalem. W.H. print "*the sun in his might*" as from Judg. v. 31 "So let all thine enemies perish, O Lord; but let them that love him be as the *sun* when he goeth forth *in his*

[**2998** (xxix)] The second vision mentioning "a son of man" (after an announcement of the fall of Babylon and of the doom of the followers of the Beast), is introduced by a voice from heaven, saying, "Write, Blessed are the dead that die in the Lord henceforth. (R.V.) Yea[1], saith the Spirit[2], that they may rest from their labours...." Then the

---

might." This agrees well with the effect of the "two-edged sword" of the Logos in this book, causing the enemies of the light to "perish," but bringing "the Sun of Righteousness" to those that "love" Him.

[**2998** (xxviii) *y*] Summing up the results of the evidence as to John's meaning when—in a book that mentions many angels and especially "seven angels" that execute the wrath of God—he describes the revelation of Jesus as conveyed through "his angel," we may illustrate it by a contrast. Ezekiel describes (**2998** (xxviii) *l—n*) "*one* man" recording the saved and "*six* men" destroying the rest. The one man is "*in the midst of*" *the six* (comp. *Enoch* 90 "that man who wrote before Him, who was one of the seven white ones"). According to John there are "seven" destroying angels, as also there are "seven" churches or "seven" candlesticks. But, as there is ONE expressly mentioned as "walking in the midst" of the seven candlesticks or churches, so there is ONE implied as being "in the midst" of the seven angels, that is to say, prompting each and all of the seven, whether to enlighten or to chastise. Yet on special occasions he seems to describe one of the seven angels, or an angel not mentioned as belonging to the seven, in such a way as to convey the impression that this particular angel specially represents the ONE.

[1] [**2998** (xxix) *a*] Rev. xiv. 13, unpunctuated, is γράψον Μακάριοι οἱ νεκροὶ οἱ ἐν Κυρίῳ ἀποθνήσκοντες ἀπ' ἄρτι ναί λέγει τὸ πνεῦμα ἵνα.... Comp. Cramer, who punctuates thus, ἡ σύνταξις οὕτως. Τὸ πνεῦμα λέγει γράψον ἀπάρτι, ναὶ γράψον,...apparently meaning—"The Spirit says, Write this moment, yea, write." This would contrast with Rev. x. 4 "Seal up, write not [yet]," and would imply that the vision in xiv. 13 was soon to be fulfilled.

[2] [**2998** (xxix) *b*] Rev. xiv. 13 λέγει τὸ Πνεῦμα. Comp. ii. 7 "He that hath an ear let him hear what *the Spirit saith* to the churches" (rep. 7 times), words recalling the words of Christ on earth (Mt. xiii. 9, &c. "He that hath ears") and best taken as uttered by Christ, speaking through His Spirit, and saying "Let each man hear what *the Spirit saith.*" This favours the view that in xiv. 13, the words "*saith the Spirit*" are uttered by Christ speaking through the "Voice from heaven." And the same will apply to xxii. 16—17 "I, Jesus, sent my messenger.... And *the Spirit and the Bride say, Come*. And he that heareth, let him

[2998] "THE SON OF MAN"

Seer continues, "I saw, and behold a white[1] cloud, and on the cloud, sitting, one *like a son of man*, having on his head a golden crown, and in his hand a sharp sickle. And another angel came forth from the sanctuary (ναοῦ) crying with a great voice to him that sat upon the cloud, Send [forth] the sickle." Here the important question is, what is meant by the "white cloud" and by "sitting" on it.

It can hardly be contended that the Seer does not distinguish this from Daniel's visions of the Figure "coming with the clouds of heaven." In O.T., the plural "clouds" has an entirely different meaning from the sing. "cloud," which signifies Shechinah. Moreover John himself has quoted

---

say, Come. And he that thirsteth, let him come"—all of which may well proceed from Jesus. "Let him say, 'Come'"—sounds like a paradox, but it is based on the truth that no man "comes" to God unless his heart asks God to "come" to him. These are the only instances where τὸ πνεῦμα is used absolutely in this book.

[1] [2998 (xxix) *c*] Rev. xiv. 14 "White," used in this book almost always as a symbol of purity. In visions that appear to represent Christ or His representative "angel," it occurs thus, i. 14, His head and His hair were "*white*," signifying (2998 (xxviii) *o*) purity of judgment in connexion with the seven churches, or "candlesticks," in the midst of which He is described as (ii. 1) "walking." Then it occurs four times in connexion with "sitting," thus, vi. 2 "Behold a *white* horse," where the Rider has a "bow," and a "crown" is "given" Him, and He goes forth "conquering and to conquer"; xiv. 14 "Behold a *white* cloud," where the Figure that sits on it, "like a son of man," "has" a "crown" on His head, and a "sickle," and is to reap the "harvest" of the world; xix. 11 "and behold a *white* horse," where "the Faithful and True," who "judgeth in righteousness," is called "the Logos of God," "King of kings" and "Lord of lords"; xx. 11 "And I saw a great *white* throne, and him that sat thereon, from whose face the earth and the heaven fled away." There appears to be a climax in these four descriptions, and perhaps the Rider in vi. 2 to whom the crown is "given" (just after the mention of the Lamb in vi. 1) is regarded not as Christ but merely as the first of the four riders mentioned in vi. 2—8. If so, the epithet "white" would appear to be used thrice in connexion with Christ or God, regarded as "sitting."

For "cloud" see 2998 (xxx), and for "like a son of man," see 2998 (xxvi) *a*.

Daniel's words as to be fulfilled hereafter, Rev. i. 7 "Behold he cometh with the clouds." It is extremely improbable that he confuses this with "sitting on the cloud."

[2998 (xxx)] The use of "the cloud"—no cloud having been previously mentioned—in such expressions as "our fathers were under *the cloud*," "were baptized in *the cloud*," "they went up to heaven in *the cloud*," shews that "the cloud" as the emblem of the divine presence had taken hold of the Jewish mind[1]. Wisdom is made by Ben Sira to say "My throne is in the pillar of cloud[2]." Philo, commenting on the words "the cloud came in the midst between the Egyptian host and the Israelite," calls the cloud "the instrument of defence and salvation for friends, but of vengeance and chastisement for foes," thus assigning to it a part like that of the two-edged sword[3]. To the same effect Origen writes about Ezekiel's "great cloud in the removing spirit, or, wind (ἐν τῷ ἐξαίροντι πνεύματι)." It has two aspects, he says, each a triad :—(1) spirit, cloud, light, (2) fire, amber, light. In both aspects, the end will be "light": but in (1), light will come to us through a baptism of "spirit"; in (2), through a baptism of fire[4]. Philo's doctrine indicates that traditions

---

[1] [2998 (xxx) *a*] 1 Cor. x. 1. In Rev. xi. 11—12, there is a previous mention of πνεῦμα ζωῆς derived from Ezek. xxxvii. 5—10, where πνεῦμα means both "wind" and "spirit" and "breath." "The cloud" may be supposed to have descended with the πνεῦμα ζωῆς.

[2] Sir. xxiv. 4.

[3] Philo i. 501. He is generally silent on other passages containing ἡ νεφέλη in this sense.

(xxx) *b*—(xxxi) *c* "CLOUDS" AND "CLOUD"

[4] [2998 (xxx) *b*] Origen (Lomm. xiv. 27) on Ezek. i. 4, Διχῶς ἐξαίρει τὰ φαῦλα ἀφ' ἡμῶν ὁ θεός, πνεύματι καὶ πυρί. Ἐὰν καλοὶ καὶ ἀγαθοὶ γενώμεθα, καὶ λόγῳ παιδευώμεθα, πνεύματι τὰ φαῦλα ἐξαίρεται, κατὰ τὸ γεγραμμένον "εἰ δὲ πνεύματι τὰς πράξεις τοῦ σώματος θανατοῦτε, ζήσεσθε (Rom. viii. 13)." Εἰ δὲ τὸ πνεῦμα οὐκ ἐξῆρε τὰ φαῦλα ἀπ' ἐμοῦ, χρεία, οἶμαι, τοῦ πυρός. On p. 23 ἐξαίρω is rendered "surgens" when Origen quotes Ezek. i. 4, but "surgens sive auferens" when he comments on it. Ἐξαίρω means "journey forth" in Gen. xxxv. 5, Exod. xiii. 20 &c., applied to men,

about the double nature of "the cloud" go back to a very early period.

[**2998** (xxxi)] The Synoptic Gospels and the text of Daniel (vii. 13) shew a chaotic confusion of traditions about the "coming" of the Son of Man—whether "*with clouds*" or "*on clouds*," or "*in a cloud*"; and the Fourth Gospel (which never uses the word "cloud") avoids them altogether[1]. Early in the second century R. Akiba was reproved by his contemporaries for heretical interpretation of the "thrones" in

---

and in Exod. xiv. 19 applied to the pillar of cloud (R.V. "removed"). It also means "remove," *i.e.* destroy, something evil, *e.g.* Deut. xvii. 7.

[**2998** (xxx) *c*] The LXX renders סערה, "storm," by ἐξαίρω, in Ezek. i. 4, xiii. 11 πνεῦμα ἐξαῖρον, xiii. 13 πνοὴν ἐξαίρουσαν, and nowhere else. But Ezekiel's meaning is the same as that of Jeremiah xxiii. 19 (rep. xxx. 23) "the tempest of the Lord, [even his] fury, is gone forth, yea, a whirling tempest; it shall burst upon the head of the wicked," where ἐξαίρω is not used. Perhaps Ezekiel's mention of the "cloud" in the context induces the LXX to employ ἐξαίρω as being applied to the "removing" of "the cloud" in Exod. xiv. 19.

[1] [**2998**(xxxi)*a*] Mk xiii. 26, Mt. xxiv. 30, Lk. xxi. 27; Mk xiv. 62, Mt. xxvi. 64, Lk. om. (see *Fourfold Gospel* "Clouds"); Dan. vii. 13. Origen (on Mt. xxiv. 30) says (Lomm. iv. 312) "forsitan super nubibus animatis et rationalibus." Comp. Deut. xxxiii. 2 (R.V. txt) "*from* (מ) the ten thousands (Heb. myriads) of holy ones," LXX "*with* (σὺν) the myriads of Kades" (s. Gesen. 873—4), Onk., Targ. Jon., and Targ. Jer. "*with him* the myriads (Jon. myriads of myriads) of holy angels (Onk. of holy ones)" [in xxxiii. 3, where Targ. Jer. has "*as* the myriads of the holy angels," the parallel Targ. Jon. has "and all of them hath he called to be holy"], *Enoch* i. 9 "He comes *with* myriads of [his] holy ones," Jude 14 "Enoch prophesied saying, Lo, the Lord came (lit.) *in* (ἐν) myriads of his holy ones" [so Judith xvi. 5 ἦλθεν ἐν μυριάσι δυνάμεων αὐτοῦ], Zech. xiv. 5 "the Lord my God shall come and all the holy ones *with thee* (LXX *with him*)."

There may have been some early confusion between מ "from," and ב "in" (see Index to Clue, ב) which might be confused with כ "as."

In Deut. xxxiii. 2, the LXX places the "*angels*" at the "right hand" of God. But the Heb. puts the "*Law*" there. Comp. Rev. v. 1 where, "on the right hand of him that sitteth on the throne," there is mentioned a "book"—the sealed book of the New Law, the Law of Redemption.

Daniel[1]. The Revelation of John, while quoting Daniel's tradition about "clouds" correctly[2], as one that is to be fulfilled, clearly expresses another and a different tradition about "*sitting on*" a "white cloud" (where "sitting" is emphasized by a previous tradition about an angel (x. 1) "arrayed in a cloud"). This appears to be based on Ezekiel's prophecy about the "cloud," and about the "wind, or spirit, of storm," controlled by what Origen calls a "charioteer." But perhaps John blends with Ezekiel's view of the cloud suggestions from "the pillar of cloud" in the Pentateuch. On the whole, the vision of "one like a son of man," sitting on the "white cloud," appears to convey a revelation of a future righteous judgment in which humanity will be seen controlling the elements and the powers of Nature so as to subdue the powers of the Beast.

[2998 (xxxii)] A Seer must not be treated as an Apologist

---

[1] [2998 (xxxi) *b*] *Sanh.* 38 *b* raises the question on Dan. vii. 9, "Why *thrones* [instead of *throne*]?" R. Johanan explained it of God's fellow-councillors, comparing Dan. iv. 17 "This sentence is by the decree of the watchers, and the matter by the word of the holy ones." Akiba said "One for Him and one for David." R. Joses, rebuking him for profanity, said that one was for God's righteousness and the other for God's mercy (somewhat as Philo above (2998 (xxviii) *u*), only that Philo introduces the Logos between the two). Another Rabbi said that one was a "seat" the other a "footstool."

[2] [2998 (xxxi) *c*] Dan. vii. 13 "*with* (עִם) the clouds." The rarity of such a phrase would naturally cause it to be corrupted to "on" (as in LXX), and perhaps Christian influence might facilitate the corruption when Christians, applying it to Christ, desired to magnify the phrase so as to mean enthronement on clouds. Dalman (*Words* p. 242) alleges Rev. xiv. 14—16 among passages indicating that the author read ἐπί in Daniel. But that is hardly a case in point since (1) the writer uses the sing. "cloud," (2) he is describing "sitting," not "coming," (3) he is probably influenced by Ezek. i. 26, where "sitting," though not mentioned, is implied by "throne." If the writer of Rev. xiv. wrote also Rev. i. 7, then we must add (4) that i. 7 quotes Daniel definitely with μετά. The two phrases are quite consistent. The Figure might first "*come with* the clouds" and then "*sit on* the *cloud.*"

or Harmonist. Hence it would be out of place to ask why the Seer did not represent Jesus as *the* Son of man "standing" (or "sitting") in heaven, at "*the right hand*" of the Supreme[1]. Our mouths would fairly be shut by the reply, "Because he did not see Him thus." But it is lawful to ask whether the Seer expresses a tradition about "the right hand" in some other way. And this he seems to do in the only passage where he uses "*the right hand*" in connexion with the "throne" of God[2]. He tells us that "on (or in) *the right hand* of him that sitteth on the throne" is a "book...sealed." The context shews that it is the "sealed" mystery of the redemption of the Universe.

"A Lamb standing as if slain" takes the book "from the right hand of him that sat on the throne," and opens its seven seals. To describe this "Lamb," the Seer uses a word that is almost non-existent in pre-Christian Greek literature; but Jeremiah once uses it of "a gentle lamb dragged away to slaughter," and Aquila uses it to describe the "lambs" whom Jehovah, the Shepherd, "carries in His bosom[3]." Whither does the Lamb "go," and where does it

---

[1] [2998 (xxxii) *a*] Acts vii. 56 "standing," Mk xiv. 62, Mt. xxvi. 64, Lk. xxii. 69 "sitting." On the difference comp. Heb. x. 11—12 "Now every high priest *standeth*...but this [high priest] having offered one sacrifice for sins for ever, *sat down* at the right hand of God." See also above, 2998 (xxv). [2] Rev. v. 1—7.

(xxxii) *b—d* THE DIFFERENCE BETWEEN ἀρνίον AND ἀμνός

[3] [2998 (xxxii) *b*] Ἀρνίον (Steph. *Thes.*) is quoted from Lysias and Philippides (also from Lucian *De Salt.* 43, where however it is not in Gesner's text (ii. p. 294)). It appears to be rare except in Christian literature (the Indices in the 7 vols. hitherto (1906) publ. by Egypt Expl. give no instance of ἀρνίον, and those in the Berlin Pap. vols. i.—iii. only one instance, and that 7th century, vol. iii. no. 377). It occurs in N.T. only in Jn xxi. 15 "Feed my *lambs*," and about 29 times in Rev. In LXX it occurs 4 times, thrice in the phrase "lambs of (Heb. sons of, or little ones of) sheep," once in Jer. xi. 19 "as a gentle lamb led to slaughter (ὡς ἀρνίον ἄκακον ἀγόμενον τοῦ θύεσθαι)." But Aquila has it in Is. xl. 11 "He shall

feed his flock like a shepherd. He shall gather the *lambs* in his arm and carry them in his bosom."

[2998 (xxxii) *c*] In the Heb. of this last passage the word for "lamb" (טלה) is the same (only masculine) as that used by Christ to the daughter of Jairus, " Talitha," meaning "*lamb*" in Hebrew, but "*young one*" (boy or girl, according to the termination) in Aramaic. The Heb. occurs (Gesen. 378 *a*) only in Is. lxv. 25 "wolf and *lamb*," Is. xl. 11 "gather the *lambs*," and 1 S. vii. 9 where Samuel sacrifices a "sucking *lamb*" (lit. lamb of milk, ἄρνα γαλαθηνόν), as a burnt offering in a time of special emergency. In his short summary of the lives of the heroes of Israel, Ben Sira says xlvi. 16 "When he [*i.e.* Samuel] offered up a sucking *lamb* (ἐν προσφορᾷ ἀρνὸς γαλαθηνοῦ) and the Lord thundered from heaven." The Tosephta on *Aboth* i. 2 quotes 1 S. vii. 9 as a proof of the special efficacy of burnt offering "because it is all burnt up," and *Aboda Zara* 24 *b* quotes it on the question as to the masculine or feminine termination of " lamb."

[2998 (xxxii) *d*] These details may have some bearing on the very important question as to the origin and meaning of Jn i. 29 " Behold, the Lamb (ἀμνός) of God that taketh away the sin of the world." Many recognise that John the Baptist could hardly have used these words with a direct reference to the ἀμνός of the continual morning and evening sacrifice. But if the author of Revelation supplied the author of the Fourth Gospel with his groundwork, it is possible to see how the tradition of the former about the "(*gentle*) *lamb*," ἀρνίον, may have been developed into the tradition of the latter about the "(*sacrificial*) *lamb*," ἀμνός. Origen (*Comm. Joann.* vi. 35) connects (as elsewhere) Isaiah's (liii. 7) prophecy about the Man who "was led as a sheep to the slaughter and as a lamb (ἀμνός) dumb before the shearer" with Jeremiah's (xi. 19) "I was as a gentle *lamb* (ἀρνίον) led away to be slaughtered (θύεσθαι)"— which he regards as uttered by Christ concerning Himself through the prophet. It is not at all improbable that John the Baptist would call his disciple, in whom he foresaw his successor, "the *young child* of Jehovah," or "the *lamb* of Jehovah," playing on the ancient meaning of the word, in contrast with himself and his own more austere character and doctrine, and also as an expression of his belief that the younger prophet was (like the lamb in Nathan's parable, 1 S. xii. 1—6) "in the bosom" of God. Receiving this tradition from John the son of Zebedee the author of Revelation, John the Elder—or whoever else composed the Fourth Gospel in the name of " the beloved disciple "—might interpret it, in the light of subsequent events, as including a prediction about the lamb of sacrifice. Interpreting it thus, he would naturally change ἀρνίον to ἀμνός and would explain that the latter was used in a sacrificial sense. Elsewhere, retaining the *meaning* expressed by ἀρνίον (*i.e.* "darling," "cherished one"), he expresses it by quite different words, Jn i. 18 εἰς τὸν

abide, after it has opened the seven-sealed book? We may find an answer in the last of the Seer's visions (xxii. 1) "And he shewed me a river of water of life, bright as crystal, proceeding out of *the throne of God and of the Lamb*." What is the picture before the Seer? Some passages of *Enoch* suggest the thought that God vacates His throne for His Elect One, or shares it with the latter. Are we to try to think of the Lamb thus, as filling God's place, or as sitting on a portion of the throne and by the side of the Supreme? Either notion would be alien from Hebrew thought, which would rather regard the Lamb as in the "arms," or "bosom," of the Shepherd of Israel. And this—the Lamb "in the bosom" of the Father—was probably the vision, the final vision, seen by the disciple that had lain "in the bosom of Jesus[1]." Or rather, it was a *feeling*. He *saw* the water of life proceeding from the throne. He *felt* that no solitary God sat there. It was (Rev. xxii. 3) "the throne of God and of the Lamb."

There is a whole world of difference between this and the view that regards Christ merely as the sacrificial Lamb on the altar on earth, before which the redeemed stand looking up to God in heaven. The sacrificial aspect is not indeed omitted; but it is subordinated or merged in the thought that all life proceeds from an omnipotent tenderness revealed through such homely associations and images that the disciple whom Jesus loved feels almost compelled to resort to a homely word—as though Bunyan were to venture to speak of the Darling of God. All the more would such a word force itself upon the Seer if he had been in his youth a disciple of John the Baptist, and if the first words that he had heard from

---

κόλπον. In a different way Origen (*loc. cit.*) gives two aspects of the sacrificed lamb, (1) "the lamb was not other than the Man (οὐκ ἄλλον τοῦ ἀνθρώπου)," (2) "He that brought this lamb to the sacrifice was the God in the Man (ὁ ἐν τῷ ἀνθρώπῳ ἦν θεός)." On κόλπος, s. *Ephraim's Quotations from the Gospel* (ed. Burkitt) p. 49.   [1] Jn xiii. 23.

his former Master about Jesus of Nazareth declared the latter to be "the gentle lamb of Jehovah[1]."

[2998 (xxxiii)] But it may be urged that when John actually saw Christ represented—as he did twice—by a human figure, it would have been natural for him to use the words used by his Master—"*the* Son of man," not "*one like unto* a son of man." The answer is that, in fact, "*one like unto*" better expressed Christ's meaning, for the Western Churches, where (as we shall presently see) the question early arose (Jn xii. 34), "Who *is* this 'Son of Man'?" John may well have felt that by this phrase "one like unto a son of man" he was expressing his Master's conception of humanity as being exalted by God above the forces of Nature and above the forces of evil, in accordance with the language of Ezekiel and the Psalms[2]. It meant "man according to the

---

[1] [2998 (xxxii) *e*] There are indications in the gospels that Jesus may have dwelt more than is generally supposed on the metaphor of the Lamb, as representing the type of patience and gentleness, which the disciples must keep before themselves, and which they must regard as representing Himself. Thus Lk. x. 3 "I send you as *lambs* in the midst of wolves" (parall. Mt. x. 16 "sheep") suggests that they go forth to bear persecution as their Master bore it (Mt. x. 24 "A disciple is not above his teacher"). Hence the warning against the "wolves in sheep's clothing." These are "false prophets," and might be called false imitators of the Lamb.

[2] [2998 (xxxiii) *a*] Contrast the more definite use of "man" in Dan. x. 5 "Behold *a man*." There Sym. has "*as it were* a man." But the context indicates an angelic companion of Michael, probably (see Jerome's comm. and comp. *Enoch* ch. 40) Gabriel, whose name means Man of God. In Daniel, the repeated mentions of Gabriel and Michael are more definite than the single mention of Michael in Rev. xii. 7. Also, if we bear in mind that the same Hebrew noun occurs in the "four *living-creatures* (ζῷα)" in Ezekiel's vision (i. 5) and the "four *beasts* (θηρία)" in Daniel's (vii. 3), we shall see how the later prophet narrowed down to nations what the earlier intended to include the universe. Later still, the author of Revelation includes both these thoughts, expressing them by their separate Greek words. He sees in the "*four living-creatures*" of Ezekiel (Rev. iv. 4—7, v. 6—14) four ζῷα, celestial representatives of the animate and inanimate Universe—apart from the twenty-four Elders who represent the Old Church transformed into the New. At the same time he finds in

likeness of God": but another aspect of the meaning was "God according to the likeness of man." From either point of view, "like" was appropriate. This "likeness," then, John introduces twice:—once as "walking" amid the Churches to reprove and chasten them, once as "seated" on a "white cloud" to reap the harvest of the world. But both are inferior revelations. A far superior revelation is conveyed through "the Lamb." Moreover it is implied that all these visionary images are but images. None of them are to be worshipped. They are all sent by "Jesus." Jesus Himself is not seen. Nowhere does the Seer say, "I saw the Lord Jesus," or, "Behold, the Lord Jesus." Jesus speaks through His Spirit ("I was in the Spirit on the Lord's day") under various forms, or without any form, and is never beheld in the form He wore in Galilee. The warning is given, and repeated, that the Seer must not worship a visible representation of God, however awe-inspiring: "See thou do it not. Worship God." But it is God as revealed by Jesus. Apart from the final salutation, we may say that with Jesus the book both begins and ends, "The revelation of Jesus Christ... Come, Lord Jesus."

§ 12. *The Gnostics, Ignatius, and Barnabas*

[2998 (xxxiv)] This spiritual view of Christ as Humanity on earth exalted to be Humanity in heaven, by the fulfilment of Christ's law of suffering and service, became obscured when Christians came to analyse "Son of man" as a technical term

---

the "*four beasts*" of Daniel a suggestion of brutal tyrannies which he represents by θηρίον. But his θηρίον and ἄλλο θηρίον do not make war against one another as is the case in Daniel. They always make war against righteousness, and are never spoken of in the plural. Though there are more than one, they are treated as one, as in the last passage where the word occurs, describing (xx. 10) "the lake of fire and brimstone where are also *the beast* and the false prophet."

and to discuss it controversially—a proof that Christ used the term, since heretics as well as the orthodox took such great pains to explain it in accordance with their several views. The most ancient misconstruing is that of the early Gnostics, who were loth to believe that Christ had really come in the flesh. Yet how could they explain away " Son of man "? Some of them (it is hardly credible, yet it is twice averred by Irenæus i. 12. 4, i. 30. 1) declared that the Propator or First Father was called Anthropos, or Man, and hence that the Saviour styled Himself the Son of Man (or Second Man, as being Son of the First Man)[1].

[2998 (xxxv)] On the other side stood those who disliked the term "*Son of man*" (1) because it might mean "*Son of a human father,*" or (2) because it described Christ as in His humiliation, and they preferred to regard Him as the Lord in glory. We have seen that (apart from quotations of the Psalms and allusions to Daniel or Ezekiel) no book of N.T. except the Gospels (and the single instance above alleged from Stephen's martyrdom in the Acts) ever mentions "the Son of man." The Epistle to the Romans (i. 3—4), even in an antithesis, instead of saying that Christ "became Son of man after the flesh, but was manifested as Son of God through the Spirit," says "*born of the seed of David* according to the

---

[1] [2998(xxxiv)*a*] What follows (i. 30. 1) is still more portentous, namely, the generating of "an incorruptible light, a third male, whom they call Christ"—"Postea, dicunt, exultante Primo Homine cum Filio suo super formositate Spiritus (hoc est Foeminae), et illuminante eam, generavit ex ea lumen incorruptibile tertium masculum, quem Christum vocant, filium Primi et Secundi Hominis et Spiritus Sancti, Primae Foeminae." But the portent had a basis of mystical thought that was not portentous. For we shall find Origen contending that, in a certain sense, God is "man," so that from eternity there was, in a certain sense, a Man, and the Son of the Man, and the Spirit. And these Gnostics spun their cobweb out of a logical argument that the Man, and the Son of the Man, and the Spirit, cooperated with a view to the incarnation that resulted in Christ. As to Origen, see 2998 (xliii—v).

flesh," thus leaving the question of parentage undecided, since "the seed of David" might be taken by some to apply not to Joseph but to Mary. Ignatius, in his zeal against the Docetics, uses the phrase once, antithetically, "Jesus Christ, [born] according to the flesh, of the family of David, who was [at once] Son of man and Son of God (τῷ υἱῷ ἀνθρώπου καὶ υἱῷ Θεοῦ)." This is not quite the same as the evangelistic use, and even this is removed in the longer recension of Ignatius[1].

[2998 (xxxvi)] Barnabas, after introducing Joshua as "Jesus the Son of Nun," that is, *son of a human father*, quotes a Targumistic version of Exod. xvii. 14—16 in which it is said "*the Son of God*[2] shall destroy Amalek" (where Jer. Targ.

---

[1] [2998 (xxxv) *a*] Ign. *Eph.* 20. See Lightf. "This (τῷ κατὰ σάρκα) is inserted as a protest against Docetic error....But this emphatic mention of the human nature requires a counterbalance. Hence he adds that Christ is not only 'Son of man,' but also 'Son of God.'" The longer recension has, for the human side, merely κατὰ σάρκα δὲ ἐκ γένους Δαυείδ.

[2] [2998 (xxxvi) *a*] Barn. xii. 9 "Moses therefore saith unto Jesus, the son of Nun, having given him this name when he sent him to spy out the land, Take a book into thy hands and write that which the Lord saith, that the *Son of God* will cut down from the roots all the house of Amalek in the last days," corresponds to Exod. xvii. 14—16 "And the Lord said unto Moses, Write this for a memorial in a book, and rehearse it in the ears of Joshua, that (or, for) *I will utterly blot out* (lit. wiping I will wipe out) the remembrance of Amalek from under heaven. And Moses built an altar and called the name of it Jehovah my banner; and he said, *A hand* [*is lifted up*] *upon the throne of Jah; the Lord will have war* with Amalek from generation to generation." It will be instructive to trace the origin of Barnabas' "*Son of God*." It arises from "hand... upon the throne of Jah (כס יה)," confused by the LXX with "hand hidden (כסה)," but capable of being personified as "the Hand of the Lord," or "Arm of the Lord"—that is, "the Son of God," regarded as "[seated] on the throne of God." "Hands of God" means "*the Son and the Spirit of God*" in Iren. v. 1. 3 (and elsewhere) where see Grabe's note. Targ. Jon. has "The Word of the Lord hath sworn...that He *by His Word* will fight," and sim. Targ. Jer. "The Lord hath said *by His Word* that the memory of Amalek shall perish." Iren. iii. 16. 4 applies Is. viii. 4 and Exod. xvii. 16 (LXX) "hidden hand" to the child Jesus, and Justin (*Tryph.* 49) applies the latter to the Incarnation.

mentions Saul, with Mordecai and Esther, as the destroyers) and proceeds, "Behold, [here] again [is] Jesus, *not* [*now*] *son of man* (οὐχὶ υἱὸς [v. r. ὁ υἱὸς] ἀνθρώπου) *but Son of God* (ἀλλὰ υἱὸς [v.ˆr. ὁ υἱὸς] τοῦ θεοῦ)." It goes on to say that David, knowing that men were destined to call Christ "*the son of David*," and fearing their consequent error, took care to address Him as "*his Lord*." "See," says the writer, "how David calls Him Lord, not son." The whole passage shews that the writer shrank from applying the term "son" to Christ except in the phrase "Son of God" for fear of "the delusion of sinners (τὴν πλάνην τῶν ἁμαρτωλῶν)[1]."

§ 13. *Justin, Irenæus, and Tertullian*

2998 (xxxvii)] Justin Martyr uses the expression "*man* [*born*] *from men* (ἄνθρωπος ἐξ ἀνθρώπων)" two or three times, as representing what "some of our race[2]" believed

---

[1] [**2998** (xxxvi) *b*] Barn. xii. 8—10. Schmidt (*Enc. Bibl.* 4715) says, "The most natural interpretation of *Barn.* ii. 10" [an error for xii. 10] "is that the author alludes to it [*i.e.* the title "Son of man"]....The inference may be drawn that about 130 A.D. the title was known in some circles...." I should have thought it legitimate to infer more than this, namely, that when the author wrote (perhaps before 130 A.D.) the title was known *so widely and so authoritatively* that he felt it desirable to subordinate it, since he could not deny its authenticity.

[2] [**2998** (xxxvii) *a*] *Tryph.* 48 "*Of our* [*own*] *race*" ἀπὸ τοῦ ἡμετέρου γένους, *i.e.* of our belief. This must be distinguished from *ib.* 120 "*of my own race*," ἀπὸ τοῦ γένους τοῦ ἐμοῦ, which he explains (λέγω δὲ τῶν Σαμαρέων) as being Samaritan. The former may be roughly paraphrased as *ib.* 48 ταὐτά μοι δοξάσαντες "holding the same opinions as I do." He calls Christians "our race" as being mostly Gentiles, contrasted with the "race" of the Jews. Comp. *ib.* 120 τινὲς τοῦ γένους ὑμῶν "some of your race [*i.e.* some Jews] will be found [real] children of Abraham." And (*ib.*) τὸ ἐν τῷ γένει ὑμῶν πολὺ πλῆθος is distinguished from the Gentiles, with whom Justin identifies himself by the use of the first person plural ("we Gentiles") thus, πάντες οἱ ἀπὸ τῶν ἐθνῶν πάντων οὐ προσδοκῶμεν.

[**2998** (xxxvii) *b*] Justin was not "a Samaritan" in the sense of being a Samaritan by religion. Comp. *Apol.* 53 where he uses the word "our-

about Christ, but what he himself did not believe[1]. Later on, he says that Christ has revealed to us from the Scriptures that He is the first-begotten of God and "*son of the patriarchs*, having been made flesh through the Virgin who sprang from

---

selves," subsequently explained by "those from among the Gentiles," in contrast with "the Jews and Samaritans" ("seeing *our own selves* and knowing that *the Christians from among the Gentiles* are both more numerous and more true than those from among the Jews and Samaritans, ἑαυτοὺς ἡμᾶς ὁρῶντες, πλείονάς τε κ. ἀληθεστέρους τοὺς ἐξ ἐθνῶν τῶν ἀπὸ Ἰουδαίων καὶ Σαμαρέων Χριστιανοὺς εἰδότες)." He uses γένος in various senses, *e.g. Apol.* 53 τὰ μὲν γὰρ ἄλλα πάντα γένη ἀνθρώπεια ὑπὸ τοῦ προφητικοῦ πνεύματος καλεῖται ἔθνη, τὸ δὲ Ἰουδαϊκὸν κ. Σαμαρειτικὸν φῦλον Ἰσραὴλ κ. οἶκος Ἰακὼβ κέκληνται—where he uses γένη for "races" in the ordinary way, but *implies* that the prophets recognised *two* races, (1) that of the Gentiles, (2) that of the Jews and Samaritans. He compares Is. liv. 1, describing the Mother of the former, and the Mother of the latter. Justin had studied (*Tryph.* 2) philosophy in his youth, but makes no mention of the study of the Bible, and (*ib.* 29) he had not been circumcised.

[1] [2998 (xxxvii) *c*] *Tryph.* 48. The Jew, Trypho, who introduces the discussion, begins with the singular, "man," ridiculing the notion that the Christ pre-existed as God and endured to be begotten (becoming man) and was not *man from man* (τὸ γὰρ λέγειν σε προϋπάρχειν...εἶτα καὶ γεννηθῆναι, ἄνθρωπον γενόμενον, ὑπομεῖναι, καὶ ὅτι οὐκ ἄνθρωπος ἐξ ἀνθρώπου...μωρόν). Justin replies that He will still be the Christ, "though He should be demonstrated to be born as *man from men* (ἐὰν φαίνηται ὡς ἄνθρωπος ἐξ ἀνθρώπων γεννηθείς)." And he makes the following statement, "There are some of our race who confess that He is Christ but *maintain that He was born man from men* (ἄνθρωπον δὲ ἐξ ἀνθρώπων γενόμενον ἀποφαινόμενοι), with whom I do not agree, nor indeed would very many holding the same opinions as I do say [as they do], since it is not in teachings of men that we have been bidden by Christ Himself to place our trust, but in the truths proclaimed by the blessed prophets and taught by [our Lord] Himself." In his reply, Trypho falls into the plural ("men"). "We [Jews] (ἡμεῖς) all expect that the Christ will be born (γενήσεσθαι) *man from men* (ἄνθρωπον ἐξ ἀνθρώπων)." The plural occurs, rather curiously, in *Apol.* 21 (p. 67 B) Ἡρακλέα δέ..., τοὺς ἐκ Λήδας δὲ Διοσκούρους, καὶ τὸν ἐκ Δανάης Περσέα, καὶ τὸν (ἐξ ἀνθρώπων δὲ) ὑφ' ἵππου Πηγάσου Βελλεροφόντην, where Bellerophon is classed with others that have ascended to heaven, but is differentiated from them because they were from Zeus, by the father's side, whereas he was "from men," that is, from human parentage on both sides.

their race (διὰ τῆς ἀπὸ γένους αὐτῶν παρθένου σαρκοποιηθείς)...." For this reason, says Justin, Christ said, " *The Son of man* (τὸν υἱὸν τοῦ ἀνθρώπου) must suffer many things...." But he proceeds to drop "the" and to offer an alternative explanation thus : " So He called Himself *son of man* (υἱὸν οὖν ἀνθρώπου ἑαυτὸν ἔλεγεν), either (1) *from His birth through the Virgin*—who was, as I said, from the race of David and Jacob and Isaac and Abraham—or (2) *because Abraham himself* was the father of those enumerated, from whom Mary derives her race." This is so perplexing that at least two commentators have altered "Abraham," in the last sentence, into "Adam," and the alteration has found some acceptance ; but " Abraham " is probably the correct reading, and Justin uses " Abraham himself " to mean what may be called " the Patriarchs of Promise," as being the Man to whom the Promise was made, the *real* " father " of the promised "Seed[1]."

[2998 (xxxviii)] Justin's oscillation is probably to be explained by his doubt whether his explanation of υἱὸς

---

[1] [2998 (xxxvii) *d*] *Tryph.* 100. Comp. *Tryph.* 119 where he points out the superiority of Abraham, as being the recipient of promise, to Noah, although Noah was "the father of Abraham and in fact of all men." The same thing might have been said by Justin about Adam as about Noah, namely, that Adam was inferior to Abraham ; and Justin speaks of Adam elsewhere (*Tryph.* 88) as the origin of the Fall, and as (*Tryph.* 40) merely a " house of the inbreathing of God."

[2998 (xxxvii) *e*] Some, retaining "Abraham," would read αὐτοῦ for αὐτόν, thus, διὰ τὸ εἶναι αὐτοῦ τὸν Ἀβραὰμ πατέρα καὶ τούτων τῶν κατηριθμημένων ἐξ ὧν κατάγει ἡ Μαρία τὸ γένος· καὶ γὰρ πατέρας τῶν γεννωμένων ταῖς θυγατράσιν αὐτῶν τέκνων τοὺς τῶν θηλειῶν γεννήτορας ἐπιστάμεθα, " Because Abraham is the father of [*Christ*] *Himself and* of these [above] enumerated as Mary's ancestors ; for we know that the progenitors of female offspring are regarded as the 'fathers' of the children [in their several generations] born to their daughters." But, to justify αὐτοῦ, the sentence ought to run, "Abraham is the father of Christ, *as being the father* of Mary's ancestors," not "*and* the father of Mary's ancestors." Clark's translation has "because Adam was the father *both* of Himself and...." Had that been the meaning, Justin would probably have written καὶ αὐτοῦ.

ἀνθρώπου would apply to ὁ υἱὸς τοῦ ἀνθρώπου—which he has just quoted from our Lord's own words. Υἱὸς ἀνθρώπου—like "filius hominis"—might conceivably mean "son of a human being," "son of the Virgin." Ὁ υἱὸς τοῦ ἀνθρώπου, "the son of the [*masculine*] human being," could not have that meaning. Perhaps ὁ υἱὸς τοῦ pointed (so Justin might argue) to a particular man, and, if so, to no one more probably than Abraham; or τοῦ ἀνθρώπου might be used collectively, not indeed as representing all men, but as suggesting all the patriarchs of promise, from whom the Virgin was descended[1].

[2998 (xxxix)] Irenæus does not oscillate like Justin, but unhesitatingly adopts the solution that the latter seems merely to prefer. His argument (as preserved in the Latin version) is, in effect, this. Christ, being shewn by the Scriptures to be, beyond all men, God and Lord and eternal King, could not have been a mere man. It is proved from the Scriptures that He had a preeminent generation from the Father on High, and also that He underwent generation from the Virgin. Now *the Virgin was a human being, "homo." Hence the Saviour could be called "filius hominis," "Son of man."* So far, Justin would probably have agreed with him. But Irenæus prefixes to this argument a quotation from the Fourth Gospel—from which Justin never quotes—in order to

---

[1] [2998 (xxxviii) *a*] The conjecture of commentators that "Adam" ought to be substituted for "Abraham" may help us to explain why Luke carries up the genealogy in Mt. from the latter to the former. "Adam"—so Luke, or the author of the genealogy in Lk., may have argued —"is not only the first man, but is used in the Bible to mean 'man.' If I trace up the Messiah to Adam, I shall shew that He is 'Son of man.' If, further, I add that Adam is son of God, I shall shew that the Messiah is also, by lineal descent, 'Son of God' as well as 'Son of man.'" This may not seem satisfactory arguing now. But all sorts of unsatisfactory solutions might well be current in the first century when people had drifted into a misunderstanding of that mysterious combination of self-humiliation and self-trust (self-trust based on trust in God, with whom He felt at one) and trust in human nature, which led Jesus to adopt as His habitual title, "the Son of man."

shew how the birth of Christ was differentiated from that of all "mere men" (Jn i. 13): "*He* (sic) *who was not born either by the will of the flesh or by the will of man (viri)*." This is a misquotation. It should have been "*who were not born*." John applied these words to *all* real Christians, who were born, he taught, so far as the flesh went, of the flesh, but, as regards the real and spiritual birth, "from God." Irenæus, however, takes the words intended to describe that kind of spiritual birth which is common to all believers, and uses them to prove that Christ's material birth was unique[1].

[1] [2998 (xxxix) *a*] Iren. iii. 19. 2. It has been seen (2998 (xxxvii) *c*) that Justin says, about those who deny the Virgin birth, merely that he does not "agree" with them, and that "not very many" Christians would deny it. Irenæus goes further (iii. 19. 1) "Those who assert that He was simply and merely a man begotten by Joseph (nude tantum hominem eum dicunt)...*are in a state of death*....Not receiving the incorruptible Word they remain in mortal flesh and are debtors to death." Then he quotes Isaiah (liii. 8) (LXX) "Who shall declare his generation?" and the erroneous LXX version of Jer. xvii. 9 "He *is a man*, and who shall recognise him?" (Heb. "It [*i.e.* the heart of man] *is sick* : who can know it?")—in order to prepare the reader for the fact that the miraculous "generation" of Christ was not "declared" or "known" at first.

[2998 (xxxix) *b*] Then Irenæus proceeds to say (iii. 19. 2) that whosoever has received the revelation of the Son from the Father (Mt. xi. 27, Lk. x. 22, comp. Mt. xvi. 17) understands that (Jn i. 13) "*He who was not born from the will of the flesh nor from the will of* [*the*] *man* (viri) [is] the Son of man, that is, Christ, the Son of the living God." Although Irenæus, or the authority followed by him, has changed John's pl. into the sing., a believer in the non-miraculous incarnation of the eternal Son of God would accept this, *in the sense in which John wrote it*, and would say that the Eternal Son of God became incarnate as the son of Joseph and Mary, being begotten "not from the will of the flesh nor from the will of [the] man [viri] (ἀνδρός) (*i.e.* the husband, 2269, 2371, 2722) but from God." But Irenæus uses his misquoted version in order to materialise what John wrote in a spiritual sense, and to pronounce unique what John declared to be a divine law of origin for all true believers.

[2998 (xxxix) *c*] Though Justin has not quoted Jn i. 13, he has alluded to a tradition that mentions "blood" in connexion with "the will of God," in a strain of thought quite antagonistic to that of John. Justin's view, freq. repeated (2269 *b—d*), is that Christ's "blood" was not created

[2998 (xl)] In a second passage Irenæus, attacking certain heretics, who asserted that Jesus (but not the Christ) was born from Mary, says (iii. 16. 2) "The Holy Spirit, foreseeing corrupters [of the truth] and fortifying [us] by anticipation against their fraudulence, says, by Matthew (i. 18) 'Now the birth of *Christ* (W.H. txt [Jesus] Christ, marg. Christ Jesus) was on this wise,' and that He is Emmanuel, lest perchance we should suppose Him to be merely man—for (Jn i. 13) 'Not from the will of the flesh nor from the will of [the] man (viri) but from the will of God was the Word made flesh.'" This is of interest, because it suggests three things, (1) Irenæus habitually used Jn i. 13 to prove the unique generation of Christ after the flesh, (2) he habitually misquoted it, (3) he had not the least suspicion that there was

---

"from the will of man" but "from the will of God," *i.e.* miraculously. John's view is that the true spiritual birth has nothing to do with material "blood." It would appear that (Gen. xlix. 11) "the blood of the grape," being connected by Christians with Christ, originated many traditions, some false, against which John may have found it necessary to guard his readers at the outset of his gospel.

[2998 (xxxix) *d*] The passage asserting that "Son of man" means Son of the Virgin is printed by Grabe (p. 250) as follows (Iren. iii. 19. 3) "Hic igitur Filius Dei Dominus noster, existens Verbum Patris, et filius hominis: quoniam ex Maria, quae ex hominibus habebat genus, quae et ipsa erat homo, habuit secundum hominem generationem, factus est Filius hominis." This is transl. by Clark "He therefore, the Son of God, our Lord, being the Word of the Father, and the Son of man, since He had a generation as to His human nature from Mary—who was descended from mankind, and who was herself a human being—was made the Son of man." But how could Irenæus say "He...being...the Son of man... was made the Son of man?" This difficulty caused Grabe to suggest the deletion of "et filius hominis." And the difficulty is all the greater because "existens" represents ὑπάρχων in Irenæus i. 4. 1 and ii. 26. 1, so that it would not apply well to "Son of man." Moreover in iii. 19. 1, where the Greek has, εἰς τοῦτο γὰρ ὁ λόγος ἄνθρωπος, ἵνα ὁ ἄνθρωπος τὸν λόγον χωρήσας κατὰ τὴν υἱοθεσίαν λαβὼν, υἱὸς γένηται θεοῦ, the Latin has "Propter hoc enim Verbum Dei homo; et qui Filius Dei est, filius hominis factus est, commixtus Verbo Dei, ut adoptionem percipiens fiat filius Dei."

any doubt about his reading—since in the context he speaks of the "fraudulence" of heretical "corrupters" of the truth ("depravatores"). That he misused the text in this way habitually is almost demonstrated by a third passage where he misquotes it for the same argumentative purpose in order to shew that "the doctrine of the Ebionites is vanity[1]."

[2998 (xli)] About Tertullian little need be said except that he not only follows the precedent of Irenæus in misquoting Jn i. 13, but also (*De Carne Chr.* xix.) accuses heretics of having tampered with it by substituting the plural for the singular. In effect, he declares the plural—the correct reading—to be impossible, by asking "How can this be?" Later on, he says that Scripture (*ib.* xxiv.) "in the words 'Not from blood nor from the will of the flesh and the man but from God *was He born*,' has given Ebion his refutation." Earlier (*ib.* xv.), refuting a Valentinian, he assumes the same erroneous text, "If His flesh were like ours it would needs be similarly born, not of the Spirit, nor 'of God,' but 'of the will of [the] man.'" More definitely, against Marcion, he argues (1) that "Son of *man (hominis)*" must mean "son of a *human parent*"—either father or mother—(2) that it cannot mean "son of a *human father*," since God was Christ's Father, (3) that consequently "*filius hominis*" must mean "son of a *human mother*," namely, of the Virgin. Here he does not quote Jn i. 13, but he assumes that whoever is "[begotten] from God is consequently not [begotten] from man," that is to say, he assumes the untruth of what John asserted, that ordinary, non-miraculous men may be "begotten from God."

---

[1] [2998 (xl) *a*] Iren. v. 1. 3 "Vani autem et Ebionaei....Et propter hoc in fine non ex voluntate carnis, neque ex voluntate viri, sed ex placito Patris manus ejus vivum perfecerunt hominem, uti fiat Adam secundum imaginem et similitudinem Dei."

As regards "the Hands of God" (2998 (xxxvi) *a*) comp. Iren. iv. 1. Pref. "Homo...per manus ejus plasmatus est, hoc est, per Filium et Spiritum, quibus et dixit Faciamus hominem." Comp. Iren. iv. 20. 1, v. 6. 1, v. 28. 4.

§ 14. *Clement of Alexandria and Origen*

[**2998** (xlii)] No early Greek authority is alleged for the Irenæan version of Jn i. 13. But Clement of Alexandria apparently dissents from the opinion that Christ is referred to in the "man" and "the son of man" in the eighth Psalm (566), "And what else (ποτε), I ask, is the point in which man excels (διαφέρει) beasts, and again the angels of God are [still] wiser than man (τούτου τε αὖ οἱ τοῦ θεοῦ ἄγγελοι σοφώτεροι)? [What, I say, is the meaning of] 'Thou madest him a little lower than the angels'? For [people] do not accept this Scripture as meaning [ἐπὶ] the Lord—although He also bore flesh—but as meaning the perfect man and the gnostic, who in respect of the [brief] time and [frail] vesture [of mortality] is made inferior as compared with the angels[1]."

[**2998** (xliii)] Origen, commenting on Ps. viii. 4 "What is man (ἄνθρωπος) that thou rememberest him and the son of man (v. ἀνθρώπου) that thou visitest him?" says, "If he uses these words because he wonders (θαυμάζων) that the Lord remembers (?) *the man* (τοῦ ἀνθρώπου) and visits [*the*] *son of man* (κ. ὅτι ἐπισκέπτεται υἱὸν ἀνθρώπου) it is clear that the visitation is beneficent." By "if" he seems to mean "since." So far, he takes the passage as referring to man; and, like Clement, he touches on "knowledge" as being the characteristic of the "man" here mentioned[2]. But he adds "Paul

---

[1] [**2998** (xlii) *a*] Καὶ τί ποτ' ἐστὶν ᾧ διαφέρει θηρίων ἄνθρωπος τούτου τε αὖ οἱ τοῦ θεοῦ ἄγγελοι σοφώτεροι; "ἠλάττωσας αὐτὸν," φησί, "βραχύ τι παρ' ἀγγέλους"; οὐ γὰρ ἐπὶ τοῦ κυρίου ἐκδέχονται τὴν γραφήν—καί τοι κἀκεῖνος σάρκα ἔφερεν—ἐπὶ δὲ τοῦ τελείου γνωστικοῦ τῷ χρόνῳ καὶ τῷ ἐνδύματι ἐλαττουμένου παρὰ τοὺς ἀγγέλους. The punctuation in Klotz's text seems confused. Clark's transl. renders ἐκδέχονται "*some* interpret," but, if that had been the meaning, would not Clem. have inserted "some" or "some of our people," as in 499 ἢ γὰρ οὐχ οὕτως τινὲς τῶν ἡμετέρων... ἐκδέχονται?

[2] [**2998** (xliii) *a*] On Origen's "the man," substituted for the LXX "man," see **2998** (xliii) *c*. His remark about "visitation" he inserts

tells the Hebrews that these words (Ps. viii. 5) are uttered about Christ." Apparently he would say that the Psalmist meant "man in God's intention," "man as made in God's image and destined to be completely conformed to it"; but that the inward inspired meaning was "Christ." Accordingly, after warning his reader in reference to the words "thou hast crowned him with glory and honour," that there are two kinds of "honour," one of which results in "having no understanding[1]," he proceeds, "We then are first in the works of

---

because, he says, the word often means "punishing." He paraphrases "Thou hast made him a little lower than *angels*" thus, Καὶ αὐτὸς γάρ, σου γνῶσιν ἔχειν πεφυκώς, οὐκ ἀπολείπεται λίαν, (?) "For he, too [like the angels], having a nature created to have knowledge of thee, does not fall far behind [angels]." But if Origen had in view the Hebrew, as (see Field) is not improbable ("a little lower than *God*"), then we should have to add at the end, "[thee]," instead of "[angels]," and to suppose that σου is to be repeated after ἀπολείπεται. Or we might say that γνῶσιν ἔχειν πεφυκώς is treated as a compound verb governing the genit. so that σου is governed both by it and by ἀπολείπεται.

[1] [2998 (xliii) *b*] On Ps. viii. 5, Καὶ ἔσθ' ὅτε τιμῇ ἐστεφανωμένος τις οὐ συνῆκεν, ὡς ἐν τῷ (Ps. xlix. 12) "ἄνθρωπος ἐν τιμῇ ὤν, οὐ συνῆκεν." Οὐκ "ἐπὶ τὰ ἔργα σου" δὲ εἶπεν, ἅπερ οἶμαι εἶναι τὰ μὴ βλεπόμενα...πρῶτοι μὲν οὖν ἐν "ἔργοις" ἐσμὲν "χειρῶν" θεοῦ, τουτέστι "τοῖς [μὴ] βλεπομένοις." ταῦτα δὲ καὶ μετὰ τὴν ἐνανθρώπησιν νοεῖται τοῦ θεοῦ κ. σωτῆρος ἡμῶν... συνήγειρε γὰρ ἡμᾶς.... I have ventured to bracket μή so as to bring out an apparently intended contrast between "*the things that are seen*" (*i.e.* the visible bodies of men)—which St Paul calls (2 Cor. iv. 18) "*temporal*"—and "the things that are not seen," the invisible body, which St Paul calls eternal (*ib.*, and comp. 2 Cor. v. 1 "If the earthly house of our tabernacle be dissolved, we have a building from God, a house not made with hands, *eternal*, in the heavens"). Origen distinguishes between "the works of *God* (τὰ ἔργα σου)," which are invisible and eternal, and "the works of *God's hands* (χειρῶν θεοῦ)," which are visible and temporal. But the latter, he says, "are also—after the Incarnation—regarded [as the works] of our God and Saviour...for He hath raised us up with [Himself]." By "works of *God*" Origen means the ideals or patterns of things; by "works of *God's hands*" the visible Cosmos made by the Father the Son and the Spirit, when God said "Let *us* make." On "*hands*," signifying the Son and the Spirit, see **2998** (xxxvi) *a*.

the hands of God—that is, in '*the things that are* [? not] *seen.*' But these are also, after the Incarnation, conceived as the works of our God and Saviour. For with glory and honour hath *the Man* (ὁ ἄνθρωπος)[1] been crowned. For He (comp. Eph. ii. 6) 'raised us up with [Himself] and made us to sit with [Himself] in the supercelestial regions,' as the Apostle says."

[2998 (xliv)] In Origen's N.T. commentaries, the first point to note is that when he enumerates more than twenty of Christ's titles, he omits "*Son of man*[2]." Yet many of them resemble "Son of man" in being given to our Lord only by Himself. Why does he insert the many, yet omit the one—and the one most frequent in the Synoptists? The reason is

---

[1] [2998 (xliii) *c*] "The Man." We have seen above (2998 (xliii) *a*) that, in referring to the LXX "*man*," Origen used "*the man.*" Either would represent "mankind." It might be suggested that Origen preferred "the Man" because he had in view the saying of Pilate, peculiar to John, (xix. 5) ἰδοὺ ὁ ἄνθρωπος, "Behold *the Man*!"—in connexion with "the crown of thorns"; but Origen does not connect Ps. viii. 5 ("thou crownest him") with the "crown of thorns" in any of his works, so far as I have found.

[2998 (xliii) *d*] As regards "the beasts of the field" distinguished in this Psalm from the "cattle," Origen says, "Where *clean* sheep and oxen [are in question] he [*i.e.* the Psalmist] adds 'all.' But where he takes in also unclean things, as in the 'beasts of the field,' 'all' is not used. So too about the birds of the air and the fishes of the sea." This is worth noting in connexion with the Christian use of "beasts" or "serpents" to denote evil spirits, commonly called by Mark "*unclean* spirits." In the Parable of the Sower "*birds of the air*" means the agency of Satan destroying the good seed. And our Lord speaks of "catching *fish*" as a metaphor for "saving souls from the sea of sin."

[2] [2998 (xliv) *a*] *Comm. Johan.* tom. i. 24 foll. Light, Resurrection, Way, Truth, Life, Door, Shepherd, Teacher, Master, Son, Vine, Bread, First and Last, Sword, Servant, Lamb of God, Paraclete, Sanctification &c. "Son of man," though so often used by Christ about Himself, is very rarely used about Him by others. Note the exceptional use in Acts vii. 56 where Stephen beholds "the Son of man" in heaven (see 2998 (xxv)). Origen's commentary is lost on Mt. ix. 6 "But that ye may know that the Son of man hath authority on earth to forgive sins," and on many other interesting instances of "the Son of man."

suggested in the course of a long commentary on Mt. xvi. 27, "For *the Son of man* is destined to come in the glory of his Father." On this, he quotes Isaiah liii. 2—3 (LXX) "For we saw him, and he had no form or beauty, but his form was without honour, deficient beyond [the deficiency of] the sons of men...." The Son of man, he implies, is seen by two classes in two different ways. To "those who are being brought into [the Church] (τοῖς μὲν εἰσαγομένοις)" He has "no form"; but to the "full-grown (τελείοις)" He "comes in the glory of his father" (as Matthew says) since they would say (with John) (i. 14) "And we beheld"—not "*shall* behold" —"his glory, glory as of the only begotten of the Father...[1]." Afterwards (**2998** (xliv) *d*), distinguishing between Matthew (xvi. 27—28), Luke (ix. 27 (D)) and the parallel Mark (ix. 1) "the kingdom of God having come in power," he implies that the revelation of the Logos triumphing over obstacles is expressed by "the Son of man coming in his own

---

[1] [**2998** (xliv) *b*] Comm. Matth. tom. xii. 29 foll. (Lomm. iii. 176—7) (Is. liii. 2—3) εἴδομεν γὰρ...ἐκλεῖπον παρὰ τοὺς υἱοὺς τῶν ἀνθρώπων...ἐὰν δὲ δυνηθῆς...ὄψει τίνα τρόπον ὁ Λόγος τοῖς μὲν εἰσαγομένοις ἔχει δούλου μορφήν, ὥστ' ἂν εἰπεῖν αὐτούς· "εἴδομεν αὐτόν, καὶ οὐκ εἶχεν εἶδος οὐδὲ κάλλος," τοῖς δὲ τελείοις ἔρχεται "ἐν τῇ δόξῃ τοῦ πατρὸς αὐτοῦ," λέγουσιν ἂν τό "καὶ ἐθεασάμεθα τὴν δόξαν αὐτοῦ, δόξαν ὡς μονογενοῦς παρὰ πατρός, πλήρης χάριτος καὶ ἀληθείας. Καὶ γὰρ τοῖς τελείοις φαίνεται ἡ δόξα τοῦ Λόγου, καὶ τὸ μονογενὲς αὐτοῦ τῷ πατρὶ θεῷ, καὶ τὸ τῆς χάριτος πλῆρες, ὁμοίως δὲ καὶ τῆς ἀληθείας. In τελείοις, "full-grown," Origen is referring to 1 Cor. ii. 6.

The quotation is given at full length because it seems to shew that in Jn i. 14 Origen took πλήρης, if not in agreement with δόξαν, in some unusual absolute construction (contrary to the rendering given in *Johann. Gram.* **2180**). If Origen is right, John may have been influenced by a vernacular πλήρης nom.—used to mean "full measure" even when grammar requires accusative. Comp. Berl. Pap. 707. 15 (A.D. 151) ἀπέχομεν παρά σου...πλήρης, *ib.* 373. 13 (A.D. 298) ἥνπερ τιμὴν ἀπέσχεν ὁ πεπρακὼς παρὰ τοῦ πριαμένου πλήρης, comp. *ib.* 411. 12 (A.D. 314). But it is perh. more prob. that Origen himself, and some scribes of Jn, were thus influenced than that John should use such an idiom.

[**2998** (xliv) *c*] Origen expressly disclaims the desire to set aside the Second Coming (Lomm. iii. 178) ταῦτα δὲ λέγομεν οὐκ ἀθετοῦντες καὶ τὴν ἁπλούστερον νοουμένην δευτέραν ἐπιδημίαν τοῦ υἱοῦ τοῦ θεοῦ.

kingdom," but the higher revelation of the Logos bestowing its gifts is expressed by the addition of "the glory" to "the kingdom." This kingdom, he says, is spiritual. It is a kingdom of righteousness and "within" us[1]. Origen's view seems to have been that "the Son of man" was a title of Christ adapted for the gradual instruction of those who were "being brought into" a higher revelation, and who could not at once discern beneath the humiliation of Christ's humanity that "glory" which was revealed to "the full-grown."

[2998 (xlv)] Elsewhere, commenting on Mt. xxii. 1 foll. (Lomm. iv. 119 foll.) "The kingdom of heaven is likened unto *a man, a king*," Origen finds occasion to explain why Christ calls Himself "Son of man." "Some one before our time," he says (Lomm. iv. 124), contrasted Deut. i. 31 "the Lord thy God endured thy ways (Orig. ἐτροποφόρησέ σε) as if *a man* should endure the ways of his son," with Numb. xxiii. 19 "God is *not a man*[2]." After explaining the anthro-

---

[1] [2998 (xliv) d] Lomm. iii. 188—9 ὁ θεωρῶν κ. καταλαμβάνων τὴν τοῦ Λόγου ὑπεροχήν, λύοντος καὶ διελέγχοντος πάσας τὰς ὑπὲρ τῶν ψευδῶν μέν, ἐπαγγελλομένων δὲ ἀλήθειαν, πιθανότητας, βλέπει τὸν υἱὸν τοῦ ἀνθρώπου (κατὰ τὸν Ἰωάννου λόγον, τὸν Λόγον τοῦ Θεοῦ) (comp. Mt. xvi. 28) ἐρχόμενον ἐν τῇ ἰδίᾳ βασιλείᾳ· εἰ δὲ βλέποι ὁ τοιοῦτος τὸν Λόγον, οὐ μόνον λύοντα πᾶσαν τὴν τῶν ἐναντίων πιθανότητα, ἀλλὰ καὶ τὰ ἴδια τρανότατα παριστάντα, βλέποι ἂν αὐτοῦ πρὸς τῇ βασιλείᾳ καὶ (Lk. ix. 27 (D) τὴν δόξαν. Καὶ ὁ τοιοῦτός γε ἐν αὐτῷ βλέποι ἂν (Mk ix. 1) "τὴν τοῦ θεοῦ βασιλείαν ἐληλυθυῖαν ἐν δυνάμει." καὶ τοῦτο βλέποι ἄν, ὡς οὐδαμῶς ἔτι ὑπὸ ἁμαρτίας βασιλευόμενος, βασιλευούσης ἐν τῷ θνητῷ σώματι τῶν ἁμαρτανόντων, ἀλλ' ἀεὶ τεταγμένος ὑπὸ βασιλεῖ τῷ τῶν ὅλων θεῷ, οὗ ἡ βασιλεία δυνάμει μὲν "ἐντὸς ἡμῶν ἐστι," ἐνεργείᾳ δὲ (καὶ ὡς ὠνόμασεν ὁ Μάρκος, ἐν δυνάμει) καὶ οὐδαμῶς ἐν ἀσθενείᾳ ἐντὸς τῶν τελείων μόνων.

[2] [2998 (xlv) a] Origen here indicates that Numb. xxiii. 19 "God is not a man that he should lie nor *son of man* that he should repent" was quoted by an earlier writer than himself ("some one before our time") in discussions about God's nature. It is quoted by Irenæus but only in a fragment (24, Grabe p. 471) and the context simply contrasts God's truth with man's falsehood. On the anti-Christian use of this quotation see 2998 (xviii) foll. Origen's "some one before our time" is Philo, as is clear from his reference to Philo's "allegories of sacred laws." But Origen quotes Deut. and Numb. not as Philo does, but as LXX (see

pomorphic metaphors of O.T. he says that now, after this explanation of "*a man, a king*" (Lomm. iv. 128) "We can discover the reason why the Saviour has [in the Gospels] continuously named Himself 'Son of the [above-mentioned] man,' or 'Son of man' (υἱὸν τοῦ ἀνθρώπου ἢ υἱὸν ἀνθρώπου ἑαυτὸν ὠνομακέναι). He thereby shews that, as God, in His dispensations with men (ἀνθρώπους οἰκονομῶν), is called Man in the language of (ὡς ἐν) parables—yes and perhaps in a certain sense [actually] becomes Man—so also the Saviour... in accordance with the dispensation of Him who though in parables called Man is really God, becomes Son of Man (οὕτως καὶ ὁ Σωτήρ...γίνεται—κατ' οἰκονομίαν τοῦ ἐν παραβολαῖς λεγομένου ἀνθρώπου, ὄντος δὲ θεοῦ—υἱὸς ἀνθρώπου)...." Hence, says Origen, "We *ought not to seek some particular man and to say that the Saviour is that man's son.* But we ought to take our stand on the conception of God, and on the parables that say He is Man (λεγουσῶν αὐτὸν εἶναι ἄνθρωπον), and thus intelligently to take in His meaning when He calls Himself Son of the Man (συνετῶς ἀκούειν αὐτοῦ λέγοντος ἑαυτὸν υἱὸν τοῦ ἀνθρώπου)[1]."

2998 (iv) *b—d*). He contrasts Philo's use of "one saying (ἑνὶ μὲν ῥητῷ)" about the human aspect of God (*i.e.* Deut.), and "one (ἑνὶ δέ) [saying]" about the non-human aspect of God (*i.e.* Numb.), with the "abundance of examples in the gospels (ἡμεῖς δὲ πολλὴν ἀφθονίαν ἔχομεν ἀπὸ τῶν εὐαγγελίων περὶ τοῦ θεοῦ παραδειγμάτων)."

[1] [**2998** (xlv) *b*] It may be urged that Origen does not quite meet the difficulty. For Christ is represented as calling Himself ὁ υἱὸς τοῦ ἀνθρώπου, with a twofold use of the article. Origen explains υἱὸς ἀνθρώπου and υἱὸς τοῦ ἀνθρώπου, but not the Gospel phrase. Perhaps he omits the article because the phrase is used predicatively. Thus, in the context, he says υἱὸς ὢν τοῦ θεοῦ, not ὁ υἱός, and so υἱὸς τῆς ἀγάπης αὐτοῦ, and εἰκὼν τοῦ θεοῦ —all predicative. Comp. Jn v. 27 "He hath given authority to him to do judgment because he is *man's son* (ὅτι υἱὸς ἀνθρώπου ἐστίν)," and x. 36 "because I said *I am God's son* (ὅτι εἶπον, Υἱὸς τοῦ θεοῦ εἰμί)," and Heb. i. 3 ὢν ἀπαύγασμα τῆς δόξης κ. χαρακτὴρ τῆς ὑποστάσεως αὐτοῦ.

§ 15. *Conclusion*

[**2998** (xlvi)] The use of the term "Son of Man" in the gospels has not been discussed in this Appendix. That is reserved for *The Fourfold Gospel,* which will take the instances in Mark's order and compare them with Synoptic and Johannine parallels. The present discussion is intended to facilitate the comparison by collecting and classifying facts, bearing on the title, from Hebrew, Jewish, and early post-Christian writings. Looking forward from Hebrew and Jewish traditions, we ought to be prepared to find the expression of what is purest and noblest in them when we come to our Lord's teaching in the gospels. Looking backward from the Acts, the Apocalypse, Ignatius, the Epistle of Barnabas, Justin Martyr, Irenæus and Tertullian, we ought to be prepared to find in the gospels themselves divergences indicative of early obscurities and misunderstandings. Noting how Origen strives to make matters clear and to bring out what—on our hypothesis—was the original and spiritual significance of the title, we shall not be surprised if we find traces of the same effort apparent in the Fourth Gospel.

[**2998** (xlvii)] Provisionally we are justified in taking—only as a working hypothesis, but with strong claims to careful consideration—the view suggested by the consensus of Ezekiel, Daniel, the Psalms, the Apocalypse, and the Fourth Gospel, that "the Son of Man" implied man in his physical weakness, man seemingly inferior to the beasts of the field, man represented by "the babes and sucklings" on whom "the mighty" look down with contempt. This "man," or this "son of man," the Psalmist regards as but "a little lower than God," and destined to have lordship over the beasts.

The dominion of the human over the non-human living creature is avowed in Genesis (i. 26—8) as part of God's creative intention along with His intention to make man in His own "image" and according to His own "likeness." If we remember that the Hebrew for the *four* "*living creatures* (ζῶα)" in Ezekiel is the same as that for the *four* "*wild beasts* (θηρία)" in Daniel (**2998** (xxxiii) *a*), and is mostly rendered in LXX by θηρίον which repeatedly means "beast" in Revelation, we shall realise more clearly how the Bible, from the beginning to the end, suggests that "man" is bound to control the "beast" in a spiritual as well as in a literal sense, and that "trampling on the lion, the adder, and the scorpion" could hardly fail to convey to spiritually minded Jews the notion of subjugating in one's own heart the evil spirits of ferocity and malignity. As Christ actually goes back to Genesis (Mk x. 6, Mt. xix. 4) to define the relation between man and woman, so it is antecedently probable that He would go back to Genesis, as interpreted by the Psalms and Prophets, in order to inculcate the right relation between Man and God.

[**2998** (xlviii)] Christ's view of the "son of man," and even of the "suckling," as being, not (so to speak) promoted unexpectedly and paradoxically to be Son of God, but destined from the beginning to be His Son and His Glory, may help to explain many things in the gospels. For example, in Jn ix. 35 "Believest thou in the Son of man?" very many authorities alter "man" to God. But they are probably in error, not having understood the Johannine conception (appreciated by Origen above, **2998** (xlv)) that God is, in a sense, Man, that the "Son of Man" is "Son of God," and that the Son of Man (Jn iii. 13) "descended out of heaven."

[**2998** (xlix)] Christ's doctrine about "the Son of man" may be illustrated by His doctrine about the "*babes and sucklings*" mentioned in the same Psalm. And both may be illustrated by Isaiah's doctrine about the Suffering Servant who is described by Aquila and Theodotion as "growing up like a *suckling* before Jehovah," and as "despised and rejected[1]." The word "suckling" is used by the Jews to mean a "pupil" or beginner. No teacher was to teach "more than twenty-five sucklings[2]." Our Lord was addressing a professional class of Teachers of the Law, some of whom talked (Rom. ii. 19—20) about being "guides to the blind," "trainers of fools," "teachers of babes." In a spirit of pedantry, some of them despised these "babes," and those whom they called "the people of the earth," and "the sons of men," and every "son of man"—so far as the term represented mere humanity —while, all the time, they themselves were "blind" and "fools," far indeed below the "babes." The one thing they needed (according to Christ's doctrine) was to become "babes," and to "believe in the Son of man." It cannot be matter for surprise that, among this class, Christ's doctrines about "babes" and about the Son of man sounded paradoxical and absurd. They refused to learn from "the suckling." As to "the Son of man," they understood it in the popular sense,

---

[1] [2998 (xlix) a] Is. liii. 2 (R.V.) "He grew up before him as a *tender plant* (יוֹנֵק)." Gesen. 413 gives abundant instances of יוֹנֵק as subst. "suckling," but no instance, except this, of its use as "sucker," *i.e.* sapling. Aq. has τιθηνιζόμενον (s. τι[τ]θιζόμενον), Theod. θηλάζον. The LXX completely misunderstands the sentence, thus, "We made announcement *as a little child* (παιδίον) in his presence (ἀνηγγείλαμεν ὡς παιδίον ἐναντίον αὐτοῦ)." But it agrees with Aq. and Theod. in giving יוֹנֵק the meaning that it has invariably in the rest of O.T. And it makes excellent sense. The parallelism to "as a root out of a dry ground" indicates that the despised "suckling" had everything against it. No doubt there is a play on the meaning of "suckling," יוֹנֵק, as compared with יוֹנֶקֶת which freq. means (Gesen. 413 b) "sucker." But the frequency of the latter makes it difficult to believe that Isaiah, here alone, used the former for the latter. Origen (*Comm. Rom.* viii. 5, Lomm. vii. 219, and comp. *Cels.* vi. 75) has some difficulty in deciding in whose person "we made announcement" is uttered, but he follows the LXX in reading παιδίον.

[2] [2998 (xlix) b] Levy ii. 247 b. Targ. on Cant. viii. 1 represents the Jews as saying to the Messiah, "Come, be our Brother, and let us go up to Jerusalem and suck with thee the doctrine of the Law, as the infant sucks the mother's breast." Schöttg. on 1 Pet. ii. 2 gives abundant instances of "suckling" used in the rabbinical sense.

and in Daniel's sense; but in Christ's sense it probably drew the same question from them as from the multitude (Jn xii. 34), "Who is this Son of man?"

[2998 (1)] So, too, in many of the Christian Churches, there would be a natural tendency to smooth the edges of Christ's words, sometimes to literalise, sometimes to de-orientalise them, sometimes to make them more definite—often resulting in making them less spiritual. This would affect traditions of His teaching on all the deepest subjects, such as (1) "bearing the yoke" or "taking up the cross," (2) "bearing" or "forgiving" sins, (3) "becoming a babe[1],"

---

[1] [2998 (1) *a*] The Pauline warning against (1 Cor. xiv. 20) "becoming little children in mind," and against continuing to live on (1 Cor. iii. 2) "*milk*," should be contrasted with 1 Pet. ii. 2, "as newborn babes desire the sincere *milk* of the word," where there is not the least suggestion that there is to be an advance to "meat." Both utterances were (no doubt) needed. The readers of the Pauline epistle may have literalised Christ's sayings about "babes" and "sucklings" and needed a warning not to reduce them to an absurdity. The readers of the Petrine epistle seemed to the writer to need a caution never to forget that they must be Christ's "newborn babes."

[2998 (1) *b*] The connexion between "sucklings" and "son of man," perceived by the Psalmist, is very difficult for modern readers to trace in the gospels. Yet it extends all through them, ramifying into many verbally divergent doctrines about the necessity of "receiving a little child" in the name of the Son of Man, or "becoming as little children," or "being born from above," or about "the Son" being "able to do nothing except that which he sees the Father doing." No doubt, the Psalmist, when he sang of "the son of man," did not lay any great stress on "son." He simply placed "sucklings" and "sons of men"—the ordinary specimens of humanity, weak in comparison with the beasts of the field—on one and the same level. "What are they that God should regard them?" But our Lord—who answers this question by Himself becoming, as Origen says (Lomm. iii. 341—2), a babe or suckling—replies, in effect, "This son of man, this little one, this babe or suckling, whom the great men of this world despise, is in truth God's greatest glory, because his face is always turned towards the Father in heaven receiving the light reflected from His face."

[2998 (1) *c*] There is no passage in which this connexion is so strangely half-revealed—this link between the doctrine of "sonship" and the

and (4) " believing in," or accepting the " authority " of, " the Son of man." In the last of these doctrines we have endeavoured to trace the gradual corruption of Christ's meaning, brought about by two causes (both compatible with honesty), 1st, by the love of definiteness, resulting in the desire to answer the question " son of what human being ? " 2nd, by the desire to elicit such a meaning as would magnify Christ and shew that He was something more than " a mere

---

doctrine of "babes," and this assumption that the "babes" are God's "glory," which He has "set" above, or on, "the heavens"—as in Christ's exultation over the revelation to babes (Mt. xi. 25—7, and sim. Lk. x. 21—2) (R. V.) " I thank thee, O Father, Lord of heaven and earth, that thou didst hide these things from the wise and understanding, and didst reveal them unto babes : yea, Father ; for so it was wellpleasing in thy sight. All things have been delivered unto me of my Father : and no one knoweth the Son, save the Father ; neither doth any know the Father, save the Son, and he to whomsoever the Son willeth to reveal [him]."

[2998 (1) *d*] What is the meaning of, " No one knoweth the Son save the Father"? It means that the true nature of the Son of Man, as designed in the mind of God, is known only to God, who is also (2998 (xlv)) Man. The context implies that the two Divine Powers, the Father and the Son, cannot be known directly from either One, but must be known indirectly through the Spirit that is (so to speak) between the Two. It also implies that none can receive this Spirit unless they become "babes."

[2998 (1) *e*] Is there here—in these parallel passages of Matthew and Luke—any allusion to the eighth Psalm with its combination of " *babes*," and " *glory*," and " *heaven*," and " *beasts of the field* " over whom the "son of man" is to rule, all things being " *subjected* " to him ? None whatever in Matthew. But there may be in Luke. Luke tells us that just before this utterance of the Lord, the Seventy returned, exclaiming, "Even the devils are *subjected* to us." Christ replies, " I have given you authority to trample on *serpents and scorpions*." But they are not to boast of this. Their joy is to be that their "names are *written in the heavens*." Then the Saviour exults in this revelation to His " *babes*," who are exalted above "the wise and understanding." Finally He claims for Himself universal authority : "All things have been delivered to me by my Father." These may be mere coincidences or parallelisms of thought between Luke's Gospel and the Psalm, but they are at least worth noting.

man." The probable influence of these two motives in evangelists and scribes, as well as the probability of an original doctrine of the highest and purest spirituality taught by Christ Himself, must be taken continually into account, when we come to a detailed examination of Christ's utterances about "the Son of man" in *The Fourfold Gospel*.

§ 16. *Addition on the "Similitudes of Enoch"*

[2998 (li)] The evidence from the *Similitudes* (*Enoch*, ch. 37—71) is weakened by the uncertainty as to their date[1], by the certainty of interpolations, and by the possi-

---

[1] [2998 (li) *a*] "Uncertainty as to their date." Comp. Dalman p. 243 "It cannot be proved that they [*i.e.* the *Similitudes*] originate from a pre-Christian period." The *Similitudes* constitute one of several documents embedded in what is called *The Book of Enoch* (see *Enoch* ed. Charles pp. 24—33). The following paragraphs will occasionally refer to other parts of *Enoch*, besides the *Similitudes*. Dr Charles (pp. 107—8), for his theory of the pre-Christian date of the *Similitudes*, relies on three passages.

(1) *En.* 38 "Then will the kings and the mighty perish and be given into the hand of the righteous and holy." "The kings etc.," he says (*ad loc.*), are "decidedly" indicated to be "native rulers and Sadducees," *i.e.* (p. 108) "the later Maccabean princes and their Sadducean supporters."

(2) *En.* 47 "And in those days the prayer of the righteous and the blood of the righteous will have ascended from the earth before the Lord of Spirits. In those days will the holy ones who dwell above in the heavens ...supplicate...and bless the name of the Lord of Spirits on account of the blood of the righteous which has been shed, and the prayer of the righteous, that it may not be in vain before the Lord of Spirits, that judgment may be done unto them, and that they may not have to suffer for ever. And in those days I saw the Head of Days when He had seated Himself on the throne of His glory....And the hearts of the holy were filled with joy...and the blood of the righteous was required before the Lord of Spirits."

(3) *En.* 56 "And in those days will the *angels* return and hurl themselves upon the East, upon the *Parthians* and Medes, to stir up the kings ...that they may break forth as lions....And they will march up to, and tread under foot, the land of His elect ones...."

Dr Charles considers (3) to be an interpolation from a document

bility of their having received a partial and inconsistent revision. They open with a prediction (*En.* 38) that "*the Righteous One*" will "appear before the eyes of the *elect righteous*...and light will appear to the *righteous and the elect* who dwell on the earth...and when the secrets of *the righteous* shall be revealed, then will the sinners be judged...and from that time those who possess the earth will no longer be powerful and exalted." This vision of what will happen "on the earth" is succeeded by a vision in which Enoch is transported to heaven (*En.* 39) "I saw...the mansions of the holy ...and the *Elect One of righteousness and of faith,* and how *righteousness* shall prevail in his days...and I saw his dwelling-place under the wings of the Lord of Spirits." We are afterwards told abruptly that (*En.* 42) Wisdom found no place on earth and returned to heaven. As for those who (*En.* 45) "deny the name of the dwelling of the holy ones and the Lord of Spirits," they will be punished, and "mine Elect One

---

earlier than 64 B.C. depicting (p. 148) "the last struggle of the heathen powers against the Messianic kingdom established in Jerusalem."

[2998 (li) *b*] But, as to (3), comp. Rev. ix. 14 " Loose the four *angels* that are bound at the great river Euphrates," and Swete's note as to "the greatly dreaded resources of the *Parthian Empire*," and Rev. xvi. 12 "He poured out his bowl on the...river Euphrates...that the way of *the kings* that [come] *from the sun-rising* might be prepared." These passages indicate that a fear of "*the Parthians*" might be felt in the first century A.D. And, as to (1) and (2), indicating oppression by "native rulers," comp. Mt. xxiii. 35, Lk. xi. 50, Jas. v. 1—6, Rev. vi. 10, which—like abundant passages in the Psalms and the Prophets—indicate that there were many periods in Jewish history when the poor and pious might complain of oppression at the hands of the rulers and the rich. There is nothing in (1) or (2) that seems to attach the utterances to a period B.C., or to any particular "kings" or "rulers." For example, *En.* 38 mentions "*the kings and the mighty*" just after "*those who possess the earth*." As in Jas. v. 1—6, the outburst is against the rich, as much as against the rulers. Any nation might call an extortioner in some sense a "murderer," especially a nation whose laws forbade usury, and enjoined periodic remission of debts, and declared that to take a poor man's millstone as security for debt was to "take life in pledge" (Deut. xxiv. 6).

will sit on the throne of glory" and judge men's deeds; "and on that day I will cause mine Elect One to dwell among them and I will transform the heaven...and I will transform the earth...and cause mine elect ones to dwell upon it."

[**2998** (lii)] Up to this time no mention has been made of the *nature* of the Righteous or Elect One—whether divine, angelic, or human. But Enoch now proceeds to develop the view that He is, in one aspect, *a human being*, thus: (*En.* 46) " And there [*i.e.* in heaven] I saw One who had a head of days, and His head was like wool; and with Him was *another being whose countenance had the appearance of a man, and his face was full of graciousness, like one of the holy angels.* And I asked the angel, who went with me and showed me all the hidden things, concerning *that Son of Man*, who he was, and whence he was, and why he went with the Head of Days?" The answer is, " This *is the Son of Man who hath righteousness, with whom dwelleth righteousness*, and who revealeth all the treasures of that which is hidden, because the Lord hath *chosen* him....And *this Son of Man* whom thou hast seen will arouse the kings and the mighty ones...and loosen the reins of the strong and grind to powder the teeth of the sinners."

[**2998** (liii)] Here the first sentence is obviously from Daniel, and it is from Daniel (with perhaps a touch of Ezekiel) that the writer borrows " the appearance of a man." But what follows is consistent with the view that "*that Son of man*" has, at first, no technical meaning, but means "that human being yonder." This would be the natural meaning in Hebrew and Aramaic. If that is the meaning here, Enoch says, in effect, " How comes it to pass that I see *yonder human being—a mere man, if I may believe my eyes—full of graciousness like that of an angel,* seated on the throne of God?"

Then the reply is, in effect, " True, this figure is human; but it is a particular form of humanity. It is one of the sons of men, but '*that* [*particular*] *Son of Man who hath righteousness.*'" After describing (*En.* 48) "a fountain of righteousness"

—from which "the thirsty drank," and "had their dwellings with the righteous and holy and elect"—Enoch continues, "And at that hour that Son of Man was named in the presence of the Lord of Spirits....And before the sun and the signs were created...his name was named before the Lord of Spirits. He will be a staff to the righteous...and he will be the light of the Gentiles....And for this reason has he been chosen and hidden before Him before the creation of the world and for evermore....And the wisdom of the Lord of Spirits hath revealed him to the holy and righteous....And... the kings of the earth and the strong...will fall and not rise again...for they have denied the Lord of Spirits and *His Anointed* [i.e. *His Christ*]."

[**2998** (liv)] There is nothing in all this to indicate that the writer or editor presents to his readers "*the* Son of man" as a Being already defined in their minds, and as though they were familiar with the term as a technical title in the Messianic sense, or in any sense. The ideal that the writer has before him seems to be "the Righteous One," and, next to that, "the Elect One." These two titles he has bestowed on one supernatural and celestial Person round whom all the righteous and elect are to be concentrated and in whom they are to find Redemption and life. This Being has been (*En.* 48) "chosen (or, elected) from the creation of the world" and "hidden" in heaven, but he is apparently to dwell on earth "with the elect." Is he God or Angel or Man? That question is answered (*En.* 46) in the course of a vision of One, on the throne of God, whose "countenance had the appearance of a man." Enoch, in astonishment, repeats, in effect, a question like the last part of the Psalmist's question, "What is *the Son of man* that thou honourest him?" There is no indication whatever that "*asked concerning that Son of man*" means "asked concerning *the Son of man* mentioned *by Daniel*," or "concerning *the Messiah.*" The meaning appears to be, "Among all the sons of men, who is the one that is thus honoured? Whence did he come? Why has he a place by the side of God?" When this "son of man" has been defined as "the son of man who has righteousness," then, but not till then, is he regularly spoken of as "that (or the) son of man[1]."

Whence did the writer of the *Similitudes* derive his ideal of "the Righteous One"? And what bearing has it on the use of "righteous" in N.T.? These questions there is no space to discuss: but a few notes are given below on points to which it may be convenient to refer in *The Fourfold Gospel*[2].

---

[1] [2998 (liv) *a*] The phrase, thus used as a title, might be printed with capital initials, and Dr Charles prints it Son of Man (I think) almost always. I have printed it similarly when quoting from him, but not always in other cases.

Most frequently, the expression is "*that* Son of Man" (once "*this*"), especially perhaps where the demonstrative is emphatic, xlvi. 2 "I asked concerning *that* S. of M.," *ib.* 4 "And *this* S. of M. whom thou hast seen," xlviii. 2 "And at that hour *that* (*i.e.* ille) S. of M. was named in the presence of the Lord of Spirits," etc. "*The* S. of M." is not used absolutely (s. Dalm. *Words* p. 243) till lxii. 7 (Dalm. "62[72]" by error) (but it is naturally used in xlvi. 3 "the S. of M. who hath righteousness" (where emphasis is thrown on the last words) and in lxxi. 14 "Thou art the S. of M. (so Charles in p. 184 n., but "s. of m." in p. 185 txt) who art born for righteousness").

[2998 (liv) *b*] Similarly in the Syr. of 2 Esdr. xiii. 1 foll., "son of man" is introduced (Dalman, *Words* p. 244) in the same way as in the *Similitudes*, namely, 1st, "as the likeness of a son of man" (om. in Lat. by error) and then *ib.* 3 "*ille* homo" (Syr. "*that* son of man"), *ib.* 5 "homo (Syr. "son of man") qui ascenderat de mari," *ib.* 12 "ipse homo" (Syr. "*that* son of man"). Later on, *ib.* 25, 51, comp. 33, it is "*vir* (not "homo," Syr. also "vir") ascendens de corde maris." Here, as in the *Similitudes*, the writer first introduces *a son of man* in mysterious surroundings and then goes on to speak of *that son of man* as the Redeemer.

[2] [2998 (liv) *c*] "*The righteous* [*one*]," as צדיק, occurs only in Exod. ix. 27, Deut. xxv. 1, Ezek. xviii. 20, xxxiii. 12, Hab. i. 4, Eccles. iii. 17—where "unrighteous" is expressed in context—and in Is. lvii. 1 "The righteous perisheth and no man layeth to heart...none considering that

the righteous is taken away from the evil to come." Even in this last passage there is an implied antithesis: "*The unrighteous man* does not realise God's mysterious wisdom when He causes *the righteous man* to die." Comp. *Wisd.* iii. 2 "In the sight of the unwise they [*i.e.* the righteous (pl.)] seemed to die," and *Wisd.* iv. 7—10 "Though *a righteous* [*man*] be prevented with death, yet shall he be in rest....Wisdom is the gray hair...and an unspotted life is old age. He pleased God and was beloved of Him, so that *living among sinners* he was translated (μετετέθη)." The writer is here alluding to the patriarch Enoch, who (Gen. v. 22, 24 LXX) "pleased God" (Heb. "walked with God") and (LXX) "God translated him"; and he implies that this is true of any "righteous man" dying early. Noah however—not Enoch—is the first man called "righteous" in Scripture. Philo (ii. 3—5) followed by Origen (Lomm. vi. 330) implies that Enoch *did not please God till after he "begat Methuselah."* Then, they say, he *repented*. According to this view, Enoch would be "a righteous man that needed repentance," Noah "a righteous man that did not need repentance." Sir. xliv. 16, in LXX, says, "Enoch pleased the Lord and was translated, *an example of repentance* to the generations." The Heb. has, "Enoch was found perfect and walked with the Lord *and was taken, a sign* of knowledge to all generations." This is an instance of Heb. confusion. Gen. v. 24 says "*For* God *took him* (כי לקח אתו)." The MS. of Sir. has ויני לקח אות, shewing that the writer confused אתו "*him*" with אות "*sign*" and then adapted the context to make sense.

[2998] (liv) *d*] Possibly Philo and Origen may have been aware of traditions based on a corruption of this kind. In any case, Gen. v. 21—31 raises an interesting question as to the patriarchs that preceded Noah. Did they all escape the deluge or not? It will be found that Lamech, Noah's father, died five years before the deluge; that Methuselah, Noah's grandfather, died in the actual year of the deluge; and that Enoch did not die at all, because God "took him." Presumably Methuselah died a natural death; for the refrain, "and he died," which is applied (Gen. v. 5, 8, 11) to all the patriarchs whose genealogy is given, is applied also to him without change. And *Beresh. R.* ad loc. takes this view, containing a tradition that the Lord delayed the deluge till the death of Methuselah. But the Scripture leaves it doubtful. And the doubt makes Enoch's "translation" all the more intelligible from the point of view indicated in *Wisdom* and Philo. Enoch begot Methuselah while still in sin. Then he repented. What followed? Methuselah lived on to be a proverb for old age. But he only just escaped, if he did escape, being destroyed by the deluge. Enoch died early—but he was taken by the Lord. *Wisdom* says (iv. 11) it was "lest wickedness should alter his understanding." This was also the Rabbinical doctrine, taught however with considerable variations (see *Beresh. R.* on Gen. v. 24, and Kimchi's commentary). Origen (Lomm. vi. 330, and sim. on Gen. v. 22) says "Metusalem...interpretatur emissio mortis."

(liv) *e—j* "THE RIGHTEOUS ONE"

[2998 (liv) *e*] "The righteous one," in N.T., occurs mostly in quotations. Of these, Rom. i. 17, Gal. iii. 11, Heb. x. 38 (with [μου]) are from Hab. ii. 4 "His soul...is *not upright*...but *the righteous* [*one*]...," and 1 Pet. iv. 18 "if *the righteous* [*one*]...where...*the godless* [*one*] *and the sinner?*" from Prov. xi. 31. In the original of these, "the righteous [one]" is opposed to "the guilty [one]"; so, in English, we might use "the accused (sing.)," implying antithesis to "the accuser." Comp. Exod. ix. 27 "the Lord is *the righteous* [*one*], and I and my people are *the guilty* [*ones*]," and Deut. xxv. 1 "If there be a controversy among men...and [the judges] judge them, then they shall pronounce righteous *the righteous* [*one*] and pronounce guilty *the guilty* [*one*]"—where the former passage assumes what the latter expresses, that there are two parties to a dispute, and that one is "*the* right," the other "*the* wrong." In such antitheses, "*the* righteous" may not be conspicuously "righteous," but merely "the righteous one of the two." In Gen. xviii. 25 "righteous [one]" with "guilty [one]," without article, is followed by "*the* righteous [one] as *the* guilty [one]" (Heb. and Gk). In 2 Pet. ii. 7—8 δίκαιον Λώτ ...[ὁ] δίκαιος, the adj. may contain an allusion to Gen. xviii. 25, implying that Lot, though not a very good specimen of righteousness, was at all events "*the* righteous man" in Sodom. Even concerning Noah, some Rabbis gave a similar interpretation to Gen. vi. 9 "righteous...perfect in his generation" (*i.e.* considering what his generation was, s. *Beresh R.* ad loc.).

[2998 (liv) *f*] "The righteous [one]," in N.T., apart from quotations, occurs in Mt. xxiii. 35 "Abel *the righteous*" as a type of persecuted prophets. Heb. xi. 4 and 1 Jn iii. 12 both use "*righteous*" in connexion with Abel or Abel's works, and both also introduce a comparison between him and Cain. Taken together, the three passages indicate that "the righteous" in Mt. xxiii. 35, somewhat like "the martyr," means "*the righteous*, as is often the case, persecuted by *the unrighteous*." Jas. v. 6 "Ye have condemned, ye have murdered, *the righteous* [*one*]"—when read with the next words, "he resisteth you not"—seems to mean "Ye are continually pronouncing sentence in favour of *the guilty oppressor* [such as Ahab] against *the righteous* [i.e. *the innocent*, such as Naboth]." In Rev. xxii. 11 "he that is unrighteous...he that is righteous" is antithetical.

1 Jn ii. 1 (R.V.) "We have an Advocate...*Jesus Christ the righteous* ('I. X. δίκαιον)" is not a correct translation. Δίκαιον is predicative; and the meaning seems to be, "Jesus Christ, righteous [yet Advocate for us who are unrighteous]." It is strange that Origen, who quotes this text

about a dozen times, never explains the force of δίκαιον. Westcott's translation is "being as he is righteous." This is not clear to me.

"The Righteous [one]," in Acts, denotes Christ thrice, namely, in public utterances of Peter and Stephen and in a private utterance of Ananias to Saul. First, Peter says to the Jews (Acts iii. 13—15) "The God of our fathers hath glorified his *Servant* Jesus whom ye *delivered up* ...ye denied *the Holy and Righteous One*, and asked for a murderer to be granted unto you, and killed the Prince of life." There is antithesis here (as above) but the primary reference is not to any antithesis between "the guiltless" and "the guilty" but to God's "*righteous servant*" mentioned in Isaiah (Is. liii. 11) who was to be "*delivered up*" (ib. liii. 12 (LXX)). This is proved by (1) the verbal coincidences, (2) the closely following sentence (Acts iii. 18) "the things which God foreshewed by *the mouth of all the prophets, that his Christ should suffer*, he thus fulfilled," (3) the repeated use of παῖς, "*servant*," applied to Christ in the following context (Acts iii. 26, iv. 27, 30) and in Mt. xii. 18 (from Is. xlii. 1), but nowhere else in N.T., and characteristic of Isaiah both when applied to individuals and when used absolutely (Is. xliii. 10, lii. 13, liii. 11). The same meaning—namely, "the righteous servant" predicted by Isaiah—is probably intended in Stephen's speech (Acts vii. 52) "Which of the prophets did not your fathers persecute? And they slew those that *announced beforehand the coming of the Righteous One*—of whom now ye have become betrayers and murderers." The reference is less clear in the utterance of Ananias to Saul (Acts xxii. 14) "The God of our fathers hath appointed thee to know his will and to see the Righteous One"; but "his will" probably means God's will and purpose about His "righteous servant" (Is. liii. 11—12).

In Acts iii. 14, 26, iv. 27, 30, R.V. marg. has "Child" (comp. Lightf. on Clem. Cor. 59): "This designation [*i.e.* παῖς for Christ] is taken originally from Is. xlii. 1 quoted in Matt. xii. 18...where παῖς is 'servant, minister' (עבד). Comp. Acts iii. 13, 26, iv. 27, 30. But the higher sense of υἱός was soon imported into the ambiguous word παῖς." Later writers (*ib.*) sometimes defined παῖς (erroneously) as "son" by adding μονογενής or ἀγαπητός. Tertullian (*Marc.* iv. 22) renders Is. l. 10 "servant," παιδός, by "filii." Perhaps "Righteous One" may have arisen out of "Righteous servant," from a desire to dispense with the ambiguous παῖς.

[2998 (liv) *g*] "The Righteous" in *Aboth* i. 2, "Simon the Righteous" (commonly called "Simon the Just") was probably a title of honour like "Aristides the Just." So in Euseb. ii. 23. 15 (quoting Hegesippus), the Jews cry out concerning James—who was called "righteous"—"Even the *Righteous [one]* has gone astray." The Jews did not intend to say "the righteous one predicted by the prophets." Yet Hegesippus (*ib.*) proceeds, "And they fulfilled the Scripture in Isaiah iii. 10 (LXX), 'Let us slay (LXX bind) *the righteous one* because he is not for our turn'" (where

Heb. has " Say ye of *the righteous* [*one*] that [it shall be] well [with him]; for they [*i.e.* all the righteous] shall eat the fruit of their doings"). Comp. *Wisd.* ii. 10 foll. " Let us oppress a poor righteous man; let us not spare a widow...let us lie in wait for *the righteous* [*man*], because he is not for our turn....He pronounceth the end of the righteous (pl.) to be blessed and maketh his boast that God is his Father....If *the righteous* [*man*] be the son of God, He will help him....Let us condemn him with a shameful death...." The context indicates that "the righteous" observer of the Law is contrasted with open or secret apostates from the Law. These are "the unrighteous," and persecute "*the righteous one*," whose very existence is a reproach to them. Origen (Lomm. ix. 59, *Exod. Hom.* vi. 1) quotes *Wisd.* ii. 20 as predicting Christ's condemnation, and it is hardly surprising that other Fathers do the same. Yet the passage may be explained, without hypothesis of interpolation, from pre-Christian Jewish history.

[2998 (liv) *h*] No single and special "righteous" man is mentioned in *Wisdom*. But the book teaches us that, up to the time of the Exodus, the Wisdom of God acted through the Patriarchs. None are mentioned by name. But in the descriptions of them (x. 4—20) five are called "righteous." These five are brought safe by Wisdom, through dangers, trials, or conflicts—Noah, Abraham, Lot, Jacob, Joseph. The end is that (x. 20) " righteous ones," *i.e.* Israel, made spoil of " impious ones," *i.e.* Egypt. The article distinguishes the two "righteous ones" with whom covenants were made. Wisdom " piloted *the righteous one* (τὸν δίκαιον) on a frail tree," *i.e.* Noah on the Ark. Wisdom " found *the righteous one* (τὸν δίκαιον)," *i.e.* Abraham. Philo (ii. 6) commenting on Gen. vi. 9 ἄνθρωπος δίκαιος—the first use of "righteous" in the Bible—says that Noah is here called "man" not in a general way but "preeminently (κατ' ἐξοχήν)" and that he is also called "righteous" because "an unrighteous man is really a man-shaped beast." This saying illustrates the contrast in Daniel and Revelation between the Son of man and the beasts, or the Beast. The fourth book of Esdras says of Noah that from him came "all righteous ones" (iii. 11 " dereliquisti autem unum ex his Noë cum domo sua, et ex eo justos omnes"). It briefly mentions Abraham, Isaac and Jacob, but does not call any of them "righteous."

A Noah-Apocalypse inserted in the *Similitudes* (*En.* 65—9) represents Enoch as saying to Noah (*En.* 65) " Thou art pure and guiltless of this reproach concerning the secrets," and God as saying (*En.* 67) " Thy lot has come up before me, a lot without blame, a lot of love and uprightness." Also, from Noah's seed there is to spring (*En.* 65) " a fountain of the righteous and holy without number for ever." But he is not called " the Righteous One."

[2998 (liv) *i*] There are indications that the Hebrew word *Tsaddîk*, "righteous," went out of fashion, so to speak, and then became fashion-

[2998 (lv)] The occasional difficulty of distinguishing in the gospels between "the Son of Man" when used individually and when used collectively may be illustrated by several apparently collective uses of "the righteous one" in *Enoch*[1]

able again. Onkelos (see Brederek's *Concordance*) in the first century habitually renders צדיק by זכי "pure." He never uses צדיק (except in his paraphrase of Gen. xlix. 11). Levy *Ch.* gives abundant instances of צדיק in the later Targums. A natural explanation is, that in the first century the word was disused by some for a time because it had degenerated so as to imply formal righteousness, especially formal almsgiving. The only instance in Mark where Jesus uses it is Mk ii. 17 "I came *not* to call *the righteous*, but sinners"; Matthew and Luke contain protests against the misapplication of the term.

[2998 (liv) *j*] These facts will explain the abundant use of "righteous" in pre-Christian Jewish works and its disuse in some Christian writings, especially in the Pauline epistles which emphatically subordinate the "righteous" to the "good" (*e.g.* Rom. v. 7). Yet δίκαιος was a noble word, endeared to Greek-speaking Jews by the saying of Plato that "a righteous man" was the thing most like God. Philo, after quoting Gen. xii. 3 "In thee shall all the tribes of the earth be blessed," says (i. 454) "For indeed *the righteous* [*man*] is a prop to the whole race of men." So, too, in Jn (xvii. 11, 25) when the Son prays to the Father, after ἅγιε, there comes, as a climax, δίκαιε. The same feeling pervades *Wisdom* and large parts of the Enoch literature, not the *Similitudes* alone. The author, or rather perhaps the author of parts, and reviser of the whole, of *The Book of Enoch*, is imbued with the conviction that the redemption of the world is to be accomplished by righteousness, apparently meaning justice and equity as well as the observance of the Law of Israel. The first section of the book (*En.* 1) opens with "the blessing of Enoch wherewith he blessed the elect and *righteous*, who will be living in the day of tribulation when all the wicked and godless are to be removed." The last chapter of the last section says "I will bring forth clad in shining light those who have loved my holy Name, and I will seat each on the throne of his honour...for *righteousness* is the judgment of God; for to the faithful He will give faithfulness in the habitation of upright paths."

---

[1] [2998 (lv) *a*] *En.* 91 "*The righteous one* will arise from sleep, and wisdom will arise and be given unto *them*," *En.* 92 "The Holy [and] Great One has appointed days for all things. And *the righteous one* will arise from sleep...and all his path...will be in...grace. He [? the Holy

—and these, too, where there is no antithesis between "the righteous one" and "the unrighteous one" to make the meaning clear (**2998** (liv) *c*). Moreover one passage in a late section of *Enoch* identifies "the Son of Man" with the Patriarch Enoch himself[1]! These and other non-Scriptural

One] will be gracious to *the righteous* [? *one*] and will give *him* eternal uprightness, and will give *him* power, and he will live in goodness and righteousness and will walk in eternal light." In *En.* 92 there are vv. r. (1) "*wisdom* shall arise," (2) "*righteousness* will arise from its sleep, will arise (*sic*)." "The righteous one," not being followed by "them," might be supposed by some to mean a single person, and might be altered by them to make better sense.

[1] [**2998** (lv) *b*] *En.* 71 "And I fell on my face and my whole body melted away, but my spirit was transfigured...and he [*i.e.* the Head of Days] said unto me, ' *Thou art the Son of Man* (**2998** (liv) *a*) *who art born unto righteousness,* and righteousness abides over thee, and the righteousness of the Head of Days forsakes thee not...from thence proceeds peace since the creation of the world.'...And so there will be length of days with that Son of Man and the righteous will have peace, and the righteous his path of uprightness in the name of the Lord of Spirits for ever and ever."

This is regarded by Dr Charles as an interpolation by the same (pre-Christian) editor that interpolated the Noachic fragments elsewhere. It follows (*En.* 69) a description of "the Son of Man" as judging on the throne of glory, and a statement that (*En.* 70) "After this, his [*i.e.* Enoch's] name was *carried aloft during his lifetime* to the Son of Man and to the Lord of Spirits." Then the interpolated passage (*En.* 71) begins, "And it came to pass, after this, that my spirit was hidden, and it ascended into the heavens...and he said unto me, 'Thou *art the Son of Man....*'" What could the editor mean by retaining the statement that Enoch (1) was *carried to* the Son of Man and interpolating, after it, a fragment to the effect that Enoch (2) *was* the Son of Man?

Did he think that when Enoch's (*En.* 71) "whole body melted away" and his "spirit was transfigured," he passed *into* the Son of Man? If so, the thought illustrates the Galilæan notion, in the days of Christ, that the latter was John the Baptist risen from the dead, and perhaps, also, some literalistic traditions that John the Baptist "*was* Elias." This identification of the Son of Man with Enoch is the last instance of the title in the whole book (so far as Dalman's *Words* p. 243 indicates).

The "melting away" of the "body" would favour the view that the writer of the passage did not accept the resurrection of the "body" in the popular sense. See **2998** (lvi) *f* foll.

traditions, when combined with the language of the Scriptures about "the Righteous One," "my Elect One," "my Servant," and "the Son of man," may enable us better to understand how, in our Lord's time, the last of these titles might be used in more than one sense[1].

Another point of interest in *Enoch* is its mystical doctrine about "hiding," as a necessary condition of revelation—a thought that forms the foundation of some of Christ's deepest sayings in the Fourth Gospel as well as in the Three; and it is also embedded in the Pauline epistles. But no part of the book throws much light on Christ's doctrine about the righteousness that is "in hiding" or "in secret," ἐν κρυπτῷ, being as it were a secret between the righteous man and the righteous Father in heaven[2].

---

[1] [2998 (lv) c] Comp. Is. xxiv. 16 "glory to the *righteous* [*one*]" with xxvi. 2—7 "the *righteous nation*...the way of *the righteous* [*one*] is uprightness: thou that art upright dost direct the path of *the righteous* [*one*]." In these passages, "the righteous [one]" appears (Gesen. 843 a) to mean "the righteous worshipper of Jehovah," and hence to imply "faithful Israel." But the fundamental instance is (**2998** (liv) ƒ foll.) Is. liii. 11 "*my righteous* servant shall make many righteous." From this, and from Is. xli. 8 "my servant Jacob whom *I have chosen*," xlii. 1 "my servant...*my chosen*" (comp. lxv. 9, 22) Enoch might well call Israel, or the Redeemer of whom Israel was the type, "*the* Righteous and Chosen (*i.e.* Elect)."

(lv) *d—m* THE DOCTRINE OF "HIDING"

[2] [2998 (lv) d] The following passages illustrate various traditions in *Enoch* about hiding, some of which appear to be confused:—*En.* 10 "the Most High sent Arsjalâljûr (Gk (1) Uriel, (2) Istrael) to the son of Lamech [*i.e.* Noah]...'Tell him in my name, *Hide thyself*,'" *En.* 12 "And before all these things fell out, Enoch *was hidden*...and all his activities had to do with the holy ones," *En.* 40 "The angel that came with me shewed me all *the hidden things*," *En.* 46 "I asked the angel who...shewed me all *the hidden things*...he said unto me, This is the Son of Man...who reveals all the treasures of *that which is hidden*," *En.* 48 "Before the sun and the signs were created...his [*i.e.* the Son of Man's] name was named before the Lord of Spirits. He will be a staff to the righteous...the light of the Gentiles....All who dwell on earth...will bow the knee before him. And for this reason has he been chosen and *hidden*

before Him before the creation of the world and for evermore...," *En.* 62 "And the kings and the mighty...will glorify...*him who rules over all, who was hidden.* For *the Son of Man was hidden before Him* [*i.e.* before the Lord of Spirits] and the Most High *preserved him in the presence of His might*, and revealed him to the elect. And the congregation of the holy and elect will be sown...," *En.* 70 "his [*i.e.* Enoch's] name was carried aloft...and the name vanished amongst men [lit. them]," *En.* 71 "my spirit *was hidden* and it ascended into the heavens."

[2998] (lv) *e*] In some of these passages, there appears a notion that "*hiding*" *not only precedes but also causes, or prepares the way for, revelation.* *E.g.*, on *En.* 10, Dr Charles comments thus, "*Hide thyself* [addressed to Noah] : *i.e.* in order to receive further disclosures from the angel." He compares *En.* 12 "Enoch *was hidden.*" It is easy to see how the writer could say that Enoch "was hidden," but how was Noah "hidden"? Comp. *En.* 89 which refers to Noah as a "bull," only "becoming a man" in order to build the ark, "And one of these four [angels] went to that white bull and *instructed him in a secret*, as he trembled" [*i.e.* feared God's judgments] ; "he was born a bull and became a man, and built for himself a great vessel and dwelt thereon ; and three bulls" [Shem, Ham, and Japheth] "dwelt with him...and *they were covered in.*" These last words refer to Gen. vii. 16 "the Lord *shut him in*," *i.e.* shut Noah in the ark. The expression is paraphrased by Onkelos "the Lord *protected them by his Word,*" Samaritan (Etheridge), "the Lord *sealed them over,*" Jer. Targ. "the Word of the Lord *was merciful unto him.*" Rabbinical traditions vary as to the nature of the "*protection,*" or "*covering.*" The variations shew how the Lord might be said to "*hide,*" "*cover,*" or "*protect,*" one of His messengers or prophets, in order that he might in due time deliver his message or perform his allotted task, according to many sayings of the Psalms, *e.g.* xvii. 8 "*Hide me* under the shadow of thy wings," xxvii. 5 "In the day of trouble...he shall *hide me.*"

[2998] (lv) *f*] But a different kind of "*hiding*" is contemplated in Isaiah (xlix. 2—3) "The Lord hath *called me from the womb* ; from the bowels of my mother *hath he made mention of my name*...*in the shadow of his hand hath he hid me*...*in his quiver hath he kept me close* ; and he said unto me, Thou art my servant, Israel, in whom I will be glorified.... And now saith the Lord that formed me from the womb to be his servant to bring Jacob again to him...I will also give thee for a light to the Gentiles." Here—although the context indicates that the "Servant" will be (xlix. 7—8) one "whom man despiseth" and "the nation abhorreth" but whom God "will preserve" from persecution—yet the main object of the "hiding" seems to be, not preservation from peril, but *hiding like a seed in the ground with a view to the preparation of a mysterious and divine growth.* This is just possibly contemplated in the above quoted passage (*En.* 48) which closely resembles Isaiah as to the "naming" of the Son of Man before the Lord, and his having been "chosen and *hidden* before Him from the creation of the world," and prepared to be "the light of the Gentiles." But, except for such expressions as (see Charles on *En.* 10) "plant of righteousness," (*En.* 62) "the congregation... sown" by God, (*En.* 93) "plant of uprightness," etc., there is very little, in *Enoch*, to indicate that the "hiding" implies growth, as of a seed.

[2998 (lv) *g*] Nor is there any notion of growth or development in 4 Esdr. xiii. 2, where all versions, except the Latin, represent "the likeness of a man" as "coming up *out of the heart of the sea.*" There the writer explains it thus (*ib.* 26) "The same is he whom God the Highest hath *kept a great season,*" and (*ib.* 52) "Like as thou canst neither seek out nor know the things that are in the deep of the sea, even so can no man upon earth see my Son, or those that be with him, except *in* (?) *the time of his day* (nisi in tempore diei, but Syr. Aeth. Ar. Arm. diei eius)," which seems to mean "in the appointed time, for which men must patiently wait."

[2998 (lv) *h*] "*Hiding*" was interpreted by some early Fathers as "*hiding from Satan.*" Comp. Ign. *Eph.* 19 on the "three mysteries of the cry," which "*escaped the notice of the ruler of this world.*" Among these are the παρθενία Μαρίας. Lightf. quotes many patristic passages indicating a belief that "the Deceiver was himself deceived by God's mysterious reserve," *e.g.* Hippol. *Op.* p. 38 (Lagarde) ἰδοὺ ὁ Κύριος παραγίνεται λιτός...κρύπτων δὲ τὸ τῆς θεότητος ἀξίωμα ἵνα λάθῃ τοῦ δράκοντος τὸ πανούργημα—which suggests a somewhat different picture from that in Rev. xii. 4, where "the dragon" is waiting in expectation to devour the child, but the child is snatched away. Origen (*Hom. Luc.* vi., Lomm. v. 104) quotes Ign. and says, "Disposuerat Salvator dispensationem suam, et assumtionem corporis ignorare diabolum: unde et in generatione sua celavit eam, et discipulis postea praecipiebat, ne manifestum eum facerent. Et cum ab ipso diabolo tentaretur, nusquam confessus est Dei se esse Filium." These three mysteries, says Ignatius, "were wrought in God's quiet way (ἐν ἡσυχίᾳ θεοῦ)," and he describes Christ as (*Magn.* 8) "God's Logos having come forth from silence (ἀπὸ σιγῆς προελθών)."

[2998 (lv) *i*)] Lightf. (Ign. *Eph.* 19) quotes 1 Cor. ii. 7 foll. Θεοῦ σοφίαν ἐν μυστηρίῳ, τὴν ἀποκεκρυμμένην, ἣν προώρισεν ὁ Θεὸς πρὸ τῶν αἰώνων εἰς δόξαν ἡμῶν, ἣν οὐδεὶς τῶν ἀρχόντων τοῦ αἰῶνος τούτου ἔγνωκεν· εἰ γὰρ ἔγνωσαν, οὐκ ἂν τὸν κύριον τῆς δόξης ἐσταύρωσαν, and says, "it is probable indeed that by οἱ ἄρχοντες τοῦ αἰῶνος τούτου S. Paul means earthly rulers, such as Pilate and Herod; but very many ancient commentators (*e.g.* Marcion in Tertull. *adv. Marc.* v. 6; Origen *Sel. in Psalm.* ii., II. p. 538; τινές in Chrysost. on 1 Cor. ii. 6; Ambrosiaster *ad loc.*), and some modern, have interpreted the words of spiritual powers, and Ignatius is likely to have done the same." The "hiding," or non-recognition, of a deliverer of Israel, in the beginning of his career, may be illustrated from the lives of Moses (Exod. ii. 2), Gideon (Judg. vi. 9—15), and David (1 S. xvi. 11). Comp. Jn i. 33 " And I knew him not."

[2998 (lv) *j*] Christ's doctrine about the unperceived, gradual, and widespread growth of God's "seed" is illustrated by two parables, one peculiar to Mark, the other belonging to Matthew and Luke. Mk iv. 26—29 describes "a man" sowing seed, and finding that, while he sleeps and wakes, the seed shoots up, "how—he himself knows not." The earth, "of its own accord (αὐτομάτη)," brings forth fruit—blade, ear, corn. A very similar saying about the gradual development of the vine is alleged, from unknown "scripture," by Clem. Rom. 23, where Lightf. quotes Epict. iii. 24. 86, 91, and M. Anton. xi. 35. Add Epict. iv. 8. 35—6, enjoining not only patience, but also self-suppression, ἀγνοεῖσθαι μελέτησον πρῶτον τίς εἶ· σαυτῷ φιλοσόφησον ὀλίγον χρόνον, οὕτω καρπὸς γίνεται· κατορυγῆναι δεῖ χρόνον τὸ σπέρμα, κρυφθῆναι, κατὰ μικρὸν αὐξηθῆναι ἵνα τελεσφορήσῃ. Origen (*Jerem. Hom.* 5) says concerning spiritual "seeds," that they will *seem* to spring up "*of their own accord* (αὐτόματα)" but that God really gives the increase. Then he quotes Mk iv. 28. Some objection to αὐτομάτη—and perhaps a difficulty in giving an allegorical meaning to the "man," and his "sleeping and waking"—may have caused the omission of this beautiful parable by Mt.-Lk. Jn, in very different language (iii. 8), "thou knowest not whence it cometh and whither it goeth," describes "everyone that is born of the spirit"—and this birth is really the subject of Mark's parable.

[2998 (lv) *k*] Mt. xiii. 33, Lk. xiii. 21 "The kingdom of heaven is like unto leaven, which a woman took and hid (Mt. ἐνέκρυψεν, Lk. ἔκρυψεν *v. r.* ἐνέκρυψεν) in three measures of meal till the whole was leavened." There is only one other mention of "three measures" of meal in the Bible, and that is in Gen. xviii. 6 where Sarah, just before receiving from the Three Persons the promise of a child, is told by Abraham to "knead *three measures of fine meal* and make cakes (ἐγκρυφίας)." Philo i. 173 allegorizes the "three measures" in Genesis as being the three elements of human nature corresponding to the Three Divine Persons; and he plays on the word "*cakes*" (lit. "hidden [in the embers]") as indicating that the holy word must needs be "hidden" from the uninitiated. Clem. Alex. 694, commenting on the "three measures" in the Gospel, says, "Either it means the saving of the soul that is tripartite in obedience [to the Three Divine Powers] (ἤτοι γὰρ ἡ τριμερὴς καθ' ὑπακοὴν σώζεται ψυχή)," or else it denotes simply "the compactness and invisibly attractive power of the Word on every one that takes it into himself"—a power to draw everything to itself and to make him an organic unity. Origen's comment on "the leaven" in the Gospels is lost, but his comment on Gen. xviii. 6 says "totum sacramentis repletum est," and he interprets ἐγκρυφίας as "absconditos ac mysticos panes." Also a scholium on

[2998 (lvi)] Dr Charles thinks that the doctrine of the *Similitudes* as regards the Resurrection does not include the Gentiles, but only all Israel, and that "the resurrection is

Lk. xiii. 21 (Cramer) says, "Origen takes the '*Woman*' as the Church, the '*leaven*' as the Holy Spirit, and the '*three measures*' as body, spirit, and soul." This makes the parable of the leaven a link between Mark's parable of the seed, and John's quasi-parable of the Wind or Spirit. The three parables represent the spiritual growth of the soul in three different aspects; but each aspect expresses, or implies, that man grows—"how he himself knows not."

[2998 (lv) *l*] The precepts (Mt. vi. 1—6) about giving and praying "in secret (ἐν κρυπτῷ)" are not recorded by Lk., perh. as being too oriental in expression (*e.g.* "let not thy right hand know") for western churches. It should be added that ostentatious giving is repeatedly and severely condemned in the Talmud, see Wetst. on Mt. vi. 1—6. All the gospels breathe the spirit of what 1 Pet. iii. 4 calls "*the hidden man* of the heart (ὁ κρυπτὸς τῆς καρδίας ἄνθρωπος)." Comp. Rom. vii. 22, 2 Cor. iv. 16, Eph. iii. 16 "the inner man (ὁ ἔσω ἄνθρωπος)."

[2998 (lv) *m*] Compare :—

Mk iv. 22	Mt. x. 26	Lk. viii. 17 (comp. xii. 2)
"For there is not [anything] hidden except *in order that* (ἵνα) it may be manifested."	"For there is nothing covered *that* (ὅ) shall not be uncovered."	"For there is not [anything] hidden *that* (ὅ) shall not become manifest."

This passage of Mark is separated from the preceding Parable of the Sower by a saying about a "candle," which comes very abruptly there, and which Matthew dissociates from that parable. But for that intervention, Mk iv. 22 might mean, "Nothing is hidden [by God for the mere purpose of keeping men in ignorance or perplexity. Nothing is hidden] except that [by being hidden and given time to mature] it may be manifested [as a living and growing truth]." If that were the meaning, it would be similar to the Johannine saying (Jn xii. 24) that the seed of corn must die in order that it may bring forth fruit. The thought is briefly and obscurely expressed by Mark; but for that very reason Mark ought perhaps to be supposed to be closer than Matthew and Luke to the original. Christ may well have uttered the saying in both forms. The form adopted by Mark indirectly inculcates patience, modesty, and a reverence for nature's slow and unobserved methods. It harmonizes with the saying, "The kingdom of God cometh not with observation," and with Matthew's emphasis on doing good deeds "in secret" since God "seeth in secret." On Is. xlv. 15 "thou art a God that hidest thyself, O God of Israel, the Saviour," see *Fourfold Gospel*, "Hide."

a resurrection of the body¹." But this appears uncertain.

(lvi) *a—d* THE RESURRECTION

¹ [2998 (lvi) *a*] In a long and valuable note on *En.* 51, Dr Charles specifies several distinct Jewish beliefs as to the Resurrection as affecting (1) all Israel, (2) righteous Israel, (3) Israel and a few pious Gentiles [this asserted only by "individual voices"], (4) all mankind. He considers *En.* 51 and 62 to assert "a resurrection of the body" (whereas in *En.* 91—104 "it is only a resurrection of the soul and spirit") and "of all Israel, but not of the Gentiles."

[2998 (lvi) *b*] But *En.* 51 "In those days will the earth also give back those who are treasured up within it, and Sheol also will give back that which it has received, and hell will give back that which it owes" is so manifestly of a universal character that Dr Charles himself says that the passage "would seem to point to" it. "But," he adds, "the whole history of Jewish thought points in an opposite direction." Is it not possible, however, that (1) the author of this particular book may have had exceptionally cosmopolitan views, or (2) the passage may result from late revision?

[2998 (lvi) *c*] The other passage alleged, *En.* 62, says that "The righteous and elect will be saved on that day...and with that Son of Man will they eat and lie down and rise up for ever and ever...and the righteous and elect will have risen from the earth...and will have been clothed with garments of glory." These words, following a highly metaphorical context that speaks of the Lord's "sword" being "drunk with the blood" of the oppressors, do not seem to me to prove a resurrection of the *body* (as distinct from a resurrection of the soul and spirit that are to be "clothed with garments of glory"). It is true that "eating" is mentioned, as also it is mentioned or implied in many of our Lord's parables; and the author may possibly use the word literally like the man that exclaimed (Lk. xiv. 15) "Blessed is he that shall eat bread in the kingdom of God!" But that this is not probable appears from *En.* 51 "And in those days will the mountains leap like rams, and the hills will skip like lambs satisfied with milk, and *they will all become angels in heaven.*" Neither *En.* 51 nor *En.* 62 seems to exclude righteous Gentiles.

[2998 (lvi) *d*] By Philo (i. 164) angels are expressly called "bodiless," where he says that "Abraham 'left' mortality, and was 'gathered to' (Gen. xxv. 8) the people of God, reaping immortality and becoming *equal to angels* (ἴσος ἀγγέλοις γεγονώς). For angels are God's army, *bodiless* and blessed souls (ἀσώματοι κ. εὐδαίμονες ψυχαί)." To the same effect, Christ says that those raised from the dead are (Mk xii. 25, Mt. xxii. 30) "as angels in heaven" or (Lk. xx. 36) "equal to angels (ἰσάγγελοι)," in this respect that there is no "marrying" or "giving in marriage" among

In any case, there is no indication that the doctrine of the gospels on this subject is based on *Enoch*, although the book may copiously illustrate both what Christ taught as true and what He attacked as false.

The doctrine of Redemption in the *Similitudes* appears to be that the Elect and Righteous One, being beheld with the eye of faith and love by the elect and righteous, will draw them into His glory; but He will not be beheld by the godless, and when at last they are forced to behold Him, they will behold Him with fear and without love, and their end will be shame.

The earlier part of *Enoch* (ch. 1—36) is justly described in Dr Charles's valuable edition (p. 27) as containing "naive and sensuous views of the kingdom" of God. But the rest, taken as a whole, and especially the *Similitudes*, is of a much more spiritual character. Even though all of it should prove to be pre-Christian, it would have some bearing on our Lord's time, indicating that there might exist in others besides John the Baptist aspirations after a higher righteousness than that of those Pharisees whom the gospels so bitterly condemn.

---

them, apparently indicating non-sensuous existence incompatible with "eating." Against the inference that this view extends to the extract from *Enoch*, there may be urged the following words (*En.* 51) "Their faces will be lighted up with joy because in those days the Elect One has appeared, *and the earth will rejoice and the righteous will dwell upon it, and the elect will go to and fro upon it.*" Does not the mention of "the earth"—it may be asked—imply earthly, or sensuous existence? The answer is, 1st, that the sensuous "earth" cannot "rejoice," 2nd, that, according to *En.* 45, God will "transform the earth." It would seem, then, that both "the earth" and the earthly bodies of the sons of Adam are to be "transformed" into something beyond the region of the senses and into the region of angels.

So far as concerns the two passages alleged above from the *Similitudes*, it does not seem to me proved that they refer to a resurrection of the "body" in the popular sense of the term, or that they contemplate a resurrection restricted to Jews.

NOTE II

THE SELF-MANIFESTATIONS OF CHRIST

§ 1 "*Touching*" *and* "*drawing near*"

[**2999** (i)] The object of the following paragraphs is, not to compare and discuss the gospel accounts of the self-manifestations of Christ after the Resurrection, but to collect and classify facts with a view to comparison and discussion in *The Fourfold Gospel*.

It was pointed out in **2889** that the dropping of ἄν might convert an account of a woman *desiring to touch* the risen Saviour (such as we find in John) into an account of women *actually touching* Him (such as we find in Matthew). But a much more potent cause of confusion might be found in the fact that in Hebrew (both old and new) and in Aramaic, the same word may mean "touch" and "draw near to[1]." And the same ambiguity exists in the Syriac versions of the Gospels[2].

---

[1] [**2999** (i) *a*] In Daniel ix. 21, where the LXX has προσήγγισέ μοι, Theodotion has ἥψατό μου (and comp. Dan. x. 10). In Gen. iii. 3, xx. 6, xxxii. 25 (and freq.) where Heb. has נגע and LXX ἥψατο, Onkelos has קרב, which in Heb. would mean "*draw near to*," but, in later Heb., Aram., and Syr., would also mean "*touch.*" In Numb. iii. 10, xvii. 28, "*cometh nigh*," LXX has "*toucheth*," comp. Numb. iii. 38 "*cometh nigh*," LXX "*toucheth*" but A "*approacheth* (προσπορευόμενος)." The non-LXX translators have "draw nigh" in Numb. iii. 10, 38, but in Numb. i. 51, LXX ὁ προσπορευόμενος, Field gives ᾽Αλλος· ὁ ἁπτόμενος.

[2] [**2999** (i) *b*] Thus in Jn xx. 17 "*touch* me not," μή μου ἅπτου, SS (Burk.) has "Do not *draw near to* me," whereas Mrs Lewis has "*Touch*

[2999] THE SELF-MANIFESTATIONS OF CHRIST

But the reader must not suppose that any mere confusion of similar words sufficed to produce the divergent accounts of Christ's Resurrection. Here, as almost always, the rule holds good, BEWARE OF SINGLE CAUSES. Theological motives would naturally be at work; anthropomorphism and antanthropomorphism; differences between Hebrew and Jewish (*i.e.* post-captivity) thought (or, at all events, Hebrew and Jewish expression), and the influence of these differences on early Christian thought comparing Hebrew scripture with Jewish interpretation; Semitic and non-Semitic conceptions of matter, spirit, body, angelic nature, divine nature—so that where one writer might say "the Lord," another might prefer "an angel"; and, where one might describe an angel as "bodiless," another might reserve that epithet for disembodied spirits (**2824*** foll., **2998** (lvi) *d*).

[**2999** (ii)] In considering the tradition peculiar to Matthew, that the women "approached [Christ] and *held fast* his feet and worshipped him," we have to bear in mind that this ambiguous word, "approach" or "draw near to," or "touch," may become, when applied to "feet," more than usually ambiguous, because the meaning may be (1) "fall as suppliants at a person's feet," (2) "touch and grasp his feet." And the story of Zipporah (Exod. iv. 25)—who is regarded by some of the translators of O.T. severally as "falling before the feet" of Jehovah (or Jehovah's angel) or as "touching" them, or as "holding" them—shews how easily the mere act of prostra-

---

(Murdock "*touch*," Etheridge "*touch*, or *approach*"). In Mt. xxviii. 9 (where SS is missing) ἐκράτησαν αὐτοῦ τοὺς πόδας, the Syr. (Walton) has a non-ambiguous word ("*grasped* his feet"). But in Mt. ix. 25 ἐκράτησεν τῆς χειρὸς αὐτῆς, SS has "*touched*" or "*drew near*" (Walton "*grasped*"), which might be ambiguous if the context, "hand," did not make the meaning clear. Mk i. 31 "*approached*...and *grasped* her hand" is parall. to Mt. viii. 15 "*touched* her hand." On the parall. Lk. iv. 38—9 (Syr.) containing the phrase "a great fever was grasping her," and omitting the "grasping" of the "hand," see *Fourfold Gospel*, "Touch."

tion might be taken to mean "touching" or "grasping[1]." Also the fact that elsewhere Matthew has a tradition (peculiar to himself) that Jesus "*drew near and touched* the disciples," when combined with the present instance of "*drawing near and holding fast*" (also peculiar to Matthew) suggests that both of these traditions may be "conflations," omitted by other evangelists because of the uncertainty of the text[2].

§ 2. *God "meeting" man*

[**2999** (iii)] It has been objected (*Apologia*, p. 68) that Matthew's mention of "*meeting*" (Mt. xxviii. 9 "Jesus *met* them") is inconsistent with the hypothesis of a spiritual

---

[1] [**2999** (ii) *a*] Compare the different versions of Exod. iv. 25 (R.V.) "cast [it] at his feet," marg. "made [it] touch his feet," as given by Field: Heb. "Et tangere fecit (s. 'et tetigit')," LXX προσέπεσε [the word used in Mk iii. 11 of the demoniacs "falling against," or "at the feet of," Jesus], Ἄλλος· ἤγγισε, Aq. Theod. ἥψατο, Sym. ἀψαμένη. Here the Syr. has "and grasped his feet." Onkelos—who uses a form of קרב, "bring near," or "offer"—is rendered by Walton "and offered it before him," but by Etheridge "and approached before him." Thus, in one and the same Hebrew original, this ambiguous verb is rendered "touch," "fall before (as a suppliant)," "approach" and "grasp." "At the feet of," if referring to the feet of Jehovah, or an angel (as the Targumists appear to think) may mean little more than "in the presence of," which Onkelos substitutes. I am informed by Dr Büchler that in *Nedarim* three rabbis of 2nd cent. differ as to whether Zipporah touched the feet of (1) Moses, (2) the angel, (3) the child. For the double meaning of קרב (act. and mid.) in Syr. see *Thes. Syr.*; and for inferences from the confusion of "touch" and "draw near," see *Fourfold Gospel*, "Touch."

[2] [**2999** (ii) *b*] Comp. Mt. xvii. 7 "Jesus approached (προσῆλθεν) and touched them and said, 'Arise...,'" not in the parall. Mk ix. 8, Lk. ix. 36. Also comp. Mt. iv. 24 "*they brought*," SS "*were drawing near* (קרבין)," Palest. "*drew near* (קרבו)," which might be confused with "*touched*"; the parall. Mk (which shews signs of conflation) and Lk. are as follows:—

Mk iii. 10—11 (lit.)
"They kept *falling upon* (ἐπιπίπτειν) him that they might *touch* him...*falling against* (προσέπιπτον) him."

Lk. vi. 19
"kept seeking to *touch* him" (Etheridge, "*approach* to him," SS "*touch*," hithp. of קרב).

[2999] THE SELF-MANIFESTATIONS OF CHRIST

presence. But on the contrary the notion of God as "*meeting*" Israel, in what we should call a spiritual manner, underlies the whole of the Mosaic Law, though disguised in A.V. under the mistranslation "tabernacle of *testimony*" instead of "tabernacle of *meeting*[1]." The particular word here used by Matthew, ὑπήντησεν (v.r. ἀπήντησεν) is rather rare in LXX[2]; but συναντάω is used in various forms to describe God, or angels,

---

[1] [2999(iii)a] "Of meeting," regularly rendered μαρτυρίου, "of testimony," by LXX, but συνταγῆς, "of meeting," by Aq. in Numb. iii. 7, iv. 25. Συντάσσω in N.T. is used by Mt. alone (xxi. 6, xxvi. 19, xxvii. 10 quoting Zech. xi. 13) but only in the active. The middle τάσσομαι, however, is used by Mt. (and only once elsewhere in N.T., Acts xxviii. 23 ταξάμενοι...ἡμέραν) in Mt. xxviii. 16 "the mountain where Jesus had *appointed* [*meeting*] for them." Here the Syriac (Walton) (SS is lost) has וַיַעַד, the equiv. of Heb. יָעַד, "arrange meeting."

[2999(iii)b] Matthew probably had some form of יָעַד in his original, and it was rendered ἐτάξατο as it is by LXX in 2 S. xx. 5 "appointed time." But יָעַד is rendered by the middle συντάσσομαι in Exod. xxv. 22 (so Aq. etc., but LXX mistransl.) "there will I *meet with* thee," and by Aq. in Amos iii. 3 "agreed" or "made an appointment."

[2] [2999(iii)c] Ὑπαντάω occurs (7) in LXX, but not in canon. LXX exc. Dan. x. 14 (LXX) ὑπαντήσεται (Theod. ἀπ.) "shall befall." Wisd. vi. 16, Sir. xv. 2 ὑ. ὡς μήτηρ describe Wisdom as "anticipating (Sir. Heb. קדם, Vulg. obviabit)" those who love her, as the father anticipates the returning prodigal son by running to meet him. In Sir. xii. 17 it means "befall." In Tob. vii. 1 καὶ ἦλθεν...[κ. Σάρρα δὲ ὑπήντησεν αὐτῷ] κ. ἐχαιρέτισεν αὐτὸν κ. αὐτὸς αὐτούς, the masc. αὐτός (as well as the context) shews that the clause I have bracketed is corrupt. It is om. by א and the other versions. It may be a conflation of an ambiguous clause in the context like that in the Itala "haesit cordi eius" (Chald. "the love for Sarah entered his heart," Heb. "his soul was knit to the soul of Sarah," B ἡ ψυχὴ αὐτοῦ ἐκολλήθη αὐτῇ σφόδρα) in the form "*obviam venit eius cor cordi*," taken literally and referred to Sarah instead of to Tobit (see Tobit ed. Neubauer).

[2999(iii)d] Ὑπαντάω differs from ἀπαντάω in that the former mostly has more of voluntariness—"*going* to meet" a friend, or enemy; whereas ἀπαντάω may mean "meet with [an accident]," "light upon [evil]." Comp. Ammon. (Steph. viii. 121) ὑπαντῆσαι ἐπὶ ὁδοῦ λέγεται, ἀπαντῆσαι δὲ τὸ περιτυχεῖν δίκῃ· οἷον, ἀπήντησε κατὰ τὴν δίκην, ἀντὶ τοῦ περιτυχεῖν. Ἀπάντημα is used with δαιμονίου in Tob. vi. 8 (א), and (*ib.*) ἀπάντημα by itself means "mischance."

as "coming to meet" man¹. Sometimes συναντάω ought to have been used, but has not been used, apparently because the LXX did not like to speak of God as "coming to meet" anyone. "The *real meaning*"—so the translators perhaps argued—"is that God, or rather God's angel, *appeared* to man." And accordingly they substituted "*appeared*." It is of special importance that the tradition, above (**2999** (ii) *a*) mentioned, about Zipporah at the "feet," or "touching" the "feet," of God, or of God's angel, is preceded by a statement that God "met" Moses². This makes the parallelism between the

---

¹ [**2999** (iii) *e*] Comp. Gen. xxxii. 1 "And there *met him* (ויפגעו־בו) the angels of God," LXX [κ. ἀναβλέψας τοῖς ὀφθ. ἴδεν παρεμβολὴν θεοῦ παρεμβεβληκυῖαν] κ. συνήντησαν αὐτῷ οἱ ἄγγελοι τοῦ θεοῦ, where LXX interpolates the words I have bracketed. Apparently the text is a conflation placing (1) first, a paraphrase shewing that the "meeting" was a vision, (2) next, a literal translation.

² [**2999** (iii) *f*] The manifestation of God to Moses in the burning bush is variously referred to, thus : (*a*) Exod. iii. 16 "The God of your fathers *hath appeared* (נראה) to me...." (*b*) *ib*. 18 "Jehovah the God of the Hebrews *hath met us*" (lit. "*lighted upon us* (נקרה עלינו passive)"), (*c*) Exod. v. 3 sim. omitting "Jehovah."

[**2999** (iii) *g*] Three causes have contributed to confuse the renderings of (*b*) and (*c*) above, namely, (1) the fact that Exod. iii. 16 shews the "meeting" to have been really an "appearing," (2) the frequent oscillation (**472** *c*, **474** *a*) between "meet" and "call," (3) the doubt whether the passive "call" (if adopted as the rendering) was to be rendered as middle or passive. Hence the following variations:—(*b*) Exod. iii. 18 προσκέκληται ἡμᾶς "hath called us' (*v. r.* ἐπικέκληται, perh. meaning "hath been called on us" as Onk.). Onk. and Jon. have אתקרי עלנא. This Walton has rendered, in Onk., "invocatus est super nos," but in Jon. "occurrit nobis" (Etheridge, Onk. "hath called us," *al. cod.* "hath revealed himself to us," Jon. "hath called us") Levy *Ch.* ii. 383 *a* "wird über uns genannt." The Syr. has "hath revealed himself (אתגלי) to us (or, on us) (עלין)" (Walton "apparuit nobis").

In (*c*) Exod. v. 3, Heb. and LXX as before, Onk. now has "hath revealed himself (אתגלי) to us (or, on us) (עלנא)" (and sim. Syr. Walton "apparuit nobis"). But Walton mistransl. Onk. "invocatus est super nos."

[**2999** (iii) *h*] In Exod. iv. 24 "And there met him (ויפגשהו) Jehovah," LXX retains the literal anthropomorphism, but substitutes "angel of the

[2999] THE SELF-MANIFESTATIONS OF CHRIST

story in Exodus and that in Matthew very striking indeed, and greatly increases the probability that the latter, in the original Semitic, was intended to describe what might be called, in ancient times, "the coming (or sending) of an angel of the Lord," or "the appearing of an angel of the Lord," or "the appearing of the Lord," or, in modern times, a "spiritual meeting," "vision," or "revelation." If Matthew misunderstood

---

Lord," συνήντησεν αὐτῷ ἄγγελος κυρίου, and so do Onk. and Jon. (Syr. "occurrit ei Dominus").

[**2999** (iii) *i*] In Numb. xxiii. 3 (Heb. lit.) "Perhaps there will *come to meet* (יקרה) Jehovah to my meeting (לקראתי)," εἴ μοι φανεῖται ὁ θεὸς ἐν συναντήσει, Onk. is rendered by Walton "si forte *occurrat* (ערע) Sermo Dei a facie Domini *in occursum meum* (לקדמותי)," but this conceals the fact that Onk. departs from the Heb. double use of "meet," and has (1) "meet," (2) "anticipate." Walton translates the Syr. "si forte occurrat (נקרא) Dominus in occursum meum (אורעי)" where Walton takes Syr. נקרא as "occurrat" (not as "clamabit," see *Thes. Syr.* 3713 *init.* "*clamabit* in meum occursum"). The Targum of Jonathan has (Walton) "si forte *veniat* (Etheridge "shall be discovered") (יזדמן) ("shall come to meet," see Levy *Ch.* i. 224) verbum Domini mihi obviam (לקדמותי)." It is to be noted that, in the noun "meeting," both Onk. and Jon. adopt a form of קדם, "go before," or "anticipate."

LXX does not here substitute "angel of God" for "God," but it renders "meet" freely by "appear" so as to shew that a "vision" is denoted.

[**2999** (iii) *j*] In Numb. xxiii. 4 (lit.) "And there went to meet (ויקר) God to (אל) Balaam," LXX has καὶ ἐφάνη ὁ θεὸς τῷ B., Onk. "et *occurrit* (ערע) verbum a facie Dei ad ipsum (לות) B.," Jon. "et *occurrit* (וארע) verbum a facie Dei in (ב) B.," Syr. "and God *revealed himself* (ואתגלי) to (or, on) (על) B." But in Numb. xxiii. 16, though Heb. is as in xxiii. 4, LXX has κ. συνήντησεν ὁ θεὸς τῷ B., Onk. as before (with ל for לות), Jon. as before, and Syr. as before. This illustrates the probability that, in a Gk transl. of a Semitic document, "met" might be *correct in word but misleading in fact—if the narrative described a vision.*

[**2999** (iii) *k*] In Numb. xxiii. 15 "and I [*i.e.* Balaam] will go to meet [Jehovah] yonder," the LXX paraphrases the presumptuous-sounding words as "But I will go *to enquire* of God," Onk. has "but I *will go as far* (אתמטי) *as thither* (עד-כא)," and sim. Jon. with אתארע, and Syr. with אמטא.

it, that would only be on a level with his misunderstanding of other Semitic expressions, as, for example, the Hebrew parallelism that mentioned an "ass" and "a colt the foal of an ass"—which he, alone of the evangelists, regards as representing two animals.

§ 3. "*Going to meet," "going before," and "drawing near"*

[**2999** (iv)] The facts above stated have a direct bearing on other passages connected with Christ's resurrection, and in particular with the mention—omitted by Luke—of "*going before* (προάγω)" the disciples into Galilee (**1233** foll.). It has been seen above (**2999** (iii) *i*) that Onkelos once substitutes a form of "*go before*," for Heb. "*meet*." So in Sir. xv. 2 ὑπαντήσεται αὐτῷ ὡς μήτηρ, the recently discovered Hebrew is קדם, lit. "*anticipate*," where the Gk has the same rare compound of ἀντάω as in Mt. xxviii. 9 (and Wisd. vi. 16). In Exod. xix. 3 "the Lord *called* (קרא) unto him [Moses] out of the mountain," Targ. Jer. has "the Lord *anticipated* him from the mountain," probably taking קרא as קרה, "*meet*" (**472** *c*, **474** *a*) and meaning that God "*came to meet*" Moses. Now קדם is ambiguous. It may mean absolutely (1) "do a thing beforehand," (2) "go before a person to a certain place," (3) "go to meet a person[1]." Hence we can better understand how a tradition that might be interpreted by Mark and Matthew as meaning, in effect, *Christ said I will go before you to Galilee*, might seem to Luke to refer to what *He said beforehand in Galilee* (Lk. xxiv. 6 "the things that he said unto you still being in Galilee").

[**2999** (v)] Luke in the passage just quoted (xxiv. 6), adds—what is not found in the parallel Mk-Mt.—a prediction of the Passion and Resurrection. This (though it may

---

[1] [**2999** (iv) *a*] Trommius gives קדם as (*pih.*) καταλαμβάνω (2), προκαταλαμβάνω (1), προπορεύομαι (1), προφθάνω (15), συναντάω (4), (*hiph.*) ἀνθίστημι (1), ἔρχομαι (1).

[2999] THE SELF-MANIFESTATIONS OF CHRIST

be explained as merely the result of Luke's desire to define what Jesus said "in Galilee") makes it worth while to remark that קדם "anticipate," or "go to meet," is easily confused with קום "stand," "arise," and that Gesen. 870 a recognises the confusion in 1 S. xx. 25, favouring LXX προέφθασεν "*anticipated*," against Heb. "stood." The word generally used by Luke to denote angelic appearance, or sudden entrance, is a form of ἐφίστημι. The renderings of this by SS suggest either that the translator was perplexed by the Greek ἐπί (which may have suggested to him "upon," "up," and therefore "standing up") or else that he was influenced by some Semitic traditions confusing קדם with קום[1].

---

[1] [2999 (v) *a*] Here are the renderings of ἐφίστημι in Luke as given by R.V. and SS:—ii. 9 "an angel *stood by them*," SS "*appeared to them...standing*" (comp. ii. 13 "*there was* (ἐγένετο)...a multitude of the heavenly host," SS "*appeared*"); ii. 38 "she [Anna] *coming up* at that very moment," SS (Burk.) "*stood up*"; iv. 39 "he [Jesus] *stood over her* (ἐπιστὰς (D ἐπισταθεὶς) ἐπάνω αὐτῆς) and rebuked the fever," SS "and he ⋀ rebuked her fever" [for ἐπάνω, comp. Gen. xviii. 2 "and lo, three men stood *over against* (על) *him*," ἰδοὺ τρεῖς ἄνδρες ἱστήκεισαν ἐπάνω αὐτοῦ], Mk-Mt. differ; x. 40 "(Martha) *came up to him* and said (ἐπιστᾶσα δὲ εἶπεν, D ἐπισταθεῖσα)" SS "*came* and saith to him"; xx. 1 "*there came upon him* the chief priests (ἐπέστησαν οἱ ἀρχ.)," SS "*stood up* (קמו) *against him*"; xxi. 34 "and [lest] that day *come on you* (ἐπιστῇ ἐφ' ὑμᾶς) suddenly," SS "and [lest] that day *come up* (ניקום) *upon you* (עליכון) suddenly"; xxiv. 4 "behold, two men *stood by them* (ἐπέστησαν αὐταῖς)," SS (Burk. txt) "they saw two persons (lit. men, אנשין) *standing* (דקימין) *over them* (לעל מנהין)," but SS, for "they saw," has "there appeared."

[2999 (v) *b*] The two passages just quoted (Lk. xxiv. 4 ἰδοὺ ἄνδρες δύο ἐπέστησαν αὐταῖς and Gen. xviii. 2 ἰδοὺ τρεῖς ἄνδρες...ἐπάνω αὐτοῦ) should prepare us for a version parallel to Lk., with ἐπάνω in it. Moreover, the analogy of Jon. Targ. on Gen. xviii. 2 "And *he lifted up his eyes* (LXX ἀναβλέψας τοῖς ὀφθ.) and looked, and behold, *three angels* in the resemblance of men were standing before him," should prepare us for versions parallel to Lk. with "*looking up*" in them, and with "*angel*" instead of "*man*." Accordingly, Mk xvi. 4 has ἀναβλέψασαι (2909), while Mt. xxviii. 2 has ἄγγελος and ἐπάνω (not however ἐπάνω αὐτῶν but ἐπάνω αὐτοῦ, *i.e.* above the stone of the sepulchre).

§ 4. *Different words employed by the evangelists*

[**2999** (vi)] Luke only once applies his peculiar word, ἐφίστημι, to Jesus, and there, as we have seen, SS omits the clause. Elsewhere if he wishes to describe Jesus as "drawing near" or "approaching," he mostly uses ἐγγίζω or ἐγγύς (once προσέρχομαι) when Jesus is drawing near to save (or, on rare occasions, to judge)[1]. Herein Luke agrees with LXX which,

---

[1] [**2999** (vi) *a*] Ἐγγίζω is applied by Luke alone to Jesus, as follows:—
(*a*) vii. 12 "He drew near to the gate of the city" [before restoring the widow's son to life]; (*b*) xviii. 35 "and when he drew near to Jericho" [before healing the blind man]; (*c*) xix. 29 "and when he drew near to Bethphage" [a little before the weeping over the City], SS here has "arrived" מטא, "came as far as" (=φθάνω freq. in Daniel), and repeats it "and arrived by the mount," Mk-Mt. have the pl. "*they*"; (*d*) xix. 37 "And when he drew near to the descent..." [also a little before the weeping over the City], D and SS have the pl. "*they*"; (*e*) xix. 41 "And when he drew near and saw the city" [immediately before the weeping over the City]; (*f*) xxiv. 15 "and...Jesus himself having drawn near was going with them" (SS, מטי *i.e.* "came quickly up to them" or "reached them," as in Dan. iv. 8, 17, 19, 21, 25, vi. 24, vii. 13, 22 φθάνω).

Ἐγγύς is applied to Jesus as follows:—Lk. xix. 11 "because he was near Jerusalem," where the next words are, "and they thought that the kingdom of God would immediately be shewn forth (ἀναφαίνεσθαι)," Jn vi. 19 "and when he drew near unto the boat" where the parall. Mk vi. 49, Mt. xiv. 26 have words indicating that the disciples thought they saw "a phantasm."

In all these instances the word introduces some act of healing or of divine judgment or of self-manifestation.

[**2999** (vi) *b*] Προσέρχομαι in LXX is mostly represented by קרב, "draw near," *e.g.* Exod. xii. 48, xvi. 9, xxii. 8 etc. In xii. 48 "he shall come near" means he shall "come near *to God*," and in xvi. 9, xxii. 8 "God" is expressed. Generally προσέρχομαι, Heb. קרב, is used of *approaching superiors*. So is προσέρχομαι in the gospels (where the regular Syr. for it is קרב). For example, in Mt., προσέρχομαι occurs about 50 times and very often of people coming *to* Jesus. But it is applied to Jesus only twice. The first instance is xvii. 7 προσῆλθεν ὁ Ἰησοῦς κ. ἁψάμενος "Jesus *approached* and *having touched them*" (at the Transfiguration) where SS has "*drew near* (קרב) and *raised them up*" (Mk-Lk. omit this). The other instance is xxviii. 18 προσελθὼν (SS

[2999] THE SELF-MANIFESTATIONS OF CHRIST

on the very rare occasions on which God is said to "draw near" to men, uses ἐγγίζω, not προσέρχομαι[1]. In the gospels, as in LXX, προσέρχομαι is mostly used of inferiors "approaching" superiors. When Jesus "approaches" the disciples or others, He mostly comes as a helper or a healer. On more than one of these occasions, they think He is "a phantasm," or they have previously "doubted," or their eyes are "holden that they should not know him."

---

missing, Syr. Walton קרב) ὁ Ἰησοῦς ἐλάλησεν αὐτοῖς. This refers to the period after the resurrection. Thus, προσελθών is not applied to Jesus by Mt. except during some manifestation *of a spiritual nature.* Mt. xxvi. 39 (Mk xiv. 35) is excluded because the text has προελθών, marg. προσελθών. Mk i. 31 uses προσελθών of Jesus only once, before the raising up of Peter's mother-in-law (where, as we have seen, Lk. has ἐπιστάς); Lk. vii. 14, only once, to introduce the raising of the dead at Nain.

[2999 (vi) c] Note that in three of the four instances of προσελθών applied to Christ, there follows a healing, or helping, "touch," or "grasp," or "raising up," (a) Mk i. 31 προσελθὼν ἤγειρεν αὐτὴν κρατήσας τῆς χειρός, parall. to Mt. viii. 15 ἥψατο τῆς χειρὸς αὐτῆς...καὶ ἠγέρθη, Lk. iv. 39 ἐπιστὰς ἐπάνω αὐτῆς...ἀναστᾶσα, (b) Mt. xvii. 7 προσῆλθεν ὁ Ἰησ. κ. ἁψάμενος (where SS has "drew near and raised them up"), (c) Lk. vii. 14 προσελθὼν ἥψατο τῆς σοροῦ. In the fourth there is a self-manifestation, after the resurrection, following a mention of some that had doubted, (d) Mt. xxviii. 17—18 κ. ἰδόντες αὐτὸν προσεκύνησαν, οἱ δὲ ἐδίστασαν, κ. προσελθὼν ὁ Ἰ. ἐλάλησεν αὐτοῖς....

[1] [2999 (vi) d] Gesen. (897 b) mentions the verb קרב "draw near," as applied to God only in Lam. iii. 57 ἤγγισας. But it mentions (898 b) the adj. as used in Ps. xxxiv. 18, cxix. 151, cxlv. 18, Jer. xii. 2 (all ἐγγύς), also in Deut. iv. 7, Is. l. 8, lv. 6 (all ἐγγίζω). It is very natural that Luke should prefer ἐγγίζω to προσέρχομαι, when applied to Jesus. Lk.'s only instance of προσέρχομαι thus used is in the raising of the Widow's son—where Jesus is called (vii. 13) "the Lord," and where there are signs of Semitic tradition and allegory.

[2999 (vi) e] "Draw near," קרב, may be used in a hostile sense, of an enemy "taking one by surprise"; and it is so used by SS in Mt. xii. 28, Lk. xi. 20 of the kingdom of God, ἔφθασεν ἐφ' ὑμᾶς, where φθάνω prob. combines the meaning "come right up to," "reach to" and also "come before it is expected."

§ 5. *Matthew's unique use of "anticipate"*

[2999 (vii)] The facts above collected may help us to interpret the story, peculiar to Matthew (xvii. 24–7), about Peter's "*finding a stater*" after catching "*the first fish that came up* (τὸν ἀναβάντα πρῶτον ἰχθύν)" and "opening its mouth." This story is preceded, at a little interval, by the words, "And when Peter had come to the house, Jesus came to meet him (προέφθασεν αὐτόν) saying...." If we assume, hypothetically, that προφθάνω represents "meeting" in the Hebraic spiritual sense frequently illustrated in the preceding paragraphs, it would follow that the story was of a Petrine vision. If so, it would find a natural place after the resurrection, when Peter (according to Jn xxi. 3) took the initiative in "fishing." It is worth noting that "*first*," applied by Matthew to the "*fish*," is applied by Clem. Alex. (in referring to this story) to *Peter*, as "the first of the disciples." Origen, also, says that Jesus "gave Peter power to *catch* (*a*) *fish first*," implying, shortly afterwards, that this primacy gave rise to discussion among the disciples as to who should be greatest[1]. These facts would

---

[1] [2999 (vii) *a*] Clem. Alex. 947 ὁ μακάριος Πέτρος ὁ ἐκλεκτὸς ὁ ἐξαίρετος, ὁ πρῶτος τῶν μαθητῶν, ὑπὲρ οὗ μόνου καὶ ἑαυτοῦ τὸν φόρον ὁ σωτὴρ ἐκτελεῖ. Elsewhere he implies that the catching of the fish implies the drawing up of a soul out of vice to virtue (172) ὁ γοῦν ἰχθὺς ἐκεῖνος, ὃν κελεύσαντος τοῦ κυρίου ὁ Πέτρος εἷλεν, εὔκολον καὶ αὐτὸς καὶ θεοδώρητον καὶ σώφρονα αἰνίττεται τροφήν· ἀφαιρεῖν γέ τοι ὑποτίθεται διὰ τῶν ἐξ ὕδατος ἀνιόντων ἐπὶ τὸ τῆς δικαιοσύνης δέλεαρ, τὴν ἀσωτίαν καὶ τὴν φιλαργυρίαν, ὡς τὸ νόμισμα τοῦ ἰχθύος.... He proceeds ἵνα χωρίσῃ τὴν κενοδοξίαν καὶ τὸν στατῆρα τοῖς τελώναις δοὺς τὰ Καίσαρος ἀποδοὺς τῷ Καίσαρι φυλάξῃ τὰ τοῦ θεοῦ τῷ θεῷ· ἔχοι (sic, but ? ἔχει) δὲ καὶ ἄλλας ἐπιλύσεις οὐκ ἀγνοουμένας ὁ στατήρ, ἀλλ' οὐχ ὁ παρὼν ἐπιτήδειος τῆς ἐξεργασίας καιρός. Apparently he finds a contrast between two coins, one paid to Caesar, the other to God (as also does Origen). Clement is allegorizing. Doubtless, he found no difficulty in accepting the narrative as literal. But the important point for us is, that even in those early days there were "other solutions" of the allegorical problem presented by this extraordinary story.

[2999] THE SELF-MANIFESTATIONS OF CHRIST

[2999(vii)*b*] Origen speaks of Peter as being "comforted," or "consoled," over the fish that came up, and connects the consolation with "Caphar-nahum," which he interprets as "village of consolation" (*ad loc.* Lomm. iii. 232—3 καὶ ὡς ἐν χωρίῳ γε παρακλήσεως—οὕτω γὰρ ἑρμηνεύεται ἡ Καφαρναούμ—παρακαλῶν τὸν μαθητὴν καὶ ἐλεύθερον αὐτὸν εἶναι καὶ υἱόν, δίδωσιν αὐτῷ δύναμιν τοῦ ἁλιεῦσαι ἰχθὺν πρῶτον, ἵνα ἀναβάντος αὐτοῦ παρακληθῇ ὁ Πέτρος ἐπὶ τῷ ἀναβάντι καὶ ἁλιευθέντι, καὶ ἀπὸ τοῦ στόματος εἰληφθαι τὸν στατῆρα, ἀποδοθησόμενον τοῖς οἰκείοις τοῦ στατῆρος, καὶ ἀπαιτοῦσιν ὡς ἴδιον τὸ τοιοῦτον νόμισμα. Like Clem., he regards the fish as (Lomm. iii. 230 foll.) being "benefited" and says ἀπὸ οἰκείου τόπου τῆς θαλάσσης τὴν εἰκόνα Καίσαρος λαμβάνει. The tax levied by the Jews for the Temple while standing had to be paid in a special sacred coin, but, after the destruction of the Temple, it was levied from the Jews by the Romans for their own purposes. Some confusion as to the meaning of this story might arise from this change. Madden, *Jewish Coinage* p. 238, quotes Origen's *Letter to Africanus* ed. De la Rue, vol. i. p. 28, καὶ νῦν 'Ιουδαίων δίδραχμον αὐτοῖς (sc. 'Ρωμαίοις) τελούντων.

[2999(vii)*c*] The following facts bear on Mt.'s use of δίδραχμα and στατήρ.

Exod. xxx. 12 foll. "When thou takest the sum of the children of Israel, according to those that are numbered of them, then shall they give every man a ransom for his soul unto the Lord, when thou numberest them; that there be no plague among them, when thou numberest them. This they shall give, every one that passeth over unto them that are numbered, half a shekel after the shekel of the sanctuary : (the shekel is twenty gerahs :) half a shekel for an offering to the Lord. Every one that passeth over unto them that are numbered, from twenty years old and upward, shall give the offering of the Lord. The rich shall not give more, and the poor shall not give less, than the half shekel, when they give the offering of the Lord, to make atonement for your souls."

A shekel (Joseph. *Ant.* iii. 8. 2) was four drachmae, or a *tetradrachm* or a stater (Madden's *Jewish Coinage* p. 239), so that each man was bound to pay *two* drachmae. But the LXX renders Exod. xxx. 13 "The half of the *didrachm*, which is according to the holy *didrachm*." The LXX also habitually renders "shekel" (where not σίκλος) by "*didrachm*" instead of "*tetradrachm*." On the other hand Aq. and Sym. have "[half of the] stater," *i.e.* "half a *tetradrachm*," correctly, and Josephus *Ant.* xviii. 9. 1 speaks of "the *didrachm* which they were wont to pay as a national poll-tax to God (τό τε δίδραχμον ὃ τῷ θεῷ καταβάλλειν ἑκάστοις πάτριον)," comp. *Bell.* vii. 6. 6 δύο δραχμὰς ἕκαστον, and Dion Cass. (qu. by Madden) lxvi. 7 δίδραχμον.

[2999(vii)*d*] Whatever may be the cause, the fact is certain, that the collectors were called "collectors of the *shekels*" (not, *the half shekels*) (*Hor. Heb.* on Mt. xvii. 24 qu. *Shekal.* 1)—which would literally mean

indicate that τὸν ἀναβάντα πρῶτον might be applied by some to *Peter's* "going up," if only we could find any gospel narrative connecting Peter's "going up" with "fishing." Such a connexion actually occurs in Jn xxi. 11 ἀνέβη οὖν Σίμων Πέτρος καὶ εἵλκυσεν τὸ δίκτυον εἰς τὴν γῆν[1].

[2999 (viii)] Moreover Ephrem Syrus, commenting on the finding of the Stater, quotes thus (Moes. p. 161) "But that thou mayest not cause them offence, go to the sea and cast the *net* there" (not "*hook*"). He proceeds, "When therefore Simon...took his *net* and went to cast it into the sea, *they also went with him.*" Ephrem uses "they also" to mean the Pharisees, as his context shews. Presumably he thinks that the Pharisees, and their agents the collectors, accompanied Peter to the shore to behold the result of his fishing, and to be convinced of the reality of the miracle, if

---

"*tetradrachms.*" Matthew calls them collectors of "*didrachms.*" But Madden (239—40) says that "*didrachms*" were obsolete coins and would hardly have been accepted if tendered. Either Matthew used "*didrachm*" in its monetary sense (as Josephus above) for "*two drachms,*" or in its official sense, as the LXX does, to represent the official phrase "collectors of the *shekels, i.e.* of the *tetradrachms.*"

[2999 (vii) *e*] The Talmud provides (*Shekal.* i. 3, Schwab v. 263—4) that "children shall be free from this tax," and that if a man pays for his neighbour (a whole shekel instead of a half) there shall only be one surcharge instead of two ("soumis à un seul droit pour les deux"), but R. Meir dissented. The levying was to begin from the 15th of Adar. On this point *Hor. Heb.* frankly admits a difficulty on the hypothesis of a literal interpretation. "But here this objection occurs, which is not so easy to answer. The time of the payment of the half shekel was about the feast of the Passover: but now that time was far gone and the feast of Tabernacles at hand." He fills nearly a page with attempts (very unsatisfactory, it seems to me) to answer this, concluding thus, "But if any list to understand this of the tax paid the Romans, we do not contend."

[1] The connexion would be still closer if Clark's transl. of Origen were correct (p. 481 *b*) "caught in the *net* of Peter," (p. 482 *b*) "sends Peter to drag up the fish into the *net.*" But neither Huet nor Lommatzsch gives this reading. It is however given by Ephrem Syrus (2999 (viii)).

there was to be a miracle. So Ephrem makes Christ say 'Let the sea teach them that I am...king."

Did Ephrem invent this tradition, "*they also went with him*"? Such "invention" is scarcely credible. Much more probably there were various traditions to the effect that Peter received "power to catch fish first of the apostles," or that Peter "caught the first fish," or "first, of all the apostles, drew the fish to land." Some of these would add, "*for they also went with him*," *i.e.* the other apostles also took part in the fishing. But if "*they also went with him*" was used with reference to the apostles, it would need only to be put into the mouths of the apostles in the first person in order to obtain the tradition of John (xxi. 3) "*We also go with thee.*"

Thus Ephrem's comment increases the number of links between Matthew's and John's accounts of the Petrine fishing; (1) the interchange of "net" and "hook," (2) the mention of "going up" in connexion with Peter or the fish, (3) the mention of some "going with" Peter. These agreements suggest that Ephrem had before him a tradition that blended Matthew's account of the one fish caught by Peter, and John's account of the 153 fish caught by the Seven disciples, but drawn to the land by Peter. The Johannine narrative includes an account of the *one* "*fish*" previously prepared to be the food of the disciples, and manifestly representing the ΙΧΘΥC, the Saviour Himself. This—in a Johannine sense, widely different from the Matthæan—might be called the fish that "first" came up; and Peter might be said (in Origen's words) to be "comforted" over it, as in O.T. people are said to "comfort their souls with bread[1]."

---

[1] [2999 (viii) *a*] As regards the connexion between "Peter" and "going up"—and this in a context mentioning a boat—it should be added that there is one other passage in the gospels, besides Jn xxi. 11, where ἀναβαίνω is thus used, not indeed of Peter alone, but of Peter with Jesus. It is the account (peculiar to Mt.) of Peter's attempt to walk upon the waves. Lk. is wanting. Jn, like Mk, makes no mention of Peter:

Mk vi. 51	Mt. xiv. 32	Jn vi. 21
καὶ ἀνέβη πρὸς αὐτοὺς εἰς τὸ πλοῖον καὶ ἐκόπασεν ὁ ἄνεμος.	καὶ ἀναβάντων αὐτῶν εἰς τὸ πλοῖον ἐκόπασεν ὁ ἄνεμος.	ἤθελον οὖν λαβεῖν αὐτὸν εἰς τὸ πλοῖον καὶ εὐθέως ἐγένετο τὸ πλοῖον ἐπὶ τῆς γῆς εἰς ἣν ὑπῆγον.

See **1735** *b—c*. Syr. Burk. txt has in Mt. xiv. 32 "when *he* went up into the boat" (but SS "*they*"). Ephrem has (p. 136) "Cum venisset Dominus et cum Petro navem ascendisset." The Latin versions (exc. *a*) mostly have "ascendisset."

[**2999** (viii) *b*] Steph. *Thes.* does not give any instance of ἀναβαίνω in the sense of "being drawn up" (as Mt. xvii. 27) but Wetst. on Mt. xvii. 27 quotes from Semitic sources *de Naziraeis* v. 1 "Denarius aureus qui *ascendit in manum meam primus*. Dolium vini quod *ascendit in manum meam primum*, h. e. quod veniet in potestatem meam." He also quotes *Beresh. R.* v. 8 "Piscis *ascendens* ex Acco, *ascendenti* ex Zidon, et *ascendenti* ex Apamia sapore similis est." But this, so far as the words quoted go, might mean "The fish that comes up [to Jerusalem]" from these places. So ἀναβαίνω in Epictet. i. x. 2 (and freq.) used absolutely, means "go up to Rome."

[**2999** (viii) *c*] The Syr. of Mt. xiv. 32—4 (Burk. txt) has "And when *he went up into the boat* the wind ceased...And when *he went up to the dry land*...." The Semitic active is often confused with the Semitic causative, so that "he went up" might be confused with "he caused to go up." And the Syr. "*went up* to the dry land," closely following a mention of "the boat," suggests that the former might be interchanged with "*caused [the boat] to go up* to the dry land," *i.e.* caused the boat to be immediately on the dry land, which is, substantially, the meaning of the parall. Jn vi. 21.

[**2999** (viii) *d*] It should be noted that, although Jn does not say expressly that Peter was "first" in catching the fish, yet he implies it—while at the same time implying that the other disciples laboured with him. Jn xxi. 10 "Jesus saith unto *them*, Bring *ye* of the fish that *ye* have now caught," implies a statement that all the disciples fished, and a command to them all to bring the fish to Him. We can hardly suppose that they disobeyed Him and sat still. Peter, it is true, is alone mentioned as drawing in the net, but Ammonius the Elder is probably giving Jn's meaning correctly in the words (Cramer) "The spiritual net is drawn by Peter *with the others*."

[**2999** (viii) *e*] What is likely to have been the historical basis for a tradition connecting "Peter" and "going up"? Matthew's story of the walking on the water suggests that the "going up" might refer originally to Peter's being "lifted up" from the deep waters of sin, after he had repented of his denial of his Master. But perhaps a more likely

§ 6. *Matthew's account of Peter's "fishing" illustrated from John*

[**2999** (ix)] Several convergences of evidence point to the conclusion that John is substantially right if he regards Matthew's narrative as allegorical and as referring to the period after Christ's resurrection, when Peter, as Origen says, received "power to catch [a] fish first." In the first place, the phrase "*find a stater*" appears to have been part of an old Jewish proverb, "Everyone that looks into his possessions shall *find a stater*[1]." But Jesus gives to a similar phrase, "*the*

---

explanation would base itself on the absolute use of ἀναβαίνω to mean "go up to Jerusalem," especially noticeable in the last words of Chronicles "The Lord his God be with him, and let him *go up*," *i.e.* to Jerusalem, to build the new City and the new Temple.

 [**2999** (viii) *f*] Luke, it is true, omits all mention of leaving Jerusalem or "going to Galilee" in order to see the risen Saviour, or before the preaching of the gospel began. But there are many indications that the disciples did, as a fact, "go to Galilee" before they preached the gospel in Jerusalem. If so, the truth may have been that Peter "*having gone up* [to the City] was the first to preach the gospel with effect, or, in the language of his Master, to prove himself *a fisher of men*." It may be a mere coincidence that Luke, in a different sense, applies ἀναβαίνω to the first meetings of the disciples—merely as meaning go up to an upper room, or go up to the Temple (Acts i. 13, iii. 1). Later on, when Luke speaks of Peter as opening the Church to the Gentiles, he describes him as (Acts x. 9) "going up" to the house-top where he receives a vision, and afterwards as (xi. 2) "going up" to Jerusalem to advocate the admission of the Gentiles. If there is anything more than a mere casual coincidence, we may suppose that Luke's Petrine narratives may have been influenced by traditions of the Petrine "going up," though he did not quite accurately interpret them. See **2837** (iii) *c* on the apostles "going up to the temple" and standing "on the steps."

[1] [**2999** (ix) *a*] Levy iii. 494 *b* qu. *Chull.* 105 *a*, "Samuel said, 'In many things I am behind my father, for he used to search his possessions twice a day, I only once a day....Whoever searches his possessions every day earns (verdient, מרווח, v. v. משׁכח) a stater.'" I am informed by Prof. Bacher that the context mentions two men as looking about their property and detecting an agent cheating, or a leak in an aqueduct. The searcher used to say, "Where are Samuel's staters?" After stopping the leak, he

finding of a drachma," a moral application, making it parallel to "the finding of a lost sheep." As the shepherd rejoices over the sheep, so does the woman in Christ's parable rejoice over the drachma, after she has swept her house and sought diligently, and found it. Both "sheep" and "drachma" represent a "lost soul," rescued from sin (Lk. xv. 4—10).

[**2999** (x)] Before passing to John, it will be well to add a word about a writer who has a good deal to say about the didrachm, and from whom John often borrows. Long before Clement and Origen, Philo speculated about "the half of the didrachm" in mystical doctrine by which those Fathers may well have been influenced. Philo (i. 498–9) speaks of the "half" of the "didrachm," in connexion with (Exod. xxiv. 6) "half of the blood," as implying an "equality" of division and also a twofold human nature. The Holy Word, he says, pours some of the blood into the "vessels" that are the receptacles of our sensual faculties "insisting (ἀξιῶν) that our non-logical part should become soul and as it were logical (τὸ ἄλογον ἡμῶν μέρος ψυχωθῆναι κ. τρόπον τινὰ λογικὸν γενέσθαι)." Then he continues, "Is it not the fact that in this manner also the *holy didrachm was divided,* in order that we might purify the one half, the drachma, paying down the ransom of our own soul (τῆς ἑαυτῶν ψυχῆς)? Thus, from a

---

exclaims "Now I have found them, Samuel's staters!" There may be a play on the words "search" and "stater." At all events the ithp. אסתער of סער (=סור "search") resembles אסתירא "stater" (Levy *Ch.* ii. 178) and the ithp. may mean either "search oneself" or "be violently moved," "disturbed." There is also an interchange between סער "search" and סעד (Levy iii. 560, 562) of which the latter means "comfort," or "support (with food)" στηρίζω, so that the proverb lends itself to many applications. There is no evidence that Samuel's proverb was borrowed from dialogue between defaulters and shekel-collectors—"I have not got the stater," "Search and you will find it." But any student of LXX meeting with a tradition that spoke of the "didrachm" and the "stater" might naturally connect it with the passage in Exodus where LXX uses the former and Aq. the latter to denote the "shekel" of which a half was paid for the redemption of the soul (**2999** (vii) *c*).

cruel and bitter servitude to the passions, the only free and freedom-giving God, at our supplication, and sometimes even without our supplication, rescues our soul by force." We have seen above that Clement and Origen appeared to suppose two payments, the payment of one coin to Cæsar or to "this world," but of another to God. Philo seems to make a similar distinction when he continues, "But the other portion of our nature [*i.e.* the other half of the didrachm] let us abandon to the slavish tribe that is unfit for freedom." This Philonian passage, besides illustrating many other points in Matthew's narrative—and in particular the notions of "ransom" and "freedom"—casually mentions the occasional spontaneousness of God's intervention (ἔστι δὲ ὅτε καὶ χωρὶς ἱκετείας) in a manner that accords with Matthew's use of προφθάνει.

§ 7. *Different symbolisms of "fish"*

[2999 (xi)] To understand John's divergence from Matthew we must put ourselves in the position of Christians about 70—80 A.D. when the Greek notion of Christ as the FISH (**2703**) was taking hold of the Western Churches. In the Galilæan Church, for some time after Christ's death, "fish" would always suggest something quite different—namely a *convert*. When Christ said, "I will make you fishers of men," He meant that the apostles were to raise up human souls out of the silence and darkness of the deep waters of sin. The convert was "born again," born into a new life. A Jewish tradition says that when a child is born into the light, the eye and the ear that were open in the womb must be closed, and the eye and the ear that were shut in the womb must be opened[1]. So with a convert. He was to be "enlightened," to "receive sight," to have "his eyes opened." But he was also (though that is much less seldom expressed) to have all his

---

[1] Levy iv. 154*b*, quoting Levit. r. sect. xiv. 158*a*. (Dr Büchler adds *Nidda* 30*b*.)

senses renewed, including the sense of speech. Speech was given to man (such at least was the Hebrew feeling) that man should "glorify God." A "dumb" man could not do this, and dumbness, in the west even more than in the east, was symbolized by fish. But when the fishers appointed by the Saviour had drawn him up from the water and "*opened his mouth*"—according to the saying of David "Deliver me from bloodguiltiness, O God...O Lord, *open thou my lips*, and my mouth shall shew forth thy praise"—then he could offer up the sacrifice of "thanksgiving" and utter speech as "the oracles of God[1]."

---

[1] [2999 (xi) *a*] Comp. 1 Pet. iv. 10—11 ἕκαστος καθὼς ἔλαβεν χάρισμα... εἴ τις λαλεῖ ὡς λόγια θεοῦ, and Origen (Lomm. iii. 233) who says concerning the fish, ἀναβεβηκέναι δὲ ἀπὸ τῆς θαλάσσης ἐν τῷ λογικῷ ἀγκίστρῳ συνειλημμένον, καὶ εὐεργετούμενον ὑπό τινος αὐτὸν διδάξαντος Πέτρου τὴν ἀλήθειαν, μηκέτι ἔχειν ἐν τῷ στόματι τὸν στατῆρα, ἀλλὰ ἀντ' ἐκείνου τὰ ἔχοντα τὴν εἰκόνα τὰ λόγια τοῦ θεοῦ, which seems to be a quotation from 1 Pet. describing the new speech bestowed as a gift (χάρισμα) on the convert. Comp. also Heb. xiii. 15 "let us offer up the sacrifice of praise (θυσίαν αἰνέσεως) the fruit of lips that make confession to his name." On this, Westc. refers to Lev. vii. 12 etc. The word rendered "praise" by LXX is habitually rendered εὐχαριστία by Aq. but ἐξομολόγησις by Sym. (see Lev. vii. 12, Ps. xlii. 4, cxlvii. 7). The author of Heb. xiii. 15, though quoting as LXX, explains as Symmachus.

[2999 (xi) *b*] The point is, that the converts of an apostle, when "their mouths are opened," offer up "sacrifices" to the glory of God which may be called, in some sense, the sacrifices presented by the apostle. Thus, although Rom. xii. 1 says "present *ye* your bodies a living sacrifice," yet Col. i. 28 says "that *we* may present every man." So a convert, though "begotten" by God, is sometimes said to be "begotten" by the apostle. 1 Pet. i. 13 foll. after mentioning redemption (*ib.* 19) "by the blood of the Lamb," calls on the converts to long for the (ii. 2) "milk" of the word, coming to the Lord as (ii. 4) "a living stone," and being built into Him as "living stones" so as to be a "holy priesthood" and to "offer up spiritual sacrifices acceptable to God through Jesus Christ." He adds (ii. 12) the hope that the converts will lead such pure lives that the Gentiles "from your good works beholding them, may glorify God in the day of visitation." The epistle also speaks of (iii. 19) Noah brought safe out of the deluge as a type of the world brought up out of sin by baptism.

§ 8. *The original meaning of the story of "the stater"*

[**2999** (xii)] Now, returning to Matthew's narrative, let us endeavour to ascertain what was the original meaning of the story, and to what time and place it must be referred. First, as to place, Matthew locates it at Capernaum, but this may easily be explained. Peter is said to have come to "*the* house," but some versions have "*his* house." Even without "his," readers might naturally assume the house to be Peter's. "If so, since Peter's house was at Capernaum, Capernaum would seem to be the place"—so Matthew may have argued. But the Arabic Diatessaron has "And when Simon *went forth without*," which would be in Greek ἐξῆλθεν ἔξω. Now on what occasion did Peter "*go forth without* (ἐξῆλθεν ἔξω)"? According to Matthew and (bracketed) Luke (Mt. xxvi. 75, [Lk. xxii. 62] ἐξελθὼν ἔξω) only after he had finally denied his Master[1]. In that denial, Peter had "*gone forth without*" in a spiritual as well as a material sense. He had gone outside the circle of the disciples. He had become as it were a

---

This rapid succession, or combination, of metaphors, shews how full of metaphor an early Petrine vision might be, and how some phrase (differing only a little from Origen's) about Peter's "being comforted over the first fish that came up" might come to be interpreted—quaint though the interpretation appears to us—as referring to the FISH, Christ the Son of God, after He had gone up to heaven.

[1] [**2999**(xii)*a*] Mark differs. Mk xiv. 68 ἐξῆλθεν ἔξω εἰς τὸ προαύλιον is parall. to Mt. xxvi. 71 ἐξελθόντα δὲ εἰς τὸν πυλῶνα (without ἔξω) while Lk. xxii. 58 makes no mention of "going out" at this point. Thus Mark defines locally the "going forth outside" and does not make it final; Matthew mentions one "going forth," local, and another, "going forth outside," final; Luke (bracketed in W.H.) mentions only the final "going forth outside."

For the metaphor, comp. 1 Jn ii. 19 "they went out from us," where Origen's interpretation (**2110***b*) is confirmed by *Chag*. ii. 2 Mishna "Menahem *went out*" compared with *ib*. 16*b* "Whither did he *go out*?" Abajje answers, "To an immoral life" (Levy iv. 667*a* תרבות); Raba, "To the king's service." Jn xiii. 30 describes a "going out" of Judas, but no "going out" of Peter is mentioned in Jn xviii. 27.

" heathen and a publican." Jews were familiar (**616** c) with the expressions Beth Hillel, Beth Shammai, to mean the "house," " school," " circle of disciples " of Hillel or Shammai. A Jew might therefore say that Peter " went forth," for a time, from his Master's "house," and afterwards "returned" to it. According to this view, the place of the " going forth " was, literally, the Highpriest's palace, but in fact the Church of Christ[1].

[**2999** (xiii)] According to this view—that " house " meant " the circle of Christ's disciples "—the " house " would really be independent of place but (when the narrative of " fishing " was literalised) might well be supposed to be in Capernaum— perhaps Peter's house in that town. And here, according to Matthew, when Peter " came to the house," Jesus " *anticipated him*." This, interpreted in accordance with Hebrew traditions, would mean that when Peter turned in prayer and in con-

---

[1] [**2999** (xii) b] The parall. Mk ix. 33 makes no mention of the Stater incident, but has (lit.) " And *they came to Capernaum, and being* (γενόμενος) *in the house, he* [*i.e.* Jesus] began to question them, About what reasoned ye on the way? But they were silent, for they had talked on the way, Who was the greatest?" Mt. xvii. 24—xviii. 1 has " But *when they came to Capernaum*, (lit.) *there approached* (προσῆλθον) those that collected the didrachms...(25) and when *Peter had come to the house*... thou shalt find a stater. Give that for me and thee. In that hour *there approached* the disciples to Jesus, saying, Who after all (ἄρα) is the greatest in the kingdom of heaven?" Lk. ix. 46—7 has " But there entered a reasoning among them, Who of them should be the greatest? But Jesus, knowing the reasonings of their hearts...." The facts are best explained by supposing that there was no mention of "Capernaum" or of a *literal* "house," but a statement of this kind, "It came to pass that *when there entered into the* (or *his*) *house* [that is, *Christ's disciples*] *a questioning*, Jesus knew it...." Καὶ ἐγένετο ἐν τῷ εἰσελθεῖν εἰς τὴν οἰκίαν διαλογισμὸν ἦν εἰδὼς Ἰησοῦς.... This was taken by Mk as meaning "when he entered into the house, Jesus knew of their questioning." Then it came to be thought that "the house" must be at Capernaum, and probably Peter's house. But if it had been so, and if it had been known to Luke, the latter—who takes pleasure in adding circumstances of time and place—would hardly have omitted " Capernaum."

trition to Christ, the Master *came to meet him*, and helped and comforted him. And at this point a curious verbal detail confirms the hypothesis of a parallelism between the story of the Stater and that of Peter's repentance, namely, that the Syriac word used to render προφθάνω "anticipate," קדם, occurs in Isaiah (xxxvii. 33) where Aquila and the rest have προφθάνω correctly, but LXX ἐπιβάλλω. Now ἐπιβάλλω is the very word—not yet satisfactorily explained by any agreement of critics—used by Mark in connexion with Peter's "weeping," where the parallel Mt.-Lk. omit ἐπιβαλών, but have "*went forth without.*" The context of the parallel Luke says that the Lord "turned and looked on Peter," and Cramer, on Mark, prints a paraphrase, which says that Peter wept bitterly, "the Lord having given heed to him[1]." These small verbal points indicate that in the very earliest traditions there were divergences about the manner and circumstances in which Peter "went out," and his Master helped him to return.

[2999 (xiv)] What then was the original tradition? Few will expect that in its exact form the first-hand impassioned and poetic Petrine narrative can ever be reproduced. But it appears to have referred to the ransom to be paid for the apostle's denial. Perhaps a vision of the "exactors[2]," to whom

---

[1] Mk xiv. 72, Mt. xxvi. 75, Lk. xxii. 62. Cramer has ἐξελθὼν ἔξω, φησίν, ἔκλαυσε δεινῶς, προσεσχηκότος αὐτῷ τοῦ Χριστοῦ.

[2] [2999 (xiv) a] For "exactors," see Lk. xii. 58 τῷ πράκτορι (Mt. v. 25 τῷ ὑπηρέτῃ). The meaning seems to be a chastisement, or visitation, for sin, regarded as an angelic (Lk.) "exactor" or (Mt.) "minister." Sir. xxxv. 15—17 suggests that the prayer of the oppressed widow goes up to God and brings down "judgment" on the oppressor from "the Most High." Comp. *Aboth* iii. 25 "*the bailiffs* (הנבאין) *go round continually every day and exact from a man* whether he wills or not...and the judgment is a judgment of truth." In Lk. xii. 58, πράκτορι is rendered by SS נבא, the word rendered by Dr Taylor, in *Aboth*, "bailiffs." Levy i. 293 quotes a passage calling God Himself, in some circumstances, גבאי.

THE SELF-MANIFESTATIONS OF CHRIST [2999]

our Lord once refers, had come to Peter asking whether his Master would indeed pay the tax for the redemption of his soul. Then the Lord "came to meet" Peter, assuring him that he was forgiven and that there was no need of any sacrifice, or payment of ransom or tax, since the Father did not take taxes from His Son nor from the Son's brethren. Notwithstanding, that there should be no stumbling-block—as though the Father forgave and favoured Peter but not Judas—let him toil for his Master and prove himself a true "fisher of men." The apostle had felt sore misgivings about his own soul. He had "lost his drachma." What was he to do? The proverb said, "Look into thine own possessions and thou shalt find a stater." Christ *"came to meet" him* saying, in effect, "No, do not look into thine own possessions. Toil for others, toil for my converts. Catch the fish. Open their dumb mouths to the praise and glory of God. *Thus shalt thou find a stater*[1]."

---

[1] [2999 (xiv) *b*] The explanation above given of "opening its mouth" labours under this disadvantage, that it cannot (as far as I know) be supported by any instance, from the Talmud, of a teacher "opening the mouth" of a convert. If the original was simply "catch fish and [thus] shalt thou find a stater," the detail may have been supplied for clearness. In most stories of finding pearls etc. in fish, the finder discovers the treasure *when cutting open the fish*. Instead of this, feeling that something of the kind was needed, the Greek translator may have inserted "opening its mouth." SS, D and most Latin versions define "thou shalt find" by adding "there," *f* "in it," *e* "into it." Perhaps the original was "Go down to the sea and catch fish and *there* shalt thou find a stater"; and "opening its mouth" was an addition, which has supplanted "there" in Greek MSS.

[2999 (xiv) *c*] In view of the possible confusion (2999 (xv) *b*) between "shekel" and "scandal," it should be added that in New Hebrew there is another way of expressing "scandal" when it means "occasion for slander." Levy iv. 156—7 quotes several passages where so-and-so is said to be done "that there may not be given *opening of the mouth* to heretics." The phrase is also Biblical, occurring (Gesen. 836 *a*) in Ezek. xvi. 63 where it means "*opening of the mouth* in boasting," and Ezek. xxix. 21 where it means "*the opening of the mouth*" of a prophet to declare the will of God. In the present instance, if an evangelist recording this tradition believed the meaning of Christ's alleged words to

[2999 (xv)] Assuming the story to have had some such an origin, it would be necessary to suppose that Matthew has literalised it as he has literalised "the ass and the foal of an ass"—being the only one of the four evangelists to suppose that the phrase meant two animals. Another instance is perhaps Peter's walking on the waters, which he alone records and which may be parallel to the Johannine account of the penitent Apostle coming to Christ through the waters, where SS says that Peter "fell in the sea." Why should we be surprised at such literalising? Many passages in our extant "Matthew" reveal an acquaintance with Semitic traditions that is not balanced by a corresponding power to interpret them. And surely this particular tradition would be difficult to interpret. If the above-mentioned Jewish proverb was in vernacular use during the first century ("Toil at your work, look to your own affairs, *so shall you find a stater*")—is it surprising that the author or editor of our present "Matthew" interpreted the saying, not from the point of view of a Galilæan peasant, but from that of a Greek familiar with the LXX? Then he would naturally assume that the "didrachm" or the "stater" (for two versions might well be current) referred to the "sacred didrachm," called by Aquila a "stater," which

---

be, not, "lest we should cause them to stumble and fall," but "lest we should give them an occasion, or, *opening of the mouth, [against us]*" he might write "*opening of the mouth*" in the margin. This might be erroneously transferred to the text.

[2999 (xiv) *d*] Taking the other view of the opening of the mouth (comp. Ezek. xxix. 21 "I will give thee opening of the mouth"), we might compare 2 Cor. vi. 11 "my mouth is open to you," Eph. vi. 19 "that the word may be given to me in the opening of my mouth." In that case, some slight change would be required, *e.g.* of αὐτοῦ to αὐτός, thus: ἀνοίξας τὸ στόμα—αὐτὸς εὑρήσεις στατῆρα, "Having opened thy mouth [to preach the gospel] thou thyself shalt find a stater." But the abrupt transition from the fish to the fisherman—"catch a fish and having opened the mouth," *i.e.* thy mouth—would be very harsh. Any one of the conjectures above mentioned seems preferable to this. The best seems to be that in **2999** (xiv) *b*.

each Jew offered "to redeem his soul," and which was devoted to the maintenance of the temple. The collectors of this tax in Capernaum, would (he argued) naturally come to Peter for it as being the householder, with the question, Did not his Master pay the tax? Then the Lord might naturally reply, Why ought He to pay the tax to keep up the temple of God, being Himself God's Son? Nevertheless, not to create a stumbling-block, Peter was to go and catch a fish and find the tax—yes, twice the tax, a coin sufficient to pay for two. Here seemed to be a miracle worth recording, and as such it has been recorded by Matthew[1].

[2999 (xvi)] In John's narrative, the question, "Which of the disciples was *first* in catching fish?" is answered in such

---

[1] [2999 (xv) *a*] A vestige of Matthew's tradition is perhaps to be found in the well-known story of Peter, where Peter "*went out*"—but from Rome—and the Lord "*met*" him, saying, "I go to be crucified in Rome," and then "I saw thee fleeing from death and I desire to be crucified for thee." Peter's martyrdom, as well as his preaching, might be regarded as "coin of redemption for the soul," and Peter might be said to have "found" that "stater," and to have paid it for himself and for his Master, in the strength that his Master gave him, "Fear not, I am with thee until I bring thee into the house of my Father." Another version says, "*Follow me*, for I go to be crucified again in Rome"; and John xxi. 18—22 mentions the "following" of Christ by Peter in connexion with the apostle's future crucifixion, as though the following were on "the way of the cross." It was very natural that the beautiful words of the Lord, "Pay that for thyself and for me" should be interpreted by some as referring to a sort of joint crucifixion of Master and Disciple, united in a common death. See *Acta Petr. et Paul.* Lipsius, pp. 170, 215.

[2999 (xv) *b*] As regards the introduction of the word σκάνδαλον, "offence," into Matthew's story, it is worth noting that Levy *Ch.* ii. 551 *b* gives the same letters תקלא as meaning the common shekel *i.e.* the "half of the holy shekel" (LXX "half of the didrachm," really "half of the tetradrachm") and also "trap," "stumbling-block." In Deut. vii. 16, Jon. Targ. has תקלא to represent Heb. מוקש which = σκάνδαλον in Josh. xxiii. 12, Judg. ii. 3, I S. xviii. 21 etc. This might indicate a play on the words "shekel" and "scandal" such as one might expect in a very old tradition of this kind based on a vernacular proverb.

a way as to shew the pointlessness, or at least the relative unimportance, of such comparisons. The apostles were *together*, he says, in going forth ("We also go with thee"). They were also together in toiling and in catching fish. But they caught nothing till the Word of the Lord came to help them. As for what followed, if Peter was "the first" that came to Jesus, John was "the first" to recognise Him. Peter would not have come, but for John's exclamation "It is the Lord." That Peter was in no mood now to claim primacy over the disciples is indicated by his humble reply to Christ's question "Lovest thou me more than these?" True, it is said that Peter "*went up* and drew the fish to land," when Christ gave the command to all, "Bring ye of the fish that ye have by this time caught." But the others must have taken part in unloading the vessel. Moreover another *fish*, THE FISH, was already on the shore, and it was on this—which might be called THE FIRST FISH—that the disciples fed; and this, no other, could be said to contain in itself the redemption of souls, suggested by the "finding of the stater."

For the rest, though there is scarcely a word in common between the Matthæan and the Johannine narrative, there is much common thought. In John, Christ "anticipates" the disciples—though the word is not used—by spontaneously addressing them when they did not know Him, and by helping them in their helplessness. Also, besides the precept to all the disciples, "cast the net on the right side of the ship," a special one is given to Peter, later on, which he is to obey in order to shew his love for his Master, "feed my sheep"—thrice repeated in various forms. This is better adapted for Western ears than "catch fish for me": but it has precisely the same spiritual meaning. The rule was, "Give, and it shall be given." The disciples could not partake of the one FISH until they had caught fish. They could not belong to the flock of the Shepherd unless they themselves shepherded His sheep.

[2999 (xvii)] Many other points in the Johannine story would well repay investigation¹, but space does not allow it.

The re-clothing of Peter

¹ [2999 (xvii) a] On one of these a few remarks will be made because it may illustrate the variations of Petrine traditions as well as (2837) the Law of Divergence from obscure metaphor. Among a multitude of metaphors describing the apostle's Denial and Restoration one may have been that of "garments" or "linen." This is frequent in O.T.—partly, perhaps, because of the white "ephod" worn by an ordinary priest (Gesen. 65)—and also in Revelation, *e.g.* iii. 18 "Buy of me *white garments*...that the shame of thy nakedness be not made manifest," xvi. 15 "Blessed is he that watcheth and *keepeth his garments*," xix. 8 "the *fine linen* is the righteous acts of the saints." Zechariah (iii. 1 foll.) describes a vision in which he sees a high priest "clothed with filthy garments" to whom the Lord says "I have caused thine iniquity to pass from thee" and he is reclothed. Let us examine how far such a parent-metaphor would explain difficulties in the following passage.

[2999 (xvii) b] Mk xiv. 50 foll. "And they all left him and fled. And a certain young man was following along with him clothed with a linen garment on his naked body, and they seize him, but he, leaving his linen garment behind him, fled naked."

If taken metaphorically, the passage might refer to Peter—unnamed as also in Mk xiv. 47 "*a certain one of them that stood by*...smote the high priest's servant"—relating how even Peter fled with the rest in the hour of trial and did not "watch and keep his garments." "Naked" is twice repeated. He had nothing but the linen garment "over his nakedness." He left it with his enemies and fled "naked."

But, if taken literally, the passage appears an intrusive detail, calling attention away from Christ Himself in order to say that some one of His companions was a little less timorous than the rest. Moreover no one has explained the "linen garment," which certainly (as Dr Swete says *ad loc.*) "would excite attention," and of which Bengel says that "the wearer was rich" (an inference approved by Dr Swete), while Epiphanius (*Haer.* lxxviii) says that it was a mark of asceticism. Agreeing with Epiphanius, *Hor. Heb.* takes about two pages to shew that "this young man, out of religion, or superstition rather, more than ordinary, had put on his *sindon*, and nothing but that, *upon his naked body.*" Of what interest was it for Christians to be informed in the earliest gospel that in the moment of Christ's arrest, a rich disciple left a night-shirt, or a superstitious ascetic left a *sindon*, in the hands of the arresters?

The νεανίσκος (says Dr Swete) "has been identified with St John (Ambr., Chrys., Bede), James the brother of the Lord (Epiph. *Haer.* lxxviii.), a resident in the house where the Lord had eaten the Passover (Thpt.), the Evangelist himself (many recent commentators)." If the νεανίσκος was any one of these, there would seem little reason for mentioning the fact, and none at all for omitting the name. If it was Peter, the name might be omitted here for reasons similar to those that caused its omission in Mk xiv. 47.

[2999 (xvii) c] In the passage in which Epiphanius connects James with Mk's "linen garment" he describes him as one who never trimmed his hair or bathed and (*Haer.* lxxviii. 13) "*did not put on a second garment* (χιτώνιον δεύτερον)...one who used (lit.) a light mantle of linen *absolutely alone* (τριβωνίῳ ἐκέχρητο λινῷ μονωτάτῳ), as it says (φησί) in the Gospel, *The young man fled away and left the linen garment with which he was clothed* (ἔφυγεν ὁ νεανίας καὶ ἀφῆκε τὴν σινδόνα ἣν ἦν περιβεβλημένος)." James and the two sons of Zebedee, says Epiphanius, shared this ascetic life (οἱ τρεῖς οὗτοι ταύτην τὴν πολιτείαν ἐσχήκασιν)—*i.e.* they literally obeyed the precept of the Lord (Mk vi. 9 and parall., comp. Lk. iii. 11) "Do not put on two coats." Epiphanius adds the astounding statement, "Only to this James was it permitted once in the year to enter into the holy of holies."

Compare the much earlier statement of Hegesippus about James as one who never trimmed his hair or bathed and (Euseb. ii. 23. 5 foll.) "he *alone* (or, *by himself*) *was permitted to enter into the holy places; for indeed he did not wear wool but linen garments* (τούτῳ μόνῳ ἐξῆν εἰς τὰ ἅγια εἰσιέναι, οὐδὲ γὰρ ἐρεοῦν ἐφόρει ἀλλὰ σινδόνας) and he *alone* (or, *by himself*) used to enter into the sanctuary (κ. μόνος εἰσήρχετο εἰς τὸν ναόν)."

But the Greek version of a quotation of this passage by Jerome *Catal. Script. Eccles.* ("Jacobus") says, "Now it was his custom to enter into the holy of holies *not using woollen clothing but linen* and to him alone was it lawful to enter into the sanctuary (ἔθος δὲ ἦν αὐτῷ εἰσελθεῖν εἰς τ. ἅγια τ. ἁγίων ἐσθῆτι ἐρεΐνῃ μὴ κεχρημένῳ ἀλλὰ λινῇ μόνῳ τε αὐτῷ ἐξῆν εἰς τὸν ναὸν εἰσιέναι)." Comparing the three passages together we see that the manifestly false tradition about James as going into the holy of holies alone once in the year—like the high priest on the day of atonement clothed in linen alone—may be explained by (1) a love of the marvellous, (2) a verbal transposition of a statement that James "wearing linen *alone* used to go into the temple."

This is an excellent instance of myth, springing from verbal corruption, wherein a comparatively late author, Epiphanius, unconsciously gives a hint towards the correction of an error that he himself repeats. The same author may perhaps help us to explain Hegesippus' statement (**2837** (iii)) that James was killed with "a fuller's club." Epiphanius (lxxviii. 14) is represented by the Latin of Petavius as mentioning "fullo quidam," but the Gk is ὑπὸ του (?τοῦ or του) γναφέως τῷ ξύλῳ παισθεὶς τὴν κεφαλήν, and this might conceivably represent an allusion to the *coup de grâce* given (Suidas) by he γνάφος or κνάφος, which was like a fuller's carding instrument, δι' οὗ τοὺς βασανιζομένους κτείνουσιν. Hegesippus gives the words in an expanded form suggestive of an error based on a misunderstanding of ὁ γνάφος or κνάφος (comp. Euseb. ii. 1. 5, quoting Clem. Alex., ὑπὸ γναφέως, v.r. τοῦ γναφέως and κναφέως).

[2999 (xvii) *d*] Comp. Jerome *loc. cit.* "The Gospel called *According to the Hebrews*, lately translated by me into Greek and Latin,...after the resurrection of the Saviour, says, Dominus autem quum dedisset sindonem servo sacerdotis ivit ad Jacobum et apparuit ei." The Gk transl. has, ὁ δὲ Κύριος δεδωκὼς σινδόνα τῷ δούλῳ τοῦ ἱερέως, ἀπελθὼν πρὸς Ἰάκωβον ἤνοιξεν αὐτῷ (where ἤνοιξεν is a rendering of "apparuit" as "aperuit" which the translator perhaps regarded as meaning "opened the eyes," or "the scriptures," or "the door of salvation").

[2999 (xvii) *e*] The difficult phrase "when he had given the linen garment to the servant of the priest" is omitted (or replaced) in later versions thus (ed. Nicholson pp. 63—4) : Gregory of Tours (*Hist. Franc.* i. 21) "At last on the third day, *returning with triumph from the spoil of Tartarus*, showing Himself to James," (Abdias *Hist. Apost.* vi. 1) "Wherefore He chose to appear to him [James] first of all, *as also to Mary of Magdala and Peter*," (Jacobus de Voragine, *Legenda Aurea* lxvii) "The Lord appeared to the same [James] and said to *them that were with him....*" The context in Abdias curiously resembles Epiphanius above (**2999** (xvii) *c*) in making James one of "three" (but not the same "three"), the other two being Simon the Canannæan and "Judas of James."

[2999 (xvii) *f*] The priority of Peter in seeing the risen Saviour is attested by 1 Cor. xv. 5 and by Lk. xxiv. 34 (where, however, the reading of D (λέγοντες, not λέγοντας) suggests that Simon and Cleopas saw Him together). An attempt appears to be made by Abdias ("and Peter") and perhaps by Jacobus ("them that were with him") to save this priority. Certainly, some mention of Peter here would make good sense. But, if his name ought to occur, how can we explain its omission? For future as well as for present use, it will be convenient to set down here some facts bearing on the insertion or omission of "Simon" or "Peter" in the gospels.

[2999 (xvii) *g*] "Simon" or "Peter" is sometimes parallel to, or added to, "those with him" or "the disciples," or "the multitude," in such a way as to suggest that the name might be confused with one of these phrases.

Mk i. 36	Mt. iv. 23	Lk. iv. 42
Σίμων κ. οἱ μετ' αὐτοῦ	om.	οἱ ὄχλοι

Mk xvi. 7	Mt. xxviii. 7	Lk. xxiv. 9 (in diff. context)
τοῖς μαθηταῖς αὐτοῦ κ. τῷ Πέτρῳ	τοῖς μαθηταῖς αὐτοῦ	τοῖς ἕνδεκα κ. πᾶσιν τοῖς λοιποῖς.

Parall. to Mk-Mt. is Jn xx. 17 τοὺς ἀδελφούς μου.

[2999] THE SELF-MANIFESTATIONS OF CHRIST

In the account of the Transfiguration, Lk. ix. 32 ὁ δὲ Πέτρος κ. οἱ σὺν αὐτῷ ἦσαν βεβαρημένοι is peculiar to Lk. "*They that were with him*" are James and John. These are previously described as (Mk ix. 1) "some *here* (ὧδε) of those *standing*," parall. Mt. xvi. 28 "*standing here* (ὧδε)," Lk. ix. 27 "*standing* (?) *on the spot* (αὐτοῦ)," but Mk ix. 1 (D) has "*stand with me*." Comp. Ezra x. 15 "*stood up*" (marg. "*were appointed*") עמדו, LXX μετ' ἐμοῦ (leg. עמדי). Also, for a parallelism between (1) "*standing by*," (2) "*with*," and (3) "*Peter*," compare

Mk xiv. 47	Mt. xxvi. 51	Lk. xxii. 49—50
εἷς δέ τις τῶν παρεστηκότων	εἷς τῶν μετὰ Ἰησοῦ	οἱ περὶ αὐτόν...εἷς τις ἐξ αὐτῶν

where Jn xviii. 10 has Σίμων οὖν Πέτρος.

In the following, Luke first mentions "Peter" in one of W.H.'s doubly bracketed passages (where the parallel Jn has "Peter" and the unnamed "other disciple") and then afterwards refers to the disciple as "*some of those with us*."

Lk. xxiv. 12	Jn xx. 3	Lk. xxiv. 24
[[ὁ δὲ Πέτρος ἀναστὰς ἔδραμεν...]]	ἐξῆλθεν οὖν ὁ Πέτρος κ. ὁ ἄλλος μαθητής	κ. ἀπῆλθάν τινες τῶν σὺν ἡμῖν ἐπὶ τὸ μνημεῖον

Above, Mk xvi. 7 contained the *command* to make announcement τοῖς μαθηταῖς αὐτοῦ κ. τῷ Πέτρῳ, and Jn xx. 17 τοὺς ἀδελφούς μου. But the Mark Appendices and Jn describe the *actual announcement* as follows:

[Mk xvi. 10 App. A]	[Mk App. B]	Jn xx. 18
ἀπήγγειλεν (D + αὐτοῖς) τοῖς μετ' αὐτοῦ γενομένοις	τοῖς περὶ τὸν Πέτρον συντόμως ἐξήγγειλαν	ἀγγέλλουσα τοῖς μαθηταῖς

Here, then, in Mk, "*those that had been with him*, i.e. with Christ," is parall. to "*those with Peter*," and to "*the disciples*," and points back, in Mk, to a previous "his disciples and Peter." It has been shewn (**2875**) that "those with Peter" might mean "Peter and his friends." On this point compare the description of Christ's bidding the disciples "handle" Him, where the circle of disciples is described by Luke as "the eleven and those with *them*," but by Ignatius differently, as follows:

Lk. xxiv. 33	Ign. *Smyrn.* 3	Comp. Jn xx. 26
τοὺς ἕνδεκα κ. τοὺς σὺν αὐτοῖς	ὅτε πρὸς τοὺς περὶ Πέτρον ἦλθεν	οἱ μαθηταὶ αὐτοῦ κ. Θωμᾶς μετ' αὐτῶν

Some combination of "Simon" with "and those with him" may explain:

Mk i. 29	Mt. viii. 14	Lk. iv. 38
"they came into the house of Simon and of Andrew with James and John"	"coming (sing.) into the house of Peter"	"he entered into the house of Simon."

In the story of the fig-tree, where Mark (xi. 21) has "*Peter*," the parall. Matthew (xxi. 20) has "*the disciples*"; and in Mark's immediately preceding verse (xi. 20) "they passed by," k has "prætereuntes *illi qui cum eo erant.*"

[**2999** (xvii) *h*] The causes of these interchanges are doubtful. In Syriac (*Thes.* 4216—8) the same letters, but for the final letter, might mean "*disciples*" (lit. "hearers") or "*Simon*," and there is the same similarity in Heb. and Aram. Some interchanges might also arise from confusions of עַם meaning "with," and עַם meaning "multitude" or "people." Again, in New Heb. שֶׁעִמּוֹ, "those with him," might be confused with שִׁמְעוֹן, "Simon." There might also be a tendency to attribute to a central figure (like Peter) the sayings of subordinates clustered round that centre—especially if there were documents called the *Preaching of Peter*, or *Teaching of Peter*, in which "those with him" sometimes meant Peter's companions and sometimes the disciples of Christ. Again, it is possible that some divergences might arise from Galilæan appellations now utterly or nearly lost. For example, Ephrem on Mt. xvi. 28 τῶν ὧδε ἑστώτων (Mk ix. 1 ὧδε τῶν ἑστηκότων) speaks of the three as "*pillars*" (alluding to Gal. ii. 9). But the same word, עַמּוּ(ו)דִים, is used by Delitzsch to render "standing" in Mt. xvi. 28 and "pillars" in Gal. ii. 9. And a "pillar," עַמּוּד, is easily confused with the Heb. "with him," עִמָּדוֹ. "Pillar" (Levy iii. 660) freq. means "great man" or "great teacher." The metaphor may explain the legend of Samson's casting down the "pillars" of Philistia. Comp. the tradition (Levy *ib.*) that "the *pillars, i.e.* teachers, of Cæsarea wept," with Euseb. *De Mart. Pal.* ix. 12 κιόνων οἱ...ἀπέσταζον, where "pillars" are regarded as literally dropping tears.

[**2999** (xvii) *i*] The important thing to remember is that the name "Peter" may be latent, in different forms, under many very early Christian traditions. If the phrase under consideration ("*gave the linen garment to the servant of the priest*") could be explained of Christ's appearing to Peter, then the *Gospel according to the Hebrews* would fall into line with the general Christian tradition that Christ appeared first to that apostle (1 Cor. xv. 5).

"The servant of the priest" seems to refer to Mk xiv. 47, Mt. xxvi. 51, Lk. xxii. 50 "*the* (A.V. *a* except in Lk.) servant of the high priest." *Hor. Heb.* on Mt. v. 25 "*the* officer," explains the article as meaning the "*executioner*," "*whipper*," "*verger*," or "*scourge-bearer.*" Without some explanation, "*the* servant of the high priest" is perplexing. Jn xviii. 10 says "*the* servant of the high priest...the servant's name was Malchus." Now the Talmudic treatise on scourging, or *Maccoth* (22 *b*), says that the Chazan or overseer of the synagogue was also "the scourger," *Maccah*. And Levy iii. 136—7 says that *Malcouth* (from a different root) meant "scourging." Rodkinson renders *Maccoth* 22 *b* "*Chazan* of the synagogue" by "*messenger* of the court"—loosely, no doubt, but still instructively for our purpose. For it shews that either of two glosses, attempting to explain that "*the* officer" acted as the high priest's "scourger" or "messenger," *malacha*, might give rise to a statement that "the man was called *Malchus*."

[2999 (xvii) *j*] It might seem incredible that this "servant, or scourger, of the (high) priest" could be substituted for "Peter" in a translation by Jerome of the *Gospel according to the Hebrews*. But there remains one small loop-hole through which we may discern a possibility that *this gospel might use about Peter an allusive phrase that Jerome might take as referring to the servant of the high priest*. The loop-hole must be looked for in Mk xiv. 47 εἷς δέ [τις] τῶν παρεστηκότων and Jn xviii. 22 εἷς παρεστηκὼς τῶν ὑπηρετῶν. These two are the only instances in the gospels (or in N.T.) of εἷς with παρεστηκώς. In Mk, it is generally, if not universally, interpreted as meaning "*Peter*"; in Jn it certainly means "*an officer of the high priest*." We have seen above that עמד in various forms and in various ways might be connected with "*Peter*." But it is also very frequently represented in O.T. by the LXX παρίστημι (Trommius gives 36 instances) and Delitzsch uses עמד to represent παρίστημι both in Mk and in Jn here.

[2999 (xvii) *k*] According to this view—suggested by the double use of this phrase, containing εἷς and a form of παρεστηκώς—the *Gospel according to the Hebrews* did not speak of "the servant of the priest" but spoke allusively about "*him that stood by* [the Lord] *and smote*." This Jerome took to mean "the servant" mentioned in Jn xviii. 22, who was in waiting on the high priest and *smote the Lord*. But the writer meant (Mk xiv. 47) the unnamed "bystander" (whom John called "Peter") who stood by the Lord and *smote His enemy*. The writer may have called Peter by this allusive periphrasis because he had in view the metaphor of the "linen garment," and because Peter, by shedding blood, might be said to have stained "the linen garment." He needed to have it cleansed and restored to him by His Master. He could not come into the presence of the risen Saviour without receiving what Christ had described as "the wedding garment." Or it might be called the garment of approach, the white linen ephod (Gesen. 65) with which the priests were girt.

[2999 (xvii) *l*] Keeping before us this view of "the linen garment," we are in a position not only to explain the stress laid by Hegesippus and Epiphanius upon the "linen" clothing of James but also to point out that the Hebrew Gospel assumes a similar emphasis, meaning in effect, "After Jesus had given the white linen of forgiveness and holiness to Peter he came to do the same thing for James." And now, too, passing to John's description of Peter's "reclothing," we shall find this metaphorical interpretation confirmed by the fact that he uses—and he alone in N.T.— the very word employed by Aquila to render "ephod," namely ἐπενδύτης.

[2999 (xvii) *m*] Jn's unique use of ἐπενδύτης (xxi. 7) is all the more remarkable because it does not appear to be a vernacular word in contemporary Greek, being non-occurrent in the Indices to the Papyri of the *Egypt. Expl.* and the Berlin Urk. up to the beginning of this present year (1907). Wetstein (on Jn) and Steph. *Thes.* allege it from Greek tragedy and from Greek scholiasts but not from intervening literature. Westcott says "the word was adopted in later Hebrew for the 'frock' of labourers." But he alleges no evidence. Krauss' index does not give it; nor does Wetstein's long note on its various and disputed meanings. *Acts of Philip in Hellas* § 1 τὸ γὰρ ἔνδυμα ὅπερ ἔδωκεν τοῖς ἀποστόλοις ὁ Ἰησοῦς ἐπενδύτης μόνον ἦν καὶ λέντιον is perhaps taken from Jn, since Jn, alone of the gospels, uses these two words for clothing. If Jn had meant merely the "upper garment" used by Christ's disciples and mentioned by Christ in His precepts, why should he not have used the regular Synoptic word?

[2999 (xvii) *n*] A commentary printed by Cramer says τὸ μὲν οὖν διασώσασθαι (leg. διαζώσασθαι) τὴν αἰδῶ ἐπεδείξατο (and simil. Chrys.). This, if it means that Peter felt "shame" for "nakedness," in the sense of sinfulness, probably points to the evangelist's meaning. And then a special force will be perceived in ἐπενδύτης. For Aquila is known to have used it in 1 S. xiv. 3 to represent "*ephod*"—LXX mostly ἐπωμίς, seemingly a short surplice fastened round the body with a girdle. For the most part Aquila uses ἐπένδυμα as in Exod. xxv. 7 (and so Sym. and Theod.), 1 S. ii. 18 (where LXX, Sym. and Theod. have ἐφούδ or ἐφώδ), 2 S. vi. 14 (where Sym. has ὑποδύτην, but Field fort. ἐπενδύτην and so Oxf. Conc. without comment, LXX στολήν). Ἐπενδύτης, therefore, is exactly the word to represent Peter, after repentance, "girding himself" anew in the "linen garment" that he may be no longer "naked." Compare the repeated use of ἐπενδύσασθαι "to clothe oneself additionally" (unique in N.T.) in 2 Cor. v. 2—4 "longing (lit.) to *clothe ourselves additionally* with our habitation from heaven, if so be that having clothed ourselves (ἐνδυσάμενοι) we shall not be found *naked....*We desire not to unclothe ourselves but (lit.) to *clothe ourselves additionally.*" As to the girding, the first epistle of St Peter says (1 Pet. v. 5) "Yea all of you...gird yourselves (ἐγκομβώσασθε) with humility to serve one another." Having regard to the unique N.T. use of λέντιον in the Washing of the Feet, we can have little doubt that the *Acts of Philip* had a metaphorical meaning in the passage above quoted, "For the clothing that Jesus gave the apostles was the *ephod* (ἐπενδύτης) alone [wherewith to approach God] and the linen napkin [to serve one another]."

[2999 (xvii) *o*] From this metaphorical interpretation several small details in the Johannine narrative receive a fresh significance—especially when compared with narratives of Lk., Mt., and Mk, describing how Peter, after a miraculous draught of fishes, said, "Depart from me, for I am a sinful man, O Lord"; and how he tried to walk on the water to

[2999] THE SELF-MANIFESTATIONS OF CHRIST

Indeed, these notes on the words "touching," "drawing near," "meeting," "anticipating," etc. have already taken up more space than might seem fit in such a volume as this. However, they

Jesus but his faith failed him and he began to sink; and lastly, if Mk xiv. 51—2 refers to Peter, how he fled from his Master and abandoned his linen garment "naked."

Taking up these stories, point by point, the Fourth Gospel seems to say, "Yes, these things were true once, but now all is altered. Instead of crying '*Depart from me*,' the Apostle eagerly hastens towards the Saviour. Instead of '*sinking*,' he passes safely through the waters and reaches Him. He *was* '*naked*,' it is true (ἦν γὰρ γυμνός): but as soon as he hears, 'It is the Lord,' he girds himself with his ephod." Every phrase, almost every word, seems to have its allegorical significance—the "loaf," the "coal fire" (nowhere else mentioned in N.T. except (Jn xviii. 18) where Peter denied his Master (s. **1711** *g* quoting Ephrem), the FISH (that is, the Lord Himself) and the command to "bring" Him their "fish" (the result of their labour for Him, before they could receive from Him the result of His labour for them). The allegory may possibly extend even to matters that modern readers would think incapable of being allegorized, such as the number of fish (according to the well-known interpretation of Augustine) and the number of cubits of the distance through which Peter and the rest have to pass in order to reach Jesus. They are "not far" from Him. It is only "about two hundred cubits." This number of years (according to Philo on Gen. v. 21—4) represents the length of the penitence of Enoch, "bis centum [anni] in quibus pœnitentia exercita fuit."

As to the "girding," it is alluded to by Jesus a little afterwards, perhaps (**2796—7**) implying that Peter has now adopted a new service, *His* service. When he was a raw youth, Peter girded himself and "walked" where he himself "willed." But now (xxi. 18) "Another (**2796—7**) shall gird thee and carry thee where thou willest not." Also, as in the parable of the Wedding Garment, and as in the *Gospel of the Hebrews*, the clothing with linen is followed by a feast or the gift of the "loaf" or "bread." The Lord (Ps. xxiii. 5, lxxviii. 19) "prepares a table" for the disciples. If we may substitute "*Peter*" in that Gospel, as above suggested, the passage will then run: "And when the Lord had given the linen garment to *Peter* he went to James and appeared to him....Bring ye (adferte), said the Lord, a table and bread." This "*bring ye*" appears parallel to the mystical precept in the Fourth Gospel, "Bring ye." Whether the food first "brought" be "bread" or "fish" the spiritual meaning is the same. The disciples were to "bring" their offering to Christ, before Christ fed them with His offering, that is, with Himself.

deal with subjects of great importance, some of which may not come directly under consideration in *The Fourfold Gospel*. Hence they have been given in outline here, as otherwise there might be no opportunity of publishing them at all.

The present state of the evidence makes it impossible to regard the above suggestions as established conclusions; but some may regard them as at all events more probable than the literal view; and, in any case, the considerations advanced may indicate how these apparently definite narratives of actual events may have arisen—without any dishonesty in those who have recorded the narratives in their present shape—out of visions, metaphors, parables, and songs.

I add "songs," because we perhaps lay too little stress on the influence of the earliest Christian hymnology. The Pauline Epistles (Eph. v. 14) have preserved no more than three lines of those "psalms and hymns and spiritual songs" which they commended to the Ephesians and Colossians, and which St Paul himself sang by night in the prison at Philippi. That the songs vanished may be explained on the supposition that they seemed to the second generation of Christians, and especially to plain Gentiles, too "oriental," or "florid," or "prone to treat history as poetry[1]." Such matter-of-fact western readers would be in danger of innocently converting the metaphorical into the literal and poetry into history. As the poems of Israel influenced the chronicles of Israel, so—it can hardly be doubted—the poetry of the first generation of Galilæan and Jewish believers must have left its impress on subsequent prose narratives of the life of Christ throughout the Roman empire.

---

[1] A friend suggests that the use of "linen garment" and of other above-mentioned metaphors is "too transcendental" for the simple folk of the earliest Christians. But perhaps my friend ought to have said "too oriental and poetic for our occidental and prosaic minds to accept with ease—even with the *Revelation of John* open before us."

INDICES

INDICES

I. NEW TESTAMENT PASSAGES 291
II. ENGLISH 298
III. GREEK 309

I

INDEX (NEW TESTAMENT PASSAGES)

[*Black Arabics refer to paragraphs* [2]800–[2]997 (*the* 2 *not being printed*). *Ordinary Arabics refer to the sections of* 2998–9, *the two "Longer Notes"*.[1]]

MATTHEW

		PAR.
1	8	**882**
	16	**881**
	18	**40**
	18–25	**880**
	21	**881**
	24–5	**881**
2	1 foll.	17 *b* foll.
	9	17 *e, i*
	15	**883**
	18	**883**
	22	**942*** (xxiv) *b*
3	7	**937** *f*
4	3	20 *a*
	6	20 *a*
	24	2 *b**
5	1	**887**
	3	**888**
	6	**888**
	25	14 *a**, 17 *i**
	41	**887** *a*
	44–5	**816**
6	1–6	55 *l*
8	14	17 *g**
	15	1 *b**, 6 *c**
	17	**964**
	21	**872**
9	6	44 *a*
	13	**837** *c*, **840**
	25	1 *b**
10	6	**861** foll.
	8	**905**
	10	**888**
	16	32 *e*

MATTHEW

		PAR.
10	24	32 *e*
	26	55 *m*
	28	**819**
	41	**886**
11	2–3	**841, 888**
	5	**995**
	11	**880**
	25	**842**, 23 *a*
	25–7	50 *c–e*
	27	27 *f*, 39 *b*
	28–30	**844–9**
	29	**842–9, 963–4**
12	7	**840**
	10	**961** (i) *d*
	18	54 *f*
	28	6 *e**
13	9	29 *b*
	13 foll.	**913**
	31	**852**
	33	55 *k*
	55	**879**
14	12	**942*** (xxii) *b*
	26	**824*** (i) *b*, 6 *a**
	29–30	**979**
	32–4	8 *a** foll.
15	11	**841**
	24	**860–71**
16	17	39 *b*, 44
	19	**887**
	24	**841**
	27	**850**, 24 *e*, 44
	28	25 *a–b*, 44, 17 *g–h**

MATTHEW

		PAR.
17	2	28 *w–x*
	7	2 *b**, 6 *b–c**
	17	**913**
	20	**851–6**, **942*** (xxiv) *b*
	22	**857**, 23 *d*
	24–7 foll.	7* foll., 12 *b**
	27	8 *b**
18	3–4	**885**
	10	**824*** (i) *g*, 15 *b*
	11	**861**
	12	**864** foll.
	17	**887**
	18	**887, 979**
	20	**887**
19	4	**984** *c*, 47
	8	**984** *c*
	10–12	**888, 974**
	20	**834** *a*
	26	**858**
	28	8 *b*
20	23	**935**
	28	**829, 964, 996**
21	1 foll.	**848**
	9	24 *f*
	15	**874** *c*, 24 *f*
	16	**840**, 23 *a*, 24 *f*
	18–21	**873**
	20	**875**, 17 *g**
	21	**851**
22	1 foll.	45
	14	**914**

[1] *Black Arabics refer to paragraphs* [2]800–[2]997, *ordinary Arabics to the sections of* 2998, *or, if starred, to the sections of* 2999. *For example*, 872 = 2872, 16 = 2998 (xvi), 16* = 2999 (xvi).

INDEX

MATTHEW		MARK		MARK	
	PAR.		PAR.		PAR.
22 30	56 d	1 34	839	11 20	17 g*
44	22 b–c, 23 b, e	36	17 g*	21	875, 17 g*
23 35	51 b, 54 f	38	839 c	22–3	851 foll.
24 6	26 b	2 10	839	24	857, 873
8	874 d	17	837 c, 840, 54 i	25	840, 857, 873
15–16	874 e–f, and Pref. p. xii. foll.	27	840	12 25	56 d
		3 1	961 (i) d	36	22 b–c, 23 b
		10–11	2 b*	13 7	26 b
16	942* (xiii) e	11	2 a*	8	874 d
21	984 c	17	969 foll.	14	837 (iii) d, 874 e–f, 942* (xiii) e, and Pref. p. xii foll.
28	942* (xxii) b	21	883		
29	16 a	4 12	913		
30	26 s, 31 a	22	55 m		
32	874	26–9	55 j		
25 1–11	942* (xv) c	28	876	19	984 c
31–46	850	5 35	859	26	31 a
26 26	891	6 3	879	28	874
26–8	828	8	888	14 22–4	828, 891
30	897–903	9	17 c*	26	897–903
39	6 b*	12	840	27	869
51	934, 17 g–i*	29	942* (xxii) b	35	6 b*
54	26 b	34	866, 869	36	858
61	985	49	824* (i) b, 6 a*	47	17 b–k*
64	23 b, 31 a, 32 a	51	8 a* foll.	50–2	17 b* foll.
71	12 a*	7 7	857	58	985
75	12*, 13*	15	841	62	23 b, 31 a, 32 a
27 45	910	27 foll.	859	68	12 a*
46	910, 917 foll.	8 34	841	72	13*
49	987	38	850	15 22	930 foll.
50	910, 917 foll.	9 1	25 a–b, 44, 17 g–h*	34	910, 917 foll.
53	909			37	910, 917 foll.
28 2	909, 5 b*	7	850	43	942* (xxii) b
5	909	8	2 b*	16 3	908–9
7	17 g*	19	913	4	5 b*
9	889, 979, 1 b*, 3*, 4*	23	858	7	17 g*
		29	851 foll.	8	878
16	3 a–b*	31	857	9	878
17–18	6 c*	33	12 b*	10	17 g*
18	23 d, 6 b*	35 foll.	857		
20	887	36	885–6		
		49–50	858		
		50	857		LUKE
	MARK	10 6	984 c, 47		
		13–14	859	1 1–2	980–4
1 3	839 b foll.	15–16	857, 885–6	13–14	881 a
4	839 c	20	834 a	16	936 a
7	839 c	21	857	26–35	880
11	850	27	858	2 8 foll. 13, 17 f foll.
14	839 c	39	935 foll., 28 a	9	17 i, 5 a*
15	839 a–d, 857	45	829, 857, 964, 996	13	16, 5 a*
22	839			14	24 g
29	17 g*	11 12–14	873	38	5 a*
31	1 b*, 6 b–c*	13	874 a, 878	40	840* g

Black Arabics refer to paragraphs [2]800–[2]997, ordinary Arabics to the sections of 2998, or, if starred, to the sections of 2999. For example, 872 = 2872, 16 = 2998 (xvi), 16 = 2999 (xvi).*

NEW TESTAMENT PASSAGES

LUKE			LUKE			LUKE		
		PAR.			PAR.			PAR.
2	41	961 (i) *a*	12	4	819	24	24	17 *g**
	48	883		58	14 *a**		32	908
	52	840* *g*	13	6–9	874		33	17 *g**
3	7	937 *f*		21	55 *k*		34	17 *f**
	11	17 *c**	14	1–2	961 (i) *c–d*		36	897–907
	23	882, 994		15	56 *c*		37	824* (i) *b*
	36	20 *c*	15	4	861 foll.		39–40	824* (i)
4	3	20 *a*		4–10	9*		44–9	903
	9	20 *a*	17	6	851–6, 873			
	18	839 *a*		21	996			
	22	840* *g*, 879	18	17	885			JOHN
	38	17 *g**		21	834 *a*			
	38–9	1 *b**		35	6 *a**	1	1–2	980
	39	5 *a**, 6 *c**	19	10	865		3	27 *f*
	41	839		11	6 *a**		13	39–42
	42	17 *g**		29, 37	6 *a**		14	942* (xii) *a*,
5	32	837 *c*, 840		38	24 *f–g*			24 *e*, 28 *f*,
6	6	961 (i) *d*		41	6 *a**			44
	17	887	20	1	5 *a**		14–17	840* *g*
	19	2 *b**		36	56 *d*		18	32 *d*
	20–1	888		42	23 *b*		29	32 *d*
7	12	6 *a**		43	22 *b–c*		33	55 *i*
	13	6 *d**	21	9	26 *b*		39	977
	14	6 *b–c**		20	837 (i), (iii) *a*,		41	21 *a*
	19	841, 888			874 *e–g*, and		45	979
	22	995			Pref. p. xii.		49	20 *a* foll.
8	10	913			foll.		50	20 *b*
	17	55 *m*		21	874 *e–g*, 942*	2	19–21	942* (xii) *a*,
9	3	888			(xiii) *e*			985
	23	841		27	31 *a*		20	962
	27	25 *a–b*, 44,		29	874		22	875
		17 *g**		30	874	3	3	978
	32	17 *g**		34	5 *a**		8	26 *d*, 55 *j*
	36	2 *b**	22	17–20	828		13	48
	41	913		25	829		16	870, 23 *e*
	44	23 *d*		27	829, 963–4, 996		29	806
	45	908		30	8 *b*	4	7	968
	46–7	12 *b**		32	923 *c*, 936 *a*		18	961 (i)
	47	885		44	986		24	27 *q*
	55	942* (xvii)		49	875		25	21 *a*
	59	872		49–50	17 *g**, 17 *i**		35	961 *a*
10	1	888		58	12 *a**	5	1	961 foll.
	3	32 *e*		62	12*, 13*		2	800 *a*, 959–62
	8	887		69	23 *b*, 32 *a*		5	961 (i)
	19	23 *a*	23	31	875		19	806, 858
	20	942* (viii) *g*,		45–6	910, 917 foll.		27	28 *s*, 45 *b*
		15 *b*		53	908		30	858
	21	23 *a*, 50 *c–e*	24	4	5 *a–b**	6	12	870
	22	23 *d*, 39 *b*,		6	4*, 5*		19	6 *a**
		50 *c–e*		9	17 *g**		21	8 *a** foll.
	40	5 *a**		11	890		39	870
11	20	6 *e**		12	17 *g**		64	984 *c*
	50	51 *b*		15	6 *a**			

Black Arabics *refer to paragraphs* [2]800–[2]997, *ordinary Arabics to the sections of* **2998**, *or, if starred, to the sections of* **2999**. *For example,* **872**=2872, 16=2998 (xvi), 16*=2999 (xvi).

INDEX

	JOHN			JOHN			ACTS	
		PAR.			PAR.			PAR.
7	24	28 w	16	22	874 d, 881 a,	1	13	8 f*
	37	968			942* (xii) b		15	942* (viii) g
8	17	26 k		24	806		24	888
	18	26 k		25	875	2	2	970
	44	984 c		32	923		35	22 c
	57	989–90	17	3	985		41	942* (viii) g
9	35	48		7	803	3	1	8 f*
10	1	985		11	54 j		13–15	54 f
	1–18	871		12	870		18	54 f
	10	870		13	806		26	54 f
	11–12	985		21	28 i	4	13	879
	28	870		24	806		27	54 f
	36	20 a–b, 45 b		25	54 j		30	54 f
11	33	985	18	9	870		36	860
	35	806, 985		10	17 g–j*	5	29	958
	39	909		11	875	7	52	54 f
	44	28 w		18	17 o*		55–6	25
	48–52	962 a		22	17 j–k*		56	32 a, 44 a
12	16	875		32	927	9	7	890
	23–4	856, 55 m	19	5	43 c	10	9	8 f*
	27	985		28	806		9–16	841
	28	26 c		30	923 d, 967		13	887
	31	26 p		35	925, 987		41	895 foll.
	33	927		37	26 s	11	2	8 f*
	34	850, 21, 33, 49	20	3	17 g*		5–10	841
	40	24 d		8	977		7	887
	43	24 d		17	805 a, 979, 1 b*,	12	1–2	937 b–c
13	5	963–4			17 g*		13–15	15 b
	21	985		18	17 g*	13	5	983–4
	23	32		23	887	15	10	843
	33	805 a, 978		26	892 b, 17 g*	16	25	898
	34	858, 924	21	2	925, 978	17	23 foll.	996
14	2	942* (xiii) e		3	7*, 8*	18	25 foll.	942* (xxii) d
	9	984 c		5	978	19	3	942* (xxii) d
	18	805, 978		7	934, 977, 17 m*	20	27	984 a
	20	28 i		10	8 d*	22	14	54 f
	23	899, 27 f		11	7*, 8*		20	26 j
	26	875		13	895 foll.	23	10	937 d
	30	26 p		15	978, 32 b	26	14	984 d
15	3	985		17	978		16	826 a, 983–4
	4	978		18	930 foll., 17 o*	28	23	3 a*
	5	978		18–19	936 foll.			
	6	877		18–23	962 b, 15 a*		ROMANS	
	11	806		19	926 foll.			
	12	858		20	925, 936 foll.	1	1 foll.	823
	26	26 c		23	941		3	26 o
	27	984 c		24	925, 941 foll.		3–4	35
16	4	984 c					16	825
	17	881 a, 942*		ACTS			16–18	942*
		(xii) b					17	54 e
	21	874 d, 881 a,	1	3	892 a foll., 904		20	28 b
		942* (xii)		4	892–5			
		a–b						

Black Arabics refer to paragraphs [2]800–[2]997, ordinary Arabics to the sections of 2998, or, if starred, to the sections of 2999. For example, 872 = 2872, 16 = 2998 (xvi), 16* = 2999 (xvi).

NEW TESTAMENT PASSAGES

ROMANS

		PAR.
2	16	825
	19–20	49
4	3	825
	9	825
	13	839
	24–5	820
5	7	54 *j*
	14	814
6	6	841
7	7	815
	18	815
	22	55 *l*
8	13	30 *b*
	23	814
	28	826
	32	918
	35	814
9	3	823, 942* (xviii)
	27–9	820
	33	908
10	6	908–9
	20	820
11	2	826
	8	913
	26	942* (xviii)
	32–3	942* (xviii)
12	1	828, 11 *b**
	14	909
13	4	942* (xviii) *a*
	9	815
15	12	820
	13	814
	19	824

1 CORINTHIANS

1	17	825
	17 foll.	814
	25	883
2	3	824
	4	814
	7 foll.	55 *i*
	10	814
3	2	50 *a*
	16–17	811
4	1	983, 984 *e*
	9–13	811
	15	823
5	4	887
6	2–3	8 *b*
	5	28 *h*
	19	811
7	1	888

1 CORINTHIANS

		PAR.
7	1–40	888
	35	811
9	20	829
	22	829
10	1	30
	17	895
	27	887
	31	811
11	22	811
	23–4	827–8
13	12	826
14	20	887, 978, 24 *e*, 50 *a*
15	3–8	892 *b*
	4	823
	5	17 *f**, 17 *i**
	27	22 *a*, 24 *c*
	27–8	839
	35–45	824*
	54	820

2 CORINTHIANS

3	6	828
	14	828, 908
	17	824* (i)
4	7	883
	10	26 *i*
	16	55 *l*
	18	43 *b*
5	1	43 *b*
	1–2	824*
	2–4	17 *n**
	14	814
	15	841
	17	823
	21	924
6	3 foll.	811
	11	14 *d**
	16	28 *f*
	17	28 *h*
	18	27 *i*
11	2	942* (xv) *f*
	28–9	824
12	2–3	953
	5	824
	9	824
	10	824

GALATIANS

1	10	803
	11 foll.	826
	13–14	823

GALATIANS

		PAR.
1	15	984 *d*
	16	823
2	1	826
	2	984 *d*
	6	803
	9	941, 17 *h**
	20	841
3	6	825
	11	54 *e*
4	4	880, 23 *c*
	13	824
	19	805 *a*, 978
	24	828
	25	826
5	1	843
	12	823
	13	23 *e*
6	1	840
	2	840, 924
	14	841

EPHESIANS

1	19–22	22 *a*
	21	27 *l*
	22	839
2	6	43
3	16	55 *l*
4	1	811
6	10	814
	14	28 *l*
	19	14 *d**

PHILIPPIANS

1	17	823
	23	826
	25	997 *a*
2	6–9	23 *d*
	7	923 *b*, 23 *c*
	11	26 *e*
3	2	860
	5 foll.	823
	20–1	22 *a*
	21	839, 858
4	3	942* (viii) *g*
	13	814

COLOSSIANS

1	11	814
	28	11 *b**
2	5	884
4	14	879
	15–16	28 *e*

Black Arabics refer to paragraphs [2]800–[2]997, ordinary Arabics to the sections of 2998, or, if starred, to the sections of 2999. For example, 872 = 2872, 16 = 2998 (xvi), 16* = 2999 (xvi).

INDEX

1 THESSALONIANS
PAR.
- 2 18   824
- 4 15   826

2 THESSALONIANS
- 1 8   942* (xviii) *a*
-   11   811

1 TIMOTHY
- 1 15   823
- 6 15   27 *h*

2 TIMOTHY
- 2 4   811
- 4 7   824, 826

PHILEMON
- 9   955

HEBREWS
- 1 3   27 *g*, 45 *b*
-   13   22 *c*
- 2 6   24
-   6–9   24
-   8   839
-   12   898
-   13   978
-   14   978
- 4 11–12   28 *t*
- 5 14   942* (xii) *b*
- 7 23   997 *a*
- 8 4–5   28 *d*
- 9 23–4   28 *d*
-   25   961 (i) *a*
- 10 1   961 (i) *a*, 980–1
-   3   961 (i) *a*
-   11   26
-   11–12   32 *a*
-   13   22 *c*
-   38   54 *e*
- 11 1   980
-   4   54 *f*
-   23   978
-   37   937 *d*
- 12 23   942* (viii) *g*
- 13 4   942* (xv) *b*
-   15   11 *a**

JAMES
PAR.
- 5 1–6   51 *b*
- 6   54 *f*

1 PETER
- 1 13   11 *b**
-   19   11 *b**
-   24–5   839 *b–c*
- 2 2   50 *a*, 11 *b**
-   4   11 *b**
-   4–6   908
-   12   11 *b**
- 3 4   55 *l*
-   19   11 *b**
-   20–1   942* (i) *k*
- 4 10–11   11 *a**
-   12   948
-   18   54 *e*
- 5 1   954, 26 *j*, 28 *a*
-   5   17 *n**

"2 PETER"
- 2 5   942* (i) *f, k*
-   7–8   54 *e*
- 3 4   984 *c*

1 JOHN
- 2 1   978, 54 *f*
-   7   984 *c*
-   12   978
-   14   978
-   18   962 *a*
-   19   12 *a**
- 3 12   54 *f*

JUDE
- 9   27 *p*
- 14   31 *a*

REVELATION
- 1 1   27 *q*
-   1–2   26
-   4   27 *f*
-   4–7   26
-   7   29, 31 *c*
-   8   26 *p*, 27
-   9   944
-   9–16   28
-   10   942* (iii) *b*

REVELATION
PAR.
- 1 12   942* (xxii) *a*, 26 *c–d*
-   13   26 *a*
-   14   7 *e*, 27 *h*, 29 *c*
-   15   26 *a*
-   16   28 *n*
-   17   27 *a–e, n*
-   20   28 *e*
- 2 1   28 *c, f, g, i, p*
-   6   942* (iii) *b*
-   7   29 *b*
-   8   27 *a–b*
-   10   26 *n*
-   12   28 *t*
-   13   942* (iii) *c*, 26 *i–j, n*
-   14   942* (iii) *b*
-   16   28 *t*
-   17   942* (xv) *a*
-   18   26 *a*, 28 *p*
-   20   942* (iii) *b*, (xv) *f*
-   23   27 *e*
-   24   942* (iii) *b*
-   26–7   942* (xvii)
-   27   942* (xiv)
- 3 1   942* (iii) *b*, (viii) *i*
-   4   942* (viii) *a, i*
-   14   26 *i, n*
-   17   942* (v) *b*, 28 *h*
-   18   28 *h*, 17 *a**
-   19   28 *h*
-   20   899
-   21   8 *b*, 28 *i*
- 4 1   26 *b–c*
-   4–7   33 *a*
-   5   28 *e*
-   6   28 *i*
-   7   942* (xiii) *d*
-   8   942* (i) *j*
- 5 1   942* (i) *h*, 31 *a*, 32
-   2–7   32
-   2   26 *c*
-   2 foll.   27 *q*
-   5   26 *f*
-   6   942* (i) *j*, 26 *f*, 28 *e, i, p*
-   6–14   33 *a*
-   7   8 *c*
-   11–13   942* (i) *j*
- 6 2   28 *d*, 29 *c*

Black Arabics refer to paragraphs [2]800–[2]997, ordinary Arabics to the sections of 2998, or, if starred, to the sections of 2999. For example, 872 = 2872, 16 = 2998 (xvi), 16* = 2999 (xvi).

NEW TESTAMENT PASSAGES

REVELATION			REVELATION			REVELATION		
		PAR.			PAR.			PAR.
6	6	942* (v) a, 28 i	12	1-17	942* (xi)-(xv)	17	14	26 n, 27 h
	9	26 i		3	942*(i) c, i, (xv)		16	942* (xv) f
	10	942* (iii) c, (xviii)a, 51 b		4	942* (xiii) b, 55 h	18	5-9	942* (xv) f
							9	948
	11	942* (iii) c		5	942* (xii) b, (xiv)		18	948
	16	28 w				19	5-9	26 c
7	2	942* (i) h		6	942* (xiii) e		8	17 a*
	2 foll.	26 c, 28 n		7	24 g, 27 p, 33 a		10	26 e, i, 27 n
	2-8	942* (i) c		9	942* (xiii) b		11	26 n, 28 d, 29 c
	4	942* (iv) c		11	26 i		12	28 p
	15	28 f-g, j		12	28 g		13-15	28 t
	17	28 j		14	942* (xiii) d-e		15	942* (xiv), 28 t
8	3-4	15 b		17	26 i		20	942* (xx) a
9	1	16	13	1	945		21	28 t
	3-11	942* (vi) a		3-4	942* (i) j	20	4	8 a, 26 i
	12	942* (viii)		6	28 f-g		10	942* (xx) a, 33 a
	14	51 b		8	942* (iii) d		11	28 w, 29 c
	15-18	942* (viii)		11	942* (xx) a		14	942* (xviii)
10	1	27 q, 28 w, 31		16	942* (i) h	21	1 foll.	942* (xx) c-d
	4	975, 29 a		18	942* (i) k-m		3	942* (xii) a, 28 f, g
	8	26 c	14	2	28 r			
	9	26 c		3	942* (xv) c		5-6	27 a, e-f
	11	942 foll.		4	942* (xv) b-f		9	26 b, c
11	1-13	942* (ii) a, (x), (xix)-(xxii)		7	27 n		10	942* (ii) b
				8	942* (xv) f		12	942* (xv) b
	2	942*(iv) c, (vii) foll.		13	29 a-b		14	942* (xv) b
				13-15	29 foll.		22	26 f, 27 h
	3	942* (iv) b-c, 26 i		14	26 a		23	26 f, 28 e
			15	1-3	942* (xv)	22	1	28 j, 32
	4	942* (iv) b, (xxii) a		5	28 f		2	28 i
				6	28 l		3	32
	7	26 i	16	12	51 b		4	28 w
	8	942* (i) c, (ii) a-c, (iii) b, (xxii) b		13	942* (xx) a		5	28 x
				15	17 a*		6	26 b, e, 27 h
				19	942* (ii) b		6-16	26 e
	9	942* (xxii) b	17	1	26 c		8	26 e, 27 n
	11-12	30 a		1-4	942* (xv) f		11	54 f
	13	942* (vii) foll., (esp. (viii) c-i), (xiii) f		1-15	28 r		13	27 a-f
				3	942* (i) i, (iv) b		15	860, 942* (xviii)
				5	942* (iv) b		16	26 g, 27 e
	14	942* (viii)		6	26 i, j		16-17	29 b
	19	942* (xii) a, (xiv)		7	942* (i) i		18	942* (xix) a
				9-11	942* (i) d foll., i		18-19	942* (xix)
12	1	942* (xv)		11	942* (i) j-l		20	26 h

Black Arabics refer to paragraphs [2]800-[2]997, *ordinary Arabics to the sections of* 2998, *or, if starred, to the sections of* 2999. *For example,* 872 = 2872, 16 = 2998 (xvi), 16* = 2999 (xvi).

II

INDEX (ENGLISH)

[*Black Arabics refer to paragraphs* [2]800–[2]997 (*the* 2 *not being printed*). *Ordinary Arabics refer to the sections of* 2998–9, *the two "Longer Notes"*[1].]

Abbahu 18–19
Abel 54 *f*
Abomination **942*** (i) *m*; of desolation, the **837** (iii), **874** *e*; s. also Pref. p. xvi foll.
"Above" and "below," mystically interpreted 7 *d–e*
Abraham **839**, **963**, 28 *v*, 54 *h*, 56 *d*; and Adam 37; superior to Noah 37 *d*; A., Isaac, and Jacob, the three feet of God's throne 14
Acts, the Son of Man in 24–5
Acts of John, the **902**, **988**
Adam, meaning "man" in Heb. but not in Aram. 2, comp. 20 *c*; son of A. 20, 23 *b*; A. and Abraham 37
Adjuration to scribes **942*** (xix) *a*
Ailam 28 *j*
Akiba **842**, 31 *b*
Almighty 27 *f–m*
"Alone," transposition of, error caused by 17 *c*** foll.
Alpha and Omega 27 *a* foll.
Alphabet, Gk **942*** (i) *l*
Am, "I AM," applied to God 27 *e*
"Ambassador" and "elder" **954–5**
American revisers **840*** *f*
Ananus the high-priest **942*** (ii) *d*
Ancient of Days, the 28 *o*
"Angel" interch. w. "voice" 26 *c–d*; of great counsel 27 *l, q*; meant by "watcher" 17 *h*; the recording **942***, 28 *n*; "angel of God," substit. for "God" 3 *h**; "his angel" (Rev. i. 1) 26 *c–g*; s. also "Angels"

Angelology, influence of 15 *f*
Angels **942***, 26 *c* foll.; ascension of **909**; ascending and descending 13; opposing Moses 11 foll.; guardian 15 *b* foll.; interch. w. "sons of God" 16; at the right hand of God 31 *a*; associated with "stars" 28 *e*, comp. 16 foll.; song of the 24 *g*; myriads of 31 *a*; not to be worshipped 27 *n*; "three a." (Gen. xviii. 2, Targ.) 5 *b**; "a little lower than the a." 24, 42 foll.; "their a." (Mt. xviii. 2) called by Ephrem "orationes" 15 *b*
Anthropomorphic metaphors 45
Anthropos 34
"Anticipate" 4*–5*; Mt.'s unique use of 7* foll.
Antiochus Epiphanes **942*** (i) *e*, (xiii)
Antipas, Herod **942*** (xxii)
Antipas, the martyr **942*** (iii) *c*
Antithesis, the principle of **942*** (i) *g* foll.
Anytus, Socrates on **808**
"Aperuit" and "apparuit" 17 *d* *
Apocalypse, s. "Revelation"
Apollos **942*** (xxii) *d*
"Apparuit" and "aperuit" 17 *d**
"Appear" and "meet" 3*
"Appoint" and "shew" **888**; "were appointed" and "stood up" 17 *g**
Aramaic 20, 23 *b*; how it expresses "man" 2
Ark of the Covenant, the **942*** (xiv)
"Army," parall. to "wing" **837** (i); s. also Pref. p. xvi foll.
Arrian **800–1**, **813**

---

[1] *Black Arabics refer to paragraphs* [2]800–[2]997, *ordinary Arabics to the sections of* 2998, *or, if starred, to the sections of* 2999. *For example*, 872 = 2872, 16 = 2998 (xvi), 16* = 2999 (xvi).

ENGLISH

Artemidorus, on "carrying" and "being carried" 931; on "dragon" and "serpent" 942* (xiii) b; s. also 929
Article, the, in Revelation 942* (xix)–(xx); s. also ó in Gk Index, and 984
Ascension, to heaven 18; of angels 909; and resurrection of Christ, events between 892–907
Ass and colt 846–8; "Ass's Jawbone" 873
"Assembled with" 892–5
Astrologers, called "Chaldæans" 17 a
Ath (Heb.), meanings of 27 c
Atonement, the Day of 961 a
Authority and goodness, Philo on 28 u

"Babes and sucklings" 23, 24f, 49
Babylon 942* (ii) b–c, (xv) e–f
Balaam's song 3, 4
Baptism, (metaph.) 935; (lit.) 27w; a place of 961; of spirit or of fire 30
Baptist, the, s. "John the Baptist"
Barnabas, on the Son of Man 36; s. also 843, 890, 914, 942* (i) a, (iv) c, 994, 28 o
Beast, the 942* (xx) a; the number of 942* (i) l foll.
"Beasts," in Heb., identical with "living creatures" 33 a, 47; "the b. of the field" 840, 43 d
"Beginning, from the" 984 c
Bellerophon 37 c
"Below" and "above," mystically interpreted 7 d–e
Beryl, in Ezek. and Dan. 28 m
Bethesda, the pool of 959 foll.
Between 28 j; in Heb., ambig. 28 i; "b. [the two sides of]" 28 k; "judge b. his brother" 28 k
Bildad 10
Blood, Christ's, Justin on 39 c
Blotting out 942* (viii) h
Boanerges, the name 969–77, comp. 942* (ii)
"Bodiless," ambig. 824* (i); s. also 56 d
Body, resurrection of the 56 a; Enoch's, melts away 55 b; "a spiritual body" 824* foll.
"Bones, a spirit hath not" 824* (i) d
Book, of Life, the 942* (viii) g; the sealed b. 32
Bosom of the Father, the 32
"Bow" and "truth" 837 (ii)
"Branches" and "daughters" 837 (ii)
Bride, the 942* (xv) c–f
Brutus, Marcus, in Shakespeare 830 foll.

"Call" and "meet" 3 g*, 4*
Candlestick, in the Temple, the 28 b foll.; placed by Vespasian in the Temple of Peace 28 e
Candlesticks, the seven 28 c foll.; "seven" and "two" 942* (xxii) a
Capernaum, 12*, 13*; "village of consolation" 7 b*
"Carrying" and "being carried," Artemidorus on 931
Catherine of Siena 966, 996
Cause, "Beware of single causes" 1*, s. also Pref. p. xi
Celibacy, ascetic 942* (xv) b
Chaldæans, i.e. astrologers 17 a
"Charioteer, the," Origen on 31
Cherubim, the 28 u
"Child," an error for "servant" 54f; receiving as a little c. 885–6; little children 978
Christ, birth of 880–2; preexistence of 37 c; blood of, Justin on 39 c; titles of 44 a
Christians, the, mentioned by M. Antoninus 813, by Tacitus 807
Chrysostom 823, 849, 895, 917, 936 a, 980, 990, 995, 20 a–b
Churches, the Seven 942* (iii)
City, the great 942* (i) c, (ii) a foll.
Clemens Alexandrinus, on the yoke 843; on the ass and colt 847; on the Son of Man 42 foll.; s. also 824* (i) g, 837 (iii), 854, 865, 918, 937 f, 942* (i) l, (xv) d, 985, 996, 27 f, u, 55 k, 7 a*, 10*, 17 c*
Clemens Romanus 845, 26 j, 55 j
Clement, Recognitions of 837 (iii) c
Cloud, a white 29; were baptized in the 30; the pillar of 30, 31; Rashi on the pillar of 4 c
"Clouds" and "cloud" 30 b–31 c; Origen on 31 a; of heaven, the 29; "with the clouds" 31 c
Coal fire, the 17 o*
Colt and ass 846–8
"Comfort with food" 9 a*
Compilation 942* (xix)
Confessors or martyrs 939 a
Conflation 837 (ii), 17 j, 3 e*
"Convivo" and "convivor" 897
Creatures, s. "Living creatures"
Cross, the 926 foll.; stretch out hands on 926 foll.; "tree" i.e. "cross," Ephrem on 933, comp. 942* (ii) b; cross and yoke 842–9
Crucifixion, not a Jewish punishment 927; of Peter 926 foll.

Black Arabics refer to paragraphs [2]800–[2]997, *ordinary Arabics to the sections of* 2998, *or, if starred, to the sections of* 2999. *For example,* 872 = 2872, 16 = 2998 (xvi), 16* = 2999 (xvi).

299

INDEX

Cry (n.) "three mysteries of the c." 55 *h*
Cry (vb.) *i.e.* "proclaim the gospel" 839 *b*
Cup, metaph. 935

Daniel, the Aramaic portion of 8; *ben adam* in 8; influence of, on Revelation 942* (i) *e*, (xviii), 26–33 *passim*
"Daughters" or "branches" 837 (ii)
David, son of 23 *b*, 36
"Dawn" (vb.) applied to God 27 *t*
Dead, first-born of the 26 *o*; "the dead are raised" 995
Delocalisation 28 *i*
Delos 942* (xi), (xiii) *b*
Denarius, a day's wage 942* (v) *a*
"Depart," ambig. 938–9
Desolation, the abomination of 837 (iii), 874 *e*, comp. 942* (i) *m*
Didaché, the, i.e. The Teaching of the Twelve Apostles 895, 26 *s*, 27 *w*
Didrachm 7 *b** foll., 9 *a**, 10*
Digamma 942* (i) *l*
Diogenes, in Epict. 814; Jerome on 824
"Disciples," "those with him" &c., parallels to 17 *g*–*h**
"Distrahitur," not "beheaded" 937 *d*
Divergence, caused by obscurity 837 foll.; caused by metaph. 17 *a** foll.; s. also Pref. p. xiv foll.
Divider, God as 28 *v*; the Logos as 28 *u*
Docetics, the 35
Domitian 942* (i) *a*, *b*, *e*, *m*, 27 *k*, 28 *a*; "a bald Nero" 942* (i) foll.; prohibits new vineyards 942* (v) *a*; on a white horse 28 *d*
Door, metaph. 985
Drachma, finding a 9*
Dragon, the 942* (xii) *c* foll., (xx) *a*
"Draw near" and "touch" 1*–2*; "draw near," "go to meet," and "go before" 4*–5*
Dropsical 961 (i) *c*

Eagle, the great 942* (xiii)
Earthquakes 942* (v) *b*, 946
Eating, attributed to Christ after the Resurrection 896–907; metaph. 56 *c*
Ebion and the Ebionites 867, 40, 41
Eclipse, an, Origen on 910
Egypt, "the iron furnace" 950
Eight hundred and eighty-eight 942* (i) *k* foll.
"Eighth," only twice applied to persons in N.T. 942* (i) *f*; "Noah the e. person" 942* (i) *f*, *k*

Elchasai 942* (xxiv) *a*, *b*
"Elder, the," meaning of 915, 954–5; "elders," mentioned by Irenæus 958; "twenty-four e." 942* (xv) *b*, 33 *a*
Elect, the 51
Elect one, the 51 foll.
Eliezer, the name 994
Elihu 10
Emmanuel 40
"End," parall. to "fig-time" 874 *a*–*b*
Enoch, the Patriarch 54 *c*; called the Son of Man 55
Enoch, the Book of 51 *a* foll.; a compilation 942* (xix); compared w. Revelation of John 942* (xix); quoted as Scripture 914; earlier part of 56
Enoch, the Similitudes of 19, 51; date of 51 *a* foll.; on the throne of judgment 8 *c*; doctrine of "hiding" in 55 *d* foll.
Ephod, the 17 *a*–*n**
Ephrem, on the "tree" *i.e.* "cross" 933; s. also 15 *b*, 24 *g*, 7 *e**, 8*, 17 *h**, 17 *o**
Epictetus, alleged lameness of 801; agreements of, with John 805–6; anecdote about 912; on the Galilæans 813; on repentance 815; on profit 816
Epictetus, Dissertations of:—
  Bk. I. i. 7 (802), i. 10 (802), ii. 12 (802), ii. 19 foll. (801), ii. 21 (818), ii. 29 (801), iv. 11 (814), iv. 24–7 (913), ix. 10–12 (954), ix. 15 (801), ix. 29 (810), ix. 30–2 (814), x. 2 (8 *b**), xii. 3 (822), xii. 16 (804), xii. 24 (801–2), xiv. 7–10 (822), xiv. 12 (804), xiv. 15–17 (807), xvi. 1 foll. (822), xvii. 1–4 (822), xviii. 19 (913), xix. 6 (807, 824, 840), xix. 8–9 (801), xix. 11 (816), xix. 12–15 (807), xxii. 1 (807), xxiv. 1 foll. (825), xxiv. 6 (823, 840), xxiv. 15 foll. (913), xxv. 1 foll. (825), xxvii. 4–6 (813), xxix. 1 foll. (812), xxix. 3–4 (817), xxix. 4 (815), xxix. 9 foll. (801), xxix. 18 (808), xxix. 46 (811), xxix. 50 foll. (801), xxx. 1 foll. (812), xxx. 6–7 (801)
  Bk. II. ii. 1 foll. (913), ii. 15 (808), ii. 22 (879), v. 15 foll. (828), v. 15–20 (913), vi. 10–13 (825), vi. 26 (840), vi. 27 (818), vii. 10–12 (814), viii. 2 (819), viii. 10 foll. (804), viii. 12 foll. (807, 811), viii. 18–20 (807), viii. 21 foll. (827), viii. 28 (818), ix. 1 foll. (801), ix. 3 (801,

---

Black Arabics refer to paragraphs [2]800–[2]997, *ordinary Arabics to the sections of* 2998, *or, if starred, to the sections of* 2999. *For example,* 872 = 2872, 16 = 2998 (xvi), 16* = 2999 (xvi).

997), ix. 19 foll. (812), x. 1 (997), xi. 1 (985), xii. 20-1 (819), xiii. 10 (913), xiii. 14 (801), xiii. 21-7 (801), xiv. 11 foll. (802), xiv. 15 (879), xv. 6 (939), xvi. 1 (812), xvi. 27 foll. (817), xvi. 33 (807), xvii. 19 foll. (827), xvii. 26 (827), xvii. 38 (818), xviii. 29 (814), xix. 20 foll. (827), xix. 23-4 (811 b), xix. 26 (807), xix. 32-4 (827), xx. 7 (827), xx. 22 (815), xx. 32 (807, 992), xxii. 15 (807, 816), xxiii. 13 (827), xxvi. 1 foll. (817)

Bk. III. i. 16 (913), i. 19 (913), i. 36 (818), iii. 2-4 (819), iii. 5 (913), iii. 6 (807), iii. 7 (913), vii. 4 (819), vii. 33-4 (825), vii. 34 (840), x. 13 (824), xii. 6 (813), xiii. 1 foll. (819), xiii. 4 (807), xiii. 13-15 (819), xiii. 23 (811), xv. 14 (822), xvi. 13 (813), xvii. 1 foll. (822), xxi. 11-12 (814), xxii. 5-8 (804), xxii. 21 (818), xxii. 23 (823), xxii. 30 foll. (801, 812), xxii. 35 (985), xxii. 45 foll. (801), xxii. 49 (884), xxii. 54 (811, 884), xxii. 56 (814), xxii. 58 (824), xxii. 69 (811), xxii. 72 (801, 820, 840), xxii. 73 (840), xxii. 78 (978), xxiii. 21 (808), xxiii. 30 (812), xxiv. 8 (818), xxiv. 14-20 (805-6), xxiv. 18 (913), xxiv. 18-20 (985), xxiv. 19 (804, 913), xxiv. 48 (801), xxiv. 64 foll. (814), xxiv. 64-8 (913), xxiv. 86 (55 j), xxiv. 91 (55 j), xxiv. 111-15 (804), xxv. 5 (813), xxvi. 22 (929)

Bk. IV. i. 79 (887 a), i. 103 (817), i. 153 (887), i. 169 (828), iv. 7 (815), v. 3 (913), v. 16 (801), v. 28 (818), vi. 5 (802), vii. 6 (813), viii. 35-6 (55 j), viii. 36-43 (876), ix. 6 foll. (817), ix. 12 (817), ix. 16 (814, 817), x. 14 foll. (801), x. 16 (803), x. 31 (818), xi. 4 (985), xii. 10-11 (803), xii. 19 (818), xiii. 4-19 (827)

Epictetus, Manual of (or *Encheiridion*) i. 3 (817), i. 5 (812), v. (817), viii. (817), x. (815), xi. (817), xv. (806), xvi. (913), xviii. (913), liii. 4 (808)

Epiphanes, Antiochus 942* (i) e
Epiphanius, on James the Just 17 c^*; s. also 824* (i) b, 865, 942* (xxiv) b, 994, 17 b^* foll.
Esdras, Fourth (or Second) Book of 942* (i) a, 993, 54 h, 55 g

Essenes, the 27 r–w
Eucharist, the, implies incorporation 895
"Euergetes," assumed as title 829
Euphrates, the 51 b
Eusebius, on "two tombs of John" 957; s. also 828, 837 (iii), 879, 915, 937 b–c, 939 a, 940 a, 942* (i) b, (v) a–b, (xiii) e, (xxii) c–d, 957-8, 960, 961 (i) a, 967 a, 984, 997 a, 25, 54 g, 17 c^*, 17 h^*
Evangelium Infantiae Arabicum 17 g, j
Exactors 14 a^*
"Eyes of God (or the Lord)" 28 b, p; connected with "stone" 27 v
"Eyewitnesses" 984
Ezekiel 942* (viii) h, (xv) e, (xvi); influence of, on Revelation 942*, also 942* (iv) a and (xviii), and 28-33 *passim*; parallelism of, with John 942* (ii); *ben adam* in 7

Faith 992; as a grain of mustard-seed 851-6
Famine 942* (v)
"Favour," "grace," "kindness" &c. 840*
Feeding with (?) συναλιζόμενος 893
Feet, washing of the 963-5
Fever and Cholera, divinities 807, 824
Field, beasts of the 840, 43 d
Fifty, "thou art not yet f." 989
"Fig-time," parall. to "end" 874 a–b
Fig-tree, the barren 874-8
Finding a stater 7* foll.; a drachma &c. 9*
Fire, the Stoics on 819; martyrdom by, legends of 948-51; flame of 28 p; baptism of spirit or of fire 30; confused with "man" 7 c
First 7* foll., 16*; "First" and "Last" 27 a foll.
Firstborn of the dead 26 o
Fish, different symbolisms of 11*; the first 7* foll., 16*
Fishing 8*-9*
Flame, meant by "Ur" 949; of fire 28 p
Flesh, sons of 3
"Flocks" and "waking up" 17 g
Following, metaph. 936 a
"Footstool" 22 b–c, 31 b
Forsaking 917 foll.
"Forty-six years" (Jn ii. 20) 962
Fountain of righteousness 53
Four "beasts" and four "living creatures" 33 a

Black Arabics refer to paragraphs [2]800–[2]997, *ordinary Arabics to the sections of* 2998, *or, if starred, to the sections of* 2999. *For example,* 872 = 2872, 16 = 2998 (xvi), 16* = 2999 (xvi).

INDEX

Fulfilment, in Jn and Epict. **806**
"Fuller, the," term given to a rabbi **837** (iii) *c*
"Fuller's club, a" 17 *c**
"Furnace, the iron," *i.e.* Egypt **950**

Gabriel and Michael 33 *a*
Galilæans, the **813**
Galilee 4*, 5*
Garment, reaching to the feet 28
Garments, white 17 *a** foll.
Genealogy, Christ's, in Mt. and Lk. 38 *a*
Genitive, defining, force of 20
Gird **926–34**, 17 *n** foll.
Girdle, the golden 28 *l*
Glorifying 23 *e*
Glory of God, the, "above the heavens" 12, 24 *e*, 50 *c*; "a living man" 28 *b*
Gnostics, the, on the Son of Man 34–6
Go, "going out" 12*; "going up" 8*; "going to meet," "going before," and "drawing near" 4*–5*
God, "is not as man" 4; why called "man" 45; "repents" 3; said "not to repent" 45 *a*; "meeting" man 3*; said to "dawn" 27 *t*; rendered by τὸ θεῖον 27 *u*; dividing 28 *v*; "hands" of 40 *a*; "the right hand of," s. "right"
Gold, metaph., meaning of 28 *l*
Golden girdle, the 28 *l*
Goodness and authority, Philo on 28 *u*
"Gospel," in Mk. referring to Isaiah **839** *c*; fourth, date of **962** *a*; s. also Hebrews
Gospels, Irenæus on the number of **916**
"Grace," "favour," "kindness" &c. **840***
Great City, the **942*** (i) *c*, (ii) *a* foll.
Greatness **992**
"Greeks, are always boys" **888**

Habit, Epict. on **813**
Hadrian **942*** (viii)
Hair, white 27 *o*, 29 *c*; as wool 28 *o*
Hand, "stretch out the hand" and "stretch out the hands" **928**, **932–4**; "upon the throne of Jah" and "hidden" 36 *a*
Hands, of God 36 *a*, 40 *a*, 43; of an idol **837** (iii) *d*; "stretch out the h. on the cross" **926** foll.; "spread abroad the h." **928**; "works of God" and "works of God's h." 43 *b*
Hannah, the mother of Samuel **880**

"Head, rested his" **967**; "a h. of days" 52; s. also 8 *c*
"Heads," prophetic meaning of **942*** (i) *a*, *c*
Healing **995**
Heaven, hosts of 16
Heavens, glory above the 12, 24 *e*, 50 *c*
Hebrew, Matthew wrote in **916**; parallelism, Matthew misunderstood 3*
Hebrews, Epistle to the **839**; on the Son of Man 24
Hebrews, Gospel of the **824*** (i), 17 *d** foll.
Hegesippus, on James the Just **837** (iii), 25, 17 *c**; s. also **967** *a*
"Heli," connected with "sun" **917** foll.
Heracleon **938**; on martyrdom **941**
Hercules, as a son of God **806**
Hermas, author of the *Shepherd* **981**, 28 *m*
Hermas, an imaginary character **838**
Herod the Tetrarch 17 *a*
Hesperus 17 *d*
Hiding, the doctrine of, in *Enoch* 55 *d* foll.; a means to manifesting 55 *m*; Noah "was hidden" 55 *e*; "a hand hidden" and "a hand upon the throne of Jah" 36 *a*
High, the Most, a name of God 26 *p*
High priest, the, clothing of 27 *t–v*
"Him" and "sign" 54 *c*
Hippolytus **852**, **920**, **942*** (xii) *a*, *b*, (xiii) *d*, (xxii) *d*, (xxiv) *a*, 27 *f*, *t*, *v*, 55 *h*
"Hold fast" and "draw near" 2*
Honour, two kinds of 43
"Hook" and "net" 8*
Horse, a white 28 *d*, 29 *c*
Hosts, of heaven 16, 27 *m*; the Lord of 27 *m*
"House" = "School" 12*
Husbands, five **961** (i)
Hymning **897–907**

I AM, applied to God 27 *e*
Ignatius, on the Son of Man 35; s. also **824*** (i), **891**, **894–5**, **942*** (xv) *d*, **962** *a*, 17 *d*, 55 *h*, 17 *g**
"Immolatur," how used by Tertullian **937** *d*
Incorporation, implied in the Eucharist **895**
Infanticide, Tertullian on **911**
Inkhorn, a writer's 28 *m*
Irenæus, mentions "elders" **958**; on

Black Arabics refer to paragraphs [2]**800**–[2]**997**, *ordinary Arabics to the sections of* **2998**, *or, if starred, to the sections of* **2999**. *For example,* **872** = **2872**, 16 = **2998** (xvi), 16* = **2999** (xvi).

the number of the gospels **916**; on "Titan" **942*** (i) *l–m*; on the Son of Man, misquotes Jn i. 13, 39–40; s. also **882, 895, 917, 920, 923** *a*, **942*** (i) *k*, *l*, *m*, *o*, (xii) *a*, **961**, **984** *a*, *e*, **986, 989, 994, 996, 997** *a*, 15, 27 *d*, 28 *b*, 34, 36 *a*

Isaac, son of Sarah **880**; metaph. "laughter" **881** *a*, **942*** (xii) *b*

Isaiah, and Mark, continuity between **839** *a–d*; *ben adam* in 5; in LXX, peculiarities of 27 *b*

Israel, house of **860**; the name, meaning of **987**

Jacob's Ladder, Jewish tradition about 14

James the Just, or Righteous **837** (iii), 54 *g*, Hegesippus on 17 *c**; called the brother of the Lord 25; s. also **937** *d*

James the son of Zebedee **937** *d*, **942*** (xxii) *c*

Jeremiah, *ben adam* in 6

Jerome, on John's old age **952**; on Jewish interpretations **942*** (i) *o*, *q*, (xiii) *f*; s. also **823, 824*** (i), **960, 961** (i) *a*, **995, 997** *a*, 7 *d*, 22 *c*, 17 *c–d**, 17 *j–k**

Jerusalem, the fall of **942*** (vii) foll.; the spoils of 28 *d*; the surrounding of **837** (i), (iii), **874** *f*; going up to 8 *e**

Jesus, the age of **989–90**; not seen in the visions of Revelation 33; verbs of motion applied to 6*; s. also "Christ"

Jesus, the kinsman of Ananus **942*** (ii) *d*

Jesus, the son of Nun **942*** (ii) *b*

Jezebel **942*** (iii) *b*, (xv) *f*

Job 10, 12

John the Apostle, son of Zebedee, confused with John the Baptist **937**; tradition about **948**; old age of **952**; parallelism between, and Ezekiel **942*** (ii); s. also "Revelation"

John the Baptist **942*** (xxii) *b–d*, **995**; confused with John the son of Zebedee **937**; described by Origen as an "angel" **942*** (xxii) *d*, comp. 15 *f*; the Spirit said to have "ceased" in **942*** (xxii) *d*

John the Evangelist, intervenes in Synoptic Tradition **965**, comp. **936**; on the Son of Man 21; use of χάρις by **840*** *g*

Joseph (husband of Mary), son of **979**

Joseph (son of Jacob), Targumistic tradition on **837** (ii)

Joseph, The Prayer of, an apocr. work 15 *f*

Josephus, on the Galilæans **813**; illustrated by Targums **837** (ii); interpolation in **837** (iii); illustrations of Revelation from **942*** (vi) *a*; s. also **839, 890, 942*** (ii) *d*, (ix), (xxii) *d*, **971**, 27 *r–v*, 27 *w*, 28 *d–e*, 7 *c–d**

Joshua 36

Judah, Targumistic tradition on **837** (ii)

Judging 28 *s*

Judgment, the throne of 8 *b–c*

Justin Martyr, not a Samaritan by religion 37 *b*; on the Son of Man 37–9; s. also **846, 880, 882, 898–907, 917, 942*** (and **942*** (xxii) *d*), **986, 994**, 28 *a*, 36 *a*

"Kindness," "grace," "favour" &c. **840***

Kingdom, the, is within 44

"Kings" and "kingdoms" interchanged **942*** (i) *a*

Know s. "See"

Lamb, two Gk words for 32 *b–d*; *talitha* in Heb., not in Aram. 32 *c*; "lambs" parall. to "sheep" 32 *e*

Lamb of God, the 32 *d*; in the bosom of the Father 32; the sacrificial aspect of 32; the throne of 32; the Bride of **942*** (xv) *c*

Lamech 54 *d*

Laodicea **942*** (v); the Church of 28 *h*

Last, "first and last," applied to God 27 *b–c*

Latona **942*** (xiii) *b*

Laughter, meant by "Isaac" **881** *a*

Law, the, at the right hand of God 31 *a*

Leaven 55 *k*

Leper, the Messiah to be a **995**; "cleanse the lepers" **995**

Letters, ignorant of **879**

Life, the Book of **942*** (viii) *g*

"Lifting up" 23 *e*

"Likeness," of a son of man, meaning of 33

Linen 17 *a** foll.

Living creatures, the four **942***, 33 *a*

Loaf, one **895**

"Locusts with the hair of women" **942*** (vi) *a*

Logos, the, between Goodness and Authority 28 *u*; the universal

---

Black Arabics *refer to paragraphs* [2]800–[2]997, *ordinary Arabics to the sections of* 2998, *or, if starred, to the sections of* 2999. *For example*, 872 = 2872, 16 = 2998 (xvi), 16* = 2999 (xvi).

INDEX

divider 28 *u*; comes forth from silence 55 *h*
Lord, of hosts 27 *m* ; of Spirits 51
Lord's Day, the **942*** (iii) *b*
Lost, ambig. **863** ; save the **861** foll.
Love (n.), never mentioned by Mark **924**
Loving-kindness **840*** *d–e*
Lucifer 16
Luke, "inseparable from Paul" **984** *e*; his use of χάρις **840*** *g*; his tradition about Christ's eating **897–907**; his omission of "Why hast thou forsaken me?" **917** foll.; his preface to his gospel **980–4**; on Christ's genealogy 38 *a*
Luther, on repentance **800** *c–d*
Lyons, the Martyrs of **939**, **942*** (xxii) *d*

Maccabean princes 51 *a*
Magi, the 17
Malchus, the name 17 *i**
"Man" and "the man" 43 *c*; dominion of 47; God is not as 4; God meeting 3*; ? "man" or "Adam" 20 *c*; "man" and "men" 23 *c*, 37 *c* ; Son of Man, definite or indefinite 19, 37–45 ; s. also **998** *passim*
Man-child, the, birth of **942*** (xi) foll.
Manna, the hidden **942*** (xv)
Marcion **824*** (i) *d*, 55 *i*
Mark, Papias on **915**, **965**, **983–4**; never mentions love (n.) **924**; his gospel, how concluded **924**; continuity of, with Isaiah **839** *a–d*
Martyr, or witness **935**, 26 *h–k*; or confessor **939** *a* ; s. also "Martyrs"
Martyrdom **940** foll., 28 *a* ; by fire, legends of **948–51**
Martyrs **942*** (iii) *c*, 25 *a* ; variety of **937** *d*
Mary, **881–2**, s. also "Virgin"
Matthew, misunderstands Heb. parallelism 3*; literalises 15*; on Christ's genealogy 38 *a*
"Meant" and "said" **837** (iii) *a*, **874** *f*
Measures, three 55 *k*
Measuring for the Temple **942*** (ii) *a*, (iv)
"Meet," and "appear" 3*; and "call" 3 *g**, 4*; God "meeting" man 3*; "meeting" Moses 3*–4*; "go to meet," "go before," and "draw near" 4*–5*
Meeting, the tabernacle of 3*
Mercy **840*** *a–f*
Messiah, the, birth of **942*** (xi) foll. ; to be a leper **995**; in N.T. 21 *a*; to go forth from Rome 28 *v*
Metaphors, converted to prose **837** foll.; anthropomorphic 45 ; cause divergence 17 *a** foll.; s. also Pref. p. xiv foll.
Methuselah 54 *d*
Michael 27 *p* ; and Gabriel 33 *a*
Midst, standing in the **897** foll.; walking in the 28 *f–k*
Ministers, in N.T. **983**; of Christ **984** *e*
Miriam, the song of 27 *s*
"Mirror, the enigma of the" **826**
Mistranslation **830** foll.
Moon, the, a witness 26 *n*
Moses **942*** (xiii), (xv), 28 *v*; opposed by angels 11 foll.; being met by God 3*–4*; the song of 27 *s*
Mother, the Berecynthian **942*** (xi)
Motion, verbs of, applied to Jesus 6*
Mountains, an uprooter of **873**; seven **942*** (i) *d*
Mouth, the, a sword 28 *t*; "opening the mouth" 14 *b–d**
Muratorian Fragment, the **956**
Musonius Rufus **810**, **944**
Mustard-seed, faith as a grain of **851–6**
Myriads of angels 31 *a*
"Mysteries of the cry, three" 55 *h*
Myth, springing from verbal corruption 17 *c**

Nakedness, lit. and metaph. 17 *b** foll., comp. 28 *h*
Name, "for my name's sake" **816**; s. also below
Names, variations of **942*** (i) *q*; "names of men" ? used for persons **942*** (viii); "men of name(s)" **942*** (viii) *i*
Nebuchadnezzar, the dream of 15; "the true N." 24 *e*
Nero **942*** (i) foll.; said to be "avenged" **942*** (i) *e*, *m*
"Net" and "hook" 8*
Nicolaitans, the **942*** (iii) *b*
Nile, the **942*** (xiii) *c*
Noah, "the eighth person" **942*** (i) *f*, *k* inferior to Abraham 37 *d*; hidden 55 *e*; Philo on 54 *h*
Number, the, of the Beast **942*** (i) *l* foll.; of a man **942*** (i) *m*
Numbering **942*** (viii) *g*
Numbers, antithetical **942*** (i); mystical **942***, **942*** (i) *d* foll., (vi)–(x), **994**; stress on 28 *k*

Black Arabics refer to paragraphs [2]**800**–[2]**997**, *ordinary Arabics to the sections of* **2998**, *or, if starred, to the sections of* **2999**. *For example,* **872** = **2872**, 16 = **2998** (xvi), 16* = **2999** (xvi).

ENGLISH

Obscurity, causes of **837** (ii); divergence caused by **837**; s. also Pref. p. xv foll.
Offerings, bringing 17 *b*
Oholah and Oholibah **942*** (xv) *f*
Olive-tree, the sacred, in Acropolis **820**
Omega, Alpha and 27 *a* foll.
"Omnitenens," Origen's use of 27 *g*
"Opening the mouth" 14 *b–d**
Oracula Sibyllina **942*** (i) *a*, (ii) *b*, (v) *b*, **946**, 27 *w*
Origen, on ἀσώματος **824*** (i) *e*; quotes interpolation fr. Josephus **837** (iii); on the ass and colt **848**; on mustard-seed **853** foll.; on the fig-tree **878**; on little children **885–6**; on an eclipse **910**; on the forsaking of Christ **919–23**; on the sword 28 *t*; on the removing spirit 30; on clouds 31 *a*; on the Son of Man 43–5; refers to Philo 45 *a*; s. also **801**, **805** *a*, **824*** (i) *a–f*; **845**, **857**, **867**, **874** *d–f*, **881** *a*, **890**, **892** *a–c*, **896**, **909**, **937** *c*, **941**, **942***, **942*** (i) *c*, (ii) *c*, (viii) *h*, (xii) *b–c*, (xiii) *d*, (xv) *d*, (xvii), (xviii), (xxii) *c–d*, **961** *a*, **961** (i), **963–4**, **967**, **972**, **974–5**, **978**, **980**, **982**, **984** *b–c*, **989**, **995**, 7 *d–e*, 13, 15 *b, f*, 16, 17 *a*, 20 *b*, 22 *c*, 23 *e*, 24 *e–f*, 26 *k, m*, 27 *f, g, l, q*, 28 *a, m, o, t, w, x*, 30, 32 *d*, 34 *a*, 48, 49 *a*, 50 *b*, 54 *c–g*, 55 *h–k*, 7 *a–b**, 7 *e**, 9*, 10*, 11 *a–b**
Orphans, in Epict., Jn, and Talmud **805**
Osiris **856**
Oulai 28 *j*

Papias, on Mark **915**, **965**, **984**; s. also **879**, **937**, **941**
Papyri, the **811** *a*, **875**, **879**, **923** *d*, **942*** (viii) *b* foll., **982**, **997**, 32 *b*, 44 *b*, 17 *m**
Parables, anthropomorphic 45
Parthians **942*** (xxiv) *a*, 51 *a* foll.
Patmos **942*** (xiii) *b*, **942-7**
Patriarchs, the 54 *h*; of promise 37; son of 37
Paul, "inseparable from Luke" **984** *e*; an "eyewitness" **984** *a*; mentioned in the *Recognitions of Clement* **837** (iii) *c*; does not mention the Son of Man in his epistles 22
Pella **837** (iii) *a*, **942*** (xiii) *e*
Peter, death of **926** foll.; martyrdom of 26 *j*; primacy of 7*; in Rome, legends of 15 *a**; the first to see the risen Saviour 17 *f**; the "reclothing" of 17*
Peter, the name, parallels to 17 *g–h**, comp. **875**
Peter, the Teaching of **824*** (i)
Pharaoh **942*** (xiii) *a, c*
Philo, referred to by Origen 45 *a*; on the Therapeutae 27 *r* foll.; on Noah 54 *h*; on "the half of the didrachm" 10*; s. also **806**, **880**, **881** *a*, **888**, **908**, **923** *b*, **942*** (i) *k*, (xii) *b*, **961** *a*, **965**, **987–9**, **994**, **996**, 4 (esp. 4 *b, d*), 26 *d*, 28 *d, e, j, n, u, v, x*, 30, 31 *b*, 54 *c, d*, *h, j*, 55 *k*, 56 *d*, 10*, 17 *o**
Philosophers, pretended **811**
Pillar, metaph., errors caused by 17 *h**; of cloud 30, 31; of cloud, Rashi on 4 *c*
Pinnacle, of the Temple **837** (iii); s. also Pref. p. xvii foll.
Planets, s. "Stars"
Plant of righteousness 55 *f*
Pleasing, Epict. on **803**
Pliny **944**, **946**, **960**
Plummet, metaph. 26 *m*, 28 *b*
Polycrates **958**
Pompey **942*** (xiii) *a*
Pool of (R.V.) Bethesda **959** foll.
Poor, metaph. **942*** (xv)
Porch, the, of the Temple 28 *j*
Power, the **824**
"Pray," "stand," and "with," confusable 27 *t*
Prayer, not entirely forbidden by Epict. **814**; prayers, perhaps personified 15 *b*
Prayer of Joseph, the, an apocr. work 15 *f*
Precocity, human, illustrations of **876**
Priests, metaph. 26 *r*
Proclaim, *i.e.* preach the gospel **839** *b*
Profit, Epict. on **807**, **816**
Promise of the Man, the **997**
Propator, the 34
Prophecy, adaptation of **942*** (i) *o*
Prose, substituted for metaphor **837** foll.
Psalms, the Son of Man in 9–10
Python **942*** (xiii) *b*

Quarries in Patmos **947**

Race, *i.e.* Gentiles, as opposed to Jews 37 *a*
Raising the dead **995**
Rashi, on the pillar of cloud (Deut. i. 31) 4 *c*
Receiving as a little child **885–6**

Black Arabics refer to paragraphs [2]800–[2]997, *ordinary Arabics to the sections of* 2998, *or, if starred, to the sections of* 2999. *For example,* 872 = 2872, 16 = 2998 (xvi), 16* = 2999 (xvi).

A. 305 20

INDEX

Recorder, in Ezekiel, the 28 *n*
Regeneration **885**
"Relegatio" **941, 944**
Remnant, the faithful **942*** (viii), (xiii) *f*
Repent, God does and does not 3, 45 *a*
Repentance **815, 992**; Luther on **800** *c–d*
Rephaim **942*** (i) *m*
"Rested his head" **967**
Resurrection, the 56; of the body 56 *a*; different beliefs as to 56 *a*; and ascension of Christ, events between **892** foll.
Revelation of John the Apostle, the, date and authorship of **942*** foll.; moral character of **942*** (xvii) foll.; parallelism between, and Ezekiel **942*** (ii); influenced by prophets **942*** (i) *e*, (iv) *a–b*, (xviii), 26–33 *passim*; on the Son of Man 26 foll.
Right hand of God 23 *b*, 25 *a*, 32; the Law or the angels at 31 *a*
"Righteous," first use of in O.T. 54 *h*; Heb. (*tsaddîk*) used and disused 54 *i*; "the righteous one" 51 foll., 54 *c*, 55 *a*; in N.T. 54 *e, f*; the Righteous Servant, in Isaiah 54 *f*
Righteousness, fountain of 53; plant of 55 *f*
Ripeness **874**
River **942*** (xiii)
Roman Empire, the **942*** (i) *h*
Rosh Hashanah **961, 961** (i)
Rufus, Musonius **810**
Rufus, Tineius **942*** (i) *q*
Rulers, oppressive 51 *b*

Sabaoth 27 *b*, *k* foll.
Sacrifice **963-4**
Sadducees 51 *a*
Salt, metaph. **858**
Samaritan, Justin not a, by religion 37 *b*
Samaritans **868**, 37 *b*
Samson **837** (i)
Samuel, son of Hannah **880**
Sapphire 7 *e*; s. and "writer" 28 *m*
Sarah **881** *a*; Isaac son of **880**, 55 *k*
Scapegoat, the 28 *o*
Scorpion, the constellation **942*** (xiii) *g*
Scribes, adjuration to **942*** (xix) *a*
Scripture, *Enoch* quoted as **914**
Scriptures, opening the **908**
Sea, the **942*** (xiii) *a*, **961, 992**, 55 *g*
Sealing, the, of the faithful 28 *n*
See, "he that seeth" **987**; "I know (*οἶδα*)" rendered "I saw (*vidi*)" **824*** (i) *c*

Seer, a **942*** (ii), (xiii) *c*, 26 *g*, 32; s. also "Vision"
Self-suppression, taught by Epict. 55 *j*
"Servant," in Is. l. to rendered "son" by Tertull. 54 *f*; the righteous, in Isaiah 54 *f*; the suffering, a leper **995**; of the priest 17 *e**, 17 *i** foll.
Seven, mystically used **942*** (i), 26 *m*, 28 *e*, *k*, *y*; angels, kings, hills, mountains, seals, spirits, stars, torches &c. **942*** (i) *d, i*; churches, the **942*** (iii); candlesticks **942*** (xxii) *a*; signs **991**; confused with "seventy" 26 *m*
Seven thousand **942*** (viii), (xiii) *f*
Seventy, confused with seven 26 *m*; disciples, the 50 *e*
Shaddai 27 *j*
Shakespeare, misled by North's Plutarch **830** foll.
Shechinah, the **969-71**, 27 *c*, 28 *f*
Sheep, the lost **860-71**; parall. to "lambs" 32 *e*
Shekel of the sanctuary, the 7 *c**
Shema, the, recitation of 27 *t*
Shepherd, in the gospels **869-71**
Side, "by the side of" = ἐπὶ χεῖρα **961** (i) *d*
"Sign," confused with "him" 54 *c*
Silence, the Logos comes forth from 55 *h*
Siloam **961**
Similitudes, the, s. "Enoch"
Simon, the name, parallels to 17 *g–h**
Simon Magus **852**
Simon the Righteous 54 *g*
Six **942*** (i) *k* foll.
Six hundred and sixty-six **942*** (i) *k–m*
"Snow" and "wool" 28 *o*
Socrates, on Anytus **808**; saying the same things **809**; zealots of **840**
Solomon **942*** (xv) *f*
Solomon, the Wisdom of **956**
Son, in Heb., = specimen of a class 4; in classical Gk, metaph. 20 *d*; s. of David 36; of the Patriarchs 37
Son of God 36; "a" or "the" 20
Son of Man, the **998** *passim*; the term, why disliked 35; "one like a" 26 *a*, 28 *l–r*, 33; in *Enoch* 52 foll.; def. or indef. 19, 45; s. also "Man"
Sons, of flesh 3; of God, interch. w. "angels" 16; of men 20 *f*; of Zeus **880** *a*; "s. of oil" (Zech. iv. 14) **942*** (xxii)
Song, of Miriam and Moses, the 27 *s*
Sophia, the Valentinians on **917, 923** *a*
"Soul," in Heb., = "self" **966**

Black Arabics refer to paragraphs [2]800–[2]997, *ordinary Arabics to the sections of* 2998, *or, if starred, to the sections of* 2999. *For example*, 872 = 2872, 16 = 2998 (xvi), 16* = 2999 (xvi).

ENGLISH

Sow, the congregation sown by God 55 *f*
Spirit, the, used absolutely 29 *b*; said to have "ceased" in John the Baptist **942*** (xxii) *d*
"Spirit," interch. w. "wind" 837 *a*, 30; the removing wind or spirit 30; baptism of spirit or of fire 30
Spirits, bodiless, evil **824*** (i); the Lord of 51; the seven 26 *m*; three, unclean **942*** (xx) *a*
Spiritual body, a **824*** foll.
"Spread abroad the hands" 928
Springs, medicinal and intermittent 960
Staff, perh. metaph. 888
Stand 25; in the midst 897 foll.; "stand," "pray," and "with," confusable 27 *t*; "stood up" or "were appointed" 17 *g*
"Stars," and "angels" 16 foll., 28 *e*; and "sword" 28 *s-x*; singing 16; the seven s., *i.e.* the planets 28 *u*
Stater, finding a 7* foll., 12* foll.
"Staters, Samuel's," proverb about 9 *a**
Stephen 937 *c-d*, 24–5
"Stoic, a genuine" 811 *b*
Stone, meaning "plummet" 26 *m*; connected with "eyes of God" 27 *v*; "rolled away" 909
"Stretching out the hand(s)" 928, 932-4; on the cross 926 foll.
Subjecting 22, 24 *c*, 50 *e*
Suckling 49; confused with "sucker" 49; used by Jews="pupil" 49; connected with "Son of Man" 50 *b*
Sucklings, s. "Babes"
Sun, the 28 *x*; one of the seven stars 28 *u*; worshipped **942*** (i) *m*, (xxiv) *b*; not worshipped by the Essenes 27 *r-v*; connected with "Heli" 917 foll.; with "God" 920, with "tabernacle" 918-20, **942*** (xiii) *d*
Sunrise, a time of prayer 27 *t*
Sweat, metaph. 986
"Sword," and "stars" 28 *s-x*; the mouth a s. 28 *t*; Origen on 28 *t*; two-edged **942***, **942*** (xvii), (xxii), 28 *n*
Symbolism **942*** and **942*** (i)–(xxiv) *passim*, 26–33 *passim*
Syrophœnician woman, the 862, 867

Tabernacle (n.) 28 *f*; of meeting or of testimony 3*; "in the sun he placed his t." 918-20, **942*** (xiii) *d*
Tabernacle (vb) 28 *f*
Tacitus, on the Christians 807

Talitha = (Heb.) "lamb," (Aram.) "young one" 32 *c*
Targums, 837 foll., **949-51**, 4, 28 *v*; s. also *Pref.* pp. vii-viii and xiii foll.
T(e)itan, Irenæus on **942*** (i) *m*
Temple, the 962, metaph. 839, **942*** (xv); measuring for **942*** (ii) *a*, (iv); destruction of **942*** (xi) *a*
Tertullian, on infanticide 911; on the Son of Man 41; renders "servant" in Is. l. 10 "son" 54 *f*; s. also **824*** (i) *d*, 918, 924, 937 *d*, 939 *a*, 940, **942*** (i) *b*, *m*, (xxii) *d*, 948, 960, 996, 17 *c*, 41
Testimony, or meeting, tabernacle of 3*
Tetradrachm 7 *c** foll.
Theophany 998 *passim*
Therapeutae, the, Philo on 27 *r* foll.
Third part, a **942*** (viii), (xiii) *f*
Thirst, metaph. 966; in Jn and Epict. 806
Thirty, "a son of t. years" 994
Thirty-eight, only twice in Bible 961 (i)
Three, measures 55 *k*; unclean spirits **942*** (xx) *a*
Three and a half years **942*** (i) *o*, (viii)
Threshold 28 *j*
Throne 8 *a*; metaph. **942*** (xv); of judgment 8 *b-c*; of God and the Lamb 32; of glory 8 *c*, 51; a white t. 29 *c*; the face of the 12; "a hand upon the t." 36 *a*
"Throne" or "thrones" 31 *b*
Thunder 972 foll.
Titan **942*** (i) *m*
Titus **942*** (i) *a*; the name, how used **942*** (i) *m*; in the Talmud **942*** (i) *m*, *q*
Tobit 15 *f*
"Touch" and "draw near" 1*-2*
Trajan, the third year of **942*** (xxiv) *a*
Transfiguration, the **942*** (i) *l*
Translations, Targumistic 837 foll.; s. also "Targums"
"Travail, in" **942*** (xii), (xiv)
"Tree," *i.e.* "cross," Ephrem on 933, comp. **942*** (ii) *b*
"Truth" or "bow" 837 (ii)
"Truth is always right" 828
Turnus, *i.e.* tyrant **942*** (i) *q*
Twenty-four Elders, the **942*** (xv) *b*, 33 *a*
Two, divine powers, Philo on 28 *u*; witnesses, the **942*** (ii) *c-d*, (xix) foll.
Two-edged, s. "Sword"
Two hundred, perh. mystically used 17 *o**
Tyre **942*** (xv) *e-f*

Black Arabics refer to paragraphs [2]800–[2]997, *ordinary Arabics to the sections of* **2998**, *or, if starred, to the sections of* **2999**. *For example,* 872=2872, 16=2998 (xvi), 16*=2999 (xvi).

INDEX

Ulai 28 *j*
Ur, = "flame" **949**

Valentinians, the **917, 920, 942*** (i) *k–l*; on Sophia **923** *a*
Vespasian **942*** (i) *a*; placed the golden candlestick in the Temple of Peace 28 *e*
Vines, planting of, prohibited **942*** (v) *a*
Virgin, the **881–2, 942*** (xii), 37–9
"Virgin," in LXX,=Aq. "young woman" **880**
"Virgins," meaning of, in Rev. xiv. 4 **942*** (xv) *b–f*
Vision, mixed with fact **953**; s. also **942***, **942*** (i)–(xxiv) *passim*, 26–33 *passim* (esp. 26 *g*, 32), and *Apologia* pp. v–vi and 80
Visitation, Origen on 43 *a*
"Voice," interch. w. "angel" 26 *c–d*; "seeing the voice" 26 *d*
Vowel points, not written in anc. Scriptures **839** *a*

"Waking up," confused w. "flocks" 17 *g*
Walking, metaph. **890**; in the midst 28 *f–k*
Washing of Feet, the **963–5**
"Watcher," meaning "angel" 17 *h*
"Watchers by night," astrologers are 17 *f*
Water, by the side of **961** (i) *d*; "running w." 27 *w*
Waters **942*** (xiii) *c*, **961** (i) *d*, 28 *r*; gathering of **961** (i) *c*; many 28 *r*
"Week of years, a" **942*** (i) *o*

Weeping, in Jn and Epict. **806**
White, a symbol of purity 29 *c*; w. garments 17 *a** foll.
"Wind," interch. w. "spirit" **837** *a*; "the removing wind, or spirit" 30
"Wing," in Dan. ix. 27 **837** (i), (iii); parall. to "army" **837** (i); s. also Pref. p. xvi foll.
Wisdom, Philo on **923** *b*
Wisdom of Solomon, the **956**
"With," "pray," and "stand," confusable 27 *t*; "those with him" 17 *g–h**
"Witness" and "martyr" 26 *h–k*; the faithful 26 *n–q*
Witnesses, the two **942*** (ii) *a, c*, (xix) foll.
Woman, born of a **880**
Wool, scarlet 28 *o*; and snow 28 *o*
Works, (1) of God, (2) of God's hands 43 *b*
Worship, of symbols, deprecated 27 *o*
"Written, it is" **914**
"Writer" confused with "sapphire" 28 *m*

Year, the New **960–1**; year by year, ambig. **961** (i)
Yoke and Cross **842–9**

Zealots of Socrates **840**
Zechariah, influence of, on Revelation **942*** (iv) *b*; "sons of oil" (Zech. iv. 14) **942*** (xxii)
Zeus, sons of **880** *a*
Zipporah 2*, 3*

Black Arabics refer to paragraphs [2]800–[2]997, *ordinary Arabics to the sections of* **2998**, *or, if starred, to the sections of* **2999**. *For example,* 872=**2**872, 16=**2998** (xvi), 16*=**2999** (xvi).

III

INDEX (GREEK)

[*Black Arabics refer to paragraphs* [2]800–[2]997 (*the* 2 *not being printed*). *Ordinary Arabics refer to the sections of* 2998-9, *the two* " *Longer Notes* "[1].]

Ἀγάπη : not in Epict. 814; not in Mk 924
ἀγγαρεία, -εύω : in Epict. and Mt. 887 *a*
ἀγγέλων and ἀγελῶν 17 *g*
ἀγνοέω : ἀγνοεῖσθαι μελέτησον 55 *j*
ἀγράμματος "unlettered" 879
αἰλάμ 28 *j*
Αἰλείμ 28 *j*
αἴνιγμα : ἐν αἰνίγματι 826
αἴρω ζυγόν 843
ἀλίζομαι and αὐλίζομαι 893-5
Ἄλλος 17 *o**
Ἄλφα καὶ Ὦ 27 *a* foll.
ἀμνός and ἀρνίον 32 *b–d*
ἄν : dropped in LXX 889
ἀναβαίνω 7* foll., 8 *a–f**
ἀναβλέπω : of "seeing visions" or "recovering sight" 909, 3 *e*, 5 *b**
ἀναιρέω "kill" 937 *a–b*
ἀναλαμβάνω : ἀναληφθῆναι 939 *a*, 942* (xxii) *d*
ἀνατέλλω "dawn," applied to God 27 *l*
ἀνήρ and ἄνθρωπος 942* (xii) *b*, 2 ; ἀνήρ and πῦρ 7 *c*
ἄνθρωπος : denoting the female parent 1 ; a human being, masc. or fem. 8; interpr. by Irenæus as the Virgin 39; with and without ὁ 43 *c* ; ἄνθρωπος and ἀνήρ 942* (xii) *b*, 2 ; ὡς ἄνθρωπος 4 ; υἱὸς ἀνθρώπου and ὁ υἱὸς τοῦ ἀνθρώπου 38 ; ἄνθρωπος ἐξ ἀνθρώπων 37 *c*
ἀνοίγω 14 *b–d**, 17 *d**
ἀπαντάω 3*
ἀπάντημα 3 *d**
ἀπ' ἄρτι 29 *a*

ἀπερίσπαστος κ. ἀπαρενόχλητος 811 *a*
ἀποκαίω, καίω, and ξηραίνω 876-7
ἀποκαλύπτω : ἀποκαλυφθῆναι, how expressed, s. 3 *f–j**
ἀπόλλυμι : ἀπολέσας, parall. to πλανηθῇ 864
ἀπορικός 942* (viii) *e*
ἅπτομαι, ἐγγίζω, κρατέω, προσεγγίζω, προσπορεύομαι &c. 1 *a–b**, 2 *a**, 6 *c**
ἆρα : εἰ ἆρα 878
ἀρνίον and ἀμνός 32 *b–d*
ἀρρην : superfl. 942* (xii) *b*
ἄρτι : ἀπ' ἄρτι 29 *a*
ἀρχή : ἀπ' ἀρχῆς 984 *c–e*
ἀσώματος 824* (i) *a–g*, 56 *d*
αὐγή : how used by Josephus 27 *u* ; w. Διός &c. 27 *v* ; pl. may mean " rays " or " eyes " 27 *v*
αὐλίζομαι 894
αὐτοκράτωρ 27 *k*
αὐτόματος 55 *j*
αὐτόπτης κ. ὑπηρέτης 983-4

Βαστάζω and φέρω 931
βοάω and κηρύσσω 839 *a–c*

Γαλιλαία 4*-5*
Γαλιλαῖοι, οἱ 813
γένος : *i.e.* Gentiles opposed to Jews 37 *a*
γίνομαι : " am born " 880 ; γενόμενα parall. to τέκνα 880 ; γ. ἐκ γυναικός 880
γνάθος : Ὄνου γνάθος 873
γναφεύς and γνάφως (κνάφος) 17 *c**

---

[1] *Black Arabics refer to paragraphs* [2]800–[2]997, *ordinary Arabics to the sections of* 2998, *or, if starred, to the sections of* 2999. *For example*, 872 = 2872, 16 = 2998 (xvi), 16* = 2999 (xvi).

INDEX

γνάφος s. γναφεύς
γυμνός 17 ο*
γυνή: γενόμενον ἐκ γυναικός 880; γυναῖκα...τροφόν,?"wife" or "nurse" 912; μετὰ γυναικῶν μολύνεσθαι, metaph. 942* (xv) b–f

Δαιμόνιον 824* (i) b
διά: w. gen. of time 892 a–b; διὰ 'Ιωάννου, ambig. 937 f
διάγω 899 foll.
διαγωγή, δίαιτα, and διατροφή 905
διαζώννυμι: διασώσασθαι and διαζώσασθαι 17 n*
δίαιτα s. διαγωγή
διάκονοι 983
διασώζω s. διαζώννυμι
διατροφή s. διαγωγή
δίδραχμον and στατήρ 7 b* foll.
δίδωμι and παραδίδωμι 828, 23 e
δίκαιος 54 j; ὁ δίκαιος 54 e foll.
δικαιώματα "claims" 942* (viii) c
δοξάζω: ταὐτά μοι δοξάσαντες 37 a
δραχμή 7 c*
δύναμις, ἡ 824; ἡ δ. μου 923 b; ἐν μυριάσι δυνάμεων αὐτοῦ 31 a
δωρέομαι: in Aq. 840*

'Εβδομάς 28 d
ἐγγίζω 6* (esp. 6 a*, 6 d*); ἑ., ἅπτομαι, κρατέω, προσέρχομαι &c. 1 a–b*, 2 a*, 6 a–d*
ἐγγύς 6 a*
ἐγκομβόομαι: ἐγκομβώσασθε 17 n*
ἐγκρύπτω: ἐνέκρυψεν v.r. ἔκρυψεν 55 k
ἐγκρύψιαι "cakes" 55 k
ἔθος: ὑπὸ ἔθους 813
εἶδος s. ὁμοίωμα
εἰμί: applied to God 27 e
εἰς: προσεύχεσθαι εἰς "to pray towards" 942* (xxiv) b
εἷς παρεστηκώς 17 j*
εἶτα (Epict.) and εἶτεν (Mk) 876
ἐκδίκησις 942* (xviii) a
ἐκεῖ "thither" 942* (xxiv) b
ἐκλείπω 910 a, 923 c
ἐκτείνω χεῖρα(s) 926 foll.
ἔλεος, -έω 840*
ἐμπεριπατέω 28 f–h
ἐνιαυτός: κατ' ἐνιαυτόν 961 (i) a
ἐνοικέω 28 f
ἔνσαρκος 942* (ii) b
ἐξαίρω 30 b–c; ἐξαῖρον πνεῦμα 30
ἐξᾶς 942* (i) l
ἐξέρχομαι: ambig. 938–9; w. ἔξω 12*
ἐξομολόγησις and εὐχαριστία 11 a*

ἔξω s. ἐξέρχομαι
ἑορτή: appl. to Day of Atonement 961 a; ἡ ἑ. τῶν 'Ιουδαίων 961 a
ἐπαγγελία 997
ἐπαείδω, ἐπαοιδός 17
ἐπάνω 17 i, 5 a–b*
ἐπένδυμα 17 n*
ἐπενδύομαι 17 n*
ἐπενδύτης 17 l* foll.
ἐπί: w. gen. = "referring to" 42; ἑ. and ἐπάνω 5*
ἐπιβάλλω 13*
ἐπικαλέω: ἐπικέκληται and προσκέκληται 3 g*
ἐπίκρισις 942* (viii) c
ἐπίσημος 942* (i) l foll.
ἐπιστρέφω: in Epict. 815; ἐπιστραφείς and ἐπιστρέψας 936 a
ἐπιτίθημι and προστίθημι 942* (xix) a
ἐπιφαίνω and ἀνατέλλω 27 t
ἑπτακέφαλος 942* (xiii) b
ἑτοιμάζω τόπον 942* (xiii) e
ἔτος: κατ' ἔ. 960, 961 (i) a
εὐημερία 27 s
εὐχαριστία and ἐξομολόγησις 11 a*
εὐχή 27 r foll.
ἐφίστημι: w. ἐπάνω and w. dat. 17 i; in Lk. 5* (esp. 5 a*), 6*
ἐφούδ 17 n*
ἔσωθεν εὐχόμενοι 27 t
ἕως "dawn": πρὸς τὴν ἕ. στάντες 27 r–t

Ζυγόν 843 foll.
ζῷα and θηρία 33 a, 47

'Ηλί, ἠλί 917 foll.
ἥλιος 917 foll.
ἡμέρα: ταξάμενοι ἡμέραν 3 a*
ἡνίοχος: used by Orig. in Ezek. i. 26 7 d
ἡσυχία θεοῦ 55 h

Θεῖος: τὸ θεῖον, when used for "God" 27 u
θέλω: in Epict. and Jn 806
θεός: υἱὸς τοῦ θεοῦ, υἱὸς θεοῦ, and ὁ υἱὸς τοῦ θεοῦ 20 a–b; ὁ θεός, absol., alleged to mean "the sun-god" 27 v; w. ἀνατέλλω 27 t
θέρος "fruit-time" 874
θηλάζον 49 a
θηρίον: θηρία and κτήνη 840 a; and ζῷα 33 a, 47
θύρα: διὰ τῆς θ., κατὰ θ., παρὰ θ. &c. 985

'Ιαώ 27 d
'Ιησοῦς: the name 942* (i) l
'Ισαάκ: the name 881 a, 942* (xii) b

Black Arabics refer to paragraphs [2]800–[2]997, ordinary Arabics to the sections of 2998, or, if starred, to the sections of 2999. For example, 872=2872, 16=2998 (xvi), 16*=2999 (xvi).

GREEK

Ἰσραήλ : interpr. as ὁρῶν θεόν 15 f
ἵστημι : ἑστηκότων ὧδε 17 h*
ἰσχύς : ἡ l. μου ἐξέλιπεν 923 b
ΙΧΘΥΣ 8*

Καίω, ἀποκαίω and ξηραίνω 876-7
καλέω 839 a foll.
κανών 28 b
κατά=ὅμοιος 26 a; κατ' ἔτος, κατ' ἐνιαυτόν 960, 961 (i) a
κεράννυμι : κραθέντες τῇ σαρκὶ αὐτοῦ 895; κραθῆναι and κρατηθῆναι 895
κηρύσσω 839 a foll.
κνάφος s. γνάφος
κόλπος 32
κρατέω 1 b*; κρατήσας τῆς χειρός 6 c*; s. also ἅπτομαι and κεράννυμι
κρυπτός : ἐν κρυπτῷ 55 (esp. 55 l)
κρύπτω : ἔκρυψεν v.r. ἐνέκρυψεν 55 k
κτήνη and θηρία 840 a
κύριος and ὁ κύριος 26 e-f, 27 h

Λέγω : ἔλεγε "meant" or "said" 837 (iii) a, 874 f
λέντιον 17 m-n*
λίμναι 960
λόγος, ὁ : ἀπὸ σιγῆς προελθών 55 h; τομεύς 28 n, t, u
λούομαι 27 w
λυχνία, λύχνος 28 e foll.

Μάγος : "magician," in bad sense 17 a foll.
μαθηταί, parallels to 17 g-h*
μαρτυρέω 26 h
μαρτυρία 26 i foll.
μαρτύριον 28 a; and συνταγή 3 a*
μάρτυς 26 i foll.
μέγας : μεγᾶ (i.e. μέγαν) perh. read as μέγα 833; μεγάλη πόλις, how applied 942* (ii) b
μέν : ἐδώκαμεν or ἔδωκα μέν 802
μέσος : ἀνὰ μέσον 942* (i) e, 28 j, k; ἐν μέσῳ 942* (i) e, 28 i-k
μετανοέω, -νοια 800 c-d
μονώτατος ambig. 17 c*

Νεφέλη 30 a

Ὁ, ἡ, τό : ins. and om. with ἄνθρωπος 43 c; with κύριος 26 e, f, 27 h, with νεφέλη 30; υἱὸς ἀνθρώπου, υἱὸς τοῦ ἀνθρώπου, and ὁ υἱὸς τοῦ ἀνθρώπου 24 b, 38, 45 b; υἱὸς θεοῦ, υἱὸς τοῦ θεοῦ, and ὁ υἱὸς τοῦ θεοῦ 20 a-b; s. also 942* (xix) (xx), 984

ὀγδοάς 942* (i) l
ὄγδοος 942* (i) f, k
οἶδα rendered "vidi" 824* (i) c
οἰκτείρω 840*
ὅμοιος : parall. to κατά 26 a; foll. by accus. 26 a
ὁμοίωμα ἀνθρώπου, ὁμ. ὡς εἶδος ἀνθρ. &c. 7 c
ὀνειδίζω : ὠνίδισας in D 923 c
ὄνομα : ἐπίσημον ὄ. 942* (i) l foll.
ὀνόματα ? meaning "persons" 942* (viii) a foll.
Ὄνου γνάθος 873
ὄντως ? corr. of ὁ ὡς 825
ὁράω : ὁ ὁρῶν 987; "Israel" interpr. as ὁρῶν θεόν 15 f; passive of 997 a, comp. 3 f-j*
ὀρφανός : in Epict. and Jn 805 a
ὀστᾶ 824* (i) b, d
οὔδει = "on the ground" 837 (iii) d
ὄψις 28 w

Ξηραίνω, καίω, and ἀποκαίω 876-7

Παιδεύω : for τροποφορέω 4 d
παιδίον 49 a; and τεκνίον 978
παῖς "servant" 54 f; supplanted by υἱός 54 f; ambig. 24 f
παντοκράτωρ 27 b, f-m
παρά as abbreviation 942* (viii) c
παραδίδωμι 828, 23 e
παρακαλέω 839 b
παράκειμαι 942* (viii) c
παραμένω 997 a, 27 t
παρθένια Μαρίας 55 h
παρθένος : ἐκ (or ἀπὸ) παρθένου γεννητός 880 a; παρθένοι appl. to men (Rev. xiv. 4) 942* (xv) b-f
παρίστημι : εἶς παρεστηκώς, εἶς [τις] τῶν παρεστηκότων 17 j*
πεδίον "field" 840 a
περί : οἱ περί, parallels to 17 g-h*
περιπατέω 28 f-g
Πέτρος, parallels to 17 g-h*; οἱ περὶ τὸν Π. 17 g-h*
πιστός 26 n
πλανάω : ἀπολέσας parall. to πλανηθῇ 864
πλήρης : vernacular use of 44 b
πληροφορέω 980-2
πληρόω 806, comp. 982
Πνεῦμα, τό, used absolutely 29 b, comp. 824* (i) b
πνεῦμα "wind," "spirit," "breath" 30 a; v.r. φάντασμα 824* (i) b
ποδήρης 28 l-n

Black Arabics refer to paragraphs [2]800-[2]997, *ordinary Arabics to the sections of* **2998**, *or, if starred, to the sections of* **2999**. *For example,* 872=2872, 16=2998 (xvi), 16*=2999 (xvi).

311

INDEX

ποιμαίνω : an error in LXX **942*** (xiv)
πολιαί 28 ο
πόλις : μεγάλη π. how appl. **942*** (ii) b
πολίτης 20 e
πράγματα " facts " **980, 984** b
πράκτωρ 14 a *
πρεσβύτερος s. below
πρεσβύτης and πρεσβύτερος **954–5** ; and γέρων **955**
προάγω 4*
προβάλλω ? " put forth leaves " **874**
προσεγγίζω and ἅπτομαι (q. vid.) 1 a*
προσέρχομαι 6* (esp. 6 b–d*)
προσεύχομαι : with εἰς **942*** (xxiv) b
προσκαλέω : προσκέκληται and ἐπικέκληται 3 g*
προσπίπτω and ἅπτομαι 2 a–b*
προσπορεύομαι and ἅπτομαι (q. vid.) 1 a*
προστίθημι and ἐπιτίθημι **942*** (xix) a
πρόσωπον : not used by Jn 28 w
προφθάνω 5*, 7*, 13*
πτερύγιον " pinnacle (of temple)," "wing (of army) " **837** (iii,
πτῶμα **942*** (xxii) b
πῦρ **819**, 7 d; and ἀνήρ 7 c
πύρωσις **948**

'Ρομφαία 28 s foll.

Σαβαχθανεί **923** c
σαβαώθ 27 b
σιγή : ὁ λόγος ἀπὸ σιγῆς προελθών 55 h
σίκλος 7 c*
Σίμων : parallels to 17 g–h*
σινδών 17 b* foll.
σκάνδαλον 15 b*

σκηνόω 28 g
στατήρ 7 c* foll.
στηρίζω " comfort with food " 9 a*
συμπαραμένω (LXX) = Heb. "fear" 27 t
συναλίζομαι and συναυλίζομαι **892–5**
συναντάω 3*
συναυλίζομαι s. συναλίζομαι
συνταγή and μαρτύριον 3 a*
συντάσσω, -ομαι 3 a–b*
σφάζω : ὡς ἐσφαγμένον, -ην **942*** (i) j
σφραγίς and χάραγμα **942*** (i) h

Τάσσω : ταξάμενοι ἡμέραν 3 a*
Τ(ε)ιτάν[1] : Irenæus on **942*** (i) m
τεκνίον **805** a ; and παιδίον **978**
τέλειος **44**
τελέω : τετέλεσται **923** d
τιθηνιζόμενον 49 a
τομεὺς λόγος 28 n, t, u
τριμερής 55 k
τροποφορέω v.r. τροφοφορέω 4 d, 45 ; παιδεύω for 4 d
τροφοφορέω s. τροποφορέω

Ὑδρωπικός **961** (i) c
ὕδωρ : ὕδατα πολλά 28 r
υἱός[2] : supplanting παῖς 54 f ; υ. ἀνθρώπου, υ. θεοῦ &c. ambig. 20, 24 b ; υ. ἀνθρ., υ. τοῦ ἀνθρ. and ὁ υ. τοῦ ἀνθρ. 38, 45 b ; υ. θεοῦ, υ. τοῦ θεοῦ and ὁ υ. τοῦ θεοῦ 20 a–b ; υ. γερουσίας, υ. πόλεως &c. 20 d
ὑμνέω **902** foll.
ὑπαντάω 3* (esp. 3 c* foll.), 4*
ὑπηρέτης **983–4**, 14 a*, 17 i*
ὑπό, ὑποκάτω, and ὑποπόδιον 22 b–c

---

[1] Comp. Plato 701 C (*Legg.* iii. 16) τὴν λεγομένην παλαιὰν Τιτανικὴν φύσιν as the last and worst of the stages of evil in human nature.

[2] Υἱός in Mt. xxi. 5 " son of an ass (ὑποζυγίου) " (from Zech. ix. 9 LXX πῶλον νέον) may help to explain Lk. xiv. 5 τίνος ὑμῶν υἱὸς (א, a, ὁ ὄνος, D πρόβατον) ἢ βοῦς (Syr. Burk. " son or ox or ass," but SS "ox or ass "). In the latter, " son " may have arisen from " whose *foal* ?" lit. "whose *son of an ass*? " taken by some as " whose *son or ass* ?" Misspelling may have facilitated corruption. Υἱός, besides being regularly abbreviated as υς, is spelt υος in *Oxy. Pap.* ii. 211 l. 50 (1st or 2nd cent.) ; οιειωι in *Fayûm* 113 l. 2, 114 l. 2 (A.D. 100) ; υειος freq. in a census, *Berl. Urk.* 392 (A.D. 207–8) and *ib.* 948 l. 16. Ps. xvii. 4 (R.V.) " they are satisfied with children (υἱέων, v.r. υἱῶν and ὑῶν) "—where the meaning is disputed, and Origen gives two explanations, (1) fed on their " *children* " (Lev. xxvi. 29), (2) fed on " *abomination* " (lit. " *swine's flesh* ")—has little bearing on Lk. xiv. 5, though a connexion between the two has been suggested. It should be added that the Aramaic for " young ass " is derived (Levy *Ch.* ii. 211 b) from Heb. "suckling," שׁוּל, and that very similar forms in Syriac (*Thes. Syr.* 2833) mean both " puer " and "pullus."

Black Arabics refer to paragraphs **[2]800–[2]997**, *ordinary Arabics to the sections of* **2998**, *or, if starred, to the sections of* **2999**. *For example,* **872 = 2872**, 16 = **2998** (xvi), 16* = **2999** (xvi).

GREEK

ὑποδύτης 17 n*
ὑποκάτω, s. ὑπό
ὑποπόδιον, ὑπό, and ὑποκάτω 22 b–c

Φαίνομαι 3 i*; ἐφάνη ὁ θεός 3 j*; φ. and ἀνατέλλω 27 t
φαντασία: κατὰ φ. 980, 984 b
φάντασμα 824* (i) b, d; v.r. πνεῦμα 824* (i) b
φέρω and βαστάζω 930–1; φέρων (Heb. i. 3) 27 g

φθάνω 6 a*, 6 e*

Χαλκολίβανον 28 q
χάραγμα and σφραγίς 942* (i) h
χάρις 840*; in Lk. and Jn 840* g
χείρ: ἐπὶ χεῖρα="by the side of" 961 (i) d; ἐκτείνω χεῖρα(s) 926 foll.
χωρέω 974

Ὦ : τὸ Ἄλφα κ. τὸ Ὦ 27 a foll.

Black Arabics refer to paragraphs [2]800–[2]997, *ordinary Arabics to the sections of* 2998, *or, if starred, to the sections of* 2999. *For example*, 872=2872, 16=2998 (xvi), 16*=2999 (xvi).

www.ingramcontent.com/pod-product-compliance
Lightning Source LLC
Chambersburg PA
CBHW050430240426
43661CB00055B/2329